DISPOSED OF
BY LIBRARY
HOUSE OF LORDS

INTRODUCTION TO THE LAW OF THE UNITED STATES

General Editors of the Series: Tuğrul Ansay and Don Wallace, Jr.

Introduction to the Law of the United States (1992)
Introduction to Greek Law (second edition 1993)
Introduction to the Law of Israel (1995)
Introduction to Swiss Law (second edition 1995)
Introduction to German Law (1996)
Introduction to Turkish Law (fourth edition 1996)
Introduction to Hungarian Law (1998)
Introduction to Belgian Law (2001)
Introduction to the Law of the United States (second edition 2002)
Introduction to Italian Law (2002)

Introduction to the Law of the United States

Second Edition

Edited
by

David S. Clark
Maynard and Bertha Wilson
Professor of Law
Willamette University

Tuğrul Ansay
Professor of Law

2002

KLUWER LAW INTERNATIONAL
THE HAGUE – LONDON – NEW YORK

Published by:
Kluwer Law International
P.O. Box 85889, 2508 CN The Hague,
The Netherlands
sales@kli.wkap.nl
http://www.kluwerlaw.com

Sold and distributed in North, Central and South America by:
Kluwer Law International
101 Philip Drive, Norwell, MA 02061, USA
kluwerlaw@wkap.com

Sold and distributed in all other countries by:
Kluwer Law International
Distribution Centre,
P.O. Box 322, 3300 AH Dordrecht,
The Netherlands

A CIP catalogue record is available from the Library of Congress.

Printed on acid-free paper.

ISBN 90-411-1701-6 (HB)
ISBN 90-411-1748-2 (PB)

Kluwer Law International incorporates the imprint of Martinus Nijhoff Publishers.

For my peregrine family:
Marilee, Lee, Susanna, Eliina,
Liisa, and David

– D.S.C.

To my children Arpa and Can

– T.A.

List of Contributors

Editors

TUĞRUL ANSAY
Rechtsbeistand (Legal Adviser), Hamburg; Formerly Professor of Law, University of Ankara

DAVID S. CLARK
Maynard and Bertha Wilson Professor of Law, Willamette University College of Law

Authors

HERBERT L. BERNSTEIN†
Late Professor of Law, Duke University School of Law

CHRISTOPHER L. BLAKESLEY
J.Y. Sanders Professor of Law, Louisiana State University Law Center

JONATHAN C. CARLSON
Professor of Law, University of Iowa College of Law

DAVID S. CLARK
Maynard and Bertha Wilson Professor of Law, Willamette University College of Law

ALFRED F. CONARD
Henry M. Butzel Professor of Law Emeritus, The University of Michigan Law School

VIVIAN GROSSWALD CURRAN
Associate Professor of Law, University of Pittsburgh School of Law

WILLIAM B. FISCH
Isidor Loeb Professor of Law, University of Missouri (Columbia) School of Law

JOHN G. FLEMING†
Late John G. Shannon Cecil Turner Professor of Law Emeritus, University of California at Berkeley School of Law

WILLIAM F. FRATCHER†
Late R.B. Price Distinguished Professor of Law Emeritus, University of Missouri (Columbia) School of Law

MICHAEL WALLACE GORDON
Chesterfield Smith Professor of Law, University of Florida College of Law

WILLIAM B. GOULD IV
Charles A. Beardsley Professor of Law, Stanford Law School

JOHN O. HALEY
Wiley B. Rutledge Professor of Law, Washington University School of Law

FRIEDRICH K. JUENGER†
Late Edward L. Barrett, Jr., Professor of Law, University of California at Davis School of Law

HARRY D. KRAUSE
Max L. Rowe Professor of Law Emeritus, University of Illinois College of Law

JOHN C. REITZ
Professor of Law, University of Iowa College of Law

EDWARD M. WISE†
Late Professor of Law and Director, Comparative Criminal Law Project, Wayne State University Law School

A.N. YIANNOPOULOS
Eason-Weinmann Professor of Comparative Law and Director, Eason-Weinmann Center for Comparative Law, Tulane University School of Law

JOACHIM ZEKOLL
John Minor Wisdom Professor of Law and Director, European Legal Studies, Tulane University School of Law

Preface to the Second Edition

The success of *Introduction to the Law of the United States* in the context of the rapid globalization of legal education and law practice calls for the book's renewal. The splendid group of American comparatists who participated in the first edition have agreed to update and in some cases substantially rewrite their chapters. They have also added recent suggested books for further reading to their selected bibliographies. In this second edition we bring the contributions of professors Jonathan C. Carlson, Vivian Grosswald Curran, Michael Wallace Gordon, John O. Haley, and Joachim Zekoll. At the same time we pause to remember our departed colleagues: Herbert L. Bernstein, John G. Fleming, William F. Fratcher, Friedrich K. Juenger, and Edward M. Wise.

David S. Clark
Tulsa

October 2001

Tuğrul Ansay
Hamburg

Preface to the First Edition

The aim of this book is to provide an authoritative description of the major elements of the American legal system. We are fortunate to have a distinguished group of American law professors write about fields in which they are expert. At times their commentary goes beyond historical development and explanation of the law and legal institutions to encompass critique. In that sense the 18 chapters presented here involve an historical, systematic, and critical introduction to the law of the United States.

The authors are special in another way. In addition to their areas of expertise in American law, each is also knowledgeable about a legal system outside that of the United States. They are comparative lawyers, who bring to their writing the perspective of an outsider as well as that of an insider. They thus see features of American law that are invisible to insiders, who breathe and live the law in which they work. Only strangers will see that certain aspects of the legal system in the United States are unusual, even perverse.

The 18 chapters are ordered in such a manner as, first, to acquaint the reader with the basic structural and cultural elements defining law in the United States: federalism, pragmatism, liberty, and individualism. Distinctive to the United States is also its method of legal education and its unitary legal profession, as well as the ways in which this profession makes use of its sources of law. Second, the authors describe the principal fields of public law: constitutional law, administrative law, labor law, and criminal law. Third, the traditional core of private common law in America is presented: contracts, torts, and property. The remainder of civil and commercial law follows, including family law, inheritance law, commercial transactions, and business enterprises. Finally, procedure rounds out the book with a description of criminal procedure, civil procedure, conflict of laws, and a discussion of an illustrative American case.

This book is intended primarily for two audiences. First, it is directed at the growing international audience interested in learning about the law of other countries. It provides students, lawyers, judges, scholars, business persons, and administrators outside the United States with the basic information required to understand America's principal legal concepts and institutions. Each chapter ends with a selected bibliography so that the interested reader can pursue further research in specific legal areas. Second, the volume is aimed at the American law student or general student perhaps interested in law, who desires a reliable overview of the American system of law.

Introduction to the Law of the United States has a number of features to facilitate its use. The 13 page table of contents presents a detailed outline to acquaint the reader with the major divisions in American law. For a specific inquiry the lengthy index exhaustively covers the contents of the various chapters. It includes, for instance, an alphabetical listing of all the statutes cited.

Finally, within each chapter there are liberal cross-references to related material found elsewhere in the chapter or even in other parts of the book.

The editors would like to thank the authors for their superb efforts in making this volume possible. We note with sorrow the passing of our colleague, William F. Fratcher, on 24 June 1992. We are grateful to the secretarial staff at the University of Tulsa – Ann Hail, Sharon Miller, and especially Michele Schultz – for their expert production of the manuscript. *Virtus probata florescit.*

David S. Clark
Tulsa

July 1992

Tuğrul Ansay
Hamburg

Summary of Contents

Table of Contents

List of Abbreviations

A.	*Atlantic Reporter*
AALS	Association of American Law Schools
ABA	American Bar Association
ADR	alternative dispute resolution
AFDC	Aid to Families with Dependent Children
AIDS	acquired immune deficiency syndrome
ALI	American Law Institute
ALJ	administrative law judge
ALR	*American Law Reports*
APA	Administrative Procedure Act
app.	appendix
art.	article
ATLA	American Trial Lawyers Association
CFR	*Code of Federal Regulations*
Ch.	Court of Chancery
chap.	chapter
Co.	Company
CISG	United Nations Convention on Contracts for the International Sale of Goods
C.M.L.R.	*Common Market Law Reports*
Const.	Constitution
D	defendant
D.C.	District of Columbia
DEA	Drug Enforcement Agency
DMCA	Digital Millennium Copyright Act
DWI	driving while intoxicated
EC	European Community
E.C.R.	*Report of Cases before the Court of Justice of the European Communities*
EEOC	Equal Employment Opportunity Commission
ERISA	Employee Retirement Income Security Act
EU	European Union
Ex.	Court of Exchequer
F.	*Federal Reporter*
FAA	Federal Aviation Administration
FACA	Federal Advisory Committee Act
FBI	Federal Bureau of Investigation
F.Cas.	*Federal Cases*
Fed.R.App.P.	Federal Rules of Appellate Procedure
FELA	Federal Employers' Liability Act

FLSA	Fair Labor Standards Act
FOIA	Freedom of Information Act
FRCP	Federal Rules of Civil Procedure
F.Supp.	*Federal Supplement*
FTC	Federal Trade Commission
FTCA	Federal Tort Claims Act
GAO	General Accounting Office
H.L.	House of Lords
ICC	International Chamber of Commerce
ILP	*Index to Legal Periodicals*
IRS	Internal Revenue Service
IVF	*in vitro* fertilization
J.D.	doctor of jurisprudence degree
K.B.	*Law Reports* (King's Bench)
LL.B.	bachelor of laws degree
LLC	limited liability company
LL.M.	master of laws degree
LLP	limited liability partnership
L.R.	*Law Reports*
LSAT	Law School Admission Test
LSU	Louisiana State University
M.B.A.	master of business administration degree
MBCA	Model Business Corporation Act
MPC	Model Penal Code
NAACP	National Association for the Advancement of Colored People
NAFTA	North American Free Trade Agreement
NCCUSL	National Conference of Commissioners on Uniform State Laws
N.E.	*North Eastern Reporter*
NGO	non-governmental organization
NLRA	National Labor Relations Act
NLRB	National Labor Relations Board
N.W.	*North Western Reporter*
N.Y.S.	*New York Supplement*
OCSE	Office of Child Support Enforcement
OMB	Office of Management and Budget
OSHA	Occupational Safety and Health Administration
P	principal
P.	*Pacific Reporter*
para.	paragraph
PEB	Permanent Editorial Board (UCC)
PKPA	Parental Kidnapping Prevention Act
pt.	part
Q.B.	*Law Reports* (Queen's Bench)
RICO	Racketeer Influenced and Corrupt Organizations Act
RULPA	Revised Uniform Limited Partnership Act
SEC	Securities and Exchange Commission
So.	*Southern Reporter*

S.W.	*South Western Reporter*
T	testator
TIAS	*Treaties and Other International Acts Series*
TV	television
UCITA	Uniform Computer Information Transactions Act
UETA	Uniform Electronic Transactions Act
U.L.A.	*Uniform Laws Annotated*
U.S.	United States; *United States Reports*
U.S.C.	United States Code
UST	*United States Treaties and Other International Agreements*
UCC	Uniform Commercial Code
UCCC	Uniform Consumer Credit Code
UCCJA	Uniform Child Custody Jurisdiction Act
UCP	Uniform Customs and Practice for Documentary Credits
UFTA	Uniform Fraudulent Transfer Act
UIFSA	Uniform Interstate Family Support Act
UMDA	Uniform Marriage and Divorce Act
UMPA	Uniform Marital Property Act
UPA	Uniform Parentage Act; Uniform Partnership Act
UPAA	Uniform Premarital Agreements Act
URESA	Uniform Reciprocal Enforcement of Support Act
USA	Uniform Securities Act
V	victim
WTO	World Trade Organization
§	section

Chapter 1
The American Legal System and Legal Culture

David S. Clark[*]

The idea of America as it relates to law has always been more powerful than the reality of law in America. The Declaration of Independence (1776), the United States Constitution (1787), and its first ten amendments, the Bill of Rights (1791), early stated the ideal in law and government. The voice from these documents was soon heard in Europe and Latin America, later in Asia and Africa, and more recently in eastern Europe and the former Soviet Union. But what about the United States itself? Conceived in hope and dedicated to opportunity, it has to an astounding degree over its short history accommodated different races, ethnic groups, and religions. However, unlike the few modern nations whose wealth and homogeneity have allowed their legal systems to merge the ideal and the real, the United States is a land of vast contrasts.

* Maynard and Bertha Wilson Professor of Law, Willamette University College of Law; Vice President, American Society of Comparative Law.

David S. Clark and Tuğrul Ansay (eds.) Introduction to the Law of the United States, 1-11

I. The Original Vision

Four elements of the founding fathers' vision for the United States of America are especially significant for the evolution of its legal system and legal culture: liberty, distrust of government, tolerance, and optimism.

A. Liberty

The Declaration of Independence states:

> We hold these truths to be self-evident, that all men are created equal, that they are endowed by their Creator with certain unalienable Rights, that among these are Life, Liberty and the pursuit of Happiness. That to secure these rights, Governments are instituted among Men, deriving their just powers from the consent of the governed.

A fundamental aim of the American Revolution was to assert, at least for white males, a natural and inalienable right to "Liberty and the pursuit of Happiness." The history of the 19th and 20th centuries is a story about the gradual extension of this and other rights to black slaves, women, native Americans, and even resident foreign citizens. This process of greater inclusion was assisted by the outcome of the Civil War (1861-1865), which abolished slavery and established the equality principle in the Constitution through the 14th Amendment (1868).

The natural right of liberty was to the pursuit of happiness; it was not a guarantee of happiness. An individual had the liberty to contract to improve his welfare, the liberty to marry whomever, the liberty to travel wherever, the liberty to worship God in his own way, the liberty to speak his mind, the liberty to do nothing. The physical environment of North America facilitated the exercise of this right. It was a spacious continent, less densely inhabited than Europe. It invited mobility, independence, and enterprise. Liberty realized breeds optimism. Americans felt that they had a personal stake in the future; they were inclined to experiment, to gamble, to waste. Whatever promised to increase wealth was considered good. Americans resented government if it tried to interfere with private enterprise. The negative side of liberty, however, led to vast environmental despoliation and tragic human exploitation.

Nevertheless, the symbol of liberty was and is a positive beacon to Americans and to many throughout the world. The word "liberty" appears as a reminder on the front of all American coins. It takes physical form in New York Harbor as the Statue of Liberty. A gift from the French to commemorate the centennial of American independence, it was placed to face arriving voyagers from Europe, about to disembark on the loneliness of a strange land, as the monument to freedom and opportunity offered by life in the United States.

B. Distrust of Government

The signers of the Declaration of Independence did not believe all government was bad, since "to secure these rights, Governments are instituted among Men." Some government was necessary to secure liberty. But government had to be watched, as the Declaration implied:

> That whenever any Form of Government becomes destructive of these ends, it is the Right of the People to alter or to abolish it, and to institute new Government, laying its foundation on such principles and organizing its powers in such form, as to them shall seem most likely to effect their Safety and Happiness.

One mechanism early favored to moderate the tension between the need for government and the potential for its tyranny was the rule of law. The Fifth Amendment (1791) guarantees that no person shall "be deprived of life, liberty, or property, without due process of law." The U.S. Constitution itself is an intricate design to secure a government of laws and not of men.

The details of the Constitution make it clear that the framers distrusted government. Government actions, in the framers' reading of history, were as likely to bring human misery as to promote human happiness. It was better to design an inefficient governmental machine to unite the 13 states. The trick was to increase the power of national government, after the failure of the Articles of Confederation (1777), but to avoid creating a centralized authority so effective that it threatened a return to tyranny. First, the Constitution only creates the national government, which is limited to certain enumerated powers. This *federal* structure of government is confirmed by the Tenth Amendment (1791): "The powers not delegated to the United States by the Constitution, nor prohibited by it to the States, are reserved to the States respectively, or to the people." Therefore, government was divided between a national government of restricted powers and 13 original states, each with its own constitution and divided powers.

Second, national government is separated into three branches, each with a primary function: legislation, administration, and adjudication. No one person can participate in more than one branch, unlike the parliamentary system where the prime minister is at once head of the executive and of the majority party in the legislature.

Third, the Constitution sets out an elaborate framework of checks and balances among and within the three branches of government. Within the Congress, for instance, there exist two chambers: one to satisfy small states that wanted equal representation (the Senate), and the other to accommodate the populous states with membership based on population (the House of Representatives). Federal district courts are checked in their power by the process of appeal to the Supreme Court. In general, no new governmental action can proceed without the assent of at least two branches. A bill only becomes law if both the Senate and the House of Representatives pass it by majority vote and the president does not veto it. The Congress can control or terminate executive programs by denial of funds. The president as commander in chief may only initiate war upon its declaration by Congress. The president may make a treaty, but only if two thirds of the Senate provides its advice and consent. The president appoints justices to the Supreme Court, but they must be confirmed by a majority of the Senate. And so on. Other checks were soon implied from the Constitution, such as the power to stop legislation or executive acts by judicial review.[1]

Fourth, the Constitution calls for fixed elections to promote accountability to the people of the government's principal political leaders: every two years for representatives, every six years for senators, and every four years for the president and vice president. Fifth, the Constitution is a written document – not unwritten as in England – and it is difficult to formally amend.

Finally, those who believed that the above cited barriers to tyranny were inadequate succeeded in adding the Bill of Rights in 1791 as a set of external restraints on the national government. The Supreme Court later made the Bill of Rights something more than a mere hortatory document, enforcing its provisions against all branches of government.

Americans in the first century of the republic were ambivalent about law. There is the image of the wild West, associated with the task of taming a frontier, but many today *remain* ambivalent. On the one hand, the Constitution is the supreme law. Along with the flag, it stands for national unity. America has no royal family, no timeless heritage, no national church. Since the federal judiciary emerged as the ultimate arbiter of what the Constitution means, for much of the past 200 years the judiciary and especially the Supreme Court has been America's most respected legal institution. It is surely the contemporary world's most powerful judiciary.

On the other hand, Americans are notoriously lawless; their attitude toward authority and rules is in general disrespectful since these are often seen as a threat to liberty. People also realize that the framers' vision for the Constitution has not always been implemented. The president commands a war without obtaining a declaration from Congress. Congressmen remain in office for long periods of political malaise by controlling the monetary levers of electoral power. The Supreme Court makes a widely unpopular decision. But it is more than only a recognition that the law on the books is different from the law in action. Rules represent tradition, the past. This is the New World; action is what matters most. Any problems this attitude generates can be sorted out later. Perhaps that is why there are 900,000 lawyers and judges – about one third of the world's total – in the United States today.

C. *Tolerance*

The European settlers of the 13 colonies that formed the new republic came from many lands under different circumstances. But one common element characterized their situation: they were dissenters and nonconformists. They either could not get along with the political or religious authorities in their homeland or their social or economic condition was sufficiently unacceptable that they packed their bags and made the long voyage across the Atlantic. They dissented with their feet.

1. *Marbury v. Madison*, 5 U.S. (1 Cranch) 137 (1803), *see* Chap. 4, pt. III.A.

The United States itself was born of dissent, as the complaints against King George III in the Declaration of Independence make clear. Moreover, the nation's fathers saw dissent as a positive force – or at least as an attitude that could not be eliminated from the American psyche. The right of religious conscience and the freedom to express an opinion were enshrined in the capstone amendment to the Constitution, the First Amendment (1791):

> Congress shall make no law respecting an establishment of religion, or prohibiting the free exercise thereof; or abridging the freedom of speech, or of the press; or the right of the people peaceably to assemble, and to petition the Government for a redress of grievances.

The right of dissent in a political community requires tolerance of dissenters. The First Amendment mandates tolerance, at least by the government: there would be no national religion, no governmental ideology, no state newspaper (certainly not with the pompous name "Truth").

D. Optimism

Americans were restless in a way that linked dissent to optimism. Pioneers who pulled up stakes and rode to the frontier were dissenting from the past while at the same time expressing their confidence in an unknown future. This was the New World and there was a continent to settle. Liberty was their right. Government would not stand in the way.

Europeans lived in the past, bound by the remnants of feudalism and nurtured by cultural nationalism. Those who emigrated to America escaped this past and marveled at the bounty of natural resources. The right to pursue happiness led not to just the philosophical idea of progress, but to the experience of progress: the conversion of wilderness into farms, the growth of villages into cities, and the emergence of America as a world power.

The American character was infused with optimism, stemming from the sense of space and the possibilities of human action. People could design legal institutions to improve society; there was no need to simply emulate the past. America was blessed by God. (*Annuit coeptis* according to the great seal of the United States, reproduced on each one dollar bill: *novus ordo seclorum.*) For many, optimism turned toward a feeling of moral superiority, which in turn fed a notion of manifest destiny. Some contemporary lawyers believe, to illustrate, that other nations would improve if they adopted American legal institutions associated with constitutionalism, judicial review, or human rights.

II. Unity out of Diversity

E pluribus unum, the motto of the United States adopted by Congress in 1782, found on the reverse of all its coins, sums up the central challenge facing the

American legal system. By the time of the Revolution, settlers had arrived from many parts of Europe. There were about half a million black slaves living in the southern colonies. Native Americans, of course, already inhabited the continent. Each group had its own culture, religion, language, and institutions. In spite of this rich diversity, among those colonies that revolted from Great Britain, English became the dominant language.

Along with English came the common law tradition, especially as it related to private law. But Americans selected among English legal institutions and decided which to retain as suitable to their new political and social conditions. They rejected, for instance, the parliament, the division between barristers and solicitors, and the doctrine of primogeniture. They maintained, on the other side, the jury, the division between law and equity, and the English style of legal argument and thought. Consequently, the common law tradition provided a measure of unity throughout the new nation. As additional states were admitted to the union, each (except for Louisiana) accepted the common law.

Federalism, as adopted in the Constitution, was another mechanism to bring a degree of unity out of diversity. *See* Chap. 4, pts. IV, VI. The U.S. Congress has legislative competence only in enumerated fields, but they cover the crucial concerns of national government: immigration and citizenship, taxes and excises, currency, bankruptcy, patent and copyright, weights and measures, foreign affairs, armed forces, maritime law, and the regulation of foreign and interstate commerce. The remaining fields of law were left to the states, which in their diversity could regulate most of private law as they wished.

The legal structure, however, is more complicated than this description suggests. Each state has a full set of legal institutions: a governor and executive agencies and staff, a legislature, and a complete hierarchy of ordinary courts with the power to adjudicate state law questions and even to hear most federal cases (the latter subject to appeal to the U.S. Supreme Court). States have further indulged in political decentralization by creating smaller governmental units, such as counties, cities, and districts – for water, fire protection, schools, and other special concerns – some with their own taxing and regulatory power and even with their own police force. *See* Chap. 15, pt. I.A. Local accountability is the populist slogan. Today there are an astounding 87,500 governmental units in the United States, which employ 20 million persons. State and local government employs 86 percent of these workers. The states, then, within this federal structure are like 50 huge social laboratories with plenary authority over their own administrative and tax law, as well as over property, contracts, torts, families, inheritance, and most commercial matters. States and cities create and enforce thousands of mundane rules that affect the daily life of average citizens and businesses. States are in competition with each other. A state's legal policies, along with its climate, economic situation, and other factors, attract or repel citizens, who are free to stay or to leave.

The flow of immigration in the late 19th century up to the present has further increased the degree of diversity, since many of the newer settlers have come from central and southern Europe, Latin America, and Asia. Often these new immigrants are attracted to the neighborhoods, cities, or states where people of their same ethnic heritage reside.

The American legal system has remained responsive to the social need for national unifying elements in the law. For instance, the commerce clause in article I, section 8 of the Constitution has been a major instrument for extending federal power, and thereby restricting state power, over matters that have only an indirect effect on interstate commerce, such as racial discrimination in restaurants and hotels. The Supreme Court early on had interpreted the necessary and proper clause in section 8 to provide a broad doctrine of national implied powers for the Congress.[2] The full faith and credit clause[3] similarly serves a unifying function by requiring each state to recognize and in appropriate cases to enforce "the public Acts, Records, and judicial Proceedings of every other State." Congress by statute has further required that federal courts respect state acts, records, and judicial proceedings to the extent that they are valid in state courts.[4]

The end of the American Civil War in 1865 brought renewed efforts to address the question of unity. The succession effort of the southern states was defeated; slavery was abolished; blacks became citizens. The 13th, 14th, and 15th Amendments to the Constitution gave special importance to the equality principle. Each amendment granted additional power to Congress to enforce its provisions. In addition, the Supreme Court has read section 1 of the 14th Amendment (due process and equal protection clauses) in a way to dramatically shift power away from states to be diverse in a manner that would violate certain provisions of the Bill of Rights or would infringe a person's equality rights. *See* Chap. 4, pts. IX, X.

Other elements promote unification in American law. Law schools in the United States are normally part of universities, which are financed by state government as public entities or are created by state law as private organizations. Nevertheless, law schools have a national focus since most are accredited by national groups. The professors teach from national casebooks that emphasize a common American law, and most prestigious schools attract students from throughout the country. *See* Chap. 2, pt. II. Concern about the disorder of American common law long ago led judges, lawyers, and professors to join together in an effort to promote legal unification. These efforts resulted in the National Conference of Commissioners on Uniform State Laws (1892), which publishes uniform laws that it hopes state legislatures will adopt, and the American Law Institute (1923), which publishes Restatements summarizing the legal rules found in the major fields of common law. These Restatements are frequently used by lawyers in advancing a legal argument before a court. *See* Chap. 3, pt. V.A, B.

Finally, unity has been aided by the enormous growth in the size of the federal government. Particularly since President Franklin Roosevelt's New Deal program began in 1933, people have demanded a national response to various social and economic problems that state and local governments seem unable to solve. Federal law and legal agencies today are much more important than they were at the beginning of the 20th century: for taxation, social security, business and labor regulation, civil rights, and environmental protection.

2. *McCulloch v. Maryland*, 17 U.S. 316 (1819); *see* Chap. 4, pt. IV.A.
3. U.S. Const. art. IV, § 1.
4. 28 U.S.C. § 1738 (1994); *see* Chap. 17, pts. III.A.4, IV.A.

III. Pragmatism in Law

A group of lawyers and judges trying to come to a consensus about the dominant American philosophy of law could probably not agree on anything more specific than the notion of Common Sense. The most often quoted aphorism from America's greatest jurist – Oliver Wendell Holmes, Jr. (1841-1935) – sums up this attitude: "The, life of the law has not been logic: it has been experience."[5] Grant Gilmore, in his Storrs Lectures on Jurisprudence at Yale Law School, reaffirmed this view:

> [T]he principal lesson to be drawn from our study is that the part of wisdom is to keep our theories open-ended, our assumptions tentative, our reactions flexible. We must act, we must decide, we must go this way or that. Like the blind men dealing with the elephant, we must erect hypotheses on the basis of inadequate evidence. That does no harm – at all events it is the human condition from which we will not escape – so long as we do not delude ourselves into thinking that we have finally seen our elephant whole.[6]

Americans in general tend to have little interest in philosophy or metaphysical abstractions. From a European perspective, Americans vulgarized philosophy in the same way that they debased language, food, or manners. From an American perspective, alternatively, this is acceptable so long as it serves some useful purpose. In an unbridled democracy, every person is entitled to an opinion. Intellectuals are often distrusted; professors, characterized as absent minded, are the objects of humor.

Pragmatism in the law is supported by several structural features of the American legal system. First, the judge, not the scholar, is the protagonist in the development of legal doctrine, most visibly at the level of the U.S. Supreme Court. Holmes, himself a justice on the Court, said: "The prophecies of what the courts will do in fact, and nothing more pretentious, are what I mean by the law."[7] In the civil law world, by contrast, scholars have played the predominant role since the Roman empire. Second, law schools use the case method of instruction, which de-emphasizes theory and doctrinal coherence and focuses on the facts of individual disputes. A new lawyer graduating from law school knows lots of twigs and trees, but does not have a clear view of the forest. European legal education, on the other side, teaches the grammar of the law, promotes through lecture a panoramic view of doctrine, and believes in a right answer to a legal problem. Finally, pragmatism, with its elements of relativism and instrumental reasoning, is buttressed by the original vision discussed in part I: liberty and its connection to equalitarian individualism, distrust of government (or really any *a priori* system of thought), tolerance, and optimism.

5. O.W. Holmes, Jr. *The Common Law* 5 (Mark DeWolfe Howe ed. 1963; first published 1881).
6. Grant Gilmore, *The Ages of American Law* 110 (1977).
7. O.W. Holmes, "The Path of the Law," 10 *Harv. L Rev.* 457, 460-61 (1897).

IV. INDIVIDUALISM

Although *e pluribus unum* – unity out of diversity – supports a tradition based on civic republican virtue, duty, and the common good, a conflicting American tradition, based on natural rights, fosters individualism. Lawrence Friedman, characterizing modern legal culture, found that Americans have created a "republic of choice," which has replaced an earlier balance between liberty and restraint, right and duty.[8] Liberty today means autonomous individualism; it increasingly has been separated from previous notions of the common good. This is clearly visible in the Supreme Court's decisions of the past three decades with regard to privacy and free speech rights. *See* Chap. 4, pts. IX.C.3, XI. The legal order is premised on each individual's capacity to freely choose among values without constraint by others or by the state. This requires that the many conceptions of the good all be treated as equally legitimate. Individualism recognizes no hierarchy of values outside personal choice. It is skeptical of historically or culturally deduced values – or of those communally selected – since these might impose a conception of the good on persons who did not choose it for themselves.

Even the 1960s civil rights revolution – extending rights to blacks and other ethnic minorities, women, and other disadvantaged groups – grew out of individualism. At the core of each liberation movement is the desire for the majority in society to treat each person as an individual human, not as a member of a race, gender, or group. *See* Chap. 4, pt. X.C.1. Individualism is also behind the success in the 1970s of divorce on demand. The family's communal interest is worth less than a persons's individual interest. Marriage loses the prestige of permanence; it is no longer seen as supported by religion or even as furthering any public interest. The end of marriage is simply a matter of individual choice, perhaps even between two persons of the same sex. *See* Chap. 11, pts. III, X.

Atomistic individualism, with its lack of commitment to the community, is associated with the increasing privatization of American life. Cars and guns are both appropriate metaphors for an American's liberty and autonomy, and the law protects his right to both. The automobile offers inexpensive, individualized transportation to a highly mobile people. Americans do not walk places or support community enhancing mass transit. With a car, one can drive quickly past the homeless, past the decay and violence of the inner city, toward the epitome of isolation: suburbia. Once at home – increasingly a one-person household – a gun becomes the instrument to protect one's rights: rights in privacy and property. Private citizens today possess 200 million firearms, one third of which are handguns. There is no safety or repose in community.

8. Lawrence M. Friedman, *The Republic of Choice: Law, Authority, and Culture* 2-3, 193-94 (1990); *see* John Phillip Reid, *The Concept of Liberty in the Age of the American Revolution* 2 (1988): "If people had rights they also had duties, owed less to the state than to society – to their fellow members living under the contract."

V. Disquieting Factors: Diversity as Divisiveness

Mixing the factors of race and poverty in America have produced a social development inconsistent with republican government: a substantial underclass, cut off from mainstream America by discrimination, underemployment, homelessness, lack of education adequate for participation in the community, and since the 1990s an increasing separation by imprisonment. While many legislatures and the federal courts were accentuating a rights-oriented individualism, the majority lost sight of a subculture of poverty substantially congruent with urban ghettos populated by black and Hispanic Americans. This underclass is likely to replicate itself since a larger percentage of children (17 percent) live in poverty than the general population or even retired persons (both ten percent). Of the founding fathers' vision, only distrust of government rings true for this subculture. Too many governmental programs have failed to accomplish their purposes; for many poor the primary governmental presence in their lives is the police. Liberty is a broken promise; tolerance and optimism are in scarce supply.

However, significant progress was made in the 1990s to reduce the size of this underclass and to diminish one of its most visible manifestations: crime. Thus the overall child poverty rate declined from 23 percent in 1993 to 17 percent in 1999, which is its lowest rate since 1979. While this current rate is nine percent for white children, it is 33 percent for blacks and 30 percent for Hispanics. Even so the improvement for the two major minority groups over those six years was more dramatic: 13 and 11 percentage points for blacks and Hispanics respectively.

At the same time crime declined rapidly in the last half of the 1990s. Victimization surveys reveal that crime overall fell from a rate of 326 to 232 per 1,000 persons over age 12 (with about 15 percent of the 1999 criminal activity against persons and the remainder property crime). Moreover, the worst types of crimes dropped the most. From 1993 to 1999 the number of homicides declined from 24,500 to 15,500 and crimes involving guns from 582,000 to 339,000. The 1999 homicide rate was the lowest since 1966. The reduction in crime has been attributed to various factors: increased police forces and criminal incarceration; economic expansion, especially with its employment opportunities for ethnic minorities and teenagers; and decline of the crack cocaine market and police confiscation of teenagers' guns.

Historians show us that high crime rates in the United States go back almost as far as the collection of statistics. Lawlessness is part of American legal culture, a part of the wild West mystique, a part of individualism somewhat too rugged. The recent trend toward reduced crime may reveal an improvement in community and the success of a legal system to maintain order and justice. But the level of crime is still high compared to many other developed nations, especially for homicide. It is not that the United States ignores its legal system. There are 877,000 lawyers and judges. In 1997 all governmental units spent $130 billion on the justice system: 15 per cent by the federal government, 33 per cent by states, and 52 per cent by localities. This illustrates the extreme decentralization of the American legal system. Of the $130 billion, police forces cost $58 billion, courts and legal services cost $29 billion, and corrections (for example, prisons, parole) cost $43 billion.

The unknown factor in this equation of law and order is the social consequence of turning to a more severe form of criminal justice than that used in most other democracies. Thus, the number of adults in jail or prison, or on probation or parole, expanded from 1.8 million in 1980 to about 6.2 million in 2000, which represents an increase from one to three percent of the total adult population. This three percent of the American community under some form of criminal justice supervision is unevenly distributed, so that it constitutes only two percent of the white population, but nine percent of African Americans, and only one percent of women, but five percent of men.

The harshest punishment is incarceration in prison or jail. This population has grown from 1.1 million in 1990 to 1.9 million in 2000, a rate of 7 per 1,000 persons (48 and 17 for blacks and Hispanics respectively), which is not matched in any other wealthy democracy.[9] In fact, there are only about eight million people imprisoned worldwide. The ultimate atavistic punishment in America is execution, society's sentence of death that was seemingly destined to disappear in the 1960s, but returned in the mid-1980s to reach a level in 2000 of almost 100 (of whom about one third are black).

Selected Bibliography

Robert E. Calvert, ed., *"The Constitution of the People": Reflections on Citizens and Civil Society* (1991).

E. Allan Farnsworth, *An Introduction to the Legal System of the United States* (3d ed. 1996).

Lawrence M. Friedman, *A History of American Law* (2d ed. 1985).

Grant Gilmore, *The Ages of American Law* (1977).

Kermit L. Hall, *The Magic Mirror: Law in American History* (1989).

Peter Hay, *U.S.-amerikanisches Recht: ein Studienbuch* (2000).

Theresa J. Lippert et al., eds., 1-12 *West's Encyclopedia of American Law* (1998).

Forrest McDonald, *Novus Ordo Seclorum: The Intellectual Origins of the Constitution* (1985).

Arthur Taylor von Mehren, *Law in the United States: A General and Comparative View* (1988).

Alan B. Morrison, ed., *Fundamentals of American Law* (1996).

Peter H. Schuck, *The Limits of Law: Essays on Democratic Governance* (2000).

9. The rate for black men aged 25 to 29 is an astonishing 131 per 1,000 persons that age.

Chapter 2
Legal Education and the Legal Profession

*David S. Clark**

I. A Brief History

A. Legal Education

Prior to 1865 the intellectual origins of American legal training were predominantly English. Most attorneys in the 19th century learned law through the English apprenticeship approach. William Blackstone (1723-1780) had established a place for student and practitioner use of legal treatises with his four volume *Commentaries on the Laws of England*, which was widely used in American editions and emulated in commentaries on American law. Henry St. George Tucker (1780-1848), a professor at William and Mary College, for instance, published an edition of Blackstone's *Commentaries* in 1803 with copious notes adapting it to American usage. James Kent (1763-1847), professor at Columbia and chancellor of the New York Court of Chancery, began publishing his four volume *Commentaries on*

* Maynard and Bertha Wilson Professor of Law, Willamette University College of Law; Vice President, American Society of Comparative Law.

David S. Clark and Tuğrul Ansay (eds.) Introduction to the Law of the United States, 13-33

American Law in 1826. Joseph Story (1779-1845), United States Supreme Court justice and professor at Harvard, published nine *Commentaries* on various aspects of American law between 1832 and 1845. He frequently cited, in addition to English and American cases, Roman and civil law sources.

The first law schools evolved out of law offices that took in apprentice clerks for a fee. Clerks copied by hand legal documents, conversed with and observed the attorney, and read legal treatises and other law books. A few attorneys preferred instructing clerks rather than practicing law and gained a reputation for teaching. The Litchfield Law School, which operated from 1784 to 1833 and attracted students from several states, or the 20 other law office-type schools patterned on it, clearly show their English parentage. Tapping Reeve (1744-1823), Litchfield's founder, administrated the school like a law practice. Students drafted pleadings and conveyances. This practical education was supplemented with lectures roughly following Blackstone's *Commentaries* and with periodic examinations.

Two additional currents beyond the English influence were also significant. First, Jacksonian Democracy (1829-1837) belittled the need for formal education, putting fledgling law schools and universities under economic pressure. The judiciary in many states was made subject to popular election; some states abolished or reduced apprenticeship requirements for bar membership. Formal education fell into disrespect. Second, civil law doctrines and methods were trumpeted as a supplement to, if not a substitute for, those of the common law. Some law professors and lecturers preached the civilian virtues of reason and order; they translated European treatises into English and published law journals emphasizing civil law themes.

Instruction at Harvard Law School, which opened in 1817, was only slightly more intellectual than instruction at a Litchfield-type law school. Professors used – in addition to lectures – a textbook or recitation method for which students had to memorize assigned portions of textbooks. During recitation sessions, a teacher explained the text and quizzed students to determine how accurately they had memorized their assignments. By 1869 the Law School curriculum had been reduced to 18 months, examinations had been abolished, and less than half the students graduating in law possessed college degrees.

Harvard Law School's rise to prominence is attributable primarily to the appointment of Charles Eliot (1834-1926) as university president in 1869 and Christopher Columbus Langdell (1826-1906) to the newly created post of law school dean in 1870. Of the two men, Eliot was easily the more important. He actively initiated and supported reform throughout the university, especially in the undergraduate science curriculum and in the law and medical schools. Eliot presided over most law school faculty meetings and pushed for the appointment of professors who lacked a background of professional practice. The initial 15 years of Langdell's deanship institutionalized five important changes. Langdell, with the help of Eliot's leadership, established: (1) a law school entrance examination; (2) a two year and later a three year progressive curriculum, leading to an undergraduate bachelor of laws degree (LL.B.); (3) requisite annual examinations before students could proceed on to the next year's subjects; and (4) the beginnings of a research function at the Law School similar to that existing in

German universities. Langdell contended that he was by example trying to put American law faculties on a level with universities in continental Europe.[1]

Langdell's most significant innovation, however, was the introduction of an instructional method utilizing Socratic dialogue to discuss appellate court cases. Justified as a scientific process to elaborate general, organic principles of the common law, it supplanted lecturing and recitation based on treatises. Professors and students, the idea ran, should together work through questions and answers to discover common law principles, aided by classroom research manuals called casebooks. *See* pt. II.C.1.

Legal science promised a complete and orderly system of norms; it offered determinate answers in an increasingly complex world. The American Bar Association Committee on Legal Education and Admissions to the Bar accepted this model in 1879. While Germans looked to professors to ascertain the true content of law, Americans could turn to judges, assisted of course by the professorate. This became the *usus modernus americanus*.

Harvard's success in institutionalizing legal education within a European university tradition established the model followed almost everywhere in the United States by the first decades of the 20th century. Legal science brought order, system, and prestige. Apprenticeship was in decline. The Harvard curriculum was founded on certain basic required private law courses from the common law – contracts, real property, and torts – coupled with criminal law, civil procedure, evidence, and equity; these were followed by elective courses. *See* pt. II.B. By 1909 Harvard successfully transformed the three year study of law into a graduate program, requiring a college degree for admission. The professors were hierarchically organized as full time scholars. Even students participated as junior scientists; those with distinction as shown by performance on examinations edited and published notes and comments in the scholarly *Harvard Law Review*, founded in 1877.

The American law school student population from 1870 to 1900 grew from 1,650 to 12,500 while the number of law schools increased from 31 to 102. At the turn of the 20th century three quarters of the schools were affiliated with a college or a university. But there were also 20 night law schools catering to the urban masses and emphasizing local law and practice much more than university law schools. Elite lawyers began to worry about standards and the influx of immigrant attorneys trained at the night schools. State bar associations began to tighten up qualifying examinations. The schools themselves in 1900 created the Association of American Law Schools (AALS), which together with the American Bar Association (ABA) went into the standards and accreditation business. The AALS initially accepted 32 schools as charter members. A school that failed to qualify for either list was at a competitive disadvantage in attracting students.

1. *See* David S. Clark, "Tracing the Roots of American Legal Education – A Nineteenth-Century German Connection," 51 *Rabels Zeitschrift für ausländishes und internationales Privatrecht* 313 (1987).

B. The Legal Profession

No elite profession of the bench and bar arose in the early American republic to parallel the profession in England. Requirements for admission to the bar were loose and became looser toward the middle of the 19th century. In 1840 only 11 of 30 states prescribed a definite period of apprenticeship to become a lawyer; some states required that a person pass an examination (which might involve a few formal perfunctory questions). While formal restrictions were weak, the informal constraints of an open market for legal services – where social and geographic mobility was high – remained an efficient control. Lazy, incompetent, or ineffective lawyers simply had too few clients to survive.

Judges, similarly, varied in training and ability. A majority of judges in the early republic were laymen, especially on the lower courts. These men often came from prominent families or had made their fortune and were active in politics. Once Jacksonian Democracy succeeded in broadening suffrage and the popular control of public office, almost all states abandoned an appointive selection method for judges (often through the legislature or in combination with the governor) and adopted the method of popular election for a term, typically four to eight years. Federal judges, by the U.S. Constitution's mandate, are nominated by the president for life tenure, subject to confirmation by a majority of the Senate. *See* Chap. 16, pt. I.B. Virtually all federal judges were lawyers and the trend in states was to elect lawyers to the bench (except for the position of justice of the peace, which remained with laymen until late in the 20th century). Most high court judges by the end of the 19th century were successful or ambitious lawyers, who reflected the values of America as an industrializing society run by businessmen and politicians. They were conservative but not aristocratic, an attribute promoted by the elective system. At the lower levels of the judiciary were many examples of venality and incompetence, fostered by the dependence of courts on local politics. The toughest assignments, however, were for federal territorial judges in the West, who accepted the four year patronage job in an often hostile, lawless environment.

In 1850 there were about 24,000 lawyers and law-trained judges in the United States. After the Civil War the great economic transformation from an agricultural to an industrial society increased the demand for lawyers, which together with judges reached 64,000 by 1880 and topped 114,000 in 1900. Judges had more cases to process and the work became more diverse. Lawyers prospered because they were able to adapt in a profession with little governmental or self-regulation. The profession offered upward social and economic mobility to ambitious immigrant and middle class sons. Law was not so stuffy that practitioners could not move in and out of business and politics. Bar associations did try to limit entry by raising standards, but their dream of an elite guild, an English-style bar, could not be imposed on such a porous profession.

The appearance of law firms with more than three partners was the most significant structural development of the post-Civil War period. In 1900 about 70 firms had five or more lawyers, with the majority on or near Wall Street in New York City. The largest firm had ten attorneys. These lawyers avoided lawsuits and left that work for traditional practitioners. Firms grew up to service powerful corporations; they specialized in corporate securities and finance. Other developments included the emergence of salaried lawyers, who worked as in-house counsel to corporations, especially insurance companies and railroads, and government lawyers, who worked for various agencies in the federal government and for city or state governments. For instance, the U.S. Attorney General employed 13 lawyers and the New York City Law Department had 28 attorneys.

II. Legal Education

Law schools in the late 1960s faced many of the same social changes that precipitated student revolutions and opened up universities in the United States, Germany, France, and elsewhere in the Western world. The agents of change in America were the civil rights movement and student hostility toward the Vietnam War; feminism, consumer rights, and environmentalism added to these in the 1970s. Many young people saw law not only as a bulwark of order, but also as a mechanism to promote needed change in American society.

Table 1 details the increase in law student enrollment from the middle of the Great Depression (1935) to the present.

Table 1 Law Students Enrolled in ABA Approved Schools, by Division, 1935 to 1999[2]

Year	*Total*	*Full Time*	*Part Time*	*Part Time (percent)*
1935	19,834	16,778	3,046	15
1950	41,575	32,918	8,657	21
1960	37,715	27,355	10,360	27
1965	56,510	44,014	12,496	22
1970	78,339	62,376	15,963	20
1975	111,047	90,268	20,779	19
1980	119,501	98,396	21,105	18
1985	118,700	95,640	23,060	19
1990	127,261	106,440	20,821	16
1995	129,397	107,397	22,000	17
1999	125,184	103,768	21,416	17

The enormous jump in enrollment occurred during the 15 year period 1960 to 1975, when the number of students in the standard three or four year degree program at ABA approved schools grew 194 percent. From 1982 (121,791 students), enrollment was flat until 1989 when it began a slow climb that topped at 129,580 students in 1991. The 1990s overall was a decade of enrollment stability tending toward decline, even though seven new ABA schools entered the market. A 2,000

2. Enrolled in J.D. (and before 1980 LL.B.) degree programs during the fall semester.

student increase in post-J.D. programs during the 1990s to about 7,000 in 1999 compensated for that decline.

A. Uniformity and Diversity

The ABA and the AALS from 1900 until about 1970 brought a substantial degree of uniformity to American law schools by setting national standards and in the case of the ABA by achieving accrediting power. Urban proprietary night law schools either affiliated with a university or went out of business. Legal education finally became a graduate program; in 1952 the AALS established three years of college education as a prerequisite for law school admission and today virtually all law students hold a bachelor's degree in arts or science. Law schools switched to the J.D. (juris doctor or doctor of jurisprudence) degree to reflect this change.

In 2001 the ABA approved 183 law schools, while 162 of these were members of the stricter AALS. Both organizations have detailed standards for student admission, duration of the J.D. program, faculty and student body diversity, faculty qualifications and development, law school governance, curriculum, library, physical facilities, and financial resources. Only about one percent of those who become lawyers now attend a non-ABA school (most of which are located in California), so that there no longer is open access to law study as there was at the turn of the 20th century. The ABA, however, continues to approve new schools – seven during the 1990s – even with the stable enrollment pattern of that decade. In part this is to accommodate geographic population redistribution in the United States.

For the past four decades all ABA schools have used selective admission standards to maintain their class size in proportion to their building and faculty capabilities. Admission decisions are based on an applicant's university accomplishments along with his or her score from the national Law School Admission Test (LSAT). In 1990 44,104 students enrolled in the first year of a J.D. program, while 138,865 persons took the LSAT. As the lawyer market became saturated in the 1990s, the number of LSAT takers dropped to 104,236 for the 43,152 first year students enrolled in the class of 1999. The emphasis on exclusivity led to a decline in the proportion of law students who study part time in a four year program from 27 percent in 1960 to a stable 17 percent today. *See* Table 1. All ABA schools for the 1998 academic year budgeted $2.1 billion for expenses, which averages $11.6 million per school or $15,940 per student. The average size school enrolls 727 students taught by 31 full time professors and 30 part time teachers.[3]

Beneath the facade of uniformity implicit in a successful effort to raise the nationwide standards for legal education lies a rich diversity unequaled in any

3. An important development in the 1990s is the significant decrease in the student-faculty ratio, particularly in larger law schools. Using a calculation based on full time student equivalents, from 1990 to 1999 large schools (over 1,100) reduced the ratio from 27 to 19, medium schools (divided between 700 to 1,100 and 500 to 700) from 26 or 24 to 19 or 17 respectively, and small schools (300 to 500) from 22 to 16.

other country. The evidence of this diversity flows from several sources. First, America has a large number of *private* university law schools. Virtually all the states have a public university law school, and some larger states such as California, Florida, Illinois, Ohio, and Texas have several. But there is no federal ministry of education (or even state department of education) that sets out the law curriculum, faculty salaries, or research projects. A certain level of diversity is present among public law schools that parallels the differences among American states. *See* Chap. 1, pt. II. But the, greatest diversity stems from the existence and competition of private law schools, which because they are not subsidized by state government must charge students a higher tuition. In 1999 this tuition averaged $20,600 compared to $7,200 for public law schools (which, however, charge out-of-state residents $14,800). Students will pay this higher cost, even if it is deferred through federal government or private loans (which totaled over $1.6 billion in 1999), only if the educational product or the prestige of the degree they receive is superior to the public alternative.

Second, the historic pattern of law school development established a hierarchy of prestige among law schools that further stimulates competition: for the best students and faculty, for the best library, or for selling points such as the best environmental law or clinical training program. Students (and law firms that hire them) learn about the pecking order, which ranges from national schools – such as Harvard, Stanford, and Yale – to regional schools that attract students from several states, to local schools that focus on a constituency largely from one state. Students who plan to enter politics, for instance, often attend the local state law school. Part time divisions, which usually detract from prestige and are located at urban private schools, serve working-class students and those who desire to enter law as a second career. Local schools tend to emphasize the technical aspects of law and the knowledge needed to pass the state bar examination.

Third, beginning in the 1960s schools experimented with methods of instruction beyond Langdellian appellate case analysis. In addition, curricular developments eroded what was left of a scientific study of law and opened law schools to a cornucopia of electives. *See* pts. II.B, C.

Finally, the composition of the typical student body and faculty changed from essentially a group of white males to more closely represent the diversity of the American population. Table 2 shows the dramatic increase in the number and percentage of women attending law school beginning in the late 1960s. As a proportion of the total J.D. enrollment, women increased from 3.4 percent in 1960 to almost achieve parity at 47.4 percent in 1999. In fact most of the total enrollment growth in law schools since 1970 is accounted for by the admission of women. *See* Table 1. The affirmative recruitment of ethnic minority students began in the 1970s and the proportion in law schools rose from 6.1 percent in 1970 to 20.2 percent in 1999. African Americans, constituting the largest minority presence in law school at 7.4 percent (in 1999), are still disproportionately underenrolled since they constitute 12 percent of the American population.

A similar improvement in the diversity of law school teachers and professional staff has occurred, illustrated in Table 3. Of the full time professorate in 1999, 29 percent are women and 13 percent are from minority groups. This change, in particular, has altered the discourse about law and legal institutions in

America that is shaping law school communities and to some extent the larger legal profession in the 21st century.

Table 2 Women and Minority Law Students in ABA Approved Schools, by Type, 1960 to 1999[4]

	1960	*1970*	*1980*	*1990*	*1999*
Women	1,296	6,682	40,834	54,097	59,362
% of Total	3.4	8.5	34.2	42.5	47.4
Minority		5,520	10,575	17,330	25,253
% of Total		6.1	8.8	13.6	20.2
Black		3,744	5,506	7,432	9,272
Mexican American		883	1,690	1,950	2,483
Puerto Rican[5]		94	442	506	646
Other Hispanic		179	882	2,582	3,991
American Indian		140	415	554	978
Asian		480	1,640	4,306	7,883

Table 3 Law Teachers and Professional Staff in ABA Approved Schools, by Type, 1999

	Total	*Women*	*Minority*
Full Time	5,586	1,631	743
Part Time	5,510	1,593	473
Deans & Administrators	3,413	2,174	624
Librarians	1,493	995	215

B. Curriculum

Harvard Law School set the curricular pattern for American legal education in the 19th century. *See* pt. I.A. The goal was to develop students' legal reasoning rather than to learn the law of a particular jurisdiction. Harvard offered only 22 subjects in the 1890s, even after the elective course system was adopted in 1886 to supplement a core of mandatory courses. The core curriculum consisted of contracts, real property, torts, criminal law, civil procedure, evidence, and equity. Public law dominated the significant additions in the 1920s and 1930s: administrative law, labor law, and taxation. Seminars in advanced subjects were by then taught at many schools.

4. Enrolled in J.D. degree programs during the fall semester. Minority student numbers exclude the Puerto Rican law schools. The 1970 figures for minority students are from 1971.
5. Excludes Puerto Rican students enrolled in the three ABA schools in Puerto Rico: 1,711 in 1980, 1,511 in 1990, and 1,800 in 1999.

The modern round of curricular reform began in the 1960s when less acquiescent students – concerned about civil rights and more socially relevant courses – flooded into law schools. In the next decades schools whittled back or sometimes thoroughly reformed the core mandatory courses, providing more time in a three year program for electives and seminars. The most successful innovations were in courses using the problem method, legal clinics, and professional skills courses focusing on negotiation, conciliation, drafting, and counseling. Responding to the increased complexity of American law, many law schools created or expanded joint degree and post-J.D. programs, usually lasting one year and awarding the joint degree or an LL.M. (master of laws) degree. In 1990 there were 5,172 students in these programs, which grew to 7,092 in 1999.

Globalization has fostered curricular change pushed by foreigners, many already lawyers, studying in American law schools, and by Americans studying law abroad. Most of the foreigners enroll in an LL.M. degree program (and now represent more than half of the total LL.M. enrollment). On the other side, American law students and lawyers do not tend to study in foreign universities, but rather use a summer or semester abroad program at one of the 81 American law schools now offering these courses in 44 countries. In 1980, in contrast, only 18 schools had such a program.[6]

The curricula of four law schools are described to illustrate the variety in American legal education. Two of these schools are public (the University of Michigan and Louisiana State University – LSU) and two schools are private (Stanford University and Willamette University). Two have a national reputation for their professors' scholarship and attract students from throughout the country (Michigan and Stanford) and two are regional schools (LSU and Willamette). Table 4 profiles these schools.

All four of the law schools profiled organize the first year students in larger classes for the mandatory curriculum (*see* Table 4), with the exception of legal research and writing classes and one of the other required courses, which are usually half the size of the normal first year courses. This slight decrease in efficiency was initiated to promote collegiality between faculty and students.

1. Michigan

The first year required curriculum covers contracts, torts, property, criminal law, civil procedure, constitutional law, and legal practice. This last one year course is designed to teach legal writing, research, and advocacy, skills that future lawyers will need no matter which branch of the profession they choose. Students are permitted to enroll in one elective course during their first year. The second and third years are freely open to student selection, except for a required course on professional responsibility (which most schools mandate) and enrollment in at least one seminar.

6. *See* David S. Clark, "Transnational Legal Practice: The Need for Global Law Schools," 46 *Am. J. Comp. L.* 261 (Supp. 1998).

Table 4 Selected Law School Profiles, 1999.

	Michigan	*Stanford*	*LSU*	*Willamette*
J.D. Enrollment[7]	1,067	545	637	407
% Women	43	45	48	45
% Minority	23	32	9	11
% Foreign	1	3	1	1
Full Time Teachers	72	39	32	24
Annual Tuition	$19,116	$26,358	$6,154	$18,380
Nonresident	$25,086	$26,358	$11,994	$18,380
Library				
Volumes	845,000	485,000	577,000	285,000
Current Serials	9,800	7,600	3,000	3,300
Curriculum				
First Year Course Size	86	59	81	74
Elective Courses	112	129	93	62
Seminars	50	47	12	11
Student Enrollment				
Clinics	162	68	0	22
Simulated Skills	141	359	477	123
Externs	34	28	0	31
Law Journals	365	390	42	44
Practice Competitions	67	46	124	128

Michigan is unique among public law schools in that it enrolls only a minority of students (27 percent) from its own state. This is politically possible since the law school has raised its own endowment, which partially funds the cost of operations and thus relieves the state legislature of that burden. It is economically possible since the school charges most students a high tuition similar to that of an elite private law school. Table 4 reflects the large number of elective courses and seminars (162), which include almost every conceivable legal topic and many interdisciplinary offerings. Examples include Blood Feuds, Constitutionalism in South Africa, and Using Social Science in Law.

Michigan has a large number of centers, joint degrees, and other programs. The Center for International and Comparative Law is the focal point for the school's substantial number of visiting foreign faculty and graduate students as

7. Michigan had the largest post-J.D. enrollment, with 38 full time students.

well as for the home faculty and students interested in those subjects. In addition, there is the Olin Center for Law and Economics, the Program in Refugee and Asylum Law, several clinical programs with over 15 percent of the student body participating in any given year, and 11 joint degree programs.

Over a third of the students participate on one of the school's six journals: the *Michigan Law Review*, *Michigan Journal of Law Reform*, *Michigan Journal of International Law*, *Michigan Journal of Race and Law*, *Michigan Journal of Gender and Law*, and *Michigan Telecommunications and Technology Law Review* (online).

2. Stanford

The first year curriculum consists of seven prescribed courses together with two to four electives taken in the spring term. The mandatory courses are contracts, torts, property, criminal law, civil procedure, constitutional law, and a one year research and legal writing course. This latter course is taught by teaching fellows; students take one of their required courses in a small group of 30. The objectives in the first year are to develop analytic ability, familiarity with the entire substantive legal terrain, basic working skills (assembling, organizing, and communicating information), familiarity with legal institutional contexts (litigation, negotiation, and counseling), awareness of the nonlegal environment, and professional ethics. The upperclass curriculum includes 176 courses and seminars, including those offered as electives to first year students.

Stanford promotes professional skills training through simulation, with up to two thirds of the student body participating in these practice courses. A similar proportion serve on one of the school's eight journals: the *Stanford Law Review*, *Stanford Environmental Law Journal*, *Stanford Journal of International Law*, *Stanford Journal of Law, Business and Finance*, *Stanford Journal of Legal Studies*, *Stanford Law and Policy Review*, *Stanford Technology Law Review*, and *Stanford Agora* (online). The school also has a large number of programs: environmental and resources law and policy; international law, business and policy; law, science and technology; and international legal studies. There are several joint degree programs with other departments or schools in the university and even with two other universities, as well as the Gould Center for Conflict Resolution, the Olin Program in Law and Economics, and the Roberts Program in Law, Business, and Corporate Governance.

3. LSU

LSU has a profile typical of a public state university law school, with the unusual difference that it is in a mixed civil law-common law jurisdiction. This difference is reflected in the first year required curriculum, which includes the civil law subjects of obligations, civil law property, and Louisiana civil law system, in addition to the types of courses offered in the other profiled schools: contracts, torts, criminal law, civil procedure, constitutional law, and legal writing and research. Louisiana also requires criminal procedure.

LSU mandates some study during a summer session or a seventh semester. With fewer full time professors than the national law schools, it offers fewer elective courses and seminars (105). In lieu of a clinical program it has an unusually large simulated professional skills enrollment (up to three quarters of the student body). LSU students participate more often in moot court, advocacy, and counseling competitions than do students at the two profiled national schools, but have less opportunity for a law journal experience with the single *Louisiana Law Review*. The tuition cost is low by American standards, but there is a high first year student attrition rate of 25 percent.

4. Willamette

Willamette is a small private regional law school with most of its students from the west coast, who nevertheless represent 22 states. The first year required curriculum includes contracts, torts, property, criminal law, constitutional law, civil procedure, legal research and writing, and dispute resolution. As an experiment one third of the first year students take a merged course, Lawyering Process, which includes the last three courses listed above. This coincides with the school's emphasis on the theme of dispute resolution (with a center and certificate program) to counteract the perceived overemphasis on litigation courses in American legal education.

With fewer professors Willamette offers only 73 elective courses and seminars (although one must remember that the typical student can only enroll in 20 such courses during the second and third years of study). There is a relative emphasis on externships in government offices, since the school is located in the Oregon state capital, and the practice competitions support the dispute resolution program. Willamette's law and government program includes the Oregon Law Commission, created by the state legislature in 1997 to promote law reform. The international and comparative law center supports exchanges in Shanghai, Quito, and Hamburg.

About 11 percent of the students participate on one of the school's three journals: the *Willamette Law Review*, *Willamette Journal of International Law and Dispute Resolution*, and *Willamette Law Online*.

C. *Methods of Instruction*

1. Case method

The case method in legal education began with the publication of Dean Langdell's casebook on contracts and its use at Harvard in 1871. Casebooks used actual appellate cases and arranged them to show scientific principles of law. Langdell argued that these principles transcended local law and could reveal faulty judicial reasoning in a specific instance. The teacher using a casebook became a Socratic guide, who posed questions to students that revealed concepts as essences hidden in appellate opinions. Professors replacing the traditional lecture method with the case or Socratic method required students to truly prepare for class by studying the cases in depth before meeting.

By the 20th century the case method of instruction was the *usus modernus americanus*. By moving from the particular to the general and then the abstract to the concrete, this technique replicates the dialectical common law method itself. Its advantage is that it provides students with an understanding of the evolution of legal doctrine and the capacity to evaluate and compare concrete fact patterns for legal relevance. Its disadvantage is that it is too narrow. Professors ignore economic, political, and social issues and emphasize abstract doctrine. Even after legislation was added to teaching materials, it was obscured by pretending it had no meaning until a judge interpreted it. The case method atomized American law compared to the more systematic study in England of law through textbooks. It is notoriously inefficient in teaching much of the detail of legal doctrine.

Today the remnants of Langdell's innovation can probably better be described as the discussion method. Casebooks include statutes, court rules, regulations, excerpts from journals and books – even from disciplines outside the law – and other legal materials such as contracts or pleadings. The discussion method in its purest question-and-answer form works best for first year students in the mandatory curriculum. As novices in the analytic reasoning of lawyers, they are more willing to prepare for class. For examples of the type of questions asked, *see* Chap. 18, pt. III.

2. Lecture

The traditional lecture method has found new popularity – especially in the upper division curriculum – as professors strive to explain the complexity of contemporary American legal materials or how these materials might best be utilized in a diverse social matrix. New electronic classrooms, wired to the Internet and with computer generated displays, facilitate the visual side of lecturing. Another motivation is to undercut the moral relativism that adheres to the contemporary case or discussion method, by which students learn to find good legal arguments for either side of any case. Students come to believe, as the pragmatism in American law would suggest, that what wins lawsuits is the most sophisticated or instrumental argument, not necessarily what is just. *See* Chap. 1, pt. III. For those professors who hold some *a priori* conceptualist philosophy, such as natural law, law and economics, Marxism, or some variants of feminism or critical race theory, lecturing provides the avenue to try to develop a coherent view among their students regarding American law.

In seminars, with 15 to 20 students, the professor generally will lecture for the initial class meetings until students have settled on topics to use in writing their papers. At the end of the term students typically make a presentation summarizing their papers to the class.

3. Problem method

Some advanced courses and seminars with small enrollment emphasize the solution of current problems. Students study a complex factual situation – for instance, related to the environment, business organizations, estate planning, or human rights violations – and propose solutions using legal rules and institutions. These courses provide a convenient opportunity to combine nonlegal with legal materials. For example, a seminar at Michigan, Globalization and Labor Rights, looks at freedom of association, collective bargaining, employment discrimination, and child labor issues, some in the context of the WTO or NAFTA. It also questions the use of economic sanctions by the United States against countries that violate labor rights, and the effectiveness of corporate codes of human rights practice.

4. Professional skills training (simulation) and clinical methods

Students complained in the 1960s that legal education was too theoretical and did not offer enough practical experience in the law. The issue had been raised since the days when legal apprenticeship first fell into disfavor, but more professors listened this time to the calls for relevance. The Ford Foundation set aside funds to encourage law schools to experiment with clinical studies. Certain bar committees discussed requiring particular practice courses, such as trial advocacy.

Practical education today takes many forms, but can be divided between simulated exercises in the classroom and live experience with real clients in administrative and judicial proceedings. Student performances are sometimes video-taped for subsequent discussion and evaluation. The idea is to replicate the roles and responsibilities of practicing attorneys. Students prepare pleadings, briefs, and motions. They present oral argument. They learn to interview and counsel a client, examine a witness, and negotiate with another lawyer. They draft documents. These exercises may occur in specific simulation or clinical courses or in courses as divergent as real estate transactions or welfare law.

5. Externship

Some law schools permit upperclass students to spend a semester serving as a law clerk for a state or federal judge or working in a governmental agency, public interest law firm, or non-profit organization. Judges or attorneys supervise the students' activities.

D. *Student Activities*

There are a plethora of organizations and activities available to students at a typical law school. In the early 1960s the most prestigious organization was the law review, based on the Harvard model. The review chose student members at the end of their first year on the basis of high grades. Review editors selected articles submitted by law professors and occasionally by judges or lawyers and the staff helped to edit them. The student members themselves wrote case notes or comments. Supporters of student journals saw them as an excellent learning device to supplement the case method of instruction. It is peculiar to law as an academic discipline in America that students control the primary organs of current scholarly communication within the profession. In fact it is unique in the world, where scientists and scholars themselves make decisions about quality, orthodoxy, and innovation.

By the 1970s as a more diverse student body entered law school, the few organizations representing interests such as international law or moot court expanded in number to reflect new concerns. At Stanford today, for example, there are distinct associations for Asians, students with disabilities, bisexual, gay and lesbian (queer) students (OUTLAW), blacks, Jews, Native Americans, parents, Christians, Latinos, and women. Issue organizations exist for Chinese law, entertainment and sports law, environmental law, international law, moot court, business law, prisoners' rights, global challenges, zymurgy (homebrewing and winemaking), street law, law and technology, and public interest law. Political groups support civil liberties, a more diversified faculty, progressive causes (National Lawyers Guild), and conservative causes (Federalist Society). In addition, as detailed in part II.B, the number of student-run law journals has proliferated into specialized fields so that many more students have an opportunity to benefit from journal participation.

Many law students obtain legal work during the summer after their first and second years to help pay the steep costs of education, to obtain practical experience, and to facilitate employment upon graduation. Some students work during the academic year, but the ABA attempts to limit this to 15 hours per week. The employment search has been institutionalized in the past three decades through the school's office of career services. Michigan, for instance, hosts 745 employers each year to interview its students.

E. The Bar Examination

Under the American federal system, admission to and regulation of the legal profession falls to the states. All states except eight require an applicant to graduate from an ABA approved law school (California is the main exception), to satisfy the criteria of an ethics committee, and to pass a written examination of two to three days duration. All but three states use the standardized Multistate Bar Examination as part of this process. Since the remainder of each state's examination process tests for local law, candidates normally pay for a private four to six week cram course on bar subjects. About 75 percent of first-time test takers pass bar examinations nationwide.

To practice in another state a lawyer normally must either take its bar examination or, if she has practiced for five years, apply for admission on motion. About 30 states permit this later option. Bar admission includes the right to litigate in federal courts. In response to the globalization of legal services 23 states permit foreign lawyers to take their bar examination (sometimes also requiring an American LL.M. degree) and thus to become an attorney in that state. New York dominates this trend, passing 977 foreign lawyers (43 percent of their total) in 1999.

III. The Legal Profession

A. A Unified Profession

Admission to a state bar carries with it a license to practice law anywhere within the state and to engage in all types of practice: in a law firm, as an employee of a corporation, or with the government as a prosecutor, judge, or state attorney. There is no distinct judicial or prosecutorial career; there is no division of private practice between barristers and solicitors.

Law graduates in the United States tend to view the legal profession as a single entity, a unified bar. The principal national organization is the ABA, open to any lawyer in good standing in her state. Today the ABA is, on the one hand, a federation of state and local bar associations and other important legal organizations such as the American Law Institute and, on the other hand, a social, educational, and political organization with about half the country's lawyers as members. The ABA's House of Delegates sets ABA policy and elects officers for one year terms. Many educational and social functions are carried out through a large number of sections and committees, such as the International Law and Practice Section, which has over 13,600 members and publishes its own journal, *The International Lawyer*. Since ABA members come from all sectors of the legal profession, its policies and programs have a homogenizing effect. It promulgates a model ethics code that influences state rules, but the ABA itself has no disciplinary power over lawyers.

Table 5 illustrates how the lawyer market prefers privatized lawyering. Most law graduates initially took a job in the private sector, where they typically earned more than the 1998 overall median salary of $45,000. Business paid $50,000 and attorneys who worked in firms with more than 25 lawyers began at over $50,000. It is also apparent that larger law firms have a more expensive clientele and gain efficiency from size, so that those with more than 250 lawyers could pay beginning attorneys – one out of eight of the total – $87,000. Geography also matters. For example, nine percent of the total law jobs were in New York City; employers there paid a median salary of $93,000 in private practice and $66,000 for business. Lawyers in Houston, by comparison, earned $67,000 and $51,200 respectively.

Another factor that acts to unify the profession is the high mobility among the various types of lawyers, which is promoted by two structural circumstances. First, the existence of big law firms, which pay large starting salaries to young graduates, allow the firms to choose which associates they will retain and promote to partner after a six year or so probationary period. Since only about one associate out of three becomes a partner, there is a large pool of experienced attorneys who leave firms, many of whom then work for federal, state, or local governments or for corporations as in-house counsel. Others stay in private practice, either with specialty firms, new firms composed of former associates, or in solo or small firm practice. A second variable that stimulates mobility is the political nature of the appointment or election process for certain attractive government lawyer jobs, including federal judges, state high court judges, and chief prosecutors (U.S. attorney, state attorney general, or local district attorney).

Attorneys after ten or so years experience with an interest in politics will often consider switching careers to enter government or judicial service. There is also a cultural element that emphasizes freedom of movement. *See* Chap. 1, pt. I.A. Many young law graduates will begin their employment as an appointed state trial court judge or as an assistant district attorney to determine whether they enjoy that type of work or to gain experience. After a few years they transfer to the private sector to work as an attorney, usually to earn more money.

Table 5 Employment and Median Starting Salary for the Law School Graduation Class of 1998, by Type[8]

Employment Type	*Percent*	*Median Salary*
Academic[9]	1.4	$38,000
Business	13.8	$50,000
Judicial Clerkship	11.3	$37,500
Government	13.3	$36,000
Public Interest	2.6	$31,000
Private Practice	55.0	$60,000
1-10 Attorneys	19.1	$37,000
11-25 Attorneys	6.6	$43,500
26-50 Attorneys	4.4	$52,000
51-100 Attorneys	4.6	$62,000
101-250 Attorneys	7.7	$72,000
250+ Attorneys	12.6	$87,000
All Types	100.0	$45,000

8. "All Types" includes those employed in a category not listed, 2.6 percent of the total.
9. Includes law school and university administration jobs. Assistant law professors earned a starting salary of about $60,000.

B. The Number and Type of Lawyers

Table 6 Total Lawyers, 1910 to 2000

Year	*Number*	*Women (Percent)*	*Per 100,000 Population*
1910	114,704		124
1930	160,605		161
1950	214,000	3	141
1960	285,933	3	159
1970	349,000	3	171
1980	513,623	8	226
1990	746,000	19	299
1995	815,258	24	310
2000	877,000	28	319

Table 6 sets out the growth of the American legal profession in this century. The greatest expansion began in the late 1960s and paralleled the student enrollment in law schools. Between 1970 and 1990 the profession more than doubled in size. In 1990 there were 299 lawyers per 100,000 population, a 75 percent increase since 1970 in the relative availability of law-trained persons. During the 1990s the decade's growth rate in the relative number of lawyers declined to a much slower seven percent to reach a ratio of 319 per 100,000 population in 2000, but the absolute number of active lawyers still increased by 131,000 although not yet passing the one million mark. It took a generation for the entry of women in law schools to have a significant impact on the profession. Between 1970 and 2000 the percentage of women lawyers rose from three to 28 percent of the total.

The most striking feature in Table 7 below is how little the basic distribution pattern of law work appears to have changed since World War II. While the number of lawyers almost quintupled, the relative shrinkage in private practice was about equally met by the expansion of employment by corporations and non-profit organizations. The ratio of lawyers working in the judiciary, for the other branches of government, or in education stayed about the same. For further information about law professors and judges, *see* pt. II.A (Table 3); Chap. 16, pts. III.A, XI.A. Within the private practice sector, however, there was a dramatic decline in the relative position of sole practitioners from 1951 to 1970 (from 55 to 37 percent of the legal profession) and a shift toward the use of law firms to provide legal services. This shift occurred with the large expansion of employed lawyers within firms (associates) from four to 19 percent of all lawyers in 1991, although that percentage declined in the mid-1990s as the average lawyer was older in the later period. The ageing bar was reflected in more lawyers becoming partners by the end of the century. The organization, consequently, whether a firm or a corporation, has gradually replaced the entrepreneur within the legal profession.

Table 7 Percentage Distribution of Lawyers by Position, 1951 to 1995[10]

	1951	*1970*	*1980*	*1991*	*1995*
Private Practice	81.4	73.2	72.1	76.4	77.8
Sole Practitioner	55.4	36.9	35.3	34.4	36.5
Associate	4.3	7.6	12.4	19.0	13.7
Partner (or Of Counsel)	21.8	28.6	24.4	23.0	27.6
Corporate Counsel (or Executive)	5.4	11.3	11.5	10.0	9.4
Government Lawyer	9.2	11.1	11.4	9.7	9.1
Federal	3.8	5.8	3.9	3.6	3.3
Judge (or Clerk)	3.4	3.2	3.7	2.8	2.7
Law Teacher (or Administrator)	0.6	1.2	1.3	1.1	1.0

The law firm excels in functional specialization for the delivery of private legal services, which accommodates the increased complexity of modern society. The United States, the world's leader in the absolute and relative size of its legal profession and in the number of private practitioners, also leads in taking the law firm to its logical extreme. In 1995 there were 702 firms with 51 or more lawyers and the largest firms had over a thousand attorneys. Firms with more than 50 attorneys employed 105,000 lawyers, although the growth rates in these larger firms stalled in the 1990s. As recently as 1960 American law firms were clearly identified with a particular city. Nowadays large law firms operate on a national and increasingly an international basis with branch and affiliate firms. In 1995 77 percent of the firms with over 100 attorneys had multistate or global branches. In the mid-1990s the largest 100 firms generated fees in the United States over $15 billion, about ten percent of which came from foreign clients.

American law firms come in all sizes; attorneys in private practice are a very heterogeneous group. In urban centers one likely will find large firms (representing major corporations, banks, and governments), specialty firms (handling matters such as patent applications, labor relations, or white-collar criminal

10. *See* Clara N. Carson, *The Lawyer Statistical Report: The U.S. Legal Profession in 1995* 1-2, 6-9, 14 (1999); David S. Clark, "The Legal Profession in Comparative Perspective: Growth and Specialization," 30 *Am. J. Comp. L.* 163, 169-72 (Supp. 1982). The percentages exclude retired and inactive lawyers, which are also excluded in Table 6 (and constituted about three percent in 1950, four percent in 1960, and five percent in the other years).

defense), small firms (with a general practice based on probate, real estate, and small business matters), and solo practitioners either waiting for the personal injury client or divorce case to walk into the office or more aggressively seeking business at the criminal court. In rural areas private practice is basically one of small firms and solo practitioners carrying on a general practice of whatever the community demands.

Some lawyers and organizations have established legal clinics to process routine matters relying on standard forms and extensive use of non-lawyer paralegals. Since the U.S. Supreme Court ruled that bar association minimum fee schedules violate federal antitrust law and bans on advertising violate the Constitution's First Amendment freedom of speech, clinics have advertised widely and competed vigorously by setting low prices. Some clinics have established chain operations with 100 offices in several states. In the 1990s there were over 1,000 clinics, which concentrate on wills, bankruptcy, divorces, and traffic offenses. Finally, public interest lawyers litigate to promote certain causes, such as protection of the environment (Sierra Club Legal Defense Fund) or promotion of individual liberties (American Civil Liberties Union).

To fully appreciate the distinctive American distribution of lawyers, it is instructive to compare it to that of Germany. In the United States the legal profession as a whole is more highly privatized than in Germany. Only 13 percent of the profession in the U.S. serves as judges or works as government lawyers compared to 42 percent in Germany. The ratio of judges to attorneys in the two countries also shows the much greater role in Germany that judges play to make the procedural system function properly: one judge for 3.4 attorneys in Germany compared to 27.3 attorneys in the United States.

Table 8 Lawyers in Germany and the United States, by Type, 1990s[11]

	Germany		*United States*	
	Number	*Percent*	*Number*	*Percent*
Attorneys (& Notaries)	75,900	41	587,300	76
Corporate Lawyers	30,000	16	76,900	10
Judges	22,100	12	21,500	3
Government Lawyers	55,400	30	75,000	10
Law Teachers	2,100	1	8,200	1
Total	185,500		768,900	

11. David S. Clark, "Comparing the Work and Organization of Lawyers Worldwide: The Persistence of Legal Traditions," in *Lawyers' Practice and Ideals: A Comparative View* 9, 69-70, 100-05 (John Barceló III & Roger Cramton eds. 1999); *see* id., "The Selection and Accountability of Judges in West Germany: Implementation of a Rechtsstaat," 61 *S. Cal. L Rev.* 1795, 1806-08 (1988). German notaries are fully trained lawyers and are included; retired and inactive lawyers are excluded.

Several factors account for the existence of a large private practice sector in the United States, which is also the situation in other common law countries. One, the emphasis in sources of law on judge-made rules leads to a proliferation of legal materials that makes resolution of legal issues complex and time consuming. *See* Chap. 3. In civil law nations, by contrast, codes and scholarly treatises are more efficient organizing tools for quick solution of most legal problems. Two, the common law system of procedure puts a heavy burden on attorneys to discover the facts in a case and even to brief the complicated legal issues for the judge. *See* Chap. 16, pts. II, VI. Civil law countries, alternatively, staff the judiciary and prosecutor offices more fully so that the ratio of judges to attorneys is much higher. In this sense, common law countries have a more privatized judicial procedure. Three, many common law nations are federal in political structure, further complicating legal analysis and stimulating demand for more attorneys. *See* Chap. 1, pt. II.

SELECTED BIBLIOGRAPHY

Richard L. Abel, *American Lawyers* (1989).
J.M. Balkin & Sanford Levinson, *Legal Canons* (2000).
Clara N. Carson, *The Lawyer Statistical Report: The U.S. Legal Profession in 1995* (1999).
Virginia G. Drachman, *Sisters in Law: Women Lawyers in Modern American History* (1998).
Lawrence M. Friedman, *A History of American Law* (2d ed. 1985).
— & Harry N. Scheiber, eds., *Legal Culture and the Legal Profession* (1996).
Donald B. King, ed., *Legal Education for the 21st Century* (1999).
Anthony T. Kronman, *The Lost Lawyer: Failing Ideals of the Legal Profession* (1993).
William P. LaPiana, *Logic and Experience: The Origin of Modern American Legal Education* (1994).
Law School Admission Council, *The Official Guide to U.S. Law Schools* (2000).
Sol M. Linowitz, *The Betrayed Profession: Lawyering at the End of the Twentieth Century* (1994).
Rick L. Morgan & Kurt Snyder, eds., *Official American Bar Association Guide to Approved Law Schools: 2001 Edition* (2000).
Robert L. Nelson, David M. Trubek & Rayman L. Solomon, eds., *Lawyers' Ideals/Lawyers' Practices: Transformations in the American Legal Profession* (1992).
Steve Sheppard, ed., 1-2 *The History of Legal Education in the United States: Commentaries and Primary Sources* (1999).
Roy D. Simon & Murray L. Schwartz, *Lawyers and the Legal Profession: Cases and Materials* (3d ed. 1994).
Robert Stevens, *Law School: Legal Education in America from the 1850s to the 1980s* (1983).

Chapter 3
The Sources of Law

David S. Clark[*]

I. Formalism and Realism

"The law is what an authoritative decision maker says the law is." This statement supports two distinct perspectives about the sources of law, both of which are widely held in America. Each perspective, however, presupposes a very different way of thinking about legal rules.

* Maynard and Bertha Wilson Professor of Law, Willamette University College of Law; Vice President, American Society of Comparative Law.

David S. Clark and Tuğrul Ansay (eds.) Introduction to the Law of the United States, 35-52

First, a formalist would construct a hierarchy of the sources of law that might resemble the list in Figure 1.

Figure 1 Hierarchy of the Sources of Law in Oregon

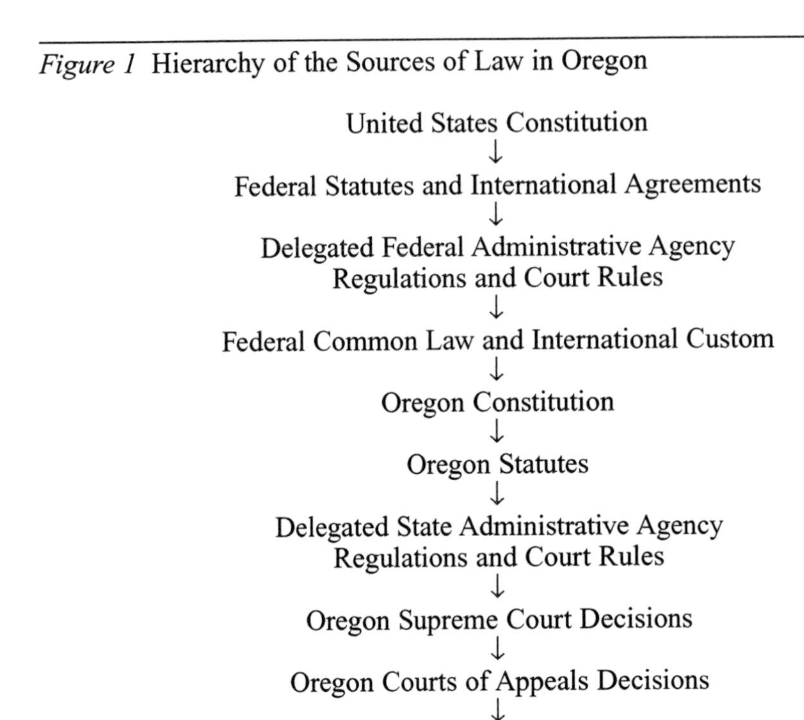

Each state, as the basic lawmaking political unit, has its own hierarchy that acquiesces only to superior federal law and in turn considers sister state common law as persuasive if no higher norm exists to resolve a legal question. The advantage of conceptualizing a hierarchical framework of legal norms is that it facilitates identification of *who* is the authoritative decision maker and, with the maxim that the superior controls the inferior, resolves conflicts between contradictory norms on different levels. The interplay between levels within the hierarchy of sources of law, however, is complicated by a variety of factors considered elsewhere. *See*, e.g., Chap, 4, pt. IV.B.4 (treaties and executive agreements); Chap. 11, pt. II (family law); Chap. 13, pt. I (commercial law); Chap 17, pt. III (choice of law).

Who is the authoritative speaker regarding the *meaning* of a legal norm? To a formalist the answer is straightforward. The framers in 1787 authoritatively determined what the provisions of the U.S. Constitution should mean. They used particular language, which they juxtaposed into a coherent, structured document. In addition, they left us further information from their debates and from contemporaneous writings. In the same manner the members of Congress authoritatively determine what federal statutes should mean and agency bureaucrats determine the meaning of regulations. The primary mechanism to communicate meaning in the law, of course, is language. It is only when we reach the level of federal common law that courts take on responsibility as the authoritative decision makers in providing legal norms with their meaning. This same analysis applies for the various levels of state legal norms.

The formalist position is the dominant one among those countries that belong to the civil law tradition. In the United States most lay persons would also subscribe to this perspective: it certainly makes sense and seems legitimate to give the makers of legal norms the power to determine what those norms should mean. Furthermore, constitutional framers, legislators, and administrators must believe that they are giving meaning to the norms they create. However, in law schools and among lawyers and judges this view is held by only a minority.

The dominant perspective among law-trained persons is one of realism. The realist looks at Figure 1 and sees the numerous levels of legal norms, but asks what happens if a citizen disagrees with the manner in which a norm is applied against him. In this situation the citizen can petition a judge for relief – money damages or an injunction, for example – that will validate the *judge's* interpretation of the norm. Since courts have plenary jurisdiction over all types of governmental acts and officials – police, administrators, legislators, and judges – it is what a judge says the law means that ultimately matters. It is precisely this problem that led the French to remove judicial review of administrative and legislative acts from the jurisdiction of ordinary courts and to prohibit judges from making a general ruling interpreting the law in a specific case. Chief Justice John Marshall, however, early on concluded in *Marbury v. Madison*,[1] that the role of a court is to determine what the law is, including constitutional law, in order to decide cases properly before it. *See* Chap. 4, pt. III.A. Judicial interpretation thus prevails over the interpretation of the police or other public officials. In this view the appellate case becomes the most important source of law. *See* Chap. 18, pt. I.

The range of realism in American law depends on the degree of one's skepticism about the instrument of language as a mode of communication and on one's belief about the general quality of judges and their willingness to purposely subvert the obvious meaning of a text to accomplish some political aim. Thus a conservative realist believes that most judges are sufficiently competent and non-political to use the accepted methods of legal reasoning to preserve the core meaning intended for a legal text. Only a small percentage of legal questions – though sometimes important ones – activate the linguistic periphery of a rule and cannot be answered by the methods of legal reasoning. At the other extreme are radical realists – some postmodernists and members of various critical groups – who believe that judges are essentially political actors who explicitly or unconsciously base their interpretations of law and decision on their own policy preferences and ethical values. Most judges, after all, are elected. They can accomplish this political activity under the guise of law since all language is indeterminate. There are no easy legal questions; there is only legal argument.

1. 5 U.S. 137 (1803).

II. The Doctrine of *Stare Decisis*

A legal realist, to solve a problem involving the U.S. Constitution or the Uniform Commercial Code, would first search for an appellate judicial decision that interprets the provision in question. This approach is analogous to the one that would be used to solve a common law tort issue. Upon finding a decision, or many decisions made over a number of years, the doctrine of *stare decisis* (precedent) becomes important. *Stare decisis* dictates that like cases should be decided today the same way they were decided in the past. The doctrine makes use of a short statement from an earlier judicial opinion known as the *ratio decidendi* or holding of the case, which is the narrow rule necessary to resolve the dispute that emerged from a specific fact situation. All the remaining language in the opinion is referred to as (mere) *dicta*, which carries less weight in legal argument. One may contrast a *ratio decidendi* to a legal principle, which emerges from a line of decisions as a broader norm pregnant with reasons for those decisions; it therefore carries greater weight in legal argument.

Stare decisis affects three types of courts. First, all lower courts in a jurisdiction are bound to follow the holding declared by a higher court. Second, the high court is expected to follow its own precedents. The high court may avoid a previous holding by determining that the facts in an instant case are sufficiently dissimilar from an earlier case that the precedent may be distinguished. Or the high court may overrule a precedent, since the American judiciary does not follow a rigid view of *stare decisis*, and justify in its opinion why a new rule is necessary. *See* Chap. 18, pt. III. Third, courts in other jurisdictions may use a precedent as persuasive authority in fashioning a rule for their systems, which among the American states might become a majority or minority rule.

The power of precedent as a source of law depends on how broadly or narrowly courts construe the holdings of earlier cases. The doctrine furthers three goals more generally related to the process of adjudication. First, fairness requires that like cases be treated alike. A judge's written justification explaining why he failed to follow an apparently applicable precedent makes it harder to base decisions on arbitrary or impermissible criteria. Second, *stare decisis* enhances the predictability of law, which enables people to plan their lives and reduce the risks of becoming involved in litigation. Third, the doctrine improves judicial decision making by permitting judges to more efficiently resolve cases without reconsidering legal issues already decided and to create an aura of similarity among themselves that enhances the judiciary's credibility.

It is possible that the whole concept of *stare decisis* today may be in decline. This results from the computerization of the bulk of American case law, which has eliminated a natural restraint on the proliferation of available judicial opinions. Networks of computers, located in Ohio or Minnesota and accessed through fee-based telecommunications systems or Web sites, overwhelm the law with sheer masses of data. These systems have an unlimited storage capacity and an enormous ability to find things: cases, concepts, phrases, and words. Lawyers have become used to the rapid manipulation of facts and rules. They make ever more arguments to the judge, who must select from the blizzard of options. In this environment the fairness, predictability, and improved decision making behind *stare decisis* become an illusion.

III. JUDICIAL DECISIONS

A. In General

The first American court reports were published in 1789. In the early decades of the republic private reporters compiled the decisions (often from their own notes), summarized oral arguments, and sometimes added analysis. To bring more order to federal and state reporting official publication was required, but government appointment of reporters proceeded slowly in the 19th century. In 1876 John West in Minnesota began a private reporting system that by the end of the decade spread beyond Minnesota decisions to group cases from several states in a regional reporter. By the 1880s seven regional reporters constituted a national system, which became so effective in speed and accuracy that over one third of the states today have discontinued their official court reports. West added to most cases numbered headnotes, which indicated a particular subdivision of a legal topic, summarizing the court's discussion of legal points (beyond just the holding). This key number scheme became an important mechanism for lawyers to find a case on point. By 1910 there were about 8,200 volumes, private and official, of American case law.

The major innovation in case reporting in the 20th century was the introduction of computerized legal research systems in the 1970s by two competing commercial entities. Today both West Group's Westlaw and LexisNexis Group's LexisNexis store the full text of judicial opinions (with West adding headnotes) in computer networks. Lawyers access this information with a personal computer and modem hooked to a telephone line, through a dedicated terminal, or since 2000 with hand-held wireless devices communicating through an Internet site. *See* pt. III.D.3. Today the accumulated number of published and public record judicial decisions stands at approximately 5.2 million, with about 100,000 cases added annually.

In the 1990s another important development structured the delivery of legal information. Traditional American legal publishers were caught up in the publishing industry's global merger activity, so that at the beginning of the 21st century three giant media empires control most legal publishing. Thomson (Canadian) is the parent company of West Group, which itself controls Bancroft-Whitney, Clark Boardman Callaghan, and Lawyers Co-operative Publishing. In 2001 West Group purchased FindLaw, a major Internet portal to public domain primary legal materials. Reed Elsevier (English-Dutch) is the parent company of LexisNexis Group, which includes Michie, Matthew Bender, Shepard's, and Martindale-Hubbell. It is ironic that the principal access to American primary legal materials is controlled by foreign companies. The third empire, Wolters Kluwer (Dutch), owns Aspen Publishers and CCH Incorporated, but has little involvement with publishing court cases and statutes.

B. Federal Court Decisions

The decisions of the U.S. Supreme Court are published in five competing series: (1) *United States Reports* (the official edition), which appears about three years after a decision is announced; (2) West's *Supreme Court Reporter*, which issues a paperback advance sheet within a few weeks after decision and annually binds them in a volume (today with supplements A and B); (3) *United States Supreme Court Reports, Lawyers' Edition* (published earlier by Lawyers Co-op, but now by LexisNexis), first appearing in advance sheets with summaries of cases and headnotes; (4) *United States Law Week* (published by the Bureau of National Affairs), which is mailed weekly and maintained in a looseleaf binder; and (5) *United States Supreme Court Bulletin* (published by Commerce Clearing House), also appearing weekly. Westlaw and LexisNexis make Supreme Court opinions available within hours after they are handed down. In addition, Supreme Court decisions are available on two electronic databases, CD-ROM, and the Internet.

West Group prints lower federal court decisions. The *Federal Reporter*, which began in 1880, today carries court of appeals opinions. The judge who writes an opinion decides whether it will be published and about half are. The *Federal Supplement*, started in 1932, publishes about ten per cent of district court opinions. Nevertheless, in 2000 90 new volumes were added to the two reporter series. West has tried to slow the expansion of these two series by publishing specialized cases in topical reporters, such as *Federal Rules Decisions* (created in 1940 for opinions about the Federal Rules of Civil Procedure or the Federal Rules of Criminal Procedure) or the *Bankruptcy Reporter* (beginning in 1980).[2]

Other publishers, now often part of Thomson or Reed Elsevier, provide looseleaf services or bound volumes in narrow subject areas. For instance, Commerce Clearing House publishes *Copyright Law Decisions*, *U.S. Tax Cases*, and *Labor Cases*. Bureau of National Affairs publishes *International Trade Reporter Decisions* and *Environmental Reporter Cases*. And Clark Boardman Callaghan publishes *Federal Rules Service* and *Federal Rules of Evidence Service*.

C. *State Court Decisions*

Official reports of appellate court decisions are published in fewer than half the states, and the number maintaining this governmental service is declining. The primary reason for the decline is the existence of West Group, which by the end of the 19th century as West Publishing Co. had developed its national reporter system that included seven regional reporters: Atlantic, North Eastern, South Eastern, Southern, North Western, South Western, and Pacific. These reporters each include the opinions of several adjacent states. In 1888 West established a separate reporter, the *New York Supplement*, for the numerous intermediate appellate decisions in New York. Along with the *North Eastern Reporter*, it also included cases from New York's high court, the Court of Appeals. The same pattern was followed with the

2. West also has created specialized reporters for new courts, such as the *United States Claims Court Reporter* and the *Veterans Appeals Reporter*, and in particular fields for which it reprints its federal and state cases, such as *West's Education Law Reporter* and *West's Social Security Reporting Service*.

creation of the *California Reporter* in 1960.[3] All of West's reporters follow a systematic format. West's staff prepares for each case a synopsis and headnotes. They then arrange these headnotes by subject (topic and key number) in digests, which are useful in researching American case law. *See* pt. III.D.1.

The online database systems Westlaw and LexisNexis, with their retrospective entry of old cases, are today comprehensive sources for state court decisions. Certain topical reporters (bound, looseleaf, or CD-ROM) contain state as well as federal cases.[4] Each of the 50 states now has its case law available on searchable compact discs, which are a less expensive alternative for small law firms than fee-based online databases. More and more states are also posting their decisions on Web sites, which will permit Internet-based companies to inexpensively develop online or CD-ROM databases useful to the legal community.

To stem the flood of case law, some states have established programs of limited issuance to control the publication of decisions that have little or no precedential value. In a few states unpublished opinions are nevertheless published (often by the online databases), and lawyers use them in their research. Some state supreme courts have adopted depublication or decertification programs, which reduce the number of erroneous or unnecessary intermediate appellate court opinions. These initiatives are controversial with the practicing bar.

D. *Finding the Precedent: Digests, Annotated Reports, and Computerized Research*

1. Digests

By the end of the 19th century West Publishing Co. realized that lawyers needed a mechanism to locate by subject the points of law stated in their chronologically arranged case reporters. West thus developed its own classification system within which to place headnotes extracted from each reported case. The West system divides all legal circumstances into seven principal areas: persons, property, contracts, torts, crimes, remedies, and government. These areas today are alphabetically subdivided into 450 topics, such as abortion and birth control, bonds, or cemeteries. Each topic then has anywhere from a few to thousands of key numbers, so that every conceivable legal situation can be covered.

West commenced its American digest system with the 50 volume publication in 1897 of abstracts from all reported cases decided between 1658 and 1896. Known as the *Century Digest*, it paralleled symbolically the Emperor Justinian's 50 book *Digesta*, which had synthesized the best juristic opinions of classical

3. For a list of research guides and bibliographies to each state's primary and secondary legal sources, *see* Robert C. Berring & Elizabeth A. Edinger, *Finding the Law* 369-73 (11th ed. 1999). The coverage of West Group's regional and state reporters is in Morris L. Cohen & Kent C. Olsen, *Legal Research in a Nutshell* 371-93 (7th ed. 2000).
4. A list of topical looseleaf and CD-ROM services, by subject, is in Cohen & Olsen, supra note 3, at 400-11.

Rome. West's key number system was initially used by the modern American glossators in the 25 volume *First Decennial Digest*, which ordered headnotes (digest paragraphs) under the alphabetical topics and key numbers from cases included in the national reporter system (federal and state) from 1897 to 1906. Subsequent *Decennials*, each covering a ten-year period, followed the *First Decennial* (which had used 44,000 key numbers). By the *Eighth Decennial* headnotes from 1966 to 1976 filled 50 volumes, so the editors decided to commence issuing five-year cumulations. Even so the number of reported cases has grown sufficiently so that the *Tenth Decennial Digest, Part 2* (spanning 1991-1996) required 64 volumes. This is supplemented by the *General Digest*, which is now in its ninth series.

In addition to the comprehensive American digest system, West publishes separate digests of headnotes from the U.S. Supreme Court, from all federal courts, and from certain specialized federal courts. West also publishes four sets of regional digests and separate digests for 47 states and the District of Columbia.

2. Annotated reports

An alternative to the American digest system – in which West published all authorized judicial decisions, extracted the points of law, and filed the headnotes within a pre-existing analytic framework – was based on the notion that only a few of the numerous opinions written each year were of interest to most lawyers. Publishers competing with West at the end of the 19th century selected leading cases for publication, which dealt with new legal issues or changed the law, and added commentaries or annotations that described similar cases.

Selective case publication succumbed to West's comprehensive reporting, but the feature of annotations as a valuable research tool survived. Lawyers Co-operative Publishing Co. (and its related company, Bancroft-Whitney) began publication in 1919 of the *American Law Reports* (*ALR*). An *ALR* volume today consists of about 20 judicial opinions mixed with annotations. These annotations are in essence legal memoranda that discuss related aspects of the law and consider all sides of each issue in the context of summarizing the facts and holdings of all relevant reported cases the editor could find. If West's jurists are modern day American glossators, Lawyers Co-op tried to push its editors into the next level of juristic evolution as commentators. Today they are on the same team since West Group purchased Lawyers Co-op in 1997. Lawyers using *ALR* compare their own cases with the abstracted fact situations discussed in an annotation, which may vary in length from a few pages to several hundred pages. Each annotation is updated annually with references to new cases on the topic, so that old *ALR* volumes continue to be useful.

The first two *ALR* series included discussion of both federal and state cases, but the expansion of federal litigation led to the introduction of *ALR Federal* in 1969. *ALR 5th*, the current series, began in 1992 and covers general and state legal issues. The five general series and the federal series up to 2000 consist of a 715 volume library.

3. Computerized research

Both LexisNexis and Westlaw contain the full text of federal and state court opinions. *See* pt. III.A. They have revolutionized the way law students and now lawyers and judges think about finding judicial precedent, but at a price that many sole practitioners and small law firms cannot afford. Older methods of research have not been eliminated, but supplemented. Westlaw includes on its database the equivalent of the American digest system, so that lawyers can use a key number to find precedents. LexisNexis includes the Lawyers Co-op Auto-Cite, which permits a lawyer to find all supplementing or superseding annotations within the *ALR* system by typing in a citation. It also incorporates Shepard's prior and subsequent case history and citing references.

What is new about computerized research is the ability to automatically search a database of cases for particular words or phrases or adjacent combinations of words or phrases. This increases the odds of finding the needle in a haystack, but also of finding several hundred needles. Innovative strategies also now become possible. By searching document fields or segments, a lawyer can find all opinions written by a certain judge, cases involving a specific corporation, or cases handled by a particular attorney.

West, LexisNexis, and other publishers, furthermore, have issued compact disc (CD-ROM) databases, which usually are cheaper than online access since they do not require a modem or dedicated telephone line to a remote computer. Most personal computers, including portable notebook computers, have drives to read CDs. One disc holds about 150,000 printed pages. Publishers market CD-ROMs with primary legal materials for particular jurisdictions or subject matter areas as well as secondary treatises and looseleaf services. They increasingly charge monthly subscription fees for updates and supplemental fees for additional users.

The Internet contains an increasing amount of legal information, including cases and statutes. Many courts now provide access to their new opinions within hours or days of their decisions. FindLaw <www.findlaw.com> is a Web site directory to these public domain legal materials.

IV. Other Primary Sources

Most primary source materials have now been entered on the Westlaw and LexisNexis databases and are available on their Internet Web pages.

A. Constitutions

1. United States Constitution

The U.S. Constitution defines its own primacy at the apex of American sources of law.[5] Since its words so seldom resolve a legal issue, decision makers often

5. Art. VI.

search out what the framers intended their words to mean. The Philadelphia Constitutional Convention in 1787 did not create an official record of its proceedings, but James Madison and other delegates kept extensive notes.[6] Debates at state conventions, which ratified the Constitution, are also available.[7] Finally, *The Federalist*, with essays by James Madison, John Jay, and Alexander Hamilton supporting the Constitution's adoption, is considered an essential source of contemporaneous opinion.

Annotated editions of the Constitution set forth each clause followed by digests of judicial decisions that have interpreted the clause. Some editions also include commentary. West publishes a ten volume *Constitution of the United States Annotated* as part of its *United States Code Annotated* series. LexisNexis (Lawyers Co-op previously) publishes a similar four volume *United States Code Service, Constitution Volumes*. The Library of Congress prepared the eighth edition of *The Constitution of the United States of America* in 1987, which adds extensive commentary, historical background, and summaries of case law.

2. State constitutions

Each of the 50 states has its own constitution, supreme within its jurisdiction when not inconsistent with federal law. Many states have adopted several constitutions or amended them more frequently than is the case with the U.S. Constitution. The most common source for these constitutions along with judicial headnotes is each state's annotated series of statutes or codes.

B. Federal Legislation

The U.S. Congress meets in two-year periods to coincide with the terms of representatives; the First Congress met from 1789 to 1791 and the 107th Congress met from 2001 to 2003. When a bill becomes law because it has passed both houses of Congress and the president has signed it (or has not vetoed it within ten days), the law is sent to the archivist who classifies it as a private law or a public law. The former benefit only a specific individual or individuals and primarily concern claims against the government or immigration and naturalization matters. All other laws are public laws and are numbered sequentially through the term of the Congress: for example, Pub. L. No. 107-1. At the term's end all these laws are published in numerical order in a set know as *United States Statutes at Large*.

Just as the chronological publication of judicial decisions hinders the search for precedent, the numerical publication of federal laws interferes with the effi-

6. Max Farrand, 1-3 *The Records of the Federal Convention of 1787* (1911, Supp. 1987); Philip B. Kurland & Ralph Lerner, 1-5 *The Founders' Constitution* (1987).
7. Merrill Jensen, 1-15 *Documentary History of the Ratification of the Constitution* (Jensen et al. eds. 1976-2001).

cient search for statutory provisions on a particular subject. Congress first attempted to improve this situation with a compilation called the *Revised Statutes of 1875*. This initial effort was improved in the 1926 publication of the *United States Code*, which arranged all public laws still in force under 50 titles. These titles today are mostly in alphabetical order; they include topics such as aliens and nationality or judiciary and judicial procedure. The *U.S. Code* is reissued in a new edition every six years with annual supplements. The 1994 edition has 35 volumes plus annual supplement volumes.

Since the government is slow to publish *U.S. Code* supplements, and lawyers want to see judicial interpretation of statutes once they are available, two annotated editions are privately marketed. West commenced the *United States Code Annotated* in 1927, which includes abstracts of relevant court decisions and references to secondary sources. The notes following each code section refer to other West publications and to its topic and key number system to locate analogous cases. The set in 2001 consists of more than 200 volumes. LexisNexis (and formerly Lawyers Co-Op) publishes a similar product known as *United States Code Service*, cross referencing annotations in *ALR*.

To ascertain Congress's intent for a statutory provision, one can investigate the legislative documents that led to the original enactment along with subsequent amendments. These documents may include a bill's numerous versions, House and Senate committee reports, or floor debate transcripts (reported in the *Congressional Record*). Some public laws already have compiled legislative histories.[8] Frequently, however, a lawyer must construct her own history using a commercial looseleaf service such as *Congressional Index*, which Commerce Clearing House began publishing in 1937, the Congressional Information Service's *CIS/Index*, published since 1970, or West's *United States Code Congressional and Administrative News*, published since 1941.

Online databases have improved one's ability to research legislative history, including the electronic version of *CIS/Index* and specialized databases in Westlaw and LexisNexis. The Library of Congress maintains a Web site, Thomas <www.thomas.loc.gov>, with the full text of bills and the tools to track their progress.

C. *International Law*

1. Treaties and executive agreements

The U.S. Constitution, in article II, provides that the president "shall have Power, by and with the advice and consent of the Senate to make Treaties, provided two thirds of the Senators present concur." Article VI then states that these treaties (together with federal statutes) "shall be the supreme Law of the Land," which means that at a minimum treaties prevail over inconsistent state law. American constitutional practice today also permits the president to conclude international

8. *See* Nancy Johnson, *Sources of Compiled Legislative Histories* (1988-2000).

agreements on the basis of congressional authorization, his independent article II constitutional authority to conduct foreign relations, or prior authorization in an earlier treaty. These international instruments are collectively known as executive agreements and carry the same force of law as treaties.

In the 21st century the United States is a party to over 14,000 international agreements. From the beginning of the Republic until 1900, treaties outnumbered executive agreements three to one. But from 1900 to 1980, treaties represented only 13 percent of the total number of American international agreements. Since then treaties have been used to commit the United States legally for only about five percent of its international agreements, although over 90 percent of *executive* agreements have been authorized by Congress. American courts are bound to give effect to international agreements unless they are non-self-executing, in which case implementing legislation is necessary.

American international agreements since 1950 are contained in *United States Treaties and Other International Agreements* (*UST*), but are published sooner in *Treaties and Other International Acts Series* (*TIAS*). Since even *TIAS* is slow to publish, two commercial services since 1990 keep the international lawyer up to date: *UST Current Service* (Hein) and *Consolidated Treaties & International Agreements: Current Document Service* (Oceana). *International Legal Materials*, published bimonthly by the American Society of International law, contains many of the most important agreements. The principal historical source for these materials is the 13 volume *Bevans' Treaties and Other International Agreements of the United States of American 1776-1949* (1968-1975).

2. Customary international law

Customary international law, what the U.S. Constitution refers to as the "law of nations," consists of obligations inferred from the general practice of nations followed from a sense of legal obligation (*opinio juris*). The objective practice and subjective sense of legal obligation can be found in diplomatic correspondence, official government statements and acts, court decisions, and scholarly writing. Contemporary United States practice relating to international law is summarized quarterly in the *American Journal of International Law*. Relevant documents are often reprinted in the bimonthly *International Legal Materials*. The Department of State publishes a series called *Digest of United States Practice in International law*, which updates the 15 volume *Digest of International Law* (1963-1973) that M.M. Whiteman compiled to cover the period 1940 to 1973. Earlier editions by John Bassett Moore and G.H. Hackworth covered the periods 1776 to 1906 and 1906 to 1939 respectively.

The domestic legal effect of international custom in the United States is hotly debated, particularly as it relates to human rights law. Most scholars and the few court cases treating the question relegate custom to the subordinate status of federal common law, lower in the sources of law hierarchy than international agreements or federal statutes, and even lower than administrative regulations.

D. State and Local Legislation

State legislatures, which meet in annual, biennial, or special sessions, enact and generally publish statutes in a manner similar to that of the federal government. Since the states publish their session laws in chronological order, they must be rearranged by subject in compilations to be useful for legal research.

Each state has at least one annotated code, usually published in bound volumes with annual pocket-part supplements. West publishes codes for more than 20 states, providing references to key numbers, and since purchasing Lawyers Co-op, references to its *ALR* annotations. LexisNexis Group publishes codes for fewer states, with references to other publishers' research aids. Westlaw and LexisNexis databases have greatly improved research into a single state's legislation and especially comparative research. Comprehensive comparative research on the particular laws of many states is still difficult, but there are a few guides.[9]

State legislatures generally do not publish their debates or committee reports, so the compilation of a legislative history to aid in the interpretation of a statute is difficult or impossible. A few states do provide reports from law revision commissions or from selected special committees dealing with important statutory reforms.[10]

Local legislative authority, which stems from a state constitution or is delegated by a state legislature, is carried out by counties, cities, or other local political units. It is significant in the areas of taxation, zoning and environmental control, education, housing, social welfare, and municipal services. A municipality operates under a charter – its basic law – and enacts ordinances, which are only sometimes published and are inadequately indexed. Research is complicated and lawyers must often seek the assistance of the county or city clerk or a local public library.

E. Court Rules

The judiciary itself generally promulgates court rules dealing with procedural issues under the authority of a constitutional or statutory provision, although for some matters courts have their own inherent authority.

The U.S. Supreme Court, for instance, has congressional authority to issue rules of criminal and civil procedure for courts of appeals and district courts. The major sets of national rules (with the date they first went into effect) include: (1) the Federal Rules of Appellate Procedure (1968); (2) the Federal Rules of Civil Procedure (1938); (3) the Federal Rules of Criminal Procedure (1946); and (4) the Federal Rules of Evidence (1975). The texts for these rules are located in

9. *See* Lynn Foster & Carol Boast, *Subject Compilations of State Laws* (1981), with supplements by Cheryl R. Nyberg & Carol Boast (1984) and Cherly R. Nyberg (1986, 1989, 1991-2001).
10. *See* M.L. Fisher, *Guide to State Legislative and Administrative Materials* (4th ed. 1988); Berring & Edinger, supra note 3, at 369-73.

appendices to title 18 and title 28 of the *United States Code*. Each rule (and each subsequent amendment) is followed by Advisory Committee notes, which serve as a kind of legislative history.

Federal cases interpreting these rules are reported by West in *Federal Rules Decisions* (since 1940) and by Callaghan & Co. (now part of West Group) in *Federal Rules Service* (since 1939). The annotated versions of the *U.S. Code* by West and LexisNexis carry case abstracts ordered by rule number. *See* pt. IV.B.

The Supreme Court and specialized federal courts, such as the Tax Court, Claims Court, or Court of International Trade, have their own rules. The Supreme Court has also issued rules specifically for bankruptcy proceedings. Finally, each federal court of appeals and district court may establish supplementary rules for local practice. The *U.S. Code* and its two annotated versions contain all the national court rules, while *Federal Rules Service* publishes local court rules.

State court rules vary significantly in their content as well as their publication treatment. Increasingly, however, they are published along with state statutes and are incorporated within annotated versions. *See* pt. IV.D.

F. *Administrative Regulations and Decisions*

At the federal level most administrative rules and regulations are authorized by congressional delegation. The president, however, also has direct constitutional power to issue some executive orders and proclamations, but even these normally are authorized by Congress. A presidential executive order may further delegate rule-making authority to an administrative agency. This source of law has dramatically expanded in importance to parallel the general growth of the federal executive branch during the past 60 years.

Prior to 1936 federal agencies were not required to make their regulations available to the public. This changed in 1936 with the creation of the official *Federal Register*, which contains in chronological order every regulation of general applicability issued by the president or an administrative agency. Congress then provided for a compilation of these regulations under 50 titles or subjects in the *Code of Federal Regulations* (*CFR*), which began publication in 1939. Since 1968 the *CFR* has been reissued annually, with each title divided into chapters (for separate agencies), subchapters, parts (for different topics), and sections. Title 3, for example, contains presidential proclamations and orders. Frequent recompilation is necessary since the *Federal Register* typically requires 70,000 pages annually. The current *CFR* comprises over 200 volumes.

Many federal agencies also perform a quasi-judicial function by resolving individual disputes involving their regulations. The Administrative Procedure Act (1946) strengthened procedural safeguards and provided a framework for judicial review of agency decisions. Most agencies that adjudicate write formal opinions to justify their decisions, which are frequently published and used by attorneys practicing before an agency. *See* Chap. 5, pt. III.A, C.

About 25 agencies – for instance, the National Labor Relations Board and the Federal Trade Commission – publish official reports of their decisions in a wide variety of forms, such as pamphlets, paperback volumes, microform, or CD-

ROM. In addition, commercial publishers print some of these reports and those of other agencies in bound volumes or in looseleaf editions, normally with superior research aids, and more recently they can be found on Westlaw and LexisNexis.[11]

The availability and organization of state administrative regulations has improved markedly since the 1960s, when only 14 states published administrative compilations by subject. Today 40 states and the District of Columbia publish administrative codes; in the seven states with neither code nor register a lawyer must contact an agency directly to obtain a specific regulation. Most states publish some agency adjudicatory decisions, usually dealing with taxation, utilities, banking, insurance, or labor. Increasingly Westlaw and LexisNexis have added state regulations and decisions to their electronic databases.

V. Secondary Sources

A. Restatements of Law

Dean Langdell's program to bring order to the common law by training future lawyers in legal science with the use of casebooks was echoed by leading law professors, judges, and lawyers in the 1920s, who created the American Law Institute (ALI). They desired to reduce the undue complexity and growing uncertainty of case law by systematically restating legal rules and principles. Although aimed primarily at traditional common law subjects, ALI Restatements also encompassed judicially interpreted statutes that had been commonly enacted by the states.

The first series of Restatements took over 20 years to finish, covering the core law school subjects of contracts, property, torts, and judgments as well as agency, conflict of laws, restitution, security, and trusts. Each Restatement is supervised by an eminent scholar called the reporter. Beginning with the second series of Restatements in 1952 reporters' notes were published after each section (in appendix volumes for agency, torts, and trusts). The third series began in 1987 with U.S. foreign relations law, followed by unfair competition (1995), suretyship and guaranty (1996), and the law governing lawyers (2000), as well as portions of the Restatements for property, torts, and trusts by 2001.

The reception of the Restatements has varied from field to field, with some commentators criticizing the ALI for stating what the law ought to be rather than restating what it is. In general, however, courts have found the scholarship of some value, citing them by 2001 about 151,000 times.

Lawyers find Restatements useful for gaining an overview of a doctrinal area as well as for finding cases that deal with a specific point of law. For the impact of the first and second Restatement on the field of contracts, for instance, *see* its organizing role in Chap. 8. Today Restatements are divided into chapters, each

11. For a listing of sources for federal agency regulations and adjudicatory decisions, *see* Berring & Edinger, supra note 3, at 375-85.

covering a major aspect of the subject. Chapters are further divided into topics, titles, and finally continuously numbered sections (with only the section number used in citation). Each section begins with the black letter statement of a legal rule or principle. An explanatory comment follows with illustrations of the rule's application to varying situations. The reporter's note, with background information and citation to cases, statutes, and secondary materials, concludes the treatment. An appendix volume includes headnotes describing judicial citations to the Restatement and cross references to West key numbers and *ALR* annotations.

B. *Uniform Laws*

The American Law Institute and its Restatements brought greater order and system to some areas of the common law. Even earlier, leaders of the ABA pushed for the creation of the National Conference of Commissioners on Uniform State Laws. Formed in 1892 for the purpose of law reform in areas (such as commercial law) where the nation might benefit from uniform laws, it had representatives from every state by 1912. The Conference, which drafts, publishes, and promotes uniform laws, had its first major success with the Negotiable Instruments Law, which was widely enacted by 1900. States, of course, are free to ignore uniform laws, but they come cheap and prepackaged so that many have met with success.

Over 100 uniform laws have been enacted by at least one state. The big winner was the Uniform Commercial Code, jointly sponsored by the ALI, which all states have adopted (although only in part by Louisiana). *See* Chap. 13, pt. I. Since uniform laws are supposed to be interpreted uniformly (a provision so stating is usually inserted into the law), a lawyer practicing in a state that has adopted such a law may look to the case law of another adopting state as highly persuasive in the matter before her. West publishes *Uniform Laws Annotated* (45 volumes), which carries the laws' official text, commissioners' comments, variations in the versions of different states, references to secondary literature, and headnotes from court decisions interpreting the laws.

C. *Treatises*

A treatise is a commentary or summary on an area of the law – constitutional, statutory, administrative, or judicial – directed primarily to legal practitioners or law students. Treatises, such as those by Kent and Story, were especially important in America during the 19th century before legal education found its way to the university. *See* Chap. 2, pt. I.A. Distinguished jurists wrote many fine multi-volume treatises in the first half of the 20th century (for example, Wigmore on Evidence, Williston on Contracts, and Scott on Trusts), but the form never reached the status occupied by commentaries in civil law countries. There are still a significant number of excellent treatises used by attorneys, judges, and students alike – such as the 21 volume *Federal Practice and Procedure* (2d ed. 1982-2001), started by professors Charles Alan Wright and Arthur Miller, but the realist impact on law professors has tended to drive them away from broad doctrinal interests toward other concerns more appropriately published in law review articles.[12]

Nevertheless, about 50 publishers print over 1,000 treatises today. These range from student textbooks to the increasingly common looseleaf format and CD-ROM directed toward the bench and bar. Lawyers use these volumes to substitute for digests in finding cases, to obtain critical interpretation of primary sources, and to learn more about an area of the law. Beyond treatises is the vast expanse of law books in general. Thousands of publishers currently maintain about 60,000 law books and other media forms "in print."

D. Law Reviews

Law school and academic reviews are playing an increasing role in informing lawyers and judges about developments in the law. Every one of the 183 ABA approved law schools has a general interest review or journal that publishes lead articles by law professors (and occasionally by judges and lawyers) and notes and comments written by students who often discuss a recent court case or legislation. Most schools now also publish reviews on specialized subjects, such as international and comparative law. *See* Chap. 2, pt. II.D. In addition, learned societies and special sections of professional groups publish journals that follow the footnote style of student-run reviews. It is precisely these footnotes, with extensive citation and discussion of primary and secondary sources, that make reviews useful to the bench and bar. Together, counting student and professional reviews, there are about 550 periodicals of this type. Westlaw provides selective or full coverage of these periodicals plus another 200 legal newspapers and publications on its online database, while LexisNexis covers over 550 journals in full text.

The oldest continuous index to law reviews is the *Index to Legal Periodicals and Books* (*ILP*), first published in 1908. Today it is available as a bound annual volume, part of H.W. Wilson's CD-ROM disc called Wilsondisk, or through LexisNexis or Westlaw. The ILP lists over 500 periodicals, with an author and subject index, a table of cases (those analyzed in a note or comment), a table of statutes, and a book review index. In 1980 Information Access Company (IAC) began *Current Law Index*, which uses the detailed Library of Congress subject headings. Westlaw and LexisNexis feature this research tool as Legal Resources Index. Today IAC, on its CD-ROM or online version called LegalTrac, lists over 800 periodicals, newspapers, and newsletters.

12. Westwell Daniels studied the U.S. Supreme Court's citation practice between 1900 and 1978. The Court cited legal treatises more often than periodicals in 1900 and 1940, but by 1978 legal periodicals surpassed treatises. Between 1940 and 1978 the number of citations to periodicals increased from 35 to 343. Westwell Daniels, "Far Beyond the Law Reports": Secondary Source Citations in United States Supreme Court Opinions October Terms 1900, 1940, and 1948, 76 *Law Libr. J.* 1, 14-17 (1983).

Selected Bibliography

Ruggero J. Aldisert, *Logic for Lawyers: A Guide to Clear Legal Thinking* (3d ed. 1997).
Robert C. Berring & Elizabeth A. Edinger, *Finding the Law* (11th ed. 1999).
Morris Cohen, Robert C. Berring & Kent C. Olson, *How to Find the Law* (9th ed. 1989).
Morris L. Cohen & Kent C. Olson, *Legal Research in a Nutshell* (7th ed. 2000).
Kent Greenawalt, *Legislation: Statutory Interpretation* (1999).
J. Myron Jacobstein, Roy M. Mersky & Donald J. Dunn, *Fundamentals of Legal Research* (7th ed. 1998).
Christina L. Kunz et al., *The Process of Legal Research* (5th ed. 2000).
Karl N. Llewellyn, *The Case Law System in America* (Paul Gewirtz ed., Michael Ansaldi trans. 1989).
Amy E. Sloan, *Basic Legal Research: Tools and Strategies* (2000).

Chapter 4
Constitutional Law

*William B. Fisch**

* Isidor Loeb Professor of Law, University of Missouri (Columbia) School of Law; General Reporter on Contracts for Professional Services, 8 *International Encyclopedia of Comparative Law* ch. 9 (1999).

David S. Clark and Tuğrul Ansay (eds.) Introduction to the Law of the United States, 53-96

I. Introduction

This overview of American constitutional law divides the subject into two broad categories: The structure of government and individual rights. In the former we look at the principal institutions created or recognized in the Constitution, and the principles stated therein to govern the allocation and exercise of power among and by those institutions. *See* pts. III-VI. In the latter we consider the constitutional rights of persons (natural and juristic, citizen and alien), affecting primarily their relationship to government but also, to a much more limited extent, their relationships to one another. *See* pts. VII-XIII.

For reasons of space and conceptual unity the chapter also limits the scope of the topic, thus requiring three important caveats. First, it will discuss only the federal Constitution. Each of the 50 states[1] has its own written constitution which plays an important role in determining the law of that state. While the federal Constitution has served as a model for the states in some major respects, there is considerable variation among the states in structure and content, reflecting history and the rather wide range of autonomy given to the states in the American system.

Second, it will concentrate overwhelmingly on the jurisprudence of the United States Supreme Court, as the court of last resort on questions of federal constitutional law. All courts, local and state and federal, are obligated to give effect to the federal Constitution where it applies, so that thousands of decisions interpreting that document are handed down every year. However, the Supreme Court's small size (nine members who render final judgments only *en banc*) prevents it from annual full-scale treatment of more than about 100 cases, which for the Court's 1999-2000 term included 77 opinions of the Court, 50 concurring opinions, and 67 dissenting opinions. These cases are selected almost entirely at the Court's discretion from currently more than 7,000 petitions. Typically less than a majority of the Court's decisions turn on a contested interpretation of the

1. The term "state" in this chapter will be used to refer to a state of the United States, or generally to statewide and local government in such a state. The term "government," when not otherwise qualified, refers generically to federal, state, and local governments.

Constitution. From the perspective of the lawyer, therefore, much of the *working* constitutional law is left out: lower court decisions on federal constitutional law within the lawyer's territorial region; the whole of state constitutional law; and much of the interpretive practice of other branches of government in so far as it escapes judicial review.

Third, the chapter only occasionally notes a persistent feature of modern Supreme Court decisions, namely the fragmentation of the opinion-writing process, the frequent juxtaposition of hard-won majority opinions against concurring opinions with alternative rationales as well as powerful dissents. Another major task of the constitutional lawyer is thereby essentially unexplored here, that of searching for special features of one's own case that could match the sensitivities of individual justices. *See* Chap. 3, pt. II.

II. The Text

The Constitution of the United States was drawn up at a convention held in the summer of 1787 at Philadelphia, Pennsylvania, at which 12 of the original 13 states were represented, each by a delegation having a single vote (Rhode Island was the holdout). The convention was called to consider amendments to the then governing instrument of the United States, the Articles of Confederation, but it proceeded to propose an entirely new document. Pursuant to resolutions of the Convention, the document went through a complicated ratification process. It was submitted first to the Congress (the governing body under the Articles of Confederation), then by it to the legislatures of the several states, which in turn convened ratification conventions to which delegates were popularly elected. After the ninth state convention had ratified the document in 1788, it went into effect as of March 4, 1789.

The amendment process contemplated in the document itself (art. V) is similarly complicated: proposals must be made either by a two thirds vote in each House of Congress, or by a Convention called by the legislatures of two thirds of the states; ratification must be made by three fourths of the states, either through their legislatures or through conventions called for the purpose, as determined by Congress. No doubt as a result of this great concern for political consensus among the states, in its 200-year history the document has been amended on just 18 occasions, producing 27 articles of amendment.

The original document consists of six substantive articles, and a seventh which determined the process of ratification and the time of its taking effect. The first three articles establish and regulate the three branches of the federal government (legislative, executive, and judicial, respectively, drawing on Montesquieu's tripartite scheme of governmental powers). The fourth article defines mutual obligations of the states to each other, regulates the process of admission of new states to the federation, and commands the national government to guarantee to each of the states a republican form of government. The fifth deals with the process of amendment of the document, while the sixth addresses several of the document's legal effects.

Significant protections of individual rights were scattered throughout the original document, but the ratification process showed great demand for a more comprehensive statement of rights protected against encroachment by the federal government, along the lines of rights statements already adopted by a number of states to limit their own governments. As a result, the first Congress of the new national government proposed in 1789 a package of 12 amendments, ten of which (including nine primarily addressing individual rights generally referred to as the Bill of Rights) were ratified by the states and took effect in 1791.[2]

Of the subsequent 17 amendments, six deal primarily with individual rights: the 13th (1865), abolishing slavery and involuntary servitude; the 14th (1868), defining federal and state citizenship and guaranteeing due process and equal protection of the laws in relation to the states; the 15th (1870), 19th (1920), and 26th (1971), protecting voting rights against race, gender, and age discrimination respectively; and the 24th (1964), prohibiting poll taxes on the right to vote in federal elections. Nine of the remaining 11 deal with various aspects of governmental structure: the 11th (1798), jurisdiction of the federal courts over suits against states; the 12th (1804), election of the president; the 20th (1933) and 25th (1967), terms and succession, and 22nd (1951), number of presidential terms; the 16th (1913), power of the federal government to impose an income tax; the 17th (1913), election of senators; the 23rd (1961), right of residents of the District of Columbia (seat of the federal government) to vote in presidential elections; the 27th (1992), effective date of changes in the compensation of senators and representatives. Finally, the 18th (1919) imposed and the 21st (1933) repealed the ill-fated "Great Experiment" of constitutionally mandated national Prohibition, banning production and distribution of intoxicating liquors.

III. The Judicial Function

Among the most important innovations of the American Constitution was its implementation of the concept of an independent judicial power, by vesting it directly in a separate institution created by the founding document itself. The transition from distinct *function* to independent *branch of government*, which neither Locke nor Montesquieu had made, has been attributed to the writings and urging of John Adams, who became the first vice president and second president. Moreover, it was understood from the beginning, by both proponents and opponents of the Constitution, that the judiciary would have and exercise some power to declare the acts of the other branches to be inconsistent with the Constitution and therefore invalid. The Framers probably did not foresee the full scope of judicial constitutional review as it has developed in practice, and it has remained controversial

2. The first, second, and 12th proposed amendments dealt with structural issues (the number of representatives, compensation of members of Congress, and the residual powers of states and the people themselves). The first two failed to receive the required number to ratify at the time. Consequently, proposals three through 12 became the First through Tenth Amendments. The second proposed amendment, however, was revived by a popular movement 200 years later, received the 38th state approval in 1992, and was quickly declared by Congress to be ratified. It is now identified as the 27th Amendment.

throughout the nation's history. Nonetheless the judiciary, led by the Supreme Court, has become the dominant interpreter of the Constitution.

The judicial review role was acknowledged in the most influential early treatise on constitutional law, Joseph Story's *Commentaries on the Constitution of the United States* (1833). Story's preface cites Chief Justice John Marshall's judgments as one of his primary sources. Most modern coursebooks and treatises on federal constitutional law give it greater emphasis by dealing with the judicial function first, while it is third in the textual order of governmental powers. Because federal courts are the principal source of the document's reasoned, authoritative interpretation, to assess the binding force of any particular statement about the law it is essential to understand the judicial power's parameters and the institutional conditions of its exercise.

A. Power of Constitutional Review

1. The basic principle

The fullest statement of the rationale for judicial constitutional review is to be found in the first Supreme Court decision directly invalidating an act of Congress for inconsistency with the Constitution: *Marbury v. Madison*.[3] Drawing on two specific provisions of the Constitution – article III, section 2 (giving the courts jurisdiction over cases "arising under this Constitution") and article VI, paragraph 2 ("This Constitution ... shall be the supreme law of the land") – Chief Justice Marshall concluded: (1) that the Constitution is law which binds all government agencies according to its terms; (2) the role of a court is to determine what the law is, including constitutional law, to decide cases properly before it; and (3) therefore courts have the power to declare legislative and executive acts void as inconsistent with the Constitution for purposes of judicial decision. Marshall went on to hold that the legislative provision giving the Supreme Court jurisdiction over the particular case before it was invalid because it allowed a party to *begin* a lawsuit in the Supreme Court, which did not fall into the categories specified in the Constitution (art. III, § 2, para. 2) as within that Court's "original" or first instance jurisdiction.

2. Powers of state and local courts

At least with respect to direct application of the *federal* Constitution in state and local courts, the rationale of *Marbury v. Madison* is universal in character. It follows indeed from the full text of article VI, paragraph 2, the so-called "supremacy clause":

> This Constitution, and the Laws of the United States which shall be made in Pursuance thereof; and all Treaties made, or which shall be made,

3. 5 U.S. (1 Cranch) 137 (1803).

> under the Authority of the United States, shall be the supreme Law of the Land; *and the Judges in every State shall be bound thereby, any Thing in the Constitution or Laws of any State to the contrary notwithstanding* (emphasis added).

This universal applicability of the federal Constitution supported another at the time more controversial decision, which sustained the statutory provision enacted by the first Congress giving the Supreme Court appellate jurisdiction over decisions of state courts of last resort. The Court reasoned that article III, section 2 and the supremacy clause must be understood as contemplating appellate jurisdiction over any court applying federal law. In fact the principle of judicial constitutional review as an integral component of the law-finding process is recognized in most states with respect to their own constitutions as well, although some states require cases arising under their constitutions to be brought in the more important courts of first instance, or appeals based thereon to be taken directly to the highest court.

B. Limitations on Constitutional Review in Federal Courts

1. Legislative control over federal court jurisdiction

Article III, section 1 vests the United States judicial power in "one supreme Court, and in such inferior Courts as the Congress may from time to time ordain and establish." As a result it is assumed that Congress may decide not only whether or not there should be any inferior federal courts at all, and what sort there should be, but also what the scope of their jurisdiction should be. In fact Congress established a system of lower courts immediately and has maintained them (with a few major reorganizations) ever since, giving them a continually expanding competence. But it has never given them by statute the full range of jurisdiction which the constitutional definition of the "judicial Power of the United States" would allow. The Supreme Court's rule of interpretation of statutes governing lower court jurisdiction is that Congress's failure specifically to provide for federal court jurisdiction over a particular type of case is treated as a denial of such jurisdiction.

The jurisdiction of the Supreme Court itself, which was the issue in *Marbury v. Madison*, is addressed specifically in article III, section 2, paragraph 2, after listing the categories of "cases and controversies" to which the judicial power generally extends:

> In all Cases affecting Ambassadors, other public Ministers and Consuls, and those in which a State shall be a Party, the supreme Court shall have original Jurisdiction. In all the other Cases before mentioned, the Supreme Court shall have appellate jurisdiction, both as to Law and Fact, with such Exceptions, and under such Regulations as the Congress shall make.

Marbury held that the first sentence is self-executing, so that Congress is not free to enlarge upon, much less diminish, the Court's original jurisdiction (that is, its power to act as a court of first instance). The sense of the second sentence is that Congress's control over the Court's *appellate* jurisdiction is virtually complete; the Court itself went so far in 1868 as to sustain action by Congress to remove from the Court's jurisdiction a specific case already pending before it. This has remained an isolated instance for the Congress, however, and there is respectable opinion supporting the view that it could not exercise its power to control the Court's appellate jurisdiction in such a manner as to deprive persons of established constitutional rights, or to impair the Supreme Court's role as authoritative interpreter of the Constitution.

2. "Justiciability"

Despite the long-standing reputation of the U.S. for judicialization of political issues, it has been understood from the beginning that there are limitations on the types of matters which can be brought before the federal courts. In one of the very few references to the issue of judicial review in the records of the Constitutional Convention, James Madison reportedly urged that Supreme Court jurisdiction in cases arising under the Constitution be expressly limited to "cases of a Judiciary nature." He was reassured that that was the intended meaning of the clause as ultimately adopted. In the final document's article III, section 2, paragraph 1, the enumeration of categories of matters within the judicial power identifies each as "cases" or "controversies."

Out of these concepts, together with those of the judiciary as an independent branch of government, and of its need prudently to manage its institutional resources, the Court has fashioned a jurisprudence of "justiciability," or appropriateness of a particular matter for adjudication, the most striking feature of which in modern terms is a firm rejection of the "abstract norm control" which is currently practiced, for example, in the constitutional tribunals of France and Germany. The most common policy reasons for this rejection are that courts should override government acts only when necessary, and then only with the help of advocacy from parties having a genuine interest in the dispute's outcome. This jurisprudence has a strongly casuistic flavor, and it acknowledges that it is only partly commanded by the constitutional language itself. While it purports to announce general rules governing all federal courts, it often gives the impression of case-by-case discretion and is to that extent a matter of continuing dispute. We shall consider only the most important examples.

a. *Adversariness and finality of judgment.* Two of the earliest matters before the justices evoked the view that an issue is appropriate for judicial resolution only if it involves parties of concretely adversary interests, and if the judicial resolution will be final. In one matter arising in 1792 Congress had enacted a scheme for processing disabled Revolutionary War veterans' pension claims which required lower federal courts to determine the degree of disability, but left it to an executive officer to make the ultimate decision whether a pension would be granted. Three such courts, on which collectively five of the then six Supreme Court justices sat at first instance in their since-abrogated role as circuit judges, refused to act on the ground that the business given them was not "of a judicial nature," because judicial judgments could not be subject to review by another branch of government. In the next year, the justices collectively refused to give the then secretary of state, Thomas Jefferson, the benefit of their opinion on a series of questions of law, to help guide the executive in the conduct of foreign affairs; in doing so they noted the impropriety of giving extra-judicial opinions.

Over a century later the Court invalidated a statute which, after adding substantially to the number of persons entitled to a share of certain Indian lands, authorized those whose prior claims were thus diluted to sue the United States, at government expense, for a judgment determining the constitutionality of the statute. The U.S. did not have an adverse interest in the issue and the statute did not provide for joining and binding the competing claimants as adversaries, so that it in effect authorized an advisory opinion.

b. *Standing*. Among the most troublesome of the requirements for a justiciable controversy is that the party invoking the federal court's jurisdiction must have *locus standi*, a *personal* entitlement to the relief sought if the factual allegations are proven. The essential elements of a claim for relief from a violation of the Constitution for standing purposes may be stated as follows: (1) actual or threatened injury to the complaining party, (2) which is individual and concrete; (3) conduct for which the defending party is responsible, to which the injury complained of is "fairly traceable"; (4) a rule of constitutional law intended to protect against the injury; and (5) a form of relief which will redress the injury. Of these, the first, third, and fifth are said to be essential elements of the constitutional definition of the judicial power, while the second and fourth are characterized as "prudential," that is, not commanded by the Constitution but developed by the Court for the prudent management of the judiciary's institutional resources. *See* Chap. 5, pt. V.C.

A party normally fails to meet the second requirement, according to the Court, if it alleges an injury which is not individual and concrete but diffuse and widely shared – as, for example, a taxpayer suing to challenge the propriety of a particular governmental expenditure out of general revenues when the expenditure's impact on the party's own tax burden is negligible or nonexistent, or a citizen suing to require the government to perform a general constitutional duty such as making an annual accounting of expenditures to Congress when the citizen's interest is only to see that government follows the rules or to vindicate a particular political view. The one established exception, which the present Court refuses to extend, is a taxpayer's challenge to expenditures of federal funds in violation of the First Amendment's prohibition against establishment of religion, originally recognized by the Court because of the centrality of public subsidy to the intended target of that clause.

The fourth requirement, that the complaining party invoke a constitutional norm intended for his protection and not for that of third persons, is subject to two well-recognized exceptions. First, an association has standing to assert the constitutional rights of its members if they themselves would have standing, if their injuries are related to the association's purposes, and the relief sought is unitary or common to the entire membership (as in an injunction against an invalid law's enforcement) rather than specific to the individual members (as a judgment for money damages). Second, a party meeting the other standing requirements may invoke the constitutional rights of others if the denial of such third-party standing would impair the ability of the real victims to vindicate their rights. So, for an example of the latter, an alcoholic beverage seller (whose own sole interest was in serving more customers) was permitted to challenge the constitutionality of a state law setting the minimum drinking age for women at 18 years and for men at 21 years, as a denial of equal protection of the laws, because the limited period during which any one male would be disadvantaged by the discrimination might well be too short for full litigation of the claim.

c. *Timing of judicial action: ripeness and mootness.* The principle that constitutional questions must be presented to courts for final determination by parties having concrete and adverse interests also has a temporal dimension, reflecting the fact that disputes develop over time and the interests of the parties may change. A constitutional dispute is said not to be "ripe" for judicial determination if the positions of the parties on the particular issues have not yet settled, or if the necessary conditions for a full definition of the constitutional issues have not yet occurred. The dispute is said to be "moot" when one or more parties cease to have a concrete interest in its resolution, or when the conditions for full resolution cease to exist.

Perhaps the best illustration of the workings of these complementary concepts is the case in which federal civil service employees (those who cannot be dismissed at will) challenged the constitutionality of a congressional enactment prohibiting such employees from engaging in certain partisan political activity. The employees bringing the action fell into three categories: (1) those who intended at some future time to engage in prohibited activity but had not yet formed specific plans; (2) those who had intended to engage in such activity in the past, but had been discouraged from it by the statute; and (3) those who had actually engaged in such activity as a result of which their employer had initiated disciplinary action. The claims of the first group were "unripe" and those of the second were "moot," but those of the third were "ripe" and could properly form the basis of judicial resolution.

The non-justiciability of "moot" claims is subject to a significant exception, where the claim is one which is "capable of repetition yet escaping review." Thus, for example, the plaintiff in the important abortion decision, *Roe v. Wade*,[4] was allowed to pursue her claim for a constitutional right to abortion, despite the fact that before the case reached the Supreme Court she had carried her baby to term and given birth, because she could become pregnant again and never be able to get a full judicial resolution of her right if the mootness rule were applied rigidly.

d. *Non-justiciability of "political questions."* Finally, there are issues which the Court has characterized as "political," meaning that – even assuming a ripe controversy between adverse parties with concrete interests who plausibly

4. 410 U.S. 113 (1973).

invoke specific constitutional provisions – they should be resolved by the political process rather than by the courts. The category is so amorphous that some scholars have denied that any such distinct category exists; nonetheless the justices have used the label from time to time as if it were dispositive.

Typically, the claim of non-justiciability takes one of two forms: (1) that the text of the Constitution assigns to another branch of government exclusive responsibility for making the particular decision or (2) that the relevant constitutional texts do not provide "judicially manageable standards" for resolution of specific cases. A leading early example involved a challenge to certain actions of the Rhode Island government, on the ground that it was not legitimate because it did not have a republican form of government, in violation of the so-called "guaranty clause" (art. IV, § 4), requiring the United States to guarantee a republican form of government to every state. In refusing to consider the claim of illegitimacy, the Court invoked both arguments: it said that the clause itself gave responsibility to the "political" branches of government, and also that a court would be unable to make the necessary determinations to enforce the clause.

C. Principles of Judicial Interpretation

Elaboration of and careful adherence to general principles of substantive interpretation of the Constitution are tasks to which neither the text nor the modern Court seems well adapted. The text itself is written in terse and general language which does not lend itself to a plain-meaning rule. Moreover, unlike acts of the legislature which can be readily amended to correct unintended interpretations, the cumbersome amendment process makes it difficult to fine tune the Constitution in response to interpretive acts. The modern Court, given its small size in relation to the complexity of the problems with which it must deal, the absence of a work-dividing chamber structure, and the permissibility of separate concurring and dissenting opinions, cannot often muster the consistent majorities needed to develop comprehensive rules of interpretation capable of overriding the policy differences which center on specific clauses. As a result the same casuistry which often characterizes the Court's handling of procedural limitations on the functioning of the judiciary tends also to prevail with respect to principles of substantive interpretation.

Joseph Story, writing in his *Commentaries* toward the end of the Court's formative era, did devote a chapter to "Rules of Interpretation," in which he expounded a teleological approach, emphasizing the Constitution's "nature and objects, its scope and design, as apparent from the structure of the instrument, viewed as a whole, and also viewed in its component parts."[5] Aided by its preamble, he identified the nature of the instrument as a fundamental law of government and the proper interpretive approach as that which, within the range of reasonable alternatives, gives the government "efficacy and force ... rather than that which will impair its operations."[6]

5. Joseph Story, *Commentaries on the Constitution of the United States* § 183 (1933, reprinted 1987).
6. *Id.* § 88.

A leading opponent of the original document in 1788 predicted such an approach by a judiciary that is not responsible to any other agency: that the courts "will not confine themselves to any fixed or established rules, but will determine, according to what appears to them, the reason and spirit of the constitution." The Court itself articulated this view through Chief Justice Marshall in 1819, in the famous phrase, "we must never forget that it is *a constitution* we are expounding."[7] Throughout most of the 19th century, in which the controversial cases dealt overwhelmingly with the allocation of power between the national government and the states, this teleological approach appears to have prevailed and to have imposed few if any limitations on the sources of guidance to be consulted, whether the substantive results tended to favor the national government (first half of the century) or the states (second half). In practice, conforming to the ancient tradition of common law countries, prior decisions of the Court itself were given the greatest weight as they accumulated – again without precluding changes in direction for which dissenting and concurring opinions often paved the way.

While the great cases of the 19th century tended to turn on the question of which agencies or levels of government have power to act, the 20th century saw a greater portion of the controversial cases involve personal rights, where the judiciary is situated between government generally and its citizens. Here especially it is argued that the judiciary should be restrained in its interference with government by the "antimajoritarian difficulty": because the first principle of American government is the democratic one ("popular sovereignty" or majority rule), unelected judges should give politically responsible government the strongest possible benefit of doubt. A number of interpretation theories have been offered to give effect to this idea.

The theory with the longest history is sometimes called "originalism," positing that the courts are bound, in interpreting any provision of the Constitution, by the understanding of that provision held by the original framers. The Court itself invoked that theory in one portion of its opinion in the infamous *Dred Scott* case,[8] although it proceeded in another section of the opinion to invalidate congressional action by what can only be characterized as adventurous interpretation. A variant of this view appears in some very recent decisions, which hold that the Court's own interpretive analysis of certain individual rights clauses is inapplicable to a specific situation in which consistent historical practice dating to the time of the Framers conflicts with that analysis. The theory is unworkable for general use, however, due both to lack of sufficient evidence of original understanding, and to the restrictiveness of its logical conclusions; it seems doomed to no more than marginal application.

A broader variant, often called "interpretivism," would limit the courts to *values* clearly adopted by the Framers. The most ambitious exposition of this view

7. *McCulloch v. Maryland*, 17 U.S. (4 Wheat.) 316, 407 (1819).

8. *Scott v. Sandford*, 60 U.S. (19 How.) 393, 405 (1857). The case held that an African slave was constitutionally incapable of becoming a U.S. citizen, and (in *obiter dictum*) that Congress could not prohibit the introduction of slavery into new states; it helped pave the way for the Civil War.

would limit the courts to a single pervasive value, that of maximizing participation in the political process, but (as of 1980) would seem to find most of the Court's recent individual rights decisions consistent with that value! The Court has not espoused this version of interpretivism, and it is very much open to question whether its most controversial decisions are in fact consistent with it.

Among those who argue for the legitimacy of judicial interpretation based on contemporary values, the antimajoritarian objection has been answered, for example, by reference to the various opportunities which the "political" branches have for influencing judicial behavior, such as the congressional power to control the jurisdiction of the courts, and by emphasizing the special character of the popular consensus required for adoption and amendment of the Constitution ("judgment-driven") by comparison with what is contemplated by the principle of majority rule ("preference-driven").

IV. Powers of the National Government

A. In general

Two contrasting themes pervade the adoption history as well as the text of the Constitution on the question of the relative powers of state and national governments. First, the national government was conceived as one of limited powers, with the states as holders of general residual authority. Second, it was meant to be an effective government, to replace a weaker confederative structure which had proved inadequate to meet common needs such as regulating the economy, providing for defense, and conducting foreign relations. These themes are set most clearly in article I governing the legislative power, whose opening "vesting clause" confers not a general lawmaking power but "[a]ll legislative powers herein granted," and proceeds to enumerate (§§ 8-10) in terse but suggestive language both powers conferred on Congress, and limitations imposed on it and on the states. Since the legislative power extends to the implementation of all the powers granted any branch (art. I, § 8, para. 18), the themes of article I are pervasive.

We have already noted the expansive interpretive approach taken by the Court in its formative years (*see* pt. III. C.), first clearly formulated in *McCulloch v. Maryland*.[9] That opinion focused on the so-called "necessary and proper clause" (art. I, § 8, para. 18), which follows the main list of legislative powers:

> To make all Laws which shall be necessary and proper for carrying into Execution the foregoing Powers, and all other Powers vested by this Constitution in the Government of the United States, or in any Department or Officer thereof.

At issue was the propriety of Congress's establishing a central national bank by creating a corporation to operate it, a mechanism not expressly authorized in the

9. 17 U.S. (4 Wheat.) 316 (1819); *see* text at n. 5.

Constitution but intended to implement the monetary powers enumerated in setion 8. The Court found authority in the "necessary and proper" clause, which it refused to interpret narrowly as authorizing only those laws which are indispensable. Rather, it permits any mechanism "appropriate and plainly adapted to" an end which is "within the scope of the constitution," unless the means employed is prohibited by or inconsistent with the letter or spirit of the Constitution. While the opinion addressed "means" rather than "ends," it heralded an expansive interpretation of the enumerated powers themselves which prevailed in the Marshall era, lost out for some of the regulatory powers in the latter portion of the 19th and first third of the 20th centuries, revived in the later 1930s, and generally holds sway today despite some signs of weakening.

B. Specific powers

1. Taxing and spending

Article I, section 8 authorizes Congress to "lay and collect taxes," and to "provide for the general Welfare of the United States." This authority is not tied to any particular regulatory power, and it can be exercised without any direct effect on state governmental activity; it is not subject to any limitations as to subject matter. An important mechanism whereby the Congress can influence state regulation in areas not thought subject to *direct* congressional control is "conditional spending," in the form of subsidies to state and local government conditioned on their adopting certain regulatory practices or social welfare structures. Since 1937 the Court has upheld these programs when non-coercive in form, however compelling the inducement. On several earlier occasions the Court had struck down a tax or a spending measure on the ground that it was in effect a measure to regulate commerce in violation of limits set by prior decisions on the regulatory power; but those limits have been abandoned.

2. Regulation of interstate and foreign commerce

The earliest pronouncement of the Court on the scope of this power was the broadest, although it was *obiter dictum* in an 1824 decision which merely held that the term "commerce" includes not only trade in but also transportation of goods and persons across state lines. Marshall said that the power to regulate interstate and foreign commerce belongs *only* to Congress, and that it extends to any activity having a substantial *effect* on such commerce. Both claims were short lived. Marshall himself soon recognized what came to be called a "police power" of the states, coexisting with the federal commerce power, allowing regulation of economic activity in the interest of health, safety, and welfare even if the activity had an interstate character. By the 19th century's end, after Congress began for the first time to exercise its power to enact comprehensive economic regulation, the Court was finding limitations on the scope of the power itself. In particular, it found that "production" or "manufacturing" was not "commerce," and therefore not subject to congressional control, and that an activity generally had to affect interstate commerce *directly* to come within the clause.

Beginning in 1937, finally responding to legislative efforts to combat the Depression, the Court abandoned these limitations on the scope of the congressional power. In that year it held that "production" was an integral part of "commerce," and that any substantial effect on interstate commerce would be sufficient, even if indirect. In 1942 it went still further and held that individual activities whose effect on interstate commerce was insubstantial could nonetheless be regulated by Congress, if the *cumulative* effect of many such activities by many persons would be substantial.

In the 1990s a bare but firm majority of the Court found renewed occasion to articulate limitations on the commerce power. Three lines of cases have developed, analytically distinct but related in spirit, in which congressional exercise of the commerce power has been struck down. First, the Court held that the activity which Congress seeks to regulate under this power must itself be economic in character. The possession of a firearm in or near a school or the commission of a violent act against a woman were held not to be economic acts, and therefore not subject to federal regulation under this power, regardless of the economic *effects* they may have.

Second, although it had abandoned the notion it had entertained in the 1970s that states as such were exempt from generally applicable economic regulations simply because of their fiscal impact on the state, the Court held that the commerce power does not authorize Congress to coerce or "commandeer" the *governmental* functions of the states. Congress cannot force a state to take ownership of private property (specifically, low-level radioactive waste) to implement federal regulation of the disposal of such property. And Congress cannot directly force a state's law enforcement officers to administer a federal regulation (specifically, the performance of a background check on gun purchasers).

Third, the Court held that the commerce power does not authorize Congress to abrogate the states' "sovereign immunity" from the jurisdiction of federal or state courts, thereby subjecting states as such to civil damage actions by private persons for violation of federal laws enacted under this power.

The first line of cases is new, but logically consistent with even the more expansive earlier decisions on Congress's power to regulate economic activity. The second line also represents a mood change rather than a direct abandonment of earlier decisions. The third line of cases, however, represents an effective reversal of precedent.

3. War and national defense

The document gives the national government a virtual monopoly over war and national defense. While the states continue to have militias (now called the National Guard), Congress is authorized in section 8 to provide for organizing, arming, and disciplining them, leaving the states only the power to appoint officers and execute the training prescribed by Congress. The militia is subject to being called to federal service, when the president becomes its commander-in-chief as well. Article I, section 10 requires Congress's consent for states to keep troops or warships in time of peace, or to engage in war unless actually invaded or in such danger as precludes delay. The states retain an inherent power to maintain police forces and to maintain order, which includes the power to impose martial law. But that requires an actual uprising, riot, or violence uncontrollable by civil authorities.

The Court has provided little in the way of detailed interpretation of the war powers complex given to Congress and the president. It has held that they include preparation for a future war, waging a successful war, and dealing with the consequences of a past war. It will decide, however, whether a particular measure premised on the effects of a past war is still justified by such effects.

4. Treaties and foreign affairs

In this field as well, the national government has exclusive authority, the states being prohibited by article I, section 10 from entering into any agreements with a foreign power, or indeed with each other, without Congress's consent. It has been held that a state law is invalid to the extent that it purports, independently of the national government, to determine and implement a foreign policy objective.

Treaties are "made" (that is, negotiated) by the president, but must have the advice and consent of the Senate before they can be ratified and go into effect (art. II, § 2). In the hierarchy of legal norms in U.S. internal law, self-executing treaties (those which purport to and are intended to have direct domestic effect without implementing legislation) have the same status as federal legislation, meaning that for purposes of internal law they supersede prior inconsistent federal legislation, are superseded by subsequent inconsistent federal legislation, and supersede any inconsistent state law. The treaty-making power is independent of any regulatory powers of Congress, so that a treaty may deal with any subject matter of international concern, even if it were otherwise a matter for state regulation.

In addition, the president has a substantial range of authority, based on statute or inherent powers or both, to enter into so-called *executive agreements*, which are binding in international law and have the same domestic legal effect as treaties, without requiring the advice and consent of the Senate.

The power to enter into international agreements is subject, however, for purposes of internal law, to those constitutional limitations which apply to all acts of government, notably the Bill of Rights, so that an international agreement cannot deprive a U.S. citizen of due process of law. *See* Chap. 3, pts. I, IV.C.

5. Citizenship and immigration

The states are doubly precluded from regulating citizenship and the admission of aliens into their territories. First, article I, section 8, paragraph 4 gives Congress power to establish a "uniform rule of naturalization," which it has exercised virtually from the beginning. Second, the 14th Amendment, after the Court in *Dred*

Scott had denied even to the national government the power to make an African a citizen, established a minimum constitutional entitlement both to U.S. citizenship (persons born in the United States), and to citizenship in a state (born or naturalized in the United States and resident in the state).

Thus while the authority of Congress over immigration and naturalization is exclusive and plenary in relation to the states, the Constitution imposes some limits on Congress. The citizenship provision of the 14th Amendment has been held to prohibit the national government from imposing involuntary expatriation on any citizen born or naturalized in the United States. Congress has the power, however, to provide for additional bases for acquiring citizenship, as it has, for example, for persons born abroad to U.S. citizens. For such persons, the 14th Amendment does not protect against involuntary loss of citizenship, and it has been held permissible for Congress to attach as a condition to retaining such citizenship that the person reside in the United States for five consecutive years prior to his 28th birthday.

V. Separation of Legislative and Executive Powers

A. *Essential Roles and Exclusive Powers*

1. Legislative

The essential function of the Congress is to enact laws. The power to make laws is at its core the power to make policy choices. As we have seen, the "necessary and proper clause" extends that role to all powers given to government by the Constitution. Laws must be presented to the president for approval or veto, but the president's disapproval can be overridden by a two thirds majority in each House of Congress (art. I, § 7).

There are relatively few additional exclusive powers given to Congress. It has sole responsibility for the removal of judges and officers of the U.S. by impeachment for misconduct, with the House of Representatives responsible for determining whether charges should be filed and what they should be (the preferring of charges is the "impeachment," art. I, § 2, para. 5), and the Senate responsible for trial and adjudication of those charges (art. I, § 3, para. 6). Moreover, article I, section 5 gives each house of Congress authority to regulate its own internal affairs, including the determination of whether or not members have met the constitutional qualifications for election to membership.

2. Executive

Unlike the vesting clause of article I, which refers to the "legislative powers herein granted," article II, section 1 simply vests "the executive Power" in the president. This fact, along with the general language of article II's specific provisions, and the perceived needs of the time, encouraged many 20th century presidents to espouse what is often referred to as the "stewardship" theory of the presidency, which accords to that office the power to take any action deemed to further the general welfare so long as it is not prohibited by law or the Constitution. The Court has not embraced this notion of inherent executive power in its broadest form, but it has repeatedly held that there are traditional forms of executive action which do not necessarily require specific statutory authority.

Aside from the duty to "see that the laws are faithfully executed" (art. I, § 3), the Constitution accords to the president other exclusive powers, such as those of commander-in-chief of the armed forces, pardoning persons for offenses against the United States, and filling vacancies in public offices by commission while the Senate is in recess (art. II, § 2), as well as receiving ambassadors and other public ministers, and commissioning all duly appointed officers of the U.S. (art. II, § 3). The Court has held – on the cumulative basis of specific constitutional grants, the inherent role of a head of state, and long-standing congressional acquiescence and exploitation – that the president has exclusive responsibility for the daily conduct of foreign relations. The "appointment power" is clearly one of very great importance, but it is a shared one, in the sense that the Senate must approve any presidential appointment of an officer of the United States if Congress has not either dispensed with Senate approval or given appointment authority to the courts or to a department head (art. II, § 2, para. 2). The Court has held that the president has the power to remove any presidentially appointed officer without Senate concurrence, unless Congress provides otherwise.

B. Principles for Resolving Conflicts

1. Presidential policy-making generally

The leading case on the scope of the president's inherent power to make and implement policy is *Youngstown Sheet & Tube Co. v. Sawyer*,[10] which involved seizure by the president of a number of steel mills to prevent a strike, and thus maintain steel production for military needs during the Korean conflict. The Court held that the seizure of property for a public purpose does not come within the president's inherent powers, but there was disagreement as to the rationale. Of the six justices in the majority, only two clearly stated that the seizure was an inherently legislative act which required congressional authorization. The other four relied on their finding that Congress had implicitly forbidden the use of this method of preventing strikes, when it had been proposed but deliberately left out of the comprehensive statute governing labor-management conflict. These justices thereby left open the argument that the president would have such power if Congress had been truly silent on the subject. The most widely quoted and admired opinion in the case was Justice Jackson's concurrence, in which he posited a continuum of executive power, at its strongest when acting with legislative authorization, and at its weakest when acting directly contrary to the will of Congress. The Court has seldom taken opportunities to define more precisely how much power remains to the presidency at its "lowest ebb."

10. 343 U.S. 579 (1952).

2. Legislative delegation of rule-making power to the executive

If most of the president's power to take action affecting the legal rights and duties of others depends on express or implied congressional authorization, there is also a question as to how broad that authorization can be – more precisely, how much discretion in the formulation and implementation of policy can be transferred or delegated by Congress to the executive. It is most often stated that there can be no delegation of legislative power as such, in the sense of unlimited discretion to make policy choices. In reality, however, the modern administrative state has required giving executive agencies broad discretion to shape specific rules, taking advantage of their superior expertise. Courts have recognized this reality and have generally given Congress the benefit of the doubt in cases involving the permissible scope of delegation.

The leading case in modern delegation theory, not surprisingly, involved foreign affairs. Congress adopted a joint resolution (having the effect of a law) authorizing the president to determine whether or not an embargo against shipments of arms to the parties to the Chaco dispute in South America would "contribute to the re-establishment of peace between those countries." The resolution required the president to announce such a determination by formal proclamation, and to prescribe such exceptions and limitations on the embargo as might be appropriate. It went on to make it a crime for any person to violate the terms of the embargo if imposed, and to prescribe the punishment for such crime. The Court held that the resolution was a valid delegation, in large part because the discretion it left to the president took advantage of exclusive executive powers and expertise in foreign relations. On the other hand, in 1998 the Court struck down Congress's attempt by statute to give the president power to disapprove of specific items in appropriations statutes (those authorizing expenditures of money) after signing the statute as a whole into law (a so-called "line-item veto"). The Court saw such a veto as a purely legislative act, equivalent to enacting or repealing a law, which cannot be delegated.

Recently the Court has restated the general standard for the scope of legislative delegations as a requirement that Congress must determine a policy and set forth conditions for the exercise of executive authority. Particularly in light of its approach to other aspects of the delegation problem discussed next, it is to be expected that the Court will pay more careful attention in the future to whether this standard has been met in particular cases. *See* Chap. 5, pt. III.A.

3. Legislative control over exercise of delegated authority

In the era of broad delegations of rule- and policy-making authority to executive agencies, Congress used various devices to monitor and control its exercise. Two such control devices have come under judicial scrutiny recently, with results which reflect a rigid concept of separation of powers.

a. *The "legislative veto."* The most widely used control device, which is about 70 years old but enjoyed a dramatic growth in popularity in the 1970s, became known as the "legislative veto." The executive would be authorized to make certain determinations or formulate certain regulations, which were to be reported to Congress; Congress in turn could prevent their taking effect by a resolution of one or both of its houses. In 1983 the Court held such mechanisms invalid, on the ground that the "veto" is a distinct legislative act which itself must follow the procedural requirements of article I, section 7 governing the enactment of laws: adoption by both houses followed by presentment to the president for approval or disapproval.[11] The particular case chosen for this dramatic reversal of a decades-old practice was atypical, in that it involved congressional review not of rule- or policy-making action but rather of specific executive applications of a well-defined congressional policy to allow suspension of deportation proceedings when certain specified kinds of hardship are shown. Nonetheless, the Court's definition of "legislative act" for purposes of section 7 (having "the purpose of altering the legal rights, duties and relations of persons ... outside the legislative branch") was broad enough to encompass any dispositive review of executive action.

b. *Delegation to "legislative officers" and the appointment and removal of "executive" officials*. The Court has also disapproved of including among those responsible for implementing a law persons who are subject to congressional control. In 1976 it held that Congress could not, without encroaching upon the executive power of appointment, reserve to its own presiding officers the appointment of members of a commission established to oversee the conduct of federal elections. In 1986 it struck down a budget-deficit reduction law in so far as it gave important responsibilities in the implementation of the law to the Comptroller General, an officer who by law is removable only by Congress. On the other hand, it held in 1988 that Congress could, in conformity with the "appointment clause" (art. II, § 2), assign to a federal court the power to appoint special prosecutors to investigate and pursue criminal charges against certain high-ranking government officials.

VI. Residual State Power in Areas of Federal Competence

A. In general

Article VI, paragraph 2, the so-called "supremacy clause," gives that status to the "Constitution, and the Laws of the United States which shall be made in pursuance thereof." This phrasing strongly suggests that the granting to Congress of authority to make laws in a particular field does not in itself preclude the states from acting in the same field; rather, it is normally only congressional *exercise* of that power which supersedes state law. Indeed the Court has held that a federal statute will not be presumed to "preempt" or occupy an entire field (that is, supersede state law relating to the subject matter regardless of actual conflict between specific provisions) "in the absence of persuasive reasons – either that the nature of the regulated subject matter permits no other conclusion, or that Congress has unmistakably so ordained."[12]

11. *Immigration and Naturalization Service v. Chadha*, 462 U.S. 919 (1983).
12. *Florida Lime & Avocado Growers, Inc. v. Paul*, 373 U.S. 132, 142 (1963).

B. "Constitutional Preemption" of State Regulation: The Commerce Clause in Its "Dormant State"

We have noted that one of the primary tasks of the new national government was intended to be effective regulation of a national economy, and that Chief Justice Marshall initially thought that that purpose required the congressional power to regulate interstate commerce to be exclusive. *See* pt. IV.B.2. While it was soon recognized that states must retain a power to regulate economic activity for various purposes, the Court has adhered to the view that the constitutional grant of power to Congress imposes substantial limitations on state regulation, even in the absence of specific congressional enactments. As early as 1851 the Court asserted in *obiter dicta* that state regulation is excluded regarding subjects which require uniform national treatment. In an 1886 decision which helped stimulate the first burst of comprehensive congressional regulation, it held that freight rates for interstate rail transportation constituted such a subject matter. Eventually, however, the Court came to the more general view that the commerce clause (art. I, § 8) embodies a policy of fostering the free flow of trade among the states, with which state regulation may not unduly interfere.

The 20th century cases under the "dormant" commerce clause can be seen as applications, frequently controversial enough on their facts, of several basic principles. First, a state may not regulate competition as such in interstate commerce, as by requiring a license applicant who wants to operate an interstate freight route on its highways to show that the route is not adequately served by existing enterprises (though it may deny such a license on the ground that traffic congestion on the particular route threatens safety). Second, a state may not intentionally discriminate *as a regulator* against out-of-state economic interests in favor of its own, though it may do so as a "market participant" (that is, as purchaser or seller of goods or services). Third, if a state regulation, however nondiscriminatory in purpose, has a discriminatory *effect* on interstate commerce in relation to local interests, the state must show that the regulation is narrowly tailored to a legitimate state interest, and that there is no less discriminatory alternative to achieve the same objective. Fourth, if a nondiscriminatory regulation nonetheless imposes a substantial burden on interstate commerce, the state must show that it actually furthers a legitimate state interest, and that the regulation's benefits to that interest are not outweighed by the burden imposed on the flow of interstate commerce.

C. State Taxation of Interstate Commerce

Article I, section 10, paragraph 2 restricts the states' power to tax imports and exports as such, to that absolutely necessary to execute inspection laws. Goods are "imports or exports" as long as they are "in transit" into or out of the country.

Concerning state taxes on interstate economic activity generally, the Court has developed a complex test combining elements of due process (the activity must have a connection with the state, the tax must not be so excessive as to deprive other connected states of their fair share of the activity's tax-generating capacity, and the state must provide some benefits to the taxpayer) with the nondiscrimination principle of the "dormant" commerce clause.

VII. Individual Rights: General Principles

A. The Requirement of Governmental Action

1. In general

The First, 14th, 15th, 19th, and 24th Amendments, as well as many of the individual rights provisions of the original document, are explicitly addressed to government: to Congress, to the states, or to the United States or any state. The other individual rights provisions of the original document and its amendments do not identify a specific addressee, but have been interpreted as only limiting government, even if the conduct or function regulated might also be performed by private persons. The single exception is the 13th Amendment, which provides that "[n]either slavery nor involuntary servitude... shall exist within the United States," and which deals with conduct historically private in character. It has always been understood to prohibit not only state subsidy and protection for that conduct, but the conduct itself whether done by government or private persons.

Moreover, as the Court has confirmed, the Constitution – unlike the German Basic Law, for example – is understood not to impose judicially enforceable *affirmative* obligations on government for the benefit of individuals. Thus, for example, government does not violate a person's *constitutional* rights merely by failing to protect him against even a known danger from a third person.

2. Private action attributable to the government

One can identify three types of situations in which the Court has found private action to be the equivalent of government action, and therefore subject to constitutional limitations protecting individual rights. First, where the private actor is performing a public function, as a political party holding a government-sanctioned internal election called a "primary" to select its official candidate for public office, or a business company operating an entire town, with all the services of local government, for the accommodation of its employees. Second, where the state has commanded or encouraged the specific private conduct complained of, as distinguished from merely permitting it or regulating the general activity in the context of which it occurs. And third, where a private enterprise is so intimately associated with a state activity that each benefits directly from the other's presence, and the private activity complained of contributes to or affects that mutual benefit.

B. The Qualified Character of Individual Rights Protections

Most of the Constitution's individual rights provisions, including those which have generated the greatest controversy in interpretation, are qualified either by their explicit terms (Fourth Amendment's protection against "unreasonable" searches and seizures), or by virtue of their breadth or ambiguity (art IV, § 2 and 14th Amendment's "privileges and immunities of citizenship," First Amendment's "freedom of speech" or "establishment of religion," Fifth and 14th Amendments' "due process of law," and 14th Amendment's "equal protection of the laws"). At least in 20th century practice, the Court's interpretive approach to essentially all of these provisions utilized the means-ends analysis drawn early on from the language of article I, section 8 for solving governmental structure cases like *McCulloch v. Maryland*. The Court evaluates the purposes sought to be achieved by the governmental action in question and the closeness of the fit between the action and its purposes, in light of the action's impact on the complaining parties. Very occasionally a case can be disposed of by characterizing the action or its operative purpose as impermissible *per se*. For most cases, however, a burden of justification is attached to the action in question which varies in weight according to the importance of the right invoked, and the likelihood that improper purposes are actually at work.

Even the most exacting of these burdens of justification, carrying labels such as "strict scrutiny," can be met in an appropriate case. For example, the Court found racial discrimination to be justified in the first case to which the "most exacting scrutiny" formula was applied, *Korematsu v. United States*,[13] by the "pressing necessity" of wartime security against the possible divided loyalty of Japanese-Americans. Earlier, similar considerations led the Court, speaking through one of its most forceful defenders of free speech, to sustain a prohibition against advocating resistance to compulsory military service. The modern test allows advocacy of unlawful action to be suppressed if it appears likely to be successful in inciting such action. However preferred the status of the individual right, in short, it is always subject to being overridden by a sufficiently important governmental interest.

VIII. Privileges and Immunities of Citizenship

The Constitution contains two "privileges and immunities" clauses purporting to provide protection of the rights of citizenship, only one of which has acquired more than marginal significance, and that only rather recently. It is clear that both clauses protect only natural persons.

A. Article IV, Section 2

This clause in the original document is addressed to the states, and appears to require each to extend to the citizens of other states the "privileges and immunities" of its own state "citizenship." Prior to the adoption of the 14th Amendment, it received very sparse attention. The most authoritative interpretation was by a circuit court on which Supreme Court Justice Bushrod Washington sat and wrote the opinion, holding that it protected only the exercise of the most fundamental

13. 323 U.S. 214 (1944).

rights, those "which belong, as of right, to the citizens of all free governments."[14] After the 14th Amendment defined state citizenship as consisting of U.S. citizenship combined with residence within the state, the clause became in effect a prohibition against discrimination based on residence, but remained virtually unused until after World War II.

Since then it has been invoked primarily against state laws requiring residency within the state as a condition of pursuing certain occupations or professions, brought under the 19th century rubric of "pursuit of a common calling." In the first such decision, the Court held that commercial fishing licenses could not be denied to nonresidents of the state on that ground alone, and announced the applicability of means-ends analysis. There must be a valid reason for discrimination against nonresidents as such which identifies them as a "peculiar source of the evil" against which the law is directed, and a "close relation" must exist between the discrimination and that reason. Subsequent cases have found residence requirements to be unjustified with respect to a license to practice a profession such as law, private employment in occupations related to state-owned natural resources, and private employment with companies which are performing public-works contracts for government entities. On the other hand, the clause has been found inapplicable to such non-fundamental rights as that to obtain a recreational, as distinguished from a commercial, hunting license.

B. Fourteenth Amendment, Section 1

This clause prohibits the states from adopting laws abridging the "privileges or immunities of citizens of the United States." The Supreme Court interpreted it narrowly in its first appearance as protecting only rights of national citizenship as such: to travel to the seat of national government and petition for the redress of grievances; access to and use of seaports, navigable waters, and federal courts; and rights secured by treaty. It would also include the right to move from state to state and establish new residence; but other provisions, in particular the due process and equal protection clauses, have proven to be more effective protectors of these rights. The 14th Amendment "privileges and immunities" clause has seldom been invoked successfully before the courts.

IX. Due Process of Law

A. General Principles

There are two "due process clauses" in the Constitution, identical in text: in the Fifth Amendment applicable to the federal government, and in the 14th Amendment applicable to the states. Three issues of interpretation concerning the scope of these clauses appear now to be well settled.

14. *Corfield v. Coryell*, 6 F. Cas. 546, 551 (C.C.E.D. Pa. 1823).

1. "Person"

For purposes of the due process clauses, as well as for the equal protection clause of the 14th Amendment, the term "person" includes both *aliens* and *juristic* persons within the jurisdiction of the state or the federal government, as the case may be.

2. "Liberty"

After adoption of the 14th Amendment, it was argued that the term "liberty" as used in that provision includes all of the protections of the Bill of Rights, the first nine amendments otherwise applicable only to the federal government. The Court has refused to accept the proposition that all of the Bill of Rights were thus made applicable to the states, but has followed a principle of *selective* incorporation: "liberty" includes, in the current formulation, those protections which are "fundamental to the American system of justice." The result, however, has been that incorporation is the rule rather than the exception. To date, only three provisions of the original Bill of Rights have been held not applicable to the states: the Second Amendment's right to bear arms; the Fifth Amendment's requirement that prosecution of serious crimes be based on grand jury indictment, and the Seventh Amendment's jury trial right in civil (as distinguished from criminal) cases. Although a few provisions of the Bill of Rights have yet to be ruled upon authoritatively, it is likely that this list of exceptions is now complete. See Chap 15, pt. I.B.

3. "Property"

Primarily in cases involving the applicability of procedural protections, the Court has interpreted the term "property" in the due process clauses as including "entitlements," governmental benefits or privileges having a substantial value to which ordinary law or administration gives an encouraged expectation of continuation. Examples of such "entitlements" are welfare benefits, tenured public employment, and a driver's license.

B. Procedural Due Process

1. Specific provisions

The Constitution, particularly in the Fifth, Sixth, and Seventh Amendments, sets forth a number of specific procedural protections applicable to court proceedings, primarily for criminal cases. *See* Chap. 15, pts. III-VI.

2. General standard for governmental action

In addition, however, the Court has defined "due process of law" in more general terms, to describe the protections which must be afforded by any government agency whose action deprives a person of life, liberty, or property. The procedural values to be served are assuring accuracy and avoiding arbitrariness; the minimum requirement for this purpose is that the affected person must be given notice and an opportunity to be heard by the decision-maker concerning the action. With respect to particular features of the notice (what form must it take, how must it be transmitted, what information must it contain?) and the hearing (must it be public, must testimony be taken in open court and subjected to cross-examination by the affected party, must the party be allowed to have the assistance of legal counsel, must there be opportunity for appeal?), the Court has adopted a formula calling for balancing the interests of the government (for example, the cost of providing additional protection), and the interests of the affected person along with the likelihood that the particular procedural protection would reduce the risk of erroneous decision.

C. "Substantive" Due Process

1. The minimum standard: "rational basis" or non-arbitrariness

The notion that "due process of law" requires not only that governmental action follow proper procedures but also that it be defensible *in substance* had its origins in earlier natural law thinking, but first took hold in the Supreme Court in the late 19th century, when governmental corruption was a major political issue and free-enterprise capitalism the dominant economic philosophy. These views gave rise to a demand that government justify any interference with private arrangements in terms of a legitimate governmental objective, and some relationship between that objective and the particular regulation. Once the Court took it up, the issue then became, and remains, one of how strong the burden of justification should be. Much of the discussion since has the appearance of a battle of formulas.

For example, in the 1905 decision in which the Court most clearly committed itself to this means-ends analysis under the due process clause, *Lochner v. New York*,[15] three positions can be identified in the opinions dealing with the constitutionality of a law limiting the number of hours bakers could work in a week. The five-justice majority conceded that the state could regulate in the interest of health and safety, but refused to be persuaded by the state's evidence that bakers' work presented a health hazard which could be mitigated by limiting exposure to flour dust. It viewed the law as simply an interference with freedom of contract. Three dissenters agreed that evaluation of ends and means was appropriate under the due process clause, but argued that the state must be given the benefit of the

15. 198 U.S. 45 (1905).

doubt where there is room for an "honest difference of opinion." The fourth dissenter, Justice Holmes, rejected even the idea that a general regulation of the hours of work would be improper, and saw the majority as imposing a particular economic theory on the 14th Amendment without warrant. He argued that "the natural outcome of a dominant opinion" may not be judicially frustrated unless a rational person would have to admit that it "would infringe fundamental principles as they have been understood by the traditions of our people and our law." Thus the majority suspected a purpose it considered illegitimate (regulating purely economic relationships), and therefore put a heavy burden of persuasion on the state as to the appropriateness of the law for the stated, concededly legitimate, purpose (health). Three dissenters assumed the limitation on proper purposes, but gave the state the benefit of the doubt as to the "fit" between the law and the claimed proper purpose. Holmes deferred to the state on the choice of both ends and means, and seemed, by insisting on some more explicit fundamental principle, to reject the substantive dimension of "due process" altogether.

In subsequent cases the Court, though it eventually abandoned the *Lochner* majority's view, has seldom professed to go as far as Holmes would have in deferring to state policy, and has continued to insist on a minimum requirement frequently called "mere rationality": that the government have a lawful purpose, and that there be a "substantial relation" between the means chosen and the end or purpose pursued, in that a reasonable person could believe that the means chosen would further the end.

2. Heightened scrutiny: economic rights

a. *Express prohibitions: the takings clause.* One express provision which is considered to be a specific instance of "substantive due process" thinking is the takings clause of the Fifth Amendment, which has been held applicable to the states through the 14th Amendment. In that clause three terms have posed interpretive issues. "Taking" can include regulation as well as the seizure of possession or ownership, provided it virtually destroys the value of the property. "Just compensation" generally means the fair market value of the property or interest taken. And "public purpose" includes "public interest" in private property, as for example, the public interest in free alienability of land. If private property is taken for a private purpose, the taking is invalid; if it is taken for a public purpose, the taking may be valid but the owner has an enforceable right to compensation. Confiscation or forced sale of property as a sanction for its use in unlawful activity is not covered by the clause.

b. *Express prohibitions: the "contract clause."* Article I, section 10 prohibits the states from passing laws which impair the obligation of contract. This provision was originally intended to prevent states from enacting debtor relief laws, and prohibits only *legislative* impairments of the obligation of *existing* contracts. It applies only to the states, and not to the federal government, although the Fifth Amendment due process clause is understood to impose a similar but less stringent limitation on the federal government. The protection against impairment by the state includes its own public contracts as well as private ones, although the modern Court would probably limit the clause's application to those public contracts by which the state enters the marketplace as an economic actor (for example, as a borrower of funds for public works projects). Where the public "contract" is made in the context of exercising regulatory or taxing powers, the principle that a government cannot contract away its sovereign powers is likely to control. The Court's formulation of the applicable burden of justification differs slightly according to whether the affected contract obligations are private or public.

For *public contracts*, the impairing law must be necessary to protect an important state interest, and there must be no other less impairing means of protecting that interest. Thus when a state sold bonds to the public to finance construction of bridges, tunnels, and other port facilities, and promised in conjunction therewith not to use the revenues from their operation to subsidize mass transportation, the subsequent urgent need for mass transportation was insufficient to justify breaking that promise, when other revenue sources could be used.

With respect to *private contracts*, the burden of justification for impairments depends on the degree of contract obligation impairment. At least three segments of that spectrum have been identified in the cases. First, for "severe impairments," there must be an emergency threatening vital state interests and relief precisely tailored to the nature and duration of the emergency. In the Great Depression of the 1930s, the economic emergency was found to justify a moratorium on the specific remedy of forced sale of a debtor's home, while leaving all other debtor obligations intact. Second, in a more recent decision, the Court held that for "substantial" but not severe impairments, an emergency is not required, but a significant state interest and a relief tailored to the nature and duration of the need; this decision may limit the emergency requirement to the most extreme impairments. Third, "incidental" impairments of an existing obligation resulting from a generally prospective change in rules do not implicate the contract clause at all.

c. *Due process clause*. At the beginning of the 20th century, after a number of hints, the Court held that "freedom of contract" is an element of "liberty" protected by the due process clause itself against government interference, unless it could be shown that the regulation directly furthered an appropriate state concern such as safety or health.[16] In effect, as the dissenting Justice Holmes pointed out, the Court interpreted the due process clause as if it codified laissez-faire economics. Subsequent decisions in cases involving employment relationship regulation turned on the state's ability to persuade the Court that safety, health, or a comparable welfare concern was at stake rather than simply the protection of particular economic interests – successful in the case of maximum-hour legislation for women and for overtime pay requirements, but unsuccessful for statutes prohibiting employers from insisting, as a condition of employment, on

16. *Lochner v. New York*, 198 U.S. 45 (1905); *see* text at n. 15.

the employee's commitment not to join a union. In the wake of the Great Depression, the Court abandoned this presumption against the validity of economic regulation, and established the basic burden of justification as that of "rational basis" or "mere rationality." In practice, if not in theory, the Court has stopped serious review of economic regulation altogether, and thus closely approximates Justice Holmes's dissent in *Lochner*.

3. Heightened scrutiny: fundamental personal (non-economic) rights

a. *Early intimations: parental control over education.* In the 1920s the Court held, without attempting to announce a change in theoretical perspective, that it was impermissible under the due process clause for a state to interfere with parents' control over their children's education by prohibiting instruction in the German language in peacetime, or by requiring them to go to public rather than private schools.

b. *The right of "privacy" or personal autonomy.* A few decades later there emerged a more general concept of privacy or personal autonomy, at least in marriage and procreation matters. In 1942 the Court held that a state law imposing involuntary sterilization of women as punishment for certain crimes but not for others invaded this right of personal autonomy, where the discrimination could not be justified in law enforcement terms. In 1965 the Court invalidated an absolute prohibition against the use of contraceptives as applied to married couples,[17] and later extended that ruling to restrictions on their distribution to unmarried persons. Characterizing the right as one of privacy, the majority opinion in the first contraceptives case found it to be implicit in a number of specific protections. Other concurring justices found warrant in the Ninth Amendment for identifying rights to be protected which are not specifically enumerated. Dissenters characterized the law as "uncommonly silly," but insisted that that was a judgment of social policy which the courts are not competent to impose on the legislature. The majority agreed that the right was such a fundamental one that the state must have compelling reasons for overriding it. Finally, in one of those highly controversial decisions which periodically call the proper role of the courts into renewed popular question, the Court extended the right of "privacy" or personal autonomy to abortion,[18] holding it impermissible to prohibit all abortions not necessary to save the life of the mother.

In addressing the problem of abortion, the Court recognized two state interests capable of overriding that of the mother's personal autonomy: (1) that in the health of the mother; and (2) that in the *potential* life of the fetus. At the same time, however, it found that the fetus is not a "person" within the meaning of the 14th Amendment, whose right to life would be equal to that of the mother, and would take precedence over the mother's personal value-choices. Moreover, the

17. *Griswold v. Connecticut*, 381 U.S. 479 (1965).
18. *Roe v. Wade*, 410 U.S. 113 (1973).

state's competing interests could be sufficiently compelling to override the mother's choice only at certain stages of the pregnancy: that of the mother's health, justifying regulations of the manner or setting in which abortions are carried out, when the health risks of abortion are demonstrably greater than the risks of continuing the pregnancy; that of the potential life of the fetus, when the fetus is "viable," capable of living outside the womb.

Subsequent cases have addressed many detailed issues, but the Court remains sharply divided not only on the existence of the right but also on the rationale for it. In its most recent comprehensive review of the right the Court narrowly rejected determined efforts to abandon it altogether, but reduced it to the right not to have the state impose "undue burdens" on a woman's decision to have an abortion, and not to have the state forbid post-viability abortions when the continued pregnancy would endanger the mother's life or health.[19] Regulations such as those requiring physicians to present overly detailed and emotionally charged information before obtaining the patient's consent to the procedure, which are designed to discourage abortion on policy grounds distinct from those "compelling interests," have been struck down, as have laws giving other persons (a spouse, natural father, or parents of an underage but competent mother) a veto power over the mother's decision. However, the state is not precluded from non-coercive advocacy against the decision to have an abortion, and it does not have a duty to subsidize abortions. In 1991 the Court held that the federal government can, to avoid all forms of official support for abortion, prohibit government-supported family planning facilities from even supplying information concerning the availability of abortion services elsewhere.

No doubt as a result of the controversy over the abortion decision and the conscious effort of conservative presidents since then to appoint new justices who would reverse or restrict it, the Court has been unwilling to extend protection, as the concept of a right of personal autonomy might suggest, to consensual sexual activity generally.

X. Equal Protection of the Laws

A. In General

The 14th Amendment prohibits a state from denying the equal protection of the laws to any person within its jurisdiction. A similar concept is now read into the Fifth Amendment due process clause applicable to the federal government. The boundary between due process and equal protection is somewhat vague, but one can say that while due process addresses government treatment of persons as such, equal protection addresses government classification of and differentiation among persons. An example of overlap occurred where a state provided, in its law prohibiting discrimination in employment and establishing an agency to receive and resolve complaints of such discrimination, that any complaint not given a

19. *Planned Parenthood of Southeastern Pennsylvania v. Casey*, 505 U.S. 833 (1992).

hearing by the agency within 120 days would be dismissed without hearing. While the opinion of the Court struck down the statute solely on the ground that it denied due process to those complaints not heard, six justices also stated that the statute established a classification of complaints – those heard within 120 days and those not heard within 120 days – and treated the classes differently without a rational basis for the distinction, in violation of the equal protection clause. On either theory the provision was irrational, because it left the availability of a hearing solely in the control of the state.

B. General Standard

Although the Court initially thought that the equal protection clause, appearing as it did in an amendment codifying the winning ideology after a civil war ultimately fought over race-based slavery, would only be applied to discrimination against blacks, it eventually came to the view that the clause states a general principle for differential treatment of persons by government. In its normal mode the clause is now understood to prohibit distinctions which are without reasonable basis, arbitrary, or invidious. In the now familiar means-ends analysis, the requirements are a legitimate government purpose and a rational fit between the classification and the purpose. Courts have been very indulgent in identifying possible purposes, even when the legislature has failed to identify one. In two recent cases, however, operative purposes have been declared to be illegitimate: (1) rewarding citizens for *past* contributions to society, as by providing subsidies or tax relief to long-term but not to new residents; and (2) discrimination against out-of-state in favor of local economic interests, which was held to be against the spirit of the interstate commerce clause, even though in the particular case Congress had validly precluded application of the "dormant" commerce clause. The rational relationship requirement has also received indulgent application, and is sometimes called the "conceivable basis test." The Court has held that it is permissible to address part of a problem or to address it in stages. Since 1930 no economic regulation has been overturned on equal protection grounds, with a single exception which was subsequently overruled.

C. Heightened Scrutiny

1. "Suspect" classifications

The Court has identified several classifications that require especially strong justification. While it has never embraced a general definition of such classifications, scholars have frequently proposed a definition based on a footnote, offered in *obiter dicta* in a 1938 case, referring to "prejudice against discrete and insular minorities" which may require "more searching judicial inquiry."[20] The Court

20. *United States v. Carolene Products Co.*, 304 U.S. 144, 152 n.4 (1938).

appears to have closed off further additions to the list. Each such classification identifies groups subject historically to pervasive invidious discrimination in American society, justifying the suspicion that governmental use of the category to select persons for differential treatment reflects prejudice rather than rational pursuit of legitimate goals.

The "heightened scrutiny" takes the form of shifting to the government the burden of justifying its differential treatment in terms of nondiscriminatory ends or purposes. To activate the burden of justification, the challenger must show *purposeful* use of the suspect classification; the mere fact that a facially neutral action has a differential *impact* on the groups is not enough.

a. *Race or national origin: strictest scrutiny.* In its first race-discrimination opinions following adoption of the 14th Amendment, the Court spoke simply of a prohibition against discrimination as the essence of the clause, and, despite its earlier assumption that only blacks were meant to be protected, quickly extended the clause to all races. Nearly a century later the Court finally took occasion to draw the logical inference from the latter point by holding that members of the white majority are also protected against such discrimination. It was not until 1944 that the Court, faced with a claim of wartime necessity for an explicitly discriminatory action, articulated the modern standard in the form of a burden of justification.[21] That decision remains, however, the only case in which discrimination against a racial minority has been held to satisfy the requirement of "pressing public necessity."

The primary occasion for fuller elaboration of the modern standard occurred in cases in which racial classifications were used in an ostensibly neutral manner, purporting to affect all races equally. The Court's initial anti-discrimination interpretation was modified by the decision in *Plessy v. Ferguson*,[22] which held that only political, as distinguished from social, equality was meant to be enforced, and that mandatory separation of the races in public facilities (as passengers on state-owned railroad trains, in that case, or as pupils in public schools) was permissible so long as the facilities available to each are roughly equal. Ten years after *Korematsu*, having previously invalidated a number of segregation laws on the narrow ground that the facilities provided were not equal, the Court finally overruled *Plessy*, and held racial segregation in public schools invalid as "inherently unequal."[23] In doing so, however, it did not expressly invoke the *Korematsu* standard, or generalize further about "neutral" use of racial categories. That process began in 1964, in a case which invalidated a law prohibiting persons of different races from living together, even as married couples. The Court there spoke of the "heavy burden of justification" for racial classifications, presupposing an "overriding statutory purpose requiring the proscription," and said that they would be upheld "only if ... necessary, and not merely rationally

21. *Korematsu v. United States*, 323 U.S. 214 (1944); *see* text at n. 13.
22. 163 U.S. 537 (1896).
23. *Brown v. Board of Education*, 347 U.S. 483 (1954).

related, to the accomplishment of a permissible state policy."[24] By 1984 the following statement, from an opinion holding it impermissible to deny child custody to a mother who had entered into an interracial second marriage, could be regarded as typical:

> [Racial] classifications are subject to the most exacting scrutiny: to pass constitutional muster, they must be justified by a compelling governmental interest and must be "necessary [to] the accomplishment" of its legitimate purpose.[25]

b. *Alienage or non-citizenship: mixed analysis.* In the leading case on the subject the Court addressed state discrimination against aliens with a dual argument: first, "alienage" is a "suspect" classification, subject like race to strict scrutiny; second, when a state regulates or adds burdens to the status of aliens, it encroaches upon the plenary power of the national government to regulate immigration and naturalization. The first argument relied in part on earlier cases which in fact involved racial discrimination disguised as alienage discrimination. This eventually yielded (not without controversy) to the perception that citizenship as such – full membership in the political community – was a permissible consideration not only for the right to vote but also for certain types of public employment involving formulation or implementation of fundamental public policy, for which a citizenship requirement was exempted from strict scrutiny. The second argument soon led to the conclusion that alienage, unlike other "suspect" classifications, is one which the federal government may employ with virtual impunity. Thus, while states may not exclude non-citizens from welfare benefits or from their competitive civil service employment, the federal government may do both.

c. *Gender and illegitimacy: "intermediate" scrutiny.* At the same time that it was addressing alienage, the Court began to deal with the claim that gender was also a suspect classification. While the case for an historical pattern of pervasive discrimination, stereotyping, and condescension was persuasively made, resulting in drastic underrepresentation of women in most better-paid occupations as well as in political leadership, other factors militate against equating gender with race in presuming the classification to have invidious intent. In particular, the facts are emphasized that women are not a numerical minority and are no longer denied the right to vote, that physiological differences exist between men and women which justify differential treatment in respect of some occupations and roles, and that society has an especially strong interest in the unique biological role of the mother which supports protective legislation. After striking down specific state and federal gender discriminations without agreement on the strength of the applicable burden of justification, the Court in 1976 settled on a formula requiring an "important" governmental purpose, and a "substantial relationship" between the

24. *McLaughlin v. Florida*, 379 U.S. 184, 192, 196 (1964).
25. *Palmore v. Sidoti*, 466 U.S. 429, 432-33 (1984).

gender classification and the important purpose. The same decision established that the justification burden applies regardless of which gender is disadvantaged by the challenged action.[26]

In subsequent cases the Court sustained a statute punishing males for having sexual intercourse with underage females but not vice versa, sustained the male-only military conscription system, struck down a state university's female-only nursing school, and struck down a male-only state public university using a military-style instructional method. In the latter two cases, the absence of an equivalent facility for the other sex was found to destroy the argument that these single-sex institutions were designed to provide diversity of educational experience.

The Court has also applied an intermediate burden of justification to classifications based on legitimacy of birth, after a number of decisions demonstrating uncertainty and disagreement on the proper formula. In the most recent opinions, which struck down special limitations periods for bringing suits against biological fathers to establish paternity and the right to support, which were unusually short in comparison with those applicable to support claims against legitimate parents, the majority opinions did not call for an especially significant state interest or end, but did emphasize that the fit between means and end must be shown by the state to be "substantial."

d. *"Benign" or remedial use of suspect classifications*. After the decisions making racial segregation unlawful, the Court had to deal with the permissibility of judicial remedies for such violations which are themselves race-conscious. The most controversial has been the reassignment of pupils to different schools by race so as to eliminate the racial imbalance caused by prior segregative policies, which in turn often involves transportation of children by bus to schools that are a substantial distance from their homes. In the leading case on the subject, the Court held that such measures were subject to but could satisfy the "strict scrutiny" standard, because there is a compelling governmental interest in redressing the injury caused by past unlawful discrimination, and pupil reassignment could properly be found necessary to redress the injury caused by forced separation of the races in the schools. In view of the complexity of the task of undoing segregation, the same decision accorded to first instance courts a large measure of discretion in fashioning remedies to fit the particular situation.

Still more controversial have been programs introduced by legislatures and other government agencies and institutions calling for "affirmative action," the granting of various kinds of preference for members of minority groups with respect to public employment, public contracts, or admission to educational programs. The Supreme Court has addressed such programs in several decisions, without achieving a coherent majority view on all aspects of the problem. In the first such decision, *Regents v. Bakke*,[27] it held invalid a program whereby a state university's medical school set aside a specific number of positions (16 of 100) in its entering class exclusively for minority applicants. A white student who would

26. *Craig v. Boren*, 429 U.S. 190 (1976).
27. *Regents of the University of California v. Bakke*, 438 U.S. 265 (1978).

have been admitted but for this preference was held to have been the victim of unlawful racial discrimination. In his opinion for the Court, with the rationale of which no other justice agreed at the time but which has become accepted as the leading one, Justice Powell held that the policy was subject to strict scrutiny, and that it could not be sustained as a remedy for past unlawful discrimination, because (1) there was no finding or assertion that the medical school itself or even the university was guilty of past unlawful discrimination, and (2) in any event it did not appear that either institution was competent under state law to make such findings.

In 1995, after an earlier decision imposing a lighter burden of justification on *Congress* for enacting affirmative action programs (intermediate scrutiny) than is applicable to the states (strict scrutiny) because of Congress's express enforcement powers under the 14th Amendment, the Court reversed itself and settled on strict scrutiny for all racial classifications, whether "benign" toward minorities or otherwise.[28] Remedying past discrimination remains a compelling state interest which may be sufficient to sustain such preferential programs. If a *legislative* body adopts them, the Court may still be willing to accept past *societal* discrimination within the legislature's territorial jurisdiction (as distinguished from that directly perpetrated by state agencies) as a basis for such remedial action. In any event, however, it will require particularized findings of such discrimination, and of harm suffered by the *beneficiaries* of the preference because of such discrimination.

In the *Bakke* case, one of the justifications for the minority admissions program was to ensure an educational environment of ethnic diversity. Justice Powell held that this was a permissible goal under the equal protection clause, but that it could not support a rigid quota of admissions, as distinguished from simply identifying a factor to be given weight in making admissions decisions. Programs which consider minority race and ethnic background as a positive factor in admission to educational institutions have not since been seriously challenged in court. The diversity issue has arisen, however, in two subsequent Supreme Court decisions. In one, the maintenance of a racially diverse public school faculty was held to be insufficient justification for laying off more senior white teachers while retaining more junior black teachers – the especially severe impact of being laid off requires an especially strong justification. In the other, the Court sustained a policy, mandated by Congress, to favor minority-owned applicants for licenses to operate television stations, where the stated purpose was to foster diversity of programming. Since this decision applied a lesser burden of justification to Congress than to the states, and in that respect has been specifically overruled, it cannot be relied upon for the proposition that "diversity" is a sufficiently compelling state interest to survive strict scrutiny.

2. Fundamental rights

The Court has also applied strict scrutiny equal protection analysis to differential treatment of persons in respect of certain fundamental rights, in circumstances

28. *Adarand Constructors, Inc. v. Pena*, 515 U.S. 200 (1995).

where it appeared that the government action would not constitute a direct violation of the right for the group less favorably treated. In particular, two such rights have been identified and dealt with extensively: the right of interstate migration (moving one's residence from one state to another), and the right to vote.

a. *The right of interstate migration, or "the right to travel."* The target under this heading has been the formerly widespread state practice of imposing "durational residency" requirements on eligibility to receive certain benefits. The leading case involved a requirement, for eligibility to receive social welfare benefits, that the applicant have resided in the state for one year. The Court held that this requirement constituted a penalty on the exercise of the right to migrate, by putting the migrant in a less favorable position regarding essential support services after the move than before. On the other hand, the Court has held that a durational residency requirement for the right to obtain a divorce in the state was not invalid, because of the state's concern to avoid intervention in the paramount interests of another state, and because the right was not denied but only postponed. Finally, a bona fide simple residency requirement – that one be a resident at the time of obtaining city employment or at the time of receiving free public education – has been sustained as not inconsistent with the right of migration.

b. *The right to vote.* Several express provisions protect the right to vote as such against various kinds of discrimination: the 15th (race), 19th (sex), 24th ("poll tax" on the right to vote in federal elections), and 26th Amendments (age, above 18 years). The equal protection clause proved indispensable, however, in attacking a different kind of discrimination, so-called "vote dilution." When representatives having equal votes in legislative or other governing bodies represent districts having significantly different population sizes, the individual voter in the larger population has less influence over the choice of her representative than does the voter in the smaller population. In the 20th century the most common disparity was between agricultural districts and urban districts. After attacks on the problem based on the "republican form of government" clause failed on justiciability grounds, the Court finally concluded in 1964 that the equal protection clause was applicable. In 1965 it held that equal protection dictated application of the basic principle that such representative districts should have as nearly equal populations as feasible. The Court has tolerated greater disparities in state legislative districts with special historical justification than in those for the federal House of Representatives (still in the first instance apportioned by state legislatures). The principle of "one person, one vote" has been held applicable to elections for office in any entity exercising general governmental powers, especially the power to tax. School districts with such power have been included, but special-purpose units such as water-supply districts without such power have not; thus the franchise can be limited in those situations to persons who use the facilities.

In other decisions under the clause, the Court struck down poll taxes as a condition of the right to vote in state and local elections. Recently it went so far as to hold that equally apportioned districts which are defined by the dominant party in such a way as to perpetuate its dominance by dividing the opposition's voting strength could be a violation of equal protection, although it demanded a showing of long-term effects not made in the particular case and not likely to be made in others.

When the right to be a *candidate for office* is at stake, the Court has said that this is not a fundamental right in itself, but restrictions on candidacy are subject to strict scrutiny to the extent that they significantly restrict the voters' right to choose their candidates. It is permissible, for example, to require, as a condition of being placed on the ballot as a candidate, that the candidate demonstrate a minimum level of support among voters (the usual method is to require submission of a petition signed by a certain number of persons eligible to vote).

c. *Other rights*. The Court has refused to extend the strict scrutiny equal protection analysis to other concededly important rights, such as education, housing, and welfare benefits, and it appears unlikely that it will expand the category of "fundamental rights" for this purpose in the foreseeable future.

XI. Freedom of Speech

A. General Principles

1. Scope of the clause

The First Amendment prohibits Congress from making any law "abridging the freedom of speech." The Court has interpreted this provision as protecting all modes of expression, whether verbal or not, and as protecting it against any type of restriction; the right is therefore often labeled "freedom of expression." The protection is not absolute, but in the form of a justification burden which in most cases is quite heavy. It is one of the provisions of the Bill of Rights, originally addressed to the national government, which has been held applicable to the states through the 14th Amendment's due process clause. Judges and scholars often confer upon it a preferred position in the scheme of rights.

2. Prior restraints and after-the-fact sanctions

It is frequently said by the Court that "prior restraints" are the most difficult restrictions on speech to justify. These are restraints which are imposed prospectively, before the speech is uttered. They include above all licensing schemes requiring official pre-publication examination of proposed publications (the historical mechanism for censorship), but also injunctions issued by courts purporting to prohibit future violations of law (thereby making the future violation not only an offense against the state or a private wrong, but also a contempt of court). After-the-fact sanctions include criminal punishment and civil liability for damages, premised on proof of wrongful publication. This emphasis on prior restraints reflects historical concerns from the English experience, but there is uncertainty among scholars about how sharp the distinction is in modern practice.

3. Content-based and content-neutral restrictions

Another pervasive theme in the Court's analysis is the distinction between restrictions of speech based on its content or message, and those which are based on other aspects of the expressive behavior. The former are clearly more difficult to justify than the latter, and the burden of justification is usually said to be strict scrutiny. In some contexts, however, the Court has distinguished among content-based restrictions, identifying those which seek to suppress a particular viewpoint as more suspect than those based on subject matter alone.

4. Overbreadth

The Court has developed a special standing doctrine for First Amendment cases, reflecting the view that the rights thus protected have a preferred status. If a law is formulated in such a way as to restrict both unprotected behavior and a substantial range of protected speech, it is characterized as "overbroad" and treated as invalid on its face. As a result, one who is accused of violating the law may invoke its unconstitutionality, even if his own behavior is unprotected and could be restricted by a properly formulated law. The rationale for this doctrine is that such a law should be attacked at the first opportunity, to minimize the "chilling effect" which even an invalid law can have on protected speech. This variant of third-party-rights standing has been criticized by some scholars and justices as an undue hindrance to effective law enforcement, and appears to be more narrowly applied now than it was a few decades ago. In particular, the Court has recently indicated a much greater indulgence for narrowing interpretations of state laws to eliminate their overbreadth in application, however strained the interpretation might be of the actual language. Nonetheless, the doctrine remains a potentially powerful tool of advocacy.

5. Speech on government-owned property

When private speech occurs on government-owned property, the question arises whether the government may have a proprietary interest in controlling it. The Court has recognized three distinct categories of government property for purposes of the freedom of speech: (1) the *traditional public forum*, defined in one majority opinion as "public places historically associated with the free exercise of expressive activities, such as streets, sidewalks, and parks," and including, for example, the sidewalks around the Supreme Court building itself;[29] (2) the *limited public forum*, defined as property which the government has designated for or dedicated to certain kinds of expressive activity, such as a state university or a public school which allows its facilities to be used by students or other members of the academic community for extra-curricular activities; and (3) other property

29. *United States v. Grace*, 461 U.S. 171 (1983).

operated by the government for specific purposes, such as a military base, jail premises used for confinement of prisoners, or public transportation vehicles operated as a business enterprise.

The government's burden of justification for restrictions on speech is heaviest in the traditional public forum, where strict scrutiny normally applies and the cases suggest a minimum guaranteed right of access for expressive purposes consistent with the other purposes for which the property is used (for example, traffic and recreation). In the limited public forum, the primary purposes to which the facilities are devoted perhaps will be given greater weight, access may be limited to relevant groups (universities to students and faculty, or schools to pupils), and the dedication to private expressive activity may be withdrawn, but within the scope of dedication the burden of justification for restrictions remains high. On other property, the government is free to restrict speech to further the purposes to which the property is devoted, so long as it is not arbitrary or capricious. For example, it may exclude political advertising from its busses while allowing commercial ads, prohibit the distribution of political literature on a military base, and foreclose the use of a school's internal mail system by an unrecognized teachers' union.

B. *Permissible Content-Based Restrictions*

1. Subversive speech

The only American law purporting to prohibit "libelous" criticism of the government was enacted in 1798, was sustained against constitutional challenge by lower federal courts but never reviewed by the Supreme Court, and expired without renewal in 1801. In 1964 the Court characterized that law (*obiter dicta*, of course) as inconsistent with the "central meaning" of the First Amendment. In the 20th century the kind of seditious speech most often addressed by legislatures was that which advocates violent or other unlawful action to effect political change. In the 1920s the Court sustained such state statutes, including those which attributed the stated aims of an organization to all its members, even if the individual member had opposed them.

During the Cold War the Court considered several applications of a federal statute prohibiting advocacy of the violent overthrow of the government as well as knowing membership in an organization committed to such advocacy, of which three are of particular interest. In 1951, applying a "clear and present danger" test, the Court considered it sufficient to show that the defendants advocated violent action "when they thought the time was ripe," and considered it common knowledge that the Communist Party leadership did so. In 1957, however, it overturned convictions under the statute because the charges did not emphasize "incitement to action" as distinguished from abstract doctrine. And in 1961 it held that the statute's "knowing membership" provision required a showing that the member was active, and had the specific intent of furthering the organization's unlawful ends. As a result of this gradual toughening of the advocacy proof standards, convictions under that statute ended. Finally, in a 1969 decision striking down a state statute similar to those it had sustained in the 1920s, the Court formulated the current test, which presumes that even advocacy of the use of force is protected unless "such advocacy is directed to inciting or producing imminent lawless action and is likely to incite or produce such action."[30]

2. "Fighting words" and the hostile audience

In 1942 the Court held that a speaker could be charged with breach of the peace if he addressed language to someone in a public place which is likely to cause the average addressee to fight. A subsequent case held it permissible for police to restrain a sidewalk speaker whose advocacy of an uprising against racial injustice produced threats of violence *against the speaker* from some listeners. This led some to infer that audience hostility to the speaker's ideas could remove First Amendment protection. In a series of decisions involving peaceful demonstrations against racial discrimination in the 1960s, however, the Court made clear that the authorities could not use audience hostility toward ideas peacefully expressed as a reason to suppress the speech, and the "hostile audience" concept appears now to be dead.

3. Defamation

While it had been traditionally assumed that the First Amendment did not protect a person against civil or even criminal liability for defamatory speech – that which tends to injure another person in his reputation, and cannot be shown to be factually true – the Court has recognized at least two important limitations. First, in 1964 it held that a public official could not recover damages for false criticism of official conduct unless he could show that it had been published with "actual malice," that is, with knowledge of its falsity or reckless disregard of its truth or falsity. Later cases extended this exceptional burden to plaintiffs who are "public figures," persons who are not public officials but have either: (1) achieved general fame and notoriety in the community through pervasive involvement in public affairs, or (2) voluntarily injected themselves into a particular public controversy which is the subject of the publication. Public interest in the controversy as such is not enough if the plaintiff is not a "public figure" with respect to it. The other constitutional limitation applies to both public and private plaintiffs. Damage awards may not exceed compensation for proven injury unless such actual malice is shown. *See* Chap. 9, pt. V.A.

4. Obscenity

The Court has frequently said that obscenity is outside First Amendment protection. Its decisions have announced a constitutional definition of obscenity, however, which makes enforcement of the prohibition difficult. The material must depict sexual conduct; it must, according to the standards of the community, be

30. *Brandenberg v. Ohio*, 395 U.S. 444, 447 (1969).

directed in a patently offensive manner to the sexual arousal of the group addressed; and it must be without serious literary, artistic, political, or scientific value to any reasonable person.

5. "Offensive speech"

Where speech is not obscene by the above definition, it cannot be suppressed solely because it is morally offensive to some persons, so long as they can avoid the message. Some regulations of time and place for such speech may be permissible, such as a requirement that pornography houses be dispersed throughout the community rather than concentrated in a single area to avoid creating a center for illegal activity, or one that offensive radio programming be confined to certain hours when children and other sensitive audiences would be less likely to tune in. Moreover, the Court has held that the state's strong interest in protecting the welfare of children permits prohibition of the production, distribution, or possession of "child pornography," defined as material depicting a sexual performance by an underage child, the production and distribution of which inevitably involves child abuse.

6. Commercial speech

Until 1975 it was assumed that advertising and other communications proposing commercial transactions were not protected at all under the First Amendment. In that year, however, the Court announced a qualified protection, which allows regulation of the content of such commercial speech to prevent false or misleading statements and the promotion of illegal transactions, but otherwise imposes a burden of justification for restrictions which is comparable to that for noncommercial speech. The government must have a substantial interest other than speech suppression, the regulation must actually further that interest, and it may not restrict the speech more than is necessary for the furtherance of that interest. Among the most significant consequences of this protection is the abrogation of rules against advertising by professionals such as lawyers, doctors, and pharmacists.

7. Student expression in the public schools

In 1969 the Court held it impermissible for a public school to prohibit the wearing of black arm bands by pupils, where the prohibition was adopted in anticipation of a specific planned demonstration against the Vietnam War, and was justified solely by the apprehension of controversy rather than by any substantial interference with the work of the school or the rights of other pupils. Two recent decisions make clear, however, that the First Amendment poses no general threat to the schools' control over pupil participation in instructional or other school-sponsored activity. It is thus permissible to discipline a student for offensive speech in a school-sponsored assembly, because inculcation of moral values is a proper function of the schools. And the faculty editor of a school-sponsored newspaper may censor student articles, where the student work is an integral part of the school's curriculum.

C. Content-Neutral (Time, Place, and Manner) Regulation

Regulations of otherwise protected speech in a public forum which do not depend on its content or viewpoint, but focus on the time, place, or manner of its expression, are permissible but also subject to an enhanced burden of justification. In particular, the regulation must be narrowly tailored to a significant governmental interest, and must leave alternative channels of communication open. Thus a law requiring a permit to hold a parade in a public place is permissible, where its sole function is to assure orderly access to such use, the permit fee is related to the size of the parade as reflecting the cost of providing police protection, and the conditions imposed are designed solely to prevent disorder. The Court also sustained a regulation requiring persons wishing to distribute literature or solicit funds at a state fair to do so only at designated booths, where the purpose was to prevent blocking of pedestrian traffic on the narrow passageways of the fairgrounds. A more controversial decision held it permissible for a city to prohibit "focused picketing" in front of or around a particular home, to protect the privacy of its residents, as applied to protesters picketing the home of a doctor who performed abortions at various clinics. The latter regulation was said to be narrowly tailored to the interest in protecting residential privacy, because it is limited to picketing directed to an essentially captive audience, and thus also leaves ample alternative means of expression open to the protesters.

XII. Freedom of Association

Although there is no express provision in the Constitution guaranteeing a freedom to associate with other persons, the Court has repeatedly acknowledged such a right. It has most often done so, however, in connection with efforts by government to restrict or control the activities of groups or associations in such a way as to infringe on fundamental rights which also belong to the individual, such as the rights to petition for redress of grievances, to gain effective access to the courts, to vote, to express ideas, and so on. A general right to associate as an element of "liberty" under the due process clause, which would be tested by government prohibition of association to engage in activities which remain lawful for the individual without being constitutionally protected, has yet to be recognized. A 1984 decision summarized the cases by identifying two types of associational freedoms: (1) a freedom of private association, which is limited to "certain intimate or private relationships"; and (2) a freedom of expressive association, to engage in activities which are themselves constitutionally protected.[31]

31. *Roberts v. United States Jaycees*, 468 U.S. 609 (1984).

So far, although the Court sought to identify general criteria of size, purpose, and selectivity, the list of protected intimate relationships is short: marriage, parenthood (bearing, rearing, and educating children), and cohabitation with relatives.

Government interference with them is subject to the strict scrutiny applied under fundamental rights due process. With respect to expressive or "instrumental" association, the government's burden of justification depends on the severity of its restriction on members' expression: if "significant," strict scrutiny will be applied, including the duty to employ the least restrictive means to accomplish the government's compelling purpose; if only "slight," it is sufficient to show that the restriction actually furthers such a purpose. In *Roberts*, the Court held it permissible for a state, in pursuit of a compelling interest in the elimination of sex discrimination in economic life, to prohibit exclusion of women from large, influential, and otherwise unselective associations of business and professional persons.

XIII. Freedom of Religion

A. *Establishment of Religion*

The first of the two religion clauses of the First Amendment, which directs Congress to "make no law respecting an establishment of religion," was seldom invoked before the courts until 1947, when the Supreme Court held that it was incorporated into the concept of "liberty" in the 14th Amendment due process clause and thus applicable to the states. By that time, although it may have been understood in 1789 simply to protect the established churches of several states from federal interference, the Court was prepared to interpret it as not only prohibiting the formal establishment of a state church but also requiring a "wall of separation" between church and government – a position espoused by Jefferson but by no means undisputed in his time.

In 1971 the Court settled on a three-part "test" for the validity of laws affecting organized religion: (1) the law must have a secular purpose (though it need not be the exclusive one); (2) the law's primary effect must be neither to advance nor to inhibit religion; and (3) the law must not involve the government in "excessive entanglement" with religion.[32] Thus, to cite some of the least complex examples from the cases: (1) a law requiring public schools, if they choose to teach the scientific theory of evolution, also to teach the religiously inspired doctrine of creationism, lacks any secular purpose; (2) a law which gives any church a veto over the granting of a liquor license to a business within 500 feet of the church, which the church may exercise or not as it wishes, has the primary effect of advancing religion; and (3) a law which assigns public school teaching staff to teach secular subjects at religious schools, and sets up an elaborate monitoring and scheduling system to assure that no religious content creeps into what those teachers teach, involves the public school administration in an "excessive entanglement" with the religion assumed to be otherwise pervasive in the sectarian school.

32. *Lemon v. Kurtzman*, 403 U.S. 602 (1971).

This three-part test is criticized by many, including some justices, as requiring government hostility toward religion, which is itself inconsistent with the spirit of the clause. It is argued, therefore, that accommodation of religion, as distinguished from favoritism toward particular religions, should be permitted. One justice, for example, takes the position that a government action does not violate the clause unless it conveys a message of endorsement of specific religious positions. While this view has not yet displaced the three-part test, the most recent decisions suggest that the second, "primary effect" prong of that test, will be a prohibition against "endorsing or disapproving" religious positions.

B. Free Exercise of Religion

The second religion clause by its terms forbids laws "prohibiting the free exercise" of religion. From 1963 until quite recently, the Court`s interpretation imposed strict scrutiny on any governmental act which "burdens" a person's observance of religious practice. Thus it was improper to deny unemployment compensation to a person merely because she had refused to accept particular work which violated religious scruples such as working on Sunday or manufacturing armaments. In 1990 the Court narrowed its interpretation dramatically, refusing to apply strict scrutiny to any nondiscriminatory criminal prohibition against a particular form of conduct merely because the prohibited conduct was required by a particular religious belief (in the particular case, sacramental use of the hallucinogen peyote by members of an American Indian religious group).

The result is a "free exercise" clause which appears to do no more than prohibit discrimination on religious grounds, a prohibition already effected by the "establishment clause" as the Court has interpreted it. An effort by Congress to reinstate the strict scrutiny test for all substantial burdens on free exercise was struck down by the Court, on the ground that Congress lacks power, even under its enforcement powers pursuant to the 14th Amendment, to override the Court's own interpretation of a particular constitutional protection's scope.

Selected Bibliography

Erwin Chemerinsky, *Constitutional Law: Principles and Policies* (1997).
David P. Currie, 1-2 *The Constitution in the Supreme Court* (1985, 1990).
Michael J. Gerhardt, Thomas D. Rowe, Jr., Rebecca L. Brown & Girardeau A. Spann, *Constitutional Theory: Arguments and Perspectives* (2d ed. 2000).
Philip B. Kurland & Ralph Lerner, 1-5 *The Founders' Constitution* (1987).
Leonard W. Levy, Kenneth L. Karst & Adam Winkler, eds., 1-4 *Encyclopedia of the American Constitution* (2000).
John E. Nowak & Ronald D. Rotunda, *Constitutional Law* (6th ed. 2000).
Norman Redlich, John Attanasio & Joel K. Goldstein, *Understanding Constitutional Law* (2d ed. 1999).

Ronald D. Rotunda & John E. Nowak, 1-5 *Treatise on Constitutional Law: Substance and Procedure* (3d ed. 1999 & Supp. 2000).
Laurence H. Tribe, 1 *American Constitutional Law* (3d ed. 2000).
—— , *American Constitutional Law* (2d ed. 1988)[individual rights].
Laurence H. Tribe & Michael C. Dorf, *On Reading the Constitution* (1991).

Chapter 5
Administrative Law

*John O. Haley**

I. INTRODUCTION

Administrative law as commonly defined encompasses the legal rules that govern the organization, activities, and relations of administrative organs within a particular constitutional structure. Administrative law in the United States, as in other industrial states, has become a leading field of law for theory and practice. At all levels of government – national, state, and local – administrative organs today make more legal rules than all legislatures and courts combined. The legal rules that determine the structure, procedure, and role of each administrative organ thus occupy as central a place within the United States as in any other country's legal system. Nevertheless, in several important respects American administrative law remains fundamentally distinctive.

*Wiley B. Rutledge Professor of Law, Washington University School of Law.

David S. Clark and Tuğrul Ansay (eds.) Introduction to the Law of the United States, 97-113

First and foremost, the particular features of American constitutional structure define administrative law in the United States. *See* Chap. 4, pts. IV, V. The United States is the only common law jurisdiction with a federal, presidential political system. Second, the United States has developed one of the world's most open and accountable political systems. Especially noteworthy are several features of the system that influence the role of administrative agencies, their procedures, and their political relationships. National party influence over political entry is negligible. Even local party control tends to be quite weak. Primary elections have expanded to allow widespread voter selection of party-affiliated candidates for elected office. With few exceptions national political leaders begin their careers at the local level and will have developed in the process strong local bases of political strength. Third, the system is characterized by a multiplicity of politically competitive organs of government at all levels. A uniquely American political structure has produced an equally unique configuration of administrative organs. One consequence is an extraordinarily varied and complex set of interactions among the legislative, executive, and judicial branches of government at the national, state, and local level. Another is the degree of concern for accountability and transparency in the administrative process and the resulting legal requirements for administrative decision making. Administrative law in the United States thus differs fundamentally from administrative law in other legal systems from both the common and civil law traditions.

Our primary focus in this chapter is administrative law at the national or federal level. The basic patterns and principles of state administrative law do not differ significantly, however, from federal administrative law. Many if not most of the observations made here thus apply to state administrative law as well. In other respects state law should not be totally ignored. State administrative law for most Americans is at least as important as federal law. States have primary responsibility for education, land use, most social services, public works, and police powers. It is indeed at the state and local level that most citizens come into direct contact with administrative authorities. Constitutional principles also restrict the authority of the federal legislature to deal with matters subject to state competence.[1]

1. A series of recent U.S. Supreme Court decisions has given new life to the reservation of powers to the states under the federalist principles of the Constitution's Tenth Amendment, which provides: "The powers not delegated to the United States by the Constitution, nor prohibited by it to the States, are reserved to the States respectively, or to the people." *Printz v. United States*, 521 U.S. 898 (1997) (federal gun control legislation is unconstitutional in requiring enforcement by state officials); *New York v. United States*, 505 U.S. 144 (1992) (low-level radioactive waste control statute exceeded Congress's constitutional powers in requiring states under certain conditions to "take title" and thereby become responsible for such undisposed waste); *see Solid Waste Agency of N. Cook County v. United States Army Corps of Eng'rs*, 531 U.S. 159 (2001). *See also Kimel v. Florida Board of Regents*, 528 U.S. 62 (2000) (right to sue in tort against age discrimination is not applicable to state employees, since the Congress's source of legislative power acted as an unconstitutional waiver of state sovereign immunity without state consent under the 11th Amendment).

II. THE STRUCTURE AND AUTHORITY OF ADMINISTRATIVE ORGANS

The U.S. Constitution recognizes three distinct but interrelated branches of government that operate within a system of checks and balances. Within this system two basic forms of administrative organs have evolved. The first is the executive department, corresponding to a ministry in most parliamentary systems. Subject to confirmation – the "advice and consent" – of the Senate, the president appoints the heads of federal departments. They are removable at the will of the president. The heads and most policy-making officials in executive departments as well as the staff in a plethora of executive offices subject to presidential direction – including many that initially developed within the president's personal White House staff – are generally political appointments that change with each presidential election rather than career civil service officials. More than 3,000 executive officers are subject to the president's discretionary, political appointment.

A second category comprises agencies that are conceptually established apart from the executive branch as "independent" agencies. Most have regulatory functions and are headed by either a single administrative official or a multiple-person commission whose members and chair are appointed by the president with the advice and consent of the Senate for terms fixed by the agency's enabling statute. They are independent in the sense that they are controlled by officials whom may be removed from office under very limited circumstances, and thus are less subject to the president's policy direction. The proliferation of such agencies reflects the competitive political tensions between the executive and legislative branches intrinsic to the U.S. presidential system.

These categories and the differences they imply are far from rigid. Many sections or divisions created within executive departments are statutorily insulated from presidential intervention and function as if they were independent agencies. Similarly, the extent of presidential direction permitted in the case of nominally independent agencies also varies. The number of administrative offices located outside of any department or independent agency with extensive administrative authority has also multiplied within the White House and state gubernatorial offices. Two examples stand out: both the Office of Management and Budget (OMB) and the U.S. Special Trade Representative (USTR) began as informal offices within the White House, without enabling legislation.

The legislative process compounds the complexity of American administrative law. All federal legislation formally originates within one or both houses of Congress. The president participates through the procedures for "presentment" and his opportunity for veto. The executive branch also is usually well represented by legislators in the president's political party on the various congressional committees responsible for the legislation, as well as by White House or departmental staff responsible for executive branch liaison with Congress. Furthermore, each department and agency has staff whose functions include liaison with their counterparts who work in congressional offices or for congressional committees. In fact, many agency heads and high-ranking agency officials served on congressional committee or office staff at the start of their government careers.

This process is not transparent. Critical provisions in a statute may be inserted at the very last moment during committee deliberations, especially in joint committees responsible for negotiating over differences in bills passed by the House of Representatives and the Senate. Nor does any central authority exist to ensure legislative coherence. Neither the executive branch nor either house of Congress has an office for systematic review and drafting of proposed legislation. One consequence of this structure is that American administrative law has a relative dearth of widely shared rules or definitions. Much of the corpus of administrative law rules – procedural as well as substantive – thus comprises the collected rules of myriad statutes and assorted agencies. They are often inconsistent. The same word used in the text of separate statutes may be defined quite differently. However, the 1946 Administrative Procedure Act (APA)[2] functions as a source of common concepts and principles. Much of the task of creating connecting threads of coherence has been left to the courts.

The role of courts in the administrative process is among the most distinctive features of American administrative law. Courts play a partnership role in the administrative process as a result of judicial contempt powers as well as the expansive availability of judicial review. *See* pt. V. As in nearly all other legal systems, they have the last word in the interpretation and application of both statutory and administrative rules.

III. Constitutional and Statutory Requirements for Administrative Procedure

A. *In General*

The emergence of the administrative state in the United States in the late 19th century initially provoked two fundamental constitutional questions. The first, the constitutionality of any administrative agency, reflected the lack of any specific provision in the U.S. Constitution for administrative authority. The issue was resolved in terms of the explicit authority of the president to see to it "that the Laws be faithfully executed" and of the Congress "To make all Laws which shall be necessary and proper for carrying into Execution" its enumerated powers.[3] The extent Congress may constitutionally delegate any of its legislative powers or interfere with executive power remains in contention even today,[4] although the

2. 5 U.S.C. §§ 551-559, 701-706 (1994 & Supp. V 1999).
3. U.S. Constitution, arts. II, § 3; I, § 8, cl. 18.
4. *See, e.g., Whitman v. American Trucking Ass'ns, Inc.*, 531 U.S. 457 (2001), in which the Supreme Court upheld the delegation of legislative power to the Environmental Protection Agency in the Clean Air Act. Only two cases have ever held delegations of *legislative* power to be unconstitutional. Both involved the National Industrial Recovery Act of 1933 (NIRA). *A.L.A. Schechter Poultry Co., v. United States*, 295 U.S. 495 (1935); *Panama Refining Co. v. Ryan*, 293 U.S. 388 (1935). For a case on congressional usurpation of *executive* power, *see Bowsher v. Synar*, 478 U.S. 714 (1986), holding unconstitutional a statute giving a legislative official, the Controller General of the General Accounting Office, review powers over the executive branch budget.

Supreme Court has defined the parameters of the delegation doctrine broadly in favor of extensive administrative discretion.[5] Delegations of legislative authority are today considered acceptable so long as the enabling statute provides sufficient direction with respect to the general standards or basic considerations intended to guide the agencies in exercising such discretion. It should be noted that American lawmakers have never adopted Cesare Beccaria's (1738-1794) principles of *nullum crimen sine lege* and *nulla poena sine lege*. *See* Chap. 7, pt. II.A. Congress's power to delegate to administrative organs the authority to define particular conduct as a criminal offense or to create a criminal penalty is not disputed.

Administrative procedure is the central concern of American administrative law. The Constitution's due process clauses set minimum procedural standards for federal (under the Fifth Amendment) and state agencies (under the 14th Amendment). *See* Chap. 4, pt. IX.B; Chap. 16, pt. III.D. The application of due process standards involves three separate questions. The first is *whether* the agency action in question affects a liberty or property interest. The identification of such an interest can be often quite difficult. If the answer to this threshold question is yes, the two remaining questions are *when* during the agency decision-making process must due process requirements be implemented and *what kind* of process or procedures are constitutionally required.

More significant in actual practice than the minimum constitutional standards, however, are the detailed statutory provisions for agency decision-making procedures of either the statute authorizing the particular agency decision or the agency's own enabling statute. In the absence of specially applicable statutory procedures, the APA applies for federal agencies. Nearly all states have similarly enacted a generally applicable statute establishing decision-making procedures for state administrative agencies. Most follow either the 1961 or 1981 version of the Model State Administrative Procedure Act.[6]

The federal APA recognizes two fundamental categories for the determination and articulation of agency policy: (1) rulemaking and (2) adjudication. These categories derive first from the distinction between a "rule" and an "order" under the APA. As defined under APA section 551(4) a rule is "the whole or part of an agency statement of general or particular applicability and future effect designed to implement, interpret, or prescribe law or policy or describing the organization, procedure, or practice requirements of an agency." Under section 551(6) an order, in effect, is any agency pronouncement that does not come within the APA definition of a rule. These categories have over time become deeply embedded in American conceptions of administrative procedure.

B. Rulemaking

Insofar as the APA is concerned, in order to adopt a rule an agency need only to comply with the procedural requirements for "informal rulemaking" set out in

5. *See, e.g., Mistretta v. United States*, 488 U.S. 361 (1989).
6. 15 U.L.A. 1 (2000); 15A U.L.A. 1 (2000).

section 553. Most rulemaking at the federal level takes the form of this relative-ly simple "notice and comment" procedure. Agencies are first required to give public notice of all proposed rules by publication in the *Federal Register*. Interested persons must also be given the opportunity to present written comments during a prescribed period, but the agency may in some instances give the parties an opportunity for oral comment. After the period for submitting comments has expired, the agency announces (again in the *Federal Register*) the final rule. Although outside comments are supposed to be taken into consideration, the discretion to determine the final rule remains with the agency. The only constraint imposed is the requirement in section 553(c) that, for all final rules, the agency must include, usually as a preamble, a "concise general statement of their basis and purpose." Courts are not free to impose procedural obligations above and beyond those provided in section 553.[7]

An agency may choose to avoid even the minimum "notice and comments" requirement in cases involving what are designated as "interpretive" or "non-legislative" rules, which do not have the force or effect of law and are therefore not formally binding or enforceable. In many instances, however, such pronouncements may have as significant an influence as a binding rule. Ordinarily, such actions are also reviewable by the courts. The categorization of the rule as interpretative, and thus the agency's failure to adopt it pursuant to notice and comment or other established procedures, may therefore be effectively challenged as inappropriate.

Congress, of course, may always establish by statute more or less elaborate procedures for any particular agency or agency action. And it has often done so as administrative rulemaking has expanded and also become more varied. Legislation authorizing trial-type hybrid rulemaking procedures was prominent in the 1970s. More recent laws require rulemaking agencies as well as the Office of Management and Budget (OMB) to conduct various kinds of "impact" or "cost-benefit" analyses. Agencies themselves have sought to develop more flexible alternative procedures, mainly to avoid delays in the promulgation or implementation of final rules caused by protracted litigation with those opposed. What is commonly referred to as "negotiated rulemaking" is one of the most widely used approaches. The APA was amended in 1990 to encourage negotiated rulemaking in suitable instances (as defined in section 563). The content of the rule in such cases is determined by negotiating committees comprising representatives of the agency and identified interests affected by a proposed measure.

Rulemaking may also take the form of an adjudicatory process, with the decision on the nature and content of the final rule made after an adversarial, trial-type hearing in which evidence is formally presented and incorporated into a written record. Such formal rulemaking procedures are rarely invoked, but they are used in proceedings involving administrative approval of pricing or rates of a highly regulated industry.

7. *See Vermont Yankee Nuclear Power Corp. v. Natural Resources Defense Council, Inc.*, 435 U.S. 519 (1978).

C. Formal Adjudication

Adjudication is the APA-designated procedure for decisions that result in orders rather than rules. An order is usually defined as an administrative action or measure that involves a determination of an individual or particular legal relation. However, the APA mandates adjudication only where the agency decisions are "required by statute to be determined on the record after an opportunity for an agency hearing."[8] The language in the statute must itself provide for an evidentiary hearing. Merely requiring a hearing is not necessarily sufficient.[9]

As in the case of formal rulemaking, the process of formal administrative adjudication resembles a common law trial without a jury. It parallels an American first instance judge trial in terms of both the procedures followed as well as the scope of judicial review on appeal. *See* pt. V.E; Chap. 16, pts. IX.A, XI.D.

An administrative law judge (ALJ) presides. The office of ALJ evolved during the second half of the 20th century as administrative hearings became increasingly judicialized and a neutral presiding official was increasingly favored over a hearing officer with expertise in the subject matter. The ALJ may be assigned to a particular agency for an indefinite period and may even serve within a single agency over the course of a career. In many states the ALJ is assigned to an agency by a separate administrative department or office responsible for administrative law judges.

To ensure the ALJ's neutrality, the separation of investigatory and adjudicatory functions is strictly observed. No person who has been involved in the investigation or prosecution of a case may preside or even participate in the decision except as a witness or counsel. An ALJ may be disqualified for bias. *Ex parte* contacts are prohibited. Most if not all of the rules of evidence will be observed. Adjudicatory decisions are to be based exclusively on the record of the hearing.

Initial decisions by an ALJ are usually subject to agency review. For administrative review the APA appears on its face to allow the agency to exercise the discretionary authority it initially enjoyed. However, once an ALJ has conducted an adjudicatory hearing and issued an initial decision, the agency is not free to disregard the ALJ's initial findings.[10]

D. Informal Administrative Action

In all legal systems most administrative actions are informal. The vast majority of all administrative decisions are reached with the consent of those involved, without the need for formal proceedings. Such agreements may lack legal force but are nevertheless effectively implemented. The forms of informality are as

8. 5 U.S.C. § 554(a) (1994).
9. *See, e.g., City of West Chicago v. United States Nuclear Regulatory Comm'n.*, 701 F.2d 632 (7th Cir. 1983). For a similar result in a rulemaking context, *see United States v. Florida E. Coast Ry.*, 410 U.S. 224 (1973).
10. *See Universal Camera Corp. v. NLRB*, 340 U.S. 474 (1951).

varied, however, as the tasks undertaken by contemporary agencies. Some agencies, such as the National Park Service and the Forest Service, have managerial responsibilities. Others, such as the Federal Trade Commission (FTC), the National Labor Relations Board (NLRB), and the Occupational Health and Safety Administration (OSHA), have investigatory and prosecutorial functions. In addition, there are an array of agencies that process claims and disburse entitlements and those that carry out promotional and educational programs. Not the least, of course, are federal, state, and local tax assessing and collecting agencies. Whatever the function, informality prevails. Even for regulatory measures, in instances where the economic stakes may be quite high, most cases are resolved by mutual agreement without resort to formal proceedings. All forms of informal measures used to carry out an agency's mandate, from public statements with respect to present or future agency policy to the negotiated resolution of an individual case – what the Japanese refer to as "administrative guidance" – are in fact as prevalent in the United States as anywhere else.

Finally the APA itself authorizes informality in the event that *de novo* judicial review is available. In American practice *de novo* review is quite rare and this provision of the law is seldom invoked. Those familiar with the more common use of *de novo* judicial review in civil law systems should note that United States law would not require detailed procedural safeguards for most of the administrative decisions made in the typical European or other civil law jurisdiction.

IV. Access to Information

Administrative agencies, those they deal with, and the general public have separate but related interests in access to information. Agency access to information is based on a variety of sources. Americans have long been subject to a vast number of record keeping requirements. Some are established by statute, and others by administrative regulation. By the mid-1990s an official compilation of record retention requirements under varied statutes and agency rules had reached over 540 pages and included over 3,000 separate items.[11] Agencies, in addition, usually enjoy broad investigatory powers. These would normally include the right to subpoena witness and documentary evidence. Under some circumstances they may conduct warrantless searches. *See* Chap. 15, pt. III.D. Agencies may be aided by reinforcing judicial subpoenas and orders subject to judicial contempt powers.

As the administrative state expanded under the New Deal in the 1930s and the need for public access to agency information intensified, Congress enacted the Federal Register Act.[12] We have already noted the key importance of the *Federal Register* in providing public notice of proposed agency actions and the concomitant opportunity to respond. The rights of private parties subject to agency regulation, as well as the public at large, to require agency disclosure of

11. *See* Office of the Federal Register, *Guide to Record Retention Requirements in the Guide of Federal Regulations* (1994).
12. 44 U.S.C. §§ 1501-1511 (1994).

information expanded greatly since the late 1960s. The 1966 Federal Freedom of Information Act (FOIA)[13] and similar legislation at the state level, including state "sunshine" laws – not to mention federal and state agency Web sites – have greatly expanded private party access to information, producing a much more transparent administrative process.

Prior to enactment of the FOIA, each agency was required under the APA to make certain information available to the public. These requirements remain in force.[14] The list includes: final opinions and orders, with dissents and concurring opinions, of any adjudication; statements of policy and interpretation that have not otherwise been made available through publication in the *Federal Register*; and staff manuals and instructions that affect the public.

What made the FOIA so radical a departure from the earlier approach was its open-ended requirement. Subject to expressly provided exceptions, the FOIA mandates that "each agency, upon *any* request for records which (i) reasonably describes such records and (ii) is made in accordance with published rules stating the time, place, fees (if any), and procedures to be followed, *shall* make the records promptly available to any person."[15] All agencies are required to establish and publish rules setting out the procedures to be followed and the fees to be charged.

Public access is denied to information that comes within the scope of nine specified exemptions: (1) national defense or foreign policy secrets as determined by executive order; (2) internal personnel rules and practices; (3) trade secrets or privileged or confidential commercial or financial information; (4) inter- or intra-agency memoranda or letters not subject to discovery in litigation with the agency; (5) personnel and medical files that would constitute, if made available, an invasion of privacy; (6) investigatory records for law enforcement under limited circumstances; (7) records of financial institutions; (8) geological and geophysical data; and (9) other information exempted from disclosure by statute.

The FOIA – like its state equivalents – is supplemented by the requirements for public access to agency meetings under the 1976 Government in the Sunshine Act[16] and similar state open meetings legislation. As in the case of the FOIA, in principle all meetings of multi-member agencies are open to the public. Agencies are required to post the times and sites for all meetings with agenda. Only meetings related to matters that are expressly excepted – a list that is nearly identical to the FOIA exemptions – may be closed to the public. In contrast to the FOIA, there has been very little litigation related to the open meetings requirement at the federal level. The open meeting requirements at the state and local levels, alternatively, have been subject to more litigation. How significant these statutes have been in making administrative decision-making processes more transparent is subject to debate.

Whatever the effect on the transparency of administrative decision making, no one should doubt the impact of the FOIA and open meetings requirements on

13. 5 U.S.C. § 552(a)(3) (1994 & Supp. V 1999).
14. 5 U.S.C. § 552(a)(2) (1994 & Supp. V 1999).
15. 5 U.S.C. § 552 (a)(3)(A) (Supp. V 1999) (emphasis added).
16. 5 U.S.C. § 552b (1994 & Supp. V 1999).

the political oversight of agency action. These reforms have contributed to the rapid growth of myriad non-governmental organizations (NGOs), with special concern or interest in specific areas of public policy. Some represent commercial and financial interests; others focus on one or more "public interest" concerns. Representing nationwide or even transnational constituencies, these special interest and often "single cause" organizations are able to monitor agency activity quite effectively and thereby exert often-determinative influence on agency policy. They provide channels of communication and the means to activate public pressure and, in turn, both congressional as well as White House responses. They have thus become significant actors in the administrative process.

V. Judicial Review of Agency Action

A. *In General*

No area of American law is more distinctive and significant in practice than the role of courts in the administrative process. In most if not all civil law jurisdictions, courts play an exclusively reviewing role. Only where an administrative agency has issued a formal decision or has acted in some allegedly wrongful fashion do the courts become involved. Otherwise administrative agencies function largely independently of any judicial scrutiny. Not so in the United States – and, it should be added, other common law jurisdictions. In American law and practice, from the initial investigation to the ultimate implementation of an agency decision, courts are partners in the administrative process.

The power of contempt is a key factor that explains the extent of judicial participation from the start of the administrative process. At all stages of the administrative process, from an initial investigation through the issuance of a final implementing decision, agencies issue orders that require at least the threat of sanction to be effective. The failure to comply with an interim administrative order, however binding as a matter of law, usually does not subject the respondent to any formal sanction. Thus, to force compliance agencies rely on judicial contempt power. In order to preclude any potential failure to comply, the agency will supplement its own measure by seeking an identical judicial order. For example, agencies quite routinely seek judicial subpoenas to require disclosure of documents and witnesses to testify. As a result, courts become active participants from the initial stages of most administrative proceedings. Although judicial proceedings at the investigatory stage of an administrative proceeding are in most instances *ex parte*, the respondents have the opportunity for appeal and review. Thus, courts become involved at all levels in response to both agencies and those affected by agency actions.

American administrative law has long been characterized by the expansive opportunity for judicial review of agency actions. A threshold constitutional concern should be kept in mind: the prerequisites for judicial jurisdiction must be satisfied.

B. Jurisdiction and Preclusion

Under the U.S. Constitution the appellate jurisdiction of federal courts, including the Supreme Court, requires statutory authorization. *See* Chap. 4, pt. III. Federal courts do not enjoy an inherent power to adjudicate appeals from administrative decisions. As courts of limited jurisdiction, they are subject to congressional direction.[17] That said, however, courts do have the last word. They thus may presume congressional intent to allow judicial review unless explicitly denied or a separate constitutional claim is presented.[18] The requisite jurisdictional authority will nearly always be found in specific legislation on the matter under review, the agency's enabling act, or the general jurisdictional statute.[19] However, the particular routes for judicial review are quite varied. Congress may have selected a particular court or circuit to review certain types of decisions by an agency and perhaps all decisions by another agency. The reasons for the varied venue choices are not always apparent.

Congress may also preclude judicial review by creating a program that commits a matter to agency discretion.[20] Whether or not judicial review is available, at least to determine whether agency discretion may have been abused, has long been debated.[21] To the extent that constitutional claims are raised, recent cases favor reviewability.[22] However, agency inaction, either by refusing to initiate the rulemaking process or to investigate and prosecute a case, is generally not reviewable.[23]

C. Standing

The authority of federal courts to review administrative action is also constrained by the Constitution's article III limitation of judicial power to "cases and controversies." In order to satisfy this requirement the party seeking judicial

17. For recent examples of judicial deference to legislative preclusion, *see Reno v. American-Arab Anti-Discrimination Comm.*, 525 U.S. 471 (1999), holding that the courts were precluded from considering a selective enforcement claim against the Attorney General; *Shalala v. Illinois Council on Long Term Care, Inc.*, 529 U.S. 1 (2000). In the first case, the Court interpreted the Immigration and Nationality Act's § 1252(g) to restrict judicial review in deportation proceedings to certain Attorney General "final orders": the decisions to commence proceedings, to adjudicate the case, or to execute a removal order. In the second case, the Court held that courts lacked jurisdiction to entertain a challenge brought by an association of nursing homes against certain Medicare-related regulations under the Social Security and Medicare Acts by virtue of a provision that required all Medicare claims to proceed through a special review channel created by the Medicare statutes.
18. *See Citizens to Preserve Overton Park*, 401 U.S. 402 (1971); *Abbott Labs. v. Gardner*, 387 U.S. 136 (1967).
19. See 28 U.S.C. §§ 1331, 1337 (1994 & Supp. V 1999).
20. 5 U.S.C. § 701(a)(2) (1994).
21. *See* Kenneth Culp Davis, 5 *Administrative Law Treatise* § 28.6 (2d ed. 1984 & Supp. 1989); Louis L. Jaffe, *Judicial Control of Administrative Action* 359 (1965).
22. *See, e.g., Webster v. Doe*, 486 U.S. 592 (1988).
23. *See Heckler v. Chaney*, 470 U.S. 821 (1985).

review must establish his or her standing to assert a reviewable claim. Until the 1960s the prerequisites for standing were relatively narrow, requiring that the party have a legal interest or legally protected right with respect to the action under review.

Beginning with the Supreme Court's 1962 decision in *Baker v. Carr*,[24] the landmark reapportionment case, the Court expanded the notion of standing to allow a much broader spectrum of parties and interests to challenge administrative actions. The Court stated that the party seeking review must have "a personal stake in the outcome" of the litigation. In two cases decided on the same day in 1970[25] the Court settled on the current test. First, the agency's action must have caused the plaintiff an "injury in fact" and, second, the plaintiff must arguably come within the "zone of interest" the statute or constitutional provision in question is designed to protect. The second prong of the test is aptly criticized for forcing courts to make what is in effect a decision on the merits of the plaintiff's claim in the context of an ostensible ruling on jurisdiction. The crux of the challenge is often whether as a matter of law or fact or both, the plaintiff's claimed interest is legally protected.

The standing of organizations claiming to represent their members has been among the most important questions the Court has faced in the wake of the 1970 decisions. In *Sierra Club v. Morton*,[26] the next case to raise this issue, the Court held that the Sierra Club did not have standing to assert a claim in environmental cases because the Club did not allege injury to any of its members. In 1973, however, the Court allowed an appeal in another environmental case by a law student group that merely alleged personal injury by one or more of its members to proceed, at least to an initial determination of facts to support the claim.[27] Recent cases have tended to tighten the personal injury requirement, but still allow associations to sue on behalf of their members if injury is convincingly demonstrated.[28] An association may sue on behalf of its members so long as the members would themselves satisfy the tests for standing, the interests the association is attempting to protect relate to its purpose, and neither the claim nor the remedy requires the participation of individual members in the lawsuit.[29] The first two of these three separate requirements are regarded as constitutionally mandated. The third, which would bar associational standing if the claim requires the participation of individual members, is characterized as a "prudential" requirement that can be modified by statute.[30]

Generally, standing is not recognized in taxpayer suits. Such cases typically involve challenges to legislation on constitutional grounds by persons whose claim of injury is based on their misspent tax dollars. In a 1968 case involving Department

24. 369 U.S. 186 (1962).
25. *Ass'n of Data Processing Serv. Orgs. v. Camp*, 397 U.S. 150 (1970); *Barlow v. Collins*, 397 U.S. 159 (1970).
26. 405 U.S. 727 (1972).
27. *United States v. SCRAP*, 412 U.S. 669 (1973).
28. *See, e.g., Lujan v. Nat'l Wildlife Fed'n*, 504 U.S. 555 (1990).
29. *See Warth v. Seldin*, 422 U.S. 490 (1975); *Hunt v. Washington State Apple Adver. Comm'n*, 432 U.S. 333 (1977).
30. *United Food & Commercial Workers Union Local 751 v. Brown Group, Inc.*, 517 U.S. 544 (1996).

of Health, Education and Welfare payments to religious schools, the Supreme Court carved out a narrow exception.[31] The Court limited such suits to cases where the plaintiff can show that the measure in question actually spends taxes, and such expenditures violate a closely related constitutional or legislated prohibition.

In recent years an increasing number of regulatory statutes, particularly legislation designed to protect the environment, such as the Clean Air Act, include "citizen suit" provisions that allow "any person" to bring suit against persons in violation of the statute or the agency responsible for its implementation. Such actions may be maintained so long as the constitutionally required elements for standing are present.

D. Timing

Timing is an equally important consideration in determining the availability of judicial review. As in the case of standing, both constitutional "case and controversy" as well as prudential constraints have led to the development of several closely related principles that preclude judicial review. An administrative measure is not reviewable until it is sufficiently final or "ripe" for review. Similarly, courts will also refrain from review if, without jeopardizing the plaintiff's interests, the agency still has an opportunity to alter the challenged action and thereby correct any error. Thus plaintiffs will be required to "exhaust" their existing administrative remedies. Moreover, an action will cease to be reviewable if the issues raised have become "moot" as a result of corrective administrative action, the challenger's change of status or position, or other factors.

The APA explicitly authorizes judicial review of any "final agency action for which there is no other adequate remedy in a court."[32] An agency's own regulations often establish when its actions become final. The APA further provides that "preliminary, procedural, or intermediate" actions or rulings are reviewable concomitant with review of related final agency actions. These provisions of the APA control in the absence of some other statutory basis for review.[33]

E. Scope of Review

The Congress's APA and judicial decisions have established the basic parameters for what courts are authorized to do when they review agency actions. As in the case of judicial review of judicial acts, the reviewing court will possibly face three types of issues: questions of fact, questions of mixed fact and law, and questions of law. Needless to say, courts exercise the most discretion with respect to questions

31. *Flast v. Cohen*, 392 U.S. 83 (1968).
32. 5 U.S.C. § 704 (1994).
33. *See, e.g., Franklin v. Massachusetts*, 505 U.S. 788 (1992) (the Secretary of Commerce's report to the President based on the population census tabulation by state did not constitute a final agency action, and therefore was not subject to judicial review).

of law. The APA, for example, allows the court to "decide all relevant questions of law, interpret constitutional and statutory provisions and determine the meaning or applicability of the terms of an agency action."[34] Indeed, the thrust of recent cases is to require a reviewing court to accept the agency's reasonable interpretation of an ambiguous statute.[35] Nevertheless, courts will consider agency interpretations of their own enabling legislation, as well as the rules they have promulgated. The degree of deference depends, however, on a sometimes-subtle combination of factors that relate to the court's sense of agency performance. Courts are also expected to review the entire record related to the contested agency action. In reviewing agency findings of fact three standards are used: *de novo* review, the "substantial evidence" test, and a residual "arbitrary and capricious" test.

De novo review involves potentially a full rehearing of the evidence submitted to the agency. In the United States *de novo* review is rare. As indicated previously (pt. III.C), formal rulemaking and adjudicatory agency proceedings today resemble a first instance trial without a jury. Similarly, courts on appeal treat the administrative decision as they would a first instance judgment. In such cases courts on review would hardly ever engage in a *de novo* fact-finding process, but instead limit the scope of review to legal issues, accepting the conclusions of fact reached by the agency so long as they are supported by "substantial evidence" in the record. In instances of serious agency error, courts are much more likely to remand for rehearing by the agency than to rehear the case themselves.

In cases involving less formal agency action, and by the same token more agency discretion, the "arbitrary and capricious" test is the usual standard. That language used in the relevant statute was long regarded to signal congressional intent to allow less intense judicial oversight of agency decision making. The courts' responses have been more varied, especially since Antonin Scalia's opinion questioning the distinction between the "substantial evidence" and "arbitrary and capricious" tests.[36] The courts' experience with the agency seems particularly important. Irrespective of the language used, to the extent that the reviewing judges respect an agency's past performance and trust its expertise and judgment, they can be expected to show considerable deference to its decisions. The less trusted an agency, the greater the intensity of judicial scrutiny.

VI. Damage Suits against the Government and Government Officials

Private damage suits provide a second, but more limited, indirect channel for judicial review of administrative actions. Such cases might be brought either against the federal or a state or local government or against government officials at whatever level as individuals. Historically, both federal and state governments

34. 5 U.S.C. § 706 (1994).
35. *See Chevron U.S.A., Inc. v. Natural Res. Defense Council*, 467 U.S. 837 (1984).
36. *Ass'n of Data Processing Serv. Orgs., Inc. v. Bd. of Governors of Fed. Reserve Sys.*, 745 F.2d 677 (D.C. Cir. 1984).

and all public agencies, including public schools, hospitals, and other service providers, were absolutely immune from private suits based on contract as well as those for tort damages for negligent or even willful conduct. Officials were similarly shielded. The federal government first waived its immunity in 1887 in the Tucker Act to allow contract actions.[37] But the federal government's waiver of immunity was not expanded to cover tort actions for nearly a half-century until the 1946 Federal Tort Claims Act (FTCA).[38]

The FTCA allows tort suits against the federal government for harms to persons or property caused by the negligent or wrongful acts or omissions of any federal employees. The employee must have been acting within the scope of his or her office. Moreover, the government is liable only to the extent that a private employer would be similarly liable in tort under the law of the place where the act occurred (*lex loci delicti commissi*). *See* Chap. 17 pt. III.C. No punitive damage claim is permitted nor can pre-judgment interest be awarded. Claims that resemble punitive damages may be recovered, however, to the extent they are recognized by state law. In *Molzof v. United States*,[39] for example, the Supreme Court recognized a claim under the FTCA for future care and "enjoyment of life" to the extent that Wisconsin law would recognize such relief. The plaintiff in the case suffered permanent brain damage as a patient in a veterans hospital located in Wisconsin when his oxygen was negligently cut off during lung surgery.

Tort claims against the federal government are further limited under the FTCA to preclude injury caused by activities that occurred outside of the United States,[40] related to tax collection, or where other statutes bar the claim. Also excluded are claims arising from libel, slander, misrepresentation, deceit, interference with contract, assault, battery, false imprisonment, false arrest, malicious prosecution, or abuse of process.[41]

The most troublesome immunity cases are those where the employee is performing *discretionary* rather than *ministerial* tasks. The ostensible aim for insulating the federal government and government officials at all levels from liability for actions that come within the scope of discretionary responsibilities has been to allow them to perform policy-making tasks without concern for potential tort claims.

Government officials are similarly immune from suit to the extent that they are performing official tasks. However, in perhaps the best known case of the 1990s, *Clinton v. Jones*,[42] the President of the United States was denied temporary immunity for the duration of his term of office from a civil damage action that arose out of alleged misbehavior prior to his taking office.

37. The Tucker Act, as amended, permits suits against the federal government when based "either upon the Constitution, or any Act of Congress, or any regulation of an executive department, or upon any express or implied contract with the United States, or for liquidated or unliquidated damages not sounding in tort." 28 U.S.C. § 3146(a) (1994).
38. 28 U.S.C. 1346(b) (1994 & Supp. IV 1998).
39. 502 U.S. § 301 (1992).
40. *See United States v. Smith*, 499 U.S. 160 (1991) (a military doctor was held not subject to a malpractice suit brought against him where the injuries occurred outside of the United States).
41. 28 U.S.C. 2680 (1994).
42. 520 U.S. § 681 (1997).

The greater the official role involves discretionary authority, the greater her immunity from suit. Judges top the list. Their immunity is absolute unless the actions at issue are nonjudicial or taken in the complete absence of all jurisdiction. In *Mireles v. Waco*,[43] for example, the Supreme Court recognized the absolute immunity of a judge deemed to be acting in his judicial capacity when he ordered police officers to use excessive force to bring a public defender to his courtroom. In contrast, in *Forrester v. White*,[44] the Court denied the immunity of a judge who was charged with gender discrimination in an employment context. In that case, the Court determined that in hiring and discharging probation officers the judge had been acting in his administrative capacity. Prosecutors also enjoy absolute immunity when deemed to be performing their traditional functions as the state's advocate. In *Kalina v. Fletcher*,[45] for example, the Supreme Court denied immunity for a prosecuting attorney who had made allegedly false statements of fact in a certification of probable cause to support an arrest warrant. The Court concluded that she was performing the function of a complaining witness in making the certification rather than the function of an advocate.

The function of the office is not always determinative, however. A qualified immunity from suit has even been extended to prison guards to the extent that the prison is managed by or under the direct supervision of the government. Alternatively, there is no immunity for a private concern, managing the prison for profit under a contract with a state or local government.[46]

VII. Conclusion

For more than two decades the extent of state ownership and direct administrative control over economic activities – including over such archetypical "public" facilities as prisons – has been greatly reduced in nearly all countries around the globe. This process continues unabated today in the United States as well as elsewhere. Yet, as paradoxical as it may appear, administrative activity and its law may have changed but has not diminished. In the United States at least, the result of privatization and deregulation have been less to reduce the extent of administrative involvement in the economy than to alter its manner or means. As enterprises as varied as electric utilities and prisons are entrusted to "private" managers, administrative regulation is altered but not eliminated. In place of managerial responsibility, direct ratemaking, or direct controls, these enterprises are now subjected to less direct but still extensive oversight by contract, antitrust, or other market regulating devices. The central role of administrative law is thus equally likely to continue.

43. 502 U.S. 9 (1991).
44. 484 U.S. 219 (1988).
45. 522 U.S. 118 (1997).
46. *Compare Procunier v. Navarette*, 434 U.S. 555 (1978) (granting qualified immunity to government-employed prison guards) *with Richardson & Walker v. McKnight*, 521 U.S. 399 (1997) (denying immunity to private prison guards).

SELECTED BIBLIOGRAPHY

Alfred C. Aman, Jr. & William T. Mayton, *Administrative Law* (1993).
Kenneth Culp Davis & Richard J. Pierce, Jr., 1-3 *Administrative Law Treatise* (3d ed. 1994 & Supp. 2000).
Christopher F. Edley, Jr., *Administrative Law: Rethinking Judicial Control of Bureaucracy* (1990).
William F. Fox, Jr., *Understanding Administrative Law* (4th ed. 2000).
Jerry L. Mashaw, *Due Process in the Administrative State* (1985).
Richard J. Pierce, Jr., Sidney A. Shapiro & Paul R. Verkuil, *Administrative Law and Process* (3d ed. 1999).
Susan Rose-Ackerman, *Rethinking the Progressive Agenda: The Reform of the American Regulatory State* (1992).
David Schoenbrod, *Power without Responsibility: How Congress Abuses the People through Delegation* (1993).
Peter H. Schuck, ed., *Foundations of Administrative Law* (1994).
Bernard Schwartz, *Administrative Law* (3d ed. 1991).
Peter L. Strauss, *An Introduction to Administrative Justice in the United States* (1989).

Chapter 6
Labor Law

William B. Gould IV[*]

I. Introduction

Labor law takes a wide variety of forms in the United States. The principal feature of labor law for more than six and a half decades has been the National Labor Relations Act of 1935, which focuses primarily upon labor-management relationships and the development of the collective bargaining system. However,

* Charles A. Beardsley Professor of Law, Stanford Law School; Former Chairman of the National Labor Relations Board, Washington, D.C. 1994-1998. This chapter is based in substantial part upon William B. Gould IV, A *Primer on American Labor Law* (2d ed. 1986, 3d ed. 1993).

David S. Clark and Tuğrul Ansay (eds.) Introduction to the Law of the United States, 115-138

in contrast to the private sector where labor law is federal or nationwide, labor law for the public sector is governed by state and local laws – except that which regulates federal employees and their employer. But the principal vehicle for the resolution of labor disputes in the United States is private arbitration, which operates outside the formal legal system of courts and administrative agencies. A kind of common law relating to the relationship between labor and management has emerged as a result of this system, in the form of decisions by both arbitrators and the courts which attempt to define the rights and obligations of the parties.

In recent years, however, more attention has been given to labor law as it relates to the relationship between the individual employee and his or her employer. The first area where this is true involves fair employment practices legislation, which initially developed in the 1940s. Since the 1960s decisions of both administrative agencies and the courts have emerged as a result of the enactment of comprehensive legislation at the federal level and the promulgation of a series of executive orders.

A principal forum for disputes between individual employees and employers has been the state courts, in which a common law of wrongful discharge has developed. In addition to this common law, made by judges, Congress enacted the Employee Retirement Income Security Act of 1974 (ERISA),[1] which is a statute designed to promote the interests of employees and their beneficiaries in employee benefit plans. Finally, labor law cannot be discussed in the United States without consideration of legislation at both the federal and state level regulating health and safety of the workplace and establishing both minimum wage and maximum hours for employment during a day and workweek.

II. The National Labor Relations Act

The National Labor Relations Act of 1935 (NLRA)[2] forms the basis of legal regulation of collective bargaining in the private sector, although collective bargaining in the railroad and airline industry is governed by the Railway Labor Act of 1926.[3]

The constitutional basis for the National Labor Relations Act is the commerce clause of the United States Constitution. This provision allows Congress to enact legislation when it regulates commerce among the various states of the Union. The constitutional theory on which the NLRA is predicated is that statutory regulation of labor and management is necessary to diminish industrial strife that could disrupt interstate commerce among the states.

In order to accomplish this objective, the Act created an expert agency, the National Labor Relations Board (NLRB), whose principal headquarters are in Washington, D.C. The Board has responsibility for the administration of representation procedures through which employees designate – generally through a secret ballot box election – a union as exclusive bargaining representative. Moreover, the Act creates certain unfair labor practices for management and labor.

1. 29 U.S.C. §§ 1001-1461 (1994 & Supp. IV 1998).
2. 29 U.S.C. §§ 151-169 (1994).
3. 45 U.S.C. §§ 151-188 (1994 & Supp. IV 1998).

Through both, the representation elections and the unfair labor practice system, the statute attempts to protect employee free choice and the organization of employees into unions and representatives of their own choice. The NLRA also protects workers from retaliation for protest of working conditions deemed by them to be unfair. Moreover, it obliges management to bargain in good faith with a union that represents a majority of the workers in an appropriate group or unit. This system contrasts rather vividly with the laissez-faire philosophy adopted by Congress in the Norris-La Guardia Act of 1932,[4] enacted as an attempt to eliminate a potential for judicial abuse associated with the antitrust laws and labor injunctions. In effect, the National Labor Relations Board provides for expert regulation and protection.

The Board is split into two separate sections by virtue of the 1947 Taft-Hartley amendments to the National Labor Relations Act.[5] On one side, there is a five-member board with its principal offices in Washington, D.C. (the "judicial" side of the Board). On the other side, also with its principal offices in Washington, is the "prosecutorial" side of the Board, which is headed by the general counsel. (It cannot be regarded as "prosecutorial" in the strict sense of the word, because it cannot seek criminal penalties or sanctions.) The general counsel's side of the Board investigates and litigates unfair labor practice charges before the judicial side which, as its title implies, adjudicates these matters prior to appeals that may be taken to federal appellate courts.

The peculiar federalist system of the United States is the wellspring of the doctrines of preemption and primary jurisdiction, which are applied in the NLRA's unfair labor practice provisions. The reason for the doctrine of preemption is that conflicting interpretations of a law by state courts or other entities may frustrate the objective of the national legislation. That is, even if state courts interpret the very same National Labor Relations Act that Congress enacted, they may interpret it in a different way than the Board would interpret it.

In applying the doctrine of preemption to the NLRA, the U.S. Supreme Court has stated that usually, before the courts intervene, the Board has primary jurisdiction to determine the question of whether the subject matter involved in a labor controversy is protected or prohibited by the NLRA.[6] The Board is the expert agency entrusted with special responsibility to interpret the statute, and, if the courts were to step in without the benefit of the Board's interpretation, their exercise of jurisdiction or interpretation of the statute and national labor policies would cause mischief for the uniform federal scheme Congress intended to apply in labor-management relations.

While the Board's jurisdiction over commerce is broad, it does not extend to foreign crews employed by foreign ships operating under flags of convenience.[7]

4. 29 U.S.C. §§ 101-115 (1994).
5. 29 U.S.C. §§ 153-157 (1994).
6. *San Diego Bldg. Trades Council v. Garmon*, 359 U.S. 236, 245 (1959). But some exceptions exist where conduct is marked by violence and imminent threats to the public order. *See, e.g., Int'l Union v. Russell*, 356 U.S. 634 (1958).
7. *NLRB v. Fainblatt*, 306 U.S. 601, 605-07 (1939); *NLRB v. Reliance Fuel Oil Corp.*, 371 U.S. 224 (1963). For the foreign crews exception, *see, e.g., McCulloch v. Sociedad Nacional de Marineros de Honduras*, 372 U.S. 10 (1963).

There must be an affirmative intention by Congress to regulate such employers, given the delicate consideration of international relations involved. However, the Supreme Court has approved the NLRB's assertion of jurisdiction over foreign flag vessels where the dispute between labor and management focused upon wages paid to American residents who did not serve as members of the crew, but rather performed casual longshore work.[8] Similarly, where the International Longshoreman's Association refused to load or unload cargo destined for or originating in the Soviet Union, in protest against that country's invasion of Afghanistan, the dispute was held to be in "commerce" and within the NLRB's jurisdiction.[9]

One of the ironies involved with the preemption doctrine is that it has expanded because the Taft-Hartley amendments broadened the Board's jurisdiction. These statutory provisions, aimed at restricting labor, have deprived what was in many instances a more hostile state judiciary of jurisdiction over labor – jurisdiction that could be devoted to restraining strikes, picketing, and other actions through damages and criminal prosecution.

A. Coverage

The coverage provided by the National Labor Relations Act is narrow. Public employees at the federal, state, and local levels are excluded, as are agricultural workers, domestic servants, and supervisory and managerial employees. This exclusion does not mean that it is illegal for such workers to engage in collective bargaining. Indeed, as noted below, collective bargaining for public employees and legislation at the federal, state, and local levels protecting the right of workers to join unions has become part of the American labor landscape. *See* pt. III. For example, although most states do not protect the right of farm workers to engage in collective bargaining, California has a comprehensive statute that is in many respects superior to the NLRA in the protection that it affords to workers.[10]

There is no logical basis for the exclusion of the workers referred to above. Essentially their exclusion from the NLRA's protection relates simply to the fact that they had little political clout when the legislation was enacted or that collective bargaining was late in coming to such workers. As a result, American labor law has traditionally excluded large groups of workers from its coverage.[11]

Additionally, certain workers besides those mentioned above are excluded from the definition of "employee" within the meaning of the Act; for example,

8. *Int'l Longshoremen's Local 1416, AFL-CIO v. Ariadne Shipping Ltd.*, 397 U.S. 195 (1970).
9. The National Labor Relations Board so held in *Allied Int'l, Inc.*, 257 NLRB 151 (1981). This view was confirmed by the Supreme Court in *Int'l Longshoremen's Ass'n v. Allied Int'l, Inc.*, 456 U.S. 212 (1982). *See Coastal Stevedoring Co.*, 323 NLRB 1029, 1031-36 (1997) (Chairman Gould dissenting).
10. Agricultural Labor Relations Act of 1975, Cal. Labor Code §§ 1141-1166.3 (West 1989 & Supp. 2001); see Herman M. Levy, "The Agricultural Labor Relations Act of 1975: La Esperanza de California para el Futuro," 15 *Santa Clara L. Rev.* 783 (1975).
11. Derek C. Bok, "Reflections on the Distinctive Character of American Labor Laws," 84 *Harv. L. Rev.* 1394 (1971).

independent contractors are specifically excluded by section 2(3).[12] Because the First Amendment to the Constitution provides for separation of church and state, the Supreme Court has held that lay teachers of religious and secular subjects are not covered by the NLRA, in the absence of an explicit indication by Congress that it intended to give the NLRB jurisdiction over such individuals.[13] Although the statute does not provide explicit exclusionary language, the Supreme Court in *NLRB v. Bell Aerospace* held that managerial employees who formulate and implement company policy are also excluded from the bargaining unit.[14] Such employees, of course, are not eligible to vote in NLRB conducted elections. On the other hand, the Board has rejected contentions that medical interns and university student teaching assistants are impliedly excluded.[15]

In 1980 the Supreme Court held that, at least under certain circumstances, faculty members in universities are properly excluded from the definition of "employee" because they are managerial employees.[16] The Court's reasoning, expressed by Justice Powell's majority opinion, is based on a presumed identity of interest between the faculty and the administration. The decision, like *Bell Aerospace*, was by a vote of 5-4. At the same time, a unanimous Court held that paid union organizers employed by a firm are employees, notwithstanding the contention that they have dual loyalties.[17]

Free choice, protected by the NLRA, is implemented through the right of workers to file a petition with the Board requesting an election to determine whether a particular labor organization represents the majority of workers within an appropriate group or unit of employees. More than half of the workers who actually vote – not those who are eligible – must vote for the union if the employer is to be required to bargain with it. Although in some countries organizations seeking to represent workers must register and be screened, no such situation exists in the United States.

However, in order for a labor organization to file a petition requesting representation, to be on the ballot, and to impose bargaining obligations upon management, it must be a "labor organization" as defined in the Act: an organization

12. NLRA § 2(3), 29 U.S.C. 152(11) (1994). Independent contractors were excluded under the Taft-Hartley amendments. *NLRB v. Hearst Publ'ns, Inc.*, 322 U.S. 111 (1944). Illegal aliens are employees within the Act's meaning, *NLRB v. Sure-Tan, Inc.*, 467 U.S. 886 (1984); so are nonresident aliens who are in the United States lawfully, *NLRB v. Actor's Equity Ass'n.*, 644 F.2d 939 (2d Cir. 1981). However, in *Sure-Tan* the Supreme Court held, by a 5-4 vote, that the court of appeals had exceeded its authority by awarding a minimum amount of back pay to illegally discharged illegal aliens without regard to their availability for work. Subsequently, the Board and the court of appeals held that undocumented workers are entitled to back pay. *A.P.R.A. Fuel Oil Group, Inc.*, 320 NLRB 408 (1995), enforced 134 F.3d 50 (2d Cir. 1997).
13. *NLRB v. Catholic Bishops of Chicago*, 440 U.S. 490 (1980).
14. 416 U.S. 267 (1974). Nonmanagerial "confidential" employees are also excluded when they are engaged in labor relations functions. *NLRB v. Hendricks County Rural Elec. Membership Corp.*, 454 U.S. 170 (1982).
15. *Boston Med. Center*, 330 NLRB no. 30 (1999); *New York Univ.*, 332 NLRB no. 111 (2000).
16. *NLRB v. Yeshiva Univ.*, 444 U.S. 627 (1980).
17. *NLRB v. Town & Country*, 516 U.S. 85 (1995).

"of any kind, or any agency or employee representation committee or plan, in which employees participate and which exists for the purpose, in whole or in part, of dealing with employers concerning grievances, labor disputes, wages, rates of pay, hours of employment, or conditions of work."[18] Again, in contrast with some other countries, there is no requirement of involvement in any particular industry or company, and the collective bargaining experience of another (perhaps larger) labor organization does not freeze out an organization that may seek to represent workers in the same industry. It is for the workers to decide who will represent them. Most secret ballot elections are conducted on the employer's property by an NLRB representative. In recent years, however, more elections have been conducted by mail.[19]

The statutory scheme is designed to confer exclusivity on a labor organization. That is, once an organization receives majority support in an appropriate unit, the employer is under a statutory obligation to bargain with no other organization for the workers in that unit. All of the workers covered by or included in the unit, whether they are members of the union or not, have their wages, hours, and working conditions regulated by the collective bargaining agreement between the union and employer unless the contract between labor and management states otherwise.

In professional sports, where contracts allow for bargaining between employers and individual players, there are good examples of such special contracts between labor and management. In prior years, stars such as Fred Lynn, the Red Sox's erstwhile centerfielder, who subsequently negotiated new contracts with the California Angels, the Baltimore Orioles, the Detroit Tigers, and the San Diego Padres, were able to command handsome salaries on the basis of individual bargaining. At the turn of the 21st century, notables such as Mike Hampton and Randy Johnson have moved from team to team. And in 2000 shortstop Alex Rodriguez secured a long term contract reputed to be worth a quarter of a billion dollars. Indeed, the decade of the 1990s seems to have been one in which it was the marginal or poorer baseball player who was a mere millionaire! But these kinds of rules, practices, and compensation are hardly the pattern outside professional sports.

B. *The Appropriate Unit*

The appropriate unit is formulated by the Board among the group of workers who have a "community of interest" with one another. The principal forum for collective bargaining in the United States is an appropriate unit of workers established at the plant based upon a number of criteria. But the statute and numerous decisions of the Board and the courts make it clear that an appropriate unit can be established at the company level and sometimes – where there is consent from

18. NLRA § 2(5), 29 U.S.C. § 152(5) (1994). A union may be disqualified as a labor organization if supervisors play an active and leadership role in the union. *See Sierra Vista Hosp., Inc.*, 241 NLRB 631 (1979); *Bausch & Lomb Optical Co.*, 108 NLRB 1555 (1954).
19. *San Diego Gas & Elec.*, 325 NLRB 1143, 1146-49 (1998) (Chairman Gould concurring).

both parts – on a multiemployer or industrywide basis. In order for an election to be conducted among the workers in the unit, 30 percent of the employees within it must indicate their desire to have an election resolve the recognition issue.

Ever since the passage of the Act, there have been conflicts between craft and industrial unions about the unit for representation. The problem is particularly troublesome in the United States because there are large numbers of both craft and industrial unions.[20]

In the United States, craft unions are able to survive where the appropriate unit is fashioned on an occupational basis. Conversely, a broader unit is more to the liking of the big industrial unions. Where the question of craft or industrial unit is extremely close, the desires of employees are to govern according to the rarely used "globe election process," which pools votes into two units when the smaller or craft group provides the majority vote for the union seeking two units.[21] If those pooled votes give that union a majority of the voters, it is certified; if there is no majority, the Board orders a run-off election between the highest vote getters.

C. *Unfair Labor Practices*

Certain employer unfair labor practices were written into the NLRA in 1935 and have remained unchanged. An employer is prohibited from interfering with, restraining, or coercing employees in any way in connection with their right to engage in concerted activities, to protect working conditions, and to join labor organizations for the purpose of collective bargaining (or to refrain from any of these things, a right provided by Taft-Hartley). The union may not restrain or coerce workers in the exercise of their rights protected under the statute. Surveillance of union activities, use of union "spies," interrogation of employees about union activities, threatening employees for being involved in the union, and promising benefits if employees desist from union activity are among the actions prohibited to employers.

Although there is a broad prohibition against discrimination on account of the presence or absence of union membership, a union may negotiate a collective bargaining agreement with an employer that includes a "union security clause" requiring that workers pay periodic dues and initiation fees as a condition of employment. If a worker refuses the union's request for pay, he may be dismissed from employment. This form of union security agreement is frequently referred to as a union shop or agency shop – as distinguished from a closed shop, which requires a worker to become a union member prior to being hired. States may prohibit the negotiation of any such union security agreements through a "right to work" law. (The closed shop was outlawed by the Taft-Hartley amendments.)[22]

In no situation is the union security agreement imposed by law. When there is no "right to work" legislation, labor and management are free to enter voluntarily into such agreements.

20. In contrast, industrial unions are dominant in Germany and Scandinavia, while Great Britain and Australia have a preponderance of craft unions.
21. *The Globe Machine & Stamping Co.*, 3 NLRB 294 (1937).

D. Organizational Activity

A large number of the unfair labor practices filed with the Board involve union organizational activity. Clearly, representation petitions involve the same subject matter.

One of the very first issues arising in this area relates to discrimination against workers on account of union membership and how such discrimination needs to be proved. In 1980 the Board said:

> we shall require that the General Counsel make a *prima facie* showing sufficient to support the inference that protected conduct was a "motivating factor" in the employer's decision. Once this is established, the burden will shift to the employer to demonstrate that the same action would have taken place even in the absence of the protected conduct.[23]

The Board stressed that the general counsel still has the burden of proving the preponderance of evidence to establish a violation – the burden that the general counsel assumes in any unfair labor practice proceeding before the Board.

The Supreme Court unanimously affirmed the Board's position in *NLRB v. Transportation Management Corp.*[24] Justice White, the author of the Court's opinion, specifically approved the Board's burden-shifting rules relating to the employer's obligation to produce evidence subsequent to a showing that illegal conduct was a substantial and motivating factor in the treatment of the worker. Said the Court:

> The employer is a wrongdoer; he has acted out of a motive that is declared illegitimate by the statute. It is fair that he bear the risk that the influence of legal and illegal motives cannot be separated, because he knowingly created the risk and because the risk was created not by innocent activity, but by his own wrongdoing.[25]

One of the major problems confronting a union in the United States relates to its ability to communicate with employees whom it seeks to organize. The leading case on this issue is *Republic Aviation Corp. v. NLRB*,[26] where the Court held that employees have the right to pass out application cards to other workers on their own free time at lunch break and to wear union caps and steward buttons in the plants. In this case the Supreme Court approved the NLRB's conclusion that the

22. However, the lawfulness of the exclusive hiring hall frequently establishes *a de facto* closed shop. *Local 357, Teamsters v. NLRB*, 365 U.S. 667 (1961).
23. *Wright Line*, 251 NLRB 150 (1980).
24. 462 U.S. 393 (1983). *Cf. Paper Mart*, 319 NLRB 9, 12 (1995) (Chairman Gould, concurring, expressing the view that adverse action based in part upon valid reasons relates to the question of remedy rather than liability).
25. 462 U.S. at 403.
26. 324 U.S. 793 (1945); William B. Gould, "The Question of Union Activity on Company Property," 18 *Vand. L. Rev.* 73 (1964); *id.*, "Union Organizational Rights and the Concept of 'Quasi-Public' Property," 49 *Minn. L. Rev.* 505 (1965). *But see Hale Nani Rehabilitation & Nursing Center*, 326 NLRB 335, 361-68 (1998) (Chairman Gould, dissenting).

employer had no business justification for precluding the activity outside of work hours and that such a rule could therefore be presumed to be an "unreasonable impediment to self-organization."

However, the Court has not accorded non-employee union organizers with the same access to company property. There has been a presumption of the propriety of the denial of access to organizers unless "the location of the plant and the living quarters of the employees place the employees beyond the reasonable reach of union efforts to communicate with them" elsewhere.[27]

For a number of years, the Board and the Court have struggled with the question of the protected status of both soliciting and picketing in so-called quasi-public property which is open to the public, generally retail outlets, fast food restaurants, and particularly shopping centers as well as banks and office buildings. In *Hudgens v. NLRB*,[28] the Court, confronted with peaceful primary picketing within a privately owned shopping center, said:

> The context of the [section] 7 activity in the present case was different in several respects which may or may not be relevant in striking the proper balance. First, it involves the lawful economic strike activity rather than organizational activity.... Second, the [section] 7 activity here was carried on by Butler's employees (albeit not employees of the shopping center store), not by outsiders.... Third, the property interests impinged upon in this case were not those of the employer against whom the [section] 7 activity was directed, but of another.[29]

In *Jean Country*[30] the Board attempted to fashion guidelines for the protected status to be accorded union activity on private property and rights of the employers on private property. The Board here said that the burden was always on the general counsel to establish that without access to property, there would be "no reasonable means of communicating with the audience that exercise of that right entails." But a divided Supreme Court reversed this view in 1992.[31]

One practical limitation on union access to private property exists because of the role of state tribunals. Despite the doctrine of preemption, unions may encounter obstacles to access from state criminal trespass statutes. The Supreme Court has held that criminal trespass statutes may be used by owners against union organizers.[32] Since the Board's administrative process moves less quickly than those of the state courts under such circumstances, the employer may prevail regardless of how strongly the union activities are protected by the Act.

27. *NLRB v. Babcock & Wilcox Co.*, 351 U.S. 105, 112 (1956).
28. 424 U.S. 507 (1976).
29. *Id.* at 521-22.
30. 291 NLRB 4 (1988).
31. *Lechmere, Inc. v. NLRB*, 502 U.S. 527 (1992). The Board held that the Court's opinion also excludes union organizers from private property where they are attempting to reach the public. *Loehman's Plaza*, 316 NLRB 109 (1995), review denied 74 F.3d 292 (D.C. Cir. 1996); *Leslie Homes, Inc.*, 316 NLRB 123 (1995), review denied 68 F.3d 71 (3d Cir. 1995).
32. *Sears, Roebuck & Co. v. San Diego County Dist. Council of Carpenters*, 436 U.S. 180 (1978).

Another obstacle exists by virtue of a provision of the statute which was adopted along with the Landrum-Griffin Act amendments in 1959, which prohibits organizational picketing after a reasonable period of time, not to exceed 30 days.[33]

The theory behind this provision is that unions ought to utilize the ballot box rather than economic pressure to resolve the issue of a majority status which obligates an employer to bargain.

There are two particular difficulties with the restrictions on organizational picketing. On the one hand, Congress was deeply concerned with prohibiting "blackmail" picketing, which was often engaged in by labor. On the other hand, organizational picketing occurs in a significant number of legitimate situations, particularly in the South and in rural areas, where the union has a genuine concern with the plight of workers who need protection. Employer counterattacks against organizational drives, sometimes involving unlawful practices, frequently make it difficult for a union to demonstrate majority support through the ballot box. Under such circumstances, picketing to dissuade employees from working and others from doing business with the employer may be a legitimate weapon.

Another tactic used by unions in the United States is secondary picketing and boycotts. The 1947 Taft-Hartley amendments revived the American common law prohibitions against secondary boycotts and are designed to prohibit economic pressure against a third party who is presumed to be innocent or wholly unconcerned with the dispute, but who does business with the employer with whom the union has the dispute. Since 1947 there has been considerable litigation about what kind of economic pressure is prohibited as a result of the secondary boycott provisions.

The way in which unions obtain recognition is either through a secret ballot box election, which takes place as a result of a petition filed with the NLRB and consequent certification by the Board of the union's exclusive bargaining representative status within the appropriate unit, or without certification through the use of authorization cards signed by employees who expressed their intent to be represented by the union. Prior to the 1947 amendments, the NLRB permitted unions to be certified for the purpose of representing employees on the basis of authorization cards. But Taft-Hartley eliminated certification through any method other than an election conducted by the Board. A bargaining order issued by the Board compelling the employer to bargain without certification will be issued where unfair labor practices have made it extremely difficult to test employee free choice through the ballot box.

E. The Established Bargaining Relationship

Once the question of recognition has been resolved, the parties are still faced with problems negotiating a collective bargaining agreement between them. There is no requirement that either side enter into a collective bargaining agreement covering wages, hours, and working conditions. But each side is obliged to bargain in good faith and the duty to bargain in good faith means that the parties must

33. 29 U.S.C. § 158(b)(7) (1994).

have an intent to consummate an agreement between them.

Both sides, labor and management, may use economic weaponry to pressure the other to come to an agreement. The union's right to strike in the private sector is governed by the NLRA, while public employees are prohibited from striking in most jurisdictions. But there are a number of limitations upon the right to strike in the private sector. For instance, the Taft-Hartley Act not only prohibits secondary activity as noted above, but also prohibits strikes (as well as lockouts) which would create an emergency affecting the nation's safety and health. In such a situation, Taft-Hartley authorized the appointment of a board of inquiry by the president. Subsequent to the board's submission of a report to the president, the attorney general is authorized to seek an 80 day injunction in federal district court. Fifteen days prior to the expiration of the 80 day period, the workers vote on the employer's last offer.

Although the right to strike is protected by the statute, the significance of this is that employees may not be discharged or disciplined for engaging in such conduct. However, ever since the Supreme Court's 1938 decision in *NLRB v. Mackay Radio & Telegraph Co.*,[34] the employer may permanently replace striking employees with strikebreakers. This is a problem that has become particularly vexatious for organized labor during the past two decades as major corporations have utilized the tactic with increased frequency. In 1990 the *New York Daily News* used the permanent replacement tactic in a widely discussed dispute. The same was true in the 1992 strike by the United Auto Workers against Caterpillar Tractor Company.

One particularly pernicious consequence of *Mackay* is that it provides employers with an opportunity to rid themselves not only of workers and pension rights, but also to eliminate the union itself. The employer, it must be remembered, is entitled under Taft-Hartley to file a petition with the Board requesting an election where there is a question about whether there should be union representation.

The employer may also engage in a lockout of workers. In *American Shipbuilding Co. v. NLRB*[35] the Supreme Court held that, under certain circumstances, lockouts by employers are lawful under the NLRA. Where the employer uses this weapon to avert harmful economic circumstances and where it possesses apprehension about the union's intentions – that is, a concern that the union will utilize pressure when the employer is vulnerable – the lockout may be used as a kind of preemptive response. In *American Shipbuilding*, the Court stressed the absence of evidence that the employer was hostile to the employees' interest in organizing for the purpose of collective bargaining and noted that the lockout was not used to "discipline" them for engaging in the bargaining process. Thus, the Court noted that it could not be said that the employer's intention was to "destroy or frustrate the process of collective bargaining," and that there was no indication that the union would be diminished in its capacity to represent the employees in the bargaining unit. Although the issue has not yet confronted the Court, the Board, with appellate court support, has held that the employer may utilize temporary replacements during the lockout so as to continue production.[36] However,

34. 304 U.S. 333 (1938).
35. 380 U.S. 300 (1965).
36. *Harter Equip. Inc.*, 280 NLRB 71 (1986), enforcement granted 829 F.2d 458 (3d Cir. 1987).

the Board has also held – this time without judicial approval – that the permanent replacement of locked out workers is unlawful.[37]

Employers and unions are obliged to bargain about so-called mandatory subjects of bargaining. The Supreme Court, in the landmark *Borg-Warner* case,[38] held that there are three categories of subject matter that might be raised by the representatives of the union or the employer at the bargaining table: mandatory, nonmandatory, and illegal subjects of bargaining.

With regard to mandatory subjects, both sides have an obligation to bargain to the point of impasse.[39] This does not mean that the parties must be deadlocked on all issues or items, but rather that they must be deadlocked in the negotiations generally. Under the NLRA the party that refuses to bargain on mandatory subjects to the point of impasse is unlawfully refusing to bargain. A nonmandatory subject is "permissive," that is to say that either party may raise the subject at the bargaining table for the purpose of discussion. It is perfectly lawful to discuss such an issue. However, when a party insists upon a discussion in such an area to the point of impasse, an unlawful refusal takes place under the Act. The purpose of the rule is to exclude frivolous subjects from the bargaining table and to infer bad faith on the part of the party that clogs the table with such subjects.

Some mandatory subjects for bargaining are layoffs and recalls, sick leave, incentive pay, paid holidays, vacation schedules, hours of work, and such fringe benefits as cost of living adjustments and profit-sharing plans.

A major point of contention in defining what is mandatory and nonmandatory in the United States relates to conflicts about so-called management prerogatives. For instance, in a case involving an employer's subcontracting of maintenance work previously performed by employees in the bargaining unit, the Supreme Court attempted to come to grips with this issue and identified three governing considerations in its conclusion that the subject was mandatory. The first was whether the subject was within the literal definition of "conditions of employment." Since workers' jobs were affected by subcontracting, it was not difficult to reach the conclusion that their conditions of employment were not being affected. The second consideration was whether industrial peace was likely to be promoted through negotiation of this issue. Third, the Court stated that the practice in the industry was important. Since many unions and employers have negotiated clauses and collective bargaining agreements providing for limitations or prohibitions on subcontracting, it was thought that this factor weighed in favor of making subcontracting a mandatory subject of bargaining.

Two decades ago, a 7-2 majority of the Court concluded that closings which produce layoffs are not a mandatory subject of bargaining, although the employer is

37. *Int'l Paper Co.*, 319 NLRB 1253 (1995), enforcement denied, 115 F.3d 1045 (D.C. Cir. 1997); *see Anchor Concepts, Inc.*, 323 NLRB 742, 744 (1997) ("An employer's use of permanent replacements is inconsistent with a declared lawful lockout in support of its bargaining position").
38. *NLRB v. Wooster Div. of Borg-Warner Corp.*, 356 U.S. 342 (1958).
39. An employer may not unilaterally alter merit pay conditions of employment, even subsequent to impasse, where it would result in carte blanche authority over wage increases without regard to objective procedures or criteria for determining merit. *McClatchey Newspapers, Inc.* 321 NLRB 1386 (1996), enforced 131 F.3d 1026 (D.C. Cir. 1997).

obliged to bargain about the effects of such a decision and, if covered by the Worker Adjustment and Retraining Notification Act of 1988,[40] to provide 60 days notice.

With regard to the decision to close, the Court established three categories:

> Some management decisions, such as choice of advertising and promotion, product type and design and financing arrangements have only a direct and extenuated impact on the employment relationship.... Other management decisions, such as the order of succession of layoffs and recalls, production quotas, and work rules, are almost exclusively "an aspect of the relationship" between employer and employee.... The present case concerns a third type of management decision, one that had a direct impact on employment, since jobs were inexorably eliminated by the termination, but had as its focus only the economic profitability of the contract [between a maintenance company and a nursing home] ... a concern under these facts wholly apart from the employment relationship. This decision, involving a change in the scope and direction of the enterprise, is akin to the decision whether to be in business at all, "not in [itself] primarily about conditions of employment, thereby affecting the decision may be necessarily to terminate employment".... At the same time, this decision touches on a matter of central and pressing concern to the union and its member employees: the possibility of continued employment and the retention of the employees' jobs.[41]

The test in these cases, which involve a balance between these competing concerns, is whether the subject matter is amenable to the collective bargaining process or whether the employer's decision "turns" on labor-cost considerations.

F. Remedies

In recent years delays in the length of time required to resolve disputes through the Board have focused greater attention on the effectiveness of remedies. One of the difficulties with the NLRA has its origin in the Supreme Court's holding that because the Act is designed to perform a remedial function, punitive sanctions may not be imposed for violations.[42] The idea here is that if an employee receives more than he or she has lost, the remedy is punitive rather than remedial. In line with this approach, the Act provides that interim earnings or those which would have been obtained with "reasonable diligence" be deducted from any back pay the employee receives from the employer, although unemployment compensation and social welfare benefits are not deducted, for public policy reasons.[43]

40. 29 U.S.C. §§ 2101-2109 (1994 & Supp. IV 1998).
41. *First Nat'l Maint. Corp. v. NLRB*, 452 U.S. 666, 677-78 (1981).
42. *Local 60, United Bhd. of Carpenters v. NLRB*, 365 U.S. 651 (1961); *NLRB v. Unbelievable, Inc.*, 71 F.3d 1434 (9th Cir. 1995).
43. *NLRB v. Gullet Gin Co.*, 340 U.S. 361 (1951).

In 1977 the House of Representatives, acting with the support of President Carter, passed the Labor Reform Bill which was designed to both expedite the administrative process and to provide damage awards with a bigger bite. But the Senate filibustered the matter to death and, while the problem of delay and ineffective remedies remains an important one and could be addressed in years to come, this issue has not been considered seriously since 1978.

G. Dispute Resolution Machinery

Dispute resolution machinery, whether it is devised by private parties (voluntary) or imposed by legislation (compulsory), generally focuses on two quite different problems. The first relates to disputes that arise during the term of the collective bargaining agreement, usually involving its interpretation. These are so-called "rights" disputes; the question is what resolution should be made where the parties disagree as to the application or interpretation of the agreement. The second are "interest" disputes; that is, disputes that arise over the terms of the new collective bargaining agreement (generally after the expiration of the old one).

In the United States the most frequently used kind of arbitration is the product of private voluntary negotiations involving an interpreter of the agreement, a third party arbitrator chosen by mutual consent. The attractiveness of arbitration is rooted in five principal reasons. The first is that the system, for the most part, has been a voluntary one devised by the parties to deal with their own problems. The American system is intended to fit the parties' peculiar needs. This feature accounts for its rich diversity but creates difficulty in making generalizations about it.

Second, in most relationships grievance arbitration machinery resolves problems before arbitration has to be invoked as a last resort. Most contracts provide for three to five steps in which discussion takes place between increasingly high-ranking labor and management representatives without outside involvement.

A third reason for the acceptance of arbitration is its relative informality. The principle of *stare decisis*, which American courts use to bind parties to legal doctrines established in the past, is not applicable to arbitration proceedings. In other words, what another arbitrator has previously decided when the same facts are in evidence may be persuasive authority, but a second arbitrator has discretion to consider the matter anew. At the same time, arbitrators will often adhere to the "law of the shop" in the form of past practices, settlements, or arbitration awards in the plant in which the dispute arose.

Fourth, the principal attraction of arbitration for both sides is that it is more expeditious than litigation, although the American arbitration system has recently developed some deficiencies: delay, expense, and difficulty in coping with issues of employment discrimination.

Finally, arbitration, to some extent, serves as a substitute for the right to strike for a period of time. This reality influences legal theory. Although the American system has by no means eliminated unauthorized stoppages in breach of contract, it has reduced the inclination to strike – particularly in discipline and discharge disputes, where workers know that an impartial arbitrator will determine cases on the merits. Unions with negotiated peace machinery rarely make the strike weapon the mode of dispute resolution in the first resort, even when no-strike clauses permit them to strike after an exhaustion of procedures over certain subject matter.

Although the law is on the periphery of some aspects of the labor arbitration process, it nevertheless is important. Except under the Railway Labor Act and in states with legislation requiring arbitration in public-sector disputes, the law becomes involved only where the parties voluntarily negotiate agreements. In the former situation arbitration is sometimes mandated, but generally it is for the parties to decide.

The Court addressed the difficult issue of the relationship between the role of the courts and arbitration in the landmark *Steelworkers Trilogy* cases.[44] The issue confronted in those cases related to the circumstances under which the judiciary would order the parties to go to arbitration and the extent to which the courts could review the arbitrator's award. The Court concluded that Taft Hartley's public policy promoting arbitration required that all doubts about whether the dispute was arbitrable should be resolved by the courts in favor of arbitrability.[45] Moreover, the Court concluded that an arbitrator's award could not be reversed by the court unless it manifested clear infidelity to the contract. And though most arbitrators write opinions, as the parties expect, the Court stated that an opinion is not necessary as a matter of federal labor law.

The Court concluded that all doubts should be resolved in favor of arbitrability, and that a detailed examination of the arbitrability issue should be avoided. The Court also noted that the processing of frivolous grievances has a therapeutic effect on the relationship between labor and management and gives each employee his "day in court." Additionally, Justice Douglas noted that the parties, through negotiating an arbitration clause in their contract, had bargained for the arbitrator's expertise. (Some arbitrators would hardly recognize themselves from Douglas's glowing characterization of their abilities; however, the arbitrator's expertise is an important theme in the *Steelworkers Trilogy* rationale.) As Justice Douglas wrote:

> The labor arbitrator's source of law is not confined to the express provisions of the contract, as the industrial common law – the practices of the industry and the shop – is equally a part of the collective bargaining agreement although not expressed in it. The labor arbitrator is usually chosen because of the parties' confidence in his knowledge of the common law of the shop and their trust in his personal judgment to bring to bear considerations which are not expressed in the contract as criteria for

44. *United Steelworkers v. Am. Mfg. Co.*, 363 U.S. 564 (1960); *United Steelworkers v. Warrior & Gulf Navigation Co.*, 363 U.S. 574 (1960); *United Steelworkers v. Enter. Wheel & Car Corp.*, 363 U.S. 593 (1960).
45. "Final adjustment by a method agreed upon by the parties is declared to be the desirable method for the settlement of grievance disputes arising over the application or interpretation of an existing collective bargaining agreement." 29 U.S.C. § 173(d) (1994).

> judgment. The parties expect that his judgment of a particular grievance will reflect not only what the contract says but, insofar as the collective bargaining agreement permits, such factors as the effect upon productivity of a particular result, its consequence to the morale of the shop, his judgment whether tensions will be heightened or diminished. For the parties' objective in using the arbitration process is primarily to further their common goal of uninterrupted production under the agreement, to make the agreement serve their specialized needs. The ablest judge cannot be expected to bring the same experience and competence to bear upon the determination of a grievance, because he cannot be similarly informed.[46]

The Court was also influenced by the argument that arbitration of labor disputes is essentially different from commercial arbitration involving business relationships and other matters. The Court stated that the collective bargaining agreement is "more than a contract; [it is a] generalized code to govern a myriad of cases which the draftsman cannot wholly anticipate."[47] The Court's view was that the mature labor agreement contained manifold ambiguities and gaps because of the nature of the agreement. In essence, since the law compels the parties to bargain with one another and imposes a relationship (if not the contract itself) upon the parties, it can be called a "shotgun marriage" dictated by economic force or law. In such a situation, more than the usual number of unforeseen contingencies and ambiguities remain to plague the parties. Sometimes the parties will be aware of the problem and yet recognize that it makes more sense to submit a dispute to an effective resolution process because of the cost of disagreement at a particular time.

The Court said that collective bargaining is an effort to "erect a system of industrial self government," that the compulsion to reach agreement and the "breadth of the matters covered, as well as the need for a fairly concise and readable instrument" produce a relatively peculiar contract for which the arbitration process is available to the parties in the event of the disagreement about interpretation.[48]

H. The No-Strike Clause

In a 1970 decision, *Boy's Market v. Retail Clerks, Local 790*,[49] a 5-2 majority of the Court concluded that injunctions against violations of no-strike clauses could be issued by the federal courts where the underlying grievance that had given rise to the controversy over which the strike was taking place was itself arbitrable under the collective bargaining agreement. In a subsequent decision, the Court refused to extend injunctive relief to sympathy strikes in violation of no-strike

46. *United Steelworkers v. Warrior & Gulf Navigation Co.*, 363 U.S. at 581-82 (1960).
47. *Id.* at 578.
48. *Id.* at 580.
49. 398 U.S. 235 (1970).

clauses where there was no underlying grievance which could be resolved through the arbitration process.[50]

I. The Duty of Fair Representation

The duty of fair representation, under which a union as exclusive bargaining agent has an obligation to deal fairly on behalf of all of a bargaining unit's employees (union and non-union) has been inferred from the NLRA's grant of authority to the unions to negotiate on behalf of all workers. That other nations, aside from Canada, do not have the exclusivity concept and all its consequences make this kind of litigation peculiar to the United States.

In 1944 the Supreme Court held that the failure of a union to meet its duty of fair representation constituted a violation of federal labor law, and the NLRB subsequently held that it constituted an unfair labor practice as well. However, the Supreme Court held that the individual employee had no "absolute right" to initiate arbitration where there was a disagreement between the employee and the union about whether the matter should proceed to arbitration.[51] If the employee is able to show that the union's refusal to process the grievance is "arbitrary, discriminatory, or in bad faith," she can obtain resolution of the merits of the grievance either in court or arbitration.

J. Individual Rights

Unions may discipline union members for a variety of reasons. For instance, the Supreme Court has held that a union may fine strikebreakers who cross picket lines.[52] However, the Court has held that it is an unfair labor practice for a union to fine a nonstriker who resigns from the union, thus establishing a right-to-resign under federal labor law.[53]

The Labor Management Reporting and Disclosure Act of 1959 (often referred to as the Landrum-Griffin Act)[54] contains a bill of rights for union mem-

50. *Buffalo Forge Co. v. United Steelworkers*, 428 U.S. 397 (1976); William B. Gould, "On Labor Injunctions Pending Arbitration: Recasting *Buffalo Forge*," 30 *Stan. L. Rev.* 533 (1978); *see id.*, "On Labor Injunctions, Unions and the Judges: The *Boy's Market Case*," 1970 *Sup. Ct. Rev.* 215. The Supreme Court later relied on both *Boy's Market* and *Buffalo Forge* in ruling that an injunction could not be issued against the International Longshoremen's Association for refusing to handle cargo bound to or coming from the Soviet Union in protest of the invasion of Afghanistan. *Jacksonville Bulk Terminals, Inc. v. Int'l Longshoremen's Ass'n.*, 457 U.S. 702 (1982). The Court found that the underlying dispute, "whether viewed as an expression of the Union's 'moral outrage' at Soviet military policy or as an expression of sympathy for the people of Afghanistan, is plainly not arbitrable under the collective bargaining agreement." *Id.* at 711.
51. *Vaca v. Sipes*, 386 U.S. 171, 190 (1966).
52. *NLRB v. Allis-Chalmers Mfg. Co.*, 388 U.S. 175 (1967).
53. *Pattern Makers' League of N. Am. v. NLRB*, 473 U.S. 95 (1985).
54. 29 U.S.C. §§ 401-531 (1994).

bers, largely procedural in nature, which emerged from the McClellan hearings of the 1950s in which considerable union corruption and other forms of abuse were exposed. Title I of the Landrum-Griffin Act declared the right of every union member to equal protection, freedom of speech and assembly, reasonable and uniform dues, and freedom to sue unions and their officers.

Even where a union may discipline an employee in connection with a reasonable rule in the union's constitution, procedural due process under the Landrum-Griffin Act obliges the union to provide the member with adequate notice of charges, reasonable time to prepare his defense, and a full and fair hearing. It is important to note that here, and in other contexts, the 1959 statute guarantees such rights only to union members, not to all employees represented by the union.

Another important area in which Landrum-Griffin plays a role is that of union elections. The Landrum-Griffin Act provides that members have the right to elect their officials and guarantees the right to an election every three years.

Some unions use the ballot box and some use conventions to elect their national officials. Those unions that have relied on the direct vote seem to have had the greatest amount of internal debate and controversy – for example, there have been hard-fought elections in the United Steelworkers of America and the International Union of Electrical and Radio and Machine Workers. On the other hand, the United Auto Workers, a democratic union that has established a Public Review Board to review charges by union members against officials, elects national officers at a convention and there has never been a substantial vote against the incumbents.

As a result of litigation commenced by the United States Department of Justice under the Racketeer Influenced and Corrupt Organizations Act (RICO),[55] sweeping revisions of the International Brotherhood of Teamsters' convention have been mandated as part of a consent decree between the parties. A secret ballot box procedure and direct election of national leaders are now required.

Several elements were agreed to between the United States and the International Brotherhood of Teamsters under the 1989 consent decree as part of a settlement of civil racketeering charges. The proposed rules for the 1991 Teamsters' election, based primarily on the union's constitution, federal labor laws, and the consent decree, included: the right of each candidate to have polling observers present; restrictions on campaign contributions to candidates, including a ban on the use of equipment or facilities from any employer; publication of campaign material in the Teamsters' magazine for any "accredited" candidate; the right of each candidate to inspect lists of union members eligible to vote; and a ban on campaigning while on union-paid time. The 1991 election results were dramatic: dissident Ron Carey was elected president of the union overwhelmingly.

III. The Public Sector

In recent years, state and local legislation on the subjects of collective bargaining and labor in the public sector have grown considerably. Forty-one states have

55. 18 U.S.C. §§ 1961-1968 (1994 & Supp. IV 1998).

some form of fairly comprehensive legislation protecting the right of public employees to organize and bargain collectively. (Some states provide that the public employer need only "meet and confer" with the union, but the practical result is often similar to that under the duty to bargain.) The same trend is present at the federal level for federal employees, although federal employees still may not negotiate wages. Congress replaced an executive order originally promulgated by President John F. Kennedy with the Civil Service Reform Act of 1978.[56] The Postal Reorganization Act of 1970[57] created an independent establishment within the executive branch. Postal employees are subject to the National Labor Relations Act and the Landrum-Griffin Act, but prohibitions against federal strikes apply to them, and therefore the Postal Reorganization Act contains its own dispute-resolution procedures. Striking federal employees can be punished with felony charges and dismissal.

The most difficult public-sector issue in the United States relates to whether public employees should have the right to strike. The federal government and most of the states prohibit striking by common law or statute. However, an increasing majority of jurisdictions (Hawaii, Pennsylvania, Vermont, Alaska, and Minnesota have been the leaders) have permitted a limited right to strike to be incorporated into statute. These statutes generally permit workers other than police, firefighters, and prison guards to strike, sometimes only after the utilization of impasse procedures designed to resolve disputes over new contract terms. And the California Supreme Court has articulated the following standard:

> strikes by public employees are not unlawful at common law unless or until it is clearly demonstrated that such a strike created a substantial and imminent threat to the health and safety of the public.... [This standard] allows exceptions in certain essential areas of public employment (e.g., the prohibitions against firefighters and law enforcement personnel) and also requires the courts to determine on a case-by-case basis whether the public interest overrides the basic right to strike.[58]

IV. The Individual Employment Relationship

A. Minimum Wage Legislation

There is minimum wage and maximum hours legislation throughout the United States at both the federal and state levels. The origins of federal legislation are in the Fair Labor Standards Act of 1938 (FLSA),[59] which has been amended on

56. Pub.L. 95-454, 13 Oct. 1978, 92 Stat. 1111, codified throughout 5 U.S.C. (1994 & Supp. IV 1998).
57. Pub.L. 91-375, 12 Aug. 1970, 84 Stat. 719, codified throughout U.S.C. (1994 & Supp. IV 1998).
58. *County Sanitation Dist. v. Los Angeles County Employees' Ass'n.*, 38 Cal.3d 564, 586, 699 P. 2d 835 (1985).
59. 29 U.S.C. §§ 201-219 (1994 & Supp. IV 1998).

numerous occasions. Most recently, in 1990 minimum wage legislation was enacted which increased the minimum wage in 1991 to $4.25 per hour and in 1996 to $5.15 in two steps. Nine states now have minimum wage rates that are higher than the federal rate. Twenty-six states have wage rates that equal the federal minimum, while nine states have wage rates that are below the FLSA rate; such wage rates govern employers which are not in interstate commerce. Although the 1990 amendments provided for payment of a sub-minimum wage to teenage workers during their initial six months of employment, a survey indicated that very few fast-food restaurants reduced their entry-level wages below the standard federal minimum wage requirement.[60]

B. Pension Legislation: The Employee Retirement Income Security Act

The Employee Retirement Income Security Act (ERISA)[61] is the first comprehensive pension labor law enacted by Congress, although section 302(c)(5) of the NLRA provides for the establishment of a financial trust fund for the benefit of employees. ERISA does not require the establishment of a pension plan, but it does require disclosure and reporting of financial and other information through the establishment of standards of "conduct, responsibility, and obligations for fiduciaries of employee benefit plans."[62] It is administered by the Department of Labor and the Internal Revenue Service. ERISA established a mandatory vesting requirement for workers so that they receive some entitlement to pension funds before reaching retirement age. Additionally, it restricts a plan's power to deprive a union member of all prior service that may be invested. ERISA does not provide for the transferability of pensions from one company to another (often referred to as "portability"). This is a particularly important deficiency, given the mobility of the American worker. However, in the Multiemployer Pension Plan Amendments Act of 1980,[63] amending ERISA, Congress strengthened the solvency and stability of multiemployer pension funds by circumscribing employers' withdrawals from them.

C. The Occupational Safety and Health Act

The Occupational Safety and Health Act of 1970 was enacted,[64] as the Supreme Court said, "for the purpose of ensuring safe and healthful working conditions for every working man and woman in the nation." The Court held that the Secretary of Labor, in fashioning regulations dealing with particular toxic materials or harmful physical agents, must show that an exposure limit is "reasonably neces-

60. *N.Y. Times*, 31 Dec. 1990, at 1, col. 1.
61. 29 U.S.C. §§ 1001-1461 (1994 & Supp. IV 1998).
62. 29 U.S.C. § 1001(b) (1994). The Supreme Court appeared to indicate that punitive damages are available as relief under ERISA actions. *Ingersoll-Rand Co. v. McClendon*, 494 U.S. 1078 (1990).
63. Pub.L. 96-364, 26 Sept. 1980, 94 Stat. 1208.
64. 29 U.S.C. §§ 651-678 (1994 & Supp. IV 1998).

sary or appropriate to provide safe and healthful employment."[65] But a major problem to be hammered out in the courts during the coming years is how significant a risk must be to warrant regulation under this Act. The Court has stated that the statute does not guarantee a risk-free workplace, but the Occupational Safety and Health Administration (OSHA) has not taken that position. Even though risks are often uncertain because of lack of scientific evidence, OSHA must provide some explanation for its determination that regulation is necessary.

D. Employment Discrimination Law

The most comprehensive legislation in this area is Title VII of the Civil Rights Act of 1964, which established the Equal Employment Opportunity Commission (EEOC)[66] and which prohibits discrimination in employment on account of race, color, sex, national origin, or religion.

The EEOC, initially provided authority to investigate and attempt to conciliate allegations of discrimination, has since 1972 had the power to sue defendants in federal district court for alleged discrimination, subsequent to resort to an administrative process. It now has jurisdiction and authority over virtually every kind of discrimination in employment, including age discrimination. Private plaintiffs also have the authority to initiate litigation.

Probably the most important case in the employment discrimination area has been *Griggs v. Duke Power Co.*,[67] in which the unanimous Supreme Court held that it is not necessary to show an intent to discriminate in order to prove a violation of employment discrimination law. However, in 1989 the Supreme Court substantially eroded *Griggs* by requiring more detailed proof from a plaintiff and also relaxed the burden that is placed upon the employer in the so-called disparate impact cases.[68] But Congress, reversing a series of 1989 and 1991 Supreme Court decisions dealing with employment discrimination, enacted the Civil Rights Act of 1991.[69]

Although race discrimination was the major factor responsible for the passage of the 1964 Civil Rights Act, in fact age, sex, sexual orientation, and handicap discrimination constitutes a substantial portion of the docket in both federal and state courts handling federal and state employment discrimination laws. Twenty-four states have their own fair employment practices legislation. In the

65. *Indus. Union Dept., AFL-CIO v. Am. Petroleum Inst.*, 448 U.S. 607, 614-15, 641 (1980). *See* Peter F. Stone, Comment, "The Significant Risk Requirement in OSHA Regulation of Carcinogens: *Industrial Union Department, AFL-CIO v. American Petroleum Institute*," 33 *Stan. L. Rev.* 551 (1981).
66. 42 U.S.C. § 2000e-4 (1994 & Supp. IV 1998).
67. 401 U.S. 424 (1971).
68. *Ward's Cove Packing Co. v. Atonio*, 490 U.S. 642 (1989); *see* William B. Gould, IV, "The Supreme Court and Employment Discrimination Law in 1989: Judicial Retreat and Congressional Response," 64 *Tul. L. Rev.* 1485 (1990).
69. Pub.L. 102-166, 21 Nov. 1991, 105 Stat. 1071, partly codified at 42 U.S.C. §§ 2000e to 2000e-5 (1994); *see* William B. Gould IV, "The Law and Politics of Race: The Civil Rights Act of 1991," 44 *Labor L.J.* 323 (1993).

area of age discrimination, the federal statute prohibits mandatory retirement at any time except for executives in high policy positions and university faculty members (but the latter became subject to the complete ban on mandatory retirement in 1993). Nineteen states have banned mandatory retirement altogether. Furthermore, in 1990 Congress enacted the Americans with Disabilities Act,[70] which requires employer accommodation to a wide variety of handicaps.

E. *Wrongful Discharge*

American common law has traditionally recognized that employment relationships are terminable at the will of either party, absent a contractual commitment to the contrary. Some of the federal and state statutes referred to earlier have limited the applicability of this doctrine because of their prohibition against a variety of forms of discrimination.

Since the late 1970s, an increasing number of jurisdictions have recognized the cause of action for wrongful discharge or discrimination. The state courts, rather than legislatures, are responsible for this development. Personnel manuals or handbooks, as well as conduct by an employer toward a worker indicating that good work had been performed, have led courts to find an implied contract under some circumstances protecting employees against dismissal in the absence of cause. However, a cause of action for wrongful termination does not rest only on contractual theories. Discharges which are contrary to public policy, that is, dismissals instituted because the employee refuses to act unlawfully or performs a public obligation (such as serving on a jury), or in retaliation for the exercise of a statutory right (such as free speech), have all served as a basis for imposing court liability and thus compensatory and perhaps punitive damages upon offending employers.

Nevertheless, federal and state supreme court decisions have had the effect of limiting wrongful discharge claims. Thus in *Foley v. Interactive Data Corp.*,[71] the California Supreme Court held that the covenant of good faith and fair dealing, which imposes liability upon companies (for instance, in the insurance field where a fiduciary duty is owed the insured and an unequal relationship exists), did not create tort liability in the employer-employee relationship. This has had the effect of diminishing the number of wrongful discharge actions initiated in California, which had previously led the way in the wrongful discharge arena.

Second, the U.S. Supreme Court in 1990 held that, where an employee's wrongful discharge claim alleged that the principal reason for termination was the company's desire to avoid making contributions to a pension plan, state court jurisdiction is preempted by virtue of ERISA, which is the exclusive remedy relating to litigation about the essence of pension plans.[72] No state has enacted comprehensive legislation in the wrongful discharge arena, although a 1984 California State Bar Report recommended that such legislation be enacted.

70. 42 U.S.C. §§ 12101-12213 (1994 & Supp. IV 1998).
71. 47 Cal. 3d 654, 765 P.2d 373 (1988).
72. *Ingersoll-Rand v. McClendon*, 494 U.S. 1078 (1990).

In 2000 the California Supreme Court established guidelines under which an employer may lawfully impose a mandatory arbitration procedure for individual employees. In *Marybeth Armerdariz v. Foundation Health Psychcare Services, Inc.* the Court held that antidiscrimination claims are arbitrable if the procedures meet minimum requirements relating to: (1) the arbitrator's neutrality; (2) adequate discovery; (3) a written decision that would allow minimum judicial review; and (4) reasonable limitations on arbitration costs.[73] The following year the U.S. Supreme Court held, in a 5-4 vote, that an employment contract containing an arbitration clause is enforceable under the Federal Arbitration Act.[74]

V. Conclusion

Traditional labor law remains an important part of the American scene, notwithstanding the decline of the labor movement. Meanwhile, new areas involving the individual employment relationship, such as pensions, health and safety, drug and alcohol testing, employment discrimination, and wrongful discharge litigation have become a new frontier of labor law. It is possible that these developments will dwarf the more traditional labor law in the 21st century.

Selected Bibliography

Roger I. Abrams, *Legal Bases: Baseball and the Law* (1998).
—, *The Money Pitch: Baseball Free Agency and Salary Arbitration* (2000).
Robert C. Berry, William B. Gould & Paul D. Staudohar, *Labor Relations in Professional Sports* (1986).
Julius G. Getman, Bertrand B. Pogrebin & David L. Gregory, *Labor Management Relations and the Law* (2d ed. 1999).
Robert A. Gorman, *Basic Text on Labor Law: Unionization and Collective Bargaining* (1976).
William B. Gould IV, *Agenda for Reform: The Future of Employment Relationships and the Law* (1993).
—, *Black Workers in White Unions: Job Discrimination in the United States* (1977).
—, *Japan's Reshaping of American Labor Law* (1984).
—, *Labored Relations: Law, Politics and the NLRB – A Memoir* (2000).
—, *A Primer on American Labor Law* (3d ed. 1993).
William J. Holloway & Michael J. Leech, *Employment Termination: Rights and Remedies* (1985).
Lex K. Larson, 1-9 *Employment Discrimination* (2d ed. 1994-2000).
—, 1-3 *Unjust Dismissal* (1984-2000).
Harold S. Lewis, Jr., *Civil Rights and Employment Discrimination Law* (1997).

73. 24 Cal. 4th 83, 6 P.3d 669 (2000).
74. *Circuit City Stores, Inc. v. Adams*, 532 U.S. 105 (2001).

Barbara Lindemann & David D. Kadue, *Sexual Harassment in Employment Law* (1992 & Supp. 1999).
Barbara Lindemann et al., 1-2 *Employment Discrimination Law* (3d ed. 1996 & Supp. 2000).
Henry H. Perritt, Jr., 1-3 *Americans with Disabilities Act Handbook* (3d ed. 1997 & Supp. 2000).
Mack A. Player, *Employment Discrimination Law* (1988).
Douglas E. Ray, Calvin William Sharpe & Robert N. Strassfeld, *Understanding Labor Law* (1999).
Mark A. Rothstein, *Occupational Safety and Health Law* (4th ed. 1998).
—, et al., *Employment Law* (2d ed. 1999).
Charles A. Sullivan, Michael J. Zimmer & Richard F. Richards, 1-3 *Employment Discrimination* (1998).
Paul C. Weiler, *Leveling the Playing Field: How the Law Can Make Sports Better for Fans* (2000).

Chapter 7
Criminal Law

*Edward M. Wise**

I. Introduction

Crime in the United States ordinarily is dealt with by state authorities under state law. Each state has its own system of criminal law. There is a separate system of federal criminal law. Each of these systems is formally distinct and differs from the others. Nonetheless, there are resemblances and common features. Despite great multiplicities, law in the United States is largely the product of a single national legal culture, and this holds true as well for criminal law.

Much U.S. criminal law originally derived from English criminal law, which was not codified, but rather an amalgam of statutory and judicially-created common law crimes and defenses. Until the 1960s, the typical state "criminal code" was a loosely arranged collection of statutes enumerating specific crimes and punishments – not a true code at all. The general principles, which modern codes elsewhere include in a General Part, were left to be developed by the courts as a matter of common law.

In 1881, in the second lecture in *The Common Law*, Oliver Wendell Holmes sketched an objective theory of criminal liability that has considerable power as

* Late Professor of Law and Director, Comparative Criminal Law Project, Wayne State University Law School.

David S. Clark and Tuğrul Ansay (eds.) Introduction to the Law of the United States, 139-157

an explanation of apparent anomalies in common law cases. But Holmes's theory, like the common law itself, depended on premises that are now regarded as morally obtuse, and it never received the kind of sustained elaboration that his theory of contracts did in Williston's great treatise on contracts. Until 40 years ago, criminal law was largely a backwater of legal scholarship in the United States.

During the past 40 years, over two-thirds of the states have enacted new criminal codes based, to a greater or lesser extent, on the Model Penal Code (MPC) adopted by the American Law Institute (ALI) in 1962. The ALI is an unofficial organization of eminent lawyers, law teachers, and judges. It has produced over the years a series of Restatements of the Law on basic legal subjects designed to counter centripetal tendencies in U.S. law and to maintain a common legal culture. *See* Chap. 3, pt. V.A. When the Institute took up criminal law in the 1950s, it decided against a Restatement, partly on the ground that criminal law never had been stated well enough to be restated. It decided instead to try to stimulate systematic reexamination of substantive criminal law by producing a model for states to follow in reforming their own criminal codes.

The vocabulary and formulations of the Model Penal Code have been enormously influential even in states and in the federal system where revised criminal codes have not been enacted. Yet large pockets of older law still exist. States copying from the MPC have, at various points, retained common law rules. Thus, the study of U.S. criminal law nowadays requires mastering two different but related dialects – that of the MPC and that of the traditional common law.

Meanwhile, academic writing has moved beyond the MPC to put even greater emphasis on the moral philosophy underlying criminal law and on formal abstract structures. It more and more resembles German criminal theory, by which it has, to some extent, been influenced. To theorists for whom dogmatic reasoning is the only grown-up way to talk about criminal law, both traditional common law and even the MPC are apt to seem arbitrary and incoherent.

II. General Principles

A. *The Principle of Legality*

The principle of legality requires that a crime be specifically proscribed by law in advance of the conduct sought to be punished. The classical formulation of the principle, *nullum crimen nulla poena sine lege*, comes from the great Italian and German criminologists, Cesare Beccaria (1738-1794) and Paul von Feuerbach (1775-1833). Recent state codifications incorporate this principle. In so far as the legality principle requires that crimes be defined by statute, by the legislature rather than the courts, it is not a principle of U.S. constitutional law. The federal courts, having only powers conferred by Congress, can only punish according to statute. But state courts are not so limited as a constitutional matter – although the power of state courts to punish common law crimes seldom has been used to invent wholly new ones; and, in states where crimes still are incompletely codified, to do so would run counter to current understandings of the constitutional guarantee of "due process of law." *See* Chap. 4, pt. IX; Chap. 5, pt. III.A. The U.S. Constitution (art. I,

§§ 9, 10) bars both Congress and state legislatures from enacting *ex post facto* laws (retroactive penal statutes). Further, due process has been held to require fair warning that particular conduct is prohibited. Statutes that fail to give such warning are said to be "void for vagueness." Early cases on unconstitutional vagueness spoke of the importance of giving public notice of precisely what acts are forbidden; later cases emphasize the importance of setting guidelines for law enforcement and thereby limiting the discretion of public officials to determine what counts as a crime on an ad hoc basis rather than on the basis of impersonal general rules. But due process has never been held to require prosecution of all crimes coming to official attention: apart from cases such as those involving outright racial discrimination, prosecutors have virtually complete discretion to forego invoking an otherwise valid statute.

B. Punishment

Crimes in the United States generally are divided into felonies and misdemeanors. Originally, in English law, felonies were punished by death and forfeiture; misdemeanors by fine or often long imprisonment. In the U.S., "felony" typically refers to a crime punishable by over a year's imprisonment; "misdemeanor" to a crime punishable by at most a year in jail.

Until the 1970s, punishment, at least of adult felons, seemed to have three central aims: deterrence, incapacitation, and rehabilitation. U.S. law does not distinguish between punishment and security measures. Under the traditional sentencing system, the legislature prescribes a wide range of years of imprisonment for each offense; the judge imposes an individualized sentence within statutory limits; and parole authorities are permitted to release a rehabilitated offender before the full sentence is served. The MPC's sentencing provisions were a variant of this system. But, starting three decades ago, dissatisfaction with disparity and indeterminacy in sentencing and with the idea of rehabilitation – as well as revived fascination with retribution as a penal aim – precipitated a reaction that has led to abolition or curtailment of the possibility of parole and to the use of "sentencing guidelines" that severely restrict judicial discretion in sentencing.

C. The Requirement of an Act (Actus Reus)

1. The act requirement

It is conventionally said that every crimes has two parts: (a) an objective part, the criminal act, or *actus reus*; and (b) a subjective part, a culpable state of mind, or *mens rea*. Analysis of criminal liability proceeds in terms of three questions: (1) Did the defendant (D) do the prohibited act? (2) Did D act with the requisite state of mind? (3) Does D nonetheless have a good defense° Some defenses (for example, involuntariness) are said to relate to the lack of a criminal act; others (for example, mistake) to lack of *mens rea*. But most are treated as free-standing. Conventional analysis does not try to relate defenses to abstracted requirements of wrongfulness or imputability.

As usually elaborated, the requirement of an act subsumes several different principles: (1) What D did must satisfy all objective elements of the offense: the nature, circumstances, and results of D's conduct must exactly fit the legal definition of the crime charged. (2) Bad thoughts, desires, and intentions are not in themselves punishable: there must be overt conduct – some kind of act or omission. (3) If D is to be held for bringing about a particular harmful result, the result must be attributable to D's conduct. (4) D's conduct must be voluntary.

The requirement of voluntariness derives from the moral principle that blame attaches only for conduct D could control. Self-control is often a matter of degree, and the common law has been reluctant to allow excuses based on impaired capacity for self-control. Sometimes, however, incapacity is so marked that an excuse is allowed on the ground that D's behavior was "involuntary." Behavior resulting from physical compulsion, reflex, or certain physiological or neurological disturbances is generally regarded as involuntary. Sporadic cases allow a defense based on sleep-walking or hypnosis – but these are controversial precisely because it is more difficult to be sure how far D really lacked capacity of self-control.

U.S. constitutional law would not allow a legislature to penalize a status over which D had no control. It has not been read, however, to impose a general requirement of voluntariness. In *Robinson v. California*,[1] the U.S. Supreme Court held it unconstitutional – a "cruel and unusual punishment" – to punish D for being a narcotics addict, since addiction is an illness that can be acquired involuntarily. But in *Powell v. Texas*,[2] the Court upheld the conviction of a chronic alcoholic for the offense of public drunkenness; and it generally has been taken to follow that there is no constitutional impediment to punishing the possession or use of substances to which D is addicted.

2. Omissions

A crime may be defined in terms of failure to act, for example, failing to file a tax return. It also may be defined in terms of a certain harmful result, for example, killing (causing the death of) a human being. A result can be attributed to D's inaction only if D can rightly be expected to have acted to prevent it: D's omission cannot properly be said to have caused the harm unless D was somehow under a duty to act.

The duty to act need not be imposed by criminal law. There supposedly are some seven categories of relevant legal duties to be found outside the criminal law: in statutes, status, contract, voluntary assumption of care in a manner that secludes the victim (V) from rescue by others, creation of peril to V through an unlawful act by D, D's control over the conduct of another such as a child or employee, and a landowner's duty to business invitees. These categories are not mutually exclusive, and do not have precise boundaries. Common law cases exhibit a tendency to expand legal duties to reflect moral notions about when D rightly can be expected

1. 370 U.S. 660 (1962).
2. 392 U.S. 514 (1968).

to have acted. But U.S. law has not generally imposed a duty to give reasonable assistance to those in peril whenever it can be done without risk to one's own safety; and the principle of legality operates to keep judges in criminal cases from running too far ahead of duties already recognized elsewhere in the law.

D. The Mental Element (Mens Rea)

1. Modes of Culpability

Mens rea refers both: (1) to a general requirement of some kind of culpability on the part of the accused, and (2) to the particular mental state or mode of culpability required for commission of a particular crime. In principle, D must have the requisite degree of culpability with respect to each objective element of the offense – a requirement sometimes called the principle of "concurrence."

Older cases employ a variety of expressions to refer to culpable mental states, for instance, malice, scienter, and general and specific criminal intent. Careful modern usage distinguishes three significant modes of culpability: intent, recklessness, and negligence. The difference between them is framed in terms of the extent of D's cognition: conventional analysis minimizes the relevance of D's desires, wishes, or wants.

Intent can refer either to: (1) D's purpose to engage in certain conduct or achieve a particular result, or to (2) D's awareness of the nature, circumstances, and practically certain results of his conduct. It does not include *dolus eventualis*, and so has a narrower meaning than equivalent terms in legal systems that do not treat recklessness as a distinct mode of culpability. The MPC differentiates the two senses of intent by instead using the terms "purpose" and "knowledge."

Recklessness involves disregarding a risk of which D was aware; negligence, D's acting despite a risk of which he should have been aware. There are risks which it is reasonable to take; both recklessness and negligence require D to take an unacceptable risk. The line between recklessness and negligence is mainly a matter of whether D himself anticipated the risk. In this respect, it resembles the line drawn in other legal systems between conscious and unconscious negligence. But the common law does not generally inquire whether D actually had the capacity to conform to the required standard of care: he is required, as Holmes put it, "at his own peril to come up to a certain height." The MPC asks whether D's conduct grossly deviated from the standard of conduct that an ordinary or reasonable person in D's "situation" would have observed.

In common law cases, certain crimes are said to require "specific intent." This refers, by and large, to an actual intent: D's purpose to bring about a certain further consequence (for example, assault with intent to kill), or else D's knowing that he was engaged in proscribed conduct. It is therefore a defense to such crimes that D acted without the requisite purpose or knowledge, and it is open to D to argue that, because of mistake or intoxication, he lacked this specific intent.

Other crimes are said to require only "general intent." But this really means recklessness and, arguably, negligence. In the prevailing view, a general intent crime requires that D be aware of the probable nature, circumstances, and results of his conduct. (The MPC similarly adopts the interpretive convention that, if no mode of culpability is specified for a particular offense, recklessness at least is required for commission.) Yet actual awareness is not always necessary. In Holmes's view, negligence is a sufficient mode of culpability for crimes not requiring specific intent; and common law rules relating to mistake and intoxication tend to bear this out.

2. Mistake of fact

"Mistake" is loosely used to refer to both error and ignorance. The extent to which mistake of fact is a defense turns on the mode of culpability required for the particular crime. The MPC explicitly provides that mistake is a defense in so far as it shows that D did not have the requisite culpability with respect to an element of the offense. The common law rule is that mistake of fact will be a defense to a specific intent crime if it excludes the requisite purpose or knowledge. Otherwise, apart from cases of strict liability, only a reasonable mistake of fact will be a good defense; unreasonable mistake of fact is no excuse – which generally means that D is punished for negligence in making the mistake. This appears to support Holmes's view that negligence may be an adequate mode of culpability for general intent crimes – although the rule that unreasonable mistake is not an excuse applies to crimes that are not ordinarily thought of as being crimes of negligence, for example, assault, rape, kidnaping, and murder.

3. Mistake of law

Mistake of law ordinarily is not a good defense. D will not be excused on account of such mistake even though he reasonably thought his conduct was lawful. Holmes put this lapse from the general requirement of culpability on the ground that "justice to the individual is rightly outweighed by the larger interests on the other side of the scales." There are limited exceptions in cases where D relied on an official misstatement of the law. This is a very narrow set of exceptions – somewhat more extensive in the MPC than at common law. Under neither common law nor the MPC will D be heard to say that he relied on a lawyer's advice.

In cases of larceny, a mistaken claim of right will be a defense to a charge of stealing another's property. The larceny cases have led to the generalization that mistake about non-criminal law, like mistake of fact, may be a defense whenever it results in D not having the requisite culpability with respect to a material element of the offense. The MPC so provides. But how far this actually holds at common law for crimes other than larceny is not entirely clear.

4. Strict and vicarious liability

In a case of strict liability, D is precluded from relying on the defense of reasonable mistake of fact as to some element of the offense. Strict liability does not necessarily extend to all elements of an offense, but only to those as to which it is deemed desirable (in Holmes's words) "to throw the peril of action upon the person who does a certain act." Academic opinion generally is hostile to strict liability; it is said to be either irrational or unfair or both. The MPC abolishes strict liability except for "violations" as to which imprisonment is never permitted. Typically it has been imposed by the courts in connection with so-called regulatory or public welfare offenses, for instance, violations of pure food and drug, narcotics, liquor, and motor vehicle control laws, where the legislature has failed to specify any particular mode of culpability. But it also has been imposed in connection with sexual offenses involving minors (where there was reasonable mistake as to age) and, for reasons that seem somewhat more obscure, bigamy (where reasonable mistake as to continuation of a prior marriage has been held not to exculpate).

In a case of vicarious liability, D is held liable for the act of another. Usually it is someone over whose conduct he had control, such as an employee, and D's real liability is for a culpable failure to exercise control. Under some regulatory statutes, both strict and vicarious liability have been imposed on an employer for the acts of an employee.

U.S. law also permits corporations to be convicted and fined for crimes by their employees. The MPC, at least in cases of true (non-regulatory) crimes, takes the position that there has to be participation by top management, so that it is clear the crime represented corporate policy. But the prevailing view is that a corporation can be held criminally liable whenever one of its agents, to benefit the corporation, commits a crime within the scope of his employment.

E. *Justification and Excuse*

Early English law drew a distinction between justifiable and excusable homicide: the one entitled D to acquittal; the other, to a pardon. Even after acquittal for excusable homicide became a matter of course, D's property was still forfeited to the crown. There no longer is any procedural difference between the two forms of homicide. But the terms "justification" and "excuse" have been taken to correspond to the distinction in German theory between defenses excluding the wrongfulness of an act and those going to the imputability or culpability of the actor. If the terms are used in this sense, the distinction between justification and excuse is a great help in achieving conceptual clarity. It is a key distinction – sometimes a fetish – in recent academic writing, but often blurred in the case law and also in the MPC.

1. Defensive violence

Conventional common law defenses include: (1) self-defense, (2) defense of others, (3) defense of property, (4) crime prevention, and (5) apprehension of criminals.

(1) Self-defense is a justification where D really was in danger and responded accordingly; it is an excuse where he was not in danger but reasonably believed he was. Common law rules on self-defense collapse this distinction. D's use of force to defend against an attack by V is said to be warranted if D reasonably

believed that he was in imminent danger of unlawful personal injury, and that the force used was necessary to prevent such injury. The force must be proportionate to the threat; deadly force may only be used when reasonably necessary to counter a threat of death or great bodily harm.

There are technical rules about whether D can stand his ground in the face of a lethal attack, or must retreat, so far as he can, before using deadly force. The prevailing view does not require retreat on the part of one who was not the initial aggressor (although the MPC does). But even where retreat is required, D does not have to retreat if attacked in his home (or place of business).

If D was the initial aggressor, he cannot claim self-defense should V fight back. But if D withdraws from the encounter, he is entitled to defend against a renewed attack by V. Where D is the initial aggressor and V responds with excessive force, D may claim self-defense, but is first obliged to retreat if he can – even in jurisdictions that do not otherwise require retreat: since D was at fault in starting the fight, he is not entitled to stand his ground. Thus, in general, a deadly aggressor must withdraw, and a non-deadly aggressor must retreat if possible, before either can claim that he killed in self-defense.

If D kills in what he believes is self-defense, but his belief is found to be unreasonable, traditional common law treats the killing as murder. A few U.S. cases have held that D's honest belief affords a complete defense. Others allow such "imperfect self-defense" to mitigate murder to manslaughter; the MPC achieves a similar result by stating the conditions of permissible self-defense in terms of D's own subjective belief, but then stipulating that the defense is unavailable if D was reckless or negligent in having such a belief and the crime charged can be committed through recklessness or negligence.

(2) Modern common law allows D to use force to defend another person, as well as himself, against unlawful attack. But most cases hold that D acts at his peril; if the attack was lawful, D has no defense even if he reasonably believed it was unlawful. Other cases and the MPC allow reasonable mistake to excuse here, as elsewhere in the law.

(3) In defending property, D may, if necessary, use non-lethal force. Deadly force may not be used to protect property as such – although D may have some other basis for using deadly force, for instance, prevention of a dangerous felony. Occasional cases suggest there is a distinct rule permitting use of deadly force, when necessary, to defend one's habitation, but most statements suggesting such a defense seem to reduce to other grounds.

(4) Common law permits both police officers and private citizens to use non-deadly force, if necessary, to prevent a crime. Earlier common law allowed the use of deadly force to prevent any felony. Modern cases allow it only to prevent atrocious or forcible felonies – those typically involving danger of serious personal injury, for example, murder, rape, robbery, and arson. Burglary is often considered to be such a felony. The MPC requires D to believe that there is a substantial risk the actual felony he seeks to prevent will result in death or serious bodily harm, and that there is no substantial risk of injury to bystanders. At earlier common law, D's reasonable mistake as to whether a felony was being committed was no defense; but considerable authority in the U.S. holds that reasonable mistake should excuse here, as elsewhere in the law.

(5) Non-deadly force may be used to prevent the escape or effect the arrest of anyone whom D is entitled to arrest. Traditional common law permitted both police officers and private citizens to use deadly force, if necessary, to apprehend any felon – although, unlike police officers, private citizens (who have no authority to arrest unless a felony actually was committed) cannot rely on a reasonable mistake. Some, but not all, modern cases have limited the use of deadly force to cases of typically atrocious or forcible felonies. The MPC imposes further restrictions: in general, only police officers may use deadly force to apprehend felons; and only if there is no substantial risk to bystanders; and only if the felon is believed dangerous, either because his crime involved the use or threat of deadly force or because there is substantial risk he will kill or seriously injure someone should apprehension be delayed. In *Tennessee v. Garner*,[3] the U.S. Supreme Court held that the old common law rule allowing the police to shoot at any fleeing felon is unconstitutional, and that the use of deadly force to prevent escape is permissible only if there is probable cause to believe that the felon poses a continuing threat of serious physical harm.

2. Necessity

The MPC contains a residual principle of "justification": D's conduct will be justified if he believed it was necessary to avoid a harm or evil, to himself or another, greater than that which the law defining the offense seeks to prevent. This principle does not apply when the legislature clearly meant to exclude such a justification. If D was reckless or negligent in bringing about the situation requiring choice between two evils or in appraising the necessity for his conduct, the defense is not available where the crime charged is one that can be committed through recklessness or negligence.

Whether this defense exists at common law is disputed. There is some authority for it, but not extensive support. It often is taken for granted. The famous English case of *Regina v. Dudley & Stephens*[4] is sometimes cited as rejecting any such defense; but what that case actually stands for is controversial.

3. Duress

The exact requirements of the defense of duress vary by jurisdiction. In general, duress requires D to commit the crime in response to another person's threat to inflict unlawful injury if he does not. D must not be at fault for getting into a situation where he would be subject to such a threat. The threat must be one that an ordinary person in D's position could not have resisted. The MPC requires that the threat be one to use unlawful force against a person; threats to property or reputation are insufficient. Older rules restricted the defense to cases of threats

3. 471 U.S. 1 (1985).
4. 15 Cox Crim. Cas. 624 (Q.B. 1884).

against a limited class of persons: D or perhaps a close relative. Traditional common law does not allow a duress defense in cases of murder, and it requires that the threatened injury be imminent.

In the MPC, duress functions as an excuse and is superfluous where D's conduct can be justified as a choice of the lesser of two evils. Common law cases are not always clear about the basis for the defense. Sometimes duress and necessity both are treated as justifications, differing only according to whether the threat emanates from another person or from a natural event.

Even in the MPC, duress is limited to cases where D was coerced into doing what he did by another person's threat to inflict unlawful personal injury. Where D succumbs to other kinds of pressures, even though they are so great as to overwhelm ordinary powers of human resistance, neither common law nor the MPC allow a generalized excuse based on the argument that any ordinary person in D's position probably would have behaved precisely as D did.

4. Intoxication

Under common law cases, voluntary intoxication, either by drink or drugs, is a defense to a specific intent crime if the intoxication precludes D from having the requisite intent. The MPC likewise allows D to defend on the ground that, as a result of intoxication, he lacked the purpose or knowledge required for the crime charged. There are, however, recent statutes and cases that exclude the defense of intoxication even for specific intent crimes. The constitutionality of such a statute was upheld by the U.S. Supreme Court in *Montana v. Egelhoff*.[5]

Under common law cases, voluntary intoxication is not a defense to crimes requiring only general intent. The MPC likewise provides that voluntary intoxication is no defense to a crime that can be committed through recklessness. D will not be heard to argue that, because of intoxication, he failed to perceive a risk of which he should have been aware. There are some states, however, that allow intoxication as a defense whenever it precludes the existence of a mental element which the definition of the particular crime requires.

Involuntary intoxication will generally be a defense if it negates a required mental element, or so affects D as to produce the kind of impaired capacity required by the definition of legal "insanity."

5. Mental abnormality

In common law countries, the traditional test of legal insanity is that laid down in 1843 by the English judges in *M'Naughten's Case* [6]: whether, as a result of disease of the mind, D was so impaired as not to know the nature and quality of his act, or that it was wrong.

5. 568 U.S. 37 (1996).
6. 8 Eng. Rep. 718 (H.L. 1843).

There has been great controversy over the years about the *M'Naughten* rule. The principal criticism is that, by focusing on cognitive impairment, it does not allow mental abnormality to exculpate in cases where it has the effect of impairing D's self-control – cases in which D knows what he is doing, but is unable, through no fault of his own, to refrain from doing it. To cover cases of incapacity for self-control, a number of U.S. jurisdictions at one time adopted the so-called "irresistible impulse" test as a supplement to *M'Naughten*. The MPC's provision of legal insanity is a modified version of this combined test. It excludes criminal responsibility whenever, as a result of mental disease or defect, D "lacks substantial capacity either to appreciate the criminality of his conduct or to conform his conduct to the requirements of law."[7]

For a while it seemed that the MPC test might become the prevailing rule in the United States. But in the 1980s, dissatisfaction with insanity acquittals led to counter-efforts to restrict or abolish the insanity defense. In 1984, Congress enacted for the federal courts a version of *M'Naughten* that allows insanity to exculpate only where, as a result of *severe* mental disease or defect, D was "unable to appreciate the nature and quality or the wrongfulness of his acts."[8] This excludes an insanity defense based on incapacity for self-control – on the ground that there is no reliable method for measuring the extent of such incapacity, for drawing a line between those who cannot and those who will not comply with the law.

All insanity tests in the United States require that D's inability to control or appreciate what he is doing derive from some kind of "mental disease or defect." This is not an exact expression; it is left undefined in the MPC (which does stipulate, however, that so-called sociopathic personality disorders should not be considered mental disease). But it generally does operate to confine the insanity defense to cases in which D's behavior was the product of a recognized, independently definable psychiatric disorder.

Apart from a full insanity defense, evidence of mental abnormality might conceivably be used to show that D did not have the degree of culpability required for a particular crime or, as a matter of mitigation, to reduce the grade of an offense. Older common law authority did not allow it to be used for either purpose. But cases in some states allow such a showing of "diminished capacity" to negate a specific intent. Under the MPC, evidence of mental disorder may be used whenever logically relevant to rebut a required mental element. A few states also allow "partial capacity" for self-control to reduce murder to manslaughter. The MPC lends itself to the same result by providing that murder will be reduced to manslaughter if D shows that the killing was the result of "extreme mental or emotional disturbance for which there is reasonable explanation or excuse."[9]

7. Model Penal Code § 4.01(1) (1985).
8. 18 U.S.C. § 17(a) (1994); *see id.* § 4242 (1994).
9. Model Penal Code § 210.3(1)(b) (1980).

F. Harm and Attribution

1. Causation

There is considerable controversy about how to express causation rules. Most accounts seem to involve three requirements.

(1) In order to attribute a harmful result to D, his conduct must be a necessary or sufficient condition of that result: to say that D caused the result depends on being able to say that if he had behaved otherwise, the result never would have occurred.

(2) The type of harm that actually occurred must be a foreseeable result of D's conduct: it is not fair to hold D for results he could not reasonably anticipate. In criminal law, this coincides with a minimal requirement of *mens rea*.

(3) A result will not be attributed to D, even where his conduct was a necessary or sufficient condition of the result, and even where the type of harm involved was intended or foreseeable, if the result was (as the MPC puts it) "too remote or accidental in its occurrence to have a bearing on the actor's liability."[10] This will be the case where the result depended either on a subsequent extraordinary, abnormal, coincidental occurrence or on the free, deliberate, informed intervention of another human actor.

2. Attempt

Attempts to commit a crime are punishable even though they fall short of completion. In earlier common law, an attempt to commit a felony was classified as a misdemeanor. U.S. statutes prior to the MPC varied in grading schemes, but generally punished attempt less severely than the completed offense. The MPC generally punishes attempt just as severely as the completed offense. Underlying the traditional position is the view that attempts should be dealt with in terms of the harm actually done, while the MPC sees it as the object of the law on attempt to identify and confine potentially dangerous individuals.

Both common law and the MPC require a specific intent or purpose to commit the crime attempted. But, at least in Holmes's view, intent serves as an index not of culpability, but of potential harm: it is required "not to show the act was wicked but that it was likely to be followed by hurtful consequences."

Where D has done all he can to bring about the substantive crime, he clearly has done enough to be convicted of attempt. But if he is interrupted or desists before that point, there are several competing tests for distinguishing "mere preparation" from a punishable attempt. The main variants are Holmes's test of "dangerous proximity to success," which seems to be reflected in traditional case law, and the MPC's "substantial step" test.

In such cases, according to Holmes, liability for attempt is a matter of degree depending on: (1) the likelihood of success, (2) the seriousness of the crime, and (3) the apprehension it excites. It is not solely a question of proximity to success.

10. Model Penal Code § 2.03(2)(b), (3)(b) (1985).

The question is one of determining what steps toward crime are so manifestly harmful as to be of social concern.

The MPC pushes back the threshold of attempt (and, accordingly, has to introduce a defense of "abandonment," which common law cases do not always recognize). It treats the central problem as one of being sure about D's intentions. Thus, the test of whether D has gone far enough is whether he took a "substantial step" which is "strongly corroborative" of his criminal purpose. The MPC sets out a long list of conduct that may constitute a substantial step, but which has been held insufficient to constitute an attempt by courts applying traditional common law.

In a case of "pure legal impossibility," where the crime D thinks he is committing is not even on the books, neither common law nor the MPC would convict of attempt. Otherwise, the MPC allows conviction wherever, under the circumstances as he believes them to be, D's conduct would constitute a crime – although it also permits charges to be dismissed or reduced where the criminal result is "so inherently unlikely" that it hardly seems to warrant conviction. It is more difficult to come up with a formula that explains when traditional common law will or will not convict of attempt in cases where it is impossible for D to succeed. A distinction sometimes is drawn between legal and factual impossibility; the first is, the second is not, a defense to a charge of attempt. But the cases do not reflect this distinction in any meaningful way. In Holmes's view, liability for attempt here too is a matter of degree, depending on the likelihood of success, the gravity of the crime, and the apprehension D's conduct excites in the general public.

3. Complicity

Old common law distinguished, in cases of felony, between: (1) principals in the first degree (actual perpetrators); (2) principals in the second degree (aiders and abettors present at the scene); (3) accessories before the fact (instigators or aiders not at the scene); and (4) accessories after the fact. The real liability of an accessory after the fact is for obstructing justice, and this is generally recognized nowadays. Other parties to crime, as a result of 19th century statutes, are now prosecuted and punished as if principals. Since the accomplice is treated as if a principal (P), the ultimate question is or ought to be whether he so closely associated himself with P's crime as to make it fair to treat him as if it were his own.

Conventional analysis of accessorial liability separates the questions: (1) of how much help or assistance is required to make D an accomplice, and (2) of the level of culpability or *mens rea* required for complicity. Yet the two questions seem to be interrelated. In one view, ultimately adopted by the MPC, D must have a "purposive attitude" towards P's conduct – intent to promote or facilitate. In another view, D's knowledge of P's plans should be sufficient. But where an accessory aids in commission of one crime, he generally will be held liable for all other crimes which are a "natural and probable consequence" of the one he promoted or aided – which can result in liability for negligence. Each of these views has its place if the ultimate question is seen as one of whether D can fairly be treated as if he committed P's crime himself. That will be the case if D had a purposeful attitude toward the act he aided. It may also be the case if he knowingly rendered assistance and the crime is especially serious, or his aid was especially significant, or he otherwise had a particular "stake in the venture." It may be thought to be the case if D associated himself with P in an illegal course of conduct which was likely to require the commission of further crimes.

In general, P must be shown to be guilty of a crime before D can be convicted as an accomplice to it. If P's conduct is not a crime, or is justified, D cannot be liable as an accomplice. If P is excused, D may be regarded as a principal himself acting through an "innocent agent" – at least if he coerced or duped P into committing the crime, or knew that P had an excuse. It has been suggested that a secondary party can be held liable if he has the requisite *mens rea* for the crime and the principal whom he aided commits the *actus reus*: some but not all cases seem to so hold. This ought not to be the case, however, where P lacked a specific further intent that serves as an index of potential harm (for example, the intent to steal in larceny).

4. Conspiracy

At common law, conspiracy is an agreement to pursue unlawful purposes. It is itself a punishable offense: all parties to the agreement are subject to prosecution. Since the crime is complete on agreement, there is a very low threshold of criminality: conspiracy, like attempt, can serve as a device for dealing with potential criminals before they have achieved their object. This is its sole function under the MPC. But, traditionally, the object of a conspiracy did not have to be a crime: it could be anything the courts regarded as an "unlawful purpose." Moreover, in modern U.S. law (although not in the MPC), conspiracy also functions as a mode of accessorial liability in addition to aiding and abetting: all confederates are mutually liable for all crimes committed as part of the conspiracy. It also functions to enhance punishment, since cumulative punishment is permitted for both a completed crime and a conspiracy to commit it.

Conspiracy is said to require a specific intent to achieve the object of the conspiracy. This clearly is the case where conspiracy functions as an inchoate crime, like attempt. It is less clearly the case when conspiracy functions as a basis for finding D an accomplice to crimes actually perpetrated by others; here, it seems, there is support for saying that, as in other cases of complicity, the relevant question is whether D's participation is such as to make it fair to hold him for crimes committed by others. Under certain circumstances, knowledge, foresight, even foreseeability, will suffice.

Common law defines conspiracy in terms of an agreement and requires at least two "guilty" parties. The harm lies in their having combined for an unlawful purpose. D can be convicted of conspiracy even though the other parties are untriable, because at large, or unknown, or immune from prosecution. But D cannot be guilty of conspiring with a feigned accomplice who does not actually have a criminal purpose. The MPC, however, treats conspiracy primarily as a device for getting at a prospective criminal who has manifested his dangerousness by agreeing with others to commit a crime; it therefore allows conviction of anyone who thinks he has agreed with another to commit a crime.

5. Criminal Associations

Current U.S. law does not punish membership in criminal associations or organizations. A ban on membership as such is thought to pose insuperable constitutional difficulties. In any event, as a practical matter, anyone who agrees to combine with others for a criminal purpose can be prosecuted for conspiracy.

The federal RICO (Racketeer-Influenced & Corrupt Organizations) statute,[11] enacted in 1970, is specifically aimed at organized crime. Thirty-two states have enacted similar statutes. RICO was supposed to be directed primarily against the infiltration of legitimate businesses by organized crime groups. However, a crucial subsection makes it an offense (subject to 20 years' imprisonment, to forfeiture of any property connected with the offense, and to private civil suit for treble damages) for anyone associated with an "enterprise" to conduct or participate in its affairs through a "pattern of racketeering activity" (which is defined in terms of a long list of state and federal crimes.) Arguably, this subsection was meant initially to apply only to racketeers who take over a legitimate business and use it to commit crimes. But it has been interpreted to apply to anyone who commits a series of listed crimes as part of an "enterprise." Since an enterprise, according to the statute, does not have to be a legal entity, but can be a "group of individuals associated in fact," this interpretation had the effect of criminalizing participation in the activities of any organized criminal group. RICO goes beyond conspiracy in so far as it permits prosecuting together at one trial members of a large group who are too loosely connected with each other to be considered parties to a single conspiratorial agreement. Still, like conspiracy, it does not penalize group membership as such: both conspiracy and RICO violations technically are defined in terms of an act or a series of acts.

III. Specific Offenses

A. Homicide

1. Murder

Homicide is the killing of a human being by another human being. At common law, there are two main forms of criminal homicide: murder and manslaughter. Murder in the United States often is divided into two degrees: first and second degree murder – although the MPC abandons this distinction. Degrees of murder were first introduced in 1794, in a Pennsylvania statute, which was widely copied in other states. Originally this was a device for limiting capital punishment to cases of first degree murder. Nowadays, it would be unconstitutional to prescribe a mandatory death sentence for first degree murder: in those jurisdictions that retain the death penalty, there must be a separate sentencing hearing at which the prosecution demonstrates the existence of certain "aggravating circumstances" beyond those necessary to prove first degree murder. *See* Chap. 15, pt. VIII.E.

11. 18 U.S.C. §§ 1961-1968 (1994 & Supp. IV 1998).

Under the prototypical statute, murder committed by poison, lying in wait, or another kind of wilful, deliberate, or premeditated killing, or while committing certain felonies (arson, rape, robbery, or burglary) is murder in the first degree. All other murders are murder in the second degree. The definition of murder itself is left to common law.

At common law, murder is defined as unlawful killing with "malice aforethought" – an archaic expression which has come to refer to one of four states of mind: (1) intent to kill, (2) intent to inflict serious bodily harm, (3) extreme recklessness with regard to the value of human life, or (4) intent to commit a felony during which death ensued.

Under the typical statute, an intentional killing will be first degree murder if it was deliberate and premeditated. There is a difference of opinion as to whether premeditation should be taken to mean anything special, or whether any intended killing can be considered premeditated, and therefore first degree murder, if it was sufficiently horrendous.

Murder can be committed recklessly if the recklessness involves such extreme callousness and indifference to human life that it seems to warrant calling D a murderer. Older cases speak of "malice" being "implied" where D is shown to have had an "abandoned and malignant heart." Holmes took the position that murder can even be committed negligently, without D having foreseen the risk of death, if his negligence was sufficiently grotesque: "If a man should kill another by driving an automobile furiously into a crowd, he might be convicted of murder, however little he expected the result." The difference between forms of homicide then turns entirely on the degree of danger represented by D's act. There are older cases that support this view, but it is distinctly unfashionable.

Common law permits conviction for murder, even though D did not anticipate the possibility of death, if the killing occurred while D (or an accomplice) was committing another felony. If it is one of the felonies designated in the first degree murder statute, the crime will be first degree murder. The felony-murder doctrine has long been criticized. The MPC largely rejects it, but has not been widely copied in this regard. Where applied, the doctrine is subject to limitations which often tend to require that death at least have been foreseeable and D therefore negligent; it is required, for instance, that the felony must be violent, or dangerous to life, or that death be a "natural and probable" result of the felony.

2. Manslaughter

Manslaughter may be voluntary (intentional) or involuntary (unintentional). Voluntary manslaughter is an intended killing, normally murder, but mitigated to manslaughter, usually on the ground that D acted "in the heat of passion" or under "sudden provocation." This partial defense of provocation requires that: (1) D lose self-control under circumstances (2) that make his reaction reasonably explicable, and (3) which are traditionally regarded as legally adequate, such as an actual physical attack on D by V. The MPC drops the requirement of a "legally adequate" provocation.

Involuntary manslaughter has two forms. One is an analogue of felony murder allowing conviction for manslaughter if D committed an "unlawful act" which resulted in death. This so-called "misdemeanor-manslaughter" doctrine is not recognized in all states. Where it is recognized, it usually is subject to qualifications limiting it to cases in which death was foreseeable and D therefore negligent.

The other form of involuntary manslaughter involves a reckless or negligent killing. Some cases suggest that D must actually be aware of the risk of death and therefore reckless. There is a difference of opinion as to whether negligence should, in any event, be sufficient for manslaughter. But generally it is, at least at common law, although the MPC treats negligent killing as a separate new offense: "negligent homicide."

B. Rape

At common law, rape involves a male defendant using force, or the threat of force, to accomplish sexual intercourse with a woman, not his wife, against her will (or without her consent). Rape also can be committed where the woman, because unconscious or incompetent, is incapable of giving consent. Sexual intercourse with an underage female is considered rape, despite her consent; this form of rape is called "statutory rape." Obtaining consent to intercourse by fraud does not constitute rape (unless the fraud goes to the nature of the act).

Rape usually is treated as a "general intent" crime: D's mistaken belief that V consented will be a defense only if it was reasonable. But statutory rape is usually a crime of strict liability: D's mistaken belief that V was of age will not be a defense, even if it was reasonable.

During the past two or three decades, the law on rape has undergone considerable reform. Modern rape (or "criminal sexual conduct") statutes often use gender-neutral terms and proscribe different degrees of coercive sexual activity – not only intercourse – between persons of the same or opposite sex. Some allow for the possibility of marital rape. Most modify the common law rule that forcible rape can be committed only if V physically resisted her attacker (some older cases required V to "resist to the utmost"). Some eliminate the requirement of V's non-consent, in order to shift the focus from V's behavior to D's. Most do away with the rule that V's testimony must be corroborated by independent evidence; and most severely limit the extent to which the defense in a rape prosecution may bring out V's previous sexual history and reputation.

C. Theft

Apart from aggravated forms of theft such as robbery (theft accompanied by violence) and burglary (which, strictly speaking, involves breaking into a home at night for a felonious purpose, not necessarily theft), the common law, like other legal systems, distinguishes three basic theft offenses: larceny, embezzlement, and false pretenses (fraud). These roughly correspond to dishonest taking, withholding, and obtaining another's property.

Modern statutes tend, to a greater or lesser extent, to attenuate the differences between these three crimes, treating them as alternative and equivalent modes of misappropriation. Historically, however, they were not so viewed.

Larceny was an early common law crime; embezzlement and false pretenses originated in later English statutes widely copied in the United States. Larceny involves taking another's property with intent to steal (that is, to effect a permanent deprivation). But the common law also regarded certain forms of wrongful withholding and obtaining as larceny: for instance, D's retention of lost or mislaid property, or of property delivered to D by mistake, and D's obtaining possession (as opposed to title) of property "by trick." These forms of withholding and obtaining continued to be regarded as larceny even after embezzlement and false pretense statutes were enacted. Moreover, embezzlement statutes were enacted piecemeal to fill gaps in the law with regard to specific classes of defendants, and so apply only to persons falling within a specified class, such as employees, agents, or trustees.

Ultimately, these three offenses are concerned with different harms: larceny, with the possibility of permanent pecuniary loss to V; embezzlement, with breach of trust; false pretenses, with V's loss of the "chance to bargain with the facts before him."

Selected Bibliography

American Law Institute, *Model Penal Code and Commentaries (Official Draft and Revised Comments), Part I – General Provisions* (3 vols. 1985); *id., Part II – Definition of Specific Crimes* (3 vols. 1980).
Joel M. Androphy, *White Collar Crime* (1992 & Supp. 2000).
Kathleen F. Brickey, 1-3 *Corporate Criminal Liability* (2d ed. 1992-1994 & Supp. 2000).
Joshua Dressler, *Understanding Criminal Law* (2d ed. 1995).
George P. Fletcher, *Rethinking Criminal Law* (1978).
Lawrence M. Friedman, *Crime and Punishment in American History* (1993).
Richard S. Gruner, *Corporate Crime and Sentencing* (2d ed. 1997-2000).
O. W. Holmes, Jr., *The Common Law* (1881).
Sanford H. Kadish, *Blame and Punishment: Essays in the Criminal Law* (1987).
—, ed., 1-4 *Encyclopedia of Crime and Justice* (1983).
Leo Katz, *Bad Acts and Guilty Minds: Conundrums of the Criminal Law* (1987).
—, Michael S. Moore & Stephen J. Morse, eds., *Foundations of Criminal Law* (1999).
Wayne R. LaFave, *Criminal Law* (3d ed. 2000).
— & Austin W. Scott, Jr. 1-2 *Substantive Criminal Law: Criminal Practice Series* (1986 & Supp. 2000).
Gerhard O. W. Mueller, *Crime, Law, and the Scholars: A History of Scholarship in American Criminal Law* (1969).
Otto G. Obermaier & Robert G. Morvillo, 1-2 *White Collar Crime: Business and Regulatory Offenses* (1990-2000).
Herbert L. Packer, *The Limits of the Criminal Sanction* (1968).

Rollin M. Perkins & Ronald N. Boyce, *Criminal Law* (3d ed. 1982).
Michael L. Perlin, *The Jurisprudence of the Insanity Defense* (1994).
Jed S. Rakoff & Howard W. Goldstein, *RICO: Civil and Criminal Law and Strategy* (1989-2000).
Paul H. Robinson, *Criminal Law* (1997).
—, 1-2 *Criminal Law Defenses* (1984 & Supp. 2000).
Charles E. Torcia, 1-4 *Wharton's Criminal Law* (15th ed. 1993 & Supp. 2000).

Chapter 8
Contracts

*Herbert L. Bernstein**

I. INTRODUCTION

The law of contracts in general is state law and case law. In addition, legislation in the various states applies. Some state statutes in the area of contracts date back, with amendments, to colonial times – for instance, the statutes of frauds (*see* pt. III.B.3.). Most relevant state statutes, however, were enacted more recently and tend to address specific issues in a rather haphazard fashion. For example, a statute may revise the case law which holds a promise to pay for benefits received by the promisor, before the making of the promise, to be unenforceable for lack of consideration (*see* pt. II.A.5). More comprehensive and somewhat more systematic legislation applicable to contracts exists in the form of uniform laws, which are published and promoted from time to time by the National Conference of Commissioners on Uniform State Laws (*see* Chap. 3, pt. V.B.). The most important of such uniform enactments is the Uniform Commercial Code, discussed in Chapter 13.

* Late Professor of Law, Duke University School of Law.

David S. Clark and Tuğrul Ansay (eds.) Introduction to the Law of the United States, 159-187

Two very recently drafted uniform laws are designed to adapt contract law to technological innovations of the information age. The Uniform Computer Information Transactions Act (UCITA) and the Uniform Electronic Transactions Act (UETA) represent reactions to the rapidly increasing use of electronic media for information processing and business communication.

In general, federal law plays a marginal role in the area of contracts, except for government contracts. Like state legislatures, Congress, in response to pressure from interest groups, has occasionally dealt with particular issues of contract law, such as consumer product warranties or the mailing of unordered merchandise. Finally, international law provides a layer of comprehensive contract rules, which results from the U.S. Senate's ratification of the United Nations Convention on Contracts for the International Sale of Goods (CISG), which went into effect for the United States in 1988.

II. Contract Formation

A. *Consideration*

Consent is the basis of contractual liability under contemporary American law just as much as in the civil law. More than consent, however, is required for contract formation. Ordinarily, consideration must support a promise to make it legally binding. In certain instances a promise will be enforced even in the absence of consideration if there is an element of reliance strong enough to justify protection of the promisee. In addition, some American states still recognize a promise not supported by consideration or reliance as binding, if a traditional device, the seal, is used in making the promise.

1. Bargained exchange

The essence of consideration is a bargained-for exchange. Many courts describe consideration in a highly formalistic fashion as a benefit to the promisor or a detriment to the promisee. But since the end of the 19th century the prevailing view in the United States is the bargain theory of consideration.[1] It is most clearly stated in the two Restatements of Contracts.[2] The 1981 Restatement (Second) of Contracts provides in section 71:

> (1) To constitute consideration, a performance or a return promise must be bargained for.

1. Origins of the bargain theory can be traced further back than 1881, the year of Holmes's lectures on the common law. Grant Gilmore, *The Death of Contract* 19-21 (1974) argues to the contrary. But cases like *Hardesty v. Smith*, 3 Ind. 38 (1851), prove him wrong.
2. For the use of Restatements in organizing and clarifying the law of a particular field, *see* Chap. 3, pt. V.A.

> (2) A performance or return promise is bargained for if it is sought by the promisor in exchange for his promise and is given by the promisee in exchange for that promise.

Where consideration for a promise consists of a return promise, the transaction is usually termed a "bilateral" contract. Where the promise by its terms calls directly for an act of performance by the promisee, rather than for a return promise to be followed by its performance, the ensuing contract is "unilateral" in traditional parlance. (The Restatement Second has abandoned this terminology, but not the basic distinction.)

In its modern form the doctrine of consideration is ill-designed for the purpose of testing the fairness of an exchange. Rather its principal purpose is to identify the types of transactions which in most circumstances are likely to have economic significance because of their presumed social utility. On the assumption that most gratuitous promises lack this utility,[3] they are normally unenforceable under the consideration doctrine unless reasonably relied upon. Bargained-for promises, on the other hand, are generally enforceable without an inquiry into the equilibrium in the exchange. The underlying principle here is that in a market economy the parties themselves determine the value of goods and services involved in a transaction. This determination is embodied in the price (the promisee's performance) in exchange for which someone makes a promise. Thus, it is said courts should not inquire into the "*adequacy*" of consideration. The Restatement Second expresses this idea in section 79:

> If the requirement of consideration is met, there is no additional requirement of (a) a gain, advantage, or benefit to the promisor or a loss, disadvantage, or detriment to the promisee; or (b) equivalence in the values exchanged.

Yet the "adequacy" of consideration, which courts are not supposed to scrutinize, must be distinguished from the legal "*sufficiency*" of consideration, which must be shown so as to make a promise binding. This requirement has several consequences, as discussed in the following sections.

2. Preexisting duty rule

The requirement of legally sufficient consideration is not fulfilled if someone promises or does an act which he is already bound to do by a legal duty owed to the promisor.[4] The preexisting duty may have arisen from a contract with the promisor or from a general rule of law protecting the public at large or a particular group of which the promisor is a member.

3. For a critical discussion of this proposition, *see* Richard A. Posner, "Gratuitous Promises in Economics and Law," 6 *J. Legal Stud.* 411 (1977).
4. Restatement 2d § 73.

Cases in which promises are not enforced because of a preexisting duty resulting from a *general rule of law* typically involve public officials claiming a reward for the apprehension of a criminal or the return of lost or stolen property. In these cases the preexisting duty rule serves the purpose of protecting the integrity of such officials and their offices.

Cases in which a preexisting duty resulting from a *contract* with the promisor may prevent enforcement of a later promise involve problems of contract modification. Where such a modification changes the rights and corresponding duties of both parties, there is consideration and the preexisting duty rule does not apply. On the other hand, where only the duties of one of the parties are changed, for instance, a higher compensation than originally agreed is promised, the preexisting duty rule would defeat an enforcement of the modified promise, no matter how reasonable and fair the modification was in view of the circumstances. Such overkill is undesirable. Consequently, courts have sought to avoid it on sometimes spurious grounds.[5]

In a seemingly much more radical fashion the Uniform Commercial Code (UCC) provides in section 2-209(1): "An agreement modifying a contract within this Article needs no consideration to be binding." But the official comment clearly states that only a modification made in good faith and for a legitimate commercial reason will be enforced. Similarly, section 89(a) of the Restatement Second looks first of all to the fairness and equity of a modification in view of unanticipated circumstances. In addition, section 89(c) would give effect to a promise modifying a duty "to the extent that justice requires enforcement in view of material change of position in reliance on the promise." This is in line with the tendency in modern American contract law (*see* pt. II.A.6), which supplements the bargain theory of contracts by a principle designed to protect substantial reliance on promises.

3. Illusory promises

Illusory promises constitute insufficient consideration. A promise is viewed as illusory if it does not effectively limit the promisor's freedom of action in a meaningful way. However, a promise subject to a condition within the promisor's control is not necessarily illusory. For instance, if the sale of goods to be manufactured by the seller is conditioned upon the seller's purchase of a certain factory, the decision whether or not to buy the factory will in all likelihood be made on several grounds other than the sale of the goods. Thus it is not left to the whim of the seller of the goods whether he will perform. Modern courts and the UCC tend to disfavor the argument that consideration is lacking because no firm promise has been made. By implying a duty to act in good faith in the case of requirements and output contracts under UCC section 2-306(1), or by implying a promise to use best efforts in other situations, a contract can be upheld over a challenge based on illusory promise grounds.[6]

5. *See, e.g., Schwartzreich v. Bauman-Basch Inc.*, 231 N.Y. 196, 131 N.E. 887 (1921).
6. *See Wood v. Lucy, Lady Duff-Gordon*, 222 N.Y. 88, 118 N.E. 214 (1917); UCC § 2-306(2).

4. Dispute settlement

If someone promises to pay a certain amount (or tender some other performance) for the surrender of a claim, for example, a claim as a beneficiary under a will,[7] strict application of the consideration requirement would lead to quite untenable results. It would allow the promisor to refuse performance on the ground that the disputed claim did not exist so that he received nothing through the surrender of the claim. This would re-open the dispute supposedly settled. In order to further the private settlement of disputes, the consideration doctrine had to be adapted to this situation. Thus the rule was developed that there is consideration if the surrendered claim "is in fact doubtful because of uncertainty as to the facts or the law," or "the surrendering party believes that the claim ... may be fairly determined to be valid."[8] This rule facilitates the enforcement of honest compromises and thus encourages their making.

5. Past consideration

Past consideration is generally held to be legally insufficient to support a later promise to pay for it. If, however, the act constituting past consideration conferred a benefit upon the promisor, there may be a right to recover the reasonable value of the benefit under the law of restitution. A promise to pay a certain amount for the benefit received would be enforceable on the theory that the claim for restitution was surrendered in exchange for the promise. This rule clearly applies where the promisor's property has been benefitted, as, for instance, in the case of an escaped animal fed by the promisee until its return to the promisor. Where the benefit involves the promisor's person rather than property, courts disagree on the enforceability of a promise to pay, even though the promisee may have suffered serious injuries in doing an act to protect the promisor from harm.[9] The difficulty courts have in dealing with such cases stems from the fact that the law of restitution is actually not applicable and a rule comparable to the civil law doctrine of *negotiorum gestio* is alien to the common law.

Sometimes courts and writers analyze this situation in terms of a "moral obligation" owed to the rescuer, thereby analogizing the situation more closely to the restitution cases involving benefits to property. But traditionally the moral obligation analysis is applied when someone promises to pay a debt barred by a statute of limitations or after bankruptcy proceedings, where it is said a moral obligation to pay still remains so that no new agreement or new consideration is necessary to make the promise enforceable.[10] The same view is taken of a written promise to perform an earlier oral contract for which the statute of frauds

7. *Springstead v. Nees*, 125 App.Div. 230, 109 N.Y.S. 149 (1908).
8. Restatement 2d § 74(1)(a),(b).
9. *Compare Webb v. McGowin*, 27 Ala.App. 82, 169 So. 196 (1935) *with Mills v. Wyman*, 3 Pick 207 (Mass. 1825).
10. But the 1978 Federal Bankruptcy Reform Act in § 524 protects the bankrupt debtor making such a promise from a creditor's overreaching. 11 U.S.C. § 524(c) (1994).

requires a writing, and of a promise to perform a contract with the knowledge that it is subject to a defense because of mistake, fraud, or lack of capacity.

6. Promissory estoppel

Reliance by a promisee upon a promise not supported by consideration may be protected by the doctrine of promissory estoppel. The early cases from which the doctrine originated typically involved donative promises in a family context[11] and charitable subscriptions.[12] The doctrine took its name from the fact that some of the early cases enforcing promises in the absence of a bargained-for exchange held the promisor to be estopped from relying on the lack of consideration. In the course of time, however, it was recognized that the enforcement of unbargained-for promises rests not on consideration, but on an independent rationale. Its most crucial element is detrimental action in reliance on the promise. The first Restatement expressed this idea in section 90 using this language:

> A promise which the promisor should reasonably expect to induce action or forbearance of a definite and substantial character on the part of the promisee and which does induce such action or forbearance is binding if injustice can be avoided only by enforcement of the promise.

Subsequently, some courts began to protect action in reliance by enforcing unbargained-for promises even in a business relationship.[13] Others refused to do so, at least in the case of a promise not to revoke an offer made by a subcontractor to a general contractor with respect to a construction project.[14] Today the doctrine of promissory estoppel is applied to business and non-business relationships alike. Indeed, current cases involving the doctrine arise predominantly in a business context.

The only remedy available to the promisee on a promissory estoppel basis was originally expectation damages. Obviously, this is a drastic sanction from the promisor's perspective and thus calls for a high threshold of reliance. Indeed, the first Restatement specified stringent standards for promissory estoppel in section 90, as quoted above, by requiring that the promisee's action or forbearance was of a substantial and definite character, and by the proviso which makes the promise binding "if injustice can be avoided only by enforcement of the promise."

Only a few years after the promulgation of the first Restatement in 1932 the problem of measuring damages, and especially reliance in various situations as an alternative measure to expectation damages, came into sharp focus in academic discussion.[15] As a consequence, courts began to view reliance damages as

11. *See, e.g., Hamer v. Sidway*, 124 N.Y. 538, 27 N.E. 256 (1891); *Ricketts v. Seathorn*, 57 Neb. 51, 77 N.W. 365 (1898).
12. *See Beaty v. Western College*, 177 Ill. 280, 52 N.E. 432 (1898).
13. *Feinberg v. Pfeiffer Co.*, 322 S.W.2d 16 (Mo. App. 1959).
14. *James Baird Co. v. Gimbel Bros.*, 64 F.2d 344 (2d Cir. 1933). The issue of firm offers will be taken up again. See pt. II.B.3.
15. See the pathbreaking article by L.L. Fuller & William R. Perdue, Jr., "The Reliance Interest in Contract Damages," 46 *Yale L.J.* 52, 373 (1936-1937).

an appropriate remedy in cases of promissory estoppel, where the making of a promise and the degree of the promisee's reliance was somewhat in doubt, so that expectation damages appeared excessive.[16]

Following these cases the Restatement Second embraced a more flexible approach to remedies in promissory estoppel cases and simultaneously eliminated the demanding requirement of substantial and definite reliance. Section 90 now reads:

> (1) A promise which the promisor should reasonably expect to induce action or forbearance on the part of the promisee or a third person and which does induce such action or forbearance is binding if injustice can be avoided only by enforcement of the promise. The remedy granted may be limited as justice requires.
> (2) A charitable subscription or a marriage settlement is binding under Sub-section (1) without proof that the promise induced action or forbearance.

So as to remove all doubts, subsection (1) provides in sentence 2 for a "limited" remedy, obviously referring to reliance damages as an alternative to expectation damages in appropriate circumstances. Also it should be noted that in cases of charitable subscriptions according to subsection (2), detrimental reliance is no longer required.

7. Seal

Sealed promises were, historically, enforceable in an action under a writ of covenant, long before the doctrine of consideration took root in the common law. So it is historically incorrect to say that the seal serves as a "substitute" for consideration. Several American states abolished the seal in contracts, and others reduced its effect to that of a presumption of consideration; but some still enforce sealed contracts irrespective of consideration. In these states donative promises can be made enforceable easily. The formality required which originally involved the use of hot wax and an engraved signet ring or similar device, has been watered down completely. Use of the letters L.S. (for *locus sigilli*) or a scribble is enough, as long as it can be assumed it was meant as a serious formality to give effect to an unbargained-for, unrelied-upon promise. In some states which abolished the seal, a signed writing can be used to make gratuitous promises enforceable.[17]

Since the notary profession, in the form and function known in civil law countries, does not exist in the United States, the notarial form cannot be used to facilitate the making of gift promises. On the other hand, the trust is readily available to serve the same purpose as a serious notarized gift transaction in a civil law country. For instance, if as in a leading case,[18] an uncle wishes his nephew

16. *See Hoffman v. Red Owl Stores, Inc.*, 265 Wis.2d 683, 133 N.W.2d 267 (1965).
17. For tables of legislation on the seal see the statutory note preceding Restatement 2d § 95.
18. *Hamer v. Sidway*, 124 N.Y. 538, 27 N.E. 256 (1891).

to receive a specified amount of money upon the occurrence of a certain event, he can put funds in a bank, make the bank a trustee, and instruct it to turn the funds over to the nephew as beneficiary upon the specified event. To save expenses, he could also set himself up as trustee, provided the funds are kept sufficiently separate from other assets.

B. *Mutual Assent*

The distinction between bilateral and unilateral contracts (*see* pt. II.A.1) is important to the topic of mutual assent. A bilateral contract is formed by an exchange of promises. A unilateral contract is formed when performance is rendered in response to a promisor's offer calling for acceptance by performance.

1. Making an offer

An offer is the necessary first step toward contract formation under the common law as well as under the civil law. The same problems are encountered under both major legal traditions when it comes to drawing a line between invitations to bargain and, more generally, the process of preliminary negotiations on the one hand, and the making of an offer on the other. In strictly doctrinal terms an offer is easily defined. The Restatement Second supplies this definition in section 24:

> An offer is the manifestation of willingness to enter into a bargain, so made as to justify another person in understanding that his assent to the bargain is invited and will conclude it.

By contrast, section 26 provides:

> A manifestation of willingness to enter into a bargain is not an offer if the person to whom it is addressed knows or has reason to know that the person making it does not intend to conclude a bargain until he has made a further manifestation of assent.

Whether a particular communication manifests a present willingness to enter into a bargain or whether it reserves the power of final assent to be expressed at some time later is said to be a question of fact. That is, it must be interpreted in this respect from the perspective of a reasonable recipient of the communication. Relevant circumstances to be taken into account include the existence of an ongoing business relationship, trade usages, and other social practices. Advertisements, catalogues of mail-order companies, price lists, and the like are ordinarily not understood as justifying a prospective customer's expectation that the placing of an order alone will conclude the bargain. In the absence of special circumstances

19. *E.g., Lefkowitz v. Great Minneapolis Surplus Store*, 251 Minn. 188, 86 N.W.2d 689 (1957).

such communications are treated as invitations to make offers.[19] More doubtful is the effect of so-called price quotations mailed in response to a prospective buyer's specific inquiry. Courts sometimes view such an act as an offer, at least where the seller failed to use cautionary language, for instance, a reference to limited supply.[20] However, circumstances may be such that no cautionary language is needed, as where a farmer in a circular letter offers all of his crop to several potential buyers.

2. Specificity of an offer

The specificity and completeness of a proposed deal's terms stated in a communication will be considered in resolving doubts as to its being an offer or something short of an offer. The Restatement Second states in section 33(3):

> The fact that one or more terms of a proposed bargain are left open or uncertain may show that a manifestation of intention is not intended to be understood as an offer or as an acceptance.

Modern courts, however, are more inclined than courts were in the past to fill gaps in a contract. Older cases often contain language to the effect that courts are not in the business of "writing" or "re-writing" contracts for the parties and that all the "essential" elements must be agreed upon by the parties. Such essential terms were sometimes said to include the identity of the parties, the subject matter of performance by each party, and the time for performance. Today, there is broad consensus that generalizations of this kind are not very useful. Some transactions, such as land contracts, typically call for more specificity than others, for instance, contracts for the sale of goods or certain employment contracts. And then again, even within these categories, much depends on the individual circumstances.

Consequently, the Restatement Second in section 33(l) and (2) is satisfied with "reasonably certain" terms to constitute an offer and it finds such reasonable certainty to exist where the terms "provide a basis for determining the existence of a breach and for giving an appropriate remedy." In other words, in case of a dispute it must be reasonably ascertainable what a party allegedly in breach was supposed to do by virtue of the contractual undertaking, since absent such a determination it is impossible to decide whether a breach occurred and what remedy to grant. The UCC contains a rule to the same effect in section 2-204(3).

3. Termination of an offer

If the offeree does not accept within the time specified in the offer or, where none was specified, within a reasonable time, the offer is terminated. Also the rejection of an offer terminates the offeree's power of acceptance. The same is true of

20. *Fairmont Glass Works v. Grunden-Martin Woodenware Co.*, 106 Ky. 659, 51 S.W. 196 (1899).

a counter-offer, unless the offeree reserves the power to accept and wants his to be considered as an alternative proposal.

The death of the offeror terminates an offer. But an irrevocable offer or an option contract remains in effect after the death of a party, unless the promised performance would have been such as to involve a personal act by the decedent. Under the common law offers are ordinarily revocable. A statement by the offeror that the offer will not be revoked is treated as a promise and thus as not binding in the absence of consideration. If, however, consideration supports the promise to hold an offer open, a binding option contract results therefrom. Under certain circumstances the mere recital of a nominal consideration in a written option contract is sufficient to make the offer irrevocable.[21] Going even further, some state statutes dispense with consideration entirely and make certain offers irrevocable if an assurance has been given that the offer will be held open.[22] Bids to public authorities may also be irrevocable under state law.

Action taken by the offeree in reliance on the offer can make an offer irrevocable. Under the modern view an offer for a unilateral contract becomes irrevocable once the offeree begins to perform: this, however, on the implied condition that performance will be completed.[23] Sometimes acts that do not even amount to the beginning of performance are necessary to put the offeree in a position to perform or to accept by promise. If such reliance is reasonably foreseeable and substantial, the Restatement Second in section 87(2) now recognizes the need for protection of the offeree from revocation. Under the new rule this situation is treated "as an option contract to the extent necessary to avoid injustice." This means that expectation damages can be, but will not always be, awarded. Instead, reimbursement of actual losses or restitution of benefits conferred will be granted, if this appears more equitable in view of the interests of both parties.

4. Acceptance of an offer

An offer that does not clearly specify whether it is to be accepted by the making of a return promise or by rendering performance can be accepted either way. This modern rule, stated in UCC section 2-206(1) and in Restatement Second sections 30(2) and 32, replaced the traditional approach which held that any given offer could aim either at a bilateral or at a unilateral contract. This rigid approach ignored the fact that many offerors are indifferent as to the manner of acceptance.

Acceptance by performance is ordinarily effective without notification to the offeror. Where, however, the offeror can reasonably expect to be notified, contract formation may be subject to a condition subsequent of notification.[24] If, for instance, A requests B to extend credit to C and promises to guarantee repayment,

21. Restatement 2d § 87(1).
22. *E.g.*, UCC § 2-205; N.Y. Gen. Oblig. Law § 5-1109 (McKinney 1989).
23. Restatement 2d § 45.
24. Restatement 2d § 54(1); *see* UCC § 2-206(2).

and if B and C reside in a remote place, failure to notify A promptly will defeat an action brought against him as guarantor, but failure of the notice actually to arrive will not.[25]

A promissory acceptance will in most cases be communicated to the offeror so that he receives notice. In exceptional cases the offeree may have to exercise reasonable diligence to notify the offeror of acceptance after its occurrence.[26] Under the mailbox rule an acceptance takes effect upon dispatch, not upon receipt.[27] The rule is primarily designed to protect offerees from revocation arriving after dispatch of an acceptance. It is, however, also applied to cases in which an acceptance gets lost or is delayed in the course of transmission. But the offer may be interpreted to provide that a contract exists only if and when the acceptance is received; option contracts are generally subject to this provision.[28]

A purported acceptance, which states terms additional to or different from those in the offer, does not have the effect of an acceptance, but rather is a counter-offer if the offeror's assent to the new terms must be understood as a condition to contract formation.[29] But the offeree may wish to conclude the contract, and the new terms may merely be a request for a change. If the offeree's communication can thus be interpreted as an unequivocal acceptance, it will operate as such.[30] In this case the new terms are treated as a proposal for a modification of the contract. Under UCC section 2-207(2) between merchants the new terms become part of a contract for the sale of goods without the offeror's express assent if the terms are additional to, not if they are different from, the terms of the original offer. Several exceptions apply to this rule which makes it unwieldy and hard to apply. Most commentators regard the provision as poorly drafted and its policy as inadequately defined.

In general, silence does not constitute an acceptance. But in exceptional circumstances an offeree who remains silent after receiving the offer will be held bound by the contract proposed in the offer.[31] For instance, an insurance company which does not respond within a reasonable time to an application for insurance solicited by its agent and coupled with payment of the first premium is most unlikely to escape contract liability.

In an auction a bid is an offer, not an acceptance of an offer by the auctioneer, provided the auction is "with reserve," which is always the case unless otherwise stated.

Recently, new forms of marketing, communication, and packaging have presented intriguing issues of contract formation. In so-called shrinkwrap cases, a buyer of computer software may discover only after tearing the plastic wrapping from the package that, according to information inside the package, he has agreed

25. *See Bishop v. Eaton*, 161 Mass. 496, 37 N.E. 665 (1894).
26. Restatement 2d §§ 54(2)(a), 56.
27. *See Adams v. Lindsell*, 106 Eng.Rep. 250 (K.B. 1818).
28. Restatement 2d § 63(b).
29. Restatement 2d § 59.
30. Restatement 2d § 61.
31. Restatement 2d § 69(1).

to the terms of a "license" concerning the use of the software.[32] Essentially the same situation can arise with a purchase, in a store or online, involving products packaged in boxes. The buyer usually agrees to have the price charged to her credit card account or pays in cash.[33] Even though no shrinkwrap may be involved, crucial terms of the contract are frequently unknown to the purchaser until printed information including the terms is taken out of the box. If, in either case, the buyer dislikes these terms, she may have the right, under the seller's terms, to return the merchandise within a stated period of time, for instance, 30 days.

In a number of controversial cases, where the buyer failed to exercise this option, it has been held that the terms inside the box or inside the shrinkwrap package became part of the deal.[34] The judicial analysis in these cases is based on the conclusion that, as one opinion puts it, the terms must "stand or fall together," and they "all must be enforced."[35] This conclusion is predicated on the curious assumption that no contract was formed when the order was placed and payment made online or when the buyer went to a store, selected a product and took it home after arranging for credit card payment or paying in cash. Rather, the courts reason, the seller structured the transaction in such a way that the buyer expressed an acceptance, and thus formed a contract, by using instead of returning the merchandise after having an opportunity to read the crucial terms.[36] The situation resulting from these holdings has been described quite appropriately as a "pay now, terms later" transaction.

III. Validity and Interpretation

Even though consideration and mutual assent appear to be present, a contract may be invalid because the agreement process was flawed, in that it is affected by a lack of capacity, duress, misrepresentation, or mistake. Also, more general policy concerns may demand denial of a contract's intended effect. With respect to defects of the agreement process and to general policy considerations, the meaning of contract terms, and thus their interpretation, is of paramount importance.

A. The Agreement Process

The enforcement of private agreements in the law of contracts proceeds on the premise that the parties freely arrive at their agreements. Where the bargaining process is flawed, it may be necessary to deny effect to its outcome.

32. *See ProCD v. Zeidenberg*, 86 F.3d 1447, 1149 (7th Cir. 1996).
33. *See Hill v. Gateway 2000*, 105 F.3d 1147 (7th Cir. 1997).
34. *See id.*; *ProCD v. Zeidenberg*, 86 F.3d 1447 (7th Cir. 1996); *Brower v. Gateway 2000*, 246 A.D.2d 246, 676 N.Y.S. 569 (1998).
35. *Hill v. Gateway 2000*, 105 F.3d 1147, 1148 (7th Cir. 1997); *Brower*, 676 N.Y.S. at 571.
36. *Hill*, 105 F.3d at 1150; *ProCD*, 86 F.3d at 1452; *Brower*, 676 N.Y.S. at 572.

1. Capacity to contract

Minors generally are lacking in capacity to contract. Most states now fix the age of majority at 18, some at 19. Contracts entered into by a minor are not void, but can be avoided. If the contract involves so-called necessities, it cannot be so disaffirmed. The policy underlying this exception is to enable the minor to obtain necessities crucial to his existence. Courts, however, can limit the extent to which the contract will be enforced. The actual value of goods or services obtained, rather than the contract price, may be used as the measure of recovery.

A person who contracts under the influence of a mental impairment may also lack capacity to contract. But American courts tend to protect certain groups in this category more than others. Someone suffering from a mental illness affecting cognitive abilities can usually avoid a contract. If, however, an illness affects only a person's emotional processes, avoidance may depend on whether the other party knew or had reason to know of the impairment.[37] Similarly, a person who is found to be voluntarily intoxicated enjoys no great protection in American courts. Such intoxication, as distinguished from compulsive alcoholism and from medication administered by a physician, is seen as a ground for contract avoidance only if the other party took advantage of the condition.[38]

2. Duress

Duress provides a ground to avoid a contract when someone is induced to enter into a contract by a threat of which the law disapproves. There is consensus among courts and writers that certain threats are permissible and provide no ground for contract avoidance. The Restatement Second recognizes this fact by providing in section 175(l) that only an "improper" threat constitutes duress. Obviously, social mores change and with them our attitudes concerning the propriety of specific forms of compulsion in society. Threats of a criminal or tortious act or of criminal prosecution are generally seen as duress.[39] In addition, the threat to bring a civil action can amount to duress if the person using this threat acts in bad faith, and would thus commit an abuse of process by bringing the action.[40]

The most problematic situations involve what has been termed "economic duress." Here the control over economic resources is used as a means of compulsion. Undoubtedly, the exercise of economic power is considered as legitimate in many instances not only in America but throughout the Western world. The law reflects this attitude, for instance, by recognizing strikes which comply with certain rules as lawful. Similarly, the threat not to carry out a contract can be perfectly legal if, for instance, the other party is in breach. A refusal to do business with someone is lawful, provided alternative sources are available and antitrust

37. Restatement 2d § 15(1)(b).
38. Restatement 2d § 16.
39. Restatement 2d § 176(1)(a),(b).
40. Restatement 2d § 176(1)(c).

or anti-discrimination laws do not apply. But, as these provisos indicate, some uses of economic power are illegal, and so is the threat of such uses. For instance, the threat not to perform a contract, for the purpose of obtaining a promise of more compensation than originally agreed, can constitute duress. Older cases deal with this kind of situation by application of the preexisting duty rule. *See* pt. II.A.2. The modern approach looks to the good faith of the threatening party and commercial reasons for the threat.[41] Fundamentally different circumstances from those anticipated, which make the threatening party's performance more costly, may justify the threat.

More generally speaking, if the harm resulting from the threatened act would be out of proportion with the potential benefit for the party making the threat, or if the ends pursued by the use of economic power are illegitimate in themselves, there is likely to be a case of duress.[42]

If an improper threat originates not from a party to the transaction but from an outsider, the contract is still voidable by the victim unless the other party to the transaction in good faith and without reason to know of the duress gives value or relies materially on the transaction.[43]

3. Misrepresentation

An assertion that is not in accord with the facts is a misrepresentation.[44] Under certain circumstances, the nondisclosure of a fact will be treated as equivalent to an assertion that the fact does not exist.[45] A misrepresentation can go to the "factum" of a contract, as where a movie star is signing autographs and one of the fans lets her sign a promissory note in the belief it is another autograph. If there was no reasonable opportunity to know the character of the transaction, no contract is formed.[46] There would be a defense even against a holder in due course.

If a misrepresentation goes not to the "factum," but merely to the "inducement," the contract is voidable. In this situation, the victim of a misrepresentation knows that a contract is concluded. But since the false assertion supplying a motive affects the agreement process, the contract can be avoided provided the misrepresentation is either fraudulent or material.[47] This means that a fraudulent misrepresentation entitles the defrauded party to an avoidance of the contract irrespective of its materiality. Fraudulent misrepresentations include assertions which the maker knows or believes not to be in accord with the facts. In addition, if the maker has no confidence that he states or implies the truth of an assertion, or if he knows that he does not have the basis for an assertion, there is a fraudulent misrepresentation.[48]

41. Restatement 2d §§ 89(a), 176(1)(d); UCC § 2-209, cmt. 2.
42. Restatement 2d § 176(2)(a),(c).
43. Restatement 2d § 175(2).
44. Restatement 2d § 159.
45. Restatement 2d § 161.
46. Restatement 2d § 163.
47. Restatement 2d § 164.
48. Restatement 2d § 162(l).

In determining the materiality of a non-fraudulent misrepresentation, courts use a reasonableness standard. They ask whether a reasonable person was likely to be induced to agree to the deal by the false assertion. Alternatively, if the maker knows that the recipient was likely to be induced by the assertion, reasonableness of the expected reaction becomes irrelevant.[49]

A misrepresentation by someone not a party to the contract is treated exactly like duress by an outsider.[50]

4. Mistake

A belief that is not in accord with the facts is defined as a mistake.[51] Thus an erroneous assumption with respect to future events, for instance, market conditions at some time in the future, is not recognized as a mistake since it does not involve existing facts. It is termed an "error in judgment," which on principle does not entitle someone to relief.

Mutual mistake occurs when both parties share an erroneous belief as to an existing fact. Such mistake furnishes a ground for contract avoidance if it affects the "essence" or "substance" of the contract, as courts usually put it.[52] The Restatement is more specific; it provides in section 152(1) that the mistake, in order to be relevant, must meet three conditions. It must go to a "basic assumption on which the contract was made," and it must have a "material effect on the agreed exchange of performances."[53] If a violinist contracts to sell to another violinist an instrument which both believe to be a Stradivarius, when in fact it is but a clever imitation, the contract is voidable, provided that as is likely the case the agreed price and the value of the imitation differ greatly.[54] The third condition of relief for mutual mistake is that the mistaken party does not bear the risk as to the mistaken fact.[55]

A particular kind of mutual mistake involves the unintended discrepancy between the text of a writing embodying a contract and the actual agreement reached by the parties. To deal with this kind of situation, courts of equity have fashioned a special remedy called reformation.[56] By virtue of this remedy the writing is made to express the actual agreement. But the rights of innocent third parties, such as good faith purchasers, must be protected. If reformation is thus precluded, avoidance may become available.

Unilateral mistake not induced by a false assertion will not give rise to a defense of misrepresentation. If, however, the three conditions of relief for mutual mistake are present, a unilateral mistake of which the other party knew or should

49. Restatement 2d § 162(2).
50. Restatement 2d § 164(2); *see* pt. III.A.2.
51. Restatement 2d § 151.
52. *See Sherwood v. Walker*, 66 Mich. 568, 33 N.W. 919 (1887).
53. *See* UCC § 2-615(a).
54. Since the seller is not a merchant there is no implied warranty of merchantability under UCC § 2-314. *See Smith v. Zimbalist*, 2 Cal.App. 324, 38 P.2d 170 (1934).
55. Restatement 2d §§ 152(1), 154.
56. *See* Restatement 2d § 155.

have known makes the contract voidable. Even in the absence of actual or constructive knowledge of the other party, under more recent cases unilateral mistake is a ground for avoidance if it causes enforcement of the contract to be unconscionable.[57] For instance, an error in computation resulting in a bid for $150,000 rather than $200,000, and leading to a loss of $20,000 rather than an expected profit of $30,000, makes the contract voidable.[58]

Mistakes as to the identity of the subject matter of, or a party to, a contract have sometimes been seen as a separate category of mistake. More recently, such cases have come to be decided under the same rules as applied to other kinds of mistake.[59]

The fault of a mistaken party whose diligence could have avoided the mistake will ordinarily not defeat a request for relief. Only when the action is inconsistent with the principles of good faith and fair dealing is relief for mistake likely so be denied.[60] Another way of stating this exception is to say that only gross negligence will bar relief.

Misunderstanding in the agreement process can result in problems of mistake. Where the parties attach different meanings to expressions they use in that process, as for instance to the word "chicken" in a leading case,[61] it may be found by a court that none of the parties knew of any different meaning attached by the other, and only one of them knew or had reason to know of the meaning attached by the other.[62] In the absence of such finding there would be no contract.[63] But given that finding, the party who had reason to know of the other's understanding is bound by a contract based on that understanding.[64] Yet she may be entitled to avoidance because of her mistake as to that understanding. If the three basic conditions discussed before are met, the claim to relief turns on whether enforcement of the contract yields an unconscionable result, since the possibility that the other party had reason to know of the mistake does not exist here.

A. Policy Concerns

1. Public policy

American courts invoke public policy as a ground for holding a contract unenforceable in a variety of situations. In certain instances courts and writers may also characterize a transaction as illegal. But the Restatement Second rightly

57. Restatement 2d § 153.
58. *Elsinore Union Elementary School Dist. v. Kastorff*, 54 Cal.2d 380, 353 P.2d 713 (1960).
59. Restatement 2d § 153, cmt. g.
60. Restatement 2d § 157.
61. *Frigaliment Importing Co. v. B.N.S. Int'l Sales Corp.*, 190 F.Supp. 116 (S.D.N.Y. 1960).
62. *See id.*: "chicken" has a standard meaning fixed by general usage, government regulations, and so on.
63. *Raffles v. Wichelhaus*, 159 Eng.Rep. 375 (Ex. 1864).
64. *Frigaliment Importing Co. v. B.N.S. Int'l Sales Corp.*, 190 F.Supp. 116 (S.D.N.Y. 1960); Restatement 2d § 20(2) & illus. 4; *id.* § 153(b) & illus. 6.

points out that the law of contracts is concerned only with the enforceability of promises, not with other sanctions or the broader issue of illegality. Rather, unenforceability on grounds of public policy is the real issue.[65]

A public policy may have found expression in legislation in the form of not only statutes, but also constitutions, local ordinances, or administrative regulations. Sometimes legislation prohibiting certain activities, for instance gambling, will also provide that agreements made in the course of such activities are unenforceable. More often, however, there is no express provision to this effect. The courts must then interpret the legislation and determine whether it establishes a public policy whose enforcement is more important in the circumstances than the general policy in favor of enforcing promises and other terms of a contract. The Restatement Second section 178 lists the various factors to be taken into account in this balancing process.

Legislation which does not unconditionally prohibit certain activities, but requires a license, registration, or a similar act, can give rise to especially troublesome contract law problems in cases where the requirement has not been complied with. Must unlicensed brokers, plumbers, milk dealers, and others be denied compensation under contracts they made and performed? And what if a license was originally obtained, but has not been renewed upon expiration due to a clerical error? Courts and commentators agree that non-compliance with legislation requiring a license to raise revenue in the form of a license fee, but not for a regulatory purpose, does not express a public policy outweighing the interest in the enforcement of freely made bargains. If, on the other hand, the purpose of a license requirement is truly regulatory, a party acting without the required license may be barred from recovering his compensation. But the public policy behind the requirement of a license, for example, must always be balanced against considerations such as the protection against large forfeitures or the consequences of purely technical infractions unknowingly committed.

In the absence of applicable legislation public policy can be found expressed in case law.[66] For instance, long before antitrust legislation was enacted courts developed a tradition of refusing to enforce certain agreements in restraint of trade. They continue to do so today.[67]

If a contract is found to conflict with public policy, it may still be partly enforceable provided there are severable parts. Also an innocent party may be allowed to enforce a contract where the other party is the actual violator, for instance, an unlicensed contractor who may be barred from enforcement. An even stronger argument can be made in favor of a party seeking enforcement who belongs to the very class of persons which the public policy in question is designed to protect. This applies, for example, to an employee suing on a contract made in violation of minimum wage laws and similar protective labor law rules.

65. *See* introductory note preceding Restatement 2d § 178.
66. Restatement 2d § 179(b).
67. *See* Restatement 2d §§ 186-188.

2. Unconscionability

Unconscionability of a contract term or a contract in its entirely can be set up as a defense so as to resist enforcement of that term or contract. In a case where public policy arguments are advanced, considerations of the general welfare are the starting point, yet concrete circumstances of the individual case inevitably enter the picture in a process of interest balancing, as pointed out in the previous section. By contrast, unconscionability arguments are geared primarily to the equities in the concrete case before the court, but the very concept of unconscionability stems from the idea that the most fundamental purpose of courts and the legal system is to do justice in society and not to enforce specific rules, statutes, or contracts which are merely means to that end. Seen in this light, both public policy and unconscionability are manifestations of basic policy concerns. Agreements or terms that "shock the conscience" have never been enforced in courts of equity, to which a plaintiff had to turn for such relief as specific performance, injunction, or reformation. But common law courts took the position expressed in the consideration doctrine that the fairness of a transaction, the "adequacy" of consideration, was none of their concern. However, they created typified exceptions to this principle. For example, the non-enforcement of penalty clauses or of one-sided contract modifications (based on the preexisting duty rule) are clearly instances of agreements viewed as presumptively unfair.

Today courts can and do pass more directly on the unconscionability of a contract or a clause in it. The Restatement Second states a broad rule to that effect in section 208, 30 years after the UCC in section 2-302 had already adopted a similar rule with respect to contracts for the sale of goods in 1951. *See* Chap. 13, pt. III.B.

In interpreting and applying the concept of unconscionability, courts and writers have come to distinguish aspects of procedural unconscionability from those of substantive unconscionability. In most cases involving procedural unconscionability a party with superior bargaining power imposes terms of a standard contract upon a weak and ignorant party with no bargaining power. In other words, an adhesion contract is typically involved. Also from the standpoint of substantive unconscionability, the terms of such standard form contracts tend to favor the party using them and tend to be grossly unfair to the other party.[68] Thus while the distinction between procedural and substantive unconscionability helps to conduct a more focused analysis, in most cases of real significance both factors are likely to be present. Rarely will one or the other factor alone be accepted as a sufficient reason to deny enforcement of a contract or one of its terms.[69]

68. *See Williams v. Walker-Thomas Furniture Co.*, 350 F.2d 445 (D.C. Cir. 1965); *Campbell Soup v. Wentz*, 172 F.2d 80 (3d Cir. 1948); *Jones v. Star Credit Corp.*, 59 Misc.2d 189, 298 N.Y.S.2d 264 (1969).

69. For such a rare case see *Brower v. Gateway 2000*, 246 A.D.2d 246, 676 N.Y.S. 569 (1998).

3. Form requirements

Legislation commonly referred to as the statute of frauds establishes form requirements. An English statute of 1677 called "An Act for Prevention of Frauds and Perjuries" required a writing for various transactions, including certain types of contracts. In England the majority of these requirements were repealed in 1954. By contrast, legislation in most American states has expanded the scope of the statute of frauds by the requirement of a writing for many transactions not covered by the original statute and its American early derivatives. Thus, while the law in all other Western countries is characterized by the tendency to liberate the law of contracts from form requirements as much as possible, the legislative policy prevailing in America is to the contrary. Presumably, one of the reasons for this anomaly is the fact that a jury trial can be demanded in civil cases in the United States. *See* Chap. 16, pt. IX.B.

Among the contracts for which a writing is required are contracts for the sale of goods for the price of $500 or more,[70] contracts for the sale of investment securities,[71] contracts for the sale of other kinds of personal property beyond a remedy of $5,000.[72] As in other systems, including England after the reform of 1954, contracts for the sale of an interest in real property and agreements by which someone promises so pay as a guarantor or surety of a principal debtor are enforceable only if in writing. Also agreements which by their terms cannot be performed within one year, contracts to make a will, promises to pay a commission or other compensation to a real estate broker or agent are frequently included in statutes of frauds. So are promises to pay a debt barred by a statute of limitations or discharged in bankruptcy. The form requirement is fairly easy to meet. A writing must originate only from the party against whom enforcement of a contract is sought by action or defense. Only that party's signature is required. Furthermore, rejecting some older case law the UCC section 2-201(1) provides that a writing is not insufficient because it is incomplete or states a term incorrectly. *See* Chap. 13, pt. III.A. The Restatement Second section 131 has adopted a similarly liberal rule. Also the writing need not be intended as a communication between the parties; an internal memorandum can be a sufficient writing. Several writings can be pieced together to satisfy the statute where no single one of them would be sufficient.

Application of the statute of frauds in cases to which it ordinarily applies can sometimes be avoided. Part performance, especially of a contract for the sale of land, is frequently considered a sufficient ground to enforce an oral contract. Also reliance on representations that a writing will be executed or that a defense based on the statute will not be asserted may help to overcome the form requirement. In Restatement Second section 139 the reliance principle, as applied to statute of frauds cases, is now stated so broadly that it may thwart the statute's basic policy. Once the Uniform Electronic Transactions Act (UETA) is adopted

70. UCC § 2-201(1).
71. UCC § 8-319.
72. UCC § 1-206(1).

by a state, an electronic record will satisfy the writing requirement between parties who have agreed to conduct transactions by electronic means.[73]

C. *Interpretation*

1. Canons of construction

Canons of construction of a rather formalistic nature have sometimes been advocated. Samuel Williston, the reporter of the first Contracts Restatement, favored an approach to interpretation which looked more to an alleged objective standard than to the individual parties' subjective intentions when a contract or its terms called for interpretation.[74] On the other hand, Arthur Corbin and the Restatement Second want us to establish first of all the subjective meaning of contract clauses.[75]

But the Restatement Second, after stating certain formal canons in sections 202 and 203, also embraces principles with respect to interpretation which, while apparently of a formalistic nature, are in fact an expression of substantive policies. The most prominent canon in this realm is that of *contra proferentum*. According to Restatement Second section 206, that meaning of an ambiguous agreement or term is generally preferred which operates against the draftsman. This rule has counterparts in Roman law as well as in modern systems of civil law. Under circumstances prevailing today it takes into account the control over terms by virtue of superior bargaining power, which the draftsman typically possesses, especially in the context of an adhesion contract. Application of the rule occurs most frequently in insurance cases.

It is well settled now that every contract must be interpreted to impose a duty of good faith in its performance and enforcement. The UCC in section 1-203 contains a rule to this effect for all contracts to which the Code applies, not only Article 2 contracts for the sale of goods. Restatement Second section 205 states a rule imposing a duty not only of good faith, but also of fair dealing, on parties to all contracts. A bad faith breach of contract may give rise to a tort action, once again especially in the field of insurance.

2. Parol evidence

Parol evidence to establish the actual content of a contractual agreement may be inadmissible once the agreement has been reduced to a writing. In most instances, the various rules pertaining to parol evidence preclude testimony by a witness, but written evidence may also be precluded.

A strong argument for an application of the rule can be made in the case of a so-called merger clause contained not in a standard form contract, but in an

73. UETA §§ 5(b), 7(c); *see* pt. I.
74. Restatement 2d §§ 235-236.
75. Restatement 2d §§ 200-201.

individually negotiated written contract. Such clauses stipulate in essence that the writing represents the complete agreement between the parties. It characterizes the writing as something the Restatement calls an "integrated agreement."[76] Such agreements can be interpreted by extrinsic evidence, and a jury may have to pass on the credibility of such evidence or inferences to be drawn from it; in all other respects interpretation is a question of law to be decided by the judge. Under the parol evidence rule a completely integrated agreement supersedes all prior agreements within its scope, not only inconsistent prior agreements.

In the absence of a merger clause it is for the court to decide whether a writing was intended to be a completely or partially integrated agreement, that is, an agreement constituting a final expression of one or more terms of a transaction.[77] Some courts purport to make that determination within "the four corners" of a writing without ever considering the extrinsic evidence offered to establish an additional agreement. Increasingly, however, it is admitted that this very evidence must be considered by the court to make the initial determination of whether it seems plausible that an additional agreement exists. If so, the writing constitutes only a partially integrated agreement. As such it precludes evidence of an agreement which contradicts terms of a writing, but not evidence of consistent additional terms. The final decision of whether the additional agreement was really concluded must be made by the fact-finder, in jury trials by the jury.

The fact that trial by jury can be obtained in civil cases in America explains to a large extent the significance of the parol evidence rule as well as that of the statute of frauds. *See* pt. III.B.3. It is generally believed that juries are too much inclined to accept oral testimony as credible even where it conflicts with written evidence. Since this tendency may undermine the integrity of documented business transactions, the parol evidence rule in spite of its murkiness can serve an important purpose by keeping evidence which is likely to mislead away from the jury.[78]

IV. Performance and Nonperformance

A. *Conditions*

Once an enforceable contract has been formed which cannot be avoided, a duty to perform may still not arise immediately. The parties can stipulate that performance shall be due only upon the occurrence of a future event. If such event is certain to occur, as a day specified by reference to the calendar, the duty is absolute, not conditional; it will be activated at the time so specified. A true condition is an event which is not certain to occur, but which must occur before a present duty to perform exists.[79]

76. Restatement 2d §§ 209-210.
77. Restatement 2d § 209(1).
78. *See Masterson v. Sine*, 68 Cal.2d 222, 436 P.2d 561 (1968).
79. Restatement 2d § 224.

1. Express conditions

A term included in the parties' agreement may result in an express condition. No specific language is required to create such a condition. But doubts respecting the interpretation of a particular clause in a contract, especially an insurance policy, are usually resolved in favor of holding it not to be a condition because that helps to avoid a forfeiture. If, for instance, a fire insurance policy calls for the installation of a sprinkler system by the insured, interpretation of this clause as a condition might defeat recovery by the insured. As discussed before (*see* pt. III.C.1) ambiguities in a form contract are resolved against the drafter under the principle of *contra proferentum*. Therefore, in the absence of unambiguous language an insurance policy is likely to be interpreted not to contain a condition, but only a covenant.

The mutuality of obligations in a bilateral contract is also conceptualized in the form of conditions, not by the use of a discrete concept, such as the civil law idea of synallagma. Where by the terms of a contract, the exchange of performances has to occur simultaneously, each is seen as a concurrent condition to the other. Tender of one party's performance activates the other party's duty to perform in this case. Where, however, one performance must be completed before the other becomes due, the former is a condition precedent to the latter.

2. Constructive conditions

Constructive conditions are not created by the parties, but by the court. The party's failure to provide for a connection between their mutual performances does not necessarily mean that their promises are independent of each other. Rather, the interdependence of the promised performances may be so inherent in a transaction that the parties' actual purposes would not be accomplished without reading constructive conditions into their agreement.

A distinction is sometimes made between implied-in-fact conditions and constructive conditions, which are also called implied-in-law conditions. The former are said to be based on an actual, though unarticulated, intention of the parties while the latter follow from general notions of fairness and justice. It is stated also that implied-in-fact conditions as well as express conditions must be strictly complied with, while constructive conditions need only be substantially performed in order to trigger the other party's duty to perform.

To be sure, courts have developed the doctrine of substantial performance in connection with constructive conditions. In a leading case a contract to build a house called for the installation of pipes of a certain brand. One year after completion of the building it was discovered that a different brand had been installed. The court held that the builder had substantially performed and was therefore entitled to his compensation.[80]

80. *Jacob & Youngs v. Kent*, 230 N.Y. 239, 129 N.E. 899 (1921). For a list of factors used in determining whether substantial performance has occurred, see Restatement 2d § 241.

While the doctrine as such is not applied to express conditions, courts will not enforce them if this would result in an unacceptable hardship. A condition is held to be excused if its enforcement would cause an extreme forfeiture and its occurrence forms no material part of the exchange.[81]

B. Breach

After the duty to perform becomes due, nonperformance of a promise unless excused constitutes a breach of contract. Fault is not an essential element of the concept of breach. *See* Chap. 13, pt. III.C.

1. Excuses for nonperformance

Excuses can be derived from impossibility or impracticability of performance as well as from a frustration of purpose. It amounts to the same when these instances are viewed as grounds for a discharge of the promisor rather than as an excuse.

Where the existence of a particular person or a specific thing is necessary for the performance of a duty, death of the person or destruction of the thing may excuse performance. Earlier cases and writers dealt with these situations under the rubric of impossibility,[82] and some still do. But the prevailing view today is that impossibility as such does not necessarily furnish an excuse. Rather the issue turns on whether the promisor assumed the risk of the contingency, in which case he may still be liable in damages. On the other hand, performance may be excused even though it is still possible but, due to an unexpected event, has become commercially impracticable. When the Suez Canal was closed in 1956 the added expense of a voyage around Africa under a charter party providing for the carriage of wheat from the United States to Iran was held not to be so excessive as to constitute impracticability.[83]

Closely related to supervening impracticability is the case of supervening frustration of a party's purpose. The postponed coronation of King Edward II in 1902 led to a series of cases in which the frustration doctrine was argued by renters of rooms on a street in London through which the coronation procession was originally scheduled to pass. The courts in England were split on whether the renters' duty to pay was excused after cancellation of the procession due to Edward's illness. In the United States the doctrine has found the support of some courts and the Restatement. But it is not frequently applied.[84]

81. Restatement 2d § 229.
82. The leading case is *Taylor v. Caldwell*, 122 Eng.Rep. 309 (Q.B. 1863).
83. *Transatlantic Fin. Corp. v. United States*, 363 F.2d 312 (D.C. Cir. 1966).
84. Restatement 2d § 265 & rep. note.

2. Anticipatory repudiation

If a duty to perform has not yet become due and the promisor repudiates the contract, the other party can treat this act as a present breach. Repudiation consists either of a statement by the promisor that she will not perform or an affirmative act by which she renders herself unable to perform.[85] For instance, if a contract for the sale of land calls for performance on a future date and before the arrival of that date the seller either announces that she will not make the conveyance to the buyer, or if she conveys title to a third party, she has repudiated her duty to perform.

An anticipatory repudiation has various consequences. Under a bilateral contract the non-repudiating party is discharged of his remaining duties of performance once repudiation occurs.[86] Also the nonoccurrence of a condition to the repudiator's duty is excused if the repudiation contributes materially to such nonoccurrence.[87] Finally, the repudiation gives rise to an immediate claim to damages for total breach. A leading English case[88] so holding is still followed in the United States even though, unlike the other two consequences, granting a right to bring an action for damages before the due date is not necessary for the protection of the victim of repudiation.

Even where a party does not repudiate a contract by word or deed, circumstances may indicate that performance is not likely to be rendered. If, for instance, two months before delivery of the deed and payment become due, a buyer of land discovers that a third party has a dower interest in the land, clear title cannot be transferred to the buyer without cooperation of the third party. In circumstances like these a promisee, here the buyer, can demand that adequate assurance of due performance be given and can suspend his own performance until such assurance is received. Failure of the promisor to provide adequate assurance within a reasonable time can be treated by the promisee as an anticipatory repudiation.[89]

V. Remedies

A. Damages

A breach of contract ordinarily entitles the injured party to damages. Under the common law a claim to damages is always understood to be a claim to compensation in the form of money. Restitution in kind to the status quo cannot be demanded in an action for damages.

While fault is not an essential element of the concept of breach as such, in assessing and measuring damages the blameworthiness of a breach is sometimes considered.

85. Restatement 2d § 250.
86. Restatement 2d § 253(2).
87. Restatement 2d § 255.
88. *Hochster v. De La Tour*, 118 Eng.Rep. 922 (Q.B. 1853).
89. Restatement 2d § 251; UCC § 2-609.

1. Expectation damages

Expectation damages are designed to put the injured party in as good a position as performance would have done. The injured party, being entitled to the benefit of the bargain, can demand an amount of money equal to the value of the promised performance. Individual circumstances, such as the value of benefits received through part performance and expenditures incurred by the victim as well as those saved, must be taken into account.[90]

Abstract market price differentials, as well as concrete measures looking to cover or resale prices, can be used to claim damages under a contract for the sale of goods according to the UCC.[91]

If the lessee of real property promises to return the property in a certain condition and then returns it in a lesser condition, the issue arises of whether damages are to be measured by the cost of work necessary to bring about the promised condition or by the diminution in value of the property. In the case of a willful and deliberate breach by the lessee it has been held that the cost of the work to be done determines the amount of damages.[92] This represents one of the instances in which blameworthiness of a breach influences the extent of liability. The same is true of cases in which a builder renders performance which substantially, but not completely, complies with the terms of the contract. *See* pt. IV.A.2. Here, too, courts take into consideration whether the breach was willful or not; if it was unintended, substantial performance may be found and damages assessed on the basis of a diminution in value, if any.

Under the mitigation principle no damages can be recovered for a loss that the injured party could have avoided after learning of the breach. However, in order to minimize her loss the injured party does not have to enter into a substitute transaction that involves undue risk, burden, or humiliation. For instance, a movie star who is denied a promised, very significant lead role in one type of movie does not have to play a much less important lead role in a different type of movie.[93]

Under the foreseeability principle, established by the most prominent contract case of all times, which interestingly relied on the French Civil Code and the French author Domat, damages are not recoverable for losses that were not reasonably foreseeable for the breacher at the time of contract formation.[94] Foreseeability is determined by application of a dual test. It looks to the probable results of a breach which follow either from the ordinary course of events or, on the other hand, from special circumstances that the party in breach was apprized of by the other party or had reason to know of anyhow. Under the Restatement Second even compensation for foreseeable loss of profits may sometimes be denied as disproportionate and be replaced by reliance damages.[95]

90. Restatement 2d § 347.
91. UCC §§ 2-708, 2-712, 2-713; *see* Chap. 13, pt. III.D.
92. *Groves v. John Wunder Co.*, 205 Minn. 163, 286 N.W. 235 (1939). *But see Peevyhouse v. Garland Coalt & Mining Co.*, 382 P.2d 109 (Okla. 1962), preferring the diminution-in-value measure.
93. *Parker v. Twentieth Century-Fox Film Corp.*, 3 Cal.3d 176, 474 P.2d 689 (1970).
94. *Hadley v. Baxendale*, 156 Eng.Rep. 145 (Ex. 1854).
95. Restatement 2d § 351(3). See the special rule in UCC § 2-715 as to a buyer's incidental and consequential damages.

Under the certainty principle no damages are recoverable for losses that may be characterized as speculative, for which there is no stable foundation in the evidence. In applying this principle a court may be satisfied with a lesser degree of certainty in a willful breach case, another instance in which blameworthiness of a breach matters. Where courts apply the certainty principle the injured party's evidence will not be allowed to go to the trier of fact. In the past an alleged uncertainty of profits frequently affected the recovery of losses involved in a new business with no past earnings history. More recently, however, it has been held that there is no hard and fast rule that prevents every new business from recovering anticipated lost profits for breach of contract.[96] More generally speaking, the certainty requirement is gradually losing much of its significance as more sophisticated knowledge on economic and financial data becomes available and can be interpreted and applied by expert witnesses.

2. Reliance damages

Reliance damages are not designed to put the plaintiff in the position she would have enjoyed if performance had been rendered as promised. Rather, where reliance damages are granted, they are designed to restore the injured party to the position she would occupy if the transaction had never taken place.

The reliance measure of damages may be an attractive alternative to a victim of breach who finds it hard or impossible to prove expectation damages, more specifically loss of profits. However, the party in breach is allowed to show that full performance would have resulted in no gain for his opponent. In the case of such a losing contract, presumably entered into by mistake in calculation or error in judgment, breach must not leave a party better off than performance. Since no expectation damages could possibly be recovered, reliance damages must be denied too.

Several more modern rules of contracts permit courts to limit a remedy "as justice requires," or to enforce a contract only to the extent "necessary to avoid injustice." The Restatement Second provides such rules, for instance, in cases of promissory estoppel (section 90), binding offers (sections 45, 87), contract modification (section 89), and action in reliance under the statute of frauds (section 139). In applying rules like these a court may decide to limit recovery to reliance damages rather than to grant expectation damages, even though the injured party is able to prove his loss of profits. In these circumstances the reliance measure is preferred not for practical but for equitable reasons. It is used by the court and not, in the first place, by the plaintiff.

Under the reliance measure of damages, out-of-pocket expenses which are attributable to the contract can be recovered. Sometimes the injured party can recover the value of a lost opportunity. For instance, the plaintiff thinking to be bound by the contract that was later breached may not have bid on another contract that can be shown he would have won as the lowest bidder. Here profits not made in the foregone transaction may be viewed as an item of reliance damages.

96. *See Fera v. Village Plaza, Inc.*, 396 Mich. 639, 242 N.W.2d 372 (1976).

Finally, in exceptional circumstances even non-pecuniary loss has been held to be recoverable as reliance damages. When a series of three attempts by a surgeon to improve the appearance of a female entertainer's nose failed miserably, she was granted reliance damages for her expenses, the worsening of her condition, and for pain and suffering and emotional distress involved in the third operation.[97]

3. Punitive damages

While available in certain circumstances in a tort action, punitive damages cannot ordinarily be recovered for breach of contract. If, however, the conduct constituting the breach is also a tort, punitive damages may become recoverable.[98] The issue is entirely determined by tort law. *See* Chap. 9, pt. II.E.

In recent decades courts have in effect gone beyond the traditional approach to punitive damages, which requires an independent tort accompanying a breach of contract. Primarily in insurance cases, but also in employment and other cases, a breach of contract committed in bad faith is as such treated as a tort to the extent that it is a basis for imposing punitive damages. The development started in liability insurance where the rationale was advanced that the insurer in handling a third party claim was acting as the insured's fiduciary. Once the practice of imposing punitive damages for a bad faith breach of contract grew to include other lines of insurance and also non-insurance cases, the fiduciary duty rationale was tacitly abandoned. It is obvious that punitive damages are used as a sanction in contract cases because courts see a need to discourage particularly reprehensible business conduct. This new development provides the most impressive incident demonstrating that under American law the blameworthiness of a breach of contract, while irrelevant to establish liability as such, can be highly significant in determining the extent of liability, that is the amount and the kind of damages recoverable.

4. Liquidated damages

Damages agreed to in a contract clause by the parties will be enforced, provided their agreement meets certain criteria.[99] Unreasonably large liquidated damages will not be enforced. Rather, they are regarded as a penalty, and unlike other systems the common law is generally opposed to penalty clauses. It was only very recently that this policy has come under attack. It is being criticized as paternalistic and inconsistent with economic efficiency. It is also at odds with the new development pertaining to punitive damages discussed in the previous section.

97. *Sullivan v. O'Connor*, 363 Mass. 579, 296 N.E.2d 183 (1973).
98. Restatement 2d § 355.
99. UCC § 2-718; Restatement 2d § 356.

B. Equitable Relief

Remedies which in the past could not be granted by a court of law, so that the injured party had to turn to a court of equity to obtain relief, are still termed equitable remedies even though the formerly separate court systems have long been merged in most American states. *See* Chap. 16, pts. I.C, D.

1. Specific performance

Specific performance of a contractual promise will not be granted if damages would be an adequate remedy. In this respect, in theory at least, the American law of contracts differs sharply from the law of contracts in civil law countries, which grants specific performance as a regular remedy.

The American approach to specific performance is largely the product of history. Policy reasons in terms of economic efficiency, advanced by some writers in favor of this approach, have been refuted by others.

In actual practice the difference between the systems with respect to specific performance is less dramatic than in theory. Under the civil law a plaintiff will not demand specific performance unless this serves his particular interests. In case such interests exist it is quite likely that an American court would also grant specific performance, since the courts are increasingly inclined to find that there is no adequate remedy at law.

Traditionally, the concept used to determine when damages are inadequate has been the uniqueness of a contract's subject matter. For mostly historical reasons real property is always considered to be unique, so that the buyer of land is automatically entitled to specific performance. With respect to a contract for the sale of goods the UCC section 2-716(1) provides that specific performance may he decreed where the goods are unique or in other proper circumstances. This rule has been applied to long term supply contracts, especially requirements contracts. Also contracts for the sale of a business, or of an interest in a business in the form of shares to which UCC section 2-716 does not apply directly, have been found to involve unique subjects of performance.

When deciding whether to grant specific performance, in addition to considering the uniqueness of a performance, courts will take into account the difficulty of proving damages with reasonable certainty and the likelihood that an award of damages could not be collected. Reasons for which a decree may be denied include the uncertainty of contract terms. A higher degree of certainty is said to be required for a decree of specific performance than for a judgment awarding damages. It is also said that in a suit for specific performance courts can base a dismissal on a wider range of fairness and public policy grounds than in an action for damages. Finally, a decree may be denied because the character and magnitude of the performance impose disproportionate burdens in enforcement or supervision upon the court.[100]

100. Restatement 2d §§ 364-365.

If a court decrees specific performance, it has broad discretionary powers in fashioning the remedy. The purposes for which the contract was made, and not necessarily its terms, determine the details of the court's order.[101]

2. Injunctions

Injunctions can be issued in all kinds of cases, not only those involving contracts. The purpose for which injunctions are primarily used in the area of contracts is the enforcement of a duty of forbearance. Frequently such duties are implied by law, not expressly agreed upon by the parties.[102]

Contracts involving a promise to render personal services will not be specifically enforced, partly because the United States Constitution prohibits involuntary servitude. Still, injunctions are sometimes issued enjoining the promisor from rendering services for others while performance should be rendered to the promisee.[103] If, however, this would leave an employee without a reasonable livelihood, an injunction must be denied.[104]

Selected Bibliography

F.H. Buckley, ed., *The Fall and Rise of Freedom of Contract* (1999).
John D. Calamari & Joseph M. Perillo, *The Law of Contracts* (4th ed. 1998).
Arthur Linton Corbin, 1-8 *Corbin an Contract* (Joseph M. Perillo ed., rev. ed. 1993-1999 & Supp. 2000).
Richard Craswell & Alan Schwartz, *Foundations of Contract Law* (1994).
E. Allan Farnsworth, *Contracts* (3d ed. 1999).
—, 1-3 *Farnsworth on Contracts* (2d ed. 1998 & Supp. 2000).
Grant Gilmore, *The Death of Contract* (Ronald K.L. Collins ed., 2d ed. 1995).
John Edward Murray, Jr., *Murray on Contracts* (3d ed. 1990).
Harry N. Scheiber, ed., *The State and Freedom of Contract* (1998).
David H. Vernon & Alan I. Widiss, *Understanding Contract Law* (2000).
James J. White & Robert S. Summers, *Uniform Commercial Code* (5th ed. 2000).
Samuel Williston, 1-17 *A Treatise on the Law of Contracts* (Richard A. Lord ed., 4th ed. 1990-2000).

101. Restatement 2d § 358.
102. Restatement 2d § 357(2) & cmt. b.
103. The leading case is *Lumley v. Wagner*, 42 Eng.Rep. 687 (Ch. 1852).
104. Restatement 2d § 367(2).

Chapter 9
Torts

Joachim Zekoll[*]
John G. Fleming[**]

* John Minor Wisdom Professor of Law and Director, European Legal Studies, Tulane University School of Law.
** Late John G. Shannon Cecil Turner Professor Emeritus, University of California at Berkeley School of Law; Editor-in-Chief, *American Journal of Comparative Law* (1971-1987).

David S. Clark and Tuğrul Ansay (eds.) Introduction to the Law of the United States, 189-207

I. Introduction

The law of torts (civil wrongs) in the United States is state law and may therefore vary in detail from one state to the next. Relevant statutes are primarily those of state legislatures and each state supreme court has the last word without any possibility of an appeal to the (federal) U.S. Supreme Court.[1] But the principles, originally derived from the common law of England, are common to all jurisdictions, even Louisiana with its French-inspired Civil Code.

Again, most of tort law is "common law" in the sense of judge made law. Although it has undergone substantial changes in the last quarter century, this process has generally been carried out by judicial innovation, not by legislative reform. Most state legislatures have been paralyzed by opposing power groups: on one side the "defense" lobby representing the insurance industry, on the other the plaintiffs' interest represented by the American Trial Lawyers Association (ATLA). The resulting vacuum was filled by the judiciary which earned it the sobriquet of judicial activism.[2] Most of this modernization resulted in substantial improvements in the position of plaintiffs, in which certain state courts (for example, New Jersey and California) took the lead. For more than a decade, there has been a tendency for legislative roll-backs of some of these gains, in an effort to curb liability insurance rates, first in medical malpractice actions and later spreading to product liability and tort claims in general. These laws, enacted by many state legislatures, include caps on compensatory damages awards and heightened thresholds for the imposition of punitive damages. Lately, several of these enactments have been declared unconstitutional by state courts, typically because they were held to infringe the right to a jury trial.

Tort law has become big business in the United States, marked both by a swollen and highly publicized volume of claims and by what to foreign observers seem staggering awards of damages. The catalyst is a combination of the jury trial and a specialist plaintiffs' bar. Unless waived by the parties, which only rarely occurs, trial of tort actions is by jury. Although inherited from England, civil jury trial has become a peculiarly American institution, and one almost exclusive to tort actions.[3] Especially in urban areas juries are perceived as pro-plaintiff and are therefore the sheet anchor of the plaintiffs' bar. *See* Chap. 16, pt. IX.B.

The American trial bar is sharply segregated into attorneys serving either plaintiffs or defendants. The division is marked by their different kinds of fees:[4] defendants' attorneys are paid on an hourly basis, plaintiffs' on a contingent fee. Under the American legal costs structure, clients are ordinarily responsible for their own attorney's fees, whether they win or lose, since (unlike in most other countries) the loser does not have to reimburse the winner for the latter's legal

1. There are a few federal statutes in this field, most notably the Federal Employers' Liability Act (FELA) which controls railroads' liability to their employees, and the Federal Tort Claims Act dealing with the tort liability of the federal government. Constitutional law has also intruded into defamation and invasion of privacy. *See* pts. V, VI.
2. *See* John G. Fleming, *The American Tort Process* ch. 2 (1988).
3. *Id.* ch. 4.
4. *Id.* ch. 5.

costs. But in tort claims the plaintiff's attorney is prepared to work for nothing if he loses, and becomes entitled to a share of the award (a third and more) if successful. These attorneys are therefore highly motivated to win or settle the case and secure as large an award as possible. Their interests are represented in the legislative and public opinion arena by the high profile and politically influential medium of ATLA.[5] Tort law and tort reform are thus politicized and largely viewed by the bar in terms of what best promotes the cause of either plaintiffs or defendants.

II. Negligence

Tort liability is customarily divided into intentional, negligent, and strict liability torts. Central and most important is liability for negligent harm. The elements of this liability are: (1) a duty of care, (2) breach of that duty by negligent conduct (act or omission), (3) causing injury, and (4) subject to the defenses of assumption of risk and contributory negligence.

A. Duty of Care

The defendant must be under a duty of care for the benefit of the plaintiff before his carelessness can incur liability. Whether such a duty exists in the particular relationship between the parties is a question of law to be decided by the judge rather than the jury. In the absence of precedent the most important determinant is foreseeability of injury, but legal policy has the last word. One formula lists among the most important factors the closeness of the connection between the injury and the defendant's conduct, the moral blame attached to the defendant's conduct, the policy of preventing future harm, and the prevalence and availability of insurance. In most situations involving physical injury resulting from such activities as driving a car, duty goes without saying; it becomes controversial only in unusual situations.

These situations may be grouped into three basic kinds. The first relates to the particular status of either party or some peculiarity in their mutual relation. The defendant may be a government agency claiming immunity from liability in tort. *See* Chap. 5, pt. VI. While absolute immunity has disappeared, it is still prevalent in relation to the exercise of policy functions such as decisions on nuclear testing or supersonic flying. Or the plaintiff may be a trespasser on the plaintiff's land for whose safety less than ordinary care may be demanded. Or the relation between the parties is that of car driver and guest passenger, which until repealed used to engender liability only for grosser forms of misconduct such as drunkenness.

The second *discrimen* has reference to the nature of the conduct that caused the harm, in particular the difference between acts of commission and omission. A society dedicated to individualism is content to deter one person from harm-

5. *Id.* ch. 6.

ing another, but cautious about compelling a person to protect another from harm. However, duties of affirmative action have become increasingly recognized: between occupier and visitor, employer and employee, and other relations of reliance. This development has contributed to the vast expansion of tort liability in recent years, driven by the pursuit of "deep pockets" to pay for injuries inflicted by impecunious culprits. Many antecedent relations now engender a duty even to control the conduct of others, such as the duty to protect tenants against rapists[6] or for psychotherapists to warn persons threatened by their patients.[7]

The third major distinction on which a duty of care might hinge is the kind of injury for which damages are sought. One problem area has been liability for emotional harm such as nervous shock from seeing a close relative injured or endangered. Here the law has moved from the original position requiring physical impact to allowing claims without insisting either that the victim feared for his own safety or even suffered physical injury such as a resulting heart attack or miscarriage.[8]

Another problem area concerns pregnancies. It is now well settled that prenatal injuries are compensable, at any rate by a child born alive, against third parties. Claims against a parent used to be barred by an absolute immunity which now applies only to obligations specific to parenthood, not for example to dangerous driving. But what if a mother is a drug addict and causes injury to the fetus? Equally problematical are "wrongful birth" and "wrongful life" claims. The birth of an unwanted child is now widely held to be actionable in cases of failed sterilization, defective birth control devices, or a physician's failure to warn a patient against risk of congenital diseases. Mostly, however, damages do not include the cost of rearing an unwanted child, though they might the medical care of an injured child. But almost all claims by the child itself for "wrongful life" have been defeated as incompatible with our cultural affirmation of life.[9]

More divisive is the question of recovery for purely economic loss. While tort claims are generally associated with personal injury or damage to tangible property, there is no categorical bar against economic loss, standing alone. The scope of liability is, however, much more restricted for fear of imposing an undue, incalculable, and uninsurable burden on enterprise. Thus, according to the better view, an accountant is not liable to members of the general public who invest in reliance on an audit, unless he knew that it would be shown to a particular person for a particular purpose.[10] Similarly where business is interrupted by damage to an electricity cable in the vicinity. Nor can the purchaser of a defective product that is shoddy but not dangerous sue the manufacturer in tort for its lesser value; his remedy is for breach of contract against the retail seller. In these situations of purely economic loss, more than in any other, foreseeability is not enough.

6. *Doe v. Dominion Bank of Wash., N.A*, 963 F.2d 1552 (D.C. Cir. 1992).
7. *Tarasoff v. Regents of Univ. of Cal.*, 551 P.2d 334 (1976).
8. *Thing v. La Chusa*, 771 P.2d 814 (1989).
9. *Turpin v. Sortini*, 643 P.2d 954 (1982).
10. *Credit Alliance Corp. v. Arthur Anderson & Co.*, 65 N.Y.2d 536, 483 N.E.2d 110 (1985).

B. Breach of Duty

Negligence consists in conduct fraught with unreasonable risk of harm, or more simply, in failure to observe the care of a reasonable person in like circumstances. This is preeminently a jury issue. The standard is objective; individual failings do not excuse the actor from liability. There are some exceptions: for example, physical infirmities, provided the handicapped person took care to compensate for his disability. Also, children are judged by the standard of reasonable behavior of children of like age, intelligence, and experience except when engaged in adult activities like driving automobiles (*cherchez l'assurance*!).[11]

Whether the act or omission in question is one that a reasonable person would recognize as posing an unreasonable risk is determined by balancing the magnitude of the risk against the burden of eliminating it.[12] The former factor comprises both the probability of the risk eventuating and the seriousness of its consequences; the latter includes both the utility of the defendant's conduct and the cost of eliminating or reducing the risk.

Instead of using the model of the reasonable person, the standard may be supplied by a statutory prescription of the appropriate conduct, as is very common in road traffic, industrial, and other safety legislation. The question whether statutory violation is the equivalent of negligence has not been answered uniformly. In all jurisdictions it is at least evidence of negligence, but in some it is deemed to be negligence *per se*. In that event it is irrelevant whether the violation was committed intentionally, negligently, or faultlessly; it can therefore be a bridge toward strict liability. But varying defenses are allowed, such as "I could not help it," as when a car swerves into the opposite lane due to a sudden tire burst.

C. Causation

Actual injury is a necessary element of liability for negligence. For merely threatened harm damages are not recoverable, although some recent decisions have made awards for cancerphobia after exposure to asbestos.

There are two aspects. First, was the defendant's conduct a "cause in fact" of the injury in the sense that "but for" it, the injury would not have occurred? The burden of proof ordinarily rests on the plaintiff to establish this relationship on a "balance of probabilities." In a few situations it has been reversed: for example, where the plaintiff suffered an external injury during surgery but could not identify whom of the team was responsible, or where two hunters negligently fired at the plaintiff, who could not identify the culprit. Also in medical malpractice cases, loss of a chance of less than 50 percent cure has sometimes been held sufficient.

Secondly, the negligence must not only be the cause, but the proximate cause of the injury. There is no consensus on how to determine proximity. Foreseeability

11. *Robinson v. Lindsay*, 598 P.2d 392 (1979).
12. Or, liability depends on whether $B < PL$ (P=probability, L=liability, B=burden): *United States v. Carroll Towing Co.*, 159 F.2d 169, 173 (1947).

is the traditional test, but is much more forgiving in practice than as a test of negligence and often stretched beyond realistic limits. It is not required that the precise injury, its extent, or the precise manner of its occurrence be foreseeable; harm of the general kind is sufficient. Moreover, the tortfeasor must take his victim as he finds him, so that a peculiar susceptibility to harm such as hemophilia does not excuse; nor does the exceptionally high earning capacity of the victim or value of damaged property.

Multiple tortfeasors are classified as either joint or concurrent. The principal example of the first is that of two or more acting in concert, for example, to engage in a road race, in which event all are liable regardless of which one of them caused the injury. Concurrent tortfeasors are those who, acting independently, cause an indivisible injury, for example by colliding with each other and harming a passenger. Each is liable *in toto* (the so-called joint and several liability rule), but the plaintiff may collect from any one or both any amount until he has recovered 100 percent of his loss. As between themselves, they can claim contribution if one has paid more than his appropriate share. But in practice it will often happen that the "deep pocket" defendant will end up paying most, if not all, the damages. The "explosion" of tort liability in the last quarter century has brought to book many such "deep pocket" defendants whose responsibility may be quite marginal compared with that of the real culprit who as often as not is "judgment proof," like burglars and drunk drivers. The resulting unfairness has led to reform in some jurisdictions, confining the liability of concurrent tortfeasors to their share of responsibility, at least with respect to non-pecuniary loss.

In order to encourage settlements, a tortfeasor who settles in good faith is immune from claims for contribution, but only the amount of such settlement is deducted from the liability of the remaining defendant(s) who therefore carry the risk of an undervalued settlement.

D. Defenses

There are two defenses to negligence claims: contributory negligence and voluntary assumption of risk.

Contributory negligence used to be a complete bar to recovery, but has in most jurisdictions been modified so as merely to reduce damages. Where this reform of "comparative negligence" was carried out by legislation, it is mostly conditional on the plaintiff's fault being no greater than the defendant's; where accomplished by judicial decree, it mostly takes the form of "pure" comparative negligence, that is, regardless of the parties' respective shares of fault.[13]

Voluntary assumption of risk used to play a big role in defeating actions by employees against their employer or co-employees, contributing to the eventual passage of workers' compensation. Today, it is virtually confined to passengers of drunk drivers and spectators of sporting events like baseball or hockey. In some jurisdictions the defense has been merged into comparative negligence.

13. *Li v. Yellow Cab*, 13 Cal.3d 804, 532 P.2d 1226 (1975).

E. Damages

Damages are awarded in lump sums once-and-for-all, not by periodic payments subject to variation. However, modern so-called structured settlements in big cases, often against hospitals, provide annuities and free medical care.

Damages are either for pecuniary or non-pecuniary loss, known respectively as special or general damages. The former compensate for medical costs and loss of earnings, past and future. In order to allow for inflation, a low or no discount factor is applied. By virtue of the "collateral source rule," no deduction is made for benefits coming to the victim from other sources, including prepaid medical care, insurance, and even social insurance benefits.[14] This, together with the absence of a publicly funded health scheme, accounts in some measure for the much larger awards in big cases compared with damages awarded in most other countries. Loss of earnings (or earning capacity) is assessed on the basis of gross, that is pre-taxed, earnings; nor is such an award itself subject to tax. This, as well as the collateral source rule, is explained on the ground that it goes towards compensating the plaintiff for his lawyer's fees. Recent legislation in several states, however, has eliminated some of these benefits for plaintiffs.

For non-pecuniary damages, called general damages or damages for pain and suffering, juries are given a very free hand, there being no tariffs. Additionally, prior awards in similar cases are not citable as guides nor do judges give helpful instructions. Juries presumably get some inspiration from mega-awards publicized in newspapers, which thus have a snow-balling effect. Although these damages are meant to be compensatory, they often contain an element of vindictiveness, especially against corporate defendants. Not surprisingly, the plaintiffs' bar views the jury's role, constitutionally entrenched, as crucial to its own financial advantage. Some statutes in the last decade have placed "caps," ranging between $200,000 to $500,000, on awards for medical malpractice, but some of these have been struck down for violating state constitutions.

Claims for wrongful death were long limited to the pecuniary loss sustained by the surviving next of kin in being deprived of the decedent's financial support. The death of young children therefore remained largely uncompensated. Nowadays, however, half the jurisdictions also award damages for loss of companionship, usually running into several hundred thousand dollars. In recent times relatives of a person injured, but not killed, have also made claim for such compensation, but only spouses have been successful, an archaic remedy for husbands being in effect extended to wives.

General damages for emotional distress have traditionally been confined to tort. This principle has been obscured by treating "malicious breach" of certain types of contract as torts so as to allow awards of non-pecuniary damages. This sanction has been applied principally against insurers for unreasonable failure to settle within policy limits and thereby exposing the insured to excess liability.

Punitive or exemplary damages are also increasingly assuming major importance. Their avowed purpose is to punish the tortfeasor for atrocious misconduct,

14. Nor is there in general any subrogation except for first-party property insurance.

not to compensate the plaintiff for his humiliation and anger, which is the function of general damages. In the past they were mainly a sanction against personal aggression and other intentional torts like deceit. As such the awards were modest, having regard to the defendant's usually exiguous means. One aspect of the modern "tort explosion" is the extension of punitive damages against corporate defendants for mere "conscious disregard of the safety (or rights) of others." Such damages are nowadays awarded against insurance companies for unreasonable failure to pay claims promptly or within policy limits, against doctors and hospitals for medical malpractice, and against manufacturers of defective products. Because juries are encouraged to take into consideration the defendant's wealth, awards may range in the millions of dollars.

F. Special Relations

The law has developed special rules with respect to certain problem areas. Two prominent ones concern the duty of an occupier to visitors (*see* pt. II.A) and medical malpractice.

The traditional common law developed a special approach in the occupier cases by classifying visitors into distinct categories entitled to varying duties specifically defined by law rather than by the generalized standard of reasonable care. The highest class is that of "invitees," originally defined as business visitors but later also including persons entering public premises such as city halls, parks, and libraries. To them the occupier owes a duty to warn of dangers of which she knows *or* ought to know. No such duty of inspection is due to the next group, "licensees," in whose presence the occupier has no *material* interest, most prominently social guests. The lowest category comprises trespassers who can complain only of intentional or reckless injury. The original function of this stereotype was to give judges greater control over juries, but it fell into disrepute because of its fine and capricious distinctions. In recent years some reform-minded courts have introduced the ordinary standard of care for all, or at any rate for all lawful, visitors.[15]

Claims for medical negligence (or malpractice) used to be heavily discouraged by several devices. The rule was and still is that a plaintiff must prove that the physician failed to conform to the prevailing standard of skill and care among fellow practitioners. Conversely, conformity is, contrary to the general rule, *conclusive* evidence of due care, thus allowing the profession in effect to set its own legal standard. Secondly, only expert evidence sufficed to establish lack of care, and it was difficult to procure respectable practitioners to testify against another. An exception is now allowed where a jury of lay persons can form their own judgment, as in cases where the injury is outside the area of treatment or an instrument is left in the patient's body. The defendant can also be called to testify against himself and medical textbooks are admissible. The greater success of malpractice claims in recent times has entailed a dramatic rise in insurance premiums, which in turn inspired widespread reform statutes, setting caps on non-pecuniary dam-

15. *Rowland v. Christian*, 69 Cal.2d 108, 443 P.2d 561 (1968).

ages (between $100,000 and $500,000), limiting the rate of contingent fees, and introducing periodical payments.

III. Strict Liability

By the middle of the 19th century, an earlier tradition of stricter liability had been repudiated in favor of the principle "no liability without fault." A century later no-fault liability is again making big strides. One aspect of this development is the tendency to set ever more demanding standards of care especially in areas, such as automobile traffic, with a background of mandatory or widely held liability insurance. Shifting the burden of proof, or at least of producing evidence, to the defendant under relaxed conditions of *res ipsa loquitur* is a straddle between negligence and strict liability.

In addition, strict liability proper is recognized in the following situations:

A. Abnormally Dangerous Activities

Associated with the English decision of *Rylands v. Fletcher*[16] is the liability, independent of negligence, for injury caused by the miscarriage of abnormally dangerous activities such as bursting dams, "blow-out" oil wells, escaping cyanic gas in fumigating a building, testing rocket motors, or blasting on a construction site. An exception is generally allowed for common usage, which has been used to explain the refusal to extend strict liability to automobile driving. It did not, however, exonerate crop spraying with herbicide nor an explosion of a large gasoline truck on the highway. Under statute, strict liability now rests on nuclear operators and in a few states for ground damage by aircraft. A vestige from an agricultural past is the strict liability for cattle trespass (except in Western states with open grazing) and, as one of the building blocks of the general principle of abnormal dangers, the strict *scienter* liability for dangerous animals, including statutory liability for all dog bites.

B. Vicarious Liability

An employer is liable, regardless of fault either in hiring or supervision, for the torts of its employees committed in the course of their employment. The guilty employee is liable as a joint tortfeasor, though judgment is rarely executed against that party. But there is no general principle requiring the employer to reimburse the employee or preventing the employer from seeking an indemnity from the employee (or the latter's liability insurer). An exception is the statutory immunity granted to employees of the federal government.

Vicarious liability applies only to employees, not to independent contractors. The conventional test is whether the "master" can tell the "servant" not only what

16. [1868] L.R. 3 H.L. 330.

to do, but how to do it. This no longer implies the employer's ability but merely the right to do so. The employment relation thus extends to skilled and professional personnel. By contrast, independent contractors are people in business on their own, who undertake to perform a specific task such as painting a house or driving a taxi. But over time many exceptions have been engrafted on the immunity of "employers" of independent contractors in a search for the deeper pocket. Such so-called non-delegable duties are linked in the main to work involving a higher degree of risk, but not limited to activities of strict liability.

The tort must have been committed "in the course of employment." As in defining the relationship itself, so here too many factors are relevant; it has been said that in general the servant's conduct is within the course of employment if it is of the kind he is employed to perform, occurs substantially within the authorized limits of time and place, and is actuated, at least in part, by a purpose to serve the master.[17] But not even the fact that the tort was intentional or the act prohibited necessarily exonerates.

An employer may of course also incur liability for negligence in employing or supervising an employee, but such liability would be personal, not vicarious, and requires proof of negligence by the employer herself rather than by the employee.

C. Products Liability

The principal contribution of American law to tort theory is the development of strict liability for defective products, which has provided the model for the 1985 EEC Directive and is now in force in all member states of the European Union.[18] It evolved somewhat similarly to a parallel development in France, by an extension of guarantees of quality implied in the sale of goods as between buyer and seller to the relation also of manufacturers (and other sellers in the chain of distribution) and the ultimate consumer. Although at first presenting itself merely as sales warranties, now without the limiting requirement of "privity" of contract, this no-fault liability was openly recognized as a new tort by the mid-1960s. *See* Chap. 13, pt. III.B.

The initial focus had been principally on manufacturing defects and was broadly accepted as in practice not adding a great deal to prior tort liability based on negligence, reinforced by reversal of the onus of proof under *res ipsa loquitur*. But its later expansion through application to design defects and failure to warn, coupled with awards of punitive damages, has been much more controversial. A persisting problem is in defining a test for what is "defective." One is the consumer-expectation test, which is more meaningful in relation to a buyer than to third parties who are frequently among the injured. Also, in many cases the consumer has no specific expectation, without knowledge of alternative designs. The test is frequently supplemented by balancing the risk against the utility of the design. Alternatively, the product is deemed to be defective if a prudent manufacturer, knowing of the risk, would not have marketed it. Here, unlike in negligence,

17. *Wilson v. Chicago, Milwaukee, St. Paul, & Pac. R.R. Co.*, 841 F.2d 1347 (7th Cir. 1988).
18. Council Directive 85/374/EEC of 25 July 1985, O.J. L 210/29.

knowledge is assumed; but most courts have declined to hold the manufacturer responsible for knowledge available only after the product was marketed. The question relates both to knowledge of risks (as in the case of pharmaceuticals like Thalidomide) and of the technology, to which the "state of the art" defense is particularly directed. It is as relevant to claims for failure to warn as for design defects.

To what extent defenses relating to the user's conduct are available is also controversial. Mere failure to recognize the risk or defect is no defense at all. One view is that only continued use after becoming fully aware of the defect would qualify as voluntary assumption of risk or, at most, as comparative negligence, as would negligent use of the product such as speeding in an automobile with a defective windshield.

Strict liability clearly covers personal injury and damage to other property. Damage to the defective product itself is generally left to contract claims between buyer and seller, unless perhaps the product was destroyed or damaged in an accident. Loss of profits or the decreased value of the product are excluded as purely economic loss. As already mentioned, claims nowadays can carry large awards of punitive damages by treating calculated design choices as indicative of conscious indifference to the safety of the public and by taking account of the corporate defendant's wealth. On the other hand, in many jurisdictions the burden of proving a design defect is very similar to the costly enterprise of proving negligence on the part of the defendant, thus calling into question whether strict liability truly is liability without fault.

D. *Industrial Accidents*

There also exist scattered special compensation schemes either supplementary to or replacing tort liability for specific types of accidents. The oldest example is workers' compensation, which made a tardy entry and is still less than satisfactory in many states in terms of the amount of benefits and its efficiency. It provides the exclusive remedy for claims by workers against their employer and co-employees. One exception is the federal regime for railroad employees (FELA) and seamen (including waterside workers injured on navigable waters), which in theory is based on negligence but in practice comes close to strict liability and delivers the larger measure of lump-sum tort damages compared with periodical compensation payments.

E. *Automobile No-Fault Plans*

Automobile driving, though arguably an abnormally dangerous activity in terms of its 41,500 fatalities and more than 3.2 million injuries a year,[19] has remained rooted in negligence law. Until the 1960s, few states even required mandatory liability insurance, and to this day the insurance minimum rarely exceeds $15,000,

19. Nat'l Highway Traffic Safety Admin., U.S. Dep't of Transp., *Traffic Safety Facts 1998* 2 (1999).

which goes to explain the trend to expand the net of tort law to catch other, less culpable but more pecunious defendants. Even so, there is continuing complaint about escalating insurance rates.

The American alternative to the traffic problem has not been, as in most other countries, a strict liability regime based on the model of third-party liability or a centralized public compensation fund. Instead, building on voluntary first-party insurance, it requires insurance by the automobile owner with a private insurance carrier for personal injuries by occupants of the car, including the driver and pedestrians. No-fault benefits are limited to medical costs and loss of earnings, subject however to very low caps ($10,000 or less). Only a few states offer unlimited medical expenses or substantial totals. In order to keep the system in balance, its extended benefits to persons not previously covered by tort liability have to be compensated by savings in non-pecuniary damages for relatively trivial injuries. To that end, in all but a few of the 25 states which have adopted the system, tort claims must rise above certain thresholds, such as $1,000 medical expenses, loss or fracture of limbs, or serious permanent impairment. Otherwise, premiums would exceed the level of public acceptability. As a result the plans cover only the bulk of less serious injuries and leave those most in need to the vagaries of the tort system. The opposition of the plaintiffs' bar, wedded to the adversary process and its financial rewards, has stultified more drastic reform.

IV. Intentional Torts

A. *Personal Injuries*

Among the historically oldest of the intentional delicts are the *trespass* torts of assault, battery, and false imprisonment. Assault consists of intentionally putting another in apprehension of immediate physical contact, and battery consists of inflicting such a contact. In both instances protection is given a dignitary interest in as much as actual personal injury is not essential. To be a battery the contact must be unconsented, though it need not be hostile, as when a person is kissed without his or her consent, express or implied.

False (that is to say, illegal) imprisonment consists of confining a person or preventing him from leaving the place where he is. Though originally implying incarceration, it is now sufficient, for example, for a store detective to detain a suspect for interrogation. Neither actual force nor physical contact is required so long as the plaintiff's will is overborne.

Bearing some resemblance is the tort of malicious prosecution, which consists of maliciously and without reasonable and probable cause instituting groundless legal proceedings, especially criminal prosecutions. It differs from false imprisonment in that the restraint on the plaintiff's liberty is not directly imposed by the defendant but through an intermediate authority (public prosecutor). Because of the countervailing public interest in encouraging private initiative in law enforcement, however, this tort is hedged by the double requirement that the defendant acted with malice and with want of reasonable and probable cause. To complement the torts of assault and battery, a new tort of intentional infliction of emotional distress was devised to deal with reprehensible conduct other than with threats to physical safety. Such would be falsely informing a woman that her husband has been killed,[20] importuning and threatening debt collection, or even harassing an employee with racial slurs. Two safeguards are designed to set a limit beyond which the law is not prepared to intercede against uncivilized conduct. First, the misconduct must be reasonably likely to cause terror in a normal person or in one known to be peculiarly sensitive. Second, the victim's hurt must be evidenced by substantial physical symptoms to qualify as physical injury, just as where the defendant's conduct was merely negligent rather than intended to cause the distress. This requirement differentiates this tort from assault, where mere indignation is sufficient. However, in recent years a few courts have relaxed the requirement, insisting merely on the affront being calculated to cause serious distress.[21]

B. Property Wrongs

Trespass to the person (like assault and battery) had its counterpart in trespass to land and chattels (movables). Any direct interference, such as entering land without the occupier's consent or dispossessing him of a book, a hat, or picture, is thus actionable. Proof of actual damage is no more required than for trespass to the person, but nowadays the interference must have been intended, not merely negligent (for the latter, damage is essential).

A more comprehensive remedy for interference with possessory rights in chattels is the action for conversion. Besides actual dispossession it covers other deprivations, such as refusing to return a chattel originally rightfully obtained (for example, on rental), transferring them to the wrong claimant, or denying the true owner's title. Thus conversion became a remedy for trying title to goods. A successful plaintiff is entitled to the full value of the goods, so that by converting, one can say the defendant had bought them.

C. Defenses

Originally the preceding trespass wrongs were actionable without proof of fault. In the course of time, however, various justifications came to be admitted as specific defenses. (In negligence, a similar function is part of the plaintiff's case in establishing wrongfulness.)

1. Mistake

Mostly, mistake provides no excuse for intentionally violating the plaintiff's rights. For example, by cutting the plaintiff's trees believing them, however rea-

20. *Wilkinson v. Downton* [1897] 2 Q.B. 57, the seminal English case.
21. *State Rubbish Collectors v. Siliznoff*, 38 Cal. 2d 330, 240 P.2d 282 (1952).

sonably, to be your own. Having to pay for the trees prevents your unjust enrichment at the plaintiff's expense.

On the other hand, mistake excuses a police officer's arrest of somebody whom he believes to have committed a felony or when one defends himself in the mistaken but reasonable belief of being attacked. In the former case, leniency is justified by the policeman's duty to protect the public against crime; in the latter by the need for instant action.

2. Consent: *volenti non fit injuria*

Consent may be express or implied by conduct, as by participating in contact sports. But the consent must be real, though economic duress is not recognized. Misapprehension, induced by the defendant or known to him, as to the nature of the proposed interference vitiates consent; not so a mistake merely as to its consequences. Thus a doctor's failure to explain the risks of a proposed operation does not convert the treatment into a battery: "informed consent" belongs to negligence. Consent must be to the precise conduct in question or at least to acts of a substantially similar nature. A surgeon cannot ordinarily go beyond instructions, unless it is a matter of life or death, merely because he thinks it is in the patient's best interest.

3. Self-defense

An act in self-defense is justified, while an act in response to mere provocation is not. The force used, however, must be no more than reasonably necessary to ward off the attack. It is also permissible to defend others, even strangers, under the same conditions.

4. Defense of property

One may expel trespassers, though not generally with force likely to cause grievous bodily harm or death. For this purpose the occupier may use force himself or employ mechanical devices or animals (dogs). However, to evict a tenant one must resort to legal processes.

Likewise, one who has been dispossessed of chattels may recapture them without force. Otherwise, he must resort to law to regain possession.

5. Necessity

In some circumstances, one is privileged to infringe on the interests of others for the purpose of preventing or avoiding harm to oneself or third persons. A "public champion" may do so without paying for the damage he thereby inflicts, for example, when firemen tear down a building to create a fire break (such loss is covered by fire insurance). When the action is taken to advance one's own interest at someone else's expense, the action itself may be privileged, but the actor has to compensate the other for the actual loss.[22]

6. Legal Authority

Police officers, security personnel, and even private citizens have authority in some circumstances to arrest persons suspected of crime. The conditions are defined by state statutes, subject to constitutional restraints. *See* Chap. 15, pt. III.

D. Economic Torts

Several distinct torts are specifically associated with economic loss. As previously pointed out, negligence does not readily afford protection against purely economic loss. Nor is there even a recognized general principle of liability for intended economic harm, given our commitment to competition in a free market economy. In order to attract liability, there must be an additional element of either improper means or malice.

1. Fraud

Liability for fraudulent misrepresentation was admitted long before, and with less reservation than, liability for negligent misrepresentation. It confers a cause of action on any person who was intended to, and did, rely on a fraudulent statement to her detriment, regardless of whether she was a contractual promisee or a third-party, such as an investor relying on a company audit. The misrepresentation must have been known to be false, or at least been made recklessly, that is, not caring whether it was true or false. Damages are assessed on the basis of the actual loss incurred, not (as in contract law) for loss of the expected benefit. *See* Chap. 8, pt. V.A.1.

2. Passing-off

A specific form of misrepresentation is to pretend that your goods or services stem from a competitor in order to appropriate the latter's goodwill. False trademarks and deceptive get-ups are examples. Such deception is actionable not only in the suit of disappointed customers (consumer protection) but also of the competitor who has thereby lost sales. The Federal Trademark Protection Act (Lanham Act) offers an alternative, more advantageous remedy.

22. *Vincent v. Lake Erie Transp. Co.*, 109 Minn. 456, 124 N.W. 221 (1910).

3. Trade libel

Disparaging another's property or merchandise, knowing it to be false and for a dishonest purpose, is the tort variously known as slander of goods, trade libel, or injurious falsehood. It resembles defamation but relates not to the plaintiff's character but to his ability to dispose of his property, goods, or business. The same privileges are probably recognized as for defamation.

4. Interference with contractual relations

Intentionally interfering with the performance of a contract, as by persuading one party to breach it or not to renew it, is actionable in a suit by the other. This includes luring away a competitor's employee or customer. In regard to industrial action, such as strikes and secondary boycotts, however, it is largely preempted by the National Labor Relations Act. *See* Chap. 6, pt. II.

V. Reputation and Privacy

A. Defamation

Written defamation is known as libel, oral defamation as slander. The first is actionable *per se*, the second only on proof of special damage, that is, pecuniary loss. By constitutional mandate, however, even a libel plaintiff can recover only for "actual" damage, including proven loss of reputation.

At common law, liability was strict, with no allowance being made for an honest mistake of fact in what was asserted, as long as the publication itself was intended or negligent. Publication must be to a third person because defamation is concerned with reputation, not dignity as such. A lone confrontation with the plaintiff or an insult is not actionable.

Mitigating the strictness are major defenses in the interest of freedom of speech. Absolute privilege attaches to legislative and judicial proceedings and to fair reports of the same. Communications between spouses are also privileged. Qualified privilege covers communications in protection of a common interest (for example, partners) or of interest to the recipient (for instance, supplying a reference about a former employee or a report to the police). Such privilege is lost either by excessive publication (for example, to a newspaper of general circulation) or by malice, that is, an indirect motive other than to serve the purpose for which the privilege is recognized, including lack of belief in its truth. From a free speech point of view, the most important defense is that of fair comment on a matter of public interest, such as politics, entertainment, or the arts. There is a split of authority on whether the defense covers honest, if defamatory, comment based on false facts mistakenly believed to be true. This controversy has since been resolved by constitutional intervention, as discussed below.

Voluntary retraction is a common statutory defense, at least to liability for other than material loss. But a right of reply has been held unconstitutional for interfering with editorial independence.

Until 1964 defamation was not considered "speech" for the purpose of the constitutional prohibition of the First Amendment against laws "abridging the freedom of speech and of the press." The intervention in *New York Times v. Sullivan*[23] was prompted by the misuses of libel law by the Southern racist establishment against the liberal Eastern press. It was held that a public official had to prove that a libel of him was published with "actual malice," that is, with knowledge that it was false or in reckless disregard of the truth. This constitutional privilege was later extended to all public figures. An additional modification of the common law in *Gertz v. Welch*[24] prohibited liability without fault for *all* libel actions, and prohibited damages for other than actual proven injury, at least in the absence of "actual malice." Subsequently, however, this new rule was restricted to "speech involving matters of public concern."[25]

A dictum in *Gertz* proclaimed that "there is no such thing as a false idea."[26] For a time this was interpreted as immunizing all expressions of opinion; but it has now been held that the dividing line was not between fact and opinion, but between what can and cannot be proven false.[27] Ideas cannot, but an opinion may be based on false facts or imply a knowledge of facts which are false. This decision reverts to the traditional limits of the defense of "fair comment," that is, comment or opinion based on true facts.

Some federal courts have also endorsed an absolute constitutional privilege for "neutral reportage," that is, accurate reporting of newsworthy allegations even if the reporter entertains serious doubts about their accuracy. But the matter remains in doubt. *See* Chap. 4, pt. XI.B.3.

B. Privacy

Invasion of privacy became recognized as a tort in the 20th century. It may take four different forms: (a) intrusion, like bugging a home; (b) misappropriation of personality, such as commercialization of one's name or face; (c) putting someone in a false light by non-defamatory but embarrassing falsehoods; and (d) publicity of private facts. Publication of contemporary newsworthy matter is privileged. A state prohibition against publishing the name of rape victims from court records has been held unconstitutional, but otherwise the effect of the constitutional guarantee of free speech on the tort remains to be explored.

23. 376 U.S. 254 (1964).
24. 418 U.S. 323 (1974).
25. *Dunn & Bradstreet v. Greenmoss Bros.*, 472 U.S. 749 (1985).
26. *Gertz*, 418 U.S. at 339.
27. *Milkovich v. Lorain Journal*, 493 U.S. 1055 (1990).

VI. Government Liability

Government liability is based on statutes, state as well as federal. By the Federal Tort Claims Act (FTCA) of 1946 the federal government submitted to tort liability for the "wrongful act or omission of any employee of the Government while acting within the scope of his office or employment." Excepted were claims based on the exercise of a "discretionary function," a distinction between policy and operational decisions, which is often hard to draw. Exempt, for example, are acts of an agency as regulator of private individuals, such as decisions by the Federal Aviation Authority of what inspections to carry out on civil aircraft; while errors by air traffic controllers are considered operational. *See* Chap. 5, pt. VI.

Culpable government employees remained exclusively liable for intentional torts. Another important area of such personal liability consists of constitutional torts.

The Civil Rights Act of 1871 established an action (§ 1983) against anyone who, "under color" of state law, deprives another of "any rights, privileges, or immunities secured by the Constitution and [federal] laws."[28] Long dormant, the remedy was activated in 1961 by the Warren Supreme Court in *Monroe v. Pape*,[29] and has since become a major area of federal jurisdiction. Misuse of power, such as by the police, possessed by virtue of state law, was held to be action "under color" of state law although prohibited by it. Governmental entities, in contrast to the individual officer, are not liable unless the latter acted in execution of a governmental policy or custom. Section 1983 itself does not postulate any level of individual blameworthiness, but the particular constitutional violation does. Thus, racial discrimination under the equal protection clause must be committed with "invidious discriminatory purpose," cruel and unusual punishment under the Eighth Amendment with "deliberate indifference," and deprivation of life, liberty, or property under the 14th Amendment must be more than merely negligent.[30] In the course of retrenching the action in this and other ways, conservative majorities on the Supreme Court have also engrafted numerous, mostly qualified, immunities. Local police officers, prison officials, and school board members can plead "good faith," while prosecutors and judges enjoy absolute immunity.

As in the case of liability for defamation, non-pecuniary damages can be awarded only for proven injury, but may be augmented by punitive damages for outrageous conduct and by an award of attorney's fees.

By analogy to the civil rights action against persons acting "under color" of state law under section 1983, a similar remedy has been recognized against federal officials like narcotics agents or FBI officers.

28. 42 U.S.C. § 1983.
29. 365 U.S. 167 (1961).
30. *Daniels v. Williams*, 474 U.S. 327 (1986) (prisoner fell over pillow carelessly left on stairs by a guard).

Selected Bibliography

John L. Diamond, Lawrence C. Levine & M. Stuart Madden, *Understanding Torts* (1996).
Dan B. Dobbs, *The Law of Torts* (2000).
Richard A. Epstein, *Torts* (1999).
John G. Fleming, *The American Tort Process* (1988).
Fowler V. Harper, Fleming James, Jr. & Oscar S. Gray, 1-6 *The Law of Torts* (3d ed. 1995 & Supp. 2000).
Robert H. Jerry II, *Understanding Insurance Law* (1996).
Robert E. Keeton & Alan I. Widiss, *Insurance Law* (1988).
W. Page Keeton, Dan B. Dobbs, Robert E. Keeton & David G. Owen, *Prosser and Keeton on the Law of Torts* (5th ed. 1984).
Marshall S. Shapo, *Hornbook on Basic Principles of Tort Law* (1999).

Chapter 10
Property

*A. N. Yiannopoulos**

I. INTRODUCTION

Property is a word with high emotional overtones and so many meanings that it has defied attempts at an accurate all-inclusive definition. For the purposes of this chapter, property may be defined as an exclusive right to control an economic good. It is the name for a concept that refers to the rights and obligations, privileges and restrictions, that govern the relations of persons with respect to things of value. What is guaranteed to be one's own is property in a broad sense.

In the United States, the word property is frequently used to denote indiscriminately *objects* of rights that have a pecuniary content or *rights* that persons

* Eason-Weinmann Professor of Comparative Law and Director, Eason-Weinmann Center for Comparative Law, Tulane University School of Law.

David S. Clark and Tuğrul Ansay (eds.) Introduction to the Law of the United States, 209-230

have with respect to things. Thus, lands and chattels are said to be property; and rights, such as ownership, life estates, and easements are likewise said to be property. This latent confusion between rights and their objects is avoidable. Accurate legal terminology ought to reserve the use of the word property for the designation of rights that persons have with respect to things.

Neither are all things objects of property rights nor are all rights that persons have with respect to things governed by the law of property. State and federal legislation, doctrine, or judicial decisions define the things that can become objects of property rights in the United States.

The law of property may be defined as a branch of private law that deals with rights which confer a direct and immediate authority over things. This definition distinguishes property law from other branches of private law, such as the law of persons, the law of contracts, the law of torts, the law of the family, and the law of successions. These branches deal with relations which may, and frequently do, give rise to property rights. Due to their origin and purpose, however, these property rights are often subject to special rules rather than the general law of property.

With the exception of Louisiana and Puerto Rico, American jurisdictions have shaped their property systems in accordance with the common law tradition. Louisiana has a modern law of property based on the models of the French, German, Swiss, and Greek civil codes. Puerto Rico's property laws derive from the Spanish civilian tradition and certain borrowing from the Louisiana Civil Code of 1870. Unless otherwise indicated, the following discussion of property institutions refers to the laws of American jurisdictions adhering to the common law tradition.

II. Historical Development

In the long history of property law in Western civilization, simple and unencumbered ownership was known at the beginning and end of the Roman period, and again after the French Revolution. In the Middle Ages, lands in western Europe and in parts of the New World were subjected to feudal tenures, namely, to a regime of division of ownership into perpetual interests of landlords and tenants.

Feudal tenures were wiped out in France on 4 August 1789, when the representatives of the privileged classes in the Assembly renounced their privileges. Analogous developments took place in most parts of continental Europe where feudalism had prevailed. In the United States, tenures established by prior sovereigns have been largely abolished by statutes declaring all lands to be *allodial*, that is, subject to perfect ownership free of any obligations of vassalage. In a few states, in which tenures may be said to have survived, the only incident of tenures is *escheat*, that is, the reversion of lands to the state in the absence of a person competent to inherit.

Reform legislation in common law jurisdictions has not hindered further evolution. Modern legislation and judicial practice in the United States exhibit a tendency toward a limitation of the intensity of ownership in the interest of all, and, at the same time, toward extension of ownership to new forms of wealth. These developments in contemporary systems tend to indicate that ownership is an exclusive rather than absolute right, with two sides to it, one individual and the other social. The right of ownership does not confer today, as it did in the feudal period, political, social, and economic privileges. Yet, the possession of wealth still exerts much *de facto* power in society. In spite of limitations, the institution of ownership allows considerable freedom for the satisfaction of purely private interests.

The evolution of property institutions continues. Individual property rights are not only an economic necessity in civilized societies but are also sensitive to social change.

III. Acquisition of Property Rights

A. Types of Acquisition

Property rights may be acquired in a variety of ways, as by occupancy of things that belong to no one, by transfer from an owner or even a non-owner, by operation of law, by the effect of judgments, and by acts of public authorities. For systematic purposes, a distinction is made in civil law jurisdictions between *original* and *derivative* acquisition of property rights. An original acquisition involves the creation of a new property right; it is independent of any preexisting rights over the same thing. A derivative acquisition involves a transfer of a preexisting right from one person to another. American treatises on property law do not draw a distinction between original and derivative modes of acquisition. However, for the benefit of civilian readers, this distinction is applied to the following analysis of common law property institutions.

The distinction between the two modes of acquisition of property rights is important in the light of the almost universal maxim of property law that no one can transfer a greater right than one has. This means that, ordinarily, the transferor must be an owner and must transfer the property as it may be burdened with the rights of third persons. In most jurisdictions, the scope of the maxim has been narrowed by exceptions. Thus, property rights in chattels that are neither lost nor stolen may be transferred by a non-owner to a good faith purchaser for value by application of the bona fide purchaser doctrine. Lands, as a rule, must be transferred by the true owner; yet, by way of exception, a purchaser may be protected in several legal systems if he has relied on entries in land registers or other public records. These problems do not arise in cases of original acquisition of property rights.

B. Original Acquisition

There is a variety of original modes of acquisition of property rights, including occupancy, finding, accession, adverse possession, expropriation, and the establishment of property rights by acts of the public authorities.

Occupancy, namely, the taking of possession of things that belong to no one, is perhaps universally recognized. This mode of acquisition of property rights is largely limited to chattels, such as wild animals, birds, fish, and abandoned chattels. In times past, lands could also be acquired by mere occupancy or cultivation. Today, however, the acquisition of property rights in lands is subject to license or grant by the state, which is supposed to hold title to all unclaimed lands.

Akin to occupancy is the finding of lost things and treasures. Lost things have an owner, but laws in various jurisdictions ordinarily attribute ownership to the finder after the lapse of a certain period of time or upon the completion of certain formalities, such as advertisements or reports to the authorities. Likewise, laws provide for the apportionment of a treasure trove between the finder and the owner of the property in which the treasure was hidden.

Accession is another broadly recognized mode of acquisition of property rights. It is based on the principle that the ownership of a thing carries with it the right to whatever the thing produces and to certain other things that are united with it, whether naturally or artificially. The principal of accession is relevant for both lands and chattels. Thus, the fruits of the earth, whether spontaneous or cultivated, and the increase of animals belong to the owner by right of accession. The ownership of the soil carries with it the ownership of all that is directly above and under it, unless the contrary is established by provision of law or contract; therefore, buildings and other constructions erected by trespassers on the land of another become the property of the landowner. Certain fixtures attached to the land of another may become his property, even if the annexor acted in good faith and in the framework of a contractual right. Alluvion formations, created by imperceptible additions to the banks of rivers, and islands formed in the beds of non-navigable rivers, belong likewise by accession to the riparian owners.

Adverse possession is a mode of acquisition of property predicated on the possession of a thing over a designated period of time with the intention to own it. This mode of acquisition is relevant for both lands and chattels, although in jurisdictions in which a land register system has been established, adverse possession of lands has little practical significance. Acquisition of property rights in lands ordinarily requires a longer period of possession than the acquisition of property rights in chattels. The requisite period of possession may also vary with the nature of possession: a good faith possessor ordinarily acquires property rights in a shorter period of time than a bad faith possessor. Technically, and in light of the historical evolution of the institution, adverse possession extinguishes the right of the previous owner and bars his remedy against the possessor; it does not confer title upon the adverse possessor. Today, however, this technical difference has become largely a matter of form rather than substance, for in all jurisdictions those in adverse possession are well protected and are able to transfer their rights to their heirs and assigns.

Expropriation of property for purposes of public utility is known in all jurisdictions. Expropriation is distinguished from confiscation, namely the taking of property by the authorities arbitrarily or as a penalty for the violation of law. Ordinarily, constitutional provisions and other legislative texts condition the validity of expropriation upon notice and the payment of an adequate, fair, or just compensation to the owner. In effect, expropriation is a forced sale of property made for a public purpose and in favor of the state, its political subdivisions, or private utilities enjoying the so-called power of eminent domain on account of the services they render to the general public. The possibility of expropriation indicates that property rights are exclusive rather than absolute rights.

An original acquisition of property rights occurs when public authorities confer upon certain persons entirely new economic privileges or recognize privileges which heretofore existed only in fact. Examples are grants of property rights to lands of the public domain, including ownership and rights for the exploitation of mineral resources; grants for the exploitation of natural resources, such as hydroelectric energy or radio waves; and patents, registered designs, trademarks, trade names, and copyright, which form the so-called industrial or intellectual property (*see* pt. IX).

Rights of industrial property, substantially controlled by federal statutes, are highly specialized and are handled by experts in this field. They confer upon the owner a virtual monopoly, which may be either perpetual or for a limited period of time. Trademarks and trade names are ordinarily perpetual; they confer the right to identify one's business or one's products, and prevent others from usurping the advantages which go with them. The right to exploit patents, industrial designs, and copyright provides the holders thereof with temporary monopolies, which exclude competition in manufacture, trade, or the dissemination of literary or artistic works. They provide an inducement to produce goods, but, at the same time, they guarantee that the general public will be the ultimate beneficiary. A patent is the exclusive right, ordinarily granted for a number of years, of using, exercising, or vending an invention. Provisions of law establish the conditions for the grant of a patent and determine its duration. Copyright is the exclusive right to print or otherwise to multiply copies, and in the case of dramatic or musical works, to perform them.

C. Derivative Acquisition

In all jurisdictions methods are established for the acquisition of property rights by transfer from an owner. The transfer may be voluntary, as in the case of a last will and testament and in the case of an agreement between the owner and the transferee; it may be involuntary, as in the case of a judicial sale; or it may take place by operation of law, in accordance with the presumed intention of the owner, as in the case of intestate succession. A derivative acquisition of property rights may thus be based on volitional acts, judgments, or directly on law.

One of the most prevalent modes of acquisition of property rights is by the contract of sale. A sale involves the transfer of a thing in consideration of a sum of money or the promise of a sum of money; if the consideration is a thing other than money, the transaction is technically designated an exchange. In common law jurisdictions the contract of sale, upon its completion, transfers the ownership of the things sold as between the parties. Insofar as third persons are concerned, however, transfer of ownership may depend on delivery of chattels or recordation of the title of lands. Contracts of sale are free of any formalities and may be based on verbal agreement; but rules of evidence may exclude the proof of contracts the object of which exceeds a certain value. Moreover, in most jurisdictions, the sale of lands requires, either for its validity against third persons or for the transfer of rights, recordation in public records.

Another common mode of acquisition of property rights is by donation. Donations may be intended to take effect while the donor and the donee are living, or in contemplation of death. Donations of all sorts are ordinarily subject to strict requirements of form tending to safeguard the genuineness of their execution and the donor's intent. Thus, contracts or promises of donation require for their validity and effect compliance with such formalities as the execution of a notarial act or the redaction of a sealed document. Donations contained in last wills and testaments must be executed in strict compliance with the requisite formalities. Formal requirements are usually dispensed with in cases of manual gifts, namely, when the possession of tangible things is transferred to the donee.

Still another prevalent mode of acquisition of property rights is by adjudication, namely, by the effect of a judicial sale. Judicial sales take place in a variety of circumstances, as when the property of an insolvent debtor is seized and sold for the satisfaction of his creditors, when property is sold by the state or by its political subdivisions for the payment of tax claims, when property is judicially partitioned among co-owners, or when the property of a succession or of a minor is sold by the administrator or the tutor. Provisions of law ordinarily establish the requisite formalities and rules of substance for the validity of an adjudication. As a derivative mode of acquisition, the adjudication transfers to the acquirer only the property rights that the previous owner had; that is, ordinarily, the property continues to be burdened by preexisting property rights of third persons.

Derivative acquisition of property rights takes place by operation of law in cases of intestate succession, namely, when a person dies without leaving a will. State rules determine which rights are heritable and specify the order of succession. Death taxes have, to some extent, restricted the devolution of large fortunes, but the right of inheritance remains one of the fundamental precepts of law. *See* Chap. 12. The property of an intestate is placed under the authority of an administrator who pays all debts and charges of the succession, and who puts the legal heirs into possession upon completion of the administration. An almost absolute freedom of testation is characteristic of the common law. The institution of forced heirship was, as such, foreign to the common law, although there were devices destined to secure the interests of a surviving spouse. Modern legislation in common law jurisdictions has accomplished this end by granting to the surviving spouse a right of election against an unfavorable will.

IV. Types of Ownership

Rights of individuals, groups of individuals, or other entities for the exclusive enjoyment of economic goods may be designated as rights of *ownership*. The word ownership has a precise technical meaning in most civil law countries but it is seldom used in the professional literature of common law jurisdictions. In the United States, ownership is frequently used synonymously with property.

Rights of ownership may be classified according to a variety of criteria. From the viewpoint of the *subjects* of these rights, namely, the persons or entities that hold them, rights of ownership may be divided among those held by individuals, by family groups, by collectives and cooperatives, by unincorporated associations, by corporations, and by the state and its public corporations. Each right of ownership in this respect may have peculiar characteristics of its own.

Ownership may be vested in a single individual, in which case one speaks of individual ownership; or it may be vested in a number of individuals, in which case one speaks of individual co-ownership. Co-ownership has been recognized from early times and may arise by application of any of the methods available for the acquisition of property rights. Thus, it may arise from an agreement, such as the purchase of the same thing by two or more persons to be held in common, from a material act, as the finding of a treasure by several persons, or by operation of law, as in the cases of intestate succession and matrimonial regimes of community property.

In common law jurisdictions, the institution of co-ownership may assume the form of an ownership in common (*tenancy in common*), corresponding with the civilian notion of co-ownership, or that of joint ownership (*joint tenancy*), which is an original common law institution. The difference between the two forms of co-ownership relates to the devolution of an individual interest upon the death of a co-owner. If an owner in common dies, his share passes to his successors, whether by will or by intestate succession. But if a joint owner dies, his interest accrues to the remaining owners, so that when all owners but one are dead the survivor becomes the sole owner.

Lawyers have tried to explain the institution of joint ownership on theoretical grounds. They have suggested that while owners in common hold individual shares, each of which is capable of alienation, joint owners hold the whole of a thing subject to the concurrent interests of the other owners. When a joint owner dies, the others do not acquire anything new; they are merely relieved of the presence of a competing interest. It is preferable to explain the institution of joint ownership on practical grounds, as a concession of theory to the demands for an effective administration of property in trust. The right of survivorship conferred upon joint owners tends to produce anomalous results when several persons share the prerogatives of use, enjoyment, and disposition of a thing, but it is a very convenient device in the framework of the law of trusts, when ownership is split into the constituents of legal title and beneficial enjoyment. *See* Chap. 12, pt. III.

It is indeed desirable that the legal title of one of several trustees should not devolve to those who succeed him on death, but should automatically vest in the surviving trustees. If the trustees were to be regarded as a committee, all that has happened is that a member of the committee has disappeared and the remaining members are allowed to carry on the management of the property. Joint ownership is thus appropriate to the management of property and ownership in common for its beneficial enjoyment.

Property may be owned by collectives and cooperatives. These are associations of individuals, such as farmers, laborers, consumers, homeowners, or small entrepreneurs, formed for the pursuit of some productive enterprise, the benefits of which are to be shared in accordance with the capital or labor contributed by each member. The rights and obligations of members may be specified in contractual provisions or in applicable legislation. In the United States, attention has been focused on electric cooperatives formed for the production and distribution of electricity in rural areas and on cooperatives formed for the building and enjoyment of apartment units in metropolitan areas.

Rights of ownership, as indeed all rights and obligations, may exist only in favor of entities possessing legal personality. Such entities are living human beings, associations of human beings, as well as foundations established for the realization of a general interest. The United States, individual states and their political subdivisions, profit and non-profit corporations, and partnerships are examples of associations capable of possessing legal personality and of owning property. Hospitals and charitable institutions are examples of foundations likewise capable of possessing legal personality and of owning property. The underlying basis of these institutions is the pursuit of a general purpose rather than the mere association of certain individuals. Unincorporated associations formed for the pursuit of vocational, artistic, scientific, or religious purposes may or may not possess legal personality, depending on applicable laws and on compliance with requisite formalities. If they do not possess legal personality, they cannot hold property in their own name; their property belongs directly to the members of the association, usually by undivided shares. If they possess legal personality, they have property of their own which is distinct and distinguishable from the property of the members; in this case, the members have an indirect interest in the property of the association by virtue of their membership.

Unincorporated groups and associations may be regarded for certain purposes and under certain circumstances as *de facto* corporations. Though not technically persons, unincorporated groups and associations may own property by virtue of applicable legislation or case law. In these circumstances, unincorporated groups and associations may be said to possess "incidents" of legal personality rather than full personality.

Corporations are artificial entities formed by human beings to which the law attributes legal personality for the pursuit of social and economic purposes. They have no physical existence, but, as juridical persons, they participate in legal life and are capable of holding property in their own name. There are various sorts of corporations: private and public, secular and religious, and profit as well as non-profit corporations. *See* Chap. 14.

The proliferation of corporations during the 20th century reflected a movement from a regime of individual ownership of capital to a regime of collective ownership of capital. Today, industrial production is largely undertaken by corporations and the same is true of various service fields. Agricultural production, however, is still largely in the hands of individual farmers.

The corporate device allows for a clear distinction between the property of the corporation and the property of a shareholder. Technically, no one owns the corporation, which has an independent existence of its own. A share merely represents a fractional interest in the patrimony of the corporation and confers a corresponding interest in its administration; and even when all shares are concentrated in the hands of a single person, there is still a clear distinction between the property of the corporation and the property of the sole owner of its shares. When incorporation is completed and the shares are fully paid and non-assessable, the individual property of a shareholder is completely insulated from the risks of the corporate enterprise. Creditors of the corporation may not reach the property of a shareholder for the satisfaction of their claims, nor may creditors of the shareholder reach the corporate assets. The only risk that a shareholder assumes is that represented by the amount of his investment in the corporation; and it is only his shares that constitute property which may be seized by his own creditors.

The government and its political subdivisions are political corporations that have capacity to own property. The property of the federal government, states, and its political subdivisions may be of two sorts: public property, which is ordinarily inalienable and is held in trust for the benefit of all citizens; and private property, which does not differ in essence from property held by private persons. Examples of public property are navigable waterbottoms, national parks, and monuments. Examples of private property are state-owned enterprises, moneys in treasuries, and buildings that house various agencies. Public property of the government and its political subdivisions is ordinarily subject to public use; that is, it may be enjoyed by all members of the general public. Public property is frequently distinguished from common property, which is owned by no one in particular and which may be freely enjoyed by all; of this kind are the atmospheric air and the open sea.

In modern times, the federal government and states have asserted ownership over a variety of things that were previously considered to be without owner, such as running waters and wild animals. This form of public ownership, asserted in an effort at conservation of natural resources, confers mainly administrative advantages and stresses the idea that certain assets of society are not capable of private appropriation or ownership except under regulations that protect the social interest.

The government and its political subdivisions may enjoy certain economic monopolies and may directly own a variety of enterprises, whether in competition or in cooperation with private interests. Moreover, political units may undertake economic activities through a variety of public corporations.

V. Personal Property and Real Property

In common law jurisdictions, property is divided into personal property and real property, and these terms may be taken as roughly equivalent to the civilian notions of movables and immovables.

The laws governing real property tend to delimit narrowly individual rights in this species of wealth and to enhance security of title. In the past emphasis was placed on limitations imposed on the scope of the rights in real property. In modern times, however, emphasis has shifted toward security of title. But even today rights in real property may be subject to special limitations concerning acquisition, alienation, seizure, or partition.

The trend toward security of title has led to the development of systems of publicity. In certain jurisdictions, the existence of interests in real property depends on the recordation of formal acts in land registers. Acts that are unrecorded cannot produce their intended consequences. Entries in land registers are, generally, accorded full faith and credit so that innocent third parties may rely upon them. In states in which a land register system has not yet been established, the transfer or encumbrance of real property is ordinarily effective toward third persons from the time of inscription of the pertinent documents in public records. The degree of credit accorded to entries in these records varies from jurisdiction to jurisdiction.

Lines of demarcation between real property and chattels are ordinarily drawn in accordance with the natural characteristics of things and prevailing notions in society bearing on the relative significance of the elements of wealth. Since ancient times and up to the era of the industrial revolution, land was regarded as the most important species of wealth from the viewpoints of both social and individual interests. Hence, particular rules were developed to safeguard interests connected with the possession, use, and enjoyment of land. In modern times, however, economic emphasis has shifted to property other than land, and the law tends to accord to these interests the type of protection traditionally reserved for land.

The division of property into personal property and real property arose in the formative era of the common law and corresponds roughly with the distinction between feudal and non-feudal property. Furthermore, as land was the foundation of feudalism, the distinction between real property and personal property corresponds roughly to that between land and chattels.

The distinction between the two kinds of property arose in England in the framework of procedural institutions. The terms real and personal property denoted originally differences in the forms of action by which rights were enforced rather than differences among objects of property rights. Actions were distinguished into real, tending to secure the recovery of property in kind, and personal, tending to secure payment of damages for unlawful interference with one's possessions. Since the relations among persons in feudal society were usually determined by the manner in which particular tracts of land were held, it was important in case a holder of land was ousted from his domain that he recover that particular tract. Hence, real actions were largely available for the protection of interests in land, while personal actions were available for the protection of interests in chattels. In the course of time, however, the terms real and personal property came to denote the objects of property rights protected, respectively, by real and personal actions.

Real property (realty) may thus be defined as that kind of property which was recoverable in the Middle Ages by real actions, namely, interests in land other than leasehold interests. Personal property (personalty) forms a residuary category of interests in movables (chattels personal) and leasehold interests in land (chattels real). The two kinds of property were in effect governed by distinct sets of rules, one of which, applicable to real property, was of feudal origin, and the second, applicable to personal property, had largely evolved from the work of ecclesiastical courts and had been influenced by Romanist learning.

With the exception of certain technical rules of minor significance, the differences between real and personal property have been swept away as a result of statutes enacted in the first half of the 20th century. This legislative reform of the property regime and the suppression of vestiges of feudal institutions have minimized the differences between real and personal property in the United States.

In spite of differences in methodology and conceptual technique, the law of real property performs today a function essentially similar to that performed by the law of immovable property in civil law jurisdictions.

Legislation in the United States has simplified the law of real property and has transformed it into a law applicable to land. The distinction between real and personal property is still drawn in the light of history, and real property continues to be defined as a freehold interest in land. But, since tenures have been largely abolished by statutes declaring all land to be allodial, and in jurisdictions in which tenures may be said to have survived the only remaining incident of tenure is escheat, the distinction between real and personal property has lost most of its original significance. In contemporary American practice, therefore, the distinction is made between land and movables and modern treatises of property law include consideration of both elements of wealth.

The division of property into real property and personalty may carry significant legal consequences in various fields of law, such as contracts, torts, successions, and conflict of laws. Thus, according to a broadly recognized rule of choice of law, the question is whether a particular thing is movable or immovable, and most disputes concerning rights in immovable property are determined by application of the law of the place in which the property is situated, the *lex loci rei sitae*. *See* Chap. 17, pt. III.I.2. This law determines such diverse questions as the validity of a contractual transfer of land and the creation, modification, or termination of proprietary interests, such as mortgages, servitudes, and easements. The law of the *situs* is ordinarily the court's own law, that is, the law of the forum, because common law courts refuse to exercise jurisdiction with respect to claims in immovable property situated in another state or country.

Determination of rights in movable property has given rise to a variety of choice of law rules. The traditional common law rule is that movables, having no fixed location, are governed by the law of the domicile of their owner: *mobilia sequitur personam*. The validity of this rule, which is supposed to apply to contractual transactions concerning movables as well as to succession upon death, has been questioned by modern writers. According to them, courts merely pay lip service to the traditional rule while they are busily engaged in fashioning new choice of law rules calling for application of the law of the situs of tangible movables, of the law of the forum, or of the law of the place in which a transaction concerning movables is made, depending on particular facts and circumstances. *See* Chap. 17, pt. III.I.2.

VI. Tangible and Intangible Property

Analytical jurists in common law jurisdictions distinguish between tangible and intangible property. This distinction corresponds roughly with the Roman division of things into corporeals and incorporeals, but does not coincide with it. The category of tangible property includes lands and certain chattels known as *choses in possession*, that is, rights in definite tangible things over which possession may be taken. The category of intangible property is largely composed of certain abstract things such as *choses in action* and *incorporeal hereditaments*. Choses in action are rights of property which can only be claimed or enforced by action and not by taking physical possession. Of this kind are bank accounts, debts generally, stocks and shares, and industrial property, including patents, registered designs, trademarks and tradenames, and copyright.

Hereditaments are rights that are heritable, namely, capable of passing by way of descent to heirs. Using the word hereditament in this sense, jurists in common law jurisdictions reached the conclusion that hereditaments are either corporeal or incorporeal. Corporeal hereditaments are lands, buildings, minerals, trees, and all other things that are part of or affixed to land. Incorporeal hereditaments are rights such as easements, profits, and rents, classified as real property. Thus, an interest in a physical thing is itself a corporeal interest while an interest in an intangible is an incorporeal interest. This nomenclature has been subjected to criticism as it became apparent that all property consists of rights that persons have with respect to things, and which rights are, by definition, intangible.

From among the various species of intangible property, attention may be focused on easements and profits. An easement may be defined roughly as a property right in a person or a group of persons to use the land of another for a special purpose that is not inconsistent with the general property right of the owner of the land. Of this kind are rights of way, rights of diverting the course of a stream for irrigation purposes, and rights for the support of buildings. A profit, technically known as *profit-a-prendre*, is the right to use another's land by removing a portion of the soil or its products. Of this kind are rights to take fish or game, to pasture one's animals on the land of another, and the rights to take wood, sand, coal, and other mineral substances. Easements as well as profits may be "appurtenant," established in favor of an estate, or "in gross," established in favor of a designated person.

Rights of passage or of way are among the most frequently encountered easements in American states. These are rights to pass over the land of another. They are not natural rights, but they must be created by application of one of the methods that are available for the acquisition of property rights. Rights of passage or of way may be either public or private, namely, they may be rights of which every person may avail himself, or they may exist for the benefit of a designated person or class of persons.

Rights with respect to the use of waters are likewise some of the most frequently encountered easements. Landowners have certain well-defined rights with respect to surface waters, underground waters, and natural watercourses, such as rivers, streams, and lakes, traversing or bordering their lands. Modifications of these well-defined rights may take the form of an easement. Thus, the owner of an estate situated above may acquire, from the owner of an estate situated below, the right to pollute a natural stream traversing both estates or the right to obstruct the flow of the stream or the flow of surface waters; the owner of the upper estate may acquire the right to use an unreasonably great amount of water for his own purposes or to discharge upon the lower estate drain and refuse waters; and any landowner may acquire the right to divert the flow of natural water courses and to maintain on another estate an aqueduct for his needs.

Mineral rights, and especially rights for the exploitation of oil and gas, may take the form of profits. In American jurisdictions, it is only seldom that oil and gas rights are qualified as profits; ordinarily, persons undertaking such operations acquire from the owner of the surface the ownership of the minerals in place, that is, a distinct estate the object of which is tangible property.

VII. Temporal Division of Ownership

The right of ownership is susceptible of division among co-owners holding undivided interests in the same thing. In common law jurisdictions, however, what may in a general way be called ownership is susceptible of division in a great variety of ways from the viewpoint of time as well as from the viewpoint of space. The law governing temporal division was worked out in the first instance for land and later applied to funds comprising both land and certain chattel interests of a permanent nature, such as stocks and shares. It has not been applied in its entirety to tangible chattels, because, for the temporal division of ownership to be worthwhile, the object of the right ought to be capable of yielding income for a considerable period of time and its location must be readily ascertainable. These two requisite qualities are present in lands as well as certain permanent chattels.

The historical basis of common law property is that only the crown can own land. A landowner, strictly speaking, does not own land but a *time* in the land, an interest called an *estate*. Common lawyers manipulated this concept of time in the land and devised an intricate system of estates, which may be either successive in time or concurrent, in the sense that two or more persons may own property jointly or they may have separate rights of ownership in the same property at the same time.

Thus, one may own a time in the land for life or for a term while another holds at the same time a separate present ownership of a "time without end." This common law technique, giving a legal explanation to the present market value attaching to successive rights to hold property, attaches ownership not to the land itself but to an abstract entity, the estate, which is interposed between the tenant and the land. The estate is purely conceptual, yet it is treated by the law as if it were a real thing with an identity of its own. It may be said that the estate represents the fourth dimension of land: the ownership of the land is divisible in respect of time according to a coherent set of rules, and slices of the ownership representing rights to successive holdings of the land are regarded as present estates co-existing at the same time. With this development, the law of property in common law jurisdictions ceased to be earthbound.

The intricate system of interests in land was made even more complex by the rise of the law of trusts. The array of legal interests at common law was matched by a corresponding array of equitable interests created behind the ownership of the trustee. Thus, one could have an estate arising under the common law, namely, a legal estate, or an estate arising under the law of trusts, namely, an equitable estate. The main characteristic of property systems in the United States is the existence of various ownerships, concurrent but separate, legal and equitable, all built around the notions of estate and trust. This tends to be true of both real and personal property.

Three simple classifications of estates may be mentioned. The first is into estates in *possession* and estates in *expectancy*. If a person's estate gives him a right to the immediate possession of the land, it is said to be an estate in possession; if, on the other hand, he must wait for his right to possession to take effect, he has only an estate in expectancy. The second classification concerns only estates in expectancy, which are divided into *remainders* and *reversions*. A remainder is the remnant of an estate which becomes effective upon the expiration of the estate of a previous owner. A reversion is similar to a remainder in that the right to enjoy the land is postponed to a future date, but when there is a reversion the land eventually returns to the grantor, while with a remainder the land goes to some other person. The third classification is into *freehold* and *leasehold* estates, the former having an indefinite and the latter a definite duration or one which can be made definite at the will of the parties concerned. The simplest examples of freehold estates are the estates in fee simple, the estate tail, and the estate for life.

The estate in fee simple is in the ordinary course of events perpetual and the nearest thing to full ownership of land found in common law jurisdictions. It confers full rights of possession, enjoyment, and disposition during life and by will. If the owner of the estate in fee simple dies intestate, the land passes to the relatives entitled under statute in that event. Only in the event of the owner dying intestate and without relatives will the estate come to an end and the land will pass to the state. The estate tail or fee tail is an estate less than a fee simple in the sense that it is limited to the person and the heirs of his body. The tenant in tail has full rights of possession and enjoyment and the estate does not come to an end at his death; it passes to his heirs, but only a limited class of heirs, his descendants. *See* Chap. 12, pt. II.A.

The line of descent may be further limited by making the estate in tail male, namely, descending only through males, or conceivably in tail female, descending through females. If the tenant dies without leaving descendants, the estate may revert to the grantor or it may go to a remainderman. A life estate is one whose duration may be measured by the lifetime of the tenant or of another person, in which case it is qualified as an estate *pur autre vie*. It may also be cut off by the happening of a specified contingency, as for example, the remarriage of the life tenant. A life estate is thus always temporary in the sense that it will come to an end at some future time, but the time of its termination is indefinite. The owner of a time in the land for life, namely, the life tenant, has the right to obtain the profits of the property, the right to possession, and the right to dispose of his interest. When a life estate is created, there is always a corresponding estate in expectancy. The owner of this estate may be a reversioner or a remainderman.

Leaseholds or estates less than freehold are those that have a definite duration or a duration that may be made definite at the will of one of the parties concerned. Lawyers, impressed with the definite duration of a lease, designate the lease as an *estate* or a *term for years* rather than as an arrangement giving possession to the lessor.

However, not all leaseholds arise from leases in the strict sense of the word; some arise from other arrangements and are more properly called *tenancies*. The most important and the most frequent are the so-called periodical tenancies, for example, from week to week, from month to month, or from year to year. These periodical tenancies have a definite duration for the time being as they may terminate by notice given by the landlord or by the tenant only on the anniversary of the original grant. When the proper day for notice passes without notice being given the tenancy is renewed for an additional definite term. Other possible tenancies are those at will and at sufferance. A tenancy at will may terminate at any moment by notice given by either the landlord or the tenant; a tenancy by sufferance is one held by a person whose lawful term has terminated and who continues to possess without right.

When a person holds a terminable estate, such as a life estate, questions arise as to his duties toward the reversioner or the remainderman. Ordinarily, a life tenant is entitled only to the income of the property, including in this term the physical use of tangible things, but he may not touch the capital which must be transmitted intact at the termination of his interest.

It is frequently difficult to draw a clear line of distinction between capital and income, and the problem is even more complicated when the enjoyment of land is divided among several persons successively. To resolve this difficulty in a practical manner, and to afford a measure of protection to the interests of successive holders of land, courts developed remedies for waste. The ever present temptation of a temporary holder of land to exhaust the soil or to let buildings fall into disrepair may be checked by an action for damages, or even more important, by an injunction restraining the commission of waste. Around these two remedies has grown a body of substantive law, that is simple in its outlines but complicated in its detailed applications.

There is a distinction between permissive and voluntary waste, the former comprising mere omissions to act, such as failing to repair a building, and the latter comprising affirmative acts that diminish the capital value of the property or change the nature of the land, such as tearing down a building. Whether a person is to be held liable for permissive or voluntary waste depends on the nature of his estate. The liability for waste for tenants for years varies with the terms of the lease and kind of the tenancy. The life tenant is liable for voluntary waste, that is, he is under obligation not to destroy or alter the character of the buildings or of the land. He is not liable for permissive waste, however, unless the duty to keep the property in a good state of repair has been expressly imposed upon him by the grantor. As a matter of practice, instruments creating life estates frequently relieve the life tenant of liability for waste; and in this case, he may even commit voluntary waste with impunity, although he may be restrained by injunction from committing wanton or extravagant destruction.

Statutes enacted in various jurisdictions since the 19th century have worked out substantial modifications of the common law governing estates over land. In most American jurisdictions the estate in fee tail has been practically abolished, and land holdings have been declared to be allodial: that is, subject to free and unencumbered ownership.

Compared with the common law doctrine of estates, the institution of ownership in civil law systems is the essence of simplicity. A person either owns a thing or he does not; it is as simple as that. Some detraction may be made from the content of ownership, when burdens on the land such as servitudes are created, but these burdens are regarded as restrictions on the use of the land rather than as rights of separate or concurrent ownership.

VIII. Trusts as Property

The right of ownership confers on a person direct, immediate, and exclusive authority over a thing. The owner may use, enjoy, manage, and dispose of the thing he owns within the limits and under the conditions established by law. However, not all persons are capable or willing to manage their property, and the law permits management to be detached from ownership. This may be accomplished by the use of the corporate device, namely, the transfer of property to a juridical person, such as a corporation, a partnership, or a foundation. It may also be accomplished without the interposition of an artificial person between a human being and his property, as in cases of administration of the property of a minor or an incompetent.

In common law jurisdictions, detachment of management from ownership is frequently accomplished by means of a trust. A trust is a legal relationship by which a *trustee* undertakes the obligation to deal with property over which he has control, that is, the *property in trust*, for the benefit of a *beneficiary* or *beneficiaries*, of whom he may himself be one. All kinds of property, real or personal, and tangible or intangible, may be held in trust, but the things most frequently so held are lands, stocks, and bonds.

Separation of the management from the beneficial enjoyment of property is always allowed in common law jurisdictions. In civil law jurisdictions, as a rule, separation of management from the enjoyment of property without the interposition of an artificial person is allowed only when a person is incompetent to manage his own affairs on account of absence, minority, or unsound mind. Competent persons are forced, in effect, to manage their own property or at least undertake the risk of mismanagement by other persons. In common law jurisdictions, however, the use of the trust device enables competent as well as incompetent persons to have their property managed by others without much risk of mismanagement.

When management and beneficial enjoyment are separated, a question arises as to the nature of the interests of the manager and of the person having the beneficial enjoyment. It might be possible to say that the manager owns the property but he is under a duty to manage it for the benefit of another who has nothing more than a correlative personal right against the manager. It might also be possible to say that the beneficiary owns the property but the manager has the power of administration without owning the property. This second possibility has materialized in civil law jurisdictions: the property administered by the tutor of a minor or by the curator of a person of unsound mind belongs to the incompetent. Neither possibility has materialized in common law jurisdictions. In these jurisdictions, both the trustee and the beneficiary own the property but in different ways. Neither owns the property in the sense of the Roman *dominium*, but each owns an interest in it, called respectively the legal estate and the equitable interest.

Thus, in the framework of the institution of trust, there is no single object of ownership. The property in trust is fragmented into two separate abstract objects; the legal estate that the trustee owns for the purpose of managing the property and the equitable interest that the beneficiary owns for the purpose of enjoyment.

The legal estate is a way of explaining that the trustee may act as owner of the property, enjoying wide powers of administration and disposition. The equitable estate means that the beneficiary has during the term of the trust advantages of the use and enjoyment of the property. In the light of the historical development of the law of trusts, it would be misleading to ask the question who owns the property in trust, just as it would be misleading to ask the question who owns the property subject to a life estate, that is, the life tenant or the remainderman. Each of these persons owns an abstract thing, an estate, rather than the property.

Property may be given to a trustee for the benefit of a person or for the accomplishment of certain purposes, usually charitable. In either case, a trustee may not take any benefit in his capacity as such, unless he is entitled to charge for his services under the instrument creating the trust. He must obey the terms of the trust and is personally responsible to the beneficiary for the proper management of the property. Correlatively, the beneficiary has a personal right against the trustee. If the trustee fails in his duties toward the beneficiary, the beneficiary may bring an action against the trustee to have the provisions of the trust enforced.

A question has arisen in common law jurisdictions whether the beneficiary of a trust has only a personal right against the trustee, a right *in personam*, or also a proprietary interest in the trust property, a right *in rem*. The better view is that the beneficiary as well as the trustee has a proprietary interest. Thus, the beneficiary may follow the trust property that has been disposed of in breach of the trust in the hands of any person other than a purchaser in good faith for value without notice of the breach of the trust or one who acquires the property from or through such a purchaser, even with notice of a previous breach of the trust.

The fragmentation of ownership into a legal estate and an equitable interest is an original common law institution that serves a variety of functions. There is no equivalent institution in civil law jurisdictions, unless one may regard as equivalent a substitution or *fideicommissum*, whereby an instituted heir or legatee is bound to restore the succession to another person. But the analogy fails because the instituted heir, though temporary owner of the property, has both management and beneficial enjoyment as long as his right lasts. *See* Chap. 12, pt. III.

As a single device to accomplish a variety of purposes the trust has no equal, but nearly everything which the trust can accomplish may actually be achieved within the framework of civil law institutions, the policies of the law permitting. When something achievable with the trust is not achievable in civil law jurisdictions, it is usually because the result is forbidden for reasons of social policy.

Nowhere may property rights be suspended indefinitely, whether in or out of trust; the law does not tolerate a high degree of uncertainty as to who is entitled to the enjoyment of material goods, and develops devices tending to prevent goods from being kept out of the market for long periods of time. These devices relate to the *vesting* of titles. The word vesting has different meanings, and the rules concerning the vesting of property rights are more complicated than in civil law jurisdictions. All interests in property are divided into vested interests and contingent interests. For an interest to be vested, the person entitled to it need not have a right to the immediate possession of land or to draw an income immediately from a fund; all that is required is that the nature and quantum of the interest and the identity of the person entitled to it should be known. If the identity of the person or the quantum of his interest are not yet known, and will only be known upon the happening of a contingency, the interest is qualified as contingent. Contingent interests are prevented from coming into existence at too remote a time by the common law rule against perpetuities or by statutory rules designed to accomplish the same purpose. *See* Chap. 12, pt. III.F.

IX. Intellectual Property

A. Types of Intellectual Property

Intellectual property consists of trademarks, know how, copyrights, patents, trade secrets, rights of publicity, and certain other rights.

Copyright confers on authors, artists, and publishers exclusive rights over their original works. American copyright law stems from article 1, section 8, clause 8 of the U.S. Constitution (known as the copyright and patent clause), which grants Congress the power to "promote the progress of science and useful arts, by securing for limited times to authors and inventors the exclusive right to their respective writings and discoveries." Pursuant to this power, Congress completely revised the Copyright Act[1] in 1976, which protects "original works of authorship" for a limited time (up to 70 years after the author's death).

It is only the expression of an idea that can be copyrighted, not the idea itself. Accordingly, copyright covers the creation of works such as literature, music, drama, choreography, motion pictures, video, sculpture, and sound recordings. Copyright automatically protects a work from the time that it is fixed in a tangible medium, whether registered or not. Registration is a significant feature of modern American copyright law, but the basic doctrine protects authors even without any registry. The exclusive rights conferred by copyright include the right to produce and distribute the original work, to publicly display or perform the original work, and to produce derivative works. However, the "fair use" of a work does not infringe upon these rights. In general, fair use means that only an insignificant amount of the right holder's expression is used, or that a substantial amount is used under circumstances that are excused under the law (such as use for a nonprofit educational purpose).

Patent law grants inventors the exclusive right to produce, use, and sell their inventions. Stemming also from the patent and copyright clause in the U.S. Constitution, the Patent Act[2] provides for grants of patents only to new, useful, and non-obvious processes or products for a nonrenewable period of years, after which time the invention enters the public domain. Unlike copyrights, no exclusive-rights patents are conferred before the U.S. Patent and Trademark Office (PTO) issues the patent.

Trademarks protect the use of the distinctive symbols of a business that relate to its goods or services. In the absence of an explicit grant of trademark power in the U.S. Constitution, the federal trademark law stems from the constitutional

1. 17 U.S.C. §§ 101-1332 (1994 & Supp. IV 1998).
2. 35 U.S.C. §§ 1-376 (1994 & Supp. IV 1998).

power of the Congress to regulate interstate and foreign commerce. *See* Chap. 4, pt. IV.B.2. Congress has enacted the Lanham Act[3] that protects trademark owners against the use of similar marks by others if such use would result in confusion. Trademarks differ from copyrights and patents in that the underlying rights are not always exclusive. A trademark does not confer rights outside the markets in which it is known or has been used, or on products or services so unrelated to the right holder's that there is no possibility of confusion. Further, a trademark does not confer power to prevent "collateral" use of the mark by others, such as comparative advertising. However, trademark rights were expanded in 1995 by the Federal Trademark Dilution Act,[4] which goes beyond the confusion criterion to protect a mark owner from use that effectively decreases the capacity of the mark to identify and distinguish goods or services.

Trade secrets protect the compilation of information (including formulas, patterns, devices, and customer lists) that is not common knowledge and that confers on the right holder an economic advantage over competitors. Rights of publicity grant a person control over the commercial value and exploitation of his name and likeness.

B. *The Internet*

The development and widespread use of the Internet has necessitated the adaptation of traditional intellectual property law to an electronic environment: "cyberspace." The traditional rights and remedies are available to authors and inventors as well as holders on the Internet, and the copying of material from the Internet may infringe on those rights. However, there are calls for a new system of Internet-specific intellectual property law because of the tendency of cyberspace technology and e-commerce to outpace traditional law.

Novel issues of intellectual property law arise as Web site owners incorporate the copyrighted material, patented inventions, and trademarks of others into their own sites through techniques such as linking, framing, meta-tagging, cyber squatting, spamming, and caching. Infringement on the Internet is unique because data are stored electronically and can be silently pirated at the speed of light from anywhere in the world. Detection of infringement is more difficult and sanctions are rare because the holders of rights are often reluctant to pursue "fans" using the material on their personal web pages, for fear of alienating their support base.

Copyright is the most commonly used protective device on the Internet. Data embedded in computer memory, photographs, paintings, films, and other forms of preexisting works which may be incorporated into an Internet-based application have been held to be "fixed in a tangible means of expression" under the Copyright Act. In addition, the Digital Millennium Copyright Act (DMCA)[5] was enacted in 1998 to bring federal copyright law in line with the rapidly growing dig-

3. 15 U.S.C. §§ 1051-1127 (1994 & Supp. IV 1998).
4. 15 U.S.C. § 1127 (Supp. IV 1998).
5. 17 U.S.C. §§ 1201-1205, 1301-1332 (Supp. IV 1998).

ital information technologies. The DMCA implemented two international treaties of the United Nations World Intellectual Property Organization in the hope of encouraging worldwide adoption. The DMCA prohibits the use of technology to circumvent measures designed to protect copyrighted works online, limits copyright liability of Internet service providers, and extends the fair use doctrine to digital media. Similarly, the No Electronic Theft Act (NET) of 1997[6] imposes criminal liability and monetary penalties on persons who reproduce or distribute, by electronic means, one or more copies of copyrighted works valued over $1,000, even if those persons do not obtain a commercial advantage or private financial gain.

Patents are also employed for protection of interests on the Internet. Computer software and Internet business methods are often found to be patentable. Because a law of nature, including its mathematical manifestations (formulas or algorithms,) is not patentable, the computer-related patentee must demonstrate novelty independent of the law of nature.

Trademark law is implicated in cyberspace as right holders sue to prevent the unauthorized use of their marks on the Web, often in domain names. Plaintiffs use trademark law to maintain the use of a particular domain name in their Web site address, to prevent others from using the name, and to stop "cyber squatters" – individuals who register a domain name that incorporates a trademark for the purpose of selling the name to the trademark holder. Much of the problem stems from a fundamental difference between the traditional environment and the Internet. In the traditional trademark environment, identical marks can coexist in different markets; in the Internet environment, however, a mark can only be used in one commercial domain name. Thus, the use of a single mark is more limited on the Internet.

Trade secrets also give rise to important issues in cyberspace. Companies are finding the Internet useful in communicating and conducting business, but they are also finding it to be a serious threat to trade secrets unless appropriate steps are taken. To this end, the Economic Espionage Act of 1996[7] makes it a federal crime to steal a party's trade secrets or to knowingly purchase or possess stolen trade secrets. The Act explicitly includes protection for trade secrets in the form of programs or codes, even if stored or compiled electronically.

X. Restrictions on the Ownership of Property

In all legal systems, the scope, incidents, and content of ownership are subject to restrictions which give expression to the general interest of society in the enjoyment of material goods. In the light of these restrictions, ownership is ordinarily qualified as an exclusive right. Some of these restrictions are imposed by rules of public law, others by rules of private law, and still others by the effect of lawfully executed private covenants.

There are everywhere limitations as to the kinds of things that may become objects of property rights. Human beings may not be owned by other human beings.

6. 17 U.S.C. §§ 506-507, 18 *id.* §§ 2319-2320 (Supp. IV 1998).
7. 18 U.S.C. §§ 1831-1832 (Supp. IV 1998).

Contemporary legislation, jurisprudence, and doctrine, however, indicate that transactions concerning parts or members of human bodies, such as donations of blood or legacies of eyes, are valid, unless, of course, they conflict with public policy.

To protect persons injured in their physical integrity, courts have at times indicated that a human body is a thing and that one may have an ownership right in his own body. With regard to dead bodies, the possibility of private ownership is broadly admitted, although such bodies are ordinarily subject to compulsory disposal by burial or cremation. According to modern ideas, dead bodies should be regarded as things insusceptible of private appropriation; the right and duty of relatives to dispose of the body, based on customary law and controlled by provisions of public law, should not be regarded as a right of ownership.

Apart from human bodies and members or parts thereof, there are things which may not become objects of property rights either because of a physical impossibility of appropriation or because the law so provides. For example, running waters, the atmospheric air, and the open sea, may not be appropriated in their entirety by any individual or artificial person. These are things insusceptible of ownership.

The state may, and frequently does, assert primary rights to property, thus excluding from the spheres of private ownership a wide variety of elements of wealth. The state usually asserts ownership of the seashore, of the continental shelf, and of inland navigable waters and bottoms. These things are ordinarily designated as public property held by the state in trust for the benefit of all. Statutes have been enacted in some jurisdictions asserting state ownership over running waters and wildlife, namely, things which have been traditionally regarded as belonging to no one in particular. This form of state ownership is a new conception, giving expression to the demand for conservation of natural resources, which are assets of society and capable of appropriation only under regulations that protect the general interest.

In all legal systems there are limitations pertaining to the use of lands by private landowners. Before the industrial revolution, lands constituted the bulk of wealth and the foundation of the social order; hence, limitations were needed to safeguard the general interest. In spite of changed economic conditions, most of these limitations are still relevant and continue to prevail. They may derive from rules of public law, as zoning regulations and provisions concerning the expropriation of lands for purposes of public utility, from rules of private law, as provisions prohibiting excessive emissions of smoke, noise, vibrations, and odors, and from protective covenants entered into among landowners under the protection of the law.

The matter of excessive emissions is dealt with in civil law jurisdictions under the heading of neighborhood rights, because the restrictions are imposed in favor of adjoining owners. In common law jurisdictions, the same matter forms the object of the law of nuisance, a topic of tort law. Protective covenants are rare in civil law jurisdictions, because the field is adequately covered by directly applicable legislation; moreover, the scarcity of protective covenants may be attributed to the fact that restrictions on the use of lands by juridical act must necessarily take the form of a predial servitude, namely, of a charge laid on an estate in favor of another estate. In common law jurisdictions, however, protective covenants, frequently termed covenants running with the land, are quite common in subdivision developments. They are ordinarily established by a subdivider or by a group of landowners for the purpose of preserving and enhancing real property values by the maintenance of certain building standards and uniformity in the use of lands. Protective covenants designed to perpetuate racial, ethnic, or sexual discrimination in housing are null and void on constitutional grounds.

Selected Bibliography

George T. Bogart, *Trusts* (6th ed. 1987).
Ralph E. Boyer, *Survey of the Law of Property* (3d ed. 1981).
Ray Andrews Brown, *The Law of Personal Property* (Walter B. Raushenbush ed., 3d ed. 1975).
Donald S. Chisum & Michael A. Jacobs, *Understanding Intellectual Property Law* (1992).
John E. Cribbet & Corwin W. Johnson, *Principles of the Law of Property* (3d ed. 1989).
Jay Dratler, Jr., 1-2 *Intellectual Property Law: Commercial, Creative, and Industrial Property* (1991 & Supp. 2000).
—, *Licensing of Intellectual Property* (1994 & Supp. 2000).
Milton R. Friedman, 1-3 *Friedman on Leases* (4th ed. 1997).
Paul Goldstein, 1-4 *Copyright: Principles, Laws and Practice* (2d ed. 1996 & Supp. 2000).
J. Thomas McCarthy, 1-6 *McCarthy on Trademarks and Unfair Competition* (4th ed. 1996 & Supp. 2000).
Cornelius J. Moynihan, *Introduction to the Law of Real Property* (2d ed. 1988).
Melville B. Nimmer & David Nimmer, 1-10 *Nimmer on Copyright* (1963 & Supp. 2000).
Richard R. Powell & Michael Allan Wolf, 1-17 *Powell on Real Property* (2000).
Lewis M. Simes & Allan F. Smith, 1-4 *The Law of Future Interests* (2d ed. 1956 & John A. Borron, Jr. ed., Supp. 2000).
John G. Sprankling, *Understanding Property Law* (2000).
William B. Stoebuck & Dale A. Whitman, *The Law of Property* (3d ed. 2000).
David A. Thomas, ed., 1-15 *Thompson on Real Property* (1994 & Supp. 2000).
Herber Thorndike Tiffany, 1-6 *The Law of Real Property* (Basil Jones & Emily S. Bernheim eds., 3d ed. 1939 & Supp. 1996).
Athanassios N. Yiannopoulos, ed., 6 *International Encyclopedia of Comparative Law* (Property and Trust, 1973-1994).

Chapter 11
Family Law

*Harry D. Krause**

* Max L. Rowe Professor of Law Emeritus, University of Illinois College of Law. Adviser, American Law Institute's Principles of Family Dissolution (1990-2000); Commissioner (Illinois), National Conference of Commissioners on Uniform State Laws (1991-1997).

David S. Clark and Tuğrul Ansay (eds.) Introduction to the Law of the United States, 231-263

I. THE AMERICAN FAMILY IN A NEW WORLD

The last twenty years have consolidated a revolution in American family life and law. The move to no-fault divorce is complete: All fifty states offer no-fault divorce, exclusively or as an option to traditional fault grounds. The treatment of property on divorce has undergone fundamental reform – in favor of the economically weaker spouse, typically the wife. Spousal maintenance after divorce (alimony), by contrast, is now less often considered a long-term remedy. The new theme is "rehabilitation." "Rehabilitation" from motherhood – no less!

Despite the failure of the federal Equal Rights Amendment, women have achieved *legal* equality, although not always *de facto*. Children born to unmarried parents have obtained equal legal rights. Billions of dollars are successfully collected under a national child support enforcement system. A new concept of children's rights has upset many traditional notions of parental prerogatives.

With the help of modern medicine, potential parents are deciding not to parent children. Legalized abortion is a widely accepted alternative to birth control, as well as to pregnancy and childbirth, even while the age-old dispute over abortion – "life begins at conception" versus "life begins at birth" – is more alive than ever. New beginnings of pregnancy, ranging from artificial insemination to *in vitro* fertilization, embryo transplants, and "surrogate motherhood," have spawned ethical and legal questions without precedent and, so far, without universally accepted answers.

Unmarried fathers have gained custodial rights to their non-marital children. On divorce, joint custody of children has swept through legislatures and the courts, but must still prove itself to be a workable alternative to having *one* final decision-maker for the child. Grandparents have gained rights to visit with their grandchildren, sometimes even against the parent's will.

Domestic violence directed against women has garnered national attention and sympathy. While many a wife has not been prosecuted for killing her abusive husband, a husband may now be prosecuted for raping his wife.

Disillusionment with the role of law and lawyers in divorce has given rise to a wishful search for non-adversary alternatives. "Mediation" is the preferred approach, on the all too often mistaken premise that "no-fault" divorce implies a non-adversary situation. The reality remains that where important rights are at stake there must be rules – and those who are trained to interpret the rules. Divorcing ex-partners continue to need law and lawyers.

The U.S. Supreme Court emphasizes that marriage is a "fundamental human right," but new personal lifestyles are reducing the importance of that right. The opportunity for women to have full careers has reduced interest in raising children in role-divided marriage. Though nominally still a crime in several states, cohabitation without marriage now may produce legally sanctioned partnerships with serious financial consequences. Social acceptance is implicit in invitations even to formal events that are phrased in terms of the "significant other." The U.S. Department of Health and Human Services reports that one in three of all births is non-marital, with a disturbing racial imbalance: Two of three African-American children are born outside of marriage, compared with "only" one in five of white (and "Hispanic") children.

The national government has become increasingly concerned with the large-scale family breakdown witnessed in the recent past. Comprehensive, bipartisan welfare reform was enacted in 1997 with attention to a national pro-family (or at least a pro-parental responsibility) policy. A five-year lifetime limitation on receipt of benefits and strong work incentives to those on welfare has quickly succeeded in significantly reducing welfare rolls, but, when the five-year period of eligibility is up or when the economy slows, the picture may look less good.

Not to be underestimated, the AIDS catastrophe and the herpes epidemic have heralded a return to more traditional lifestyles, ending – after only three decades – history's first sexual revolution that had become possible only with scientific birth control and the legalization of abortion.

II. Sources of Family Law

American family law springs from five sources: *First*, there is the individual states' comprehensive common, statutory, and constitutional law regulating sexual behavior and ordering family relationships. Accordingly, there is no American family law in a national, unified sense. Instead, more than fifty[1] more or less sovereign jurisdictions have their own say on the subject. *Second*, there is the United States Constitution by means of which, especially in the last four decades, federal courts have made unprecedented incursions into family law, often upsetting centuries' old state laws that traditionalists had thought immune to federal challenge. An important incidental effect of this intervention has been to make the resulting law nationally uniform. *Third*, an increasing volume of federal law – ranging from child support enforcement to interstate child custody issues – quite specifically injects federal authority into family law. *Fourth*, there is the vast complex of state and federal social and tax legislation that, by providing and withholding benefits on the basis of marital status or dependency, indirectly but vitally affects, sometimes governs, many aspects of family behavior. *Fifth*, some family regulation also occurs on the local level, such as municipal zoning ordinances that restrict a large proportion of our living space to "one family residential" or multi-family uses, or "partnership" ordinances that provide benefits to unmarried couples, same-sex or heterosexual.

A. State Sources

Despite federal incursions, family law continues to remain primarily in state hands, less perhaps because of the U.S. Constitution's Tenth Amendment (reserving powers to the states) and more because of the relative scarcity of express federal legislation and a tradition-bound reluctance to enact more. Many basic rules of state family law are accepted generally. In many specifics, however, the full range of state statutes extends from one logical extreme to the other – sometimes to illogical extremes. Even within one jurisdiction, the law does not always stand out clearly, nor is it ascertained easily. Too often it still is an admixture of old

1. That is, 50 states plus the District of Columbia and Puerto Rico.

English common law tempered with flashes of modern thought – limited, narrow, occasional statutes that are directed at selected subjects. In several states, state constitutions have played a limited role in reshaping family law. For instance, about one-third of state constitutions now contain women's equal rights amendments, while the federal Constitution does not. In addition, some state equal protection clauses have been construed more broadly than the federal provision.

No state has undertaken a comprehensive review of all of its positions on the family and fashioned a comprehensive, modern family code. Help is being provided by the National Conference of Commissioners on Uniform State Laws who, although they have so far refrained from proposing a uniform national family code, have drafted and proposed uniform acts on numerous family law subjects. *See* Chap. 3, pt. V.B. Their uniform acts include the 1970 Marriage and Divorce Act (lately demoted to a model act), the 1973 Parentage Act (superseded in 2000 by a new version), the 1950 Reciprocal Enforcement of Support Act (superseded in 1992 and again in 1996 by the Interstate Family Support Act), the 1973 Abortion Act, the 1968 Child Custody Jurisdiction Act, followed in 1997 by the Child Custody Jurisdiction and Enforcement Act, the 1983 Marital Property Act (lately demoted to a model act), the 1983 Premarital Agreements Act, the 1988 Putative and Unknown Fathers Act (lately demoted to a model act), the 1994 Adoption Act (superseding a withdrawn prior version), the 1988 Status of Children of Assisted Conception Act (demoted to a model act) the conveniently forgotten Marriage Evasion Act (withdrawn by the Commissioners, but still in effect in several states), the 1998 Disposition of Community Property Rights at Death Act, the withdrawn Blood Test Act, and the 1997 Interstate Visitation Act. Various other uniform acts have incidental effects on family law, such as the 1969 Probate Code on marital inheritance rights (*see* Chap. 12, pts. II.C, IV.D) or the 1983 Transfers to Minors Act.

The Uniform Laws Commissioners have had a good measure of influence, but they have not reached the stature (or even sought the role) of a national law reform commission. That role remains unfilled, even while the American Law Institute completed a ten-year family law review and reform project in 2000, resulting in a statement of "Principles on the Law of Family Dissolution," focusing primarily on divorce and its consequences but also extending to same-sex partnerships.[2]

B. Federal Constitution

The infusion into family law of federal constitutional interpretation is a national source that supersedes state regulation and thus tends toward uniformity. The Tenth Amendment holds that "the powers not delegated to the United States by the Constitution, nor prohibited by it to the States, are reserved to the States respectively, or to the people." This had long been thought to put family law under the exclusive jurisdiction of the states. The traditional view was expressed by the late

2. Many volumes (including exhaustive commentary) will be published. Contact: The Executive Office, The American Law Institute, 4025 Chestnut Street, Philadelphia, PA 19104-3099.

Justice Black in 1971: "The power of the States over marriage and divorce is complete except as limited by specific constitutional provisions."[3] Further:

> [T]he power to make rules to establish, protect and strengthen family life ... is committed by the Constitution of the United States and the people of Louisiana to the legislature of that State. Absent a specific constitutional guarantee, it is for that legislature, not the life-tenured judges of this Court, to select from among possible laws.[4]

Justice Black's view is of the past, perhaps because so many state legislatures failed for so long to "select from among possible laws" – if Justice Black meant "possible" in terms of a livable, modern family law. Yet Justice Black's conviction still echoes uncertainly in current constitutional adjudication. With five justices concurring, Justice Rehnquist said in 1975: "[R]egulation of domestic relations [is] an area that has long been regarded as a virtually exclusive province of the States."[5] Dissenting in 1982, Rehnquist elaborated:

> [T]he majority invites further federal-court intrusion into every facet of state family law. If ever there were an area in which federal courts should heed the admonition of Justice Holmes that "a page of history is worth a volume of logic," it is in the area of domestic relations. This area has been left to the States from time immemorial, and not without good reason.[6]

Justice Powell concurred in 1978: "I write separately because the majority's rationale sweeps too broadly in an area which traditionally has been subject to pervasive state regulation."[7] Justice Blackmun said in 1981:

> This Court repeatedly has recognized that "[t]he whole subject of the domestic relations of husband and wife ... belongs to the laws of the States and not to the laws of the United States." ... Thus, "[s]tate family and family-property law must do 'major damage' to 'clear and substantial' federal interests before the Supremacy Clause will demand that state law be overridden."[8]

Notwithstanding these relatively recent pronouncements, the last time the U.S. Supreme Court resisted a serious invitation to enter family law arguably dates back to 1961.[9] In 1965, the Court actively stepped into the void with its historic decision

3. *Boddie v. Connecticut*, 401 U.S. 371, 389, 390-91, 91 S.Ct. 780, 28 L.Ed.2d 113 (1971)(Black, J., dissenting).
4. *Labine v. Vincent*, 401 U.S. 532, 538-39, 91 S.Ct. 1017, 28 L.Ed.2d 288 (1971).
5. *Sosna v. Iowa*, 419 U.S. 393, 404, 95 S.Ct. 553, 42 L.Ed.2d 532 (1975).
6. *Santosky v. Kramer*, 455 U.S. 745, 770, 102 S.Ct. 1388, 71 L.Ed.2d 599 (1982)(Rehnquist, J., dissenting).
7. *Zablocki v. Redhail*, 434 U.S. 374, 396, 98 S.Ct. 673, 54 L.Ed.2d 618 (1978)(Powell, J., concurring).
8. *McCarty v. McCarty*, 453 U.S. 210, 220, 101 S.Ct. 2728, 69 L.Ed.2d 589 (1981).
9. *Poe v. Ullman*, 367 U.S. 497, 81 S.Ct. 1752, 6 L.Ed.2d 989 (1961).

in *Griswold*,[10] "discovering" a right of family privacy in the "emanations" and "penumbras" of various constitutional provisions. The enormous power of the equal protection clause was brought to bear on family law with *Loving*[11] in 1967 and *Levy*[12] in 1968. This was soon followed by pronouncements on individual sexual rights in *Eisenstadt*[13] (1972), on abortion in *Wade*[14] (1973), on homosexual conduct in *Bowers*[15] (1986), and many other cases. While aspects of the due process clause had long been in the picture, its important presence was reaffirmed in 1971 in *Boddie*[16] and many other cases.[17] *See* Chap. 4, pts. IX.C.3, X.C.1.a.

In sum, the states' formerly all but unfettered discretion has been eroded by a rapidly growing body of U.S. Supreme Court, state supreme court, and lower court decisions that subject state family laws to federal (and state) constitutional provisions – provisions that do not speak expressly of the family, nor to subjects such as marriage, divorce, illegitimacy, birth control, abortion, adoption, neglect, and dependency, or termination of parental rights. Concern may be raised as to long-term implications for the federal-state structure, but in terms of substantive results achieved, the Court's involvement has, in the main, been forward-looking.

C. Federal Courts

Relying on a dictum in a 1858 case,[18] federal courts practiced essentially voluntary abstention from litigation relating to the family, even when all objective grounds for federal jurisdiction (diversity of citizenship, amount in controversy) were fulfilled.[19] In 1992, the U.S. Supreme Court reaffirmed and strengthened the old dictum.[20] On the other hand, recent federal legislation on child support enforcement specifically invokes the intervention of federal courts.

D. Social Legislation

A broad, conscious, and coordinated approach to dealing with social problems is necessary as an increasing interdependence of the members of the complex

10. *Griswold v. Connecticut*, 381 U.S. 479, 85 S.Ct. 1678, 14 L.Ed.2d 510 (1965).
11. *Loving v. Virginia*, 388 U.S. 1, 87 S.Ct. 1817, 18 L.Ed.2d 1010 (1967).
12. *Levy v. Louisiana*, 391 U.S. 68, 88 S.Ct. 1509, 20 L.Ed.2d 436 (1968).
13. *Eisenstadt v. Baird*, 405 U.S. 438, 92 S.Ct. 1029, 31 L.Ed.2d 349 (1972).
14. *Roe v. Wade*, 410 U.S. 113, 93 S.Ct. 705, 35 L.Ed.2d 147 (1973).
15. *Bowers v. Hardwick*, 478 U.S. 186, 106 S.Ct. 2841, 92 L.Ed.2d 140 (1986).
16. *Boddie v. Connecticut*, 401 U.S. 371, 91 S.Ct. 780, 28 L.Ed.2d 113 (1971).
17. *E.g.*, *Michael H. v. Gerald D.*, 491 U.S. 110, 109 S.Ct. 2333, 105 L.Ed.2d 91 (1989); *Santosky v. Kramer*, 455 U.S. 745, 102 S.Ct. 1388, 71 L.Ed.2d 599 (1982); *Little v. Streater*, 492 U.S. 1, 101 S.Ct. 2202, 68 L.Ed.2d 627 (1981); *Stanley v. Illinois*, 405 U.S. 645, 92 S.Ct. 1208, 31 L.Ed.2d 551 (1972).
18. *Barber v. Barber*, 62 U.S. (21 How.) 582, 16 L.Ed. 226 (1858); *see Solomon v. Solomon*, 516 F.2d 1018 (3d Cir. 1975).
19. *E.g., Cole v. Cole*, 663 F.2d 1083 (4th Cir. 1980); *Crouch v. Crouch*, 566 F.2d 486 (5th Cir. 1978).
20. *Ankenbrandt v. Richards*, 504 U.S. 689, 112 S.Ct. 2206, 119 L.Ed.2d 468 (1992).

American society has brought increased dependence on laws and government. Welfare laws, for instance, are indirectly a source of family law. Because of pervasive federal involvement in welfare legislation, these laws are largely a national source of uniformity. Traditionally, legislation dealing both with the family and with social welfare has been the product of intuitive (moral-religious-political) value judgments. Religious tradition has predominated in the family sphere. In the social welfare arena, the guiding forces have been modern liberalism, recast from the "charity"-mold, past "altruism," to the "welfare rights" and "entitlements" philosophy of the 1970s. In the 1990s there was a reaction against these themes, with a partial return back to the themes of work and self-reliance.

Important family policy issues arise under numerous social assistance laws. The classic example is the (now repealed) traditional Aid to Families with Dependent Children (AFDC) "welfare" program that assisted only *single* mothers. As an unintended effect, the program required fathers to absent themselves in order to make their families eligible for assistance. Many other areas are less visible, such as the complex relationship between the Supplemental Security Income program, Medicaid, social security insurance and "relative responsibility" laws.[21] Further illustrations involve laws regarding women's rights, public day care (freeing women for work, but with the issue of the "quality" of child rearing), public provision of the means for birth control and abortion, maternity care, and so forth. Even tax laws (income, inheritance, and gift, and especially the deduction and tax credit framework) are an important aspect of "social" legislation in that they grant or deny benefits or impose burdens on the basis of marital status or family-related dependency.

Conversely, family law affects the circumstances of welfare. For instance, the enactment of liberal divorce legislation and the concomitant relaxation of economic ties that used to survive divorce have left their mark in terms of increased dependency statistics. The reversal of the centuries-old tradition on abortion may have had the opposite effect, although Congress's *denial* of abortion funding for welfare recipients held back that outcome.[22] Amazingly, the predictable effect on welfare burdens of these changes in the law was not an operative nor even a conscious factor in their enactment.

E. Federal Legislation

Recent federal legislation has injected itself into family law more intentionally, directly or by providing funds to the states on condition that they enact laws that follow federal specifications. Prominent examples are the 1975 Child Support Enforcement Act, as frequently amended,[23] and the Parental Kidnapping Prevention Act of 1980.[24] Congress also has tried indirectly to influence state law,

21. *See Schweiker v. Gray Panthers*, 453 U.S. 34, 101 S.Ct. 2633, 69 L.Ed.2d 460 (1981); *Septuagenarian v. Septuagenarian*, 126 Misc.2d 699, 483 N.Y.S.2d 932 (1984); *Swoap v. Superior Court*, 10 Cal.3d 490, 111 Cal.Rptr. 136, 516 P.2d 840 (1973).
22. *See Harris v. McRae*, 448 U.S. 297, 100 S.Ct. 2671, 65 L.Ed.2d 784 (1980).
23. 42 U.S.C. §§ 651-69 (1994 & Supp. IV 1998).
24. 18 U.S.C. § 1073 note; 28 *id.* § 1738A note (1994 & Supp. IV 1998).

as by having the Department of Health and Human Services draft a Model Act for Adoption of Children with Special Needs, or by way of a congressional resolution admonishing the states to adopt laws granting visitation rights to grandparents.

The movement to grant working parents leave upon the birth of a child gained momentum with a U.S. Supreme Court decision upholding California's pregnancy leave law against a sex discrimination challenge,[25] even if the Court held almost simultaneously that Missouri (without a pregnancy leave law) need not pay jobless benefits to a woman who was not reinstated by her employer after an absence for childbirth.[26] Several states were in the forefront of providing unpaid leave to mothers and fathers, and Congress passed a federal law in 1993 that requires employers to grant mothers and fathers unpaid parental leave.

F. International Treaties

Numerous international conventions deal with matters of family law. Examples include adoptions, recognition of foreign divorces, and international enforcement of maintenance obligations. Because a federal treaty is national law and would bind state courts, the United States generally has refrained from acceding to such agreements, in traditional deference to state autonomy in these matters. One important exception in the area of family law is the 1980 Hague Convention on Civil Aspects of International Child Abduction. Ratification of that treaty may be explained by the great interest Congress showed to parental violation of custody orders, which was also expressed in the federal Parental Kidnapping Prevention Act. More recently, the Hague Conference on Private International Law – with considerable U.S. interest and participation – completed a treaty on the international adoption of children. The president has signed that Convention, but it has not yet been ratified by the Senate. Similarly, the 1989 U.N. Convention on the Rights of the Child was signed by the president in 1995, but it also has not yet been ratified.

III. No-Fault Divorce

All 50 states now offer no-fault divorce, about one-third exclusively. In the rest of the states, no-fault divorce is an alternative to traditional fault grounds that remain in effect. This has shifted the focus of the divorce process from "status" (whether divorce may be obtained) to the economic consequences (divorce is freely available, but not "for free"). Aside from the generalization that divorce serves to make all participants – and particularly wives and children – poorer,[27] the emphasis has

25. *California Savings & Loan Ass'n. v. Guerra*, 479 U.S. 272, 107 S.Ct. 683, 93 L.Ed.2d 613 (1987).
26. *Wimberly v. Labor & Indus. Relations Comm'n*, 479 U.S. 511, 107 S.Ct. 821, 93 L.Ed.2d 909 (1987).
27. *E.g.*, Lenore J. Weitzman, *The Divorce Revolution: The Unexpected Social and Economic Consequences for Women and Children in America* (1985).

shifted away from maintenance for spouses (alimony) to division of marital property and child support.

Recently, however, "family values" have taken the forefront in political oratory. The perceived demise of the traditional family is often attributed to the ease of divorce. In consequence, several states have played with the idea of resurrecting divorce for fault only. In Louisiana, the option of "covenant marriage" became law in 1997.[28] Covenant marriage is more difficult to enter (counseling is mandatory), and more difficult to end (divorce is available only for a limited set of traditional fault grounds). Much may be criticized about this "retro-approach" to family stability; after all, it was the ineffectiveness of traditional fault-based divorce laws that led to modern, fault-free divorce.

IV. The Cohabitation Alternative to Marriage and Divorce

A. The Emergence of Cohabitation Law

New attitudes toward marriage, family formation, and sexual companionship have become socially and legally acceptable in the United States. Many modern couples now think that the commitments and burdens of marriage outweigh its advantages. In 1998 the number of cohabiting unmarried couples stood above 5.9 million, 1.7 million of whom lived with partners of the same sex.[29]

Unmarried cohabitation has its attractions. First, potentially costly legal procedures are not needed to end the relationship, and the increasingly severe financial consequences of divorce are thus avoided. Second, "sophisticated" couples have an opportunity to define the terms of their relationship individually and precisely if they stay unmarried – an opportunity that may still be restricted by marriage laws. Third, for income-tax-conscious two-earner couples, cohabitation may spell financial savings over marriage. Fourth, for the feminist, cohabitation promises freedom from traditional male dominance in marriage. Fifth, for the unemancipated recipient of alimony derived from a first marriage or of welfare benefits, remarriage or marriage may be costly if, as is often the case, financial benefits are thereby terminated. Sixth, for same-sex partners who are denied the option of marriage, contract offers some help in legally ordering their relationship.

Not long ago, contracts involving money and sexual relations – if anyone was bold enough to sue – were struck down without sympathy. Even today, the universal theory remains that a contract providing for "meretricious sexual services" violates public policy and hence is void. Prostitution is illegal almost everywhere and often vigorously prosecuted. Fornication and adultery remain criminal offenses in about one-half of the states – even if criminal enforcement ranges from exceptional to non-existent. These prohibitions may fatally affect the

28. *See* Katherine Shaw Spaht, "Louisiana's Covenant Marriage," 59 *La. L. Rev. 63* (1998).

29. U.S. Dept. of Commerce, Census Bureau, Current Population Reports: Marital Status and Living Arrangements, March 1998 (Detailed Tables) 71 (Report P20-514u 1998); *see* <http://www.census.gov/prod/www/abs/marital.html>.

validity of cohabitation contracts, at least in theory. In short, although extensive press coverage and generally approving academic commentary have conveyed the opposite impression, in many states the legality and enforceability of cohabitation arrangements remains in question. Two now decades-old leading cases still illustrate the range of opinion.

The movie actor Lee Marvin, while still married to Betty, had an affair with Michelle, who became his companion for almost six years. When Lee stopped paying Michelle, one year and a half after he had "compelled plaintiff to leave his household," she sued. The Supreme Court of California lip-served the traditional view. The courts should enforce express contracts between nonmarital partners except to the extent that the contract is explicitly founded on the "consideration of meretricious sexual services." From there, the Court proceeded "on the principle that adults who voluntarily live together and engage in sexual relations are nonetheless as competent as any other persons to contract respecting their earnings and property rights." Indeed, absent an express contract the courts should "inquire into the conduct of the parties to determine whether that conduct demonstrates an implied contract or implied agreement of partnership or joint venture ... or some other tacit understanding between the parties."[30] The courts may also employ the doctrine of quantum meruit, or equitable remedies such as constructive or resulting trusts, when warranted by the facts of the case.

The Illinois Supreme Court's decision in *Hewitt* is the antithesis of *Marvin*. A dentist had held out a woman as his wife for fifteen years. She had borne and raised their three children. When she sought a divorce, her dentist (whom she believed to be her husband) confronted her with the information that they had never been legally married. In fact, their cohabitation had started with her pregnancy, and no marriage ceremony had ever been performed. Apparently overwhelmed by the appellate court's full-scale embrace of the *Marvin* doctrine in favor of Ms. Hewitt,[31] the Illinois Supreme Court held wisely that the situation was too complex for judicial resolution and should be left to the legislature. Unwisely and unnecessarily, the court proceeded to conclude that Ms. Hewitt had no rights whatever.[32]

The problems of policy and proof are indeed serious, but they must not lead to a solution along the lines of *Hewitt*. To reach a result fairer to Ms. Hewitt, the Illinois court did not need *Marvin*. It might have drawn on old-fashioned theories of estoppel (the dentist should not have been allowed to deny that he was married), or the court could have played loosely with the fact that the parties' original cohabitation took place in Iowa, which recognizes common law marriage. For a long time, many courts had routinely (and sometimes not a little retrospectively) used the concept of common law (informal) marriage to do "justice," when they felt that strict adherence to legal norms would produce injustice. Indeed, many of the cases that have seemingly accepted the *Marvin* doctrine may be explained in just those terms.

30. *Marvin v. Marvin*, 134 Cal.Rptr. 815, 822, 825, 831, 557 P.2d 106 (1976).
31. *Hewitt v. Hewitt*, 62 Ill.App.3d 861, 20 Ill.Dec. 476, 380 N.E.2d 454 (1978).
32. *Hewitt v. Hewitt*, 77 Ill.2d 49, 32 Ill.Dec. 827, 394 N.E.2d 1204 (1979).

The key to a sensible solution lies here: Where there has been a long-standing, marriage-like, role-divided, child-bearing and child-raising relationship between a man and a woman, a quasi-marital, legal relationship is properly thrust upon them, especially (but not only) in case of the death of one of them. In sum, nothing much short of the *Hewitt* facts should have spawned a doctrine protecting "quantum-meruit-cohabitation." The *Hewitt* situation merited protection;[33] the *Marvin* facts did not. Both leading cases were decided precisely wrong!

Nationwide, many courts still reject *Marvin* outright. Some refer to traditional policies against meretricious relationships or against common law marriage.[34] Some courts give lip service to *Marvin*, but hold cautiously that in this particular case, the contract was not proved, or not implicit, or the *Marvin* remedy not applicable.[35]

Much misunderstanding concerning the spread of *Marvin* was caused by many cases that seem to accept the doctrine by (mis)applying it to cases that do not involve facts that closely resemble *Marvin*. Since only about a dozen jurisdictions still recognize common law marriage, courts in jurisdictions that have abandoned the concept have been tempted to invoke *Marvin* as a substitute. This would give them legal justification for granting rights in long standing relationships, typically with children, or involving post-divorce relationships of partners previously married to each other, or involving premarital relationships of parties who have subsequently married.

Another group of cases nominally invokes *Marvin*, but the courts limit themselves to disentangling commingled assets. In terms of validating the *Marvin* doctrine, these cases do not mean much either. After all, *someone* must "get the waterbed," as an exasperated judge in Minnesota once put it. Yet another line of cases invokes *Marvin* with approval, but with even less relevance, in situations in which there is a direct financial, business, or special (such as nursing) service relationship between two parties, who also happen to have had a sexual relationship. While typically repeating (as indeed did *Marvin*) that meretricious relationships continue to be in violation of public policy, the courts have held (as of course they should) that a sexual relationship does not nullify the parties' otherwise valid business dealings. Recovery in these cases, however, typically is for the value of the *business* relationship and not for some undefined quasi-marital interest.[36] On careful analysis, surprisingly few cases apply the *Marvin* doctrine in its broad reach, in circumstances that cannot be explained under the "excuses" suggested above.

A quarter century later, a broad interpretation of the *Marvin* doctrine (in the sense of "quasi-marital" rights arising from mere cohabitation) remains more the plaything of theorists than a tool of practice. Ironically, in the *Marvin* case itself,

33. For similar facts and a better solution, *see Watts v. Watts*, 137 Wis.2d 506, 405 N.W.2d 303 (1987).
34. *E.g., Hewitt v. Hewitt*, 77 Ill.2d 49, 31 Ill.Dec. 827, 394 N.E.2d 1204 (1979).
35. *E.g., Marvin v. Marvin*, 122 Cal.App.3d 871, 176 Cal.Rptr. 555 (1981). The California Supreme Court denied review.
36. *E.g., Bass v. Bass*, 814 S.W.2d 38 (Tenn. 1991).

the trial court's final award of $104,000 to Michelle (unkindly termed "for rehabilitation") was struck down on appeal as not in the purview of the vast array of potential remedies suggested by the California Supreme Court. Apparently tired of it all, the latter court acquiesced in the denial of any recovery whatsoever.

Acclaim *and* criticism both have emphasized *Marvin's* perceived abandonment of traditional sexual mores. Virtually unnoticed is that acceptance of the *Marvin* doctrine would actually achieve the opposite: It would eliminate the option of cohabitation "without strings," just when society seemed ready to accept it. *Marvin* would regress "free love" to a form of forced "mini-marriage" that is imposed upon the parties without their consent or, indeed, their knowledge. Pushing this point further, *Marvin* may be seen to resurrect something akin to the legal status of "concubinage" of medieval vintage. With only a little more imagination, *Marvin* might be seen as remaking "seduction" into a compensable tort. Least pleasantly, *Marvin* has emerged as a legalized blackmail weapon for disappointed lovers, similar to but potentially more troublesome than even the old-fashioned "heart balm" actions. To underscore this last point, numerous prominent figures (including Billie Jean King, Liberace, and the Bloomingdale estate) have made expensive settlements – less perhaps because the paramour could not have been defeated in court, and more, probably, to avoid embarrassing publicity.

Aside from substantive considerations, the issue of proof is important because of the potential for fraud and imposition, as well as the cost and inconvenience on the parties and the judicial system. Dealing with that issue, current statutes, as did the original "statute of frauds" in 1677, generally require a writing with respect to *marital* agreements, to produce certainty and to eliminate fraud and imposition. *See* Chap. 8, pt. III.B.3. For identical reasons, cohabitation contracts should be treated cautiously. True, a requirement of written, formal proof would leave out many potential claimants, and might lead one to argue that formal marriage should be required as the prerequisite for the derivation of legal rights from cohabitation!

Solving the technical problem of proof does not solve more substantive policy problems. Consider: Even if there is perfect proof, is it not a fundamental substantive question whether the law should permit parties to enter into a contractual relationship resembling marriage, but providing different particulars? To rephrase the most important aspect of this issue more precisely: Should unmarried partners have greater freedom to arrange economic and other aspects of their relationship than most states now allow to married partners? Accordingly, if a cohabitation contract specifies anything significantly more or less than what is "naturally implicit" in the kind of interpersonal relationship modern law understands modern marriage to be, we should be very careful indeed to consider literal enforcement – or we should reconsider the wisdom of our marriage laws.

It *is* new and true that under the *Marvin* line of cases same-sex couples may gain a measure of legal recognition for their relationships, having thus far failed in their quest for legal marriage. *See* pt. IX. Accordingly, the law of "contract cohabitation" is developing rapidly in connection with same-sex unions. Illustrating the potential pitfalls even here, Martina Navratilova filed a malpractice suit against her attorney, blaming him for the support contract she signed with July Nelson, her lover, and claimed she had not understood the contract.[37] Here as well – or worse, for those who still desire to keep their sexual activities out of the public eye – a threat of suit under the *Marvin* doctrine provides staggering potential for blackmail.

Legitimate skepticism regarding the legalization of the cohabitation alternative to legal marriage notwithstanding, basic legal problems arising in such relationships will have to be identified and solved – and preferable not by single issue-oriented court decisions. Legislation is needed to settle these issues, no matter what a state's attitude may be on the broader topic.

In the context of heterosexual as well as same-sex cohabitants, these "inescapable" problems include: (1) identification of the paternity of the unmarried woman's children; (2) settlement of custodial rights, including rights of child visitation; (3) parental support duties toward the children; and (4) definition of the ex-partners' property rights in relation to (joint) acquisitions and gifts (express and implied) made during the period of cohabitation.

B. Public Legal Consequences of Cohabitation

A broader policy issue has not received enough attention: *Marvin* deals *solely* with the partner-to-partner relationship. To the extent that it moves unmarried cohabitation to a level of recognition resembling marriage, it does so *only between the parties*. The next question is what, if any, "public" legal consequences should attend unmarried cohabitation? For instance, should cohabiting partners be permitted to file joint income tax returns? Should they be *required* to file jointly if that would be to the advantage of the tax authorities? Should cohabitants be legally obligated to provide support to their current partners, or to their ex-partners? If unmarried cohabitants are allowed to waive their mutual support obligation, should the welfare authorities, that is, the taxpayer, be bound by such a contract and provide "welfare?"[38] Should a dependency relationship based on unmarried cohabitation trigger welfare eligibility when the "provider" leaves? Should welfare and similar benefits be terminated when a de facto "provider" enters the picture? Should cohabitants have standing to sue for loss of consortium and wrongful death benefits?

The City of Berkeley was among the first to adopt a city ordinance assimilating marriage and cohabitation in terms of social and welfare benefits. Many cities, corporations, universities, and even a few states – notably Hawaii and Vermont – now allow "registration" of domestic partners of either sex with varying legal benefits and ramifications. Notably, this move has extended primarily to marriage-similar *benefits*, and legally enforceable burdens have generally not been imposed on the non-marital partners.

37. *Washington Post*, 14 Nov. 1991.
38. Even the highly "progressive" Uniform Premarital Agreements Act, § 6(b), would not permit one marriage partner to contract the other into welfare dependence.

V. Contractual Modification of Marriage

A. Antenuptial Contracts: Progress in the Courts

The interest in unmarried, unregulated, long-term cohabitation (and not to underestimate, unrestricted exit from relationships) may be interpreted as a reaction against the traditional model of marriage, which many modern couples consider too rigid to accommodate perceived new needs arising out of the new social circumstances in which they find themselves. Even today, however, agreements between marriage partners seeking to define their respective rights during marriage and, especially, upon divorce, run the risk of being ignored by a court asked to enforce them because the traditional public policy against divorce is in clear memory.

Few courts still share the traditional concern that if the consequences of divorce are defined in advance, the parties will be encouraged to seek divorce, nor do the courts much care. In any event, the opposite argument has always seemed at least equally plausible: If people knew in advance the all too often ruinous consequences of divorce, fewer divorces might occur. The more persuasive argument remains that parties to marriage should not in advance be allowed to vary those consequences of divorce that are imposed as a matter of public policy. In addition, in cases involving marriages of long duration, the ultimate circumstances of divorce were usually so unforeseeable at the time of an antenuptial agreement as to render any such agreement potentially unconscionable.

The typical antenuptial agreement sets forth special conditions relating to the contemplated marriage. These conditions seek to rule out, vary, or supplement legal consequences that would otherwise arise automatically. Since the relationship between the parties typically is not at "arm's length," great care must be taken in the negotiation and execution of such contracts. The courts carefully scrutinize the circumstances under which such contracts were procured. Provisions regarding the support or custody of children stand on still a different footing, as the court will not feel bound by anything it may view as adversely affecting the interest of a child.[39]

Traditionally, if the wife relinquished rights that otherwise would have resulted from marriage, she was zealously protected against overreaching. Husbands have not been protected nearly as well and often have been left to live with burdensome "deals." Courts spoke in terms of the *husband's* fiduciary duty. Some still do, but others now have found a mutual duty. While this discrimination may be explainable in terms of a tradition of chivalry, it made sense insofar as gender-role-divided marriage required that the law give the wife special protection and because men were generally more conversant with financial matters than women.[40]

Concerning permissible subject matter, the simplest case involves the transfer of property to the prospective spouse in consideration of marriage. Such agreements have long been held valid. Antenuptial agreements relating to the dis

39. Harry D. Krause, *Family Law in a Nutshell* 91-92 (3d ed. 1995).
40. *Sogg v. Nevada State Bank*, 108 Nev. 308, 832 P.2d 781 (1992).

tribution of property on death have also long been upheld. Given varying requirements of independent counsel, full disclosure, and fair provision – along with a writing satisfying the statute of frauds – each spouse may renounce or promise inheritance rights regarding the other.

Until recently, however, agreements seeking to define the respective rights of the parties upon divorce were viewed as violating the traditional public policy against "encouraging" divorce, making divorce "too easy." While by definition it "restated" the law rather than looked forward, the 1981 Restatement of Contracts (Second) section 190 still held:

> (1) A promise by a person contemplating marriage or by a married person, other than as part of an enforceable separation agreement, is unenforceable on grounds of public policy if it would change some essential incident of the marital relationship....
> (2) A promise that tends unreasonably to encourage divorce or separation is unenforceable on grounds of public policy.

Note the flexible word "unreasonably!" One old rule remains true: An agreement may not give one party a "prize" for divorce. To illustrate, where a previously impecunious bride was promised a house plus half a million dollars in the event she decided to divorce, the court did not allow her the "prize" when she did divorce – after only seven months' of marriage.

Over the past several decades, courts have upheld antenuptial agreements looking to divorce,[41] when high standards of fairness were met[42] or when older parties and second marriages were involved.[43] Agreements relating to property settlements upon divorce have had a better chance than agreements affecting support obligations, because support is deemed more of the essence of marriage and involves public policy more directly.

B. Modern Legislation on Premarital Agreements

Today it is accepted wisdom that the parties' wishes, expressed in an antenuptial agreement, should be respected – up to a point. Given compliance with varying requirements of full disclosure, fair provision, and independent counsel, no rational reason continues to support the traditional, overly solicitous attitude to such contracts. Today's realities – at least in many cases – differ from the past when it was appropriate to go to extremes to protect financially dependent wives from exploitation by unscrupulous husbands.

41. *Marshall v. Marshall*, 350 N.W.2d 463 (Minn. App. 1984); *Frey v. Frey*, 298 Md. 552, 472 A.2d 705 (1984); *Gross v. Gross*, 11 Ohio St.3d 99, 464 N.E.2d 500 (1984).
42. *Osborne v. Osborne*, 384 Mass. 591, 428 N.E.2d 810 (1981).
43. *Volid v. Volid*, 6 Ill.App.3d 386, 286 N.E.2d 42 (1972). *But see Connolly v. Connolly*, 270 N.W.2d 44 (S.D. 1978).

Clear statutes, however, are needed to provide certainty and predictability, and the Uniform Marriage and Divorce Act (UMDA) did not make specific provision for antenuptial agreements, even while it allowed them to be "considered on divorce." In 1983, the Commissioners on Uniform State Laws approved the Uniform Premarital Agreements Act (UPAA). Until then, few states had passed legislation firmly establishing a reasonable, modern framework for the validity of antenuptial contracts. The UPAA covers all conceivable subjects and allows the modification of spousal support obligations, except to the extent that welfare eligibility would result.[44] By 2000, the UPAA – or a variant – had become law in 26 states, and its spirit influences the law in the rest of the states.

A crucial feature of the UPAA is that an otherwise valid ante- or postnuptial agreement may be upset *only* if it was "unconscionable when executed."[45] "Fair and reasonable disclosure," *or* notice or adequate knowledge or reasonable opportunity for knowledge of the property or financial obligations of the other spouse, is required. The Act does not specifically require counsel, although agreements no doubt gain strength from the presence of separate counsel for each party.

Significantly, the Act does not clearly define the crucial term "unconscionable" that would void an agreement, leaving that to the court to be decided "as a matter of law." Testing "unconscionability" as of the time the agreement was executed is a potentially harsh rule. Years later, an antenuptial agreement that *then* has unconscionable consequences, will, one hopes, be treated with caution, if the *current* circumstances were not foreseen or foreseeable at the time the contract was made, or even if they were. Perhaps a retailoring of contract law dealing with "frustration" and "change in circumstances" may provide the needed remedy for this unique context. *See* Chap. 8, pt. IV.B.1. Most long-term marriages involve such vast changes in "circumstances" that "frustration" may not only describe the parties' attitude, but may also be present in an equitable sense, even if not in the technical sense applied to commercial contracts. Notably, Illinois rephrased its own version of the UPAA to the effect that if any contractual modification of *spousal support* "causes one party ... *undue hardship* in light of circumstances not reasonably foreseeable at the time of the execution of the agreement, a court ... may require the other party to provide support to the *extent necessary to avoid such hardship*."[46]

C. *Agreements During Marriage and Separation Agreements*

Antenuptial contracts have traveled a rocky road, but the fate of agreements concluded during marriage has been even more troubled. The first hurdle was that traditional contracts need "consideration." When the parties are married, however, their mutual promises of, for instance, marital support or housekeeping that supply consideration to antenuptial contracts are unavailable to serve as consideration because, upon marriage, these promises have turned into legal duties. A

44. *See supra* note 38.
45. UPAA § 6(a)(2).
46. 750 Ill. Comp. Stat. § 10/7(b) (1996) (emphasis added).

safeguard that remains is that a postnuptial agreement may easily be struck down for undue influence or duress. A flagrant case is that of a husband who, after twenty years of marriage, presented his wife (who was distressed over her father's recent death) with an agreement – in exchange for which he agreed to not seek a divorce for two years – that would have given her only eight percent of the parties' $40 million assets. When the wife's first counsel advised her not to sign, her husband found her another lawyer who did. The "deal" did not stand.[47]

The type of contract most frequently executed between spouses during marriage is the "separation agreement," attendant to imminent separation or divorce. Although their usual purpose is to assure the consequences of divorce in advance, the courts have long accepted these agreements, if executed with care.[48]

Traditional law laid many traps in the way of separation agreements and considerably limited the parties' freedom to contract concerning their own affairs. As late as 1981, the Second Restatement of Contracts illustrated the difference between invalid and valid separation agreements as follows:

> A, who is married to B, promises to pay B $50,000 in return for B's promise to obtain a divorce. The promises of A and B tend unreasonably to encourage divorce and are unenforceable on grounds of public policy. The result does not depend on whether or not there are grounds for divorce or on whether or not B has performed.
>
> A, who has begun divorce proceedings against B, promises B that if divorce is granted, alimony shall be fixed at a stated sum, in return for B's agreement to relinquish all other claims to alimony. A court *may* decide that in view of the disintegration of the marriage relationship, the promises of A and B do not tend unreasonably to encourage divorce and their enforcement is not precluded on grounds of public policy.[49]

The circumstances and formalities of separation agreement execution are governed by rules similar to those applying to antenuptial agreements, that is, there must be full disclosure *or* fair provision for the wife. If anything, here the courts have been even more intent on satisfying themselves completely that no undue influence was exercised, so that an agreement stands on better ground if there is full disclosure *and* fair provision.

Under the traditional rules, it was difficult to draft a separation agreement that could not be upset. In practice, of course, most separation agreements are adhered to by both parties without question and consequently are accepted by the court. But even today, the typical separation agreement is less a contract than a proposal to the court. More precisely, actual scrutiny still runs heavily in favor of the wife, so that the separation agreement resembles an irrevocable offer by the husband to the wife which, if the wife has changed her mind or sometimes even

47. *In re Marriage of Richardson*, 237 Ill.App.3d 1067, 179 Ill.Dec. 224, 606 N.E.2d 56 (1992).
48. Krause, *supra* note 39, at 480-90.
49. § 190, cmt. c, illus. 3, 6 (emphasis added).
50. *Crawford v. Crawford*, 39 Ill.App.3d 457, 350 N.E.2d 103, 107 (1976).

if she has not, may be accepted or rejected by the court. To illustrate, the Illinois Court of Appeals held that "reviewing courts not only focus on whether such contracts are free of actual fraud and coercion, but emphasis is also placed on whether they are reasonably fair and sufficient in light of the station in life and the circumstances of the parties."[50] The Iowa Supreme Court accepted a wife's argument that she agreed to a settlement under duress and emotional stress induced by the *trial judge*, even though she had had independent counsel and the advice of her brother.[51]

A drastic illustration of the traditional gender-based "double standard" applying to separation agreements involved a high-income physician who was so eager to marry his paramour that he "bought" a no-contest divorce from his wife for an open-ended monthly alimony for literally more money than he had or could earn. When the ex-husband woke up in the arms of his new wife, he attacked the agreement as "unconscionable." The South Dakota Supreme Court agreed that the agreement was "harsh," but held that the husband got "exactly what he bargained for."[52] Another physician was so depressed about his impending divorce that he refused to obtain counsel and signed everything that his wife's attorney took to him. When he later attacked the settlement, the Michigan Court of Appeals told him that, absent fraud, he could have no relief.[53] And when a husband committed suicide – perhaps to invoke the clause calling for support payments to his ex-wife to end upon his death – it took an appellate court to overrule the trial court's holding that his suicide constituted a compensable tort upon his ex-wife.[54] Short of suicide, few husbands were given relief.

It is common practice to incorporate separation agreements into divorce decrees, either by reference or by setting forth their terms expressly. The latter, when clothed in mandatory language, gives separation agreements the status and enforceability of judgments. In most jurisdictions, the contract then ceases to exist as a contract. Among other things, this means that the parties' agreement now may be modified only in accordance with the rules for modifying judgments (or in accordance with its terms, if the court has chosen to adopt the terms of the agreement concerning modifiability). When an agreement is incorporated by reference only, the chief effect is that its validity is assured by res judicata, but the agreement does not gain the status of a judgment. To facilitate enforcement abroad, where a contract may be favored over a judgment, the Uniform Marriage and Divorce Act (UMDA) provides that even if the parties opt for merging their separation agreement into the divorce decree, their contract nevertheless continues to have independent existence alongside the divorce decree.[55]

The Act provides that a separation agreement (except for terms providing for child support, custody, and visitation) is "binding upon the court unless it finds, after considering the economic circumstances of the parties and any other relevant evidence produced by the parties, ... that the separation agreement is uncon-

51. *In re Marriage of Hitchcock*, 265 N.W.2d 599 (Iowa 1978).
52. *Jameson v. Jameson*, 90 S.D. 179, 239 N.W.2d 5 (1976).
53. *Firnschild v. Firnschild*, 67 Mich.App. 327, 240 N.W.2d 790 (1976).
54. *Wilmington Trust Co. v. Clark*, 289 Md. 313, 424 A.2d 744 (1981).
55. UMDA § 306(e).

scionable."[56] The difficulty is that "unconscionable," by and large, still means what a particular judge may think it means – and that may not offer as much predictability as the parties may want or should have. The UMDA's "official comments" refer to commercial law definitions of "unconscionable," but – as already noted in the case of antenuptial contracts – that may not be an altogether appropriate reference in the peculiar circumstance of divorce. Another question is whether the non-binding nature of stipulations regarding children is compatible with binding stipulations regarding the parties, when the agreement may be highly interdependent and concessions in one sector may have been made in response to advantages gained in the other.

Beyond the UMDA, provisions in the Uniform Premarital Agreements Act regarding post-marital contracts or post-marital modification of antenuptial contracts also may apply to separation agreements.

VI. Dollars on Divorce: Alimony

Alimony, in the sense of post-divorce spousal support, dates back to the time when legal separation (limited divorce) was the sole remedy for broken marriages. Since parties could not remarry and the inheritance relationship and other legal incidents of marriage remained in effect, alimony originally represented no more than the definition and continuation of the *husband's* marital support obligation past the termination of cohabitation.

When *full* divorce (with the right to remarry) became available, the concept of alimony had been taken over from limited divorce without much thought. Commentators long used this history to attack alimony as illogical and unjust, but it is *not* difficult to find a satisfactory modern rationale upon which to uphold, in appropriate cases, continued payments after marriage by the economically stronger ex-spouse to the economically weaker.[57] Not all of these payments should necessarily fall under the rubrics of "property" or "child support."

Traditional alimony statutes have allowed a judge to award alimony as he or she deemed "equitable and just," and no specific guidelines have fettered judicial discretion. The "wife's needs" and the "husband's ability to pay" were the common denominators, even while there was little agreement as to the meaning of this in specific circumstances. Declining, but still extant, is the notion that the wife is entitled to be maintained at the level she lived during the marriage. Obviously, that standard is an illusion – two households cannot be maintained at the same level as one, assuming a finite amount of dollars.

Traditionally, equitable notions related to the "clean hands" concept dictated that the spouse guilty of a marital offense could not receive alimony – as that would compensate her for her own wrong doing. If it was the husband who strayed, a few courts might increase his alimony obligation to provide some punishment for him and extra compensation for his wife.

56. *Id.* § 306(b).
57. Harry D. Krause, *Family Law: Cases, Comments and Questions* 578-80 (3d ed. 1990); Krause et al., *id.* at 821-35 (4th ed. 1998).

Divorce without fault quickly raised the question whether the no-fault approach should carry over to alimony. This question has generally been answered affirmatively, even while early in the no-fault era, the Minnesota Supreme Court decided that in an "irretrievable breakdown" divorce, "evidence of marital misconduct should, upon a showing of proper circumstances, be considered by the court for purposes of property division and award of alimony."[58] That decision was subsequently overruled by the legislature.[59] Some doubts, however, have surfaced abroad: In 1984, ending a decade of disregard for fault, the British House of Commons returned fault to a limited role in adjusting the consequences of divorce, if it would be inequitable not to consider it. In 1986, West Germany returned to fault-like considerations involving serious offenses against the spouse and looking to the parties' respective economic behavior, though *not* to the traditional grounds for divorce, in setting the level of post-divorce support.[60]

As do other support obligations, alimony usually terminates at the death of either the payor or the payee. However, if the separation agreement is phrased appropriately or even ambiguously,[61] an award may extend beyond death. Some courts insist that the intent to provide alimony past death be "unmistakably clear."[62] Even if alimony may not be awarded past the spouse's death, an order that he maintain insurance on his life, payable to his ex-wife, has been employed quite commonly as a means of providing continued support. Manipulation of the "death-ends-all" rule also may be possible by defining a periodic payment as a division of property by installments. Tax consequences must be considered.

In the case of the former wife's remarriage, termination of alimony is automatic or considered a "changed circumstance" that ensures success upon application to the court. Specific wording in the separation agreement controls, especially when it is incorporated into the decree.

Whether the former wife's entry into either a void or voidable new marriage ends the prior husband's alimony obligation has generally been answered to the effect that alimony is deemed "suspended" during the continuation of the new relationship, that is, arrears may not be collected after annulment. Some courts have reinstated prior alimony in the case of the later annulment or declaration of nullity of a *void* marriage. In the case of an annulment of a *voidable* marriage, on the other hand, alimony typically is not reinstated. More recently, courts have not distinguished between void and voidable marriages and do not reinstate alimony in either case.

Short of formal remarriage, many courts have *not* terminated alimony when the ex-wife opted for cohabitation, even in cases where the ex-husband's payments helped support the ex-wife's lover.[63] Other courts have strained to reach a different result, some by modifying alimony to assure that no portion of it would

58. *Peterson v. Peterson*, 308 Minn. 365, 242 N.W.2d 103, 108 (1976).
59. 1978 Minn. Laws 1062, ch. 772, § 51, codified as amended at Minn. Stat. Ann. § 518.552(2) (West 1990); *see Otis v. Otis*, 299 N.W.2d 114 (Minn. 1980).
60. Bürgerliches Gesetzbuch (Civil Code) § 1579 (as amended in 1986).
61. *Cohen v. Cronin*, 39 N.Y.2d 42, 382 N.Y.S.2d 724, 346 N.E.2d 524 (1976).
62. *Kendall v. Kendall*, 218 Kan. 713, 545 P.2d 346 (1976); *Estate of Kuhns v. Kuhns*, 550 P.2d 816 (Alaska 1976).
63. *Sturgis v. Sturgis*, 1 Fam. L. Rptr. (BNA) 2042 (Ark. Sup. Ct. 14 Oct. 1974).

go to the ex-wife's paramour[64] and others eliminating alimony for the duration of the cohabitation.[65] An Ohio case terminated a "cohabiting" wife's alimony on the ingenious theory that the parties' separation agreement contemplated the Ohio definition of marriage, which includes common law marriage. Accordingly the cohabitation, although taking place in a state not recognizing common law marriage, was deemed to be "marriage for the purpose of triggering the separation agreement's termination clause."[66]

A number of states have enacted statutes that allow a court to modify alimony upon proof that the ex-wife is "habitually living with another man and holding herself out as his wife, although not married to such man,"[67] or if the wife cohabits "on a resident, continuing conjugal basis,"[68] or upon proof of cohabitation and holding out as a spouse for a 30-day period, consecutive or nonconsecutive. California abandoned the "holding-out-as-a-spouse" requirement in 1983 and imposed a rebuttable presumption of reduced need if the recipient of alimony cohabits with a person of the opposite sex.[69] The Illinois Supreme Court ruled that "conjugal basis" need not involve sexual contact to invoke the statute.[70]

As less social stigma attaches to informal relationships, attorneys drafting separation agreements have had to be increasingly careful in dealing with this problem. Marlon Brando's separation agreement with Movita contained the following language: "'Remarriage' shall include, without limitation, [Movita's] appearing to maintain a marital relationship with any person." The Court held that Movita and James Ford had "enjoyed a relationship of substantial duration, which bore the objective indicia of marriage," and found further that, as Movita had paid for many of Ford's expenses, their "living together" fell under the phrase used in the agreement. The Court rejected Movita's argument to the effect that she and Ford were not giving the appearance that they were married, and that they were just living together.[71]

In a situation where the ex-spouse was a homosexual or lesbian and lived with a "lover" of the same sex, a Minnesota court held that "defendant's post-decree lesbianism is a material change in circumstances which justifies the termination of alimony."[72] And an ex-husband, whose former wife became a nun (thereby materially reducing her opportunity to remarry), was denied termination of his monthly alimony payment. His argument that paying the money to the convent converted his payment to a religious purpose in violation of his constitutional rights did not persuade the Illinois Supreme Court even to hear his appeal.[73]

64. *Hall v. Hall*, 25 Ill.App.3d 524, 323 N.E.2d 541 (1975).
65. *Taake v. Taake*, 70 Wis.2d 115, 233 N.W.2d 449 (1975).
66. *Fahrer v. Fahrer*, 36 Ohio App.2d 208, 304 N.E.2d 411 (1973).
67. N.Y. Dom. Rel. Law § 248 (McKinney 1999).
68. 750 Ill. Comp. Stat. 5/510(b) (1999).
69. Cal. Fam. Code § 4323 (West 1994).
70. *In re Marriage of Sappington*, 106 Ill.2d 456, 88 Ill.Dec. 61, 478 N.E.2d 376 (1985).
71. *O'Connor Bros. Abalone Co. v. Brando*, 40 Cal.App.3d 90, 114 Cal.Rptr. 773 (1974).
72. *Anonymous v. Anonymous*, 5 Fam. L. Rptr. (BNA) 2127 (Minn. Dist. Ct. 15 Nov. 1978).
73. *Lane v. Lane*, 35 Ill.App.3d 276, 340 N.E.2d 705 (1975), *appeal denied*, 63 Ill.2d 552 (1976), *cert. denied* 429 U.S. 886, 97 S.Ct. 238, 50 L.Ed.2d 167 (1976).

American courts and legislatures have mixed futuristic ideas with historical notions. In 1979, the U.S. Supreme Court removed the gender-based, wives-only limitation on alimony when a husband's constitutional attack on his disparate obligation succeeded.[74] However, antipathy to the very idea of alimony has grown among men as well as among feminists. Many courts have attacked alimony as a "free bread ticket for life," no longer consistent with married women's property acts, the new divisibility of marital property on divorce, and improved employment opportunities for women. Invoking "women's liberation" as a *fait accompli*, some courts began to deny alimony altogether, except in cases of actual need and for a limited time, sometimes termed a "retraining" or "rehabilitation" allowance. A basic change in attitudes toward alimony was in the making. Drastically, the UMDA provided a new view of alimony:

> (a) [T]he court may grant a maintenance order for either spouse, *only* if it finds that the spouse seeking maintenance: (1) *lacks sufficient property* to provide for his reasonable needs; and (2) *is unable to support himself* through appropriate employment or *is the custodian of a child* whose condition or circumstances make it appropriate that the custodian not be required to seek employment outside the home.
> (b) The maintenance order shall be in amounts and for periods of time the court deems just, *without regard to marital misconduct*.[75]

It should be noted, however, that the anti-alimony movement has run into the reality of long-term dependent wives who, even today, are usually granted alimony if their marriage had been one of substantial duration. Moreover, by reclassifying certain post-divorce claims as "property" and providing long-term payouts, substantial monies are now being transferred *instead* of alimony.

VII. Dollars on Divorce: Distribution of "Marital Property"

Along with the decline of alimony, the property rights of the non-earning spouse on divorce have been improved enormously. This, of course, helps only in the minority of cases where there is significant property to divide.

The "pure" separate property system traditional to the common law continues nowhere. First, we now count nine community property states in the United States, plus Puerto Rico, and 41 separate property states, plus the District of Columbia. Second, community property states had always empowered their divorce courts to divide property acquired by either spouse during the marriage and, in some cases, before. Third, the 41 separate property states now follow this approach.

Considerable differences remain in the separate as well as community property states' views as to whether only "marital" property, or both "marital" and "sep-

74. *Orr v. Orr*, 440 U.S. 268, 99 S.Ct. 1102, 59 L.Ed.2d 306 (1979).
75. UMDA § 308 (emphasis added).

arate" property, is before the court for division. Divergence also persists in the definition of what is "marital" and what is "separate" property, and whether "equitable" means "50/50" or "fair."

In making their break with tradition, most separate property states adopted what has been aptly termed "deferred community property." In very simplified terms, this means that, during the marriage and *until divorce* or death, the traditional separate property system continues to apply. Most states do this in a non-technical sense, others have imported highly technical rules from the community property states.

It is clear that the states that opted for the technical "marital property" approach[76] have reaped an inordinate harvest of often highly complex litigation, probably for little benefit – except to lawyers. At great expense to the parties, dozens of appellate cases have struggled with careful definition of separate and marital property. A difficult task, because separate property may "transmute" into marital property when it is "commingled" or when title is taken jointly, leaning on the older custom of presuming a gift in such cases. The irony is that many courts have ultimately fallen back on provisions that allow discretionary adjustment through disproportionate allocation of marital property, or they have exploited the statutory interdependence of alimony and property awards, by awarding more of one, if a technical rule required less of the other. In many cases, the technical analysis has thus been reduced to little more than an expensive exercise.

In 1984, Wisconsin became the first and only state to enact the Uniform Marital Property Act approved by the Commissioners on Uniform State Laws and the American Bar Association. The Act imposes essentially a community property regime by regulating the property status of spouses during their marriage. As all other state legislatures have rejected the Act, it does not appear that either it or the traditional concept of community property will become widely accepted in the United States.

VIII. Dollars on Divorce: Child Support

Federal laws have deeply involved federal initiative and authority in child support enforcement. In an area that previously had been viewed as belonging strictly to the states, state laws now must require withholding of child support from the paycheck of a delinquent parent. Employers are held responsible if they do not comply. States must establish guidelines for child support awards for use by all judges or officials who determine child support awards, and provide for the imposition of liens against the property of defaulting support obligors. Credit companies are informed of unpaid child support. Unpaid support is deducted from federal and state income tax refunds. Expedited hearings – judicial or administrative – are required in support cases. Statutes of limitation for the establishment of paternity now extend to 18 years after the child's birth, following and extending U.S. Supreme Court decisions that struck down one and two year periods of limitation

76. *E.g.*, 750 Ill. Comp. Stat. 5/503 (1999).

on constitutional grounds.[77] Less counterproductive methods of support enforcement are now employed than have been the rule, that is, wage deduction to *avoid default*, rather than jail and the loss of one's job *after default*.

In the context of federally sponsored support enforcement, the establishment of reasonable support guidelines assures less arbitrary and diverse conceptions of the "needs of the child" and the "father's ability to pay" than have been applied in the past. The 1992 Federal Child Support Recovery Act allows criminal protection for wilful failure to support a child in another state.[78] The 1994 Full Faith and Credit for Child Support Orders Act mandates interstate enforcement.[79] Pushed by federal incentives, the Uniform Interstate Family Support Act (UIFSA) has largely replaced the earlier national standard, the Uniform Reciprocal Enforcement of Support Act (URESA).

IX. Child Custody after Divorce

A. Sex, Religion, and Race

Traditional "objective" factors used to determine whom will obtain child custody, such as the parent's gender or religion, now are hotly disputed. A California statute (repealed in 1970) summed up a lost national consensus in terms of "other things being equal, if the child is of tender years, custody should be given to the mother; if the child is of an age to require education and preparation for labor and business, then custody should be given to the father." In 1973, the Supreme Court of Pennsylvania still said "that the best interest of children of tender years will be best served under a mother's guidance and control is one of the strongest presumptions in the law."[80] Past the "tender years" (which, as any parent will confirm, end at about the beginning of teenage), the rule of thumb was that – their things being equal – boys would go with the father and girls with the mother. Reluctance to separate siblings was an important additional factor.

Many states have amended their statutes along the lines of Colorado's to the effect that "the court shall not presume that any person is better able to serve the best interests of the child because of that person's sex."[81] In some states, courts have struck down the "tender years presumption" on the basis of the constitutional equality of sexes requirement.[82]

While there is lip service to the proposition that gender is not a proper criterion on which to base an award, the reality remains that the great majority of custody

77. *Mills v. Habluetzel*, 456 U.S. 91, 102 S.Ct. 1549, 71 L.Ed.2d 770 (1982); *Pickett v. Brown*, 462 U.S. 1, 103 S.Ct. 2199, 76 L.Ed.2d 372 (1983).
78. 18 U.S.C. § 228 (1994 & Supp. IV 1998). This was toughened with the 1998 Deadbeat Parents Punishment Act, Pub. L. No. 105-187, codified at *id.*
79. 28 U.C.S. § 1738B (1994 & Supp. IV 1998) (as amended in 1996 and 1997).
80. *Commonwealth* ex rel. *Lucas v. Kreischer*, 450 Pa. 352, 299 A.2d 243 (1973).
81. Colo. Rev. Stat. Ann. § 14-10-124(3) (West 1997 & Supp. 2000) (as amended in 1998).
82. *Ex parte Devine*, 398 So.2d 686 (Ala. 1981); *Watts v. Watts*, 77 Misc.2d 178, 350 N.Y.S.2d 285 (1973). *But see Cox v. Miller*, 146 Ill.App.2d 399, 166 Ill.Dec. 922, 586 N.E.2d 1251 (1992).

adjudications still run in favor of mothers. An important analysis of 1,100 divorcing California families found that mothers still outscore fathers in custody settlements by seven to one, and that fewer than two percent of divorces involving children require the judge's decision on custody.[83] On rational balance, it appears that the sex of parent and child *should* remain an important circumstance to be considered in the overall picture, though not the sole factor. At the extreme, however, one feminist scholar advocates an unvarnished return to a "maternal deference standard."

> I assess custody standards against their ability to protect the greater emotional commitments of women to children. I reject the best interest standard, joint custody, and deference to the mature child because they do not protect adequately the strong emotional bonds between children and their mothers. ... At divorce, judges should defer to the fit mother's decision with respect to custody."[84]

More moderately, but to the same end, the "primary caretaker rule" has emerged from West Virginia as a thinly disguised variant of the maternal preference rule.[85]

On the issue of race as a criterion in interracial custody and adoption cases, the U.S. Supreme Court decided a case that involved a divorced white mother who was then cohabiting with (and later married to and now divorced from) a black man. In the mother's appeal from a lower court decision giving custody of the child to the father, the U.S. Supreme Court in *Palmore v. Sidoti* held:

> It would ignore reality to suggest that racial and ethnic prejudices do not exist or that all manifestations of those prejudices have been eliminated. There is a risk that a child living with a stepparent of a different race may be subject to a variety of pressures and stresses not present if the child were living with parents of the same racial or ethnic origin.
>
> The question, however, is whether the reality of private biases and the possible injury they might inflict are permissible considerations for removal of an infant child from the custody of its natural mother. We have little difficulty concluding that they are not. The Constitution cannot control such prejudices but neither can it tolerate them. Private biases may be outside the reach of the law, but the law cannot, directly or indirectly, give them effect.[86]

Read restrictively, *Palmore* may be interpreted not to change the law, since the Supreme Court found expressly that the lower "court was entirely candid and

83. *See* Eleanor E. Maccoby & Robert H. Mnookin, *Dividing the Child: Social and Legal Dilemmas of Custody* (1992).
84. Mary Becker, "Maternal Feelings: Myth, Taboo, and Child Custody," 1 *S. Cal. Rev. L. & Women's Stud.* 133, 223-24 (1992).
85. Richard Neely, "The Primary Caretaker Parent Rule: Child Custody and the Dynamics of Greed," 3 *Yale L. & Pol'y Rev.* 168 (1984).
86. *Palmore v. Sidoti*, 466 U.S. 429, 433, 104 S.Ct. 1879, 80 L.Ed.2d 421 (1984).

made no effort to place its holding on any ground other than race."[87] As the *sole* factor, race had not passed muster on any recent appeal. Read expansively, however, the Court's opinion cast doubt on whether race may be considered under any circumstances.

B. Joint Custody

In an ongoing marriage, all custodial rights are exercised by both parents. These rights include decision-making power over all aspects of upbringing, religion, and education, so long as parental decisions and conduct stay clear of the neglect, abuse, and dependency laws. Upon divorce, however, the full parental power traditionally went solely to the one parent who obtained custody. Traditionally, the visitation rights given to the noncustodial parent constituted little more than a "possessory" interest, derisively called "entertainment time." This marked the custody decision upon divorce as a much more basic change in the noncustodial parent's relationship with his or her child than was realized by typical parents. Indeed, loss of custody on divorce might almost be compared with termination of parental rights, regarding which – outside of the context of divorce – the U.S. Supreme Court has expressed considerable constitutional reservations.[88]

Real social change is implicit in the lessening of marital role division that we commonly see today. In the ongoing family, fathers increasingly have assumed an active parental role. One result has been an increased interest of fathers in claiming custody, accompanied by the willingness of courts to grant him custody. Now it often seems unfair to fathers as well as to the child that his active participation would be terminated on divorce. Yet the traditional presumption that favors giving custody to the mother is dying a very slow death, and the great majority of custody dispositions still go to the mother. To the complaint of many a father, the legal obligation to pay child support is not affected by his loss of custody. Worse, since he has to maintain his children outside of his own household, his actual financial burden is typically increased.

The concept of "joint custody" strives to alleviate this dilemma. Joint custody, briefly, means that *legal* custody – that is, decision-making power over the child's "life-style" – remains in both parents. Only *physical* custody goes to one or the other or is being shared. The idea has been hailed as much as condemned. Obviously, if both parents are truly able to share the decisions of parenting after divorce, the unfairness implicit in traditional practice and law – all but terminating the noncustodial parent's rights and nevertheless asking him to pay support – would be avoided or alleviated. Equally obviously, joint custody will be harmful if, after the divorce, the parents continue to play out their lingering animosity, or confuse the child with conflicting directions, or are simply unable to agree on basic issues involving the child's welfare.

87. *Id.* at 432.
88. *Santosky v. Kramer*, 455 U.S. 745, 102 S.Ct. 1388, 71 L.Ed.2d 599 (1982); *Lassiter v. Dep't of Soc. Serv.*, 452 U.S. 18, 101 S.Ct. 2153, 68 L.Ed.2d 640 (1981).

Some states have enacted statutory presumptions that it is in the best interests of the child to be in both parents' joint custody. Others have established an all but opposite presumption and allow joint custody only in exceptional cases. The question is how to resolve disputes that the joint custodians cannot resolve themselves? Continuous recourse to the courts will not be in the child's nor the courts' best interests. Arbitration may provide an answer. Less formally, a "deciding vote" may be given to a person whose decision both parents are willing to follow. Two dubious alternatives are the award of sole custody either to the "more reasonable" parent, or to the parent who has had more day-to-day physical "possession" of the child. The loss-of-custody alternative may encourage *other* parents to be more reasonable – but should *this* child pay the price? If the physical possession course is taken, on the other hand, the initial adjudication of joint custody potentially becomes a mere "placebo,"[89] with day-to-day custody remaining the key to long-run rights over the child.[90]

To conclude, joint custody raises problems that may equal the solutions it offers. The appropriate judicial attitude would seem to be a careful case-by-case approach with no presumption for or against joint custody. The key remains that the best interests of the child do involve continuity and stability, but also extend to a mutually responsible relationship with *both* parents.

C. Grandparents' Visitation Rights

With increased break-up through divorce of families with young children, grandparents (especially those on the side of non-custodial parents) have registered their vital interest in continued contact with their grandchildren. In a surprisingly rapid sweep, all states now grant grandparents potential visitation. The content of these laws varies greatly, but the universal test goes to the *child's* best interest, *not* that of the grandparents.

Some states limit visitation to cases where the parent is deceased. Others specifically extend the grandparents' right to the case of divorce, annulment, or separation. The great majority hold that adoption by strangers preempts visitation, but several states hold that adoption by a stepparent is not enough to disallow visitation by grandparents. In 1983, the U.S. House of Representatives passed a resolution calling on the states to enact laws allowing visitation to grandparents.[91]

In 2000, the U.S. Supreme Court, in a conflicted and complex opinion, held that Washington's unusually broad grandparental visitation statute unconstitutionally interfered with a parent's right to raise his or her child.[92]

89. *Gordon v. Gordon*, 339 N.W.2d 269 (Minn. 1983).
90. *Griffin v. Griffin*, 699 P.2d 407 (Colo. 1985).
91. H.R. Res. 45, 98th Cong. (1983).
92. *Troxal v. Granville*, 530 U.S. 57, 120 S.Ct. 2054, 147 L.Ed.2d 49 (2000).

D. The Unwed Father's Custodial and Visitation Rights

Along with his support obligation, the *unwed* father's interest in his child has been recognized, if he is fit as a parent. He has been expressly granted visitation rights in many states. A number of U.S. Supreme Court and state court cases hold that where the father, the mother, and the child have lived in a *de facto* family setting, the father has potential custodial rights, including visitation.[93] The Uniform Putative and Unknown Fathers Act proposes statutory rules, but was enacted in only two states.

E. Custody and Kidnaping

Twenty years ago, encouraged by the non-final nature of child custody awards and the choice of 50-plus American jurisdictions, many noncustodial parents still "kidnaped" their child from the court-ordered custody of the other parent, taking the child to another state, to another court, for another ruling.

By adopting the Uniform Child Custody Jurisdiction Act (UCCJA), states accepted their long-neglected responsibility in this area. In 1980, Congress moved into the picture: The federal Parental Kidnapping Prevention Act (PKPA)[94] provides that a custodial adjudication carries "full faith and credit," if the rendering state had jurisdiction as defined in the federal law, largely paralleling the jurisdictional criteria set forth in the Uniform Act. This means that a custody adjudication in one state must be respected and enforced by all other states. Federal courts have taken jurisdiction, where previously they would have declined to do so on the basis of their long-standing refusal to get involved with "domestic relations." Beyond that, a federal "parent locator service," set up for the enforcement of child support, has been made available to aid in locating an abducting parent. Finally, if parental child-snatching is a felony in the state where it occurred – and most states have enacted felony statues to invoke this portion of the PKPA – the abducting parent is brought under the sweep of the Federal Fugitive Felon Act.

The PKPA has strengthened the hand of the custodial parent. No longer may a court in a state with a "significant connection" to the child modify an existing court order. The court that originally rendered the decree is the exclusive arbiter. Some commentators have regretted the considerable and, to the child, potentially harmful inflexibility brought along by the invocation of full faith and credit. *See* Chap. 17, pts. IV.A, C. Fine-tuning the relationship between federal and state law, the Commissioners on Uniform State Laws promulgated the Uniform Child Custody Jurisdiction and Enforcement Act in 1997 and, by 2000, that Act had been enacted in about 20 states.

93. *Michael H. v. Gerald D.*, 491 U.S. 110, 109 S.Ct. 2333, 105 L.Ed.2d 91 (1989); *Lehr v. Robertson*, 463 U.S. 248, 103 S.Ct. 2985, 77 L.Ed.2d 614 (1983).

94. 28 U.S.C. § 1738A (1994 & Supp. IV 1998) (as amended in 1998 to add visitation determinations).

F. The Hague Convention

The 1980 Hague Convention on the Civil Aspects of International Child Abduction has been implemented in the United States, along with some 50 other countries. The Convention is designed to facilitate the return of abducted children and the exercise of visitation rights across international boundaries. It is operating successfully in the United States, with numerous U.S. court decisions ordering the return of children abroad.[95]

X. Marriage or Legally Recognized Partnership of Same-Sex Couples

The current struggle over the meaning of "marriage" is reflected poignantly in the demand for marriage of hitherto excluded groups, particularly gays and lesbians. A rational analysis of what useful social functions are capable of being fulfilled by what unions, will quickly yield the answer that, in many particulars, rational law would not differentiate between unions solely on the basis of the partners' sexual orientation.[96] Rational law would differentiate only on the basis of actual differences in social functions that are or can be fulfilled by particular unions. True, in the child-rearing arena the controversy regarding "actual differences" gets hot, and that debate may best be left with citations to prominent exponents of both sides of the controversy.[97]

Several state legislatures have recently recognized same-sex partnerships as relationships with the potential of legal incidents. Varying marriage-like incidents are provided to partners, variously defined, under varying conditions. Same-sex partnerships increasingly are also being recognized in varying degrees by court decisions, by city ordinance, and by more or less voluntary actions by business and educational corporations. Indeed, Vermont's Supreme Court invoked recent laws of European countries in its pace-setting decision on Vermont's (newly discovered) constitutional requirement that same-sex partnership be offered the same legal rights as heterosexual marriage.[98]

A current glimpse of the American picture may be seen through the lenses of recent decisions of the supreme courts of Hawaii and Vermont. First, the Hawaii court ended a long period of suspense in December 1999 that had begun with a landmark decision in 1993 holding that the equality mandate in Hawaii's constitution required the recognition of same-sex marriage, unless the state could demon- strate

95. *Friedrich v. Friedrich*, 983 F.2d 1396 (6th Cir. 1993); *In re Prevot*, 855 F.Supp. 915 (W.D. Tenn. 1994); *Grimer v. Grimer*, 1993 WL 142695 (D. Kan. 14 Apr. 1993).
96. Harry D. Krause, "Marriage for the New Millennium: Heterosexual, Same Sex – Or Not at All?," 34 *Fam. L.Q.* 271, 276-79 (2000).
97. Lynn Wardle, "The Potential Impact of Homosexual Parenting on Children," 1997 *U. Ill. L. Rev.* 8330; Carlos Ball & Janice Pea, "Warring With Wardle: Morality, Social Science, and Gay and Lesbians Parents," 1998 *U. Ill. L. Rev.* 253; Lynn Wardle, "Fighting With Phantoms: A Reply," 1998 *U. Ill. L. Rev.* 629.
98. *Baker v. State*, 744 A.2d 864, 81 A.L.R.5th 627 (1999).

"that [the limitation of marriage to heterosexuals] furthers compelling state interests and is narrowly drawn to avoid unnecessary abridgments of constitutional rights."[99]

For a time, the court decision in Hawaii made gay hopes fly high. A shocked Hawaiian legislature, however, quickly reaffirmed through legislation that marriage would be reserved to heterosexual couples. But, intended perhaps more to preempt Hawaii's Supreme Court than to provide equality for gay couples, the legislature enacted near-equality by way of a same-sex partnership law that now provides many or most of the rights of marriage – but not the rite – to same-sex couples. Subsequently, the population of Hawaii voted to amend the Hawaiian Constitution to the effect that the legislature should decide whether to allow gay marriage – which essentially ratified what had already been done. Accordingly, by the time the case was finally re-reviewed by Hawaii's Supreme Court, the Hawaiian Constitution was no longer silent on the issue. The Court accordingly held that the specific conferral of legislative authority on this subject to the legislature made any further consideration of more general constitutional equality mandates moot.[100] It is worth noting, however, that the Hawaii court did not reach the question whether the partnership legislation enacted in Hawaii needed to be scrutinized under any general (Hawaiian) constitutional equality mandate.

Within days of Hawaii's final decision, the Vermont Supreme Court – at the opposite geographic and arguably demographic end of the United Sates – reignited the national debate with its decision in the *Baker* case, with many parallels to the Hawaii case. The Vermont court held:

> that the State is constitutionally required to extend to same-sex couples the common benefits and protections that flow from marriage under Vermont law. Whether this ultimately takes the form of inclusion within the marriage laws themselves or a parallel "domestic partnership" system or some equivalent statutory alternative, rests with the Legislature. Whatever system is chosen, however, must conform with the constitutional imperative to afford all Vermonters the common benefit, protection, and security of the law."[101]

It may seem eminently sensible to the observer from a civil law country that the Vermont court left it to the legislature to decide whether it wanted to implement the equality mandate by way of allowing same-sex couples to marry, or by way of providing equality with a new institution such as "domestic partnership." It cannot be overemphasized, however, that while such a show of deference to the legislative branch would be normal in European constitutional processes, it is very unusual for the American constitutional decision process. Far more typically, constitutional decisions in the United States either uphold or strike down legislative enactments, and let the "chips fall where they may."

If someone expected more from Vermont, she was disappointed. Vermont did not become the first state to allow marriage, as such, to same-sex couples. The leg-

99. *Baehr v. Lewin*, 74 Haw. 530, 852 P.2d 44, 68 (1993).
100. *Baehr v. Miike*, 92 Haw. 634, 994 P.2d 566 (1999).
101. *Baker v. State*, 744 A.2d 864, 867, 81 A.L.R.5th 627 (1999).

islature predictably followed its popular-political instincts and continued to limit marriage as such to heterosexual couples – but then proceeded to provide legal equality to same-sex couples by way of a domestic partnership law. The drafting of that law progressed amid considerable controversy and early political positioning indicated that the outcome would please neither the gay movement (which wants marriage, not partnership), nor the conservative opposition (which wants neither).[102] It now appears that most observers welcome the compromise the legislation struck.

Beyond state-level partnership legislation, heated debate continues whether gay marriage should be legalized. This debate is taking place at the state level – even while about one quarter of the 50 American states still criminalize same-sex conduct. Federal law strictly provides through the ineptly titled "Defense of Marriage Act" that, for purposes of federal law, only heterosexual marriage is to be recognized.[103] Many or most states provide the same by legislation or by having amended state constitutions.[104]

In 2000, California voted affirmatively on the much contested Proposition 22, stating: "Only marriage between a man and a woman is valid or recognized in California."[105] Despite excited controversy – a lead editorial in the *New York Times* labeled it "California's Poisonous Proposition" and a "divisive excise in wedge politics"[106] – the passing of that proposition merely meant that California joined some 30 other states that already had enacted similar laws or constitutional amendments – including Vermont.[107] In short, events at the federal level and in so many states – including California, Hawaii, and Vermont – show that full-status same-sex marriage is not yet on the United States' legal horizon, "poisonous wedge politics" or not.

As much, or more, than the right to marry, same-sex couples need a "right to divorce," in the sense of an orderly process to dissolve their *de facto* relationship. Issues that have come to the fore include the "routine" cohabitation case based on express or implied contract,[108] and range from intestate succession,[109] to taking over the lover's apartment after the latter's death under New York's rent control laws,[110] to the eligibility of a lesbian partner to act as legal guardian of her partner who suffered brain injury in an accident,[111] to a variety of child custody issues. In the latter arena, outcomes range from allowing the lesbian partner to

102. In 2000 Vermont's legislature enacted a detailed "civil union" statute to provide same-sex couples the opportunity to obtain the same benefits and protections afforded by Vermont law to married opposite-sex couples. Vt. Stat. Ann. tit. 15, § 1202 (2000).

103. 28 U.S.C. § 1738C (Supp. IV 1998).

104. *See* Harry D. Krause, "U.S. American Law on Same-Sex Marriage: Formal and Informal, Same-Sex and Heterosexual Cohabitation," in *Die Rechtsstellung gleichgeschlechtlicher Lebensgemeinschaften* 187 (Jürgen Basedow et al. eds., 2000).

105. *N.Y. Times*, 25 Feb. 2000, at A1.

106. *N.Y. Times*, 4 Mar. 2000, at A30.

107. In the very Act legalizing same-sex partnerships! *See supra* note 102.

108. *Van Brunt v. Rauschenberg*, 799 F.Supp. 1467 (S.D.N.Y. 1992).

109. *In re Petri*, *N.Y.L.J.*, 4 Apr. 1994 (no).

110. *Braschi v. Stahl Associates Co.*, 544 N.Y.S.2d 784, 543 N.E.2d 49 (1989) (yes).

111. *In re Guardianship of Kowalski*, 478 N.W.2d 790 (Minn.App. 1991) (yes).

adopt a child born to her lover,[112] to joint adoption of an unrelated child.[113] After the termination of such relationships, some courts have denied, and others allowed, visitation rights to a lesbian domestic partner.[114] Notably, custodial rights to a Dalmatian puppy were denied to a lesbian ex-lover where her ex-companion was the owner of record of the dog as well as of the apartment.[115]

If same-sex marriage is not in America's immediate future, it seems equally clear that broader legislation on "domestic partnership," extending to or specifically directed at, same-sex partners will soon become widespread. Such legislation will address a fuller range of specific, tangible concerns of same-sex couples by extending legal consequences that ultimately may be more or less equivalent to heterosexual marriage, as has now been the case in Vermont and to lesser degree in Hawaii. True, such legislation would not cede the crucial demand: Domestic partner legislation would not provide the full social and cultural legitimation of same-sex unions that same-sex marriage would provide. Precisely for that reason, however, such legislation avoids many of the political, cultural, and legal problems still associated with the proposal of extending "marriage" *qua* marriage to same-sex cohabitants.

Selected Bibliography

Homer H. Clark, Jr., *The Law of Domestic Relations in the United States* (2d ed. 1988).
Mary Ann Glendon, *Abortion and Divorce in Western Law* (1987).
—, *The Transformation of Family Law: State, Law, and Family in the United States and Western Europe* (1989).
John De Witt Gregory, Peter N. Swisher & Sheryl L. Scheible Wolf, *Understanding Family Law* (1993).
Joan Heifetz Hollinger et al., eds., 1-2 *Adoption Law and Practice* (1989 & Supp. 2000).
Harry D. Krause, *Black Letter on Family Law* (2d ed. 1996).
—, *Family Law in a Nutshell* (3d ed. 1995).
—, *Family Law: Cases, Comments, and Questions* (3d ed.1990).
Harry D. Krause, Linda D. Elrod, Marsha Garrison & J. Thomas Oldham, *Family Law: Cases, Comments, and Questions* (4th ed. 1998).

112. *Matter of Adoption of Evan*, 153 Misc.2d 844, 583 N.Y.S.2d 997 (Sur. 1992) (yes); In re *Interest of Angel Lace M.*, 184 Wis.2d 492, 516 N.W.2d 678 (1994) (no).
113. *Matter of Adoption of Jennifer R.C.*, 130 Misc.2d 461, 496 N.Y.S.2d 915 (Sur. 1985); *Petition of L.S. for Adoption of Minor T.*, 1991 WL 219598 (D.C. Super. 1991).
114. *Kulla v. McNulty*, 472 N.W.2d 175 (Minn. App. 1991); *Alison D. v. Virginia M.*, 569 N.Y.S.2d 586, 572 N.E.2d 27 (1991); *Sporleder v. Hermes (In re Interest of Z.J.H.)*, 162 Wis.2d 1002, 471 N.W.2d 202 (1991).
115. Rejecting also the ex-lover's claim for infliction of emotional harm, the court ordered her and her lawyer to pay $500 each to the dog's owner. *Malanga v. Godshein*, *N.Y.L.J.*, 30 June 1993.

Alexander Lindey & Louis I. Parley, eds., 1-2 *Separation Agreements and Antenuptial Contracts* (2d ed. 1998 & Supp. 2000).
Margaret M. Mahoney, *Stepfamilies and the Law* (1994).
J. Thomas Oldham & Marygold S. Melli, eds., *Child Support: The Next Frontier* (2000).
Milton C. Regan, Jr., *Alone Together: Law and the Meanings of Marriage* (1999).
Arnold H. Rutkin, ed., 1-6 *Family Law and Practice* (1986 & Supp. 2000).
Stephen D. Sugarman & Herma Hill Kay, eds., *Divorce Reform at the Crossroads* (1990).
John Tingley & Nicholas B. Svalina, eds., 1-3 *Marital Property Law* (rev. 2d ed. 1994 & Supp. 2000).

Chapter 12
Inheritance Law

Vivian Grosswald Curran[*]
William F. Fratcher[**]

* Associate Professor of Law, University of Pittsburgh School of Law.
** Late R.B. Price Distinguished Professor of Law Emeritus, University of Missouri (Columbia) School of Law; Reporter, Uniform Probate Code; General Reporter on Trust Law, 6 *International Encyclopedia of Comparative Law* ch. 11 (1973).

David S. Clark and Tuğrul Ansay (eds.) Introduction to the Law of the United States, 265-280

I. INTRODUCTION

A. Fifty-one Systems of Law

For inheritance purposes the United States consists of 51 autonomous jurisdictions, 50 states and the District of Columbia, each with its own legislature, courts, and independent system of law. All of these, except Louisiana, which has a code partly based on the French Civil Code of 1804, have received to some extent the law in force in England on some date between 1607, the year of the first permanent English settlement in North America, and 1792.

To bring more uniformity to the laws of so many jurisdictions, the governors of the states appoint commissioners who form the National Conference of Commissioners on Uniform State Laws. *See* Chap. 3, pt. V.B. This body drafts "uniform laws," such as the Uniform Probate Code, the Uniform Trustees' Powers Act, and the Uniform Principal and Income Act, with a view to their enactment in all of the states. A legislature of a particular state, such as New York, may choose not to enact a uniform act or to adopt it in a modified form, but the work of the National Conference has achieved some uniformity or, at least, similarity of state law.

B. Marital Rights

Under the English law in force in 1607, a husband was entitled to possession and the rents and profits of all lands of the wife and to ownership of all movables acquired by her before or during the marriage. Nineteenth century legislation in England and the American jurisdictions abolished these marital rights of the husband. Under the current law of England and most of the American jurisdictions, while both are alive, a spouse does not have an interest in property acquired by the other spouse. All property of each spouse is separate property unless it is conveyed to them as tenants by the entirety or as joint tenants, in which case on death the survivor takes the whole. The English law of separate property is in force in all but nine of the 51 United States jurisdictions.

Eight states in the United States have adopted from French and Spanish law the system of community property. Under this system, property acquired by a spouse during the marriage, other than by gift, devise (by will), or (intestate) descent, is owned by both spouses in equal shares. Property acquired before the marriage and that acquired by gift, devise, or descent is separate property. Income derived from separate property during the marriage is community property in Idaho, Louisiana, Texas, and Wisconsin. It is separate property in Arizona,

California, Nevada, New Mexico, and Washington. If the source of property is unclear there is a presumption that it is community property.

C. *Exempt Property and Allowances*

In all American jurisdictions some property does not pass at death by intestate succession or by will and is not subject to the claims of creditors. A surviving spouse and, if there is none, minor children, are usually entitled to exempt property, consisting of household goods and an automobile not exceeding a specified value, an allowance for a year's support, and a right either to occupy the family homestead or to receive a homestead allowance in land or money. The extent of these rights is usually determined by the court with jurisdiction over probate of wills. There is considerable variation among the jurisdictions as to the amounts allowed and as to how far such rights override the rules of intestate and testate succession. In small estates these rights may exhaust the estate and leave nothing for creditors, heirs, next of kin, devisees, and legatees. This is likely to be the case if the value of the property of the deceased person does not exceed the annual earnings of a typical factory worker.

II. Intestate Succession

A. *The English Common Law of Descent of Real Property*

In 1607 English law made a sharp distinction between real property, consisting of interests in land (including trees and buildings), other than those of tenants under leases for years or shorter periods, and personal property, consisting of movables and the interests of tenants under such leases of land. Immediately upon the death of a landowner who had not effectively disposed of it by will, his real property passed to his heir, subject to "dower," the right of his widow to a life interest in a third of all lands owned during the marriage. In the case of a female landowner, real property passed at death to her heir, subject if a live child had been born of the marriage to "curtesy," the right of the surviving husband to a life interest in the whole. The heir and the tenant in dower or by curtesy took without any judicial proceeding and, with minor exceptions, free of the debts of the deceased owner. A widow was entitled to occupy the dwelling house of the deceased for 40 days, during which time her dower was assigned.

The heir to real property was the eldest son, if living, and, if not, his eldest son. In the absence of a son or a descendant of a son, daughters took in equal shares. If the deceased landowner was not survived by descendants, his eldest brother of the whole blood was the heir, if living, and, if not, his eldest son. In the absence of such a brother or a descendant of such a brother, sisters of the whole blood or their descendants took. If there were no siblings or descendants of siblings, the eldest uncle who was related by blood to the ancestor from whom the deceased owner inherited the land, or his eldest son, was the heir. If there was no qualified uncle or descendant of an uncle, aunts of the blood of the ancestor took in equal shares. The eldest son of a deceased aunt took her share. More remote relatives could take but, as parents and grandparents could not, there might be no heir, in which case real property passed by escheat to the feudal overlord.

After 1285 much land was held in fee tail (usually created by a conveyance to one and the heirs *of his body*), in which case it could pass at death only to lineal heirs of the first taker. If a tenant in tail was not survived by lineal descendants of the first taker, the land passed to the creator of the estate tail or his heir or designee.

B. Distribution of Personal Property by the Ecclesiastical Courts

In 1607 distribution of personal property on death was supervised in England by the ecclesiastical courts. The court appointed an administrator (usually the widow or next of kin), who was to pay debts and distribute the balance. If a widow survived, she took a third and the children two thirds, the issue of a deceased child receiving that child's share. If no widow survived, the children took all in equal shares, the issue of a deceased child taking that child's share. If there was a widow but no descendants, the widow took half and the next of kin the other half. In the absence of widow and children, the administrator of the decedent's estate distributed to the next of kin, the persons related in the nearest degree of consanguinity to the intestate decedent, computed according to the rules of the Roman civil law. Parents were in the first degree, siblings and grandparents in the second, uncles, aunts, nieces, and nephews in the third. If there was no next of kin, personal property passed to the crown as *bona vacantia*. The rules were the same in the cases of widows and women who had never married. However, as all personal property of a married woman belonged to her husband, there was none to pass at her death.

C. American Systems of Intestate Succession

Although some 11 American jurisdictions have retained dower and curtesy, usually in a much modified form, all have abolished the English system of primogeniture and have applied to real property rules of intestate succession that are the same as or similar to those relating to personal property. Most have converted estates tail into estates in fee simple (which are alienable, devisable, and descendible on death to collateral heirs) or provided that a conveyance that would have created an estate tail under English law creates a life estate or interest in the transferee, with a contingent remainder (right to possession upon the death of the first taker) to his descendants, who take in fee simple.

The Uniform Probate Code, substantially adopted in its 1969 form in 16 states, with several more states adopting one or more of its subsequently enacted provisions, has influenced legislation in still other states. It abolishes dower and curtesy, treats real and personal property alike, and prescribes rules of intestate succession that are typical (§§ 2-101 to 2-114). Under these rules an administrator is appointed by the court with probate jurisdiction to collect the assets, pay debts, and distribute. The surviving spouse is entitled to distribution of the entire estate if there is no surviving issue or parent. If there is no issue but a parent or parents, the surviving spouse takes $200,000 plus three-fourths of the balance. If there are issue, all of whom are issue of the surviving spouse, that spouse takes the entire estate; if some of the issue are not issue of the surviving spouse, that spouse takes $100,000 and one-half of the balance. The Code provides that, in a community property state, the same rules apply to separate property but the surviving spouse takes all of the community property.

Under the Uniform Probate Code, property which does not pass to the surviving spouse passes to the children in equal shares, the issue of a deceased child to take that child's share. If there is no child, grandchildren take in equal shares, the issue of a deceased grandchild to take his share. If there are no descendants, the parents or parent take all. If there is no issue or parent, the issue of the parents take by representation. If there is no issue, parent, or issue of a parent, half of the estate passes to the paternal grandparents or grandparent or their issue and the other half to the maternal grandparents or grandparent or their issue. In the absence of a paternal or maternal grandparent or his issue, his half passes to the other grandparents or their issue. If there is no taker of the designated classes, all property passes to the state. To take by intestate succession under the Code, one must survive the intestate by 120 hours.

D. Persons Born out of Wedlock

Under the law in force in England in 1607, a child born out of wedlock was not related, for inheritance purposes, to his parents or their relatives. Marriage of the parents did not legitimate him. Hence he was no one's heir or kin and had no heir or next of kin unless he married and had legitimate children. The American jurisdictions have enacted legislation legitimating children born out of wedlock if the parents marry and permitting those who are not legitimated to inherit from and through the mother. In 1977 the Supreme Court of the United States decided that the U.S. Constitution requires the states to allow a child born out of wedlock to inherit from his father if a legitimate child could so inherit.[1] Some states have reduced the effect of this decision by making it difficult for a child born out of wedlock to establish paternity.

E. Inheritance by, from, and through Adoptees

In 1607 English law did not recognize adoption. All of the American states now permit it. In the 19th century an adoptee could inherit from his adoptive parents and they could inherit from him, but, except for that, the adoptee was deemed for inheritance purposes to be a member of his blood family, not that of the adoptive parents. The Uniform Probate Code (§ 2-109) and most states now treat an adoptee for inheritance purposes as a full member of the adoptive family and not

1. *Trimble v. Gordon*, 430 U.S. 762 (1977).

of his blood family. This occasions litigation in some cases. For example, if a son of T has died, the son's widow has remarried, and a child of the son has been adopted by his stepfather, a bequest in T's will to "my grandchildren" may require litigation to determine whether the adoptee takes as a grandchild of his former grandfather.

F. Criminal Homicide of Ancestors and Testators

An heir, next of kin, devisee, or legatee who intentionally and criminally kills the ancestor or testator forfeits his right to take. Most recent legislation on this point, for example, Uniform Probate Code section 2-803, imposes forfeiture whether or not there is a criminal conviction and provides that the property passes as if the killer had predeceased his victim.

G. Advancements

Under the English law of 1607, a substantial *inter vivos* gift to a child was treated as an advancement; that is, his share in personal property on intestacy would be reduced by the amount already received. Thus, if the father paid for one child's university education and not that of the others, the educated child might take nothing. Uniform Probate Code section 2-110 and other recent legislation would not treat a gift as an advancement affecting intestate succession unless the parent or the child characterized it as such in writing. Education in particular tends no longer to be deemed an advancement.

III. Trusts

A. Medieval Feoffments to Uses

Except as to certain lots in cities and large towns and certain lands in the County of Kent and the Principality of Wales, English law did not permit wills of real property between 1066 and 1540. By 1290 it was clear that a feudal tenant in fee simple, that is, one whose interest could descend on intestacy to collateral as well as lineal heirs, could transfer his interest *inter vivos* by "feoffment," a form of conveyance which involved a public ceremony on or near the land. A feudal tenant might not wish to have all of his land descend at death to his eldest son or *his* eldest son. In most cases he would not wish the land to escheat to his overlord. To achieve his wishes, he might "enfeoff," convey by feoffment, to a group of friends, or his lawyers, as "feoffees to uses," trustees, to hold land for the use of the "feoffor," transferor, during his lifetime and, upon his death, to transfer the land to (1) his wife or a daughter or younger son; or (2) such person as the feoffor should appoint by deed or will. By 1400 the English Court of Chancery was willing to compel such trustees to carry out the wishes of the feoffor. A 1535 statute made it possible to create such uses, since called "trusts," by delivery of a deed, without the public feoffment ceremony. It also entitled some trust beneficiaries to enforce their interests without a suit in the Court of Chancery. A "conveyance to uses" (upon trust) could not defeat dower without the cooperation of the feoffor's wife.

B. Later English Use of Trusts

English conveyancers used the trust as a will substitute for personal as well as real property. The father of a woman could defeat the marital rights of his son-in-law by conveying land or movables to trustees for the separate use of his daughter, free of any control by her husband, with a duty to convey upon her death to such persons as she might by deed or will appoint. Before abolition of the husband's marital rights in his wife's property in the 19th century, unless property was held in trust for her separate use, a married woman could not make a conveyance to uses (upon trust) without the cooperation of her husband.

C. The Trust as a Will Substitute in the United States

The use of the trust as a will substitute was relatively uncommon in the United States before the 20th century, but it is now frequently used by persons with substantial wealth. It commonly takes the form of a transfer of land or movables, or both, to a trustee or trustees, often a bank or trust company, upon trust to pay the income to the settlor (creator of the trust) for life, then to pay the income to his widow for life and, upon her death, to transfer the trust property to descendants as they come of age. *See* Chap. 10, pt. VIII. The settlor may and often does retain power to revoke, amend, or withdraw property. Such a trust has advantages over a will in avoiding publicity, probate (judicial proof of the will), and judicially supervised administration. The extent to which such a trust can override the rights of the widow and minor children to take household goods, support allowance, homestead, and a forced share varies from jurisdiction to jurisdiction and is a common subject of litigation. Such a trust is invalid to the extent that it is created in fraud of creditors.

D. Testamentary Trusts

To the extent that property is disposable by will, it may be devised and bequeathed to a trustee to manage, pay the income to designated beneficiaries until they reach a stipulated age or die, and then to distribute the property to them or to other designated beneficiaries. Although there is no requirement that trust beneficiaries be incapable of managing their property, such a testamentary trust may be used to provide for the management of property for persons who, because of minority, mental incapacity, or otherwise, are unable to manage it themselves, without the necessity of a guardian, tutor, conservator, or other court-appointed fiduciary. Trusts created by will are enforced in the same way as those created *inter vivos*, but some jurisdictions provide for more court supervision of such testamentary trusts than that required for trusts created *inter vivos*.

Roman law did not know trusts but it permitted fideicommissary substitutions, which served some of the purposes of testamentary trusts. Article 896 of the French Civil Code of 1804 prohibited substitutions. The Louisiana Civil Codes of 1808 (art. 40), 1825 (art. 1507), and 1870 (art. 1520) prohibited substitutions and did not permit trusts. Article 1520 was amended in 1962 to except interests under trusts from the prohibition on substitutions and Louisiana legislation now permits limited use of trusts.

E. Trust Beneficiaries and Purposes

To be enforceable, a trust must be for ascertainable human beneficiaries or a charitable purpose. The promotion of any religion with a substantial following is charitable. Charitable trusts may be enforced by the state attorney general. Trusts not benefitting an ascertainable person for non-charitable purposes are not enforceable but – at least in the cases of those for the erection of tombstones, the maintenance of graves, or the care of pet animals, limited in duration to 21 years – the trustee may carry them out if he is willing.[2]

F. Trustees

The trustee of a trust has *legal title* to the trust property (also known as the trust *res* or *corpus*). This means that the trustee can manage the property to the full extent permitted by the governing trust instrument. The trust beneficiaries, on the other hand, have an *equitable* interest in the property. Consequently, personal creditors of the trustee cannot reach the trust property.

G. The Rule against Perpetuities

Under the law in force in England in the 17th century, an interest under or following a trust was void if it might, by any possibility, vest in interest beyond lives in being and 21 years, plus any period of gestation involved, after the trust became irrevocable. An *inter vivos* trust is irrevocable from its creation unless the settlor reserves a power of revocation, in which case it becomes irrevocable at his death. A testamentary trust becomes irrevocable at the death of the testator, unless some living person is given a power to appoint the trust property to himself.

In order to be vested, an interest under or following a trust must be certain in extent, free from any condition precedent other than the termination of interests prior to it in time, and its holder must be in being and ascertained. Under 17th century law, in the case of a class gift, that is, a limitation of a future beneficial

2. See William F. Fratcher, "Bequests for Purposes," 56 *Iowa L. Rev.* 773 (1971).

interest to persons designated by a group name, such as "my grandchildren" or "the issue of the life beneficiary," the whole class gift was void if the interest of any possible member of the class might vest beyond the perpetuity period. This was because the extent of any member's interest was uncertain until the full membership of the class was known.

If a settlor created an *irrevocable inter vivos* trust limiting future beneficial interests to "my grandchildren, whenever born, in equal shares," all of the interests were void, even if the settlor had four living grandchildren when he created the trust and none was born thereafter. Viewing the possibilities existing when the trust was created, the settlor might have had children born after the creation of the trust, who themselves might have had children, grandchildren of the settlor, born more than 21 years after the death of the survivor of the settlor and all of his descendants in being when the trust was created. This limitation would be valid in a revocable *inter vivos* trust or a will because the settlor could not have children born more than the period of gestation after his death. Similarly, if the terms of an *irrevocable inter vivos* trust limited beneficial interests to "whatever woman may be my widow, so long as she shall live, then to my descendants in being at her death" the interests of the descendants were wholly void, even though the woman who became his widow was his wife when the trust was created and his descendants at her death were all in being at that time. The settlor might have married a woman who was not in being when he created the trust and his descendants could not have been ascertained until her death, which might be more than 21 years after the settlor's death. These dispositions also would be valid in a revocable *inter vivos* trust or a will because the settlor's widow, if any, must necessarily have been in being and ascertainable at the time of his death.

The rule against perpetuities as applied in England in the 17th and 18th centuries has been thought by some to be unduly severe, sometimes striking down dispositions which do not tie up property for very long. Recent years have seen substantial reforms of the traditional rule against perpetuities. The three approaches to reform that have been adopted by various states are (1) *cy pres*; (2) wait-and-see; and (3) total abolition of the rule.

Under the *cy pres* approach, courts will reform property interests that violate the rule against perpetuities so as to prevent the violation, while still giving as much effect as possible to the testator's intent. Under the wait-and-see approach, the rule against perpetuities ceases to be a rule of proof. In other words, a property interest will be invalidated only when it in fact violates the rule, rather than *ab initio*, merely because it *might* violate the rule at some future time. Most states have adopted one version of the wait-and-see approach. The Uniform Statutory Rule Against Perpetuities (enacted in 1986, amended in 1990) also endorses wait-and-see. Finally, a few states have abolished the rule against perpetuities completely. Other states have abolished, or are considering abolishing it, with respect to trusts of personal property.[3]

3. For the view that the rule against perpetuities is unlikely to survive in the United States, *see* Jesse Dukeminier, "The Uniform Statutory Rule Against Perpetuities: Ninety Years in Limbo," 34 *UCLA L. Rev.* 1023 (1987).

IV. Wills

A. The Form of Wills of Real Property

An English statute of 1540 permitted the devise of real property by written will. A 1676 statute required that such a will be signed by the testator, or by some person in his presence and by his direction, and subscribed in the presence of the testator by three or more attesting witnesses. Similar formal requirements are prescribed in the American jurisdictions which received English law, but most have reduced the number of subscribing witnesses to two and some 20 permit unwitnessed wills which are all in the handwriting of the testator. In some the witnesses must be persons who take no benefit under the will. Proof of due execution is required for admission to probate but, in the absence of contest, this may be made in a number of jurisdictions by an affidavit of due execution executed by the testator and the witnesses before a notary public.

B. Women's Wills of Real Property

Under English law marriage revoked a woman's will of real property and, until the 19th century, a married woman could not make such a will. Nineteenth century legislation in England and all the American jurisdictions permitted married women to make wills devising land.

C. Testaments of Personal Property in English Ecclesiastical Courts

The English colonies in North America were deemed to be in the ecclesiastical diocese of London. In 1607 the English ecclesiastical courts would admit to probate both oral and written testaments of personal property (movables and interests of tenants under leases of land for years) upon proof by two witnesses. A written testament did not need to be signed by the testator or the witnesses. A testament ordinarily named an executor to collect the assets, pay debts, and distribute in accordance with the testament; if it did not, the court would appoint an administrator *cum testamento annexo* to perform these functions. As all personal property acquired by a married woman belonged to her husband, she had nothing to bequeath by will. In the Diocese of London, if a male testator was survived by wife and children, he could dispose of a third of his personal property by will; a third passed to the widow and a third to the children by way of forced share or legitim. If he had only a wife or only children, he could bequeath half of his personal property; the other half passed to the wife or children by way of forced share or legitim.[4]

4. *See* William F. Fratcher, "Protection of the Family against Disinheritance in American Law," 14 *Int'l & Comp. L.Q.* 293 (1965); see also William Dickson Macdonald, *Fraud on the Widow's Share* 54-58 (1960).

D. Forced Share of the Surviving Spouse

Although some states permit oral wills of small amounts of personal property, the requirements for bequeathing personal property by will are the same in most American jurisdictions as those for devising real property. In nearly all of the jurisdictions that have abolished dower and curtesy, which could not be defeated by will, and in some that have not, the surviving spouse is entitled to a share in both real and personal property which cannot be defeated by will.

Under the Uniform Probate Code, in force in some 19 states, and typical of most, the surviving spouse may elect against the augmented estate (§ 2-202). The augmented estate is computed by subtracting from the property owned by the testator at his death the aggregate of his debts, the homestead allowance, the exempt property (household goods and automobiles), and the family allowance (for a year's support of the surviving spouse and minor children). To the remainder thus calculated is added, first, the value of property which the testator gave *inter vivos* to the surviving spouse, including the proceeds of insurance on the testator's life, beneficial interests under trusts, survivor benefits under annuities and pension plans, and survivorship rights under joint tenancies and tenancies by the entirety. Second, the value of property given by the testator to other persons during the marriage is also added to the remainder: (1) if the testator retained the right to possession or income during his lifetime; (2) if the testator retained a power to revoke, consume, invade, or dispose; (3) if the testator retained a right of survivorship under a joint tenancy; or (4) the gift was made within two years of death to the extent that it exceeded $3,000 (§§ 2-202, 2-204, 2-205). The Uniform Probate Code allots to the surviving spouse an elective share percentage based on the length of the surviving spouse's marriage to the decedent (§ 2-202(a)).

The State of Maine, instead of prescribing forced shares of a fixed percentage of the estate, empowers the court to grant a surviving spouse or dependent minor child an allowance from the estate. The Maine courts consider the property and needs of the widow and whether she helped the testator to accumulate his wealth. The Maine statutes, enacted between 1821 and 1871, are similar to family maintenance legislation enacted in Australia, Canada, England, and New Zealand in the 20th century.

E. Other Restrictions on Dispositions by Will

In a few jurisdictions, devises and bequests to charity in wills executed shortly before death are ineffective; some limit the proportion of the estate which may be devised or bequeathed to charity. The latter type of restriction usually applies only to a testator survived by designated relatives. There has in the past been legislation restricting the amount of property which particular charitable organizations may hold, but most of this has been repealed. A few jurisdictions limit devises and bequests to mistresses and illegitimate children. Devises and bequests to persons whose subscription as witnesses was necessary to the validity of the will are void in some jurisdictions, but not under the Uniform Probate Code (§ 2-505). No American jurisdiction permits a person who dies before the testator to take under his will. Such a devise or bequest is said to lapse. Under the Uniform Probate Code, a devisee or legatee who dies within 120 hours after the testator cannot take unless the will makes provision for this (§ 2-601). The Code provides that, if the devisee or legatee is a grandparent of the testator or a descendant of a grandparent, the devise or legacy passes to the issue of the devisee or legatee (§ 2-605). All American jurisdictions have such "anti-lapse" statutes, but they differ as to which devisees and legatees are covered and as to the persons who take if a devisee or legatee dies before the testator. If no anti-lapse statute applies to a lapsed devise or bequest, the property ordinarily passes as if the language giving the devise or legacy had not been in the will.

F. Contracts to Make Wills

Contracts to devise or bequeath property by will, to refrain from doing so, to revoke a will, or not to revoke it, are valid. Those which relate to real property are usually required to be in writing and signed by the promisor, but attesting witnesses are not required. A contract not to revoke is most often found to exist when two persons, usually husband and wife, sign a single joint will or mutual and reciprocal wills. If such a contract exists and is breached, persons taking under a will or by intestacy may be obliged to surrender the property to the promisee.[5] Such contracts tend not to be favored by the courts. A tension persists between the doctrine of permitting a testator to revise his will until his dying day and the contractual right to benefit from an agreed upon promise.

G. Revocation of Wills

The English statute of 1676 permitted total or partial revocation of wills by another will or codicil, executed in the manner prescribed for a will, "or by burning, canceling, tearing or obliterating the same by the testator himself, or in his presence and by his directions and consent." Some American jurisdictions have retained this statute. Under it, it is usually held that marriage revokes a woman's will and that marriage plus birth of issue revokes that of a man. Some do not permit total or partial revocation by cancellation. The Uniform Probate Code permits revocation "by a subsequent will which revokes the prior will or part expressly or by inconsistency; or by being burned, torn, canceled, obliterated, or destroyed, with the intent and for the purpose of revoking it by the testator or by another person in his presence and by his direction" (§ 2-507). It further provides that divorce or annulment revokes provisions in favor of the former spouse (§ 2-804). Under the Code, neither marriage nor marriage plus birth of issue revokes; the reason being that the Code itself provides an intestate share for a spouse married or child born after the execution of the will, when other provision for such spouse or child has not been made (§§ 2-301, 2-302, 2-508).

5. See Bertel M. Sparks, *Contracts to Make Wills: Legal Relations Arising Out of Contracts to Devise or Bequeath* (1956).

H. Renunciation by Heirs, Devisees, Next of Kin, and Legatees

Under the English law in force in 1607 an heir or devisee of real property was unable to renounce succession because title passed to him at the moment of death. A next of kin or legatee of personal property could renounce because title did not reach him until the administrator or executor distributed. The American jurisdictions have enacted legislation permitting heirs, devisees, next of kin, and legatees to renounce. The Uniform Probate Code provisions are typical. An heir, devisee, next of kin, or legatee entitled to a present interest may renounce by filing an instrument in court within nine months after the death of the intestate or testator; one entitled to an interest to become possessory in the future may do so within nine months after his interest becomes certain and indefeasible, which will usually be when he is entitled to immediate possession. The property passes as if the person renouncing had predeceased the intestate or testator (§ 2-801). The motive for the renunciation is usually immaterial. It may be to reduce taxes, to defeat creditors, or to bar access by a spouse.

I. Will Substitutes

The *inter vivos* trust was developed as a will substitute in England in the 13th century and it is still used for this purpose there and in the United States. Legal future interests could serve the purpose, especially after the recognition of contingent remainders about 1500. A landowner could convey to a straw party, who would convey back to the former landowner for life, with remainder in fee simple to a particular child or to all his children. This is still possible but not used very frequently. Other will substitutes have become common in the present century.

Designations of beneficiaries under life insurance policies, annuity contracts, and retirement plans are enforced without question. Joint bank accounts payable to either or to the survivor have served this purpose in some jurisdictions. Recent legislation in many American jurisdictions permits the holding of land, bonds, corporate stock, bank accounts, and other specific assets in the name of the holder "transfer on death to Jane Stiles." It is likely that there will be much litigation to determine how far such devices can be used to defeat a homestead allowance, exempt property, family allowance, and forced shares. They are not likely to be effective to defeat creditors whose claims exist at the time of designation of beneficiary, but they certainly may impede creditors, whenever their claims arise.

J. Probate and Contest of Wills

In England in 1607 the executor named in a testament of personalty presented it and his sworn statement that the testator was dead and that this was his will to the ecclesiastical court with jurisdiction. If the estate was large, this was usually the Prerogative Court of the Archbishop of Canterbury. The court would then admit the will to probate in common form. The executor was required to swear that he would account and, in some cases, to provide a bond to do so. Anyone who would benefit from revocation of probate could file a caveat. This would vacate the probate in common form and require the executor to prove the will in solemn form by the testimony of the attesting witnesses. The caveat or will contest might be based on allegations that the instrument was a forgery, that it was not executed in the manner prescribed by law, that the testator lacked testamentary capacity, or that the will was procured by fraud, duress, undue influence, or mistake. The widow and next of kin were cited to attend the proof in solemn form. The executor could not maintain actions against persons who held property of the testator or owed him money without a certificate of probate. Probate of a will of real property was not required. It could be proved in a court of common law.

Ecclesiastical courts never had probate jurisdiction in the American colonies. The 51 American jurisdictions lodge probate jurisdiction either in a special court (for example, in New York the surrogate's court; in Pennsylvania the orphans' court) or in a division of the trial court of general jurisdiction and expand it to include wills of real property and power to order the sale of real property to pay debts. Some permit only solemn form probate, that is, proof by the attesting witnesses after notice to interested parties. In such a jurisdiction, a will is contested in the initial proceeding for probate. The Uniform Probate Code (§§ 3-302 to 3-311, 3-401 to 3-414) and many states permit both common form and solemn form probate. In some the contest is an appeal from the decree of probate to a superior court. If an issue of fact is involved in a will contest, there is ordinarily a right to trial by jury.

V. Administration of Decedents' Estates

In England in 1607 real property passed to the heir or testamentary devisee at the moment of death and there was no need for judicial proceedings unless someone chose to contest the title of the heir or devisee. If no executor or next of kin sought administration, a creditor might seek appointment as administrator in order to get his claim paid. Personal property passed to the executor or administrator, who could sue in the ordinary courts to collect the assets and debts due the decedent. The executor or administrator then paid the debts of the decedent. A creditor could sue him in the ordinary courts. When the assets were collected and the debts paid, the executor or administrator transferred the remaining assets to the legatees or next of kin, whose title was based on the transfer made by the executor or administrator.

In England there were, ordinarily, no proceedings in the ecclesiastical court after the executor secured probate or the administrator letters of administration. In theory, he was supposed to account to the ecclesiastical court but he usually did not do so unless a creditor, legatee, or next of kin had him cited to do so. It was, and is, possible for the executor or administrator or someone else with an interest to commence a suit in the Court of Chancery (now the Chancery Division of the High Court of Justice) for a supervised administration of the estate. Suppose, for example, the assets were worth £100,000 and the executor had a hundred actions commenced against him in the ordinary courts for debts owed by the deceased aggregating £300,000. In such a case, the executor would do well to commence such a suit in

Chancery and secure an injunction against prosecution of the creditors' actions and an order requiring the creditors to file their claims in the Chancery. After that, the executor would not pay money or distribute assets without an order from the Chancery. Such a supervised administration has always been rare in England.[6]

During the 19th century a number of states, most of them located near the Mississippi River, imposed a requirement of supervised administration of all estates of decedents. An executor or administrator could not commence litigation, pay a claim against the estate, sell an asset, or distribute without an order of the probate judge. In that century probate judges were not lawyers and executors and administrators could apply to them directly. During the 1930s, lawyers' organizations secured legislation or rulings making only lawyers eligible to be probate judges and requiring executors and administrators to employ lawyers to request orders from a probate judge. If, when a pig was ready for market, the executor had to pay a lawyer $100 to secure an order from the judge authorizing sale of the pig for $30, the estate could not be administered economically. Most states, including those which have adopted the Uniform Probate Code (§ 3-501), now permit unsupervised administration unless there is special reason for requiring supervision.

Upon appointment, an executor or administrator must first see that known creditors of the decedent are notified by mail and others by publication in a newspaper of his appointment and warned that they must file claims against the estate within a stated period.[7] If the executor or administrator does not pay a claim, the claimant may sue him in the ordinary courts or seek allowance of his claim by the probate court. In either event, the executor or administrator need only pay with estate funds; he is not personally liable for the decedent's debts. As a practical matter, tort claimants (for example, persons injured in an automobile collision) usually prefer a jury trial in the ordinary courts; contract claimants tend to be satisfied with allowance by the probate court.

The executor or administrator has a duty to collect the assets of the decedent, if necessary by judicial proceedings against persons holding property of the decedent and persons who owed him money. Such proceedings may be conducted in the ordinary courts and, in some states, also in the probate court.

When the assets have been collected and the debts paid, a supervised executor or administrator files a final account with the court and secures a decree of distribution of the estate in accordance with the will or the intestate laws. When he has distributed, he is formally discharged by the court. An unsupervised executor or administrator does not have to seek such court action but many do, especially if the estate includes real property, because the judicial decree of distribution may be recorded in the land records and serve as a muniment of title to the land. Uniform Probate Code sections 3-1002 and 3-1003 provide for both methods of closing an estate.

6. See William F. Fratcher, "Fiduciary Administration in England," 40 *N.Y.U. L. Rev.* 12, 72 (1965); see also Sir E.V. Williams, *Williams on Executors and Administrators* 396, 746-48, 779, 860, 862, 1146-67 (George Williams Keeton ed., 14th ed. 1960).
7. Uniform Probate Code section 3-801 (providing for notice) and section 3-803 (barring claims not presented within the statutory period).

Before 1969 it was doubtful in most states whether it was possible to secure probate of a will without administration. In the absence of administration, heirs or devisees of a deceased landowner might not be able to secure clear and merchantable title to the land without open, notorious, hostile, and adverse possession for 20 years or some other long period. Under the Uniform Probate Code, probate of a will need not be followed by administration. The heirs, devisees, legatees, and next of kin own the property of the decedent, subject only to the rights of the surviving spouse or minor children to exempt property, family allowance, and homestead allowance (§§ 3-101, 3-901). In some cases a judicial proceeding to determine heirs and next of kin may be necessary to ensure their having merchantable title.

Selected Bibliography

Thomas Edgar Atkinson, *Handbook of the Law of Wills and Other Principles of Succession: Including Intestacy and Administration of Decedents' Estates* (2d ed. 1953).

George Gleason Bogert, George Taylor Bogert & Amy Morris Hess, 1-23 *The Law of Trusts and Trustees* (2d rev. ed. 1984-1999).

George T. Bogert, *Trusts* (6th ed. 1987).

William J. Bowe & Douglas H. Parker, 1-8 *Page on the Law of Wills* (1960-1965 & Jeffrey A. Schoenblum ed., Supp. 2000).

William F. Fratcher, "Trust," in 6 *International Encyclopedia of Comparative Law* (Property and Trust) ch. 11 (Athanassios N. Yiannopoulos ed. 1973).

John H. Langbein & Lawrence W. Waggoner, *Selected Statutes on Trusts and Estates* (2000).

William M. McGovern, Jr., Sheldon F. Kurtz & Jan Ellen Rein, *Wills, Trusts and Estates, Including Taxation and Future Interests* (1988).

Austin Wakeman Scott & William Franklin Fratcher, 1-12 *The Law of Trusts* (4th ed. 1987-1991 & Mark L. Ascher ed., Supp. 1999).

Thomas L. Shaffer & Carol Ann Mooney, *The Planning and Drafting of Wills and Trusts* (4th ed. 2000).

Chapter 13
Commercial Transactions

John C. Reitz
*Jonathan Carlson**

I. The Uniform Commercial Code

In the United States, the subject of commercial transactions is generally considered to be first and foremost the area covered by the Uniform Commercial Code ("UCC" or "Code"). The Code governs such matters as the sale of goods, drafts, checks, promissory notes, letters of credit, bills of lading, warehouse receipts, and security interests in movable property, and this chapter will deal primarily with these subjects.

While at first blush, the Code may appear an odd assemblage of unrelated subjects, it has a practical and conceptual unity. From the practical viewpoint, the Code unites rules dealing with all aspects of the sale of goods, including not only rules relevant to the sale itself, but also those governing payment for the goods

* Professors of Law, University of Iowa College of Law. We would like to thank our colleague Pat Bauer for his helpful comments on this revision for the second edition.

David S. Clark and Tuğrul Ansay (eds.) Introduction to the Law of the United States, 281-309

(drafts, checks, promissory notes, and letters of credit), transport and storage of the goods (bills of lading and warehouse receipts), and the financing of the sale through secured credit (security interests). Conceptually, the Code deals with contract and property rights concerning property other than real estate. For example, the Code governs the creation and transfer of contract and property rights in goods through the contracts of sale or lease and the creation and transfer of the property interests known as "security interests" in most kinds of non-real estate. Much of the Code is concerned with the priority of conflicting property claims in movable property. The Code also deals at length with the particular rights one can acquire in special documentary forms of property like commercial paper (drafts, checks, and promissory notes), letters of credit, or documents of title (warehouse receipts and bills of lading). *See* Chap. 10, pts. V, VI.

Like the Holy Roman Empire, however, which in Voltaire's witticism was neither holy, nor Roman, nor an empire, the Uniform Commercial Code has not produced uniform law, nor does it cover many subjects other legal cultures commonly consider to be part of commercial law, nor is it truly a code in the sense with which that word is used in many other legal systems. A short explanation of each of these three points provides a useful introduction to this subject.

First, the Code is state law. The federal Congress has enacted the UCC only for the District of Columbia, so there is no one version of the law for the entire United States. While the American Law Institute (ALI) and the National Conference of Commissioners on Uniform State Laws (NCCUSL) jointly proposed the UCC as a model law for state legislatures, each state enactment may differ on some points, including some important provisions. *See* Chap. 3., pts. V.A, B. On some points, the drafters anticipated disagreement among the states and included alternative provisions in the Official Draft. Nevertheless, the UCC has been one of the most successful attempts to harmonize state law. Every state in the Union has enacted a version of the UCC. Only Louisiana's version omits Article 2 on sales of goods in favor of its own codification on that subject closer to its civil law roots.

The uniformity of the state enactments has also been diminished by a series of amendments to the uniform model act itself. The oldest Official Draft which was widely adopted was the 1962 Official Draft, and since then significant revisions to the model act have come in 1972, 1977, 1987, 1990, 1995, and 1999. These revisions have been adopted by most, but not all, states.

Second, the UCC's scope differs from the scope of commercial codes in most other legal systems. On the one hand, unlike the commercial law codes of many countries, the UCC is not limited in its application to merchants. Thus, for example, the Code's rules on sales of goods apply to all sales of goods regardless of the identity of the buyer and seller, though certain provisions impose special rules for merchants. On the other hand, the UCC does not purport to cover many subjects of commercial importance which in other legal systems are thought to occupy central positions in the field of commercial law, such as the rules for corporations, business competition, insurance, and bankruptcy. Furthermore, the Code drafters wished to avoid the controversy that might be engendered by consumer protection provisions. The Code consequently contains very few measures specifically designed to protect the consumer. For such rules, one must look outside the UCC at other state and federal statutes. There is, for example, a Uniform

Consumer Credit Code (UCCC), which has provided the basis for legislation in 11 states, and a federal Consumer Credit Protection Act,[1] as well as Federal Trade Commission (FTC) regulations covering consumer credit.[2] Sales of goods to consumers are also covered by the federal Magnuson-Moss Warranty – Federal Trade Commission Improvement Act and FTC regulations issued under that authority.[3]

Third, the UCC is a far less systematic codification than many civil law codifications. Basic terms are left undefined. For example, the Code leaves "voidable title," which is crucial to the rule in section 2-403 protecting certain good faith purchasers of goods, to be defined by the common law. Basic rules are left unstated, such as the rule that a security interest is terminated by the debtor's timely payment of the debt. The "open-textured" nature of the Code is further highlighted by section 1-103, which provides that the "principles of law and equity" supplement the provisions of the UCC "[u]nless displaced by the particular provisions [of the UCC]." Unlike many civil law codifications, which represent an effort to state most or virtually all of the rules for a given subject without reference to prior law, the UCC is expressly limited to stating some of the rules for the commercial subjects it addresses, leaving the rest to be filled in by the courts in reliance on the common law, including pre-Code case law.

Each of these features of the Code is affected by the complex federal-state relationship in the United States. Under the supremacy clause of the Constitution, state law like the UCC is subordinate to conflicting federal law. Under the Constitution's commerce clause, Congress has wide power to promulgate federal commercial law and thereby preempt most, if not all, of the UCC, but Congress has traditionally left this area to the states. *See* Chap. 4, pt. VI.B. However, in recent years federal law has begun to encroach on this preserve of state power to an ever greater extent. Federal legislation and regulations in this area have thus started to impose greater uniformity on the commercial law applicable in each state. Furthermore, federal preemption determines the scope of the UCC. For example, the federal Bankruptcy Act[4] largely relies on state law to determine when secured creditors have priority over other creditors. But when Congress has not liked the results under the UCC, it has not hesitated to dictate a different rule. Thus, like common law principles and state consumer legislation, federal law constitutes an important source of law outside the Code which must be consulted in resolving problems apparently within the scope of the UCC. *See* Chap. 3, pt. I. This includes federal treaty law, which may preempt state commercial law in international transactions. For example, the United States has ratified the U.N. Convention on Contracts for the International Sale of Goods. To the extent that treaty applies by its terms to a transaction, it will displace Article 2 of the UCC, unless the parties have agreed otherwise.

The Code's genesis as a model state law, drafted by non-legislators but adopted into law by the state legislatures, poses one additional source of law problem: What is the authority of the Official Comments, which the American Law Institute

1. 15 U.S.C. §§ 1601-1693r (1994 & Supp. IV 1998).
2. 16 C.F.R. §§ 444.1-444.5 (2000).
3. 15 U.S.C. §§ 2301-2312 (1994); 16 C.F.R. pts. 700-703 (2000).
4. 11 U.S.C. §§ 101-1330 (1994 & Supp. IV 1998).

and the National Conference of Commissioners on Uniform State Laws have appended to each of the provisions of the Official Draft of the UCC? Many of these Comments provide helpful guidance in interpreting the UCC, especially by giving examples or explaining the commercial context of the rules. Some of the Comments, however, suggest interpretations of the provisions that are unsupported by the statutory text or even arguably contrary to the language of the statute. It is clear that in the event of a true conflict the statute has to take precedence over the Official Comment because the Official Comments have not been adopted by the state legislatures. It is equally clear that the courts tend to accept guidance from the Official Comments on doubtful points. They have the authority at least of a respected treatise or commentary because they are promulgated by the prestigious body which promulgated the model act. But the courts have also on occasion rejected the Official Comments on the grounds that they are misguided on the particular point. The situation is further complicated by the fact that the Official Comments have from time to time been amended even with regard to UCC sections that were not being changed. The lawyer working with the UCC therefore must pay attention to the Official Comments, but cannot accept them as definitive authority for interpreting the UCC without further research.

The Permanent Editorial Board (PEB) for the UCC, which was established by the American Law Institute and the National Conference of Commissioners on Uniform State Laws to monitor the need for amendments to the UCC, began in the 1990s issuing PEB commentaries on issues that have vexed the courts. These commentaries are published as an appendix to the Official Draft of the UCC, and the conclusions of the PEB commentaries usually, but not always, are reflected in amendments to the Official Comments. The courts are likely to treat the PEB commentaries and their associated amendments to the Official Comments as especially authoritative though they are not formally binding.

The current version of the UCC at this writing is the 1999 Official Text of the UCC, which contains 11 articles as the major divisions. The balance of this chapter will deal in some detail with Article 1 (general provisions), Article 2 (sales of goods), Articles 3 and 4 (negotiable instruments, including drafts, checks, and promissory notes), and Article 9 (security interests in personal property) because they are the most important parts of the Code and are enacted everywhere in the United States except Louisiana, as noted above. The following paragraphs briefly summarize the subject matter of the other articles and the status of their enactments as of early 2001.[5]

Article 2A covers leases of goods. It was finalized in 1987, amended in 1990, and has been adopted in one of its two versions by 47 states. Article 4A concerns wire transfers of funds. It was proposed in 1989 and has been adopted by all 50 states.

5. Many of the Articles of the Code and related model acts mentioned below or elsewhere in this chapter have also been adopted by the District of Columbia, Puerto Rico, or the U.S. Virgin Islands, but for the sake of simplicity the state adoption counts given in this chapter do not include them.

Article 5 deals with letters of credit and was substantially revised in 1995 to provide for explicit recognition of international standards of practice affecting letters of credit. As a result, international standards like the Uniform Customs and Practice for Documentary Credits (UCP) of the International Chamber of Commerce (ICC) will govern the particulars of many letter of credit transactions covered by revised Article 5. As of 2001, revised Article 5 had been adopted by 48 states, including New York, which is the most important state for international letters of credit.

Article 6 gives special rights to the unsecured creditors of a seller who sells a major part of its inventory (a "bulk sale"). Article 6 had been generally adopted except by Louisiana. In 1989, the sponsors of the UCC recommended repeal of Article 6 and, in the alternative, proposed major amendments. Four states have now enacted the revised Article 6 and 42 states have repealed Article 6 altogether. Legislatures in a few other states are considering the matter.

Article 7 deals with documents of title (warehouse receipts and bills of lading). It has also generally been enacted. Federal law intrudes substantially into Article 7 because the Federal Bills of Lading or Pomerene Act[6] preempts Article 7 for exports and interstate shipments.

Article 8 applies to the transfer of corporate securities. This article has also been generally adopted but was substantially revised in 1977 and 1994. Revised Article 8 (1994) has now been almost universally adopted. Further significant changes to Article 8 were made in connection with the 1999 revision of Article 9 (*see* pt. V), but those changes are not yet in effect. Articles 10 and 11 provide rules for the repeal of pre-Code statutes and for transition to the 1962 and 1972 versions of the UCC, respectively.

II. Article 1: General Provisions

The provisions of Article 1 are generally applicable to any transaction which is subject to any of the other articles of the UCC. It has therefore been subject to no wholesale revision, but has been amended to conform to amendments of other articles. Article 1 of the UCC does not approach the abstract nature of the "general part" of codes drafted in the style of the German Civil Code. Rather, Article 1 contains a number of rules and definitions that govern the specific rules in the other articles.

Perhaps most important are the definitions of terms set forth in 46 subparts of section 1-201. These range from statements of the obvious (§ 1-201(33): "'Purchaser' means a person who takes by purchase") to intricate rules that attempt to give a very precise meaning to specific terms, such as the elaborate definition of "value" in section 1-201(44) or the definition of "buyer in the ordinary course of business" (§ 1-201(9)). Perhaps the most elaborate and surprising definition is that of "security interest" in section 1-201(37), which in the 1999 Official Text covers over one printed page and includes 12 subparts. Under the guise of a definition the section sets forth an elaborate test for distinguishing true leases, which are subject to Article 2A, from disguised security interests, which are subject to Article 9.

6. 49 U.S.C. §§ 80101-80116 (1994).

Caution is required, however, even with this seemingly simple aspect of the Code because specific articles apply their own, different definitions to some terms. Thus, for example, section 1-201(19) sets forth a generally applicable, subjective definition of "good faith" ("honesty in fact"), but Article 2 imposes a higher standard on merchants in section 2-103 ("honesty in fact and the observance of reasonable commercial standards of fair dealing in the trade"). The 1990 revision to Article 3 (§ 3-103(4)) also applies the objective ("commercially reasonable") standard of good faith to holders of negotiable instruments, despite the longstanding tradition, reflected in the older version of Article 3, that holders of commercial paper were held only to the standard of subjective good faith. The proposed revision of Article 9 also adopts an objective standard of good faith (§ 9-102 (a)(43)).

So too, section 3-303 narrows the general definition of "value" set forth in broad terms in section 1-201(44). The Article 3 definition excludes executory promises for purposes of determining who has given value sufficient to merit the specially protected status of a good faith purchaser for value of negotiable instruments under Articles 3 and 4. But Article 4 eliminates the Article 3 variation for banks, so that a bank is deemed to have given value with respect to commercial paper to the extent it has bound itself to extend credit to the depositor (§§ 4-210, 4-211).

In addition, each of the other UCC articles contains definitions, especially at the outset of each article, so one cannot assume that terms not defined in section 1-201 are not defined elsewhere. Nevertheless, a good working rule in interpreting a Code section is to check section 1-201 first to see if any of the terms are specially defined. The Official Comments provide a helpful reference after each code section to most of the applicable definitions in the Code.

Section 1-103's incorporation of all pre-Code commercial law to the extent not displaced by the UCC has already been mentioned. The two other most important features of Article 1 are its rules on course of dealing and usage of trade and on good faith. Section 1-205 provides that in interpreting any agreement between two parties, the parties' previous course of dealing with each other as well as usages of the trade in which the parties are engaged or of which they are or should be aware are to be taken into account. To the extent not inconsistent with the express terms of the parties' agreement, the Code thus accommodates merchant practices as a modern form of *lex mercatoria*.

Section 1-203 imposes an obligation of good faith in the performance and enforcement of every "contract or duty within [the UCC]." There has been considerable dispute both in courts and commentary over the appropriate boundaries of the contractual duty of good faith. PEB Commentary No. 10 concludes that the parties should not be able to sue on a breach of the duty of good faith alone; rather, good faith is an interpretative guide for construing all the other duties imposed by the contract. There is general agreement that good faith ought to prevent a party from exercising its contractual discretion in a way that would be contrary to the sense of the parties' agreement. A number of Code provisions apply that idea to specific types of clauses (for example, §§ 1-208, 2-305, 2-306, and 2-311). The dispute over the boundaries of contractual good faith largely centers on determining when the exercise of discretion would be contrary to the rest of the parties' agreement. In general, if a contract clause or normal gap-filling rule gives express discretion to one party, most courts are loath to use good faith to limit that discretion, thus giving the other party protection for which it did not bargain explicitly. However, in certain circumstances, some courts have constructed out of the general duty of good faith such limitations on specific contract clauses as: (1) the duty of a bank not to terminate a line of credit without reasonable notice or commercially reasonable grounds despite a clause in the loan agreement making the loan payable on demand, and (2) the duty of a supplier not to raise its prices without reasonable notice despite a clause obligating the buyer to buy at the supplier's "posted price," but these decisions attract considerable criticism.

Much less attention has been given to the meaning of good faith in the sphere of property rights. Because, as discussed above, the Code's general definition of good faith is the subjective standard of honesty in fact, the primary effect of the good faith requirement on property rights has been to make it clear that a party engaging in fraud cannot qualify for the protections accorded such special property claimants as the good faith purchaser of goods or the holder in due course of a negotiable instrument. Some courts, however, have been willing to use the objective standard of good faith to fashion a duty on the part of parties claiming the special status of good faith purchaser or holder in due course to make reasonable inquiry before they can have the benefit of cutting off conflicting property claims or contract defenses of which they have no knowledge. This has been done especially to protect consumers. Other courts, however, have been reluctant to interpret good faith in this manner.

III. Article 2: The Sale of Goods

By contrast with most of the rest of the Code, Article 2 has been remarkably stable and, with the exception of section 2-318 (*see* pt. III. B), remarkably uniform throughout the United States, but that apparent stability is in a sense misleading. There is considerable agreement that Article 2 is old and in need of revision, and the past decade or so has seen substantial efforts to revise Article 2, culminating in a draft that was adopted by the ALI in 1999. However, controversies over various aspects of the draft – especially over the extent of consumer protection – led NCCUSL leadership to conclude that the prospects for uniform adoption by the States were not good. NCCUSL therefore was not asked to adopt the draft, and instead, ALI and it jointly appointed a new drafting committee in 1999 to produce a new version of Article 2, as well as a revised draft of Article 2A. At this writing in 2001, the committee was still at work.

There was also controversy over the accommodations to be made for electronic commerce. Initial attempts to handle this topic within the framework of revisions to Article 2 came to naught, and in 1995 a separate drafting committee was formed to draft a new Article 2B to cover software licensing. However, by 1999 NCCUSL had severed Article 2B from the rest of the Code and promulgated it as a free-standing act called the Uniform Computer Information Transactions Act (UCITA). As of 2000, it had been adopted by two states, Maryland and Virginia, and introduced for adoption in another five. In addition, in 1999 NCCUSL promulgated the Uniform Electronic Transactions Act (UETA) to remove barriers to electronic commerce by establishing the legal equivalence of electronic records and signatures with paper writings and manual signatures. UETA has been adopted by 17 states and introduced for adoption in another 11.[7]

From the foregoing discussion of section 1-103 and the open-textured nature of the UCC, it should be apparent that the common law of contracts applies to contracts for the sale of goods except as modified by Article 2. However, Article 2 contains a number of significant departures from the common law rules of contracting, and the description of Article 2 will concentrate on those points.

The differences between Article 2 and the common law rules have created an incentive in many cases to litigate over the scope of Article 2. By its terms, Article 2 applies to "transactions in goods" (§ 2-102), and the provisions of Article 2 make it clear that it applies principally to sales transactions. Section 2-105(l) clears up a number of definitional questions, such as whether growing crops are "goods" (they are), and the drafting of Article 2A on the leasing of goods should make clear that Article 2 does not apply to leases, at least in jurisdictions that have adopted Article 2A. However, there remains the troublesome category of transactions which involve both the transfer of goods and the provision of services, such as the serving of a meal or a plumbing repair. The majority of courts apply Article 2 to such cases only if they determine that the "predominant purpose" of the transaction is the sale of goods, but there is considerable debate about how these cases should be handled.

A. Contract Formation Rules

With respect to contract formation issues, Article 2 of the UCC is quite innovative. Without expressly abolishing the doctrine of consideration, Article 2 nullifies its effect by changing the result in the two cases in which the doctrine makes a difference in a commercial setting: firm offers and contract modifications. At common law, promises to keep open an offer to contract were not enforceable unless they were supported by consideration. *See* Chap. 8, pt. II.A. Section 2-205 changes that result in the case of firm offers by merchants. A merchant's firm offer is irrevocable during the time stated, or if no time is stated in the offer, then for a reasonable time, up to a limit of three months. Similarly, section 2-209 makes agreements to modify a sales contract enforceable despite the absence of new consideration. However, if the contract as modified is within the provisions of Article 2's statute of frauds (§ 2-201), there must be a writing sufficient to satisfy that section. Instead of using consideration doctrine to police oppressive insistence on contract modifications, Article 2 relies on the Code's general requirement of good faith (§ 1-203).

7. In June 2000 Congress passed the Electronic Signatures in Global and National Commerce Act, P.L. 106-229, 114 Stat. 464 (2000), to govern the question of validating electronic signatures in interstate and foreign commerce. The federal law does not apply, however, to signatures covered by Articles 3, 4, 4A, 5, 8, or 9. In effect, it recognizes UETA as the appropriate codification of the law governing electronic commerce, since it expressly exempts state laws enacting UETA from federal preemption.

Requirements and output contracts also arguably run afoul of the consideration doctrine by leaving one party free to determine the degree to which it is bound to perform. Section 2-306 codifies the common law solution precluding that argument by providing that the apparently free party in such contracts is always bound to act in good faith in setting its requirements or output and is not permitted to vary such quantities disproportionately from stated estimates or prior requirements or output.

Pre-Code versions of the statute of frauds conditioned the enforceability of contracts for the sale of goods on a writing signed by the party against whom enforcement is sought. *See* Chap. 8, pt. III.B.3. Section 2-201, however, which applies to all sales with a price of $500 or more, contains several important innovations. Most strikingly, it provides that the statute of frauds can be satisfied by a letter one merchant sends to another to confirm a contractual agreement within a reasonable time after oral agreement is reached. Even though the receiving merchant does not sign the confirmatory letter, the contract evidenced by the letter can be enforced against him as long as that merchant has reason to know of the contents of the writing. Of course, the sending merchant still has to prove that the oral agreement was in fact reached.

Section 2-201 also makes clear that the writing does not have to contain all of the terms of the parties' agreement in order to satisfy the writing requirement of the statute of frauds. The writing need only be sufficient to show that the parties reached a contractual agreement for the sale of the goods in question. Even the price need not be stated in the writing. In fact, if the court finds that the parties reached a contractual agreement but left the price term open, section 2-305 authorizes the court to determine a reasonable price. However, according to section 2-201, the contract cannot be enforced for any amount beyond the quantity specified in the writing.

Like the common law, however, Article 2 of the UCC contains another set of rules which pose a potential obstacle to a party seeking to prove that the parties' contractual agreement includes terms beyond those in the written contract. This rule is known as the "parol evidence rule" and it is found in section 2-202. Like its common law counterpart (*see* Chap. 8, pt. III.C.2), the rule prohibits the introduction of evidence of agreement on terms not expressed in the written contract to the extent that such terms would contradict the written terms or add terms to a writing which was intended by the parties to be the complete expression of their agreement. This rule does not, however, apply to terms agreed upon after the parties reached the contractual agreement reflected in the written contract. Whether these subsequent contract modifications are enforceable is governed by sections 2-201 and 2-209, discussed above.

One of Article 2's most controversial rules concerns the "battle of the forms" – the problem of determining which terms govern when the written offer and acceptance contain different or even contradictory terms. At common law, the "mirror image" rule requires the acceptance to contain terms identical to those of the offer with no additional terms. As a result, the parties' writings in the typical battle of the forms failed to create a contract under pre-Code law. Section 2-207 abolishes the mirror image rule for the sale of goods. Pursuant to this section, an expression of acceptance is sufficient to create a contractual obligation even though the acceptance states terms different from or in addition to those of the offer. Between merchants, the acceptance's additional terms that do not materially alter the deal become part of the parties' agreement unless the offeror objects within a reasonable time. The offeror can protect itself against this possibility by stipulating that acceptance must be limited to the offer's terms. The party who wants its reply to the offer to be viewed as a counteroffer instead of an acceptance can ensure that result by making its acceptance conditional on agreement to all of the acceptor's terms.

If each side's insistence on its own terms prevents the court from finding that the parties reached agreement based on either side's documents, but the parties have acted as if they had a contractual agreement – most typically by commencing performance – section 2-207(3) provides that the parties are bound contractually. The terms of the contract are the terms on which the parties' writings agree plus those supplied by the "gap-filling" provisions of the UCC. This is perhaps the most controversial aspect of 2-207 because it binds the parties into a contractual relationship when they have themselves explicitly declined to do so, but many see this as the most just result in view of the parties' behavior.

As this brief summary shows, section 2-207 provides a highly complex set of rules. Such complexity is no doubt inevitable in dealing with a problem as complicated as the typical battle of the forms. The cases show considerable confusion and creativity in trying to arrive at sensible results under the statute, and UCC section 2-207 has featured prominently in the debates over revisions to Article 2.

B. Contract Interpretation

Mention has already been made of the gap-filling provisions of the UCC. In addition to the general rules of Article 1 – including most importantly the rules on good faith and the customs and practices of merchants – Article 2 contains numerous rules of construction for sales contracts. These rules, concentrated in part 3 of Article 2 (§§ 2-301 to 2-328), provide standard terms and standard interpretations of words contracting parties may use in sales contracts. For the most part, these rules apply only in the absence of contrary agreement by the parties, but a few rules having to do with issues of fundamental fairness are mandatory.

One of the most important of these gap fillers is section 2-302, which authorizes the court not to enforce any contract or any part of a contract which the court finds to be "unconscionable." The rule is obviously a mandatory rule. Like the general clauses of many civilian law codes, this provision delegates broad power to the court to prevent unfairness. The clause has provoked widespread debate about the appropriate limits of the courts' power under this clause, but the courts have tended to be quite cautious in invoking this power. There is general consensus that the exercise of such extraordinary court power is most appropriate in providing relief to a contracting party who has been the victim of so-called "procedural" unconscionability, that is, contracting procedures involving surprise or coercion that result in one-sided terms. Thus courts have invoked this power to protect poor and poorly educated buyers – especially those who did not have a good command of English – who were subjected to high-pressure sales tactics. But whether the courts should use this power to police "substantive" unconscionability, that is, unfair or unwise agreements that do not appear to be the product of procedural unconscionability, is much more controversial, especially when a merchant invokes unconscionability to avoid the effect of a contract clause. *See* Chap. 8, pt. III.B.2.

Another very important group of gap fillers concerns the seller's warranty obligations. In addition to the warranty of title (imposed by § 2-312 unless circumstances indicate that title is not warranted) and express warranties (§ 2-313) based on express promises of quality, descriptions of goods, and samples or models which are part of the basis of the parties' bargain, Article 2 imposes minimum quality standards through the implied warranty of merchantability. In order to be "merchantable" the goods must, for example, be fit for the ordinary purposes for which such goods are used and be of average quality for goods of the description used in the contract (§ 2-314). In addition, if the buyer relies on the seller's skill or judgment to select goods suitable to the buyer's special purpose and if the seller has reason to know of the buyer's purpose and his reliance on the seller's judgment, the seller impliedly warrants that the goods are fit for the special purpose (§ 2-315).

The express and implied warranties are designed to require the seller to deliver goods which meet the buyer's reasonable expectations. The parties are free, however, to adjust the buyer's expectations contractually. Thus the seller may disclaim any or all of these warranties (§ 2-316). The Code also authorizes the seller to limit contractually its liability for breach of warranty, for example, by limiting the buyer's remedies to repair or replacement of nonconforming goods or by excluding liability for consequential damages (§ 2-719).

Despite the clear statutory authorization, the courts do not consistently give effect to warranty disclaimers and damage limitations. Uncertainty is bred partly by conflicting formal standards for the disclaimers. Section 2-316(2), for example, requires disclaimers of merchantability to use that word, but section 2-316(3) requires enforcement of any disclaimer "which in common understanding calls the buyer's attention to the exclusion of warranties and makes plain that there is no implied warranty." More important sources of uncertainty are the discretionary standards the UCC directs courts to apply to disclaimers and limitations of liability. Section 2-316(1), for example, renders disclaimers inoperative to the extent that they are unreasonable in light of language or actions creating express warranties. Section 2-719 applies section 2-302's standard of unconscionability to clauses excluding or limiting consequential damages and also more generally provides that limitations on remedy do not apply to the extent that the limited remedy provided by contract "fail[s] of its essential purpose." On these grounds, a number of courts have refused in certain cases to enforce clauses excluding consequential damages, even in contracts between merchants. In addition, the federal Magnuson-Moss Warranty – Federal Trade Commission Improvement Act prohibits the exclusion of implied warranties in some types of consumer sales.

The question of how far the seller's warranty liability is extended to persons other than the buyer – or stated differently, who is a third party beneficiary of the seller's warranties – involves the murky boundary between contract and tort law.

All jurisdictions in the United States have now recognized a strict liability tort cause of action against a seller for personal injury caused by defective goods. However, before strict liability for product defects was well established, injured parties had often relied on warranty, especially the implied warranty of merchantability, as a basis for strict liability. Thus warranty law was caught up in the long development by which the tort law of products liability came to abandon the "privity" limitation – that is, the requirement that the plaintiff be in a contractual relation with the defendant.

The Code drafters have found this question too controversial to admit of full harmonization. The Code therefore provides three alternatives to the section that deals with this issue (§ 2-318), and a number of states have made their own non-uniform amendments. Alternative A, which is most widely adopted, extends the seller's warranty liability to natural persons in the family or household of the buyer, including guests, but only for personal injury. This version has been interpreted to leave to the courts' common law powers the question of whether the seller is also liable to persons who buy the goods from the seller's purchaser. Alternative B broadens the statutory scope of the seller's liability for personal injury to include any natural person "who may reasonably be expected to use, consume or be affected by the goods," and Alternative C broadens the seller's liability even more by abandoning the restriction to personal injury. All of the versions expressly prohibit the seller from contractually limiting its liability for personal injury. Thus, at least for personal injury, the Code's warranty sections provide an alternative to the tort cause of action for strict liability, even for a number of parties not in privity with the seller. *See* Chap. 9, pt. III.C. For other types of injury, case law or statute may provide a warranty cause of action for non-privity claimants, but the rules vary from state to state.

C. Contract Performance and Breach

Article 2 also reflects certain innovations with regard to issues of contract performance and breach. One of the most confusing areas of Article 2 concerns the question when the buyer may terminate the contract (the UCC term is "cancel") and refuse to accept and pay for goods because of the seller's breach of the contract requirements. The Code rules are confusing because traditional and innovative versions of the rules lie uncomfortably side-by-side in Article 2.

At common law for non-goods contracts, a party's right to terminate the contract on the grounds of the other party's breach is governed by the "material breach" standard: the first party is released from its contractual obligations only by serious breaches, that is, behavior that significantly deprives the first party of the benefit of its bargain or reasonably threatens to do so. UCC section 2-601 reflects the stricter standard of much pre-Code law for sellers of goods. Under the "perfect tender" rule of section 2-601, the buyer may reject the goods and cancel the contract if the goods fail "in any respect" to conform to the contract.

Some of the Code drafters strongly advocated abandoning the perfect tender standard on the ground that it permits buyers to use minor non-conformities as pretexts to get out of unfavorable contracts. This view did not prevail in general, but the reformers succeeded in securing adoption of the material breach standard for contracts that call for delivery of the goods in separate installments though the Code uses slightly different terminology. Section 2-612 allows the buyer to reject non-conforming goods in an installment only if the non-conformity "substantially impairs the value of [the] installment and cannot be cured"; if the non-conformity "substantially impairs the value of the whole contract there is a breach of the whole," and pursuant to section 2-711, the buyer may cancel future installments as well. As a result, much might seem to turn on the term "installment contract," defined in section 2-612(1).

In addition, there are a number of other rules in the UCC restricting the buyer's opportunity to cancel for minor contract breaches even under the perfect tender rule of section 2-601. First is the seller's right to cure non-conformities set out in section 2-508. Under that section, the buyer cannot reject goods if the time for performance has not yet expired and the seller indicates that it will cure the defects. If, based on previous dealings between the parties or on trade usage, the seller could reasonably have thought that the buyer would accept non-conforming goods with a money allowance, the seller is entitled to a further reasonable time to substitute conforming goods even though the time for performance has expired.

Second, if the buyer initially accepts the goods, either by signifying to the seller through words or actions that it accepts the goods or by failing within a reasonable time to reject them (§§ 2-602, 2-606), the buyer still has an opportunity to revoke its acceptance if: (1) it accepted the goods on the seller's assurance that it would cure and the seller then fails to provide reasonably prompt cure, or (2) the non-conformities were difficult to discover and the buyer did not know of them at the time of acceptance (§ 2-608). However, the buyer can revoke acceptance only for non-conformities that "substantially impair" the value of the goods.

Third, section 2-504, which permits rejection for the seller's delay in making a proper shipment contract or giving the buyer notice of shipment "only if material delay or loss ensues," suggests that minor delays should never be grounds for rejection. Finally, some courts have invoked the good faith principle of section 1-203 to prevent buyers from rejecting goods in situations in which it appears plain that the asserted non-conformity is a mere pretext to mask the buyer's desire to get out of the contract. As a result, a number of respected commentators believe that, despite the complex structure of these provisions of Article 2, it would be more accurate to say that a buyer can cancel only for material breaches (in UCC terms, for breaches which "substantially impair the value of the goods").

Section 2-610 largely codifies the common law doctrine of anticipatory repudiation. *See* Chap. 8, pt. IV.B.2. Thus, if one party indicates that it will commit a material breach in the future, the other party has an option to await a commercially reasonable time in the hope that the first party will nevertheless perform or to treat the breach as a present one and resort to all permissible remedies for breach, including cancellation. The Code also carries forward the ancient device of the "seller's lien," so that a credit seller which discovers that the buyer is insolvent can refuse to deliver goods except against cash payment (§ 2-702(l)).

The Code's chief innovation in this regard is section 2-609, which in a sense generalizes the concept of the seller's lien by authorizing a party to demand "adequate assurance" of performance if it has "reasonable grounds" to believe that the other side will breach. This section enables a party to clarify the situation in which the other contracting party has behaved in a way suggesting that it is repudiating the contract, either intentionally or by virtue of performance difficulties it cannot overcome, but the repudiation is not clear. If the other party fails to respond to a request by giving adequate assurance within a reasonable time (not exceeding 30 days), it is deemed to have repudiated the contract. This device of a request for adequate assurance has proven popular, and some courts have applied the rule even in cases outside of Article 2.

Article 2's provisions on excuse for impracticability are arguably no different from current common law doctrine, and the chief provision, section 2-615, is often cited in non-Article 2 contracts cases. By its terms, section 2-615 excuses non-delivery or delay in delivery if the seller's performance is made "impracticable by the occurrence of a contingency the non-occurrence of which was a basic assumption on which the contract was made." The section also provides excuse for good faith compliance with orders or regulations of a foreign or domestic government in similar circumstances.

Like the general contract doctrine of excuse for impossibility and commercial impracticability, the UCC version of the rule has tempted many parties to assert the defense, but few have been successful. Before the courts will grant relief, they must be persuaded: (1) that the parties did not allocate to the seller the risk of the problem that occurred, and (2) that as a result of the problem that has eventuated, the seller's performance is either literally impossible or so greatly increased in cost that it would be unfair to insist on performance. A mere increase in cost of performance is not a sufficient reason for excuse. The only group of sellers that clearly are entitled to excuse are those who have contracted to sell specific goods ("goods identified to the contract when the contract is made") which are destroyed or damaged without fault of the seller. These sellers are excused by section 2-613 even if the risk of loss has not yet passed to the buyer. Sellers of generic goods, however, face substantial hurdles in persuading courts to excuse their non-performance. In addition, even if the seller's non-performance is excused, section 2-615 requires the seller to act reasonably in apportioning available production or supply among its customers.

The excuse provisions of Article 2 do not literally apply to buyers. The buyer's primary obligation is generally to pay for the goods, and this obligation rarely is rendered impossible or oppressively expensive by events after contracting. Nevertheless, some courts, with the blessing of the Official Comments, have applied section 2-615 to buyers by analogy. However, the buyer that has no use for the contract goods because of post-contracting events is really raising the claim of frustration of contractual purpose. Article 2 nowhere mentions frustration of contract as a possible excusing condition, but courts have found it to apply to sales through section 1-103's incorporation of the common law. Generally, however, the buyer does not qualify for excuse on either ground if the goods retain any reasonable commercial value.

D. Remedies

True to its common law roots, Article 2 conceives of money damages as the primary remedy for disappointed buyers or sellers of goods. *See* Chap. 8, pt. V.A.1. The pre-Code law generally computed the damages by reference to the market price, and Article 2 carries this method forward. The Code's assumption is that the victim of the breach will arrange a substitute transaction on the market, thereby mitigating the damages it might otherwise incur as a result of the breach. Although the Code nowhere states a general principle of mitigation, that doctrine is built into Article 2's remedies and may be thought of as a part of the principle of good faith in the enforcement of contracts (§ 1-203).

Thus a seller whose goods have improperly been rejected is normally entitled to the difference between the contract and market prices (§ 2-708(l)), plus incidental damages, which include commercially reasonable charges for transporting or storing the goods in connection with return or resale of the goods (§ 2-710). Since the seller has the rejected goods to sell in a substitute transaction at the market price, it usually needs only the differential between the contract and market prices to be put in as good a position as it would have been in had the buyer properly performed. Similarly, if the seller breaches, the buyer is normally entitled to the difference between market and contract price (§ 2-713), plus incidental and consequential damages (§ 2-715). By engaging in the substitute transaction of obtaining the same type of goods ("cover") at the market price, the buyer can normally be put in as good a position as it would have been in if the seller had properly performed, unless the market price is more than the contract price, and in that case, section 2-713 redresses the balance.

The buyer's incidental damages include reasonable expenses of caring for and returning the rejected goods and obtaining cover, as well as expenses resulting from the delay in obtaining cover. Consequential damages, as at common law, are limited to those the seller had reason to anticipate at the time of contracting. The foreseeability limitation does not apply, however, to actions for personal or property damage resulting from any breach of warranty. In any case, the buyer is precluded from recovering consequential damages which it could have avoided by reasonable action, for example, by promptly obtaining cover.

Article 2's principal innovation in this area is to provide alternative remedies to both buyers and sellers based not on the market-contract differential, but on the difference between the contract and the actual substitute transaction in which the non-breaching party engaged. Thus if the seller improperly fails to deliver, the buyer is entitled to recover the difference between its actual costs of cover and the contract price, plus incidental and consequential damages (§ 2-712). The seller whose goods the buyer has improperly rejected may recover the difference between the contract price and the actual price at which it resold the goods, plus incidental damages (§ 2-706). The actual cost of cover or the actual price of resale can serve as the basis for the remedy only if the substitute transaction was commercially reasonable. The market price may be an important factor bearing on whether the substitute transaction meets this standard, but if the substitute transaction was commercially reasonable, it is irrelevant that the market price was higher than the actual resale price or lower than the actual cost of cover.

The Code thus seeks to protect the contracting party that responds in good faith to a contract breach by arranging a substitute transaction so as to minimize its damages. Its decision to enter into the substitute transaction at a price that turns out to be different from the market price will not prevent it from being made whole by money damages as long as it has acted reasonably. In addition, the reselling seller must give the buyer notice of intention to resell if the resale is at private sale (§ 2-706(3)).

There are some situations to which these general remedies do not apply. For example, if the buyer does not reject or revoke acceptance of the goods in a timely manner despite non-conformance with the contract requirements, the buyer has no right to arrange a substitute transaction. In fact, the buyer must pay the contract price for all units accepted (§ 2-607(l)). But the buyer also normally has an offsetting claim for the amount by which the breach of contract requirements, including any applicable warranties, has reduced the value of the goods, together with incidental and consequential damages resulting from the breach (§ 2-715). In order to preserve this claim, however, the buyer must give the seller notice of the breach within a reasonable time after it discovers or should have discovered the breach (§ 2-607(3)(a)).

Similarly, if the seller cannot resell improperly rejected goods, perhaps because they were manufactured specially for the breaching buyer and have no value for any other buyer, no substitute transaction is possible, and the seller is entitled to the entire contract price (§ 2-709). Furthermore, certain types of sellers cannot arrange a substitute transaction because no other sale they might make can be said to be a substitute for the one on which the buyer has breached. Such sellers, like dealers with access to an unrestricted supply of goods in a market in which demand does not exceed supply, are called "lost volume" sellers. Such a seller could have made all the other sales it actually made even if the buyer had not breached. The buyer's breach, in effect, deprives the seller of a sale and the only remedy to make it whole is an award of lost profits. Section 2-708(2) authorizes the award of lost profits (including reasonable overhead) if the normal contract-minus-market-price differential is "inadequate to put the seller in as good a position as performance would have." Courts have awarded lost profits to "lost volume" sellers, though there is much controversy over the appropriate definition of the term.

If the buyer cannot obtain the substitute transaction of cover because the goods contracted for are unique, the buyer has a right to obtain specific performance of the contract (§ 2-716(l)). Pre-Code law limited specific performance to unique goods. Article 2 attempts, as the Official Comments say, "to further a more liberal attitude ... [toward] specific performance." Section 2-716(l) therefore authorizes the courts to decree specific performance for unique goods and "in other proper circumstances." Some courts have granted specific performance of certain contracts for non-unique goods. Following the lead of the Official Comments, most such cases base specific performance on a finding that the buyer was unable to obtain cover because of unique aspects of the breached contract, such as financing by the seller which the buyer is unable to obtain elsewhere or the length of the period in a supply contract which other sellers are not willing to match.

E. Title and Other Property Concepts

Article 2 also regulates a number of important matters relating to property rights in goods, though it by no means constitutes a comprehensive or systematic code of such rights. Foremost among the concerns of the Code drafters was the desire to prevent contracting parties from using contract provisions on title to manipulate the rights regulated in the UCC. For example, under pre-Code law buyers that wanted to be sure they could force their sellers to deliver the goods without regard to the limits on specific performance might have insisted on contract terms providing that title (ownership) passed before delivery. When the sellers refused to deliver, the buyers could then sue for replevin to enforce their property rights. Section 2-716(3) provides that the buyer can have replevin only if it can show that it is unable to effect cover. This provision effectively cuts down the buyer's right to enforce its property rights to correspond generally to the buyer's right to specific performance of contract.

Similarly, section 2-401 provides that a contract provision purporting to reserve title to the seller after the goods have been shipped or delivered results only in the reservation of a security interest. The effect of this provision is to force a credit seller to comply with the requirements of Article 9 on security interests in order to obtain priority against other creditors with regard to the specific property subject to the sale. Contractual reservation of title will not suffice to preserve the seller's priority over other creditors of the buyer, as it will in some countries.

The unpaid seller that has delivered goods to the buyer on credit without retaining a security interest can normally gain a property interest in any specific property of the buyer for the purpose of collecting the debt only by suing on its contract claim, getting a judgment against the seller, and having the sheriff levy against that specific property. Without complying with that somewhat cumbersome procedure, the unpaid seller may be able to regain its property rights in the specific goods sold if the seller can establish one of a narrow set of reasons for rescinding the transaction. The most important grounds for rescission are mutual mistake and fraud. Thus at common law the fraudulent credit buyer, for example, was said to have "voidable title" to the goods because the seller had an option to rescind the transaction and "void" the buyer's title if the seller acted with reasonable diligence. Section 2-702(2) broadens the seller's reclamation right to include any situation in which the buyer has received the goods while insolvent. But except in the case of certain written misrepresentations of solvency, the seller can preserve its reclamation right only by making demand for return of the goods within ten days after the buyer has received them. The ten-day rule severely restricts the seller's right to reclaim. Furthermore, most such cases are subject to the Bankruptcy Act, which makes no exception to the requirement of a demand within ten days.

The fundamental rule of property transfer, reflected in the first sentence of section 2-403(l), is that the transferor purporting to transfer its whole ownership interest transfers that interest, but nothing more or less. A thief thus cannot transfer any interest in stolen goods because he acquires no property interest through the theft. But the first sentence of section 2-403(l) also provides that a transferor transfers all title she has "power to transfer," which signifies that the law of agency, apparent agency, and estoppel may also apply to permit someone to transfer a greater interest than she herself had.

Perhaps the most important property rules in Article 2 are the protections accorded various types of good faith purchasers of goods (§ 2-403). Section 2-403(l) provides that a person with voidable title has the power to transfer good title to a "good faith purchaser for value." The foregoing discussion on Article 1 mentioned the broad definition of "value" (§ 1-201(44)) and the two definitions of "good faith" (§§ 1-201(19), 2-103(l)(b)) applicable here. *See* pt. II. Voidable title, as already mentioned, is the title a buyer holds even though the sale is subject to the seller's right to rescind the transaction for fraud or mistake. Thus a good faith purchaser for value will not bear the risk that someone in her chain of title acquired title by fraud. The defrauded owner must bear this risk. However, even the lowest standard of good faith, the subjective standard, is not satisfied if the claimant has actual knowledge of conflicting claims, so the good faith purchase doctrine does not permit a buyer knowingly to cut off title to goods procured by fraud or mistake.

A good faith purchaser for value who buys goods in the ordinary course of business from a merchant in the business of selling goods of that kind is defined as a "buyer in the ordinary course" (§ 1-201(9)). Section 2-403(2) affords these good faith purchasers special protection: they obtain from the merchant from whom they buy their goods all rights of anyone who has entrusted these goods to the merchant. Thus the jeweler to whom X delivers his watch, even if merely for repair, can transfer full ownership of the watch to Y as long as: (1) X owned the watch and entrusted it to the jeweler; (2) the jeweler is in the business of selling watches; and (3) Y buys in good faith, for value, and in the ordinary course from the jeweler. It should be noted, however, that unlike the rules in some other countries, the UCC does not protect any type of good faith purchaser from the risk of buying stolen goods.

IV. Articles 3 and 4: Negotiable Instruments and Bank Deposits and Collections

Article 3 applies to negotiable instruments, including drafts (also called "bills of exchange"), checks, and notes. A "draft" is an order from one person to another person to pay a certain amount of money to a third person. A "check" is a draft drawn on a bank and payable on demand. "Notes" are promissory notes, evidencing debts and consisting of a written promise by the maker to pay money to the payee when the note is due. Although notes and drafts can be either negotiable or nonnegotiable, it is in the form of negotiable instruments that they have their greatest commercial importance. Negotiability permits them to be transferred freely from person to person, thus making negotiable notes and drafts useful tools for facilitating payment and credit extension in commercial transactions. This discussion will concentrate on the check, which accounts for the greatest volume of negotiable instruments in the United States. Article 4 builds on Article 3 by providing special rules for the banks involved in the circulation of negotiable instruments.

The winds of change have been blowing particularly hard with respect to this subject. For example, federal law has increasingly asserted itself in this area. In 1988, the Federal Reserve Board promulgated Regulation CC pursuant to the Expedited Fund Availability Act[8] to speed up the banks' check collection processes. In 1990, the UCC sponsors proposed extensively redrafted versions of UCC Articles 3 and 4. As of 2000, 47 states had adopted the new versions.[9] Further extensive changes to Article 4, designed to incorporate federal check collection regulations, are currently being drafted.

The rules on negotiable instruments may seem particularly unfamiliar at first to the foreign lawyer. The Geneva Conventions, which have had such an impact on the continent of Europe and elsewhere, have had little impact on the UCC. The Geneva Conventions' device of the "crossed check" is unknown in the United States. Unlike the situation in countries which treat a check as an assignment of funds, the drawer of a check in the United States ordinarily has the right to stop payment on the check before it is paid by the bank on which it is drawn (§§ 3-408, 4-403). Moreover, checks in the United States constitute a well-established means of payment and do not compete against postal checks or a giro system of pay orders, as they do in many other countries. However, here as elsewhere checks have more recently come under competition from credit and debit cards and electronic wire transfers, none of which are regulated by Articles 3 and 4. Credit cards are subject to the federal "Truth in Lending" legislation, Title I of the Consumer Credit Protection Act (*see* pt. I). Electronic wire transfers involving consumers, including debit card transfers, are governed by the federal Electronic Fund Transfer Act and Regulation E of the Federal Reserve Board.[10] Non-consumer wire transfers are the subject of the UCC's Article 4A.

Article 3's rules governing negotiation are quite simple. A check made out to the order of a named payee or indorsed to the order of a named person is "order paper" and can be "negotiated" only by a voluntary or involuntary transfer of possession of the check, combined with indorsement by the named person through that person's signature on the back of the check (§ 3-201). A check made out in such a manner as to indicate that it is not payable to an identified person (for example, a check made out to "bearer") is called "bearer paper" and is negotiated by transfer alone. Once a check has been indorsed in blank (indorsed without indication that it is transferred to the order of a named person), it becomes bearer paper.

The person to whom the check has been negotiated is a "holder." A holder is generally entitled to enforce the check against any person who is liable on it. Thus, if the check is dishonored by the drawee bank, the holder may enforce it against the drawer (§ 3-414). However, unless the holder has the rights of a "holder in due course," the holder's effort to enforce the check will be subject to defenses of the obligated party as well as to claims of that party or others to the check itself (§§ 3-305, 3-306).

8. 12 U.S.C. §§ 4001-4010 (1994); 12 C.F.R. pt. 229 (2000).
9. In the following discussion, all citations are to the amended versions of Articles 3 and 4.
10. 15 U.S.C. §§ 1693-1693r (1994 & Supp. IV 1998); 12 C.F.R. pt. 205 (2000).

A holder who has taken the check for value, in good faith, and without notice of defenses or claims to the check is a holder in due course (§ 3-302).[11] The holder in due course is entitled to the chief benefits of negotiability: taking free of (1) all claims of property rights in the check on the part of any other party and (2) most defenses of any party obligated on the check with whom the holder in due course has not dealt (§§ 3-305, 3-306). The only defenses that the drawer can assert against a holder in due course are the so-called "real" defenses, including incapacity, duress, illegality, and the type of misrepresentation that induced the drawer to sign the check without knowledge or reasonable opportunity to obtain knowledge of the document's essential terms. Drawer's defenses based on claims that the payee breached the underlying contract in satisfaction of which the drawer gave the check, and even drawer's claim that the payee induced him by fraud to incur the debt which he has paid by issuing the check, are cut off by the holder in due course. It follows from the rules on negotiation explained above that a good faith purchaser of stolen bearer paper can become a holder in due course and therefore can cut off the claims of the rightful owner. But if the check is "payable to the order of" the rightful owner when it is stolen, no subsequent transferee can become a holder without the indorsement of the owner, and as long as he has not facilitated the theft by his negligence, no one can cut off his property interest in the check.

The chief risks a holder of a check under the UCC faces are the risks that the check will not be paid because: (1) the drawer does not have enough funds on deposit at the bank on which the check is drawn (the drawee or payor bank), (2) the drawer has stopped payment on the check, or (3) the check bears a forged signature. If the payor bank refuses to pay, either because the drawer has insufficient funds in his account or because he has issued a stop order to the bank, the holder has no right against the bank. Section 3-408 provides that a payor bank is not liable on a check until it has accepted it. That section expressly rejects the notion that a check automatically creates an assignment of funds to the holder. If the payor bank refuses to pay, the holder's only recourse will be against the drawer (§ 3-414) or prior indorsers (§ 3-415), though the rules on presentment and notice of dishonor require the holder to act with dispatch to preserve her rights, especially against indorsers.

A holder may seek to protect herself against dishonor by securing prior acceptance by the payor bank. "Certification" is one form of acceptance. Once the payor bank has certified a check, the bank itself is liable to pay the check (§ 3-413), and the drawer has lost the general right to stop payment. The only way the drawer might then prevent payment is by asserting an "adverse claim." If in the underlying transaction in which the drawer gave the check as payment the drawer was the victim of fraud or mistake sufficient to give him grounds to rescind the underlying transaction, then the drawer has a property claim to the funds represented by the certified check, and the drawer's claim is superior at least to the payee's claim to those funds. Sections 3-305 and 3-306 permit the bank to assert the drawer's property claim as a defense, but only if the drawer

11. For a discussion of the Code's definitions of "value" and "good faith," *see* pt. II.

joins the law suit to assert the defense and only as a defense to suit by a claimant that is not a holder in due course. Once the certified check comes into the hands of a holder in due course, the adverse claims are cut off like most other claims and defenses.

The rules on forgeries bear the peculiar stamp of the common law. In the case of forged indorsements, the rules operate to transfer the loss occasioned by an absconding forger who passed the check for value to the solvent party who took the check from the forger or who comes closest in the chain of transfer to the forger. The Code achieves this result by requiring each indorser to give a warranty against forged indorsements (§§ 3-416, 4-207), and this warranty survives even after the payor bank has made final payment on the check. This point is important because the UCC requires payor banks to make final payment within very tight deadlines, generally by midnight of the next business day after it receives the check. As a result of the warranty, however, if the payor bank pays the forged check before the forged indorsement comes to light, the payor bank can nevertheless within generous time limits hold any indorser liable on the warranty and so transfer liability "upstream" when the forgery comes to light. A similar rule applies in the case of a forged drawer's signature as long as the forgery comes to light before the payor bank makes final payment on the check.

But once the payor bank has made final payment over a forged drawer's signature, the famous rule of *Price v. Neal*[12] comes into play: The payor bank cannot pass the loss upstream because the warranties the upstream parties make do not include a warranty against forgeries of the drawer's signature for the benefit of payor banks (§§ 3-417, 4-208). Moreover, the payor bank cannot pass the loss on to a non-negligent drawer because the payor bank has no right to charge his account for a forged check (§ 4-401). *Price v. Neal* may be harsh on payor banks, who today rarely check drawer's signatures, but the rule obviously relieves drawers and holders of a risk they might otherwise have to bear. Supporters of the rule may thus argue that it contributes to general public acceptance of the checking system. Despite controversy over the rule, the new version of Article 3 preserves it, although possible limitations of the rule are currently under consideration.

All of the rules on forgeries are subject to further refinement in the case that the negligence of one of the solvent parties to the check contributed to the making of the forgery (§ 3-406). In such a case, the entire loss is shifted to the negligent party. The new version of Article 3 introduces the notion of comparative fault, so that the parties will share the loss in proportion to their negligence. Both the old and the new versions of Article 3 include further special rules imposing liability on drawers who negligently fail to detect forgeries on checks returned to the drawer by the payor bank (§ 4-406), as well as special rules imposing liability on drawers for checks they are fraudulently induced to issue (§ 3-404). New Article 3 includes a provision making employers strictly liable for forged indorsements by employees to whom they have entrusted the duty of signing or indorsing checks (§ 3-405).

12. 3 Burr. 1354, 97 Eng. Rep. 871 (K.B. 1762).

V. Article 9: Secured Transactions

A creditor to whom a debtor has voluntarily given a "security interest" in specific property ("collateral") has the right upon the debtor's failure to repay the debt ("default") to have the collateral sold and to apply the proceeds of the sale to pay off the debtor's unpaid debt. Article 9 undoubtedly qualifies as the greatest achievement of the Code. Out of the plethora of pre-Code security devices for various types of collateral, it has created the unified concept of the security interest, which is nevertheless sufficiently flexible to cover a wide variety of collateral. Despite this great achievement, the particular accommodations among the interests of debtors and of the various types of creditors reflected in the uniform text have been controversial, and Article 9 has been the principal target of amendments, both nonuniform state enactments and amendments to the Official Text. For example, the 1972 amendments to the Official Text chiefly concerned Article 9, and the 1977 amendments, which largely redrafted Article 8 on investment securities, also required conforming amendments mainly to Article 9.

A major revision of Article 9 was completed in 1999, with a delayed effective date of 1 July 2001. All states have adopted the new version. However, because most of the case law and literature prior to the effective date cites to the old Article 9, one cannot ignore that version completely. The following discussion focuses on general principles common to both versions of Article 9. Citations to the revised version are given in brackets if different from the old version. Changes made by the revised version are noted when pertinent to the discussion. It is worth noting at the outset, for example, that revised Article 9's scope is broader than its predecessor, covering both new kinds of collateral (for example, health insurance receivables, consignments and commercial tort claims) and new kinds of transactions (for example, sales of payment intangibles and promissory notes).

Article 9 seeks to establish a "comprehensive scheme" for regulating security interests and the transactions that create them (Official Comment, § 9-101). The scope of Article 9 is therefore quite broad. Section 9-102 [9-109(a)] applies Article 9 in principle "to any transaction (regardless of form) ... intended to create a security interest in personal property," but section 9-104 [9-109(c),(d)] excludes a number of types of security interests. Moreover, because of the difficulty in distinguishing true sales from assignments for security in the case of accounts receivable (called "accounts" under Article 9) and chattel paper (a written form of accounts receivable involving leases or security interests in personal property), Article 9 also applies to sales of these two types of property. For this reason, Article 9 codifies some of the major common law rules concerning assignment of contract rights (§§ 9-206, 9-318, [9-403, 9-404, 9-405, 9-406]), though Article 2 also includes rules on assignments (§ 2-210) in the case of transactions in goods.

The law of security interests comes with a set of specialized legal terms. For example, Article 9 refers to the debtor's creation of a security interest for a creditor as the process of "attachment." The process by which a secured creditor gives notice of its interest to other creditors and potential creditors is called "perfection." The secured creditor whose security interest has attached and has been perfected has priority over a wide array of conflicting claimants to the collateral. The security interest which has attached but has not been perfected is enforceable against the debtor but does not assure the creditor priority with respect to most other creditors. Thus the primary beneficiary of Article 9 is the "perfected secured creditor."

A. Attachment and Perfection of Security Interests

Section 9-203 regulates attachment of a security interest by providing that no security agreement is enforceable unless three events have occurred. Two require little discussion: the security interest does not attach until (1) the secured party has given value (extended credit to the debtor) and (2) the debtor has rights in the collateral (§ 9-203(l)(b), (c) [9-203(b)(1), (2)]). The other requirement is in the nature of a statute of frauds (§ 9-203(l)(a) [9-203(b)(3)]). If the collateral remains in the debtor's hands, then there must be a written security agreement signed by the debtor and containing a description of the collateral. If the secured party takes possession of the collateral (a so-called "pledge"), no writing is required. In that case, the debtor's voluntary relinquishment of the collateral constitutes sufficient evidence of the parties' intention to create a security interest. Under revised Article 9, a creditor's control over certain kinds of collateral, if exercised pursuant to a security agreement, serves the same attachment function as a creditor's possession of the collateral [§ 9-203(b)(3)(D)].

With one exception discussed below, a security interest is perfected by an action designed to put other creditors and potential creditors of the debtor on notice of the perfecting creditor's security interest. The requisite publicity is generally provided by: (1) the secured party's possession of the collateral, (2) filing a notice in public files established for this purpose, or (3) the secured party's control of the collateral. A security interest cannot be perfected unless it has also attached, but the actions necessary to both steps can take place in any order (§ 9-303 [9-308]).

Automatic perfection is the one exception to the requirement of publicity. Purchase money security interests in consumer goods constitute the most important type of collateral subject to an automatic perfection provision (§ 9-302 [9-309]). A lender that loans money to a debtor to enable her to purchase consumer goods and that can show that its loan was actually so used by the debtor, need only make sure that its security interest is properly created. Once it has attached, it is automatically perfected as well. Automatic perfection is thought to encourage consumer lending by reducing the costs of purchase money lending against consumer goods. The price of this benefit is that it discourages non-purchase money lending against consumer goods because the official records do not suffice to reveal all creditors with priorities, but that type of lending is not commercially significant.

Security interests in which the secured creditor holds the collateral (pledges) are especially easy to establish and protect. The creditor's possession of the collateral pursuant to an oral security agreement is sufficient for both attachment and perfection. The most important forms of the pledge are represented today by pawnshops, pledges of corporate stock, and warehoused goods. Every type of collateral which is sufficiently tangible to be "possessed" is subject to perfection by the secured creditor's possession. This rule includes: (1) "instruments," a term which under old Article 9 covers negotiable instruments and corporate stock certificates; and (2) negotiable documents of title, like warehouse receipts and bills of lading (§ 9-305). A security interest in most types of collateral can also be perfected by filing, but a security interest in money, negotiable commercial paper, or stock certificates can be perfected only by the secured party's taking possession (§ 9-304(l)), though the rules for stock certificates are separately stated in Article 8 (§§ 8-313, 8-321). Truly intangible collateral, like accounts receivable ("accounts" in Article 9) or other contract or tort rights ("general intangibles" under Article 9) are subject to perfection only by filing (§ 9-302).

The idea of control as a method of perfection first appeared in the 1994 amendments to Article 8, where it was applied to security interests in such investment property as securities and commodity contracts. Revised Article 9 expands "control" as a method to perfect security interests in investment property, letter of credit rights, electronic chattel paper, and deposit accounts [§ 9-314]. Although "control" is defined differently depending on the type of collateral, a secured party generally has control over collateral when the debtor cannot transfer the collateral without the creditor's consent [§§ 9-104 to 9-107]. Control thus serves the same function as creditor possession of collateral – it puts third parties who seek to take an interest in the collateral on notice of the creditor's claim.

Most forms of commercially important security interests are perfected today by filing. Part 4 of Article 9 [Part 5 of revised Article 9] governs the mechanics of this requirement. The document the secured creditor must file is called a "financing statement," and it must be signed by the debtor, give the names and addresses of both parties, and indicate the types of collateral the security interest covers (§ 9-402). The financing statement is thus intended to put third parties on notice that a particular creditor claims a security interest in certain types of collateral. The secured creditor may provide more information if it wishes, but it is not required to do so. If a prospective creditor wishes additional information, it can see from the file whom to ask.

Section 9-401, which designates where the financing statement is to be filed, comes in three alternative official versions, and each actual state enactment blends statewide or central filing with some local or countywide filing requirements. In general, the central files are maintained in the offices of the state's secretary of state, and under the first two official alternatives, this is the only office in which a filing need be made for most collateral. All three versions require local filing in the county office where mortgages on real estate are filed for certain types of collateral closely associated with real estate, such as timber to be cut, minerals, or fixtures. The issue of where to file also raises knotty questions in the context of multistate transactions. These questions are regulated by section 9-103, which determines in such cases which state's Article 9 controls questions of perfection and priority. A filing is effective for five years and must be renewed before the end of that period to maintain perfection (§ 9-403).

Revised Article 9 makes a number of important changes to these filing requirements. First, revised Article 9 permits electronic filing; paper financing statements are not required. Second, the information required on a financing statement is minimized and the requirement of the debtor's signature is abandoned [9-502]. Third, revised Article 9 centralizes the filing process. With the exception of certain security interests in collateral closely related to real property (filed in the same office as mortgages on the real property), all security interests are to be filed in a single office [§ 9-501]. Moreover, under the new choice of law rules in revised Article 9, the governing law will be the law of the state where the debtor is located [§ 9-301]. If the rules work as intended, a single search in a single office in a single state should reveal all the filings affecting the personal property of a particular debtor.

A number of types of collateral require a different sort of filing. The most important example is automobile certificates of title. Under most state statutes governing automobile certificates of title, the holder of a security interest in the automobile must have that interest noted on the certificate of title in order to perfect it.

B. Protection of the Perfected Secured Creditor

The perfected secured creditor has priority in the collateral over an impressive array of competing creditors. Of course, it has priority over all unperfected security interests in the same collateral (§ 9-301(1)(a) [9-317]). Moreover, under section 9-312(5) [9-322] perfected secured creditor X generally has priority over all other creditors with perfected security interests in the same collateral as long as X either perfected or filed a financing statement concerning the collateral before the other perfected secured creditors. The rule permits a lender who is contemplating making a secured loan in effect to "reserve" a priority with respect to competing secured creditors by filing before making the loan. The filing itself is ineffective to perfect the security interest until it attaches – which cannot happen until, among other things, the creditor has given credit in some form – but as soon as it attaches, it is also perfected, and no other creditor who perfected or filed in the interim can gain priority. The special priority, however, for perfected purchase money security interests, discussed below, forms an important exception to this rule.

The perfected secured creditor also has priority over persons who become "lien creditors" with respect to the collateral after the security interest is perfected (§§ 9-301 [9-201, 9-317]). By lien creditors, the Code means creditors who reduce their claims to judgment and use judicial process to attach or levy on the property at issue (§ 9-301(3) [9-102]). Under Article 9 and the Bankruptcy Code, the trustee in bankruptcy, who represents the interests primarily of all the unsecured creditors of a bankrupt debtor, has the powers of a lien creditor starting from the commencement of a case in bankruptcy. In principle, therefore, secured parties who had perfected prior to the filing of the petition in bankruptcy have priority over the trustee, and perfection thus saves a secured creditor's interest in collateral from falling into the general pool of assets to be distributed pro rata to all the unsecured creditors in a liquidation or to be used to continue the debtor's business in a reorganization. However, the trustee has a variety of special powers to affect even the perfected secured creditor's collateral. The filing of the petition in bankruptcy automatically freezes all of the debtor's assets, so that without leave of the bankruptcy court the secured parties cannot exercise their rights to take possession of the collateral after the debtor's default. As discussed below, the trustee's broad powers to disregard voidable preferences may render even a perfected security interest vulnerable to his lien in certain circumstances. Finally, the bankruptcy court even has the power to deprive the perfected secured party of its collateral if necessary for the proper winding up or restructuring of the debtor's business. In that case, the secured party must be given the "indubitable equivalent" of the collateral – most likely substitute collateral, but the courts' power of substitution imposes some new risk on secured lenders.

The rules on perfection do not literally exclude from their protection secured parties who perfect their interests with knowledge of competing unperfected interests, and most courts have concluded that the priority provisions of sections 9-301 [9-317] and 9-312 [9-322] are therefore "pure race" statutes. But that conclusion may in some situations be in tension with the general requirement of good faith (§ 1-203), as well as with pre-Code priority doctrines. Consequently some courts have invoked good faith or the "equitable lien" to subordinate the first filed or perfected security interest, even in favor of an unperfected creditor, in order to prevent one creditor from unfairly gaining a priority over another. Alternatively, some courts may subordinate such a perfected security interest under the state statutory or common law of "fraudulent conveyances," which permits a court to set aside a debtor's property transfers intended to defraud creditors. There is, however, considerable controversy over the proper limits of these equitable adjustments to the express priorities provided by the Code.

The perfected secured creditor is also protected against most purchasers, even good faith purchasers for value. However, there is one major exception for buyers in the ordinary course (§ 9-307 [9-320]), the good faith purchaser for value who buys goods from a dealer. As a result of section 9-307 [9-320], perfected lenders against inventory must reckon with the possibility that the debtor will sell the inventory out from under the lender's security interest. This accords with normal commercial expectation that a dealer will sell off inventory and that the inventory lender should look to the money received from such sales for repayment. Section 9-307 [9-320] of the Official Text contains an exception to this exception for farm lenders. But the federal Food Security Act[13] overrides the special farm lender rule to protect good faith purchasers who buy crops or livestock from farmers unless the lender with a perfected security interest in the crops or livestock has taken prescribed steps calculated to give actual notice of its interest to the buyers. The states can help farm lenders give notice by providing a special centralized filing system, and a small number of states have done so.

Although purchase, except by a buyer in the ordinary course, does not cut off the perfected secured creditor's priority in collateral, generous tracing rules also permit the perfected secured creditor to assert priority to most "proceeds" from the transfer of collateral (§ 9-306 [9-315]). Proceeds include whatever property, including money, the debtor received from the transfer. The courts have even per-

13. 7 U.S.C. § 1631 (1994).

mitted secured parties to trace their priority into bank accounts in which money proceeds have been commingled with funds from other sources. These tracing rules are of particular value to the perfected inventory lender, who in effect gains a priority in proceeds to substitute for the security interest in inventory which is cut off by sale to buyers in the ordinary course. Controversy exists as to whether the federal bankruptcy laws nullify section 9-306(4), which states special tracing rules for commingled accounts in bankruptcy, and the revision of Article 9 eliminates that section.

Another aspect of the extraordinary protection Article 9 provides to the perfected secured creditor is the "floating lien." While Article 9 does not provide for a blanket security interest in all of a debtor's assets, it does give effect to both after-acquired property clauses and future advances clauses (§ 9-204). As a result of one security agreement and one filing, a secured inventory lender, for example, may be perfected for a period of five years in all of the debtor's inventory, including all new inventory the debtor acquires during this period and with respect to all new loans the lender makes during the period.

To prevent a lender with such a floating lien from unduly tying up a debtor's collateral, the Code makes an exception to the first-to-file-or-perfect rule in favor of purchase money lenders. Purchase money lenders can get priority with regard to the new collateral they finance as long as they perfect according to the timing rules of the Code (§ 9-312(3), (4) [9-324]). In the case of inventory, the purchase money lender also has to give actual notice to any secured creditor that has already filed.

The power Article 9 gives the perfected secured creditor to sweep the debtor's property into its floating lien generally enables a perfected secured creditor whose collateral is insufficient to cover the debtor's outstanding debt to benefit substantially from the after-acquired property clause. For example, an under-collateralized inventory lender hopes that the debtor will invest available money in building up inventory because the build-up will reduce the lender's under-collateralization. Article 9's attempt to favor the perfected secured creditor, however, is subject to the federal law power of the trustee in bankruptcy to prevent creditors from benefitting from transfers (so-called "voidable transfers") which reduce their under-collateralization with respect to the debtor within the preference period, for most purposes the 90 days immediately before the filing of the petition in bankruptcy. Similarly, governmental tax liens, which attach to the property of a delinquent taxpayer to secure payment of taxes owed, cut down floating liens by taking priority over the after-acquired property and future advances clauses, at least after the government files notice of its tax lien and in accordance with specific timing rules.

Despite all the extensive protections Article 9 affords the perfected secured creditor, its security interest is subject to a number of creditor interests, some of which arise outside the Code. Thus section 9-310 [9-333] subordinates even the perfected secured creditor to so-called "artisans" liens, interests in property given by statute or case law to, for example, an automobile repair shop in the cars it repairs to secure the materials or services it furnishes with respect to the cars. Although Article 9 excludes them generally from its coverage, the liens for unpaid rent that state law gives landlords on tenants' personal property brought onto the premises are usually given priority over at least some perfected security interests, as are sureties' rights in the accounts receivable of a defaulting contractor. However, Revised Article 9 does provide rules for determining priority conflicts between Article 9 security interests and "agricultural liens," which include landlord liens arising in connection with land leased for farming operations. [§§ 9-102(a)(5), 9-322.]

C. *Rules upon Debtor's Default*

Part 5 of Article 9 [part 6 of revised Article 9] regulates debtors' and creditors' rights upon the debtors' default. The protections these rules give to debtors are mandatory rules that the parties are not free to vary by contract, at least until after the default has occurred (§ 9-501 [9-602, 9-624]). Upon default, the secured party normally has the right to take possession of the collateral, but only if it can do so "without breach of the peace" (§ 9-503 [9-609]). Thus a debtor who keeps the collateral inside its building can probably deny the secured creditor the self-help remedy of repossession. In that case, the secured party must obtain either: (1) a court order to enforce its rights to repossess, or (2) a judgment on the debt, which the secured party can enforce like any unsecured party by obtaining a writ of execution and requesting the sheriff to levy on any of the debtor's property.

Until the collateral has been disposed of, the debtor has a right to redeem by tendering payment of all amounts due plus the creditor's reasonable expenses (§ 9-506 [9-623]). Acceleration clauses normally provide that upon default the entire unpaid balance of the contract becomes due. In such a case, the debtor can redeem only by tendering an amount that includes the full unpaid balance.

Upon taking possession of the collateral, the secured party must normally sell the collateral at public or private sale (§ 9-504 [9-610]). The secured party must refund to the debtor the "surplus," the amount it receives for the collateral in excess of the unpaid debts and allowable expenses the creditor has incurred in handling the collateral. If the amount realized at sale falls short of the outstanding debt and allowable expenses, the debtor is normally liable to the secured party for the difference, known as the "deficiency." Alternatively, except for consumer goods on which the debtor has paid substantial amounts specified in the statute, the secured party may elect to keep the collateral in full satisfaction of the debt (§ 9-505 [9-620]). This is known as "strict foreclosure" and leaves no residual liability for deficiency on the part of the debtor or for surplus on the part of the secured party, but the debtor must be given written notice of the secured party's intention and can force the secured party to conduct a sale – thereby avoiding loss of an anticipated surplus – by giving written objection within 21 days. Except in consumer transactions, revised Article 9 also permits a creditor to retain the collateral in partial satisfaction of the debt, if the debtor consents.

Every aspect of the sale, including the price, must be "commercially reasonable" (§ 9-504(3) [9-610]). Chief among the secured party's duties is to give "reasonable notification" of the sale to the debtor and to certain junior secured creditors. Section 9-507 [9-625] makes the secured creditor liable for any loss caused by its failure to comply with the requirements of part 5 [part 6] and even imposes a penalty in the case of consumer goods. According to the statute, proof that a better price could have been obtained is not sufficient to prove that the secured party has violated these requirements, but it is equally clear that failure to give proper notice is a violation even though the debtor may not be able to show that it would have been able to bring a higher bidder to the sale if it had notice. A number of courts have assisted debtors in such situations either: (1) by eliminating judicially the secured party's right to a deficiency as a penalty for secured party misbehavior, or (2) by creating a rebuttable presumption that the collateral was equal in value to the outstanding debt and allowable charges so that the misbehaving creditor has no claim for a deficiency. Consumer protection statutes, including the UCCC, also tend to restrict or eliminate the creditor's right to a deficiency judgment. Revised Article 9 adopts the rebuttable presumption rule for non-consumer transactions, leaving to the courts or other statutes the proper rule for consumer transactions.

Selected Bibliography

Barkley Clark, 1-2 *The Law of Secured Transactions under the Uniform Commercial Code* (rev. ed. 1999).

Barkley Clark & Barbara Clark, *The Law of Bank Deposits, Collections, and Credit Cards* (rev. ed. 1995).

Grant Gilmore, 1-2 *Security Interests in Personal Property* (1965).

Robert A. Hillman, Julian B. McDonnell & Steve H. Nickles, *Common Law and Equity under the Uniform Commercial Code* (1985).

William H. Lawrence, 1-2 *Commercial Paper and Payment Systems* (1990).

William H. Lawrence & William H. Henning, *Understanding Sales and Leases of Goods* (1996).

William H. Lawrence, William H. Henning & R. Wilson Freyermuth, *Understanding Secured Transactions* (2d ed. 1999).

National Conference of Commissioners on Uniform State Laws (NCCUSL) <http://www.nccusl.org>.

James J. White & Robert S. Summers, *Uniform Commercial Code* (5th ed. 2000).

—, 1-4 *Uniform Commercial Code* (4th ed. 1995 & Supp. 2000) (practitioner treatise).

Chapter 14
Business Enterprises

*Alfred F. Conard**
*Michael Wallace Gordon***

* Henry M. Butzel Professor Emeritus, University of Michigan Law School; Chief Editor on Business and Private Organizations, 13 *International Encyclopedia of Comparative Law* (1965-1986).
** Chesterfield Smith Professor of Law, University of Florida Levin College of Law.

David S. Clark and Tuğrul Ansay (eds.) Introduction to the Law of the United States, 311-337

I. Forms of Organization

A. Preface

United States business enterprises encompass a wide variety of forms. Nevertheless, lawyers commonly use only a few of them, including: proprietorships, partnerships, limited liability companies, and corporations. The lines between some of the forms are sometimes blurred. But usually a given enterprise assumes one of the principal forms.

B. Proprietorships

A proprietorship, sometimes called an individual proprietorship, is a business organization enterprise owned by one individual. The proprietorship may be quite large, and employ many people. But it has one owner. Proprietorships are found chiefly in small retail shops and in service enterprises, such as hair salons and real estate or insurance agencies. There are far more proprietorships in the United States than all the other forms of business organization. They annually file approximately 73 percent of all business federal income tax returns, but report only about five percent of total business revenues. The large number of proprietorships exist not because the owners chose that form, but more often simply because they went into business without any thought given to forming a limited liability company or corporation. The word "proprietorship" is most likely unknown to many proprietors. If asked what form of business organization they were, they might say they were "self-employed" – the term used on their tax returns.

United States proprietorships include individual merchants who would be known in some other countries as *commerçants*, *comerciantes*, or *Kaufmänner*. They nevertheless include persons who sell services rather than goods, such as carpenters, surgeons, barbers, and brokers. Many proprietorships are operated part-time by persons who work "full-time" for a larger enterprise.

C. Partnerships

1. Simple partnerships

When two or more individuals join in an enterprise as co-owners and refrain from expressly adopting any other form of organization, they form a "partnership." If they are prudent, they record their intentions in a written agreement and adopt a firm name which they publicly file; but they are partners even if they do neither. They fall under a regime similar to that of the French *société en nom collectif*, the Latin-American *sociedad colectiva* or *en nombre colectivo*, and the German *offene Handelsgesellschaft*.

Since there are no formal prerequisites for the formation of a partnership, some businessmen become partners without knowing it. They think that they are in a "joint enterprise," or a "pool," or a "deal," but they are partners in the eye of the law. As such, they are all entitled to share in the profits of the enterprise and to participate in its management, and are all liable for its obligations.

When analysts need to distinguish the partnership from its cousin, the limited partnership, they sometimes call it a "simple" or "plain" or "general" partnership, but none of these modifiers is part of the statutory definition.

2. Limited partnerships

If some of the investors in an enterprise want to escape liability for the enterprise debts without incurring the complications of incorporation, they may form a limited partnership, in which they are designated as "limited partners." There must be at least one participant, called a "general partner," who is liable for the debts of the firm, but the general partner may be a corporation, so that no individual bears responsibility.

Investors who want to enjoy this status must enter into a written agreement, file it, and avoid active participation in the business. The resulting regime is broadly similar to that of the French *société en commandite simple* (from which it was deliberately copied in the 19th century), the Latin American *sociedad en comandita simple*, the German *Kommanditgesellschaft*, and their counterparts around the world.

An American limited partnership may have negotiable shares, in which case it resembles the French *société en commandite par actions*, the Latin American *sociedad en comandita por acciones*, and the German *Kommanditgesellschaft auf Aktien*, but will still be designated in American law merely as a "limited partnership."

3. Joint venture

A few writers and judges formerly recognized enterprises jointly owned by individuals for a temporary project as a distinct form of organization that they called a "joint venture." Most academic jurists now avoid this term, partly because the enterprises involved conform to the U.S. definition of "partnership," and partly because "joint venture" is loosely used to describe many dissimilar phenomena, including even a corporation jointly owned by two or three other corporations. Joint ventures, with partnerships and limited partnerships, constituted about seven percent of all enterprises and transacted six percent of all business done.

D. Limited Liability Companies

Lawyers long searched for some form of business that would have the limited liability of corporation shareholders, but be taxed as a partnership. The "S" corporation, formed under a special tax regime, was often used but was limited in scope. The solution was thought to be in the limited liability company (LLC). States began to adopt this form in the early 1990s, but until the Internal Revenue Service (IRS) issued a revenue ruling in 1995 affirming that the LLC would be taxed as a partnership, few were actually formed. Since 1995 their numbers have increased geometrically and it is today a very popular form for small corporations.

The IRS taxes entities as corporations unless they fail two of four tests: continuity of life, centralization of management, limitation of liability for corporate debts to corporate property, and free transferability of ownership. The LLC is designed to fail two of these tests, excluding the third one that guarantees their limited liability. Lawyers accomplish this somewhat by mirrors and illusions, since the enterprise really is intended to be a corporation in LLC clothing.

While it may be tempting to compare the limited liability company with the French *société à responsabilité limitée*, the Latin American *sociedad de responsabilidad limitada*, and the German *Gesellschaft mit beschränkter Haftung* (all of which are known in English as "limited liability companies"), because the U.S. LLC is a creature of tax law, it appears to stand alone, not as a "secondary" form of corporation. Nevertheless, it does to some degree attempt to imitate these foreign limited liability companies.

E. Corporations

1. In general

When Americans say "corporation," they usually mean a business corporation, conducting an enterprise for profit. That is the way we will use the word here, although there are other important kinds of corporations, notably *municipal* corporations like New York City, and *nonprofit* corporations like the American Red

Cross. The total number of business corporations filing income tax returns in 1996 was about 4.6 million, or slightly less than 20 per cent of all business enterprises; but they transacted 89 percent of all U.S. business.

Corporations come in all shapes and sizes. Some have millions of shareholders, some only one. Some can issue negotiable shares, while others cannot. Consequently American corporations include some that correspond to the French *société anonyme*, the Latin American *sociedad anónima*, and the German *Aktiengesellschaft*.

The most basic element that characterizes all corporations is their legal recognition as "entities" or "legal persons," which may buy and sell property, may sue and be sued separately from their members, and may own or owe obligations that are not owned and owed by their members. But not every organization with these attributes is a legal "corporation"; it is a "corporation" if formed under a law to which the legislature has attached the name "corporation."

2. Publicly held corporations

At the large end of the corporate spectrum are more than 12,000 companies whose shares are publicly traded on organized markets. Most of these companies have over a thousand shareholders, and a growing number have over a million. They are often called "public corporations," although this term must be read with care because it is used in other contexts to designate governmental or municipal corporations.

3. Close corporations

At the small end of the spectrum are "close corporations," which restrict the number of their shareholders, usually to 35 or fewer, and often forbid transfers of shares without the consent of other shareholders. They correspond in some respects to the "limited liability companies" of other nations, but their legal status is very different; many of them operate under the same statutes as public corporations.

The number of close corporations is not recorded, partly because the demarcations of the class are vague. About 2.3 million of them use the special income tax regime (known as "Subchapter S" or S corporation status) that is available only to close corporations. There are another 2.3 million corporations that may be "close" in fact, but whose precise status is unrecorded.

F. Other Forms of Organization

The menagerie of American enterprise accommodates a few species that do not fit any of the categories of proprietorship, partnership, limited liability company, and corporation. One of these is the "business trust," whereby investors entrust their money to trustees, who become the joint proprietors of the enterprise for the benefit of the investors. It flourishes chiefly in Massachusetts, and is sometimes known as a "Massachusetts trust" even when formed in other states. Although a few examples survive from earlier years, it has seen little use since World War II.

II. The Laws That Govern

A. In General

The American law of business enterprises is mystifying until one recognizes the unusual diversity of statutes, rules, and judicial decisions of which it is composed. Neither the nation nor any of its states has a comprehensive code of commerce that imposes rules of registration and record-keeping on all kinds of business establishments.

The basic norms of enterprise structure are separately prescribed by the laws of 50 different states. These laws are similar in many respects, but rarely identical. The state laws are overlaid at a few points by federal legislation and case law, but the basic elements remain within the realm of state courts and legislatures.

There are, however, a few disconnected requirements that apply to all business enterprises. State and federal tax laws require every enterprise to register with tax authorities and obtain a "tax identification number." Increasingly state laws mandate keeping accounting records, and the tax laws bear heavily on enterprises whose accounts do not prove the correctness of its tax returns. If the corporation adopts a name other than the legal name of its owners, such as a restaurant that calls itself "The Chuck Wagon," it must file the name of the enterprise and the names of its owners in a register of "fictitious" or "assumed" business names.

There are no rules of organization that apply distinctively to proprietorships.

B. Simple Partnerships Laws

The formation and structure of simple partnerships is regulated in nearly all states by the 1914 Uniform Partnership Act (UPA),[1] most recently revised in 1997.[2] Each state has adopted the UPA, usually with only minor deviations. Since its fundamentals are similar to those of the partnership laws of European and Latin American countries, we will not expand in this short chapter on its differences.

C. Limited Partnerships Laws

Limited partnerships are also governed in most states by a uniform act, the 1976 Revised Uniform Limited Partnership Act (RULPA).[3] This Act follows a trail blazed by European antecedents, and calls for no detailed analysis here.

The most troublesome questions of limited partnership law do not arise under the RULPA, but under tax law. An enterprise that qualifies as a limited partnership under the RULPA may be taxed as a corporation. This happens when a limited

1. 6 U.L.A. (Uniform Laws Annotated) 125 (1995 & Supp. 2000).
2. 6 U.L.A. 1 (Supp. 2000).
3. 6A U.L.A. 1 (1995 & Supp. 2000) (includes 1985 amendments).

partnership has too many of the characteristics of a corporation, such as negotiable shares, elective management, or perpetual duration.

A recent newcomer is the limited liability partnership (LLP). State LLP provisions are intended to offer general or limited partnerships certain liability limitations by registration.[4] Since registration was already required of limited partnerships, its greatest influence is on general partnerships.

D. Limited Liability Company Laws

Wyoming enacted the first limited liability company law in 1977. It was followed by Florida in 1982. But not until the IRS gave the concept its blessing with Revenue Procedure 95-10 did the number of states following this lead increase significantly. The adoption by the National Conference of Commissioners on Uniform State Laws of the Uniform Limited Liability Company Act in 1995[5] accelerated the passage of state limited liability laws, and they now exist in nearly every state.

One of the early concerns with these laws was whether one state, which did not have its own LLC law, would recognize and apply the LLC law of another state. Another concern, which continues, is that there is yet to develop any significant body of case law on the LLC. Much of the essence of U.S. corporation law is in case law. Many of the LLC laws were intended to track the state's corporation laws as closely as the tax laws would allow, without forfeiting favorable tax treatment. Courts were expected to consider corporation laws when the LLC law appeared deficient or ambiguous. In some instances a state would update its corporation law, but its LLC law would remain identified with the old, repealed corporation law. Despite some initial uncertainty and confusion, the LLC is clearly here to stay. It is used extensively in the formation of small business entities, especially as an alternative to the close corporation.

E. Corporation Laws

Unlike partnerships, corporations have no uniform law. The closest approximation is the 1984 Revised Model Business Corporation Act, as amended, which replaced the 1950 Model Business Corporation Act. Promulgated by what is now the Section of Business Law of the American Bar Association (ABA), the current version is published as the Model Business Corporation Act (MBCA).[6] Twenty-four states have adopted all or substantially all of the MBCA as their general corporation statute, seven other jurisdictions have statutes based on the MBCA's 1969 version, and other states have adopted selected provisions. There are a few national laws governing the formation and structure of particular kinds of enter-

4. *See, e.g.*, 3 Del. Code Ann., tit. 6, § 17-214 (1999).
5. 6A U.L.A. 425 (1995 & Supp. 2000).
6. American Bar Association Section of Business Law, Model Business Corporation Act: Official Text (1999) [hereinafter MBCA].

prise, such as "national banks" and "federal savings and loan associations," but none for broad categories of business.

Each state has its own business corporations act, which governs comprehensively the procedures of formation and decision making for the enterprises that incorporate under it. There are other state laws which regulate corporations, but the principal corporation act is what we refer to when mentioning the "corporation laws" of a state.

An enterprise does not have to incorporate under the corporation laws of the state in which it operates. It may incorporate in any state whose laws it finds more attractive. Under the prevailing U.S. choice of law rule, the internal law of the corporation is governed by the statutes and case law of the state of incorporation, even if all the corporation's offices and operations are located somewhere else. *See* Chap. 17, pt. III.I.5. Only California and New York have modified this rule, and apply certain provisions of their own corporation laws to corporations whose activities are predominantly within these states, regardless of where they were incorporated. The criterion is not the locality of the home office, as in some European countries, but the locality of a majority of the corporation's activities, measured by such factors as property, payroll, and sales.

The principal inconvenience involved in incorporating in another state is that corporations will have to pay filing fees, and sometimes legal fees, in both the state where it incorporates and the state where it operates. For small enterprises that operate mostly in one state, local incorporation is the rule. But for large corporations that operate in several states, forum shopping for the most favorable state corporation laws is common, usually leading to incorporation in Delaware.

Several states have consciously designed their corporation codes to attract the incorporation of enterprises located elsewhere. Incorporations bring income to the state treasury by way of fees for corporate filings, and bring income to lawyers, bankers, and clerks through the activities of filing and litigation that are drawn to the state. Delaware has been the most successful player in this game; over half of the corporations listed on the New York Stock Exchange are incorporated in Delaware.

Since other states are reluctant to lose their incorporations to Delaware, they liberalized their laws to match Delaware's, with a consequence variously described as the "race of laxity" or a "race for the bottom." The result is that most American corporation laws have become largely "enabling," rather than "regulatory."

A few examples of the permissiveness of state corporation laws may be illuminating. For one, most of them do not require that a minimum amount of capital be contributed, nor that the capital that has been contributed be maintained. They do not require that accounts be professionally audited, nor give creditors any right to be consulted on mergers that affect the corporation's load of debt.

F. Close Corporation Laws

Several states have adopted "close corporation acts" that authorize corporations to designate themselves as "close corporations," and when so designated to restrict the number and the identity of their shareholders, simplify their governing structure, and otherwise deviate from the suppletive rules of the corporation codes. The ABA Section of Business Law also promulgated a Model Close Corporation Supplement, which has been adopted in a number of states. Many states, however, remain with no formal close corporation statutes.

These close corporation laws are not comprehensive codes, like the limited liability company laws of many countries, but mere addenda to the main corporation codes. Organizers of closely held corporations sometimes ignore these laws even where they exist. The general corporation laws are so permissive that enterprisers can generally obtain all of the flexibility they want by adopting tailor-made charter and bylaw clauses, without invoking close corporation laws.

G. Federal Securities Acts

The most distinctive component of American laws governing business enterprises is the federal securities legislation, of which the main elements are the Securities Act of 1933, commonly known as the "Securities Act,"[7] and the Securities Exchange Act of 1934, commonly known as the "Exchange Act,"[8] and the rules issued under the authority of these acts by the Securities and Exchange Commission (SEC).

The Securities Act and the Exchange Act are closely related, but impinge on different stages of securities marketing. The Securities Act regulates principally the *issuance of new securities* to raise money for the issuing enterprise; the Exchange Act regulates the mechanisms by which investors buy and sell securities that are *already extant*. In economists' terms, the former Act regulates the "primary market," and the latter the "secondary market," including the stock exchanges.

When securities are first issued by an enterprise, the Securities Act requires that the essential facts be publicly filed in a "registration statement" and presented to buyers in a "prospectus." When the securities are subsequently quoted and traded on stock exchanges and other public markets, the Exchange Act requires that the issuers file and publish the information that a prudent investor needs to know. The Exchange Act also requires enterprises whose securities are traded on public markets to inform their shareholders about shareholders' meetings, the matters to be decided there, and to facilitate the shareholders' voting on these matters by proxy if they do not attend the meeting in person.

Although the securities laws apply most conspicuously to public corporations, they apply also in some circumstances to close corporations and limited partnerships, and potentially even to partnerships and proprietorships if they issue securities.

The Exchange Act also regulates various activities of securities buyers and sellers. It forbids traders to buy or sell securities when they possess important confidential information about the securities traded; this is called "insider trading." The Act also requires that when traders buy or propose to buy large blocks of shares of public corporations, they report to the SEC, the relevant exchange, and the issuer of the securities.

7. 15 U.S.C. §§ 77a-77aa (1994 & Supp. IV 1998).
8. 15 U.S.C. §§ 78a-78*ll* (1994 & Supp. IV 1998).

Although the federal securities laws are often called "rigorous," they do not impose rigidity on the financial structure or governance of enterprises. Their rigor is found chiefly in the requirements of information disclosure. These requirements compensate indirectly for the laxity of state corporation codes.

The norms imposed by the federal securities laws are not always revealed by the words of these Acts. Some of the most important norms, including the prohibition of insider trading and the requirement of proxy statements, are found only in the rules. The rules are codified separately from the Acts in title 17 of the *Code of Federal Regulations* (C.F.R.).

H. *Blue Sky Laws*

Alongside the federal securities laws there are state securities laws, which also require disclosure by issuers, buyers, and sellers of securities. Having originated before the adoption of the federal securities laws, they persist in spite of duplication. Their greatest utility lies in giving state officials legal authority to suppress local frauds that would escape the attention of federal officials.

State securities laws are known as "blue sky laws," following a vernacular characterization of valueless securities as "blue sky." The laws vary widely, but a majority of them are now patterned on the Uniform Securities Act of 1985 (USA).[9] At the minimum, they require some significant disclosure of the assets behind securities that are sold to the public; at the maximum, they authorize state officials to bar sales that they find "unfair or inequitable." Under this authority, state securities commissioners may forbid sales that are perfectly legal under the federal securities laws.

I. *Federal Antitrust Laws*

The federal antitrust laws relate chiefly to market behavior rather than to enterprise organization, but they affect enterprise structure in one important way. They forbid combinations of enterprises that have a tendency toward monopoly.[10] To provide the government with early warning of possible violation, the law requires that relevant government agencies be notified before a takeover or merger of some multi-million dollar enterprises is concluded.[11]

J. *The Bankruptcy Act*

The Bankruptcy Act[12] has become a major factor in the law of business enterprise in two ways, aside from its classic function of regulating liquidation. Under

9. 7C U.L.A. 1 (2000) (with 1998 amendments) [hereinafter USA].
10. 15 U.S.C. § 18 (1994 & Supp. IV 1998).
11. 15 U.S.C. § 18a (1994).
12. 11 U.S.C. §§ 101-1330 (1994 & Supp. IV 1998).

Chapter 11, regulating "corporate reorganization," shares may be cut down or wiped out, and creditors turned into shareholders.[13] The Bankruptcy Act impinges also on the amounts that may be validly distributed to shareholders by way of dividends and repurchases of shares.

K. Case Law

Many of the disputes over enterprise organization that reach the courts are not resolved by reference to legislative rules, nor even by interpretation of these rules, but by the application of principles found in judicial decisions. The open texture of the corporation laws leaves many questions to be answered on the basis of general principles that would be codified in countries with comprehensive codes, but which must in the United States be sought in the opinions of judges.

Foremost among these bodies of case law is that relating to the duty of loyalty, sometimes called a "fiduciary duty," that is owed by partners to co-partners, and by officers and directors to their corporations. The duty of loyalty is violated when officers or directors gain by actions that are detrimental to the corporation. Another significant package of case law relates to the authority of officers to involve the corporation in liabilities for actions that were never authorized, or even forbidden, by the board of directors. A third parcel of important case law relates to the valuation of enterprise shares when they are compulsorily exchanged for cash or other securities in a reorganization.

The applicable case law on these questions is the law of the state in which the enterprise has been incorporated. For a majority of the largest corporations, that state is Delaware. Although it is one of the smallest states in area and population, it is the one with the greatest influence on the internal affairs of large corporations.

In 1992 the American Law Institute first published *Principles of Corporate Governance*,[14] which was designed to guide corporate functionaries in the conduct of corporate affairs and courts in the resolution of disputes about them.

III. Formation and Finance

A. Incorporation

Creation of a corporation in the United States is surprisingly simple. The incorporators need only to pay the required fees and file a single sheet of paper containing the name of the corporation, the address of the corporation's office, the number of

13. 11 U.S.C. § 1123 (1994).
14. American Law Institute, *Principles of Corporate Governance: Analysis and Recommendations* (1994 & Supp. 2000).

shares the corporation is authorized to issue, the name and address of the registered agent, and the incorporators' names, addresses, and signatures. It may be much more elaborate than this, but does not need to be; additional provisions may be added later. An individual or corporation may be a sole incorporator. The initial document is designated by most statutes as the "articles of incorporation," but by others as the "certificate of incorporation." It is colloquially known as the "charter."

If the fees are correct and the charter appears proper, the relevant state official accepts and "files" the document. The corporation now exists as a legal entity.[15] It may lawfully transact business. If the corporation's organizers are prudent, they will defer business transactions until they have converted the bare legal entity into a functional and economic reality. To this end the organizers should first elect directors (unless the initial directors were named in the charter). The directors should appoint officers and adopt bylaws which specify the times and places of meetings, the authority of officers, and other internal matters. They should then raise funds by issuing shares before commencing ordinary business transactions.

If the managers intend to transact business in states other that the one in which they incorporated, they must file applications and obtain certificates of authority in each of these states.[16] There is no way of obtaining a national authorization by a single filing.

B. *Liability of Controlling Persons*

One of the principal objectives of incorporation is to shield the owners of an enterprise from individual liability for its debts. But the achievement of this goal is subject to conditions imposed by case law and securities laws.

1. Case law: "disregarding the entity"

Corporation laws imply that enterprise owners have no liability for corporate obligations if they conform to the laws. The only express imposition of liability declares that agents are liable when they purport to act for the corporation while knowing that it is *not* incorporated.[17] The negative implication of this section is reinforced by a declaration that shareholders are not liable for anything beyond the price of their shares.[18]

Notwithstanding these indications of legislative intention, judicial decisions have imposed liability on enterprise managers who are perceived to have abused the privilege of incorporation. The imposition is known by a variety of graphic metaphors, including "piercing the corporate veil," "disregarding the corporate entity," and "looking through the corporate fiction." The criteria of imposition

15. MBCA § 2.03.
16. MBCA §§ 15.01-15.05.
17. MBCA § 2.04.
18. MBCA § 6.22.

vary somewhat state to state, but tend to try to reach the same goal. The general rule is that the corporate veil will not be pierced unless the corporation is being used for illegal or fraudulent activities, or there is "other misconduct." Obviously what is meant by other misconduct may vary. In more conservative courts, such as in New York, the controlling persons are safe if the corporation is formally autonomous, with assets and governance of its own, rather than a mere department of a larger organization that supplies resources and gives the orders. In more liberal courts, led by California, less weight is given to formal autonomy, and more to the adequacy of the corporation's resources to meet its expected liabilities.

When courts "disregard the corporate entity," liability is usually imposed on the individuals who managed the enterprise, on a parent corporation that gave orders, or on a group of corporations that were operated as an economic unit. Although the metaphors of "piercing" and "disregard" suggest the possibility of imposing liability on the whole body of shareholders, the cases contain no examples of carrying theory to this extreme.

2. Securities laws

The federal securities laws and the Uniform Securities Act[19] impose express civil liabilities on persons who "control" the violators of the securities laws.[20] But liability is only presumptive, and can be negated by proving that the controlling person had no participation, by knowledge or inducement, in the conduct that gave offense. In addition, the federal Securities Act imposes on a controlling person a duty of registration, regardless of knowledge or participation.[21]

The meaning of "control" in these enactments is uncertain; in common usage, the term embraces everything from being physically in the seat of control to the power to muster a voting majority in an election of directors. The SEC adopted definitions embracing the broadest of these conceptions,[22] but the full extent of this definition has yet to be tested in the courts.

C. Finance

So far as statutory law is concerned, a new corporation can raise as much or as little capital as its directors choose to raise. Many corporation laws formerly required an initial contribution of a nominal amount, such as $1,000. A few still do, but none requires a substantial input like the minimum capital of a German stock corporation. The American case law on disregarding the corporate entity requires contribution only of some vaguely defined amount, that will be determined retrospectively when

19. *See supra* note 9.
20. Securities Act, 15 U.S.C. § 77o (1994); Exchange Act 15 U.S.C. § 78t(a) (1994); USA § 605(d), 7C U.L.A. 78 (2000).
21. Securities Act, 15 U.S.C. §§ 77b(11), 77e (1994 & Supp. IV 1998).
22. 17 C.F.R. §§ 230.405, 240.12b-2 (2000).

the corporation fails to pay its debts. Undercapitalization is generally not a reason to pierce the corporate veil.

The statutes are equally indeterminate on the amount to be received for each share. If the share has a "par value," it must be issued for at least that much, but most shares issued now have no par value, and may be issued for any amount, high or low. Most corporations set their issue prices between five and 100 dollars because those denominations are the most acceptable to investors, and shares priced lower are negatively regarded by regulators as "penny" shares or "sucker-traps."

Securities laws impinge on share issuance chiefly by forbidding enterprises to issue securities to "the public" without filing a registration statement with state and federal officials, and delivering an informative prospectus to each buyer.[23] But "private" issuances are exempt.[24] Under this rubric, billions of dollars worth of securities are issued each year to founders and officers of the issuing corporations, and to large professional investors such as banks, insurance companies, and pension funds.

When corporations are able to find private buyers for their securities, they generally prefer to sell privately, avoiding registration. Registration requires answering all the questions posed by securities regulators, and waiting while the regulators make up their minds about the permissibility of the issuance. In addition, the Securities Act imposes on officers, directors, and auditors the burden of proving that any material errors in a registration statement could not have been discovered by "reasonable investigation."[25]

D. Dividends and Repurchases

The liberality of American corporation law is nowhere more evident than in the rules on "distributions," which include dividends on shares and repurchases of shares. Corporations may buy back the shares that they have issued almost as freely as they may pay dividends.[26] Repurchase is a favorite way of distributing profits, because it allows shareholders who want cash to obtain it by surrendering some of their shares, while allowing other shareholders to escape the income tax that they would owe if the company paid a dividend.

With respect to the limits of distribution, there is a significant difference between the rules of the corporation laws and the rules of the Bankruptcy Act and Uniform Fraudulent Transfer Act (UFTA).[27] Most current corporation laws allow corporations to make distributions so long as they retain enough assets for two purposes: (1) to pay the debts of the corporation as they mature in the ordinary course of business, and (2) to equal the amount of the corporation's liabilities plus the liquidation preferences of its preferred shareholders.[28]

23. Securities Act, 15 U.S.C. § 77e (1994); USA § 301, 7C U.L.A. 35 (2000).
24. Securities Act, 15 U.S.C. § 77d(2) (1994); USA § 402, 7C U.L.A. 58 (2000).
25. Securities Act, 15 U.S.C. § 77k(b)(3) (1994).
26. MBCA § 6.31.
27. 7A U.L.A. pt. 2, at 2 (1999 & Supp. 2000).
28. MBCA § 6.40.

A stricter rule is imposed by the Bankruptcy Act and the UFTA. Distributions are voidable if they are made with the intent of defeating creditors, or if they leave the corporation with assets that are "unreasonably small in relation to the business" in which the corporation is engaged or about to engage. Creditors or trustees in bankruptcy may recover these distributions from the shareholders if the corporation defaults on its obligations or soon after it enters bankruptcy.[29]

Neither of these standards requires, as corporation laws formerly did, and as many foreign codes still do, that the corporation retain net assets equal to their "stated capital."

The laxity of American law in this regard does not reflect indifference to the interests of investors and creditors, but a prevalent belief that "market forces" furnish more efficient protection than rigid rules. Although this belief may be unduly sanguine, it gains in credibility as accounting and auditing standards improve, and credit reports become more readily available.

IV. Governance

A. *The Statutory Norm*

Corporation laws prescribe a system of representative democracy in which the political constituency consists of shareholders. The shareholders elect directors, who appoint executives, to whom directors delegate authority to conduct the ordinary business of the corporation.

Matters that are beyond the scope of the officers' authority remain within the directors' power, except for the most fundamental matters, which must be referred to the shareholders. These matters include significant amendments of the charter, mergers with other companies, and decisions to dissolve. Shareholders may also be called upon to vote on matters with respect to which directors have a conflict of interest, like the compensation of officer-directors; this reference is not mandatory, but shields the directors' decision from attack on grounds of conflict of interests.

This pattern is prescribed equally for close corporations and for public companies, except that close corporations are allowed under some statutes and judicial decisions to dispense with boards of directors, shareholders' meetings, and other procedures that are necessary in large corporations.

For public companies, the conception of shareholders as the ultimate constituency is reinforced by the "proxy rules" issued by the SEC under the authority of the federal Exchange Act.[30] These rules require the corporation to furnish its shareholders with detailed annual reports, notices of the matters to be decided at shareholders' meetings, and convenient proxies by which the shareholders can direct the voting of their shares without attending shareholders' meetings in person.[31]

29. 11 U.S.C. § 548 (1994 & Supp. IV 1998); UFTA § 4, 7A U.L.A. pt. 2, at 67 (1999 & Supp. 2000).
30. 15 U.S.C. § 78n(a)-(c) (1994).
31. 17 C.F.R. §§ 240.14a-1 to 240.14a-6 (2000).

Proxy rules also provide shareholders with some help from the corporation in contacting their fellow shareholders. Shareholders may propose motions to be voted on and require the corporation to circulate them at its own expense in the company's own proxy statement. Shareholders may also require the company to furnish them with a list of shareholders in order to solicit the votes of their fellow shareholders, unless the company prefers to circulate the solicitation at the shareholders' expense.

The corporations to which proxy rules apply are the 12,000 plus that are registered under the Exchange Act, by virtue of being listed on a national securities exchange, or of possessing assets exceeding $5,000,000 with 500 or more shareholders of record. In the other four and a half million corporations, shareholders are entitled to receive only the rudimentary notices required by state corporation codes.

B. *The Reality*

In close corporations, governance in reality approximates the statutory norm. A majority of shareholders generally decide who will manage the corporation; they often appoint themselves and members of their families to executive positions. Since the majority shareholders are usually close-knit, the minority shareholders have little chance of splitting the coalition, or of otherwise exerting influence.

In public corporations, the reality of governance bears little resemblance to the statutory norm. Shareholders docilely deliver their proxies to the managers, who elect directors who can be trusted to reappoint the incumbent managers or appoint successors whom the incumbents choose.

The result is a system of governance known as "managerialism." Although sometimes characterized as an advance stage of capitalism, it departs completely from the characteristic that gave capitalism its name – the supremacy of the suppliers of capital. Whether it is better or worse than a system of control dominated by investors is vigorously debated.

A complex set of obstacles dissuade shareholders from exerting authority over managers. Foremost among them is the many shareholders that doubt they would improve corporate performance by exerting more influence on the choice of managers; managerially managed enterprises are not observably less efficient than enterprises managed by major investors.

Shareholders with relatively few shares rarely attempt to organize opposition to management, even if the shareholders are dissatisfied, because the cost of soliciting and the difficulty in obtaining proxies from thousands of other shareholders outweighs any individual benefit. Dissatisfied shareholders can sell their shares at a loss and buy shares in another better-managed company more cheaply than they can organize a voting block.

Institutional investors, shareholders with large numbers of shares, have other reasons for remaining passive. Their investment managers are in a constant race to obtain better returns than their competitors, by buying and selling at strategic moments. They would gain nothing in this competition by forming a coalition of institutions to improve management, because all their competitors would share any advantage gained. Besides, the largest group of institutional investors are the corporate pension funds. These funds are generally controlled by the managers of major corporations, who would naturally oppose any movement to disturb the reign of managerialism. A few state pension funds have launched anti-managerial balloons, but their shareholdings are insufficient to prevail over enterprise managers.

C. The Case Law of Management

In view of the impotence of shareholders' suffrage, legal attention has focused on judicial enforcement of officers' and directors' duties of diligence and fidelity. These duties are matters of state law, interpreted by state courts. Since a majority of the largest corporations are incorporated in Delaware, Delaware decisions predominate in the interpretation of officers' and directors' duties. Federal securities laws do not impose standards of diligence and fidelity in management, but only in disclosure.

With respect to the duty of diligence, judges and legislators have been tolerant toward all but the most extreme cases of neglect. When the Delaware Supreme Court imposed liability on unusually supine directors,[32] the Delaware legislature responded by adopting a law which authorizes corporations to exonerate directors from virtually all errors except crimes and acts benefitting themselves.[33] This law was subsequently copied by other states, and has become the prevailing rule.

When officers' and directors' actions are not merely negligent, but self-serving, judges have been more stringent, and have frequently set aside transactions that were more beneficial to the directors who approved them than to their corporations. When these transactions that involve "conflicts of interest" are challenged by shareholders, directors bear the burden of proving that the transactions are beneficial and fair to the corporation.

But judges defer to the "business judgment" of "disinterested" directors. This deference has led managers to choose a majority of directors who are neither officers nor employees of the corporation, and are therefore regarded as "disinterested." When these disinterested directors approve a transaction that benefits other directors, it is sustained unless the challengers prove that reasonable directors *could not* consider the transaction advantageous to the corporation.

In rare cases in which officers and directors are held liable for misconduct, they may be indemnified for their liabilities by the corporation, or by liability insurance that the corporation has purchased. The corporation codes expressly authorize both forms of protection in all but the most extreme cases.[34]

D. Shareholders' Suits

Corporations are unlikely to enforce the duties of directors, because the corporations are under the control of the directors whose duties are in question. Suits by shareholders on their own behalf encounter two obstacles. First, the harm done

32. *Smith v. Van Gorkom*, 488 A.2d 858 (Del. 1985).
33. 4 Del. Code Ann., tit. 8, § 102(b)(7) (1991 & Supp. 2000).
34. MBCA §§ 8.50-8.57.

by unfaithful directors is not suffered primarily by the shareholders, but by the corporation. Second, the harm suffered by a particular shareholder is usually far less than the shareholder's costs of suing. To provide shareholders with effective means of protecting their interests, courts have developed two types of collective remedies: shareholders' derivative suits and shareholders' class actions.

In a typical derivative suit, a shareholder sues on behalf of the corporation to restrain or redress harm to the corporation done or threatened by an officer's or director's negligence or self-dealing. The shareholder may ask that millions of dollars be repaid to the corporation, although the suing shareholder's total stake may be only a few hundred dollars. The imbalance between the stake of the plaintiff shareholder and the stakes of the defendant officers and directors creates an opportunity for attorneys to harass corporations and their officers and directors in the hope of being bought off, rather than of achieving any real gain for the enterprise.

Legislatures and courts have responded to the danger of abusive suits by imposing various procedural hurdles. Suitors are generally required to have owned their shares at the time of the offenses of which they complain, and to give the directors an opportunity to correct the problem by making a demand before filing suit.[35] If disinterested directors determine that the suit will not benefit the corporation, the court may dismiss it. In some states, the plaintiffs may be required to post a bond to pay the defendants' attorney fees if the defendants win the suit. The suit cannot be settled without court approval.[36]

A class suit may be based on the same events as a derivative suit, but it proceeds on a different theory. The complainant does not sue on behalf of the corporation, but on behalf of all of the shareholders who are injured, or threatened with injury, by the officers' or directors' actions. The injury must affect the shareholders directly, rather than indirectly through harm to the corporation. Class suits escape the procedural hurdles erected against derivative suits, but incur some hurdles of their own. The plaintiffs must notify all members of the class, and give them a chance to dissociate themselves from the class. *See* Chap. 16. pts. IV.E, V.F.

The distinction between derivative and class suits is often elusive, since injuries to the corporation may injure the shareholders directly by diminishing their dividends, their votes, and other incidents of ownership. Complaining shareholders often file simultaneous derivative and class suits on closely related grounds in the hope that one of the suits will survive if the other founders.

Shareholders' suits of either type are useful to redress instances of egregious misconduct by managers, but cannot produce daily diligence and efficiency in the executive suite. For that, enterprises depend on other impulsions.

E. Self-Interest and Market Forces

Enterprise managers have material incentives for managing efficiently and faithfully. Greater profits justify higher bonuses, and enhance the value of managers'

35. MBCA § 7.42.
36. MBCA § 7.45.

stock holdings and stock options. Lower profits expose enterprises to takeover bids, which may result in the managers' losing their jobs and perquisites. The literature of management and market-oriented economics stresses the effectiveness of these forces.

Skeptics question the adequacy of self-interest and market forces to produce efficient management. Unscrupulous managers may gain more by looting their enterprises than they could extract from the shares they are able to purchase. The possibility of profits on stock trades may lead them to contrive a roller coaster of share prices, rather than steady appreciation. Takeovers may displace prudent managers with reckless speculators, who over-borrow and break up enterprises for quick gains.

If the behavior of officers and directors is not optimized by the prospect of material gains, it may be favorably affected by their desire for the good opinion of others. Corporate executives serve on the boards of one another, and are presumably sensitive to the opinions of their peers. They are probably somewhat sensitive to a broader public opinion; they like to be well regarded. Finally, they like to think well of themselves on a scale of values in which corporate prosperity occupies a high rank.

Whether managers are motivated by their interest in material gains or by their interest in being well regarded, the tendency of these motives to produce efficient management depends on the quality and quantity of information that flows to the financial community and to the general public. The disclosure regime of federal securities laws is a major factor bringing forth this information. Through this medium, securities regulation has beneficial effects on corporate governance, even though it does not specify standards of managerial behavior.

V. Structural Changes

A. Statutory Modes

When corporate owners or managers decide to make radical changes in the structure of a corporation, they have several available procedures expressly authorized by corporation laws. These procedures include amendment of the charter, merger, sale of assets, dissolution, and share exchange.

1. Amendment

By amendment, a corporation may add new provisions to its charter, or change any that are already there.[37] Amendments are most commonly adopted to increase the number or kinds of authorized shares. They are also used for an infinite variety of other purposes, from changing the corporate name to relieving directors of liability for mismanagement.

2. Merger

By merger, as the term is used in corporation laws, a corporation may simultaneously transfer all its assets and liabilities to another "surviving" corporation and extinguish itself. The former shareholders of the merged corporation commonly receive shares in the survivor, but are sometimes given bonds or cash.

In some cases, shareholders of a merged corporation receive, instead of securities of the surviving corporation, securities of a third corporation. This procedure, known as a "triangular merger," is useful for combining the merged corporation with the wholly owned subsidiary of a "parent" corporation, which issues the new securities.

If two of more corporations merge into a new corporation that is created by the merger, rather than into an existing corporation, the operation has sometimes been characterized as a "consolidation," but this term has become obsolete by being absorbed into the meaning of "merger."

The word "merger" is often used colloquially to include various other means of linking enterprises, such as takeovers and share exchanges. To distinguish the procedure authorized by corporation laws, it is sometimes designated a "statutory merger."

3. Sale of assets

A sale of assets is a short name for an operation defined in corporation laws as the "sale of substantially all the property of the corporation otherwise than in the usual and regular course of business."[38] The assets may be sold for cash or for shares or bonds of another corporation. After the sale, the selling corporation continues to exist, but conducts a very different enterprise than it did before.

4. Dissolution

Dissolution is a corporation's decision to dispose of its assets, pay its debts, and terminate its existence.[39] But dissolution does not immediately terminate corporate existence, which continues throughout the process of liquidation.

5. Share exchange

A share exchange, as used in corporation laws, is a procedure by which all outstanding shares of one corporation are transmuted into newly issued shares of another.[40] For example, shareholders of corporation *A* become suddenly holders

37. MBCA § 10.01-10.09.
38. MBCA § 12.02.
39. MBCA § 14.01-14.07.
40. MBCA § 11.02.

of new shares of corporation *B*, while corporation *B* becomes the sole shareholder of *A*. The effect is to make *A* a subsidiary, while the former shareholders of *A* become shareholders of the parent company. The procedure is of recent origin, and is seldom mentioned in legal literature.

B. Restructuring Procedures

The laws that authorize these restructuring operations prescribe procedures for effectuating them. With minor exceptions, the changes must be proposed by the directors of each corporation, approved by a vote of the shareholders of each corporation involved, and recorded in a document that is filed with the state office that holds the records of incorporations.

If any of the corporations involved in one of these restructuring procedures is a public company of a type regulated by the federal Exchange Act, it must give its shareholders a full disclosure of the purposes and the consequences of the operation on which they are asked to vote.[41]

C. Dissenters' Rights: Appraisal

Shareholders who are dissatisfied with a restructuring are not always obliged to accept the shares or bonds that are offered to them by the terms that the majority has approved. One alternative is to demand cash in lieu of securities. Nearly all corporation laws give shareholders such "dissenters" rights in cases of merger. Some award it also in a variety of other restructurings, including amendments that adversely affect the financial position or the voting rights of shareholders.[42] The right to receive cash instead of securities is sometimes called the "appraisal right," because the dissenting shareholder may have the shares appraised in a judicial proceeding if the corporation does not agree to a satisfactory price.

Another alternative for dissatisfied shareholders is to sue to enjoin or annul a restructuring on the ground that managers or majority shareholders have violated their fiduciary duties to the whole body of shareholders. But courts are reluctant to interfere with measures approved by majority vote when dissenters have a right to demand a cash payment.

D. Sale of Control

The most important restructurings at the beginning of the 21st century have been effectuated primarily by market operations, rather than by the operations described in corporation codes.

41. 17 C.F.R. § 240.14a-101, items 11-15.
42. MBCA § 13.01-13.03.

The simplest of these operations is a "sale of control." Typically, a few executives who hold shares in the corporation sell them to a buyer; simultaneously the sellers and their nominees on the board of directors resign and elect nominees of the buyer to fill their vacant seats. The sellers usually receive a price per share that is well above the price at which shares are sold on the open market.

The non-management shareholders who have not participated in the premium price received by the sellers of control sometimes complain that the sellers have taken a profit that belongs in fairness to all the shareholders. Their case is strong when they can show that the buyers of control have looted or otherwise mismanaged the enterprise, and the sellers could foresee this result, or that the buyers were prepared to buy all the shares, but were diverted into buying only the shares of the sellers at a higher price. In these situations, the sellers of control are said to have violated the fiduciary duty of controlling persons to the whole body of shareholders. But the mere receipt of a premium price with the delivery of control is an insufficient basis for liability.

E. Takeover Bids and Tender Offers

Instead of buying the shares of only a controlling group, an acquirer may make a public offer to buy enough shares to control the enterprise. This tactic is called a "takeover bid."

In practice, a takeover bid is usually framed with a complicated set of conditions. The bidder publicly invites shareholders to "tender" their shares, with the statement that if some minimum percent of shares are tendered by holders within a specified time, the bidder will accept all or a specified fraction of the tenders. A structured invitation of this kind is known as a "tender offer," the initiator is called a "bidder," the enterprise whose shares are bid for is known as a "target," and the target's shareholders are the "offerees."

There are other kinds of tender offers that are not takeover bids. Occasionally an investor will make a tender offer for a large block of shares with no intention of obtaining control. More often, a corporation will make a tender offer to its own shareholders for the purpose of defeating the takeover bid of an outsider.

Tender offers and other major acquisitions of publicly held shares are rigorously regulated by the Exchange Act. The main objective of this regime, as of other federal securities laws, is to inform investors. Even when no tender offer is made or intended, a shareholder who acquires as much as five percent of a class of shares must file a report with the issuer of the shares and with the SEC.[43] The report must include not only the identity of the acquirer, but also of the acquirer's owners and financiers, the purposes of the acquisition, and any agreements that the bidder has made about buying the shares or about operating the enterprise after acquisition.

43. Exchange Act, 15 U.S.C. § 78m(d) (1994).

When a tender offer is made, the bidder must give similar information in even greater detail to the offerees, the target, and the SEC.[44] Beside disclosing facts about the bid, bidders must observe a packet of rules designed to give offerees a fair chance to choose their course of action. The tender offer must remain open for at least 20 business days, it must be available to all shareholders on the same terms, and shareholders who tender in haste must be allowed to withdraw their tenders as long as the tender offer remains open.

State laws on takeovers, unlike the federal regime, have been clearly intended to give target-corporation managers a stronger hand in resisting tender offers that are unwelcome to them. Some of these state laws have been held invalid by reason of their burden on interstate commerce, and their incompatibility with the federal objective of a "level playing field." But the Supreme Court has sustained a type of anti-takeover statute that does not prevent the bidder from acquiring shares, but merely impedes or delays a successful bidder's exercising the control that would normally follow ownership of the shares.[45]

F. Anti-Takeover Devices of Target Managers

When managers of a target enterprise are not satisfied with the terms of a takeover bid, they often employ a variety of colorfully nicknamed defenses, known collectively as "shark repellents."

The most elementary repellent is to pay the bidder an extravagant price for the bidder's shares and the bidder's promise to drop the bid; this gambit is known as "greenmail." Another scheme is to grant other shareholders a right to exchange their shares, in case of a takeover, for much more valuable shares in any merger partner; this is characterized as a "poison pill." A third device is to give some rival of the bidder a cheap option on some of the target's most desired assets; this has earned the label "crown jewel lockup."

Since all these devices deprive the shareholders of an opportunity to sell their shares at a premium price and simultaneously protect the jobs of the target managers, they are frequently challenged as violations of the managers' fiduciary duties. The decision of this question is for the courts of the state of incorporation; federal securities laws are silent on the subject.

The prevailing judicial approach is to permit defensive devices that tend to preserve the enterprise as a viable business entity, but to forbid devices that sacrifice the integrity of the enterprise to save the jobs of the managers. Since all devices reveal some of both tendencies, the decision is not easy. The courts of Delaware, which entertain the largest volume of such litigation, seem to interpret the facts more sympathetically to target managers than do courts of some other states.

44. Exchange Act, 15 U.S.C. § 78n(d) (1994).
45. *CTS Corp. v. Dynamics Corp. of Am.*, 481 U.S. 69 (1987).

VI. Enterprises in the National Economy

A. Business Enterprises and Public Welfare

In the United States privately owned business enterprises provide virtually all the commodities used by consumers, other enterprises, and governments; they also provide a majority of the jobs held and wages paid, and generate much of the pollution of air, water, and scenery. The efficiency of U.S. enterprises in providing commodities, jobs, and wages, and in minimizing environmental degradation was increasingly challenged in the late 20th century, as other nations' enterprises were perceived to be capturing markets and rewarding their workers more effectively than enterprises in the United States.

Critics of the enterprise system offer an infinite variety of analysis and prescriptions, which may be divided for brevity into two schools of thought. On the one side stand critics who urge regulation by courts and legislatures; they may be called "institutionalists." On the other side are the critics who urge deregulation because they believe that enterprises operate best under the pressure of unchallenged market forces; they may be called "market economists."

A central factor in the debates of institutionalists and market economists is the concept of an "efficient market" for corporate securities. The term is derived from the observation that markets are efficient in reflecting available information about securities; prices rise and fall so quickly on good and bad news that traders can derive little or no advantage by trading on news breaks. This kind of efficiency has been called "arbitrage efficiency."

Market economists often ascribe to securities markets efficiency in a broader sense, such as awarding control to the managers who are best able to use it, and attracting investment to the most promising projects. This would be "allocative efficiency"; institutionalists generally doubt that securities markets are very efficient in this sense.

B. The Dynamics of Governance

One phase of the dispute between institutionalists and market economists relates to the collapse of the model of shareholder supremacy that is contemplated by corporation laws.

Some institutionalists respond to this problem by urging that courts should intervene in governance by correcting decisions that serve the interests of managers rather than the interests of shareholders, and foolish decisions that serve no one's interest. Other institutionalists urge that laws should be amended to facilitate the activism of large shareholders, such as pension funds, and thereby resurrect the model of shareholder control contemplated by the corporation laws.

Market economists, in response, contend that managerial supremacy is just as efficient as shareholder supremacy, if not more so. Some of them articulate a theory of a "market for control," whereby enterprises that are not efficiently managed are captured through share purchase by more efficient managers.

During the 1980s the "market for control" lost some of its plausibility as managers, state courts, and legislatures developed defenses against takeovers. To fill the resulting gap, market economists moved to a theory of the enterprise as a "nexus of contracts," in which shareholders buy the quality of management they want, and sell out when they are dissatisfied. Managers strive for efficiency in order to make their shares desirable and their costs of capital low. These systems of promoting efficiency are advocated as having lower transaction costs than intrusive devices like shareholders' suits and court orders.

C. *The Dynamics of Securities Markets*

The debate between institutionalists and market economists is encountered also in the regulation of trading in securities markets.

A major impact of the federal securities laws and rules is the prohibition of "insider trading." This prohibition reflects the institutionalist view that enterprise managers and their friends should not take advantage of other investors by trading on confidential information. Institutionalists argue that if insider trading is permitted, insiders will manipulate information and preempt the profits of market fluctuation. As a result, outsiders will invest less, and the costs of enterprise capital will increase.

In contrast with these views, some market economists defend insider trading. They say it rewards managers without taking money from the enterprise, and rewards other traders for diligence in discovering values. Moreover, it helps investors in general by making the market more efficient. Since prices rise and fall on insiders' purchases and sales, their trading makes prices reflect available information more quickly, and brings prices closer to intrinsic values.

D. *Social Costs*

However efficient enterprises may be in producing commodities and returns to investors, there are some social costs that market forces do not obligate enterprises to minimize. Periodic layoffs of workers and pollution of the environment are prominent examples. Economists sometimes call these costs "externalities," in contrast to "internalities" like payments for material and labor used, which managers are inherently motivated to minimize.

At the height of protest movements in the 1970s, critics proposed to "internalize" concerns about societal interests by legislation requiring corporations to install representatives of constituencies other than shareholders, such as labor, local communities, and minorities, on corporate boards of directors. These proposals made very little progress. Some corporations elected a few women, blacks, and labor union officers to their boards, but these were always the nominees of management, not of the constituencies of which they were symbols.

In the 1980s a new acknowledgment of social interests in enterprise management erupted in amendments of several state corporation laws to *permit* directors to consider "the social, economic, legal, or other effects of any action on the employees, suppliers, customers ..., communities and society .... and the economy of the state and nation."[46] But most state corporations laws were not amended to *require* directors to consider these factors, and none of them gave any of these constituencies a voice in the directors' deliberations. The purpose of the provisions was to permit directors to defeat takeover bids, even at some cost to shareholders, on the ground that the takeover would be detrimental to some of these social interests; there is no expectation that corporations will conduct other operations in the interests of employees, suppliers, customers, communities, the state, or the nation any more than they did in the past.

The protection of societal interests in enterprise behavior continues to depend principally on external pressures, including regulation by government and the bargaining power of organized employees and consumers.

Selected Bibliography

American Law Institute, *Principles of Corporate Governance: Analysis and Recommendations* (1994 & Supp. 2000).

Alan R. Bromberg & Larry E. Ribstein, *Bromberg & Ribstein on Limited Liability Partnerships and the Revised Uniform Partnership Act* (1995 & Supp. 2000).

—, 1-4 *Bromberg & Ribstein on Partnership* (1988-2000).

Alfred F. Conard, *Corporations in Perspective* (1976).

— & Detlev Vagts, eds., 13 *International Encyclopedia of Comparative Law* (Business and Private Organizations, 1972-1998).

Robert Charles Clark, *Corporate Law* (1986).

James D. Cox et al., 1-3 *Corporations* (successor ed. 1995 & Supp. 2001).

William Meade Fletcher et al., 1-20 *Fletcher Cyclopedia of the Law of Private Corporations* (perm. ed. 1991-2000).

Franklin A. Gevurtz, *Corporation Law* (2000).

Michael W. Gordon, 1-5 *Florida Corporations Manual* (1975-2000).

Robert W. Hamilton, *Corporations in a Nutshell* (5th ed. 2000).

Thomas Lee Hazen, *The Law of Securities Regulation* (3d ed. 1996).

Harry G. Henn & John R. Alexander, *Laws of Corporations and Other Business Enterprises* (3d ed. 1983).

J. Dennis Hynes, *Agency, Partnership, and the LLC in a Nutshell* (1997).

William A. Klein & John C. Coffee, Jr., *Business Organization and Finance: Legal and Economic Principles* (7th ed. 2000).

Louis Loss & Joel Seligman, *Fundamentals of Securities Regulation* (4th ed. 2001).

Jonathan R. Macey, 1-2 *Macey on Corporation Laws* (1998 & Supp. 2000).

Model Business Corporation Act Annotated (3d ed. 1997).

46. *E.g.*, Fla. Stat. ch. 607.0830(3) (2000); *see id.* ch. 608.4225(3) (managers).

F. Hodge O'Neal & Robert B. Thompson, 1-2 *O'Neals Close Corporations; Law and Practice* (3d ed. 1986 & Supp. 2000).

Arthur R. Pinto & Douglas Michael Branson, *Understanding Corporate Law* (1999).

Harold Gill Reuschlein & William A. Gregory, *The Law of Agency and Partnership* (2d ed. 1990).

Marc I. Steinberg, *Understanding Securities Law* (2d. ed. 1996).

Chapter 15
Criminal Procedure

*Christopher L. Blakesley**

* J.Y. Sanders Professor of Law, Louisiana State University Law Center.

David S. Clark and Tuğrul Ansay (eds.) Introduction to the Law of the United States, 339-371

I. INTRODUCTION

A. Federal and State Jurisdictions: Confusion for the Unwary

Substantive penal law and constitutional law are so intertwined with criminal procedure in the United States that one cannot understand criminal procedure without understanding certain aspects of these other subjects. One of the major difficulties in studying criminal procedure in the United States is that there is no one single system. Each of the 50 states, as well as the District of Columbia and the central federal government, has its own legislature, penal laws, and criminal justice system. The legislative and executive authorities which enact and implement these laws are sovereign within their respective jurisdictions, although among the 50 states the crimes punishable overlap considerably. Each state and the federal system also has its own set of courts of first instance, courts of appeal, and supreme court.

The primary responsibility of controlling criminality and defining crime, however, rests with the states, although the list of federal crimes and federal judicial jurisdiction keeps expanding. For criminal caseloads, *see* Chap. 16, pt. III.A. The Tenth Amendment to the U.S. Constitution provides that whatever the Constitution has not designated as within federal competence, or has not denied to the states, belongs to the states. Although each state has the general police power to control its residents, to proscribe, and to enforce its laws, the federal government can criminalize specific conduct (and cause the perpetrators to be punished) only pursuant to powers granted explicitly by the Constitution. See Chap. 4, pt. IV.

Every jurisdiction (each state and the federal system), furthermore, has its own police and prisons. Fragmentation is a serious problem. In a large metropolitan area there may be more than 100 separate police systems, each operating independently of, and often competing against, each other.[1] Looking from the outside, especially from nations in which there exists unity in the supervision and control in the criminal justice arena, this appears to be a *pagaille de confusion*. There is tremendous variety in types and organization of police agencies, prosecutorial agencies, and judiciaries. Although each state owes the other jurisdictions' records, acts, and judicial decisions full faith and credit, conflicts of judicial and legislative jurisdiction abound.

An additional problem relates to the very language of the constitutional Bill of Rights. It is quite vague and general, at least when applied to specific circumstances. For example, the Sixth Amendment provides the *right to counsel*. Does

1. Francis A. Allen, "The Quest for Penal Justice: The Warren Court and Criminal Cases," 1975 *U. Ill. L.F.* 518, 522.

this right obtain at the moment a person is the *focus* of suspicion? At the moment of arrest? What exactly is an arrest? It would seem that the proper way to ascertain constitutional rights is to determine what values and interests they represent and to interpret the language as applied to specific facts in a manner that promotes those interests or values. Unfortunately, many decisions interpreting specific guarantees of the Constitution do not do this, but rely on definitional analysis.[2]

B. Constitutional Criminal Procedure: Incorporation Doctrine(s)

The U.S. Supreme Court usually reviews cases of constitutional dimension, originally tried in federal or state courts. It has supervisory power over the federal judiciary, but its only role over state courts is to review issues of federal magnitude. Determination of the sources for constitutional standards has troubled the Court for most of its history. In 1883 the Court held that the Bill of Rights was adopted to limit the power of the *federal* government; there was no indication that the Bill of Rights limited the power of *states* to enforce their own criminal laws.

The 14th Amendment was adopted in 1868, after the Civil War. It prohibits any state to "deprive any person of life, liberty, and property, without due process of law." That language, so similar to that in the Fifth Amendment, has been a perennial source of disagreement in constitutional jurisprudence: what parts, if any, of the Bill of Rights are "incorporated" to the states through the 14th Amendment? The Supreme Court ultimately decided upon a process of selectively incorporating provisions of the Bill of Rights one by one and including some unenumerated rights deemed constitutionally *fundamental*. A right is "incorporated" when it is deemed required by fundamental fairness essential to or implicit in the very concept of ordered liberty. Ultimately, this *selective incorporation* approach resulted in the application of all but two of the enumerated provisions of, and several rights not listed in, the Bill of Rights, including:

freedom from unreasonable search and seizure;
notice of the nature and cause of the accusation;
privilege against self-incrimination;
right to assistance of counsel;
right to a public trial;
right to a speedy trial;
right to an impartial jury trial;
right to compulsory process for obtaining witnesses;
right to confront opposing witnesses;
guarantee against double jeopardy; and
prohibition against cruel and unusual punishment.

Only the Bill of Rights requirement of a grand jury indictment and the prohibition against excessive bail have not been incorporated.

2. John E. Nowak, "Foreword – Due Process Methodology in the Postincorporation World," 70 *J. Crim. L & Criminology* 397, 400 (1979).

Most provisions in the Bill of Rights are also found in the various state constitutions. Recently, the courts appear to be interpreting each particular provision differently, depending upon whether the action challenged was federal or state governmental action. Due to recent retrenchment by the Supreme Court, many state supreme courts have begun to interpret their constitutions more broadly to maintain the level of civil liberty protection developed prior to this federal retrenchment.

C. *Basic Characteristics of the System*

The American system of criminal procedure is "adversarial," with the burdens of evidence production and proof resting with the state, specifically with the prosecutor, not the judge. The judge functions as an impartial arbiter. Obstacles to the gathering and presentation of evidence have developed to prevent the state from abusing the criminal process. The common understanding is that the state has an overwhelming advantage over the accused in a criminal proceeding and that procedural protections are necessary to give the accused a fair chance to defend. In addition, some believe that the criminal process is an arena in which there may be a tendency for the government unrighteously to extend its power over people. The Bill of Rights has been the primary vehicle to counteract these tendencies.

D. *The Warren Court Era (1953-1969): Expansion of the Due Process Model*

One of the themes that emerged from the Warren Court was an attempt to ensure that fundamental liberties, like those enunciated in the Fourth, Fifth, Sixth, and Eighth Amendments were not hollow rhetoric; they should receive enough protection by the judiciary to be functional. The Court attempted to ensure fair treatment for rich and poor alike, especially to eliminate racial discrimination in the criminal justice process, and to protect against the unchecked power of the executive.[3]

II. Trends in American Criminal Justice: A Framework for Analysis

When Herbert Packer in 1968 wrote his significant, albeit criticized, work on the criminal justice system,[4] American society seemed to be in turmoil. Largely in reaction to abuses by the police, the United States Supreme Court (under Chief Justice Earl Warren) began reforming the criminal justice system to promote the civil liberties in the Bill of Rights. The Court's impact on penal law and procedure was without parallel. In Packer's terms, the system was moving from a *crime*

3. Stephen J. Schulhofer, "The Constitution and the Police: Individual Rights and Law Enforcement," 66 *Wash. U.L.Q.* 11 (1988).
4. Herbert L. Packer, *The Limits of the Criminal Sanction* (1968).

control model toward a more adversarial and judicial *due process* model. The American due process model is based on notions of confrontation and irreconcilable differences between the individual and the state.[5] It might be said that this due process system emphasized building safeguards against police abuse and the dangers of developing a police state, even at the expense of fact-finding accuracy in a given case. Thus, the rule had been developed and made applicable to the states, that if a police officer violated a suspect's constitutional protections and obtained evidence thereby or as a fruit of that violation, the evidence could not be used in the defendant's prosecution. In a given case, it is possible that everyone involved might know that the accused committed the offense charged, but this could not be proved in court because too much of the evidence was tainted by police illegality.

This approach might be contrasted with traditional continental models, where there are protections to ensure a fair trial, but also more emphasis on finding the "objective truth." While Europeans are now moving toward a more "adversarial" model, continental criminal justice systems traditionally have been built around the notion that penal law and punishment are designed not merely to deter, but also to educate and redeem. The due process model, on the other hand, is prepared to accept less efficiency (although this has not been proved) to minimize police power against individuals in a free society.

The Warren Court focused so much on the dangers related to police or other governmental abuse and the vindication of individual rights, that some believe it failed to resolve problems caused by the significant increases in crime.[6] This perception fueled fires of reaction and caused some to argue that European models should be adopted, but without much concern for the protections that have slowly been built into continental systems. Under Chief Justice Rehnquist, the Warren Court protections have been scaled back in a reaction to a system which had, from the point of view of many conservatives, become too lenient.

The model of a criminal justice system in a state of flux between two polar extremes – due process versus crime control – while an oversimplification, provides an analytical framework for this chapter. It is a Weberian heuristic model, which can provide an idea not only of the current status of the law in the area of criminal procedure, but also an indication of what the law might be in the near future. Developments indicate that there is a continuing trend toward the crime control polar extreme. Indicaors include the popularity of "shock incarceration," the "war on drugs," the increasing number of persons being executed for capital offenses, selective incarceration, rigid determinate sentencing, and the acceptance among the general public of vengeance as a legitimate reason for the imposition of penal sanctions. Individual rights advocates for criminal defendants have bitterly criticized the current Supreme Court for eroding protections, including the exclusionary rule, one of the major tools of the Warren Court to protect individuals.

5. Mirjan Damaška, "Evidentiary Barriers to Conviction and Two Models of Criminal Procedure: A Comparative Study." 121 *U. Pa. L. Rev.* 506 (1973).
6. *See* Allen, *supra* n. 1.

This chapter will focus on a few key areas: (1) the competition between protecting civil liberty and the need for strong law enforcement; (2) the "core" procedure amendments in the Bill of Rights, that is, the Fourth, Fifth, and Sixth Amendments; (3) the "war on drugs"; (4) pretrial detention and sentencing reform; (5) shock incarceration and new methods of serving time; (6) the death penalty; and (7) selective incapacitation. These essential areas of the criminal justice system will reveal sufficient detail to provide an understanding of the basic nature of the system, as well as some ability to assess critically the direction that the system will take in the future.

The plethora of separate concurring and dissenting opinions in Supreme Court decisions indicates that there is substantial disagreement on the meaning and application of provisions in the Constitution. It is also clear that ideological orientation and the notions of the "proper" judicial role play a large part in explaining these differences. Although the Court is supposed to be independent of the other two branches of government, the judicial appointment process provides some accountability to the winds of political change. The Court's retrenchment from certain decisions of the Warren era has reflected a change in popular opinion about crime in society.

III. The Basic Meaning and Evolution of the Fourth Amendment

A. *Seizure and Search of Persons and Places: The Rise of the "Reasonableness" Balancing Test*

The Fourth Amendment guarantees that people have a right to be secure in their "persons, houses, papers, and effects." The Supreme Court during the Rehnquist era[7] has methodically emphasized the "reasonableness" balancing test for deciding what official conduct violates the Fourth Amendment. This reasonableness approach has virtually replaced the former presumption that a search without a warrant is invalid.

In *Katz v. United States*,[8] the Supreme Court held in 1967 that the Fourth Amendment protects people not places and their "reasonable expectation of privacy" from official intrusion into their persons, houses, papers, and effects. This came to mean that a person has a "legitimate" expectation of privacy: one which society is willing to accept.

In some situations the Court found a "special need" to avoid requiring a warrant or probable cause to believe there was criminal activity before executing a search or seizure. This exception began with so-called "administrative searches" for regulatory purposes. When these searches yielded evidence of criminal activity, the Court refused to apply the review standards applicable to criminal proceedings, even though the evidence could be used in a criminal proceeding. Thus warrantless searches were upheld despite the lack of probable cause in situations where the

7. William Rehnquist became chief justice in 1986, after serving as an associate justice from 1972.
8. 389 U.S. 347 (1967).

needs of administrative authorities justified the search. For example, school officials may search students, government employers may search the offices of employees, probation officers may search the homes of probationers, and police officers may search automobile junk yards pursuant to statutory authority, even where the authorizing statute in question is later held to be unconstitutional. A special administrative warrant, which requires only that regular procedures be in place, is sometimes required. The evidence obtained may be used in the accused's criminal trial.

Another "administrative" search is the "inventory search." When persons are brought to the police station or when vehicles are impounded, police generally secure and inventory items on the person or in the vehicle. The ostensible purpose of this search is to protect the automobile and its contents and to protect the police against potential danger or charges of theft or property loss while the vehicle is in police custody. The Supreme Court found the individual's privacy interest in the car or its contents to be irrelevant because the search is "non-investigatory." The police agency must have some standardized inventory procedure, although that procedure may allow police discretion to determine which containers in an automobile ought to be opened. In 1990 the Court refined this by holding that a police officer's "uncanalized discretion" is forbidden.[9]

The current Court applies a reasonableness test, balancing the governmental interest against the individual's "legitimate expectation of privacy." It should come as no surprise that when the government's interest in preventing crime or in convicting a person for a crime already committed is weighed, the individual privacy interest pales. The Court has taken this approach, combined it with the principles and reasoning of *Terry v. Ohio*,[10] to expand considerably the situations in which government officials may search and seize without a warrant or even probable cause to believe that there is criminal activity. For instance, there is a "special need" when it would be "impractical" to require a warrant or when probable cause would "unduly interfere with the maintenance of the swift and informal ... procedures needed."[11]

The Court has never defined this category of "special needs." It functions simply as a label by which governmental interest trumps what could otherwise be considered a Fourth Amendment protection. Sometimes the special needs rule has allowed a search or seizure without any individualized reasonable suspicion. A special need has been found, and the lesser standard of protection applied, in the following illustrative situations: the health code inspection of a residential dwelling or business; drug and alcohol testing; hot pursuit of a suspect; the prevention of potential harm to officers or the public; the prevention of evidence destruction; or in a public emergency such as a fire, where the Court must draw the line between an emergency search, administrative search, or criminal search (for exmple, with suspicion of arson). The rule has been used in searches and seizures at borders, airports, public schools, and on highways at sobriety and other checkpoints as well as in the "war on drugs" and the fight against terrorism.

9. *Florida v. Wells*, 495 U.S. 1 (1990).
10. 392 U.S. 1 (1968), discussed *infra*.
11. *New Jersey v. T.L.O.*, 469 U.S. 325, 340 (1985).

Prior to 1968, when *Terry v. Ohio* was decided, a person was considered to be arrested when he was deprived "of his liberty by legal authority." Arrest brought constitutional protections. *Terry* refined this and lowered the standard by providing that a person could be detained legally by an officer when the officer has a reasonable, articulable suspicion "that crime is afoot." This is a *Terry* "stop," not an "arrest," and does not trigger the panoply of constitutional protections available to a defendant upon arrest. The officer may question the suspected person to dispel or confirm his suspicion. In addition, for protection of the officer or the general public, the officer may "pat-down" or "frisk" the outer clothing of the suspect to check for weapons and seize what feels like a weapon (or obvious contraband or evidence). The "stop and frisk" rule is now a vital part of Fourth Amendment jurisprudence and has been widely applied.

For example, the Court in *Alabama v. White* held that a stop was reasonable upon corroborating the details of an anonymous tip which indicated that a particular named person, carrying cocaine, would leave a particular apartment at a particular time and drive a particular car to a particular motel.[12] The stop was upheld, although the name of the woman and the precise apartment from which she left were not verified by the police and she was not carrying the attache case that the tipster had said she would be carrying. It apparently mattered little that many people leave particular places, get into their cars, and go to motels. Justice White, writing for the majority, called this a "close case," but Justice Stevens, in a scathing dissent, called it a "mockery" of the Fourth Amendment. In 2000 the Court drew the limits on the impact of *Alabama*. It held that an anonymous tip that a described person was carrying a gun at a particular bus stop was insufficient to justify an officer's stop and frisk.[13] The Court noted that *Alabama* reached the limit that the Court could extend the use of anonymous informants to create reasonable suspicion. Hence, the stop and frisk were unconstitutional and the gun found on the person was excludable.

An objective, "reasonable under the circumstances," test is used to determine the appropriateness of the stop and the frisk. If the detention is too long or too intrusive or coercive, evidence obtained may not be used. If suspicion develops into "probable cause" – the equivalent of common law "reasonable grounds" to believe the suspect has committed (or is attempting to commit) a crime – the officer may arrest him.

An arrest without probable cause is illegal. Any evidence obtained thereby is excluded from trial, as is any evidence that the officers are led to as a direct consequence of the illegal arrest ("fruit of the poisonous tree"). However, if the police would have found the evidence anyway in due course ("inevitable discovery"), or if they had an independent source for finding it, they may use it against the accused in court. The Supreme Court has also held that evidence may only be excluded by the person whose rights were violated.

12. 496 U.S. 325 (1990).
13. *Florida v. J.L.*, 529 U.S. 266 (2000).

B. Abduction and Warrantless Searches Abroad

An illegal arrest or kidnaping which takes place outside United States borders will not bar jurisdiction to prosecute, except possibly in the circumstances where the capture was egregiously shocking. If an extradition treaty does not explicitly mention that "official kidnaping" of an individual violates the treaty, abduction is not considered improper.[14] An extraterritorial search that would violate the Fourth Amendment, had it occurred in the United States, will not bar the use of the evidence obtained in that search. The notorious execution-style murder of Drug Enforcement Administration (DEA) agent Enrique Camarina gave rise to a warrantless search in Mexico and a subsequent U.S. Supreme Court ruling that the phrase "the people" in the Fourth Amendment (and in the First, Second, Ninth, and Tenth Amendments) "refers to a class of persons who are part of a national community or who have otherwise developed sufficient connection with this country to be considered part of that community."[15] Thus, at least some of the Fourth Amendment does not apply to a person abducted abroad by or in cooperation with U.S. agents and turned over to United States authorities to be tried, or to a search of his premises abroad without a warrant. *See* Chap. 18.

C. Seizure and Search of Persons

A person is not considered arrested until she has either been physically touched by an officer or has actually submitted to the officer's authority. Thus, if a person is running from an officer, after being approached or even shot at or chased, and throws contraband or evidence aside, it is considered abandoned and may be seized and searched without probable cause. The Supreme Court in 2000 held that there is reasonable suspicion to detain and frisk a person in "a high crime area" if she runs upon seeing a caravan of police vehicles approaching.[16]

Once a person has been arrested, she and the immediately surrounding area may be searched to remove any weapons, evidence, or contraband within reach of the arrestee. A person's seizure must be made by reasonable means. The police may also perform a cursory sweep of the house in which a party is arrested. A protective sweep is a quick and limited search of the entire premises, incident to an arrest and conducted, upon reasonable suspicion that someone else may be present, to protect evidence from destruction and the safety of the officers and others. This search may include spaces "adjoining" the area where the arrest was made.[17]

Killing a person to effect a seizure is not allowed unless it is *necessary* to effectuate a legal arrest *and* the officer has an objectively reasonable belief that he or the public may be endangered if the person escapes. The test contemplates that the officer's decision is often made in a split-second, under pressure, and that the officer may take the offense's gravity into account in making this judgment.

14. *United States v. Alvarez-Machain*, 504 U.S. 655 (1992).
15. *United States v. Verdugo-Urquidez*, 494 U.S. 259, 265 (1990); *see* Chap. 18, pt. II.
16. *Illinois v. Wardlaw*, 528 U.S. 119 (2000).

D. Places Protected

Fourth Amendment protections of privacy are strongest in the home. When an arrest requires entry into a suspect's home, an arrest warrant is required. When the arrest is to be made in a third party's home, consent or a search warrant is required. Police must generally notify the inhabitants of their purpose and authority prior to entering. They may enter a dwelling without a warrant, however, when they reasonably believe that there is an emergency, including: hot pursuit, a grave offense, serious danger to the officer or the public, or likelihood of escape.

In 1990 the Supreme Court held that an overnight guest has a "reasonable expectation of privacy" in a home and, that absent an arrest warrant or "exigent circumstances," officers may not enter to arrest him without probable cause to believe that the situation poses a risk of danger to police or to other persons inside or outside the dwelling.[18] The overnight guest, perhaps any social guest, is considered to have Fourth Amendment rights in the premises. In 1998 the Court held that individuals without any connection to the resident, merely transacting business ("renting" an apartment for a few hours to cut cocaine), have no reasonable expectation of privacy in the premises. In a dictum, however, the majority of justices noted that any social guest would have Fourth Amendment protection.[19]

Once properly inside the premises, officers may seize obvious contraband and evidence that they see in plain view. Since 1969 they cannot perform a full-blown search of the entire house, but may search the surrounding area where the arrestee might be able to reach to obtain a weapon or to destroy evidence.

E. Vehicle Searches

Vehicle searches have provided a means for the Court to erode many Fourth Amendment protections. The claimed rationale for this erosion is that vehicles are inherently mobile (thus evidence may quickly disappear) and individuals have a lower expectation of privacy since vehicles are subject to regulation and inspection. Thus the Court considers vehicles to carry an inherent exigency. When officers wish to search a vehicle they generally do not need a warrant; most searches are considered reasonable. Furthermore, if probable cause exists to search a vehicle, the entire vehicle may generally be searched. If probable cause exists to search a container placed in a vehicle, the vehicle may be searched to find the container.[20]

17. *Maryland v. Buie*, 494 U.S. 325 (1990).
18. *Minnesota v. Olsen*, 495 U.S. 91 (1990).
19. *Minnesota v. Carter*, 525 U.S. 83 (1998) (*see* Kennedy, J. concurring).
20. *See Wyoming v. Houghton*, 526 U.S. 295 (1999) (full search of back seat passenger's purse allowed, even though no probable cause for that passenger, but only for the driver of the car); *Florida v. White*, 526 U.S. 559 (1999) (warrantless seizure and search of car allowed upon probable cause that car is subject to forfeiture). *Contra Knowles v. Iowa*, 525 U.S. 113 (1998) (full search based on merely a traffic citation violates Fourth Amendment).

F. Roadblocks, Checkpoints, and Border Searches

The Supreme Court held in 1990 that the Fourth Amendment does not prohibit an initial stop and brief detention, without any individualized suspicion, of all motorists passing through a highway checkpoint established to detect persons driving under the influence of intoxicants.[21] The checkpoints, examples of "special needs" searches, must be conducted with established guidelines on how they should be selected, operated, and publicized. *See* pt. III.A.

Border searches are another instance of special needs. Nations deem the control and protection of their borders to be an essential part of their sovereignty. Thus, searches and seizures at borders and their functional equivalent (for instance, airports) are allowed with significantly less vigorous privacy protections.

G. Garbage and the Reasonable Expectation of Privacy

The Supreme Court upheld the search and seizure of a person's garbage that had been left on the street for collection in sealed, opaque bags.[22] It held that once garbage is placed on the street for collection, the person who had owned the garbage retains in it no "reasonable expectation of privacy." The Court has construed privacy to encompass what the public subjectively expects and what society deems legitimate to have.

IV. Competition between Protecting Civil Liberty and the Need for Strong Law Enforcement

Frustration and some hysteria over terrorism, drug trafficking, and organized crime have been catalysts for reaction and perhaps overreaction against civil liberty. The Fourth Amendment protection against "unreasonable" governmental searches and seizures is stated in terms so vague and broad that it is difficult to determine what government conduct in specific cases is prohibited. The current Supreme Court majority considers the operative word in the Fourth Amendment ("unreasonable") to require a balancing test to determine whether the warrant and probable cause requirements apply to different types of searches or seizures. The minority position, alternatively, begins with the warrant clause, asserting that non-consensual searches are presumptively unlawful unless authorized in advance by a warrant issued by a magistrate upon proof of probable cause.

A. The Rise and Erosion of the Exclusionary Rule

The Fourth Amendment "exclusionary rule," developed by judicial decision, provides that evidence obtained by official violation of the accused's constitutional

21. *Michigan v. Sitz*, 496 U.S. 444 (1990).
22. *California v. Greenwood*, 486 U.S. 35 (1988).

rights must be excluded from trial. In 1886 the Supreme Court held that forced disclosure of papers, amounting to evidence of crime, violated the Fourth Amendment and was inadmissible in the defendant's prosecution.[23] The Court coupled principles of the Fourth and Fifth Amendments, noting that there is no difference between allowing use of this illegally obtained evidence and forcing a defendant to be a witness against himself. The Court, however, has equivocated on this point since that time. The Warren Court in 1961 appeared definitively to adopt exclusion, holding that "all evidence obtained by searches and seizures in violation of the Constitution is, by that same authority, inadmissible in a state court."[24] This was short lived.

The exclusionary rule's erosion in recent years has been significant. Proponents argue that, although far from perfect, the rule has at least provided some official approbation of constitutional principles and disapprobation of their violation. Opponents claim that it only works to release criminals when the constable blunders. Proponents counter that attacks on the rule are often disguised assaults on the Fourth Amendment by those who wish law enforcement agencies to be unfettered by procedural obstacles that impair efficiency. Wayne LaFave, Jerold Israel, and Nancy King note that the framers felt that the restriction was better than the alternative, which they had faced under former governments.[25] The powerful symbol, "Don't tread on me," was aimed at the English crown, which abused its police power. The refrain that the exclusionary rule only helps the guilty misses the point in another way, as well. As the Supreme Court noted in 1960, the rule "is calculated to prevent, not repair."[26] Like Thomas Paine's "Don't tread on me" warning, the exclusionary rule is designed to enunciate, even dramatize, the principle that we are concerned to prevent the development of a government that has the power to do whatever is "necessary to find the truth" in the criminal process.

Whether or not it has specifically deterred individual police officers, there is no doubt that the exclusionary rule has caused police departments to become more educated about the Fourth Amendment and their proper role in the American constitutional republic. Where it has been applied, it provides a clear indication of the judiciary's respect for the Fourth Amendment. In contrast to this educative vision of the rule, the Rehnquist Court's view has been that specific deterrence is its sole purpose. Exclusionary rule proponents respond that this ignores the idea that the use of evidence obtained illegally diminishes not only the accused's constitutional rights, but also those of each member of society.

B. The War on Drugs and Terrorism

1. The borders, high seas, and airports

The government's war on drugs has been the ostensible top law enforcement priority for at least the past two decades. It has also been an utter failure. In addition

23. *Boyd v. United States*, 116 U.S. 616 (1886); Wayne R. LaFave, Jerold H. Israel & Nancy J. King, *Criminal Procedure* 112-13 (3d ed. 2000).
24. *Mapp v. Ohio*, 367 U.S. 643, 655 (1961).
25. LaFave et al., *supra* n. 23, at 114-18.
26. *Ekins v. United States*, 364 U.S. 206 (1960).

to failing to stop drug trafficking or its attendant violence, it has seriously eroded civil liberties and helped to prompt police abuse and a damaging rise in racial tension. Law enforcement entities and the courts have taken the symbolism of war literally. In 2000 the "drug czar" was a former much-decorated military general, who was charged in the media with having overseen atrocities in Iraq after the Gulf War cease-fire.

The result of law enforcement militarization is not surprising. Although drug problems have not been significantly affected, civil liberties in the U.S. and abroad have eroded. Monetary and military assistance and training abroad, often to non-democratic regimes, has been used to wage war against rebel forces and even peasant populations. This has occurred in Peru, Bolivia, Mexico, and Colombia, among other countries. A majority of the Supreme Court still presses to interpret the Constitution as vigorously as possible in favor of law enforcement to fight this "war," although some now seem ready to draw the line on further erosion of civil liberty.

The war's impact is seen in customs' procedures, police tactics (especially related to youth gangs), penal sentencing, and prison administration. Special police units have been established on a military, "quick-action" model to be used in high crime areas. These units have been extremely violent and sometimes corrupt, for instance in Los Angeles and New York City. Racial tensions are exacerbated. Long, even life, sentences are imposed on those involved in any sort of drug trafficking and even for mere possession. The federal government now has adopted the death penalty for murder in relation to drug trafficking or terrorism. Authorities have devoted massive resources for the purpose of punishing drug dealers and diminishing their profits. Forfeiture laws have been applied in a draconian manner, resulting in the forfeiture of cars, planes, boats, and even homes when they are suspected of use, even in a minor way, in drug trafficking or having been purchased with drug profits. This is often the property of family members of the drug user, possessor, or trafficker. The burden of proof is on the one who loses the property to prove that it had no connection to drugs. Congress may finally be ready to eliminate the abuse and corruption that this effort has caused.

United States jurisdiction over extraterritorial crime is expanding, especially in the arenas of narcotics trafficking and terrorism. Court decisions have approved the application of U.S. law and also the assertion of adjudicative and enforcement jurisdiction over conduct that occurred on the high seas and even within the territory of other states. The military is often used to help enforce the law and to fight the war on drugs. The invasion of Panama to arrest Manuel Noriega is an extreme example.

The problem of drug trafficking and drug addiction have provided a basis for claiming a "national emergency." The exclusionary rule arises most often in the law enforcement effort against drugs. Justice Marshall lamented the weakening of Fourth Amendment protections in those cases that have reached the Supreme Court. "[T]he majority's hasty conclusion ... serves only to indicate its willingness, when drug crimes or anti-drug policies are at issue, to give short shrift to constitutional rights."[27] Similarly, Justice Stevens opined that the "Court has become a loyal foot

27. *United States v. Sokolow*, 490 U.S. 1, 17 (1989).

soldier in the Executive's fight against crime."[28] The Court's majority has applied the rhetoric and law normally reserved for war to prompt the suspension or curtailment of some constitutional principles. Danger, of course, exists that the estimation of "emergency" is not accurate. Power also arrogates to those who make that decision and determine its duration, and may be used to promote ulterior political purposes.

2. Drug courier profiles and intrusive tactics

The effort to interdict drugs at U.S. borders has produced an unusual Fourth Amendment institution known as the "drug courier profile." The *Sokolow* case presents the typical scenario.[29] Sokolow was stopped at the Honolulu airport based on the following information: (1) he had paid $2,100 in cash for his airline ticket; (2) he was traveling under a name not matching that under which his telephone number was listed; (3) his destination was Miami, a city known to be a center of drug activity; (4) his stay in Miami was for only two days, even though the flight each way was 20 hours; (5) he appeared to be nervous; and (6) he checked no baggage. The Supreme Court upheld the stop and detention as a valid investigatory stop under *Terry v. Ohio*, which allows an officer to stop and detain a person for a short period of time to dispel or affirm the officer's "reasonable suspicion" that "crime is afoot."[30] The Court stated that the existence of drug courier profiles and their use by the Drug Enforcement Agency (DEA) was *irrelevant* to whether this particular stop was made upon reasonable suspicion supported by articulable facts. However, to suggest that these profiles are irrelevant ignores the fact that the DEA uses them to determine whether to detain a person. It did so on the very occasion at hand.

The drug courier profile is so vague and flexible that almost any passenger who comes to the special attention of the DEA fits within it. Thus the officer has virtually absolute discretion. Once detained, the suspect may be handled in a most barbarous manner with little risk of administrative sanction or exclusion of the evidence. In one case, for example, agents suspected a traveler was smuggling contraband in her alimentary canal. They held her – for more than 36 hours – at the airport, until she finally succumbed to nature. Over 150 cocaine-filled balloons were finally expelled and held to be admissible evidence.

3. Aerial searches and the use of technology

The right to privacy on one's property has also suffered. Traditionally, contraband and the fruits and tools of crime could be seized when noticed in plain view. Technology has long been allowed to enhance the senses. The Court over the past decade has held that the government may utilize any technology available to the

28. *California v. Acevedo*, 500 U.S. 565, 601 (Stevens, J., dissenting).
29. *United States v. Sokolow*, 490 U.S. 1 (1989).
30. 392 U.S. 1 (1968).

public. Thus search lights, telescopes, parabolic and other sophisticated microphones, aerial cameras, and even satellites are now permitted for surveillance and investigation on private property, perhaps even into one's home.

The Court applies the Fourth Amendment's "reasonableness" test to determine the legality of using this technology. For example, it was held to be a permissible search to use an extremely sophisticated aerial camera to photograph enclosed and otherwise protected corporate property. A helicopter was allowed to descend below 400 feet for officers to peer into a mostly covered greenhouse in an individual's backyard. Civilian satellites can now provide images of extraordinary clarity of virtually any spot on the earth's surface. State police, the DEA, or the Federal Bureau of Investigation (FBI), therefore, could do the same to investigate private property. Aerial searches, enhanced by technology, are not a violation of the Fourth Amendment as long as Federal Aviation Authority (FAA) regulations are not violated.[31] In 2001, however, the Court rejected as unconstitutional a search based on the scanning of a house with a thermal imager, a device not in general public use. The police had used the imager to detect heat that they correctly believed came from lights used to grow marijuana.[32]

4. Open fields

Even the crime of trespass has not presented a bar to the admission of evidence found by guilty police. In 1924 the Supreme Court held that the special protection accorded by the Fourth Amendment is not extended to open fields.[33] Some felt that this changed in the 1967 *Katz* decision, which held that the Fourth Amendment protects people, not places, and that it protects "reasonable expectations of privacy" wherever they might exist.[34] The current majority, however, has read "reasonable expectation" to mean what society, as read by the Court, is willing to accord a criminal. In 1984 the Court confirmed that a person *cannot* reasonably expect privacy in an open field.[35] Apparently, a person has privacy on his property only to the extent that an officer does not think that the individual is using it to commit a crime.

The Court in open field cases stated that a reasonable expectation of privacy only applies to the area that the common law called curtilage: the grounds, outbuildings (large enough to hold a person), and courtyard immediately surrounding the dwelling house. At least it is still true that this area cannot be entered physically by an officer, without some legal justification, but the expectation of privacy is generally unreasonable outside the curtilage. Whether curtilage might

31. See, e.g., *Florida v. Riley*, 488 U.S. 445 (1989); *California v. Ciraolo*, 476 U.S. 207 (1986); *DOW Chemical Co. v. United States*, 476 U.S. 227 (1986).
32. *Kyllo v. United States*, 121 S.Ct. 2038 (2001).
33. *Hester v. United States*, 265 U.S. 57 (1924).
34. *Katz v. United States*, 389 U.S. 347 (1967).
35. *Oliver v. United States*, 466 U.S. 170 (1984).

afford a reasonable expectation of privacy depends on: (1) how close the area claimed as curtilage is to the home; (2) whether it is surrounded by a fence or other enclosure; (3) whether the uses to which it is put are related to what one does in a home; and (4) whether the parties have taken steps to protect privacy. Even the curtilage or in some circumstances the home itself may be penetrated without a warrant by police in search for evidence, using technology generally available, as long as they do not personally enter, create dust or danger, or violate FAA regulations.

The open field and aerial search cases make clear the decreasing value of a person's subjective expectations of privacy and perhaps even the objectively reasonable belief that most members of society would hold relating to privacy from official intrusion onto their property.

5. The exclusionary rule's deterrence justification

Wayne LaFave and Jerold Israel note that five reasons have traditionally been argued to justify the exclusionary rule: (1) Fifth Amendment due process clause implications; (2) end the defendant's privacy violation by precluding tainted evidence; (3) restore the status quo ante as a remedy; (4) judicial integrity requires the courts not to condone police illegality; and (5) deter future police misconduct.[36]

The Rehnquist Court majority claims that specific deterrence of individual police misconduct is the sole acceptable justification for the exclusionary rule. Commentators and the Court's minority have asserted that the chief deterrent function of the rule is its promotion of institutional compliance with Fourth Amendment requirements on the part of law enforcement agencies generally. If this overall educational effect of the exclusionary rule is considered, the rule's application is appropriate and beneficial, even when individual officers act in good faith. The consequence of eliminating the other four justifications for the exclusionary rule and the narrow reading of the deterrence rationale is that the Court has deemphasized any notion that judicial integrity and the protection of privacy lie behind the rule.

6. The exclusionary rule's "good faith" exception

Justice White, dissenting in a 1976 decision, argued that the exclusionary rule "should be substantially modified so as to prevent its application in those many circumstances where the evidence at issue was seized by an officer acting in the good-faith belief that his conduct comported with existing law and having reasonable grounds for this belief."[37] Justice White's position prevailed when he wrote for the majority in 1984 that evidence obtained in a search based on a war-

36. Jerold H. Israel & Wayne R. LaFave, *Criminal Procedure: Constitutional Limitations in a Nutshell* 266-74 (5th ed. 1993).
37. *Stone v. Powell*, 428 US. 465, 536, 538 (1976).

rant that was facially valid (that is, no apparent deficiency), but constitutionally infirm, would *not* be excluded from trial.[38] This has been called the "good faith" exception to the exclusionary rule.

This exception has been extended to a variety of situations. For example, in 1987 it was held to preclude exclusion of criminal evidence discovered during an administrative search that was made pursuant to a statute that was subsequently held to be unconstitutional. Justice O'Connor expressed her recently developed worries about how far the Court had gone toward eroding the Fourth Amendment. Joined by Justices Brennan, Marshall, and Stevens, she dissented: "The Court today extends the good-faith exception to the Fourth Amendment exclusionary rule ... in order to provide a grace period for unconstitutional search and seizure legislation during which the State is permitted to violate constitutional requirements with impunity."[39] O'Connor correctly noted that the legislature's power to affect Fourth Amendment rights is more extensive and potentially devastating than that of the police. Furthermore, the majority's claimed deterrence rationale for the exclusionary rule seems nonsensical in this context. The application of the good faith exception is not justified by its underlying rationale where the legislature, not the police, provides the legal authority for the search. The conduct under a statute bears no resemblance to a reasonable mistake on the part of the police. Indeed, this case looks more like judicial approval of a writ of assistance, one of the very institutions over which the American Revolution was fought and for which the strictures of the Fourth Amendment were created.

7. The warrant requirement and plain view seizures

The Fourth Amendment requires that warrants issue upon probable cause and particularly describe the place to be searched and the persons or things to be seized. This is an obvious rejection of the "general warrant." The rule requires that a neutral and detached magistrate make the decision to search and seize, rather than the officer in the heat of ferreting out crime. It requires that a warrant provide constitutionally specific instructions to officers on how to search and arrest. It actually functions to educate officers and makes them consider the Constitution in doing their work, while providing a mechanism for objective, multilateral review and a record for later evaluation.

In 1990 the Court raised questions about the warrant clause's particularity requirement and eliminated the rule that plain view seizures be inadvertent.[40] A California jeweler described three stolen rings and two masked robbers in detail. One of the robbers was carrying an Uzi machine gun and the other a stun gun. They had handcuffed the victim and then stole jewelry and several articles of clothing. A warrant was obtained to arrest a particular suspect and to search for robbery proceeds, namely, the described the rings. When the officers executed

38. *United States v. Leon*, 468 U.S. 897 (1984).
39. *Illinois v. Krull*, 480 U.S. 340, 361 (1987).
40. *Horton v. California*, 496 U.S. 128 (1990).

the warrant, they saw in plain view the Uzi and stun gun, the clothing, and a handcuff key. All of these were admitted into evidence, despite the fact that they were not described at all in the warrant although the officers were looking for these items. It has long been held that officers may seize evidence, contraband, fruits of a crime, or weapons seen in plain view. The dissent was concerned that the majority was accepting police dishonesty or laziness to erode the warrant clause and its probable cause requirement.

V. Fifth Amendment

The Fifth Amendment provides that no person "shall be compelled in any criminal case to be a witness against himself." Obviously, confessions are important in criminal investigation. Despite the standards of the Fifth Amendment and the fact that confessions may not be trustworthy, a substantial majority of all convictions are based on the defendant's confession. In U.S. jurisprudence, however, in contrast to that in Europe, the accused should not be the central source of evidence. Since the accused cannot be compelled to be a witness against himself, the classic violation of the Fifth Amendment self-incrimination clause is governmental use of an accused's statement gained by compulsion.[41] So the Fifth Amendment has a built-in exclusionary rule. It is another reflection of the "Don't tread on me" view, which refuses to give government the power to do *whatever* is necessary to find the truth.

Until 1964, when the *Escobedo* decision held that a suspect in a station house interrogation had a right to counsel and an absolute right to remain silent, the Court appeared to feel that the constitutional right was only against being forced to incriminate oneself.[42] The common law evidentiary rule that confessions be voluntary had been constitutionalized. This "voluntariness" test originally meant that a court would determine under a totality of the circumstances whether the confession or statement was coerced by threats or violence, or motivated by promises or inducements, sufficient to render it untrustworthy or unreliable.

This approach lasted until 1966, when the Supreme Court held in the famous *Miranda* case that the privilege against self-incrimination is fully applicable during custodial interrogation.[43] *Miranda* adopted a set of rules that the police must follow in any custodial interrogation. The accused must be told that he has the right to remain silent, that anything he says can and will be used against him in court, and that he has the right to consult an attorney before any questioning can take place and an attorney will be appointed if he does not have sufficient resources. The exact words of the "Miranda warning" need not be used.

Warnings are required only when authorities interrogate a person in custody. They provide prophylactic protection against Fifth Amendment violations. Today *Miranda* is read as being broader than the Fifth Amendment, providing an irrebuttable presumption of compulsion, absent compliance with its dictates.[44] Scholars

41. Israel & LaFave, *supra* n. 36, at 258-59.
42. *Escobedo v. Illinois*, 378 U.S. 478 (1964).
43. *Miranda v. Arizona*, 384 U.S. 436 (1966).
44. Israel & LaFave, *supra* n. 36, at 258-59.

noted that this difference in the perception of *Miranda's* basis has led to a diminution of its application and might lead to its reversal. In 2000, however, the Court had an opportunity to confirm *Miranda's* constitutional basis, holding that it could not be overruled by a federal statute attempting to return to the voluntariness standard for custodial statements.[45]

The Supreme Court applies an objective test to decide when an interrogation is custodial, that is, when a reasonable person, in like circumstances, would understand that she is under arrest. Basically, the Court attempts to measure the quality of coercion inherent in the situation by considering factors like the number of officers, the place of arrest, or the amount of fire-power apparent and ready for use.[46] If a person is in custody and the police question her, the evidence obtained may not be used unless the *Miranda* warnings were given and the accused has voluntarily waived her rights. Interrogation is questioning for the purpose of eliciting an incriminating statement. If the accused is confronted with incriminating evidence, or is subjected to a colloquy between two officers or an officer and a third person, which functions to initiate a response, the response will not be admitted unless warnings were given.

In 1990, however, the Court held that an undercover officer posing as a fellow inmate is not required to give *Miranda* warnings before asking questions that may elicit an incriminating response.[47] Apparently the coercive, "police-dominated atmosphere," which the Court condemned in *Miranda*, does not pertain to a jail cell when the suspect is unaware that he is speaking to a law enforcement officer. Justice Brennan, concurring, emphasized that the decision does not intend to suggest that the Constitution condones this method of deception and manipulation, and that the police conduct raises "a substantial claim that the confession was obtained in violation of the Due Process Clause."[48] *Miranda* now does not require that a suspect be made aware of all the crimes he might be questioned about for a waiver of rights to be knowing and intelligent. The fact that a suspect was in a psychotic state when he received his *Miranda* warnings does not affect the validity of his waiver. On the other hand, the Court has recognized a defendant's right to introduce testimony about the environment surrounding his statement and tactics used by the police to elicit his confession, because such evidence is "highly relevant to [the confession's] reliability and credibility."[49]

VI. Sixth Amendment

The Sixth Amendment provides: "In all criminal prosecutions, the accused shall enjoy the right ... to have the Assistance of Counsel for his defense." This right is bolstered by the Fifth Amendment's due process and anti-self-incrimination clauses. These clauses collectively include the right of indigent defendants to

45. *Dickerson v. United States*, 530 U.S. 428 (2000).
46. Israel & LaFave, *supra* n. 36, at 207-08.
47. *Illinois v. Perkins*, 496 U.S. 292 (1990).
48. *Id.* at 300, 301.
49. *Crane v. Kentucky*, 476 U.S. 683, 691 (1986).

have counsel appointed and apply to the states via the Fourteenth Amendment. The Sixth Amendment right to counsel is of paramount importance in the American adversarial system because rights are not protected by overseeing "investigative judges" or by other systemic mechanisms for judicial protection of civil liberties as in Europe.

The Supreme Court has held that *Miranda* warnings are sufficient protection for the right to counsel, indicating that the only role for counsel is to tell the defendant that he has the right to remain silent. Given the system's complexity and most criminal defendants inability to understand the implications of what happens to them in a judicial process, such a holding grossly undervalues the significance of the right to counsel in the United States. This situation is exacerbated in capital cases.

Commentators and some Court members have noted that the Sixth Amendment right to counsel demands that it apply at the earliest point at which adversarial proceedings commence. They fear that otherwise the adversarial system is undermined with an inquisitorial type system put in its stead, run by prosecutors, not judges, and with no guard against tyranny like those protections that Europeans have built into their criminal justice systems over the years. In 1964 the right to counsel was held to obtain once the investigation focuses on a particular suspect who has been taken into police custody and released on bail.[50] However, the fairness of the process may be in the balance at an earlier point. Absence of counsel in such critical stages as interrogation and line-up, for example, can undermine the fairness of a later trial. The presence of counsel provides oversight and protection against abuse. In 1977 the Court held that the right to counsel, and the concomitant right to witness confrontation, do not attach for constitutional purposes until "the initiation of adversary *judicial* criminal proceedings," that is, the formal charge and preliminary hearing.[51] Indictment on a set of charges does not trigger the Sixth Amendment right to counsel for charges of other crimes. Thus if a defendant exercises his right to counsel for one robbery charge, that is not a bar to police-initiated questioning about an unrelated robbery.[52]

The Sixth Amendment rule is that, unless an indicted person knowingly and voluntarily waives his right to counsel, any statement deliberately elicited by the police or other government agents will not be admissible in the prosecution's case for that particular crime. Obviously, if a defendant does not know that the person eliciting a statement is a government agent, knowing waiver is impossible. Deliberate elicitation means questioning or something similar to induce an incriminating response.

Once the government brings formal charges and the defendant indicates his desire to have counsel present, no official may thereafter initiate discussion. Court decisions require the following analysis: Did the defendant invoke his right to counsel? If so, the defendant's responses to further questioning may be admitted to court only when: (1) he initiated further discussion and (2) he knowingly waived the right to counsel previously invoked. A strange twist has developed in right to counsel cases, in terms of whether the right's source is the Fifth, as opposed

50. *Massiah v. United States*, 377 U.S. 201 (1964).
51. *Brewer v. Williams*, 430 U.S. 387 (1977); *see Michigan v. Jackson*, 475 U.S. 625 (1986).
52. LaFave et al., *supra* n. 23, at 325-29.

to the Sixth, Amendment. The impact of the right to counsel seems to depend on the fortuity of which particular words the accused utilizes. The Supreme Court has held that if the accused asserts his right to remain silent, he may be interrogated without counsel and statements will be admitted so long as *Miranda* warnings were given and the statements were voluntary.[53] The police may initiate discussion if they begin with the warnings. On the other hand, if the defendant happens to indicate that he will not talk without counsel being present, no discussion may take place unless initiated by defendant.

Asset forfeiture law has affected the right to counsel. Under the 1984 Comprehensive Forfeiture Act the federal government may seize property that is connected to illicit business activity.[54] In two companion cases the Court held that assets subject to forfeiture under the Act may be frozen, and the defendant is not entitled to use those assets even to hire an attorney.[55] The Sixth Amendment required only that a defendant have the assistance of counsel, not that a defendant have the freedom to hire her attorney of choice. The majority stated that to deny a defendant the use of these funds does not upset the balance of power between the accused and the state.

The Sixth Amendment also protects a person's right to confront opposing witnesses. In 1990, the Supreme Court held that this may not necessarily contemplate face to face witness confrontation. The majority allowed one-way closed-circuit television to present a child witness (complainant) who alleged that the defendant sexually abused her. The statute allowing this requires that a judge first determine, after a factual hearing, that face to face confrontation would result in the child suffering serious emotional distress such that the child could not reasonably communicate. "We have never held," said the Court, "that the Confrontation Clause guarantees criminal defendants the *absolute* right to a face-to-face meeting with witnesses against them at trial."[56] Justice Scalia, in a strong dissent, charged that this holding subordinates "explicit constitutional text to currently favored public policy, ... but it is assuredly not a procedure permitted by the Constitution."[57]

The right to a trial by jury in serious criminal cases has long been considered the quintessential protection against government tyranny. Article II, section 2 of the U.S. Constitution commands: "The Trial of all Crimes, except for Cases of Impeachment, shall be by Jury." The Sixth Amendment provides further that, "In all criminal prosecutions, the accused shall enjoy ... trial, by an impartial jury." Although the jury trial right has an extensive and illustrious history in England, royal interference with it in the colonies was deeply resented, causing them to adopt in the First Congress of the American Colonies (the Stamp Act Congress): that "among the most essential rights and liberties of the colonists, ... trial by jury is the inherent and invaluable right of every British subject in the colonies."[58] The

53. *Patterson v. Illinois*, 487 U.S. 285 (1988).
54. 21 U.S.C. § 853 (1994 & Supp. IV 1998).
55. *United States v. Monsanto*, 491 U.S. 600 (1989); *Caplin & Drysdale, Chartered v. United States*, 491 U.S. 617 (1989).
56. *Maryland v. Craig*, 497 U.S. 836, 844 (1990).
57. *Id.* at 860, 861.
58. Richard L. Perry, *Sources of Our Liberties: Documentary Origins* 270 (1959).

Declaration of Independence declared that the king has been "depriving us in many cases, of the benefits of Trial by Jury." The constitutions of the original states included a right to a guaranteed jury trial, and since that time all state constitutions have so provided. In 1968 the U.S. Supreme Court left no doubt that the jury trial right is "basic in our system of jurisprudence, ... a fundamental right essential to a fair trial," and therefore, applies to state prosecutions as well as to federal prosecutions.[59]

The jury trial, given the jury's autonomy to do its will, protects people from prosecutorial abuse. Although generally the jury is not told of its power to do what it wishes – indeed, they have and are told they have a duty to decide the facts and to apply the law to those facts, wherever that leads them – they have the ultimate power to do as they will. Thus, the right provides a protection against laws deemed unjust or circumstances deemed inappropriate despite the law and the facts. This tradition of "jury nullification" is considered by some as anarchistic, but ultimately an unfettered jury may be essential to liberty from tyranny.

The right to a jury determination applies to the guilt or innocence decision, but not to sentencing.[60] In 1970 the Supreme Court held that a jury of 12 persons is not required.[61] The jury is to be selected from a "fair cross section" of the community; the Sixth Amendment and state constitutions also guarantee that the defendant has the right to have the jury drawn from those in the "vicinage." The defense and prosecution have the right to challenge and eliminate possible jurors, although an individual has a right to a jury from which individuals of her race purposefully have not been excluded.[62] Jury trial waiver is permitted, unless expressly prohibited by state constitutional provision or statute.

VII. Pretrial Detention and Bail

Inherent in the crime control model is the notion that limitations on individual rights are justified if crimes are thereby prevented. Two Supreme Court decisions involving challenges to pretrial detention statutes illustrate the trend toward crime control thinking since the 1980s. The Court upheld a New York law, over the objection that it violated due process, which authorized pretrial detention of juvenile offenders upon finding a serious risk that the juvenile would offend again if released.[63] The Court balanced the rights of the juvenile against those of the state, holding that the prevention of crime is a compelling state interest which justifies the deprivation of a person's liberty.

The Court also upheld the constitutionality of the 1984 Bail Reform Act, which authorizes the denial of bail under certain conditions.[64] It held that the

59. *Duncan v. Louisiana*, 391 U.S. 145, 149 (1968).
60. *Spaziano v. Florida*, 468 U.S. 447 (1984).
61. *Willaims v. Florida*, 399 U.S. 78 (1970).
62. *Georgia v. McCollum*, 502 U.S. 1056 (1992); *Powers v. Ohio*, 499 U.S. 400 (1991); *Batson v. Kentucky*, 476 U.S. 79 (1986).
63. *Schall v. Martin*, 467 U.S. 253 (1984).
64. *United States v. Salerno*, 481 U.S. 739 (1987); *see* 18 U.S.C. §§ 3141-3142 (1994 & Supp. IV 1998).

Eighth Amendment does not guarantee release on bail, but requires only that the proposed conditions of release or detention not be excessive. Further, the Court noted that the Act's pretrial detention scheme is "regulatory in nature" and not intended to impose punishment before trial, although one may wonder whether the person detained can discern the difference.

VIII. Prisons and Sentencing

All three governmental branches in the federal and state systems play a role in the sentencing of criminals. The basic institutions include the legislature, judge and jury, prosecutor, probation officer, social or behavioral scientists, parole board, and pardon or amnesty board. Within constitutionally prescribed limitations, the legislature sets the rules for sentencing and corrections, defining what conduct is criminal and determining the appropriate range of penalties. Legislatures also specify the various functions among the actors in the sentencing arena.

A. Indeterminate to Determinate Sentencing

Judges formerly had broad discretion in sentencing. This caused significant variation in sentences for the same or similar conduct, even within the same state. Indeterminate sentencing created a system rife with abuse and unfairness. Until the mid-1980s very little effort was spent to establish consistency or to set a range between maximum and minimum sentences. Each of the 50 states could possibly have a different penalty for the same conduct. Arbitrary parole decisions, great disparity of actual time served in prison by individuals similarly situated, unbridled power to manipulate inmate behavior, and disillusionment over the likelihood of rehabilitation prompted change.

Thus, diverse groups, both liberal and conservative, came together with a common aim: to draft legislation or develop a plan whereby indeterminacy and unfairness could be eliminated, or at least diminished. In most states and in the federal system, indeterminate sentencing was abandoned. For example, the California Legislature declared that "essentially, the purpose of imprisonment is punishment or, perhaps more specifically, the purpose of imprisonment is the denial of freedom and the reduction of choices that individuals can make." It provided that sentences be determinate, fixed by statute in proportion to the seriousness of the offense, thus severely limiting judicial discretion.[65]

Many states have followed suit and adopted determinate sentencing schemes, the essential character of which is that they be explicit and formulary. The convicted criminal can, at the time of sentencing, calculate the exact duration of the period of incarceration, including possible remission for good behavior. There is

65. John R. Hepburn & Lynne Goodstein, "Organizational Imperatives and Sentencing Reform Implementation: The Impact of Prison Practices and Priorities on the Attainment of the Objective of Determinate Sentencing," 32 *Crime & Delinq.* 339, 340-41 (1986).

no parole. In jurisdictions like Florida, Minnesota, Washington, and in the federal system, the sentencing judge's discretion is tightly constrained by a sentencing grid (guidelines). Social science methods, as well as penalogical and political considerations, are used to construct the grid, which sets very limited sentencing ranges for various combinations of crime severity and offender record. A judge may sentence outside the prescribed range only in extraordinary cases, and his reasons for deviation must be in the record.

B. *Sentencing Guidelines*

Sentencing occurs after prosecution and conviction of the individual in the "guilt phase" of a criminal trial. Later, in an entirely different proceeding called the "sentencing phase," a sentence is imposed. Although it has been recommended that jury sentencing be abolished, several states still allow a jury to determine the sentence. After a sentence has been rendered, the convicted criminal is given over to the executive branch for the task of carrying it out.

The 1984 Sentencing Reform Act created the Sentencing Commission to establish, "sentencing policies and practices for the Federal criminal justice system" and to promulgate presumptive sentencing guidelines. The Act explicitly rejected "rehabilitation" as a goal to be reached in the penitential setting and attempted to eliminate unjustifiable disparities and uncertainties in sentencing. It attempted to establish a single and consistent sentencing philosophy to which the entire federal system would adhere. It classified offenses and provided a narrow sentencing range for each class. It virtually abolished parole, required the judge to give reasons for deviation, and provided for appellate review when judges depart from the guidelines or diverge from a plea bargaining agreement.[66]

The advent of sentencing guidelines was revolutionary, generating great criticism. Norman Abrams and Sara Beale explain certain themes in this criticism.[67] (1) The guidelines are extremely complex and sentencing under their regime is too costly and time consuming. (2) They have not even reduced the sentencing disparity that was a major purpose for their being, but rather have created new hidden forms of disparity. (3) They deprive trial judges of the discretion necessary to distinguish crucial differences among cases, making distinctions primarily on the factual elements of crimes rather than on crucial differences among offenders. This results in palpably unjust sentences. (4) These problems are exacerbated where the guidelines implement statutory mandatory minimums, most notable in drug and gang cases. This has caused extreme prison overcrowding and corrections cost to skyrocket, despite the significant drop in the overall crime rate. (5) Only judicial discretion has been reduced. Under the Constitution's separation of powers, judges should have discretion for sentencing. Alternatively, the guidelines have greatly increased prosecutorial discretion to control sentencing.

66. 28 U.S.C. §§ 991-998 (1994 & Supp. IV 1998); *see* 18 U.S.C §§ 3551-3574 (1994 & Supp. IV 1998).
67. Norman Abrams & Sara Sun Beale, *Federal Criminal Law and Its Enforcement* 766-767 (3d ed. 2000); *see id.* at 767-778.

(6) This prosecutorial discretion is hidden and not subject to any formal or judicial review. (7) The guidelines have provided prosecutors with more power to manipulate defendants, to force them to plead guilty, even when innocent, and to become witnesses against others, who may also be innocent but are found guilty on the basis of the first person's testimony (to avoid a life sentence). This is common in drug cases. (8) Guideline sentences turn on a myriad of factual findings, made without sufficient procedural safeguards.

Over serious challenge the Supreme Court found the Commission, the underlying statute, and the guidelines to be constitutional.[68] Norval Morris noted: "We have tried better to distribute sentencing responsibilities among the legislature, the courts, and correctional authorities by shaping systems of sentencing guidelines and by developing processes for appellate review, ... [but] we are not even close to attaining a fair, just and comprehensive system for sentencing convicted offenders."[69] The constitutional challenge to the Act pressed two main arguments: (1) the delegation of authority to set sentences is excessive; and (2) it violates the constitutional separation of powers.

Opponents argued that the separation of powers requirement was violated in two ways. First, the Act limits the discretion of judges to such a degree that the legislature has improperly intruded into the judicial function. Second, the feedback mechanism whereby judges contribute to the continuing work of the Sentencing Guidelines Commission, which today is substantial, improperly involves judges in the legislative function. The Supreme Court, however, held that the guidelines and Commission do not threaten the fundamental structure of government or the existing balance of power among its three branches.[70]

State judiciaries retain the role of hearing habeas corpus petitions or other requests designed to protect prisoners' rights whenever appropriate. In addition, federal courts have the power to review the constitutionality of federal and state correctional law as well as to hear prisoners' complaints. The federal judiciary in the 1970s dramatically increased its review, at the request of inmates, of nearly every aspect of a prisoner's institutional life. This trend of expanding prisoners' rights slowed in the 1980s, as more conservative tendencies of the federal judiciary, including the Supreme Court, began to assert themselves. During the 1990s the opportunity to seek federal habeas corpus relief, even for capital cases, was severely diminished.

68. *Mistretta v. United States*, 488 U.S. 361 (1989).

69. Norval Morris, "Sentencing under the Model Penal Code: Balancing the Concerns," 19 *Rutgers L.J.* 811, 813 (1988).

70. *Mistretta v. United States*, 488 U.S. 361 (1989). "The Constitution's structural protections do not prohibit Congress from delegating to an expert body located within the Judicial Branch the intricate task of formulating sentencing guidelines consistent with such significant statutory direction as is present here. Nor does our system of checked and balanced authority prohibit Congress from calling upon the accumulated wisdom and experience of the Judicial Branch in creating policy on a matter uniquely within the ken of judges." *Id.* at 412.

C. Prisons and Alternatives

Due to draconian laws, including the sentencing guidelines, the prison population in the United States has grown tremendously to the point that some prisons are overcrowded enough to be in violation of human rights norms. In addition, new "super-max" prisons have been established for those prisoners deemed too dangerous and incorrigible to be in the regular, even maximum security, prisons. Critics call these prisons torture dens, where some inmates are held in solitary confinement for years until many go insane. Some allege that guards in prison high-security units have staged "gladiator-fights" between two inmates of enemy gangs put into the yard together to "fight to the death." In Corcoran Prison's high-security unit in California, one such incident led to a brawl in which 31 unarmed prisoners were shot, seven fatally. The prosecution of eight prison guards was unsuccessful, due to what Amnesty International called the guards' "code of silence" and threats to whistle-blowers.

D. Shock Incarceration: Boot Camp and Wilderness Survival

Former national "drug czar" William Bennett called for further experimentation with "shock incarceration" or "correctional boot camps." Boot camps, first established in 1983, are programs in which offenders are placed in a military-type environment, not generally as an alternative to jail but rather to probation. In wilderness encampments inmates are "infused" with military and survival discipline: that is, harsh physical and psychological conditions and training. Long hours of training, marching, and harassment "mould" participants in a process similar to that used for young military recruits.[71] Reports from the National Criminal Justice Reference Service have noted that, while the political appeal of subjecting offenders to harsh conditions is undeniable, the evidence on program effectiveness is inconclusive and recidivism rates have not gone down.

E. Capital Punishment

In the 1960s the National Association for the Advancement of Colored People (NAACP) Legal Defense and Education Fund and the American Civil Liberties

71. "Developments in the Law: Alternatives to Incarceration," 111 *Harv. L. Rev.* 1863, 1898-1921 (1998). A parent's description of a typical boot camp dining hall provides a glimpse of the regime: "Inmates march to the dining room entrance and stand at parade rest until the line moves forward. ... Upon being served their food, the inmates march forward, ... making precise military turns until they come to the first empty table. They place their food on the table and stand at attention until enough inmates are present to fill the table, at which point staff give them a command to sit. The inmates respond in unison, 'Sir, thank you, sir!' and take their seats. They eat in silence. When all at a table have finished eating, staff will give them permission to leave. The inmates rise in unison, march crisply to where they return their trays, and march to a line where they stand at parade rest until all have eaten. Upon command, they snap to attention and march to their housing unit." 20 *Crim. Just. Newsl.* 3 (1 Sept. 1989).

Union began a program of resistance to the application of the death penalty. The result was a moratorium on the execution of prisoners which lasted from 1967 until 1977. Not until 1984 did execution become fairly common again. In 2000 Amnesty International reiterated its condemnation, since many believe that the death penalty is still applied in an arbitrary and discriminatory fashion. The debate over the death penalty has been marked by consideration of several major questions: Is the imposition of the death penalty inherently cruel and unusual punishment under the Eighth Amendment? What procedural protections are necessary to prevent arbitrary and discriminatory capital punishment? Under what circumstances is the defendant's situation such that it would be cruel and unusual to impose a sentence of death?

Three quarters of the states and the federal government have capital punishment provisions. Under review by the U.S. Supreme Court this sentence can in general only be applied for homicide and only against those who contemplate or actually kill someone under aggravating circumstances.[72] Since 1977, more than 620 prisoners have been executed, about one third in Texas alone.

In 1976 the Supreme Court determined that a fairly rigid set of procedures was necessary to protect against arbitrary imposition of the death penalty.[73] Thus it is appropriate only for first degree murder with aggravating conditions and no mitigating circumstances. Generally, a bifurcated procedure having separate phases for hearings on guilt and on sentencing is mandated. Specifically defined statutory aggravating circumstances must be found, beyond a reasonable doubt, and an opportunity must be given for consideration of any mitigating circumstances. There must be an automatic appeal to the highest state appellate court. Extensive collateral review of capital cases is also pervasive. As a consequence, it is not uncommon for a case to take more than ten years after the commission of a murder before the state and federal appeals and habeas corpus processes are complete. Many more inmates are sent to death row than are executed each year.

Critics are still concerned that the death penalty is being administered in an arbitrary and discriminatory fashion. The Supreme Court, however, held in 1984 that death penalty cases in California were not administered in such an arbitrary fashion as to mandate that each trial court, during the sentencing phase, conduct a study to determine whether the death penalty under the circumstances would be proportionate to other like cases.[74] While proportionality review was recognized as beneficial in promoting more consistent application of the death penalty, the Court held that it was not constitutionally required. Current procedural safeguards are considered sufficient. In 1987 the Court rejected a challenge to Georgia's capital sentencing scheme.[75] It refused to give credence to a study that presented statistically significant correlations between the race of the victim, the race of the

72. *See Coker v. Georgia*, 433 U.S. 584 (1977) (death penalty unconstitutional for rape of an adult). *But see State v. Wilson*, 685 So.2d 1063, 1073 (La. 1996), *cert. denied*, *Bethley v. Louisiana*, 520 U.S. 1259 (1997), in which the Louisiana Supreme Court upheld a state statute that provided for the death penalty for rape of a child under the age of twelve years, even if the victim is not killed.

73. *Gregg v. Georgia*, 428 U.S. 153 (1976).

74. *Pulley v. Harris*, 465 U.S. 37 (1984).

75. *McCleskey v. Kemp*, 481 U.S. 279 (1987).

defendant, and the rate of imposition of the death penalty.[76] The Court held that these correlations did not show a causal relationship, that is, intentional discrimination in the administration of the death penalty. The correlations were held not to be of such a magnitude to indicate a constitutionally significant risk of racial bias affecting the outcome of specific cases.

Since the federal government and each state government must determine whether to utilize capital punishment, it has remained essentially a political issue. However, there is growing awareness that other countries maintain order and justice without using the death penalty. For instance, the *Soering* case, decided by the European Court of Human Rights,[77] caused much discussion in America since it focused on the tension between law enforcement interests and the protection of human rights. Soering was charged with murder in Virginia, found in England, and arrested pursuant to an extradition request by the United States. The European Court held that extradition to the United States would constitute "inhuman treatment" in violation of article 3 of the European Convention for the Protection of Human Rights and Fundamental Freedoms, because he might be sentenced to death and have to face the "death row phenomenon," that is, sit on death row for years. Soering, nevertheless, was eventually extradited to Virginia after the Attorney General promised that he would not seek the death penalty. United States prosecutorial authorities, in reaction, are finding ways to accommodate those European and other countries that insist on a binding promise that a capital sentence will not be imposed, so that extradition will be allowed. Thus, the European decision in *Soering* has had an impact on United States domestic criminal procedure.

Other international law pressure to change United States practice has been less successful. In *Breard v. Green*,[78] the defendant Breard, a Paraguayan citizen, was arrested in Virginia but not notified of his right to consult a Paraguayan consular officer, as required by the Vienna Convention on Consular Relations. The U.S. Supreme Court held that defendant's failure to assert his Vienna Consular Convention right in the Virginia courts procedurally waived any claim he might have had. It also held that the state government's violation of the Vienna Convention had no continuing consequences of a nature that would give Paraguay standing to sue. Paraguay protested and the U.S. Department of State requested Virginia's governor to stay Breard's execution. He refused and the U.S. Supreme Court affirmed. Paraguay filed an action against the United States with the International Court of Justice on the ground that the United States had violated article 36 of the Vienna Convention and sought an order to require the United States to vacate Breard's conviction. These efforts failed and Breard was executed.

76. David C. Baldus, Charles A. Pulaski, Jr. & George G. Woodworth, "Comparative Review of Death Sentences: An Empirical Study of the Georgia Experience," 74 *J. Crim. L. & Criminology* 661 (1983).
77. *Soering v. United Kingdom*, 161 Eur. Ct. H.R. (ser.A) (1989), 11 *Eur. Hum. Rts. Rep.* 439 (1989), 28 *Int'l Legal Materials* 1063 (1989).
78. *Breard v. Green*, 523 U.S. 371 (1998).

Although United States public opinion generally favors the death penalty, this may be changing due to efforts by groups, such as the Innocence Project, that have used DNA testing to establish the innocence of many individuals who had been languishing on death row. For instance, after it was established that there were 13 innocent prisoners on Illinois death row, Governor George Ryan in 2000 imposed a moratorium on further executions. It is notorious that most states maintain an appallingly low standard for the legal representation of defendants accused of capital crimes. This fact alone explains much of the disturbing error rate.

The U.S. Supreme Court has held that a state may not execute a person who is insane at the time of the proposed execution.[79] The Court noted that in such a case, since the condemned is unable to assist his counsel in trying to stay or avoid the execution and is unable to understand the sanction to be imposed, execution would clearly be mere vengeance. However, the Arkansas Supreme Court held in 1999 that prison officials may medicate an inmate forcibly with anti-psychotic drugs to keep him from harming others or himself, even if the collateral effect of this is to restore his competence to be executed. Similarly, the state of Arizona in 1999 enacted a law authorizing the use of anti-psychotic medication and other treatment of mentally ill death row inmates, who otherwise would be incompetent for execution.

In 1989 the Supreme Court held that the Eighth Amendment prohibition against cruel and unusual punishment poses no bar to the execution of persons who commit a capital offense at the age of 16 or 17.[80] The United States also ratified the International Covenant on Civil and Political Rights. However, it insisted on several reservations, including one providing that article 6(5) on the execution of juveniles did not apply to the United States. The United Nations Human Rights Committee found that this reservation is inconsistent with the Covenant's object and purpose, and hence void. The Supreme Court has set aside the death sentence of a 15 year old murderer, but it has been unwilling to agree to a bright line that would prohibit the execution of persons who commit murder at age 15 or below.[81] In 2001 there were more than 70 individuals on death row who committed their offenses when they were under the age of 18.

The Supreme Court in dictum has said that it may be cruel and usual punishment to execute persons who are severely retarded and wholly lacking the capacity to appreciate the wrongfulness of their actions. Nevertheless, it accepted execution of a mentally retarded person who had the reasoning capacity of a seven year old.[82]

79. *Ford v. Wainwright*, 477 U.S. 399 (1986).
80. *Stanford v. Kentucky*, 492 U.S. 361 (1989).
81. *Thompson v. Oklahoma*, 487 U.S. 815 (1988). In *Penry v. Johnson*, 121 S.Ct. 563 (2000), the Supreme court granted certiorari to determine whether Texas can execute a mentally deficient convicted killer with an IQ equivalent to that of a seven year old child.
82. *Penry v. Lynaugh*, 492 U.S. 302 (1989).

IX. Police Practices

A. Community Policing and Police Militarization

The police function includes more than just apprehending criminals and crime prevention. Police also play peacekeeping, public safety, and crime investigation roles. So-called community policing represents a positive step toward improvement in the criminal justice system, since it recognizes that there are limits to what the official criminal justice system can do. Performance is heavily dependant on citizen cooperation. The implementation of community policing programs represents an attempt to improve the effectiveness and sensitivity of the police and the criminal justice system in general through the involvement of those who are most affected by the service provided.

While researchers who have evaluated the effectiveness of these neighborhood-based crime prevention programs have not been able to point to dramatic effects in terms of crime reduction, some benefits such as increased safety and increased political participation have been documented. The importance of the growth of programs, such as "neighborhood watch," should not be understated. While the rest of the criminal justice system has become more harsh in its attitudes towards crime and criminals, adopting more of the crime control perspective, the community policing approach seems at once more sophisticated and enlightened. It is based on the notion that crime is a societal problem which cannot be solved merely through increased efforts on the part of the formal criminal justice system. The positivist focus on the individual determinants of criminal behavior is absent from the community policing approach. The focus on the needs, interests, and views of those who are affected by crime is significant.

Nevertheless, while community policing may have a fairly sophisticated and effective crime prevention side, it has also developed in a way that often bypassed conventional restraints on police abuse. Thus it has spawned special "high-intensity," aggressive policing and military-style, anti-gang, and anti-crime units, such as the infamous Los Angeles CRASH unit, the New York Street Crimes Unit, and similar units in other places. These units are notorious for corruption, drug trafficking, extortion, planting evidence, framing defendants, and even murder. The terrible killing of 22 year old Amadou Diallo, a law-abiding West African immigrant to New York, is one of the infamous examples of what can result from police militarization. Diallo was hit with 19 of the 41 shots fired by four white plainclothes officers in the Bronx when he reached for his wallet in his apartment building's vestibule.

B. Selective Incapacitation and Enforcement

Since the 1970s criminal justice policy makers have attempted to utilize future criminality predictors for purposes of imposing sentences. "Selective incapacitation" has now become popular in some circles. This process determines which criminal "types" are predictably high risks for recidivism or for committing dangerous crimes and who thus should be incapacitated. "Three-strikes" laws, which increase the incarceration period after the third crime, are a common example in this genre.

Special police surveillance programs, which specialize in watching these "types," are now widely used. In many states prosecutorial resources are concentrated on "career criminals" and "major offender" police units have evolved.[83] Within academic circles, selective incapacitation of career offenders has become an especially salient topic. All of these strategies share a common assumption about the nature of criminality: since most crimes are committed by a few offenders, their removal from the streets ought to result in the reduction of crime by an amount determined by the number of criminals "incapacitated," multiplied by the rate at which they commit crimes.[84]

Increased popularity of the selective incapacitation concept marks a unique twist in crime control thinking. Several commentators have noted that its central problem is the "false positive." The very nature of social science makes only probabilistic predictions possible; unexplained variation is unavoidable. Regardless of the predictive power of the model used to classify criminal offenders, there will always be those predicted to be violent or otherwise criminal who will not offend in the future. If perfect prediction is not possible, the application of incapacitation-based strategies of intervention will result in the imposition of punishment on the undeserving as well as the deserving. This crime control philosophy would allow a policy maker to take the risk of error, with its unjust consequences for the undeserving individual defendant, to incapacitate a larger number of criminals. The only question for the crime control devotees is how large a false positive rate is acceptable.

The connection between drug use and criminality posited by many who have done research on criminal careers makes selective incapacitation an even more appealing policy option for politicians promoting, for various reasons, the drug war mentality. Those who worry about due process and the constitutional order are appalled at the thought of knowingly taking this risk of erroneous imposition of punishment to improve efficiency; this is inherently inconsistent with the due process model of criminal justice.

Selective incapacitation's predictive instruments rely on indicators beyond past criminality: for example, socioeconomic status, family characteristics, school performance, and non-criminal behavior problems. Reliance on such sociological factors to determine whether and how heavily to apply criminal sanctions poses serious danger to the constitutional order. Furthermore, as Elliott Currie has stated: "If we can predict criminality through characteristics that are amenable to change, then there is no logical reason why we should lock up certain individuals on the basis of these characteristics rather than trying to change them."[85] Although selective incapacitation is politically popular, scholars also note that it may not be a viable criminal justice strategy, even on crime control terms. It is extremely expen-

83. Samuel Walker, *Sense and Nonsense about Crime: A Policy Guide* 139-41 (2d ed. 1989); "Symposium: Three-Strikes Legislation and Selective Incapacitation," 11 *Stan. L. & Pol'y Rev.* 1 (1999).
84. Alfred Blumstein & Jacqueline Cohen, "Characterizing Criminal Careers," 237 *Science* 985, 986 (28 Aug. 1987).
85. Elliott Currie, *Confronting Crime: An American Challenge* 96-97 (1985).

sive and fails to take into account the economic theory that others may step in to take advantage of the criminal opportunities vacated by incapacitated offenders.

X. Conclusion

In the 1960s and early 1970s the criminal justice system was characterized as influenced by a *due process* model. *See* pt. II. Since that era the system has been moving more toward a *crime control* emphasis, since it is harsher in police practices, penalties are more severe, and the death penalty is used with increasing frequency. The notion that criminals can be rehabilitated by the system has largely been abandoned. The purposes which currently guide the imposition of the criminal sanction are retribution, incapacitation, and deterrence.

The war on drugs has provided the Supreme Court numerous opportunities to reconsider procedural guarantees that were initiated by the Court under Chief Justice Earl Warren in the 1960s. The result has been a significant erosion in the protection of individual rights guaranteed by the U.S. Constitution. Despite empirical studies to the contrary, the perception that the exclusionary rule provides a significant hindrance to law enforcement has grown in strength. The prison and jail population in the 1990s almost doubled. American society is less free and less open, and, to many, a less desirable place to live. Yet it is a fact that crime rates in the 1990s dropped by one third. *See* Chap. 1, pt. V.

The concept of community policing provides a bright spot in what seems to be an increasingly vengeful society. It represents a policy guided by a progressive concept of police-public interaction, proper in an enlightened, democratic society. It represents a departure from a crime control emphasis, which is based on the notion that the only proper function of the criminal justice system is to fight crime. The symbolic importance of the use of military metaphors when discussing policy options in the criminal justice system must not be understated. One must not forget that the "us" against "them" type of thinking contributed in a material way to the abuses of the 1950s and 1960s, the reaction to which produced civil unrest and violence to a degree not frequently seen in America in the 20th century.

Selected Bibliography

Amnesty International, *Death Penalty* (2000) at <http://www.amnestyusa.org/abolish>.
Hugo A. Bedau ed., *The Death Penalty in America: Current Controversies* (1997).
Christopher L. Blakesley, *Terrorism, Drugs, International Law, and the Protection of Human Liberty* (1992).
Arthur W. Campbell, *Law of Sentencing* (2d ed. 1991 & Supp. 2000).
Elliott Currie, *Confronting Crime: An American Challenge* (1985).
Joshua Dressler, *Understanding Criminal Procedure* (2d ed. 1997).
Malcolm M. Feeley & Edward L. Rubin, *Judicial Policy Making and the Modern State: How the Courts Reformed America's Prisons* (1998).
Peter W. Greenwood, *Selective Incapacitation* (1982).

Thomas W. Hutchison et al., *Federal Sentencing Law and Practice* (2000).
Wayne R. LaFave, 1-5 *Search and Seizure: A Treatise on the Fourth Amendment* (3d ed. 1996 & Supp. 2000).
Wayne R. LaFave, Jerold H. Israel & Nancy J. King, *Criminal Procedure* (3d ed. 2000).
—, 1-6 *Criminal Procedure: Criminal Practice Series* (2d ed. 1999).
Michael B. Mushlin, 1-2 *Rights of Prisoners* (2d ed. 1993 & Supp. 1999).
Herbert L. Packer, *The Limits of the Criminal Sanction* (1968).
Austin Sarat ed., *The Killing State: Capital Punishment in Law, Politics and Culture* (1999).
Charles E. Torcia, 1-4 *Wharton's Criminal Procedure* (13th ed. 1989 & Supp. 2000).
Robert Trojanowicz et al., *Community Policing: A Contemporary Perspective* (2d ed. 1998).
Samuel Walker, *Sense and Nonsense about Crime: A Policy Guide* (2d ed. 1989).
Charles H. Whitebread & Christopher Slobogin, *Criminal Procedure: An Analysis of Cases and Concepts* (4th ed. 2000).
Larry W. Yackle, *Postconviction Remedies* (1981 & Supp. 2000).

Chapter 16
Civil Procedure

David S. Clark*

* Maynard and Bertha Wilson Professor of Law, Willamette University College of Law; Vice President, American Society of Comparative Law.

David S. Clark and Tuğrul Ansay (eds.) Introduction to the Law of the United States, 373-419

I. A Brief History of American Civil Procedure and Courts

A. The Colonial Period

The fundamentals of American colonial civil procedure were English: the writ, summons, single issue written pleading, oral testimony, and the petit and grand jury. But the process was in comparison to that of England speedy and cheap. Costs were minimal and judgment generally was given on the day of trial. Judges were usually laymen. There were, nevertheless, substantial variations among the colonies. Justice was more informal in the north. For instance, Massachusetts streamlined its summons and translated it from Latin to English. New Hampshire was known for simple and direct pleadings. In the middle Atlantic and southern colonies procedure was more formal. Everywhere, however, lawyers in the 18th century introduced more English form so that the trend was one from simplicity and innovation to greater complexity and rigidness. On the eve of the Revolution procedure had become, with its common law writs and equitable bills, quite conservative.

Colonial social and economic conditions shaped court organization. From the 17th century court structures evolved from simple, undifferentiated entities mixing executive, legislative, and judicial powers to more complex sets of institutions with specialized duties. English models and usages became increasingly influential. Massachusetts Bay provides an example. The original 1629 charter called for a general court and a court of assistants. The general court included all freemen who conducted the government affairs of the colony, but soon it became a representative body that in 1639 acted as the legislature and the highest court. The court of assistants heard the more important civil and criminal cases and took appeals from county courts, which heard minor civil and criminal matters. In addition, county courts decided administrative questions and disputes, including those concerning highway routing, fee apportionment for bridge repair, wage regulations, and the licensing of new meeting houses. They also reviewed decisions from other ad hoc and special courts.

Judicial organization retained its earlier pattern in the 18th century. The lower county court represented local rule by local authorities. It was a governing court and not solely an institution to settle disputes. In Connecticut, for instance, towns chose men to form a grand jury to assist the county court in its work, which included supervising workmen clearing the commons and reporting persons selling liquor. Counterbalancing decentralization, England become more serious about governing. Appeals from colonial courts ran to a special committee of the Privy Council. A few of the Council's decisions affected major issues, but in general it was an inefficient overseer of routine court business, averaging only three appeals a year in the 18th century. It also reviewed colonial legislation in a haphazard manner, overturning about five percent of colonial laws. England also established nine vice-admiralty courts in America by 1763. These courts enforced *English* trade policy and were doubly unpopular since cases were tried without a jury. Hostility to chancery courts, which existed in some colonies, was similarly widespread. Chancery was closely linked to executive power and in turn with the English overlords. Its lack of a jury eliminated a native barrier to the use of these courts as instruments of English imperial policy.

B. *The Early Republic*

After the American Revolution, the United States Constitution of 1787 authorized a new system of limited jurisdiction federal courts, but included both cases in law and in equity. It embodied the Enlightenment idea of separation of powers, leavened by the concept of checks and balances that exemplified the American distrust of government. *See* Chap. 1, pt. I.B. The Judiciary Act of 1789 established a two-tier network of federal trial courts. The first tier consisted of district courts, each occupied by its own district judge usually covering one state. The second tier consisted of circuit courts that did not have their own judges, but borrowed them from the districts and used circuit-riding Supreme Court justices. District courts heard primarily admiralty cases, minor criminal cases, and minor matters involving the U.S. Government as a party. Circuit courts heard diversity of citizenship cases (between "citizens" from different states) and major criminal and U.S. Government cases. In addition, they had appellate jurisdiction over district courts in most admiralty and some government cases. The Supreme Court had a small first instance jurisdiction, as the Constitution required, and appellate jurisdiction over circuit courts in cases raising a federal question.

Enlightenment ideas also influenced judicial organization in the states, which under federalism in the new U.S. Constitution retained most litigation. But the long tradition of mixing branches of government at the highest level remained in many states until well into the 19th century, when all states at last gave their highest court final *judicial* authority. Many states further failed to follow the federal example of merging law and equity jurisdiction, so that jurisdictional issues plagued civil courts in many systems.

C. The Field Code of Civil Procedure (1848)

Civil procedure by the end of the 18th century had become more thoroughly Anglicized. Some states, nevertheless, tried to simplify civil procedure. Georgia, for instance, in 1799 passed a judiciary act to unite equity and common law pleading and to eliminate the forms of action. The catalytic agent of procedural reform, however, was David Dudley Field (1805-1894). He led a movement that culminated in New York's new constitution (1846) and code of civil procedure (1848). The former abolished the chancery court and prepared the path for the code to merge law and equity and to eliminate the forms of action. One "civil action" was established, with which the parties were to plead in "ordinary and concise language, without repetition, and in such a manner as to enable a person of common understanding to know what is intended," the facts constituting the cause of action or revealing a defense.[1] In addition to simplified pleading, Field's Code promoted liberal amendment of pleadings, joinder of parties, and appeals. Field favored jury trials to counteract the potential tyranny of arbitrary, politically appointed, judges; the code extended an automatic jury trial right beyond those cases provided for in the New York constitution. By 1873 more than half the American states and territories had embraced civil procedure codes based on the New York model.

D. The Federal Rules of Civil Procedure (1938)

Until 1938 law and equity practice had not been completely merged in federal courts. Equity cases were governed by uniform federal rules, but procedure in common law cases had to conform to the procedure of the state in which a federal court sat. In 1934 Congress yielded to pressure from the American Bar Association to permit rulemaking by the Supreme Court for federal district courts in cases at law under a system similar to that in use for equity procedure. Congress was careful to reserve a veto power for itself and to limit the court to procedural rules that would not modify the substantive rights of any litigant. The Supreme Court appointed an Advisory Committee of judges, lawyers, and law professors to draft a set of uniform rules covering both equity and common law actions. These became effective in 1938 as the Federal Rules of Civil Procedure (FRCP) and have served ever since as a model for state procedural reform. Over two thirds of the states have adopted most or all of the details of the FRCP and all states have been influenced by them to some extent. Many states also now vest procedural rulemaking in their state supreme court (often with a committee) to secure more expert draftsmanship than can be expected from the legislature.

The principal features of the FRCP are: (1) the union of law and equity with the retention of a jury trial in actions formerly at law; (2) further simplification

1. Code of Procedure § 120.

of pleading to require only a short and plain statement of the claim, with authorized forms for recurring fact situations; (3) liberal amendment of pleadings; (4) liberal joinder of claims and parties using the same transaction or occurrence as the unit of litigation to avoid a multiplicity of actions and to permit complicated litigation; (5) broader use of the summary judgment motion and pretrial conference; and (6) comprehensive discovery procedures to enable parties to better prepare for trial with minimal judicial supervision.

II. The Nature of American Civil Procedure

Civil procedure in the United States cannot be understood apart from the institution of the civil jury. *See* pt. IX.B. Guaranteed as a party's right in federal court by the Seventh Amendment of the U.S. Constitution for trial of facts in "Suits at common law," and guaranteed in most state courts by state constitutions, the right to trial by jury necessitates a concentrated trial and has by custom favored an oral procedure. Since the public is invited to attend trials (and today the most interesting ones are broadcast on national cable television), concentration and orality produce a dramatic event much like a morality play about justice. These elements coupled with the adversary principle controlling the proceedings recall the medieval Germanic public assembly or moot used to hear and decide disputes. Trial by ordeal, battle, or ritual oath emphasized the sensuous and emotional character of civil justice. Germany and other countries within the civil law tradition long ago adopted the Romano-canonic procedure of periodic segmented proceedings preferring written evidence used by a professional judge or panel of judges. It is thus ironic that procedure in the United States, which conducts over 95 percent of the world's civil jury trials, with its champion lawyer, forceful cross-examination of witnesses, and lay fact-finders, is more Germanic than German procedure.

The potential presence of the jury to resolve a dispute makes a discontinuous first instance trial of the European variety impracticable, since the personal inconvenience to jurors in meeting at irregular intervals would be too great. If the trial is to consist of a single episode, pretrial procedures must be developed to handle the problem of surprise.

The 1938 Federal Rules of Civil Procedure (FRCP) were designed in part to solve this problem and to promote the goals of securing substantive justice (a decision based on the applicable substantive rules of law), procedural justice (a decision according to the true facts), and efficiency (a speedy and inexpensive determination).[2] These goals are often competing, so that more justice will likely cost more time or money. The Federal Rules dealt with the problem of surprise by providing liberal discovery mechanisms, further broadened by amendments in 1970, but then narrowed in a reaction against excessive discovery requests in 1993 and 2000. The goal remains full and mutual access by the parties to evidence relevant to the issues framed by the pleadings, with the opportunity at trial to introduce all admissible evidence discovered. *See* pt. VI.

2. FRCP 1.

Another idea in the FRCP was that the unit of litigation should be the "transaction" or "occurrence" as it actually happened, and not some part that might be squeezed into a single substantive legal theory. The liberalized rules as to claim joinder and party joinder reflect this idea, while a correlative rule of res judicata has evolved along the same path so that, in the absence of excusing circumstances, all rights and grounds for relief arising out of the same transaction must be asserted in a single action or they will be precluded in subsequent lawsuits. These developments in the FRCP have made it possible for very complicated disputes, involving many parties and complex evidence, to be adjudicated in one lawsuit. *See* pts. V, X.B.

Following large annual increases in federal civil caseloads beginning in 1969, along with the emergence of the gargantuan lawsuit, calls for improved efficiency led to reforms in federal (and also in state) procedure that emphasized greater judicial involvement in the control of discovery practices and in the search for pretrial settlement. This tendency toward isolated motion hearings is also reflected in the decreased use of jury trials, less than two percent by 2000 in state and federal courts, which empirically belies the touted American jury trial archetype. *See* pt. VII.

Another salient characteristic of the American procedural system in civil courts is its strong adversary nature. The parties prosecute litigation, investigate the pertinent facts, and present proof and legal argument. The judge's function, traditionally, is limited to adjudicating issues submitted to her by the parties, based on proof submitted, and to making appropriate procedural rulings upon motion by a party.[3]

The American adversary system combines the party-presentation principle and the party-prosecution principle. Party presentation assumes that litigants are masters of their own rights and are to assert or to waive claims or defenses. The public interest in enforcing legal rights is sufficiently served by leaving their presentation to the parties' self-interest. This principle governs not only the adjudication of private disputes, but also litigation involving government agencies (administrative law cases). The second principle, party prosecution, permits the litigants to move a case forward through its pleading, motion, investigatory, and decisional stages. The case expires prior to trial only when one party asks the court to force the other to take the next step or to correct certain defects, sanctioned by dismissal in favor of the moving party. Officials representing public agencies in administrative law litigation prosecute public interests, but are treated for most purposes as ordinary private litigants.

The structuring of civil procedure so that the judge is basically a neutral and passive arbiter promotes two ideas. First, truth is more likely to emerge from the parties' investigation at their own timing, motivated by self-interest, than from judicial investigation at an official pace motivated only by public duty. Second, the legitimacy of a decision is strongest, especially if one of the parties is the state, when it is made by an official who does not have, and does not appear to have, the type of psychological or bureaucratic commitment to the result that is implied in forming and pushing the case to its conclusion.

3. A judge may raise a question of subject matter jurisdiction on her own motion. E.g., FRCP 12(h)(3).

The ultimate fairness of the American adversary system rests on a number of additional assumptions. The most important one is that the parties through their counsel are approximately equal in their ability to present and prosecute their respective positions. This assumption is patently false in America and has led to attempts to increase legal aid for poor persons and to otherwise improve "access to justice." Much remains to be done and there are certain structural difficulties that would be costly to overcome. For instance, when the state is a party, as in social security claims or student loan collection cases, it has virtually unlimited resources to commit to litigation. In product liability cases or landlord-tenant matters, one of the parties typically is a frequent and sophisticated corporate customer of the judicial system. Another assumption underlying the adversary system is that the parties will generally tell the truth and reveal adverse evidence when requested and that their attorneys, as officers of the court, will induce their clients to so behave. In practice the rules of procedure (especially for discovery) and canons of attorney ethics are inadequate to overcome a party's strong incentive to distort the facts of a case.

The American adversary system has come under substantial attack in recent decades and there is evidence that a general shift from adjudicatory toward more administrative procedures has occurred since the beginning of the 20th century. Federal judges in particular have assumed more active roles in managing their caseloads, from delegating certain tasks and cases to masters and magistrates, to participating in settlement and pretrial conferences, to supervising complex class action suits that attempt to reorganize schools or prisons or to transform public health issues involving asbestos or tobacco into mass torts. The amendment of Federal Rule 16 in 1983 to encourage judges to actively manage and schedule the pretrial phases of their caseloads illustrates this trend. In addition, to reduce the effect of some of the imbalance in resources between parties, and to generally discourage waste, the 1983 amendment to Federal Rule 26 placed controls on lawyers to discourage them from using discovery to delay or harass opponents.[4] Subsequent amendments in 1993 limited the number of depositions and interrogatories, required attorneys to automatically disclose certain core information at the beginning of a lawsuit (since 2000 treated uniformly among all the federal districts), and in 2000 narrowed discoverable material, without a court order, to that which is relevant to a party's claim or defense. *See* pts. VI.A, VII.

III. Choosing the Proper Court

An attorney's initial consideration in any lawsuit is to determine whether more than one forum is available to resolve his client's dispute if preliminary efforts to settle it are futile. More than just a question of the proper court, a lawyer should consider the forum that offers his client the best economic and tactical advantages. This may involve, for instance, an administrative agency or arbitration or

4. The 1983 amendments to rules 7, 11, and 37 also endowed federal district courts with greater power of oversight and with responsibility to actively participate in pretrial proceedings.

mediation as an alternative to litigation. If a lawyer selects judicial determination, he must then decide between state and federal court. Federal courts have a limited subject matter jurisdiction; but, if the client's case qualifies, there may be advantages stemming from federal procedure or from less delay. Having made this selection, an attorney must choose from among the various federal districts or state courts available. A proper court will have subject matter jurisdiction, the ability to obtain territorial jurisdiction over the defendant or – for an in rem action – over the property or res, and will meet venue requirements.

To begin a civil action, the plaintiff's attorney prepares a summons and complaint. He presents the summons to the court clerk for issuance and files a copy of the complaint with the clerk, which commences the suit.[5] Valid service of this summons and complaint on the defendant must then meet state or federal rules, some of which today permit electronic service, as well as satisfy three basic jurisdictional requisites before a valid judgment entitled to full faith and credit can be entered. *See* pt. X.B. A summons first invokes a court's subject matter jurisdiction, investing a proper tribunal with power and authority to adjudicate the particular case. Second, the summons subjects a defendant or thing (res) to the territorial jurisdiction of a court, if the defendant or thing has certain minimum contacts with the state in which the court is located, such that the maintenance of the suit does not offend traditional notions of fair play and substantial justice.[6] Third, the summons gives a defendant fair notice of the suit so that he has an opportunity to defend in the chosen court.[7]

If any of these requirements are lacking, a defendant may challenge the plaintiff's summons or the location or venue of a particular issuing court. Under certain conditions he may even attack a judgment entered by the court. *See* pt. III.E.

A. Subject Matter Jurisdiction

In addition to the federal system of courts, which has a strictly construed limited subject matter jurisdiction primarily concerned with resolving "civil actions" arising under the Constitution, laws, or treaties of the United States,[8] each of the 50 states and the District of Columbia has its own court system. Most of the nation's judicial business is conducted in state courts of general jurisdiction, which also have concurrent jurisdiction over the majority of matters that might be brought to federal court. State courts can thus be seen as courts of residual jurisdiction. A separate and independent system of administrative courts – as in Germany or in Italy – never developed in America apart from civil jurisdiction ordinary courts. Ordinary federal and state courts are both civil and administrative law courts and always have been. *See* Chap. 5, pt. V.

5. FRCP 3, 4(a).
6. *International Shoe Co. v. Washington*, 326 U.S. 310, 316 (1945); *cf. Shaffer v. Heitner*, 433 U.S. 186, 207-12 (1977) (for in rem cases).
7. *Milliken v. Meyer*, 311 U.S. 457, 463 (1940).
8. 28 U.S.C. § 1331 (1994); *see* Chap. 4, pt. III.

Article III of the U.S. Constitution sets the outer limit for federal court jurisdiction and leaves to Congress decisions about the actual breadth of subject matter jurisdiction and the number and kinds of courts below the Supreme Court.

The most important first instance courts in the federal system are United States district courts, allotted 655 judgeships in 2001 (although 76 positions were vacant due to Congress's unwillingness to confirm certain nominees). In addition, many senior status judges help with case backlogs. Since 1968 they have been assisted by magistrates (appointed for eight year terms by chief district judges), who rule on non-dispositive motions such as those dealing with discovery or on dispositive motions such as those for summary judgment, and who hear certain types of cases if permitted by a supervising judge, such as social security cases.[9] In reality today's 454 full time and 62 part time magistrates have become a new lower tier in what is formally a three-tier federal system of district courts, courts of appeals, and the Supreme Court. As Table 1 reveals, magistrates – whose numbers remained about the same during the 1990s – increased their role in both civil and criminal caseload processing by 80 percent from 1990 to 2000.

In 1984 Congress established a bankruptcy court as an adjunct to each of the now 94 district courts, with bankruptcy judges appointed for a 14 year term by the courts of appeals. There were 324 bankruptcy judges working in 2000, who processed 1.3 million petitions.

Table 1 Cases and Matters Disposed of by Magistrates in United States District Courts, by Type, in 1990 and 2000

Subject Matter	*1990*	*2000*
Civil consent cases	4,958	11,481
Criminal minor jurisdiction cases	100,930	88,449
Misdemeanors	13,248	8,990
Petty offenses	87,682	79,459
Preliminary proceedings in criminal felony cases	171,092	301,810
Other cases and proceedings	171,127	404,712
Civil motions & conferences	114,968	270,876
Criminal motions & conferences	35,576	108,823
Prisoner litigation	20,583	25,013
TOTAL cases and matters	448,107	806,452

9. Source information and notes for Tables 1 to 3 in this section are contained in David S. Clark, "Civil and Administrative Courts and Procedure," 38 *Am. J. Comp. L.* 181, 189-94 (Supp. 1990). Post-1990 data are available at <http://www.uscourts.gov/judbus2000>. *See* FRCP 72-76; Table 3.

The most significant cases over which federal courts today exercise jurisdiction are: (1) those arising under the U.S. Constitution, international agreements, federal statutes, federal regulations, or federal common law; and (2) those involving diversity of citizenship, that is, parties from different states or countries where the amount in controversy exceeds $75,000. A foreign citizen, admitted as a permanent U.S. resident, is for a diversity case deemed a "citizen" of the state in which he is domiciled.[10] Most of this jurisdiction is concurrent with the power of state courts, but federal jurisdiction is exclusive in bankruptcy proceedings, patent and copyright cases, some admiralty and maritime suits, and cases involving fines, penalties, forfeitures, or seizures under U.S. statutes.

The earliest aggregate statistics for federal trial courts appeared in the 1870s. Table 2 illustrates the changing pattern of civil, administrative, and criminal caseloads since the 19th century.

Table 2 Cases Terminated in United States District Courts, by Type, 1876 to 2000[11]

Year	*Civil*	*Adminis-trative*	*Ratio Admin./Civil*	*Criminal*	*Prisoner*	*TOTAL*
1876	7,680	3,203	0.42	7,095		17,978
1900	10,459	1,602	0.15	17,033		29,094
1916	19,159	10,739	0.56	20,579		50,477
1932	26,045	29,591	1.14	96,949		152,585
1946	18,438	42,562	2.31	35,215		96,215
1967	40,536	20,147	0.50	30,350	9,489	100,522
1980	81,862	57,182	0.70	29,297	21,437	189,778
1988	137,710	65,572	0.48	42,115	35,471	280,868
2000	147,044	55,588	0.38	58,102	56,602	317,336

Only the most general characteristics of federal litigation are visible from Table 2. First, civil case terminations grew with the exception of 1946, shortly after World War II, when the number was smaller than in 1916. Second, administrative case terminations (defined as non-criminal cases with the U.S. Government as plaintiff or defendant) also expanded, but with more dramatic variations. Thus, the cases for 1900 are half of those in 1876 and the terminations for 1967 are half

10. 28 U.S.C. § 1332(a) (1994).
11. Prisoner cases involve petitions filed by state and federal prisoners, who seek either direct judicial review of prison conditions or an individualized collateral review on constitutional grounds of a prior federal court or state court conviction.

of those in 1946. This primarily reflects the discretion that the U.S. Government has to initiate suits in federal court. Consider the two years when the ratio of administrative cases to civil cases was greater than one. In 1932 the U.S. Government was involved in a public morality campaign to eradicate the consumption of liquor, so that over half its cases dealt with this field. This campaign ended with the repeal of the National Prohibition Acts under the 21st Amendment (1933) to the U.S. Constitution. In 1946 the U.S. Government was still heavily concerned with regulating the national economy stemming from its effort in World War II. Rationing and price control regulations, for instance, were invoked in 28,458 cases.

The 1990s were marked by a continuing privatization in some parts of American society, illustrated by the decline in the administrative-civil ratio from 0.48 to 0.38. However, the political pressure to reduce criminality gave the government a reason to increase criminal prosecutions – including the War on Drugs – which was reflected in the substantial increase in federal criminal cases. The ever expanding prison population's response was to bring petitions to question their convictions and sentences and to complain about prison conditions. *See* Chap. 1, pt. V.

Table 3 provides greater detail about postwar civil and administrative caseloads in federal trial courts. Between 1967 and 1980, when some commentators in America began to complain about a "litigation explosion," the civil docket increased by 102 per cent, while the administrative caseload expanded by 184 percent. From 1973 to 1980 the Department of Justice deemphasized its role in the criminal process and shifted its focus to civil suits. Much of the increase in administrative cases was due to the proactive stance taken by the federal government, particularly in attempting to recover defaulted student loans and overpaid veteran benefits (contract cases in Table 3). Dissatisfied social security beneficiaries, in addition, began to use the federal courts to enforce their claims against the government. The tremendous growth in administrative cases during the 1970s slowed in the 1980s, and most of the increase by 1988 occurred with government contract cases and social security claims. During the 1990s the government reduced its position as a litigant in all the other categories listed in Table 3 – most notably with property and labor claims – but saw the rise of civil rights actions, about 60 percent of which involved the workplace.

For civil claims most of the rise in terminations between 1980 and 1988 concerned diversity of citizenship cases, a trend that was reversed when Congress raised the required minimum amount in controversy for diversity cases in 1989 from $10,000 to $50,000 and again in 1996 to $75,000. The decline in administrative and diversity cases in the 1990s was more than compensated for by the 43 percent increase in federal question cases between 1988 and 2000. Civil rights claims encompassed most of this expansion, although the information revolution associated with the Internet brought many plaintiffs to court raising intellectual property issues. *See* chap. 3, pt. III.D.

Table 3 Civil and Administrative Cases Terminated in United States District Courts, by Subject, 1946 to 2000

	1946	*1954*	*1967*	*1980*	*1988*	*2000*
TOTAL Civil Cases	18,438	37,009	40,536	81,862	137,710	147,044
Admiralty[12]	1,057	2,897				
Federal Question		7,526	22,869	43,603	66,959	95,461
Contracts			3,785	5,687	7,088	6,113
Torts		3,425	5,809	8,689	10,493	11,710
Patent, Copyright & Trademark			1,806	3,559	5,798	8,318
Labor			1,560	6,172	11,454	13,808
Civil Rights[13]			868	11,531	17,772	38,077
Diversity		16,643	19,849	34,727	67,258	51,396
Contracts		5,806	5,605	17,174	32,990	21,064
Torts		10,224	13,535	16,472	30,172	27,113
TOTAL Administrative Cases	42,562	20,894	20,147	57,182	65,572	55,588
Tax	497	1,052	1,771	3,307	2,678	1,040
Commerce[14]	5,025	2,159	3,052	2,684	3,432	2,492
Contracts	2,373	7,614	5,539	20,707	25,151	24,025
Torts		1,669	2,145	4,005	3,204	2,821
Real Property			2,364	3,643	7,051	2,937
Labor			1,878	2,113	1,227	331
Social Security				9,584	14,102	14,731
Civil Rights						3,035
Price Control	28,458	1,539				
Admiralty	1,694	889				

Many commentators in the 1970s and 1980s were quite vocal in crying wolf about the "crushing" caseloads arriving at the steps of federal district courts, usually citing the increase in total filings or terminations as shown in Table 2. These cries in fact were successful in restructuring the federal court bureaucracy, so that

12. In 1966 the FRCP became applicable to admiralty and maritime claims. In 1967 admiralty cases were placed in functional categories such as contracts and torts.
13. Includes employment cases under civil rights statutes.
14. Includes cases involving the regulation of industry: antitrust, utilities, banks, food and drug forfeitures, and cases under the Fair Labor Standards Act.

an average individual judge's workload today of 484 cases per year may not be more arduous than the average 392 terminations in 1980 or 313 in 1967.[15] First, there are 454 full time U.S. magistrates in district courts today, while there were none in 1967. They are heavily involved in processing all types of cases, as illustrated in Table 1. These "junior judges" in 2000, for instance, handled 5,516 social security cases and made recommendations in 25,013 prisoner cases. If we add their number to the 579 district judges, their combined average annual caseload drops to 307 terminations. Second, the support staff working in the federal judiciary has expanded dramatically, from 6,000 employees in 1967, 14,000 in 1980, 22,000 in 1990, to 31,000 in 2000. The dimensions of this rapid growth create serious risks of transforming the federal judiciary into another insensitive governmental bureau.

Some federal administrative cases are adjudicated in courts other than U.S. district courts. A few statutes, such as those governing the Securities and Exchange Commission and the National Labor Relations Board, provide that a dissatisfied party should take his case directly to a federal court of appeals. There were 2,963 administrative agency cases of this type terminated in 2000. In addition, the U.S. Court of Federal Claims in the same year decided 868 cases awarding over $434 million to thousands of claimants and class members, the U.S. Court of International Trade resolved 1,057 cases, and the U.S. Tax Court heard thousands of cases sitting in at least one city in each state.

In contrast to federal court jurisdiction, only in the 1980s have we learned much about the aggregate business of state courts and its division between civil, criminal, and administrative cases. Every one of the 50 states and the District of Columbia has trial courts of general jurisdiction, but 45 states also have a variety of special jurisdiction courts limited to preliminary or lesser criminal matters or to civil cases within specified monetary limits (for example, justice of the peace), or concerned with a particular subject (for example, water law or probate). In 1996 there were 10,114 state general jurisdiction court judges and 18,301 limited jurisdiction court judges. The number of cases filed in 1996 with these judges breaks down as follows: 20.1 million civil and administrative cases (one quarter of which dealt with family law), 13.6 million criminal cases, and two million juvenile cases. These figures do not include the almost 52 million traffic and other ordinance violation cases filed.

Approximately 51 percent of the civil and administrative caseload is heard in general jurisdiction courts. From 1984 to 1996 total filings (excluding family law cases) expanded 17 percent adjusted for population growth, with the peak of 5,900 filings per 100,000 inhabitants reached in 1991, down to 5,600 in 1996. About 15 percent of this total involved state and local government as a party. *See* pt. XI.A (appellate court statistics). In addition, there are 450 tribal courts among the 556 federally recognized tribes in the United States.

15. Given the development of more retired (senior) judges handling cases in the 1990s, I use the number of 655 judgeships (even though 12 percent were vacant) to determine the 2000 ratio. Ignoring senior judges and counting only occupied judgeships, the ration is 548 cases terminated annually, about seven percent more than the average 513 cases terminated in 1988.

B. *Territorial Jurisdiction*

This topic is treated in Chap. 17, pt. II. The rules for federal district courts are in general the same as for state trial courts, since Federal Rule 4(e) requires a federal court to rely on the long-arm or attachment statute of the state in which the federal court is located for extraterritorial personal or property jurisdiction.

C. *Venue*

Both jurisdiction and venue relate to the question of the proper court in which a plaintiff may bring an action. Jurisdiction, on the one hand, deals with the power of a court to adjudicate a claim and eventually render a judgment binding on the parties. Venue, on the other hand, concerns the place where judicial authority may be exercised – the particular judicial district for federal courts and the particular county for state courts where an action may be correctly brought.

An important consequence of this difference is that a default judgment entered without territorial jurisdiction over the defendant is void and subject to collateral attack; the same judgment entered by a court only lacking venue is enforceable. Venue provisions, consequently, usually justified by the policy of litigant or witness convenience, may be waived by the defendant at an early point by simple inaction. Once venue provisions are waived, the court without venue nevertheless has the power to determine the merits of the suit. In fact, the defendant may waive in advance his objection to improper venue pursuant to a provision in an agreement. Venue (as well as territorial jurisdiction) by consent will be upheld where there has been arms-length negotiation and there is no compelling public policy to reject the forum selected. In transportation adhesion ticket-contracts, nevertheless, the Supreme Court has upheld waiver as a matter of expediency for the transportation company.[16] Alternatively, if the defendant properly objects to lack of venue, a court cannot proceed with the action. Federal and state courts also will not exercise venue (or territorial jurisdiction) over a defendant based on service of process obtained solely by fraud or unlawful force.

Early in common law history there was no venue issue in England because all actions were required to be tried in the county where the event complained of occurred. This norm – today called the local action rule – is in effect for some types of actions. Jurors were originally selected for their likely personal knowledge of the facts regarding local disputes. Later, the jury's role changed. With the power of judges to send a jury to any part of England, a fiction evolved to satisfy the local action rule and to establish venue in the county where the claim arose, but in reality to allow the case to be tried in another county. This fiction, which provided that a right of action followed a defendant from county to county, could only be used for those suits classified as "transitory." For "local action" suits, typically those directly affecting real property, the claim had to be filed in the county where the subject of the suit was located. This distinction between local and transitory actions

16. *Carnival Cruise Lines, Inc. v. Shute*, 449 U.S. 585 (1991).

has been retained in all states and federal courts.[17] Moreover, the local action rule has been equated with a court's subject matter jurisdiction. Therefore, venue in this situation cannot be waived or conferred on a court by consent of the parties. The court, in fact, on its own motion may raise the issue, even on appeal.

Today, in ascertaining appropriate venue, one should first determine whether a suit is covered by the local action rule. If it is, then venue is only proper where the subject of the action is located. In federal court, if a case is not within the local action rule, the general venue statute[18] provides that in actions based only on diversity of citizenship, venue is proper in a judicial district: (1) where any defendant resides (if all defendants reside in the same state); (2) where "a substantial part of the events or omissions giving rise to the claim occurred, or a substantial part of property that is the subject of the action is situated"; or (3) if the suit may not otherwise be brought in (1) or (2), where the defendants are subject to territorial jurisdiction. In federal question cases a plaintiff may sue in judicial districts (1) and (2) above, or if there is no available district, in a "district in which any defendant may be found." Corporate defendants are deemed to reside in any district in which they are subject to territorial jurisdiction. Foreign nonresident citizens ("aliens") may be sued in any district.

In a typical state court, if a suit is not covered by the local action rule, then under the general norm for transitory actions venue is proper in a county where the defendant resides or may be summoned. Unless a suit also qualifies under other provisions applicable to particular transitory actions, these are the plaintiff's only options. If a suit or the defendant does fall into a category of actions or defendants covered by particular venue provisions, the plaintiff has a further choice of locations for proper venue, often where the cause of action arose or the plaintiff resides. If a suit is filed in any county where venue is proper, a court cannot move the suit to another forum simply because the latter forum is "more" proper. However, the doctrine of *forum non conveniens* under some circumstances may be applied. It is a defendant's remedy to protect him and the court against plaintiff's harassment in selecting an inconvenient forum.[19]

D. *Notice and Opportunity To Be Heard*

Procedural due process requires that a defendant be provided with adequate notice and opportunity to be heard before he is deprived by government action of his liberty (for example, by injunction) or property (for example, by money damages). The United States Constitution's Fifth and 14th Amendments protect the right to notice against infringement by federal or state entities. If this fundamental requirement is not met, a court lacks jurisdiction and cannot issue a valid judgment entitled to full faith and credit.

17. E.g., 28 U.S.C. § 1392 (1994).
18. 28 U.S.C. § 1391 (1994).
19. *See* Chap. 17, pt. II.B.5, which also discusses the federal rule for change of venue under 28 U.S.C. § 1404(a) (1994).

In *Mullane v. Central Hanover Bank & Trust Co.*,[20] the United States Supreme Court stated that a "fundamental requirement of due process ... is notice reasonably calculated, under all the circumstances, to apprize interested parties of the pendency of the action and afford them an opportunity to present their objections." The Court sustained notice by publication where it was impractical to provide better notice to certain beneficiaries of a common trust fund prior to a judicial settlement of accounts. This group included those whose interests or whereabouts could not, with due diligence, be ascertained. Alternatively, the Court found publication violative of due process where the names and addresses of other beneficiaries were known. The Constitution required for these persons notice by at least ordinary mail to their last recorded addresses. This approach reaffirmed the dictum by Justice Holmes finding publication notice a constitutionally inadequate replacement for personal service of process. "[T]he substitute that is most likely to reach the defendant is the least that ought to be required if substantial justice is to be done."[21]

In addition to the jurisdictional and constitutional requisite of reasonable notification, the technical specifications of Federal Rule 4 or state rules as to the form and method of notice for service of process, publication, or posting must be satisfied. Substantial compliance with the applicable statutes is sufficient, but improper service is a jurisdictional defect that can lead the court to set aside a default judgment against the defendant even though she knew about the lawsuit.[22] Federal Rule 4(f) provides several manners for service of process in a foreign country. The United States ratified the Hague Convention on the Service Abroad of Judicial and Extrajudicial Documents in Civil or Commercial Matters, which took effect in 1969. If a reasonable method of notice is prescribed and followed, the validity of a subsequent default judgment is not affected by the fact that a defendant failed to receive actual notice. Actual receipt, however, is an important factor in deciding whether the method of notification was reasonable.

Alternatively, if a prescribed method of notice is not reasonably calculated to be received, the method is constitutionally invalid even if a defendant receives actual notice.[23] This situation commonly arises where service of process may be made upon an agent of a foreign corporation or a nonresident. The Oklahoma Supreme Court, for instance, struck down a statute that provided for service of process on the Oklahoma Secretary of State for personal jurisdiction over non-domesticated foreign corporations doing business in the state. The constitutional defect was the absence of a provision for forwarding such process to the corporation itself.

Personal service of process on a defendant presents no special problems since the process is handed to the defendant and it is the notice. The *Mullane* standard becomes an important limit for substituted service, however, where a sheriff typically hands the summons to someone closely related – by blood or otherwise – to a defendant. There is usually a high probability that the defendant will receive

20. 339 U.S. 306, 314 (1950).
21. *McDonald v. Mabee*, 243 U.S. 90, 92 (1917).
22. *See Maryland State Firemen's Ass'n v. Chaves*, 166 F.R.D. 353 (D.Md. 1996).
23. *Wuchter v. Pizzutti*, 276 U.S. 13, 18-21, 24 (1928).

actual notice, but courts must remain vigilant to the real circumstances. To illustrate, substituted service of a contempt citation on a spouse's attorney of record in a divorce proceeding to enforce alimony will satisfy due process only where it is reasonable to believe that the client will receive notice. The passage of six years since the original divorce action probably rebuts the presumption of reasonableness. The rationale for permitting substituted service is to deal with legal entities such as corporations, which must be served through an agent, and to corral defendants who are temporarily absent from the state, in hiding, or cannot be found.

In 1983 Congress authorized a simplified type of substituted service: first class mail. To ensure receipt, the plaintiff must include an acknowledgment form and a return envelope, with prepaid postage. If the acknowledgment is not returned, the plaintiff must use other means of service. To encourage defendants to accept mail service, Federal Rule 4(d) was amended in 1993 to impose upon those defendants who fail to reasonably cooperate in facilitating service the additional expense in completing another form of service.

Constructive service, which includes posting real property or publishing notice of a suit in an approved newspaper, is clearly the least satisfactory method of notification under the *Mullane* standard. The U.S. Supreme Court has reaffirmed this view by finding a forcible entry and detainer statute unconstitutional since it allowed constructive service by posting when mail service would have provided more effective notice.[24] But where a defendant is missing, unknown, or conceals himself, and substituted service is not feasible, publication meets the requirements of due process. Constructive service is frequently authorized by statute for in rem and quasi in rem proceedings. Since the basis for this type of jurisdiction is the presence of property, a court's authority is established when the property is actually or figuratively "seized" and brought within the court's power. This "seizure" is normally accomplished by publication of notice for an upcoming proceeding in an authorized newspaper. However, persons with a known interest in property who may be adversely affected must be notified by the best available method if they can be reached. A landowner whose name and address are listed on official records clearly falls within this class.[25]

E. Challenging the Plaintiff's Selection of a Court

After a plaintiff's complaint and summons have been served – in effect selecting a particular court to hear the dispute – a defendant is faced with an important choice. On the one hand, he may totally ignore the summons, perhaps in the belief that any judgment rendered would be void. In this situation, a default judgment can be entered against him with a later attempt at its enforcement. Or a default judgment may occur where a defendant has received no actual notice of a lawsuit. *See* pt. VIII.B. On the other hand, a defendant may at an early point actively contest the plaintiff's selection of a court through various procedural

24. *Green v. Lindsey*, 456 U.S. 444 (1982).
25. *Walker v. Hutchinson*, 352 U.S. 112, 116 (1956).

devices. This avenue looks to one or more defects, some of which may lead to a dismissal of the lawsuit, including: (1) lack of subject matter jurisdiction; (2) lack of adequate notice or territorial jurisdiction; and (3) improper venue. Defects in the form, issuance, or service of a summons not constituting jurisdictional questions normally are not bases for quashing the process. A court will usually accept an amendment to cure these defects.

A defendant who aims for a dismissal will desire a procedure to allow him to raise issues regarding jurisdictional deficiencies without thereby submitting to the court's authority. Many states provide such a procedure in the form of a special appearance. In some states the defendant is not permitted to introduce any other defenses prior to or at the time of the special appearance. If he does, he is deemed to have made a general appearance and to have waived the right to object to jurisdiction or venue. In other states the defendant may appear specially to challenge the court's power or venue, join other defenses, and not automatically acquiesce to its jurisdiction. If the challenge is overruled, moreover, he may continue and defend an action without waiving the jurisdiction or venue issues as long as he avoids demanding affirmative relief.

If a defendant loses on his motion or demurrer at a special appearance, in many states he may directly attack a trial judge's decision in two ways. First, he may raise the defects before the state supreme court in an application for a writ of mandamus or prohibition. *See* pt. XI.C. Second, a defendant may choose to continue and defend an action. As long as he does not demand affirmative relief on a claim that he pleads against a plaintiff, a co-defendant, or a new party, his objections are preserved and he may attack the trial judge's ruling on appeal. The rationale precluding affirmative relief prohibits a defendant from benefiting in the use of a court while at the same time denying its jurisdiction or venue over him.

If in rem or quasi in rem territorial jurisdiction is upheld, most states provide the procedure of a limited appearance, which allows a defendant to contest the merits of plaintiff's claim (but not to demand affirmative relief) without subjecting himself to unlimited personal jurisdiction. If a defendant loses on the merits, the amount of a judgment is limited by the value of the res before the court. The limited appearance in a quasi in rem action eliminates the unfairness of forcing a nonresident defendant from having to choose between: (1) protecting himself against personal liability by defaulting, thereby forfeiting his property; and (2) submitting to unlimited personal jurisdiction by appearing to protect his interest in the seized property. Federal Rule 4(n) permits quasi in rem jurisdiction only if the plaintiff cannot reasonably obtain personal jurisdiction over the defendant in that judicial district.

When the jurisdictional defect is lack of subject matter jurisdiction, it may be raised at any time, even by the court itself, regardless of whether a special appearance is used or even whether affirmative relief has been requested by a defendant. It may even be raised for the first time on appeal.

Most states that allow a special appearance also provide for a voluntary or general appearance by the defendant. The consequence of such a general appearance is to waive all service of process, venue, and territorial jurisdiction defects. Some states reward a defendant who enters a general appearance with an additional 30 days in which to answer the plaintiff's complaint. Federal Rule 4(d) encourages the defendant to waive personal service of process (but not venue or jurisdictional defects) by granting him an extra 30 days to answer the complaint.

The distinction between general and special appearances has been abolished in the federal courts and in those states that have enacted the Federal Rules. In these jurisdictions a defendant may raise an objection to the process, venue, or jurisdiction by filing a motion to dismiss or by joining these objections with his answer.[26] Since these objections – except for lack of subject matter jurisdiction – are disfavored, they are lost if a defendant does not raise them at his first opportunity. Once a defendant has made timely objections, they may be argued again on appeal if the trial judge denies the defendant's motion. They may not be argued, however, by way of collateral attack on the court's judgment, even if the prior determination was incorrect. *See* pt. X.B.2.

A default judgment presents some uncertainties for a plaintiff before he enforces it. It may be attacked for voidness at any time, either directly – for instance under Federal Rule 60(b) – or collaterally when the plaintiff attempts to enforce it. Voidness must affirmatively appear from the judgment roll, which consists of the summons and return, the pleadings, and the judgment itself; in some states it may be shown by extrinsic evidence. A judgment is void when the rendering court proceeded under a jurisdictional defect. *See* pt. VIII.B.

IV. Pleading

A. In General

Pleadings are the papers by which the plaintiff and defendant first describe a case to each other and to the court. A pleading system can be evaluated by the degree of detail it requires, by the amount of variance (amendment) permitted between a pleading and the actual proof offered, or by the extent of truthfulness promoted. This evaluation should keep in mind the two major functions served by pretrial procedure: (1) to provide fair notice to the other party of the case against him; and (2) to narrow the issues of fact and law to be tried, including the elimination of baseless claims or defenses.

At common law both functions were served by the pleadings. In fact the pleadings continued until a single issue was reached, the resolution of which determined the controversy. With the Field Code reforms in the 19th century the role of pleadings changed. A complaint was to contain a "statement of the facts constituting the cause of action, in ordinary and concise language." The primary function of code pleading was to provide notice; the issue-framing function shifted somewhat to motions and discovery. *See* pt. I.C. However, Field Code pleading retained a secondary function to narrow potential issues, illustrated by the requirements to plead "the facts" and to state a "cause of action." In code states there still are skirmishes at the beginning of a lawsuit; failure to incorporate an essential allegation leads to the end of a claim or defense unless amendment is allowed.

26. FRCP 12(b).

The Federal Rules attempted in 1938 to reduce detail even more in pleading and to further shift its function toward notice. *See* pt. I.D. Under FRCP 8(a)(2) the plaintiff need only provide "a short and plain statement of the claim showing that the pleader is entitled to relief." In light of rule 8(f)'s requirement to construe pleadings "to do substantial justice," the issue-framing function was postponed until discovery and pretrial hearings.

B. The Complaint

The principal difference between code pleading and Federal Rules pleading concerns the level of detail required. In a code state the plaintiff must plead in her complaint the ultimate facts constituting the elements of a cause of action. If she is too verbose and recites evidentiary detail, her pleading is improper. But today a complaint is rarely dismissed for this defect. Alternatively, if she pleads general and vague legal conclusions, such as the terms "trespass and assault" or "negligence," some states will grant defendant's request for a general demurrer to dismiss plaintiff's complaint. A plaintiff should also include in her complaint a demand for relief. If the demand is for money damages, a specific amount should be stated. Multiple causes of action may be claimed, and even inconsistent or alternative good faith allegations may be made, so long as they are stated in separate counts in the complaint.

The simplest pleading system is found in federal courts and in those states that have adopted the Federal Rules. The troublesome code pleading concepts of "ultimate facts" and "cause of action" were replaced by the notion that the plaintiff need only "give the defendant fair notice of what the plaintiff's claim is and the grounds upon which it rests."[27] The plaintiff can plead inconsistently and alternatively, even within the same count.[28] With a few special matters, however, such as allegations of fraud or mistake, the plaintiff must state the circumstances with particularity.[29] The rationale here is to deter certain frivolous suits that sometimes are filed solely to harass defendants. The plaintiff must also plead special damages with specificity to protect the defendant from surprise.[30] In general, nevertheless, liberalized pleading rules make it easier to sue in federal court and often require the defendant to engage in discovery to obtain enough support to win a dismissal.

C. The Answer

If the defendant challenges the plaintiff's selection of a court (*see* pt. III.E.) or contends that the complaint fails to state a claim upon which relief can be granted,[31] he may either raise these defenses in an answer or a motion to dismiss. Otherwise, a defendant normally raises his defenses in the answer.

27. *Conley v. Gibson*, 355 U.S. 41, 47-48 (1957).
28. FRCP 8(e)(2).
29. FRCP 9(b).
30. FRCP 9(g).
31. FRCP 12(b)(6).

A defendant may deny some or all of the allegations in plaintiff's complaint, admit some of the allegations (either by specifically acknowledging their truth or by failing to properly deny them), raise new facts for an affirmative defense, or add his own claim against the plaintiff (*see* pt. V.A). In a code state the defendant must plead the ultimate facts regarding his affirmative defense or counterclaim against the plaintiff. Under the federal system, enough detail "in short and plain terms" to provide general or fair notice is adequate.[32] Affirmative defenses include such matters as accord and satisfaction, contributory negligence, duress, res judicata, or statute of limitations.[33]

A defendant may select among five different types of denials for his answer. A proper denial places the matter denied in issue for future determination. A denial must be truthful and should not be misleading.[34] For instance, if the complaint in a code state alleges that "defendant owned and operated a fork lift," a defendant who owned but did not operate the lift may not make a specific denial that "he did not own and operate the lift." This is an improper conjunctive denial that misleads the plaintiff, which will be deemed an admission on both the issues of ownership and operation. Some federal courts have found that even a simple "deny" can be misleading and is improper. The five types of denial are: (1) general denial, now disfavored in the federal system since it can only rarely be used truthfully; (2) qualified denial, which denies everything in a paragraph or even in the complaint not expressly admitted; (3) specific denial, which rejects the truth of a designated portion of the complaint; (4) specific denial based on lack of knowledge or information on the defendant's part; and (5) specific denial based on information and belief. The fifth category is appropriate where the defendant has no first-hand knowledge of the matter, typically used by a corporate defendant who is sued for its employees' acts.

D. Amendments

At common law the pleadings assumed such an important role that no variance was permitted between the pleadings and proof at trial. Code states and the Federal Rules, in contrast, by promoting decision based on the substantive merits rather than on procedural technicalities, freely allow amendments to pleadings.

Under Federal Rule 15(a) the plaintiff may amend his complaint once without applying to the court for permission as long as the defendant has not served his answer. After service the defendant has a similar right to amend his answer for 20 days. Otherwise a party may amend his pleading only by leave of court or by written consent of his adversary; the rule then states that "leave shall be freely given when justice so requires." Rule 15(c) and most states permit the pleading's amendment to relate back to the date of the original pleading so that it will not

32. FRCP 8(b).
33. FRCP 8(c).
34. FRCP 11.

be precluded by the running of a statute of limitations, but only if the newly stated claim or defense arose out of the conduct, transaction, or occurrence in the original pleading. A 1991 amendment to rule 15(c) clarified this rule in its application to misnamed defendants.

If evidence is submitted at trial on an issue not found in the pleadings and no objection is raised, the court will normally conform the pleadings to the proof based on the parties' implied consent. If a party at trial requests an amendment, since the other party has objected to his presentation of evidence, the court will freely allow the amendment if it would promote decision on the merits and the objecting party fails to satisfy the court that he would be unduly prejudiced in maintaining his action or defense. The judge may grant a continuance to enable the objecting party to meet this evidence. Undue prejudice might include the disappearance of documents or the unavailability of a witness. Finally, a party may request amendment even after judgment to conform the pleadings to the proof, usually to clarify a decision for the purpose of res judicata.[35]

E. *Truthful Pleadings*

A general verification requirement, by which the pleader swears under oath as to the truth of a pleading's allegations, was omitted from the original Federal Rules. In special cases, however, such as shareholder derivative claims, the requirement was retained to discourage strike suits used to coerce corporate managers to settle worthless claims.[36] Verification adds the threat of criminal prosecution for perjury. Most code states, which previously mandated verification, have either eliminated the requirement except for special situations (such as divorce or attachment) or retained an optional verification rule. Under this latter approach, a plaintiff may verify her complaint; if she does, the defendant must also verify his answer, precluding use of the general denial.

Federal Rule 11 attempts to encourage truthfulness in the liberal federal pleading scheme with an attorney signature requirement. After years of ineffective judicial supervision, due partly to a subjective standard of intentional bad faith on the attorney's part, the rule was amended in 1983. An attorney must now make a "reasonable inquiry" into the factual and legal allegations in a pleading or motion. She will have to carefully examine her client as to the bases for his assertions, even to the extent of telephoning witnesses. An attorney is responsible for her negligent failure to make an appropriate inquiry; she is judged by an objective reasonable attorney standard. Sanctions may include the reasonable expenses (and even attorney fees) caused by the offending pleading in terms of harassment or unnecessary delay. To combat an excessive number of motions for sanctions, which often became delaying sideshows to the main lawsuit, rule 11 was amended in 1993 to eliminate discovery disputes (leaving them to rules 26(g) and 37), to constrain the imposition of monetary sanctions under certain

35. FRCP 15(b).
36. FRCP 23.1; *see* Chap. 14, pt. IV.D.

circumstances, and to preclude a motion for sanctions when potential violations are corrected within three weeks. On the other side, the amendment now permits sanctions against law firms, the attorney filing a paper, or one later advocating an untenable argument as well as against the attorney signing the improper document.

V. Joinder of Claims and Parties

The joinder of claims and parties depends on two categories of rules. First, claims or parties must be within the court's subject matter jurisdiction (an issue primarily for federal litigation) and parties must be brought within the court's territorial jurisdiction. *See* pts. III.A, B. Second, the Federal Rules and Field Code rules on joinder itself differ in their liberality.

A. Claim Joinder

1. Joinder of claims by plaintiff

At common law a plaintiff could join all actions justifiable under the particular writ purchased. He could also obtain certain combinations of writs (such as case and trover, or debt and detinue) and bring the same action under both writs or join actions of the same nature. For instance, a plaintiff could join an action for slander under the writ of case with an action for conversion under the writ of trover; this joinder was permitted since trover historically grew out of the writ of case. At equity, joinder was more flexible.

The Field Code reforms were based more on the tradition from equity. Code states use a list of categories, which permits the plaintiff to join any causes of action that fall into a single category. Modern lists include a number of subject categories – contracts, personal injury, character injury, property injury, recovery of real property, and recovery of chattels – along with a category for actions arising out of the same transaction. The defendant may contest misjoinder with a special demurrer.

Federal Rule 18(a) further liberalizes plaintiff's options by permitting her to join all claims, related or unrelated, that she has against the defendant. Problems of prejudice to the defendant, jury confusion, or undue delay are handled by the judge, who may sever claims and hold separate trials.[37]

2. Joinder of claims by defendant

A counterclaim by the defendant against the plaintiff did not exist at common law, although the more limited devices of recoupment at law and set-off at equity served some of the same purpose by reducing another plaintiff's recovery.

37. FRCP 42(b).

Counterclaims, permitting affirmative relief by the defendant, were adopted by most code states for a cause of action arising out of the contract or transaction set forth in the complaint. In addition, the defendant could join any contract action he had against the plaintiff if the plaintiff sued on a contract.

Federal Rule 13 continues the pattern described for plaintiff joinder and allows the defendant to join all claims that he has against the plaintiff. The rule distinguishes between a compulsory and permissive counterclaim. It is compulsory "if it arises out of the transaction or occurrence that is the subject matter of the [plaintiff's] claim."[38] This language is satisfied if there is a logical relationship between the two claims in terms of an overlap in legal and factual issues that will require use of the same evidence. This joinder promotes the goal of efficiency – by processing one lawsuit rather than two lawsuits – but also might further justice by uniformly assessing the evidence for the two claims instead of having two lawsuits yield opposite results. All other counterclaims are permissive.[39] The distinction between these two types of counterclaims is important because the defendant's failure to plead a compulsory counterclaim will preclude him from suing on that claim in a subsequent action due to principles of res judicata, waiver, or estoppel. *See* pt. X.B.

Most jurisdictions also permit a defendant to bring a cross-claim against a co-defendant if it arises out of the same transaction or occurrence that underlies either the plaintiff's main claim or the defendant's counterclaim.[40] Cross-claims are permissive, but they must meet the transactional requirement to prevent undue complication and to avoid claims that do not directly involve the plaintiff.

B. *Party Joinder*

Five concepts come into play in identifying who may be a party to a lawsuit.

First, only the real party in interest may sue – that is, the person who possesses a substantive right. This Field Code rule changed the common law approach, which permitted suit to be brought only in the name of the person who had *legal* title to the right of action. Law courts, which did not recognize the assignment of a chose in action, would entertain an action to enforce an assignment if the suit were brought by the assignee if the name of the assignor. Code states provided that suit should be brought by the real party in interest – the assignee. Federal Rule 17(a) adopts a similar rule to cover assignments and other prior transfers of interest. A few states prohibit assignees of non-contract claims from suing.

Second, a person or legal entity must have capacity to sue or be sued. These rules depend on the character of the party. They intend to protect certain classes of persons (for example, minors or mental incompetents) who might not be able to adequately protect their interests, or to regulate certain organizations (such as non-resident corporations) that will not be allowed to sue if they have not registered with the state.[41]

38. FRCP 13(a).
39. FRCP 13(b).
40. FRCP 13(g).
41. *See* FRCP 17(b).

Third, a plaintiff must have standing, a concept most important to federal litigation, by showing that he has suffered or imminently will suffer an injury traceable to the defendant that can be redressed by a favorable court decision. This guarantees an actual dispute between adverse parties, so that the court will not be asked for an advisory opinion. *See* Chap. 4, pt. III.B.2.b.

If these three requirements are met, one must then examine the relation of a particular person to the lawsuit to determine whether his joinder is compelled or whether it is merely permitted. The party structure of a lawsuit is initially determined by the plaintiff or plaintiffs, since they agree who will be on their side of the suit and they choose the defendant or defendants against whom to proceed. For permissive joinder (or proper parties) most code states follow earlier equity practice and permit the joinder of all persons who have some interest in the subject matter of the action and in the relief demanded. More liberal still, Federal Rule 20 allows permissive joinder for suits in which: (1) some right to relief asserted on behalf of each plaintiff (or against each defendant) relates to a single transaction or occurrence or series of transactions or occurrences; and (2) some question of law or fact is common to all parties on each side of the suit. A defendant may request that an improper party be dropped from the suit.[42] Proper parties define the maximum size of a lawsuit; their joinder primarily promotes efficiency by avoiding multiple actions.

Necessary and indispensable parties (compulsory joinder) define the suit's minimum size and their joinder is concerned more with accomplishing justice. Code states maintain the terminology of necessary and indispensable parties and interests that are joint, united, or separable. Necessary persons are those whose interests might possibly be affected by a judgment entered in their absence, but the prejudice to them or to parties already joined is minimal. Indispensable persons are those whose interests will inevitably be affected prejudicially by the court's judgment. Examples include cases involving a common trust fund, partnership, or joint tenancy. Necessary and indispensable persons should be joined. However, in circumstances where these persons cannot be joined because of the rules of venue or territorial and subject matter jurisdiction, the distinction between necessary and indispensable becomes crucial. If the absentee is necessary, the suit may in the judge's discretion proceed. But if the absentee is indispensable, the suit must be dismissed.

Federal Rule 19, by amendment in 1966, abandoned this approach. In subdivision (a) the rule defines those persons needed for just adjudication. A person should be joined if: (1) in his absence complete relief cannot be accorded among those already parties; or (2) he claims an interest relating to the lawsuit that might in his absence as a practical matter be impaired or leave persons already parties subject to a substantial risk of multiple or inconsistent obligation. If this person cannot be joined due to venue or jurisdiction problems, subdivision (b) lists four factors for the court to balance in deciding whether "in equity and good conscience" to dismiss the suit or to proceed without the absentee. The Supreme Court, in *Provident Tradesmens Bank & Trust Co. v. Patterson*,[43] characterized these four

42. FRCP 21.
43. 390 U.S. 102 (1968).

factors as interests: (1) the plaintiff's interest in the forum, and whether alternative better fora might exist; (2) the defendant's interest in avoiding multiple litigation and inconsistent relief; (3) the absentee's interest in practically protecting his rights in the subject matter, and whether the court might shape the relief to protect this interest; and (4) the social interest in an orderly and efficient administration of justice.

C. Impleader

Impleader or third-party practice allows a defendant to assert a claim against an outsider who "is or may be liable" to the defendant if the latter is found liable to the plaintiff.[44] At common law a defendant could "vouch in" an outsider obligated to reimburse the defendant for his liability to plaintiff, which involved notice plus an offer permitting the vouchee to control the defense. Code states continued this joinder device, but later adopted impleader and often interpreted it restrictively.

Federal impleader is more liberal, although the defendant must obtain the court's permission (after more than ten days from the time of serving his original answer) to file his summons and complaint as third-party plaintiff against the third-party defendant. The court will then ascertain whether joinder would unduly complicate or delay adjudication of the main claim. If so, the judge may deny impleader. Typically the defendant alleges that the third-party defendant has a duty to indemnify the defendant or to contribute to payment of plaintiff's damages. When allowed, impleader avoids multiplicity of actions and ensures consistent results in the determination of those issues common to the main claim and the third-party claim. If the person contingently liable is already a co-party, the defendant should as proper procedure assert a cross-claim against that person.[45]

D. Intervention

Intervention is a procedure by which an outsider can enter an existing lawsuit to protect her interests against the possible adverse consequences of a judgment. Code states often limit intervention to the recovery of real or personal property, or require the intervenor to line up with the original plaintiff or defendant on the issues already defined.

Federal Rule 24, as amended in 1966, clarified a division between intervention of right and permissive intervention and brought it into conformity with the distinction between persons needed for just adjudication (FRCP 19) and permissive parties (FRCP 20). *See* pt. V.B. Intervention of right concerns justice to the absentee and considers the practical impairment of an absentee's interest if he is not part of the lawsuit. An intervenor must serve a timely motion to intervene on the parties.[46] For intervention of right he must meet a three-part test: (1) the

44. FRCP 14(a).
45. FRCP 13(g); *see* pt. V.A.2.
46. FRCP 5(d), 24(c).

applicant claims an interest relating to the property or transaction; (2) disposition of the action may as a practical matter impair his interest; and (3) this interest is not adequately represented by the existing parties.[47] Permissive intervention, on the other hand, concerns judicial efficiency, terminating all facets of a dispute in one lawsuit. The applicant need merely show a common question of law or fact, making joinder even easier than the liberal standard in Federal Rule 20. The judge, however, will deny intervention if the application is not timely or if it would unduly delay or prejudice the original litigation.[48]

E. Interpleader

Interpleader allows a person (the stakeholder), who admits a potential obligation, to avoid the risk of multiple liability to two or more claimants by requiring them to assert their adverse claims in a single action. The stakeholder of property or a fund can commence interpleader as an original action or, if a claimant has already sued him, interplead via counterclaim, with other claimants brought in to respond.

Four limits were developed in classical equity practice as listed by the jurist Pomeroy: (1) the same thing, debt, or duty must be claimed by all parties; (2) all claims must be derived from a common source; (3) the stakeholder must have no interest in the subject matter; and (4) he must not have incurred independent liability to any claimant. Most code states liberalized interpleader practice and eliminated one or more of these requirements. Jurisdiction rules, however, severely restrict the use of interpleader where the claimants live in more than one state.

The U.S. Congress responded in 1917 to protect fund holders, such as banks and insurance companies involved in interstate transactions, which sue in federal court. The act led to what is today known as "statutory interpleader." It eliminated Pomeroy's requirements two to four, and modified requirement one to demand only that the claimants be adverse (that is, there must be some overlap between the conflicting claims). Statutory interpleader also relaxed diversity of citizenship jurisdiction so that there need only be diversity between any two claimants (minimal diversity), the amount in controversy may be as small as $500, process and territorial jurisdiction reaches nationwide, and venue lies in a federal judicial district where any claimant resides.[49] In addition, Federal Rule 22 provides for a similar joinder device known as "rule interpleader." With it the normal restrictions of subject matter jurisdiction (that is, complete diversity and over $75,000 in controversy), territorial jurisdiction, and venue apply.

Both statutory and rule interpleader proceed in two stages. First, the court ascertains the propriety of interpleader. If proper, and the stakeholder makes no claim to the property, he is dismissed from the suit. Second, the claimants fight out their claims to the fund or property among themselves. This procedure reduces litigation and protects the stakeholder from even the threat of multiple liability.

47. FRCP 24(a).
48. FRCP 24(b).
49. 28 U.S.C. §§ 1335, 1397, 2361 (1994).

F. Class Actions

A class action permits one or more members of a definable group, with similar grievances or responsibilities, to sue or be sued as representative parties on behalf of all class members. The class action was an invention of English equity courts, applicable where the persons affected by a decree were so numerous that it was impracticable to bring them all in as parties.

The Field Code, which eliminated the distinction between legal and equitable actions, included a succinct provision preserving class actions. American code states interpreted this section to permit legal as well as equitable cases, thereby significantly expanding the use of class actions to cover the remedy of money damages. Those states that do not follow the Federal Rules today tend to have one of two flexible approaches to class action suits, exemplified by California and New York. California has a general statute, derived from the Field Code, that avoids creating class action categories.[50] As interpreted by the California Supreme Court, it requires an ascertainable class, a common definable interest in factual or legal issues affecting class members, and adequacy of representation. New York has a more elaborate scheme, derived in part from federal experience, that specifically answers questions concerning class prerequisites, factors influencing court orders, notice, partial class actions, judicial management of the process, and attorney fees.[51]

The Federal Rules in 1938 adopted a tripartite classification based on the character of the right sought to be enforced for or against a class. In a "true" or "hybrid" class suit, all class members were bound by the judgment. In a "spurious" class suit, however, absentees were not bound by a judgment adverse to the class, but could generally come in as intervenors to take advantage of a favorable judgment. This scheme was supposed to solve the problem of determining in which situations a class action would be binding on absentees as res judicata. *See* pt. X.B. The Supreme Court took up the issue and found that the Constitution's due process clause would be satisfied only where the procedure guarantees that the interests of the representative (or named) parties are similar to those of the absentees and that the representatives will fairly protect the interests of the whole class.[52]

Federal Rule 23 was totally rewritten in 1966 due to the many difficulties federal courts had in administering the tripartite classification. The original drafters in 1938 basically saw rule 23 as just another party joinder device, which in cases of large numbers would accommodate the policies of rule 19 (necessary and indispensable parties) and rule 20 (proper parties). Some continued this view in 1966 and believed that the revised rule would improve administration of class actions. Others, however, believed that necessary social change in American society required a more flexible rule that might accommodate civil rights cases as well as consumer interests. It is from this latter vision that the peculiarly

50. Cal. Civ. Proc. Code § 382 (West 1973).
51. N.Y. Civ. Prac. Laws & Rules §§ 901-909 (McKinney 1976 & Supp. 2001).
52. *Hansberry v. Lee*, 311 U.S. 32 (1940).

American class action was born, which in part transformed the nature of the federal judiciary within a system of separated governmental powers. Class actions encouraged consumers, environmentalists, civil rights activists, and corporate shareholders, for instance, to pool their resources and successfully enforce the law against institutional violators. *See* Chap. 14, pt. IV.D. Federal judges moved from their traditional passive role to a proactive stance to protect the rights of absentees or to manage relief to reform a prison or to desegregate a school. In the 1990s plaintiffs used this joinder form in suits charging gender or race discrimination and for product liability, consumer fraud, and toxic tort cases. In the process federal judges more visibly involved themselves in public policy questions, which earlier were considered to be in the domain of the executive and legislative branches.

Most class actions involve plaintiff classes. The class must exist as an ascertainable group and the named plaintiffs must have standing (as members of the class). Federal Rule 23(a) lists four prerequisites: (1) numerosity (at least 25 members and usually more); (2) commonality of legal or factual questions; (3) typicality of the named party's claim; and (4) adequacy of representation to protect the interests of the class. If these prerequisites are met, rule 23(b) further requires that the suit fall into one of three situations: (1) separate actions would create incompatible standards of conduct for the defendant or substantially impair other class members' interests as a practical matter; (2) injunctive relief is appropriate; or (3) money damages constitute the primary relief.

Situation three is the most complex and controversial: the judge must also find under rule 23(b)(3) that "questions of law or fact common to the members of the class predominate over any questions affecting only individual members, and that a class action is superior to other available methods for the fair and efficient adjudication of the controversy." The Supreme Court found this last requirement unmet in an attempt to certify a nationwide class of future asbestos claimants. Individual class member issues, such as the use of different asbestos products and varying levels and periods of exposure, outweighed the common issue of the general health consequence from asbestos exposure.[53] A suit that meets all of these requirements will be certified as a class action.[54] Notice is mandatory in (b)(3) actions and individual notice must be mailed to all identifiable class members. Absentees may opt out of the suit; those who do are not bound by the judgment.[55] These protections are expensive. Consequently, attorneys often argue to bring their suit into categories b(l) or b(2) to avoid the cost of individual notice and the risk of losing members who opt out. Rule 23(e) controls the settlement stage of a class action, which frequently determines the final outcome, by requiring the judge to ascertain that absentee interests have not been abandoned to the self-interest of the named parties and their attorneys.

53. *Amchem Products, Inc. v. Windsor*, 521 U.S. 591 (1997).
54. FRCP 23(c)(1); *see* pt. XI.C.
55. FRCP 23(c)(2).

VI. Discovery

A. Scope and Purposes

The idea of pretrial discovery emerged in English equity practice, but did not become widespread in American courts until after the merger of law and equity in the Field Code. It only fully blossomed – if that is the correct word – under the Federal Rules. Most states today follow the federal model, but a few are more restrictive in scope or require greater judicial supervision.

The purposes of modern discovery rules fall into the two general categories of furthering procedural and substantive justice and promoting efficiency. One purpose is to preserve the testimony of witnesses (such as the ill or aged) who may not be available at trial or who one suspects may attempt to commit perjury.[56] This goes toward justice. Another purpose is to permit the parties to find out what documents and testimony exist regarding disputed factual issues. Previously the trial was often a drama of surprises, with the outcome determined by a party's access to the facts or by his ability to keep certain information secret until the adversarial duel. Full disclosure again promotes justice. Finally, modern discovery allows the parties to clarify and narrow the issues actually in controversy,[57] which is still partly accomplished in code states through more detailed pleading. Discovery today, however, goes even further and is part of the total reformulation of pretrial practice that emphasizes settlement or the resolution of the lawsuit by summary judgment. Discovery and other pretrial procedures have made both pleading and the trial less important. The goal is judicial efficiency, but debate rages about whether the benefits of this issue-narrowing function exceed the greatly increased expenditure of money and attorney time necessary for its use. The American rule places discovery expenses on the party who initially incurs them. These costs in the 1990s averaged about $5,000 per case and attorneys estimated that 13 percent were unnecessary. Discovery often becomes a tactical weapon to force a settlement on a poorer opponent, to generate large attorney fees, or for sheer harassment.

The general scope of discovery is set out in Federal Rule 26(b)(1): "Parties may obtain discovery regarding any matter, not privileged, that is relevant to the claim or defense of any party." The relevance standard was narrowed in 2000 to exclude (without a court order) claims or defenses not already identified in the pleadings. "Relevant information need not be admissible at the trial if the discovery appears reasonably calculated to lead to the discovery of admissible evidence."[58] The exclusion of privileged matters refers to communication between persons in confidential relationships, such as that between lawyer and client or doctor and patient, that the law favors more highly than truth in resolving disputes.

There are additional limitations on the scope of discovery listed in rule 26(b) to protect certain materials prepared in anticipation of litigation or for trial, facts

56. FRCP 27, 32(a).
57. FRCP 36; *see* pt. IV.A.
58. FRCP 26(b)(1).

known and opinions held by retained experts not expected to be called at trial, and mental impressions, conclusions, opinions, or legal theories of an opponent's attorney. These limits intend to preserve the adversary nature of civil proceedings. *See* pt. II.

Finally, rule 26(c) provides discretionary limits as determined by a judge to regulate discovery "to protect a party or person from annoyance, embarrassment, oppression, or undue burden or expense." The growing abuse of liberal, party-directed discovery led to rule 26 amendments in 1980 (for discovery conferences), in 1983 (to reduce excessive discovery), in 1993 (to require pre-discovery and later exchange of core information), and in 2000 (to make the 1993 amendment uniform nationally and to narrow the scope of discoverable information), which overall has increased judicial management of discovery practice.[59] In 1983 attorneys were also required to sign their discovery papers to encourage them to consider the propriety of their requests, responses, and objections.[60] Judicial sanctions for failure to cooperate in discovery – including the payment of expenses and attorney fees, dismissal, default, or contempt – are described in rule 37. Since 1972 the United States has been a party to the Hague Convention on the Taking of Evidence Abroad in Civil or Commercial Matters.

B. *Methods*

Federal Rule 26(a)(5) lists the discovery methods allowed: "depositions upon oral examination or written questions; written interrogatories; production of documents or things or permission to enter upon land or other property ... for inspection and other purposes; physical and mental examinations; and requests for admission."

1. Required disclosures

The turmoil over discovery abuse led to a major reform of rule 26 and its allied rules in 1993. The new rule 26(a) requires that parties disclose, without waiting for formal discovery requests, certain basic information needed in most cases to prepare for trial or to make an informed decision about settlement. These provisions, from which judicial districts could opt out, were further modified but made mandatory nationwide in 2000.

Required disclosures are divided into two types. Initial disclosures must occur within two weeks after the discovery plan and scheduling conference. *See* pt. VII.B. They include the name, address, and telephone number of each individual likely to have discoverable information, identifying its subject, that the disclosing party may use to support his claims or defenses, as well as copies or descriptions of supporting documents (including liability insurance contracts)

59. FRCP 26(a), (b), (f).
60. FRCP 26(g).

and things. In addition, a party must provide the basis for the computation of his requested damages. Excluded from this requirement are many administrative cases and prisoner petitions as well as actions to enforce an arbitration award.

Subsequent required disclosures include the name and other information for each witness whom the party may call at trial, or whose testimony may be presented by deposition, including expert witnesses (and their reports). Parties must also identify each document that they may offer at trial. These disclosures must be made at least 30 days before trial, unless otherwise directed by the judge. In fact, these matters are usually controlled by the discovery plan incorporated into the court's scheduling order.[61]

2. Oral depositions

A deposition upon oral examination is a private proceeding with attorneys taking a person's testimony using trial-like techniques including direct and cross-examination.[62] The person deposed appears before a presiding officer, usually a reporter authorized to administer oaths,[63] and gives sworn testimony, normally in a lawyer's conference room. Since the officer has no judicial powers, evidentiary objections are recorded along with the testimony, which is later transcribed and signed by the deponent. The principal advantage to this discovery device is that it permits an attorney to test a witness's demeanor and confidence as well as the substance of her testimony. A deposition may be used at trial. Its major disadvantage is the high cost of the attorney and reporter fees.

Since some lawyers harassed parties and witnesses with excessive depositions, rule 30 was amended in 1993 to limit the total number of depositions (oral or written) to ten on each side and to one per deponent, unless the judge permits more. In 2000 it was considered necessary to define "one deposition" as lasting no more than one day of seven hours. Local rules for each judicial district may be even more restrictive. Furthermore, in 1993 new electronic recording technologies were approved and, if the parties agree or the judge orders, depositions may also be conducted on the telephone or satellite television.[64]

3. Written depositions

A deposition upon written questions is similar to an oral deposition, except that all the questions from both sides of the dispute are written out in advance.[65] The attorneys exchange their questions and prepare follow-up questions. The presiding officer reads the questions to the deponent and records her responses. Since

61. FRCP 26(a), (f), 16(b).
62. FRCP 30.
63. FRCP 28.
64. FRCP 30(a), (b), (d).
65. *See* FRCP 31.

depositions are the only discovery device (except for production of documents or things) that can be used with non-parties, a written deposition is appropriate for a friendly witness that cannot attend the trial. It is less expensive than an oral deposition, since the attorneys need not attend.

4. Interrogatories

Interrogatories consist of written questions, which the responding party must answer in writing under oath unless his attorney objects with reasons to a specific question.[66] The party is required to search his records to find answers, but the party and his attorney may compose the answers together. Interrogatories are very useful against a corporation, especially if it is difficult to ascertain which corporate officer has the specific information desired. Alternatively, answers to interrogatories are often evasive and wealthy parties sometimes use lengthy and burdensome interrogatories to coerce an opponent to settle or drop a valid suit. Rule 33(a) was amended in 1993 to correct this latter problem by limiting the number of interrogatories to 25, unless the party can convince the judge or the other party to permit more. The evasion problem was attacked at the same time with an amendment to rule 33(b)(1) requiring the objecting party to at least partially answer an interrogatory to the extent it is not objectionable.

5. Production of documents and things

A party may wish to inspect, copy, test, or sample documents or things within another party's possession, custody, or control. Or a party may wish to enter upon another party's land or other property (for instance, machinery). Federal Rule 34 permits such a written request, which the other party must answer, either agreeing to comply or objecting with reasons. A 1991 amendment makes clear that this request may also be directed against a person not a party, but specific judicially supervised protection is provided against undue burden or expense.[67]

6. Physical and mental examinations

Upon motion and for good cause – the information must be necessary and cannot be easily obtained otherwise – the court may order a physical or mental examination of any party (or person, such as a child or incompetent, benefiting from the litigation who is in the custody or legal control of a party).[68] The physical or mental condition of the party to be examined must be in controversy, which typically is the situation for a plaintiff in personal injury litigation. In other cases judges often deny this motion as an invasion of a party's privacy.

66. *See* FRCP 33.
67. FRCP 34(c), 45.
68. FRCP 35.

7. Admissions

A request for admission offers a simple and inexpensive way to narrow issues conclusively. The request may cover the truth of statements or opinions of fact, the truth of the application of law to fact, or the genuineness of a described document.[69] The responding party or his attorney must serve a written response within 30 days (or the items are deemed admitted). In the response he should admit or deny each matter, explain why he cannot truthfully admit or deny, or object with reasons. This device is commonly used after other discovery has been completed and shortly before the pretrial conference or trial.

C. Use at Trial

The products of discovery may generally be used at trial only so far as permitted by the rules of evidence. The major impediments to admissibility are the hearsay rule, precluding out-of-court statements offered for the truth of the matter asserted, and the best evidence rule, which requires an original document rather than other evidence of its contents (that might be found, for example, in an answer to interrogatories). The hearsay rule has many exceptions, allowing the use of statements, to illustrate, that are admissions or declarations against interest.

The Federal Rules permit special use of depositions in court proceedings, since they were conducted in an adversary climate with truth encouraged by cross-examination. The deposition of a witness (including a party) may be introduced if he is more than 100 miles from the place of trial or hearing or is otherwise unavailable for reasons such as age or illness. In addition, a deposition may be used to impeach any witness whose trial testimony varies from that in the deposition.[70] A rule 36 admission establishes the facts involved; no evidence may be introduced to refute them.[71]

VII. Pretrial Judicial Management

A. The Judge as Administrator

The primary model for resolving disputes in American courts shifted during the 20th century from adjudication to administration. This shift was especially noticeable in federal courts and was the consequence of three interrelated forces: (1) the political movement for judicial reform and its emphasis on efficient caseload management; (2) the changing nature of cases processed, from those justifying substantial attention by individual judges toward those supposedly requiring only routine processing, frequently by judicial staff; and (3) the rise of

69. *See* FRCP 36.
70. FRCP 32(a).
71. FRCP 36(b).

public law litigation and large class action suits. In the former a judge might attempt to restructure a major social organization such as a prison, mental hospital, or school district.[72] In the latter, thousands or even millions of claimants ask for relief in product liability, consumer fraud, or toxic tort cases that can occupy most of a judge's time. *See* pt. V.F.

B. Pretrial Conference

Federal Rule 16 in 1938 introduced the first major pretrial conference system in the United States. It was widely copied by the states, but was generally discretionary and when used occurred immediately before trial to organize and narrow the issues to be actually tried.

In 1983 rule 16 was completely rewritten to encourage federal judges to more aggressively manage their caseloads. It was further revised in 1993 to coordinate the timing and extent of required disclosures and other discovery issues associated with the discovery plan.[73] Four objectives emerged from the 1983 rule. First, the rule promotes efficiency and reduces delay. This objective was not even mentioned in original rule 16, but now is first on the list.[74] Rule 16(b) requires the judge in most cases, after consultation with the attorneys, to issue a scheduling order within 120 days after the defendant has received the complaint. The order limits the time for further pleading or joinder, hearing motions, and completing discovery. Second, the rule encourages discovery guidelines and discourages wasteful pretrial motions.[75] Third, the rule aims to formulate and simplify trial issues and to avoid surprise.[76] This was the primary goal under the 1938 version, but remains an important objective as shown by the subjects for consideration under rule 16(c)(1) to (4) and (12) to (15). Fourth, the rule promotes settlement.[77] This last objective stirred much debate in the past two decades, since it interferes with the traditional adversary contest between two attorneys umpired by a neutral judge. Nevertheless, judges today play a more active part in forcing the parties to settle. In federal courts only about 2.2 percent of civil and administrative cases go on to trial, down from ten percent in 1988.

At the end of a pretrial conference the judge enters a pretrial order reciting the action taken. This order supersedes the pleadings and controls the subsequent course of the lawsuit. If it is the final conference, the judge and the attorneys formulate a plan for trial, including a program for facilitating the admission of evidence.[78]

72. *See* David S. Clark, "Adjudication to Administration: A Statistical Analysis of Federal District Courts in the Twentieth Century," 55 *S. Cal. L. Rev.* 65 (1981); pts. II, III.A.
73. *See* FRCP 16(b), (c), 26(a), (f); pt. VI.B.1.
74. FRCP 16(a)(1), (2).
75. FRCP 16(a)(3), 26(f).
76. FRCP 16(a)(4).
77. FRCP 16(a)(5), (c)(5), (c)(9).
78. FRCP 16(d), (e).

VIII. Adjudication without Trial

A. Dismissal of Actions

At common law the plaintiff could dismiss his case voluntarily and without prejudice anytime prior to judgment. Most code states restricted this privilege by requiring dismissal before commencement of trial. Federal Rule 41(a) provides the plaintiff in general with only one voluntary dismissal without prejudice. If the plaintiff files a notice of dismissal prior to service of the defendant's answer, no court order is required. If later, plaintiff must petition the court, which usually grants such a motion, but only on terms and conditions as the court deems proper. A plaintiff may also terminate the suit by filing a stipulation of dismissal, with or without prejudice, signed by all parties.

A defendant in a code state may file a demurrer or under Federal Rule 12(b) a motion to dismiss for certain procedural errors the plaintiff committed associated with the summons, selection of a court, or joinder of parties. *See* pt. III.E. In addition, the defendant may move to dismiss the plaintiff's complaint for failure to state a claim upon which relief can be granted.[79] Finally, the defendant may move for dismissal because the plaintiff has failed to bring the case to trial or has failed to appear at or to prepare for scheduled conferences or hearings. This involuntary dismissal carries res judicata prejudice.[80]

B. Default Judgment

If a defendant fails to plead or otherwise defend, the plaintiff may move to declare her in default.[81] Often a defendant fails to respond at all to a plaintiff's summons and complaint. In such a situation the plaintiff, after obtaining the declaration of default, requests entry of judgment by default. *See* pt. III.E. If the plaintiff requests a sum certain, a court clerk enters a judgment for that amount; if the case involves unliquidated damages a judge holds a hearing at which the plaintiff must prove the amount of damages before a judgment can be entered.[82]

When the defendant has participated in the lawsuit and then defaults, the court must send her notice prior to the damages hearing and the entry of judgment by default. Finally, the plaintiff may move for default because the defendant has failed to appear at or to prepare for scheduled conferences or hearings. The entry of judgment is res judicata.

79. FRCP 12(b)(6); *see* pt. IV.C.
80. FRCP 16(f), 37(b)(2)(C), 41(b).
81. FRCP 55(a).
82. FRCP 55(b).

C. Summary Judgment

In code states a defendant's general demurrer attacking the plaintiff's cause of action was determined solely from the face of the complaint. The defendant could not go behind the pleading with evidence to show that it was a sham; "speaking demurrers" were prohibited. Federal Rule 56 and today most states for reasons of efficiency permit a motion for summary judgment.

The summary judgment motion, especially under the federal model, has evolved to be a type of mini-trial to eliminate sham issues or claims and defenses and to test the strength of an opponent's case. The motion is generally supported by affidavits of witnesses, setting forth facts admissible as evidence, and by discovery materials that would be admissible at trial.[83] Either the plaintiff or the defendant may move for summary judgment, which should be granted if the materials "show that there is no genuine issue as to any material fact and that the moving party is entitled to a judgment as a matter of law."[84] The opposing party cannot successfully defeat this motion by simply restating the allegations or denials in her pleading; she must set forth specific facts showing a genuine issue for trial. The judge can decide the motion solely on the basis of the materials and lawyers' briefs submitted or he can hold a hearing. In the later situation the attorneys will support their briefs by oral argument. Often a judge will find that only some aspects of a claim or defense (or only some claims or defenses) are not genuinely controvertible; he will then make a partial summary judgment order and the remaining issues will proceed to trial.[85]

The U.S. Supreme Court in a trilogy of cases has encouraged the use of summary judgments.[86] They do not impinge on a party's right to a jury trial because the standard is close to that for a directed verdict at trial, which considers whether there is a legally sufficient evidentiary basis for a reasonable jury to find for that party. If there is a real factual dispute, the motion should be denied. If not, it may be granted. In making this determination, the judge should construe all factual issues, including credibility of witnesses, in the light most favorable to the opposing party and then ask whether reasonable persons could differ on the outcome. If they could differ, or if they would agree with the opposing party, the case continues.

IX. Trial

A. The Process

In federal court about one in 45 civil and administrative cases makes it to trial; the other 44 are dismissed, defaulted, settled, or adjudicated without trial. Of those cases that begin trial, perhaps two in three are before a jury. The remaining

83. FRCP 56(e).
84. FRCP 56(c).
85. FRCP 56(d).
86. *Matsushita Elec. Indus. Co. v. Zenith Radio Corp.*, 475 U.S. 574 (1986); *Anderson v. Liberty Lobby, Inc.*, 477 U.S. 242 (1986); *Celotex Corp. v. Catrett*, 477 U.S. 317 (1986).

cases are heard before a single judge. The ratio in state courts is about one in 30 cases that make it to trial, where slightly more than half are before juries.

Normally a trial will not occur until one of the parties requests that the lawsuit be placed on the trial calendar. In the federal system and in some states the judge may also set the trial date, often at the pretrial conference.[87] If the plaintiff or defendant wishes and has a right to a jury trial, she must make a demand in writing so stating, usually at an early stage in the suit.[88] If she waives this constitutional right (*see* pt. II), she will have a nonjury or judge trial. In federal court she will likely wait 20 months for either a judge or jury trial, although one in ten litigants must wait four years. The average delay in state courts to reach trial is two years.

The order of presentation is usually the same for both jury and nonjury trials, although the former have additional time-consuming elements. In a jury trial, for instance, the first step is to select the jurors, who often are retired persons, homemakers, or those who can afford to be absent from their jobs. A good trial attorney will attempt to seat jurors who will identify and sympathize with his client.

After a jury is seated, plaintiff's counsel and then defendant's counsel will each make an opening statement to explain what they intend to prove. The plaintiff's direct evidence follows, with direct and cross-examination of his witnesses.[89] In a jury trial either party then has an opportunity to move for a directed verdict (since 1991 in federal court called a judgment as a matter of law) on the ground that there is no legally sufficient evidentiary basis for a reasonable jury to find for his opponent.[90] The parties have a similar right to show legal insufficiency in a judge trial, which in some states is called a motion for involuntary dismissal, but since 1991 is known in federal courts as a motion for judgment as a matter of law on partial findings.[91]

If the party's legal insufficiency motion is denied, the defendant's direct evidence is presented. The parties are then usually permitted to introduce rebuttal evidence. At the close of all the evidence in a jury trial, either party may move for a directed verdict (or judgment as a matter of law), which if granted will keep the case from going to the jury. If denied, plaintiff's and defendant's attorney make closing arguments summarizing the evidence supporting their respective clients. In a nonjury trial the judge will evaluate the evidence, specifically find the facts, and separately state his conclusions of law.[92] Judgment will be entered on a separate document.[93] Since 1993 rule 54(d)(2) permits the trial court to delay appeal to hear the increasing number of collateral disputes concerning the amount of attorney fees and related expenses to be awarded in situations where the prevailing party may be entitled to such an award or where fees will be paid from a common fund.[94]

87. FRCP 16(b)(5), 40.
88. FRCP 38.
89. For the use of discovery materials, *see* pt. VI.C.
90. FRCP 50(a).
91. FRCP 52(c).
92. FRCP 52(a).
93. FRCP 58.
94. *See* FRCP 58; Fed. R. App. P. 4(a); pt. XI.B.

In a jury trial the judge must now instruct the jurors (who are to find the facts) concerning the correct law to be applied. In many states the supreme court or legislature has approved pattern instructions that are used for recurring types of legal issues. Sometimes, however, the judge requires the lawyers to submit instructions, which he will use to prepare a final set of instructions to read to the jury.[95] Finally, the jury retires in the custody of a bailiff, who guards them during deliberations. If the jury can agree on a verdict, it is delivered in writing in open court where it is read by the judge or court clerk. The judge then enters judgment on the verdict.[96]

The losing party still has an opportunity to make certain post-trial motions to the judge shortly after the judgment is entered, typically within ten days. If he moved for a directed verdict at the close of all the evidence, he may renew the legal insufficiency argument with a motion for judgment notwithstanding the verdict (or in federal court judgment as a matter of law).[97] This is a device to control and overturn an irrational jury. In addition, the losing party may move for a new trial on grounds, for example, that an attorney, party, or juror was guilty of misconduct, that the judge mistakenly admitted (or excluded) certain evidence, that the instructions misstated the law, or that the jury's verdict was against the clear weight of the evidence.[98]

B. The Jury

Fewer than two percent of the civil and administrative cases filed in federal or state courts end up before a jury. Nevertheless, the jury trial is a fundamental part of the American system of civil justice. Although virtually eliminated in contemporary England, its transplantation to the American colonies was firmly rooted in the U.S. Constitution and almost all state constitutions, where it was viewed as a natural right to popular justice and as a protection against the government's (formerly the crown's) arbitrary judges. The right usually extends to actions historically decided at common law and does not extend to equity cases. *See* pt. I.A.

The jury certainly has its costs. Most countries – even common law countries – have abandoned the civil jury, so that about 95 percent of all civil jury trials occur in the United States. Most of the costs are evident: fees paid to jurors, additional attorney and judicial expenses associated with selecting a jury, making directed verdict motions, and preparing instructions to the jury. Other costs are more subtle. Most evidence and trial practice law, which is very complicated, evolved in response to the presence of a lay jury. For instance, the hearsay rule – which excludes statements made out of court offered to prove the truth of the matter asserted – was designed to keep impressionable lay persons from hearing statements that had not been cross-examined. Since a rigid rule would exclude too much valuable evidence, it has been riddled with numerous exceptions that

95. FRCP 51.
96. FRCP 58.
97. FRCP 50(b).
98. FRCP 59.

keep attorneys and judges busy determining which statements are admissible and which are not. The rule applies, moreover, to affect the larger system, such as a summary judgment hearing or a judge trial. Finding educated jurors for cases with complex facts is a further problem, which becomes a cost for the party with the burden of proof. Juror bias – including racial prejudice – adds to the list.

Discontent with the costliness of the jury has led to modifications in its original form and to the increase in judicial wariness toward the jury. Several states and the federal courts today permit juries composed of fewer than the original 12 persons. Groups with as few as six members decide a matter more quickly than a larger group. In addition, non-unanimous verdicts, typically with a three-fourths majority, are used. Judges in most states and in the federal system push litigants toward settlement rather than to their "day in court" with a jury. They decide more cases by summary judgment or literally take the case away from a jury with a directed verdict. Finally, several legislatures have recently become concerned about the impact of large jury awards on American business – especially in product liability cases – or on the practice of medicine and have enacted rules as part of "tort reform" to cut back on the jury's traditional powers.

X. Judgments and Their Effects

A. Enforcement

The judgment symbolizes the final determination of a lawsuit when there is no appeal. In many cases the losing defendant pays the amount of money awarded or complies with the decree. If the defendant wins, the judgment simply provides that the plaintiff is entitled to no relief under his complaint.

Some judgments, such as those declaring rights or quieting title to land, require no further action. Judgments awarding money damages and enjoining future activity, however, may not mark the end of the lawsuit. Execution is the usual method for collecting a money judgment.[99] Typically the plaintiff asks the court clerk for a writ of execution, which directs the sheriff to attach and sell as much of the defendant's property as necessary to satisfy the judgment. The plaintiff takes the writ to the sheriff and gives him a description of the property to sell. The sheriff asks the defendant to pay the judgment; if he still refuses the sheriff holds a public sale, subtracts his costs from the proceeds, delivers the correct amount to the plaintiff, and remits any balance to the court for use of the defendant. The plaintiff must then execute a satisfaction of the claim and file it in the clerk's office. When an injunction is the plaintiff's relief, he can enforce the court's decree with a motion to hold the defendant in contempt of court for failure to comply. This sanction is direct; the defendant can be punished by fine or imprisonment.

When a sister state or foreign country judgment is involved, the forum must first recognize the judgment before it can be enforced. *See* Chap. 17, pt. IV.

99. *See* FRCP 69(a).

B. Binding Effects

It is in society's and the litigants' interest that a dispute finally end. Peace in the community is a public concern. The doctrines historically associated with the common law concept of res judicata aim toward this goal. They are judicially created and thus vary significantly in detail among the federal courts and the several states. Res judicata promotes at least two separate policies. One is repose for the litigants. Give them "a day in court" – that is, due process – and then terminate the dispute with a rule of finality. The other policy is judicial efficiency. Bring an entire cause of action, claim, or even a whole dispute arising out of a transaction or occurrence before the court in one lawsuit. Avoid the splitting of claims. Do not retry issues already adjudicated. One must recognize that these two policies have nothing to do with substantive justice: the application of appropriate legal rules to the truthfully ascertained facts. It is generally a futile defense against an argument of res judicata that justice was not done the first time around.

A party can use res judicata, normally in the context of a second lawsuit, only after the judge enters a judgment in an initial lawsuit. A judgment will be binding only if it is both valid and final. A court can render a valid judgment when it has subject matter and territorial jurisdiction and has provided the defendant with adequate notice. If the defendant litigated these issues in the first suit, however, the doctrine of jurisdiction to determine jurisdiction precludes him from questioning a judgment's validity in a second suit. *See* pt. III.E. A judgment is final when it is entered. Thus, finality is satisfied even though a motion for a new trial or an appeal is pending. If a court on appeal modifies or reverses a judgment, its preclusive effects will be determined by the appellate ruling.

1. Claim preclusion

The modern approach divides res judicata into two parts: claim preclusion and issue preclusion. Claim preclusion means that a party may not relitigate in another lawsuit the same claim against the same opponent after a judgment has been entered in a case adjudicated on the merits. Since terminology differs across American jurisdictions, some courts call claim preclusion "res judicata" or "merger and bar." Conceptually the first judgment extinguishes the whole claim, including matters the plaintiff or defendant might have litigated. If the plaintiff won the first suit, his claim merges in the judgment; he may proceed to enforcement based on that judgment without worrying about the defendant successfully raising new defenses. If the defendant won the first suit, plaintiff's attempt to sue again is barred by the judgment.

The problem of determining what constitutes the same claim explains much of the difference in res judicata law among jurisdictions. Federal courts and some states are moving toward a broad view focusing on a single transaction or series of connected transactions to define the claim. This transactional approach encourages the greatest joinder of claims and defenses in the first suit, thus avoiding multiple litigation. For instance, assume defendant negligently drove his car into plaintiff's truck, jumped from the car and punched plaintiff, and then turned to a bystander and accused plaintiff of drunkenness. In a transactional state plaintiff should join all three actions, since they have related factual origins and would form a convenient trial unit.[100] Alternatively, more traditional states retain a narrow conception of a single cause of action and seek to minimize the harsh consequence of applying res judicata. In such a state plaintiff need not join his negligence, assault, and slander actions – involving distinct legal issues – even though the claim joinder rules might so permit. Plaintiff can bring one suit for negligence. After judgment he may sue again for assault and slander; defendant will be unsuccessful in asking for res judicata on the ground that plaintiff split his claim.

Claim preclusion applies only if the first judgment was rendered on the merits. This covers most judicial decisions, with some variability among states, including an involuntary dismissal, summary judgment, and dismissal for failure to state a claim, to prosecute, or to obey a court order. A judgment is not on the merits for dismissals for lack of subject matter or territorial jurisdiction, inadequate process or its service, non- or misjoinder of parties, and most voluntary dismissals.

2. Issue preclusion

Outside the initial lawsuit, issue preclusion stops a party from relitigating against the same opponent any factual or mixed law-fact issue actually litigated in the first suit if the determination of that issue was essential to the judgment.[101] Most instances of issue preclusion occur when the second action involves a different claim from that brought in the first suit. Courts generally call this collateral estoppel. When the second action is based on the same claim raised in the initial action, some courts call the doctrine direct estoppel. This precludes, for example, relitigation of the issue of territorial jurisdiction when the court dismissed plaintiff's first suit on this ground.

A party must meet three special requirements to successfully rely on issue preclusion. First, the same issue must occur in suits one and two. Whether the defendant acted negligently in crashing his automobile against plaintiff's automobile in a suit for property damage will involve the same negligence issue in suit two for personal injuries. Second, the common issue must have been actually litigated and determined in suit one. This element is not satisfied when the judgment results from default, an admission, or consent. Parties may have valid reasons for not raising every conceivable point that might be relevant to a claim or defense. The amount in controversy in suit one may be small, a party may have difficulty in obtaining necessary evidence, or she may fear that it will divert the judge's attention in the first action away from a strong issue in her claim or defense. Thus judicial economy is likely to be promoted by not requiring a party anticipating a second suit to expand the size of action one to include all possible issues. Third, most states require that the issue be essential to the judgment. This makes it more likely that the parties vigorously litigated the issue so that it is fair

100. *See* Restatement (Second) of Judgments § 24 (1982).
101. *See* Restatement (Second) of Judgments § 27 (1982).

to bind them on this matter in suit two. For instance, facts determined against the prevailing party in suit one are not considered essential, since the winning party usually is not allowed to appeal these facts. *See* pt. XI.D.

3. Same parties or privies

The traditional rule is that only parties and their privies (those in a representational relationship with a party) in the first suit can benefit from or be bound by res judicata in the second suit. Persons in privity with a party have their interests represented and protected in the first litigation. They include: (1) successors in interest to property, for example by assignment or inheritance; (2) persons represented by a party, such as a beneficiary by a trustee, a ward by a guardian, or absent members by named parties in a class action; and (3) persons who assume actual control of litigation in the name of another.

A correlate to this rule is that a person may not benefit from a prior judgment unless he would also be bound by it. Strangers involved in similar suits (for instance, in plane crash litigation) could never be bound by an adverse judgment since that would violate the "day in court" notion of due process. Thus a stranger should not benefit from another person's judgment against a defendant in a mass disaster. For the doctrine of collateral estoppel this rule is known as mutuality of estoppel; it has significantly eroded in most states and in the federal courts since the landmark California case, *Bernhard v. Bank of America National Trust & Savings Association.*[102] The rationale for the erosion, allowing a stranger to benefit (but not be bound), is efficiency and consistency in the two suits. The common party is entitled to only one opportunity to litigate an issue. More jurisdictions have accepted the defensive use of collateral estoppel in suit two by the nonparty than have accepted its offensive use by the nonparty. Offensive use would encourage a line of potential plaintiffs to sue a tortfeasor seriatim until one won, then the remaining victims would sue and invoke collateral estoppel on the liability issue. The Supreme Court as a matter of federal common law has given lower federal courts broad discretion to use offensive estoppel when its applicability is foreseeable in action one and would not be otherwise unfair to the common party.[103]

XI. Appeal

A. Appellate Courts

A system of appeals is so clearly inefficient – since a case is processed twice – that it can only be defended for the reason that it promotes justice. There are two major functions of appellate adjudication. First, the historic basis for the intervention of an appellate court is to correct error in the trial court or administrative

102. 122 P.2d 892 (1942).
103. *Parklane Hosiery Co. v. Shore*, 439 U.S. 322 (1979).

agency. Second, appellate courts are also needed to enunciate, clarify, and harmonize rules used within the legal system. Trial courts working independently would have no capacity to assure uniformity among their decisions; there thus would be no basis on which to contend that a jurisdiction was ordered by the rule of law. Appellate justice, as a result, is today concerned with the impact of its decisions on particular litigants (review for correctness), as well as with the interpretation and creation of norms that govern the affairs of persons other than those who brought a lawsuit (institutional review).

These dual functions are preformed by the appellate system as a whole. Where there is a single appellate court – the supreme court – as in less populous states, that body assumes the entire appellate responsibility. The notion of sharing responsibility between two separate levels of appellate courts stems from the national experience with the United States Supreme Court.

The caseload of the Supreme Court remained very small until after the Civil War. During the 19th century the Court was primarily a private law adjudicator required to take appeals. By 1890 filings had expanded to 636, but average delay was two years. Given this perceived crisis, Congress in 1891 provided for a separate group of circuit courts of appeals, which eventually relieved Supreme Court justices of circuit riding duties. In 1914 Congress provided for discretionary review by writ of certiorari and passed the Judiciary Act of 1925, which further limited the court's obligatory jurisdiction. It was the premise of the 1925 reform that the Supreme Court would continue to hear cases of institutional importance, but would let stand cases of significance only to the parties involved. The latter function of review for correctness was to be the primary responsibility of the courts of appeals, which now first hear appeals. Today petitions for certiorari comprise almost all the Court's docket and since the 1960s constitutional issues have consistently comprised at least two thirds of the caseload.

As the American states faced supreme court caseload crises in the 1960s and 1970s, they looked primarily to federal experience in evolving their own structures.[104] The result is that a two-tier appellate framework exists in 39 states and the District of Columbia. Some states use a variant that sends all appeals to the supreme court, which then determines those cases to retain and those to release to the intermediate appellate court. Subsequent appeal to the supreme court is still possible from the intermediate court. All states have unitary supreme courts with plenary jurisdiction except for Texas and Oklahoma, which have a high court of criminal appeals and a supreme court for all other cases.

In 1996 198,722 cases were filed in intermediate appellate courts and 88,010 cases were filed in state supreme courts. For the former, 86 percent of the appeals were mandatory in the sense that the appellate court must hear and determine the appeal. At the supreme court level, however, only 35 percent of the cases were mandatory. Supreme courts spend much of their time reviewing the remaining discretionary petitions to decide which of these cases to hear. Rates of acceptance range from one percent for California to 23 percent for Nebraska. In the federal

104. *See* David S. Clark, "American Supreme Court Caseloads: A Preliminary Inquiry," 26 *Am. J. Comp. L.* 217 (Supp. 1978).

system there were 54,697 cases filed in the courts of appeals in 2000 and 8,445 in the Supreme Court. *See* pt. III.A (trial court statistics). Virtually all of the U.S. Supreme Court's docket is discretionary and fewer than 100 cases are decided by full opinion (with another five or so by per curiam opinion). State appellate courts and federal district courts and courts of appeals publish 100,000 opinions annually.[105]

B. The Final Judgment Rule

The federal courts and most states permit an appeal only from the entry of a final judgment.[106] This rule at common law was developed for the writ of error. Today it promotes efficiency at two levels. The trial court operates more swiftly when the parties cannot interrupt the pretrial and trial processes. And the appellate court saves time by considering one appeal that consolidates all alleged errors rather than by adjudicating multiple appeals. The final judgment rule is also likely to foster justice – in terms of the correct disposition of the case on the merits – when the appellate court has the whole record by which to ascertain the legality of a particular interlocutory order.

A few states are very liberal regarding appeals. New York, for example, allows a party to appeal as of right to the appellate division from an order that involves some part of the merits or that affects a substantial right. This approach is inefficient, but it does permit appellate courts to establish uniform law for trial courts in areas – such as discovery – that otherwise realistically cannot be raised on appeal.

C. Interlocutory Appellate Review

At equity interlocutory decrees and even orders could be reviewed before the judge rendered a final decree. This tradition remained after merger of law and equity to accommodate circumstances under which the final judgment rule would be inefficient or unjust.

There are two basic approaches to the appellate review of interlocutory decisions. First, a rigid rule provides a list of those categories of orders that are appealable, such as orders affecting injunctions, receiverships, admiralty, or patent infringement suits that are final except for an accounting.[107] This type of rule has the advantage of certainty: one usually knows when one may appeal. Second, a flexible rule provides broad guidelines of decision, where the appeal is conditioned upon the consent of either the trial or appellate court or both. A party, for instance, may appeal from a federal district judge's order if: (1) the judge certifies that the decision "involves a controlling question of law as to which there

105. *See* Chap. 18 for an example of a judicial opinion; *see also* Chap. 3, pt. III.A.
106. E.g., 28 U.S.C. § 1291 (1994).
107. E.g., 28 U.S.C. § 1292(a), (c) (1994).

is substantial ground for difference of opinion and that an immediate appeal from the order may materially advance the ultimate termination of the litigation"; and (2) the court of appeals accepts the application.[108] This type of rule has the advantage of accuracy, since it only allows those important appeals necessary to obtain justice or efficiency.

The federal All Writs Statute[109] preserves five extraordinary writs inherited from England, which evolved to accomplish justice when no other avenue of relief was available. The primary writ still used in federal litigation for civil interlocutory review is mandamus. It compels a judge to perform a non-discretionary duty, such as adjudicating a difficult case rather than delegating it to a master. Although rare in federal courts, mandamus is used more often in some state appellate systems – for example, to review decisions in California denying motions to quash service of process for lack of territorial jurisdiction. Other states use the writ of prohibition to prevent an inferior court from acting in excess of its authority or jurisdiction.

D. Scope of Review

A party who wishes to appeal generally must file a timely notice of appeal with the trial court clerk within 30 days from the entry of the relevant order or judgment.[110] With the attorney's assistance the clerk assembles and sends the record to the appellate court clerk, who files the record.[111] An appeal usually stays the proceedings in the lower court and an appellant can also take measures to suspend enforcement of the judgment until the appeal is decided.[112] The record on appeal contains the pleadings and other papers filed, at least a portion of the verbatim trial transcript, and the court clerk's docket entries.[113]

The appellant may contest on appeal prejudicial rulings that he objected to below.[114] A winning party may only appeal from decisions that were essential to the judgment, since these are the only ones that pose a future threat from collateral estoppel. *See* pt. X.B.2. When the losing party appeals, however, the appellee may respond by raising any issue that would sustain the judgment. The parties present their views to the appellate court by written briefs and often by oral argument. Intermediate appellate courts normally work with three-judge panels, while the various state supreme courts operate in a plenary session of five, seven, or nine justices.

Appellate courts vary their standard of review, which depends on whether the alleged error was an issue of law or one of fact and, if the latter, whether the trial

108. 28 U.S.C. § 1292(b) (1994). Federal Rule 23(f) was added in 1998 to permit the court of appeals to review a district judge's class certification ruling. *See* pt. V.F.
109. 28 U.S.C. § 1651 (1994).
110. Fed. R. App. P. 3, 4.
111. Fed. R. App. P. 12.
112. FRCP 62; Fed. R. App. P. 8.
113. Fed. R. App. P. 10.
114. FRCP 46; 28 U.S.C. § 2111 (1994).

was before a jury or not. Full or de novo review of trial court decisions occurs for legal issues, which satisfies the institutional function to promote uniform law throughout the jurisdiction. For rulings placed in a trial judge's discretion, such as most new trial motions, an appellate court will overturn the judge only where his decision is clearly wrong and an abuse of discretion.

Appellate courts do not follow the civil law model and in second instance adjudicate facts de novo, which would fully promote the correctness function. Rather findings of fact receive significant deference. In a nonjury trial the appellate court will let stand a judge's factual findings unless clearly erroneous; due regard must be given to the trial court's opportunity to judge the witnesses' credibility.[115] In a jury trial the appellate court allows even greater leeway to lay fact finders, to respect the parties' constitutional right to a jury trial.

An appellate court has the authority to affirm, modify, or reverse the trial court's order or judgment. If it reverses, the appellate court can enter judgment for the appellant or it can remand the case to the lower court for further proceedings consistent with its decision. Many decisions are accompanied by a written opinion supported by reasons, signed by one of the judges, that is published as a guide to the legal community. Other participating judges may file a concurring or dissenting opinion. *See* Chap. 18.

Selected Bibliography

Erwin Chemerinsky, *Federal Jurisdiction* (3d ed. 1999).

Jack H. Friedenthal, Mary Kay Kane & Arthur R. Miller, *Civil Procedure* (3d ed. 1999).

Fleming James, Jr., Geoffrey C. Hazard, Jr. & John Leubsdorf, *Civil Procedure* (4th ed. 1992).

Richard L. Marcus, "Malaise of the Litigation Superpower," in *Civil Justice in Crisis: Comparative Perspectives of Civil Procedure* 71-116 (Adrian A.S Zuckerman ed. 1999).

Christopher B. Mueller & Laird C. Kirkpatrick, *Evidence* (1995).

Roger C. Park, David P. Leonard & Steven H. Goldberg, *Evidence Law* (1998).

Gene R. Shreve & Peter Raven-Hansen, *Understanding Civil Procedure* (2d ed. 1994).

John W. Strong, ed., *McCormick on Evidence* (5th ed. 1999).

Larry L. Teply & Ralph U. Whitten, *Civil Procedure* (1994).

Charles Alan Wright, *Law of Federal Courts* (5th ed. 1994).

115. FRCP 52(a).

Chapter 17
Conflict of Laws

Friedrich K. Juenger*

I. Introduction

In the United States the conflict of laws (or, as it is called elsewhere, "private international law") comprises: (1) jurisdiction, (2) choice of law, and (3) judgments recognition. These topics correspond to three fundamental questions counsel encounter in litigating interstate and international transactions: (1) Will the court take the case? (2) If so, what law will the court apply? (3) Will the court's judgment be recognized outside the forum's territory?

* Late Edward L. Barrett, Jr., Professor of Law, University of California at Davis School of Law and President, Common Law Group, International Academy of Comparative Law.

David S. Clark and Tuğrul Ansay (eds.) Introduction to the Law of the United States, 421-449

The responses to these questions have largely been developed by the judiciary rather than by legislatures. Except for constraints imposed by the U.S. Constitution on jurisdiction and choice of law, state rather than federal law controls, unless the issue presented is federal in nature (for example, jurisdiction and choice of law in maritime cases). The rules and approaches courts have elaborated apply equally to interstate and international cases, unless peculiarities of the international setting require deviations from the norm, or international conflicts problems lack a domestic counterpart (for instance, currency or bankruptcy matters).

II. JURISDICTION

The question whether a court will hear a case ought to merit a simple answer. Attorneys must know where they can vindicate their clients' rights and should be spared the embarrassment of – and potential malpractice liability for – having sued in the wrong forum. Yet, for historical reasons, the American law of jurisdiction is highly complex and confusing.

A. Historical Evolution

The common law heritage differs from the tradition that, first codified in Justinian's *Corpus Juris*, informs the jurisdictional rules of civil law countries. According to this tradition, a person may be sued: (1) at his domicile (*actor sequitur forum rei*), and (2) in places with which the dispute has a certain nexus, for example, where a contract was made, where a person was injured, or where property is situated. Thus, in effect, Roman law already distinguished "general" jurisdiction – amenability to suit where the defendant lives – from "specific" (or transactional) jurisdiction.

1. The common law

In contrast, the English common law premised jurisdiction not on the defendant's nexus with the forum but rather on a procedural act, namely the service of summons within the realm. This approach proved to be quite unsatisfactory in the American federal system. On the one hand, it is clearly exorbitant to exercise jurisdiction over defendants whom the process server manages to slap with a summons while they are traveling through the forum state. On the other hand, such "tag jurisdiction" is also too narrow. It does not reach corporations, artificial beings that lack a physical presence, unless they appoint a human being as their agent. Nor does this catch-as-catch-can approach work satisfactorily with nimble defendants such as out-of-state motorists, whom the rule merely induces to step on the accelerator after maiming the local victim.

Once cars and corporations proliferated, American courts and legislatures looked for ways to expand jurisdiction. However, the quest for common-sense solutions ran into an obstacle: the U.S. Supreme Court decision in *Pennoyer v.*

Neff[1] had bestowed upon the English approach the status of a constitutional dogma. Deducing jurisdiction from tenets of sovereignty and territoriality, the majority concluded that courts lack power to deal with the personal rights of individuals who have not been brought under the forum state's control by serving them within the state, or with property that has not been subjected to such control by attaching it there. Hence *Pennoyer* precluded, with a few exceptions (divorce and other status matters, jurisdiction based on appearance and consent), any exercise of *in personam* jurisdiction over nonresidents that is not premised on personal service within the forum's territory. It did, however, allow plaintiffs to proceed *quasi in rem* against a nonresident's local property to effectively vindicate personal rights. According to Justice Field's majority opinion in *Pennoyer*, jurisdictional assertions that fail to abide by this territorial imperative violate the 14th Amendment's due process clause.

2. "Minimum contacts"

It took the U.S. Supreme Court almost 70 years to free itself from this fateful precedent. Initially the Court resorted to fictions, such as corporate "presence' and "implied consent,' to broaden jurisdiction over foreign corporations. Along similar lines the Court allowed the states to assert jurisdiction over nonresident motorists premised on the idea that driving within the forum implies consent to jurisdiction for any injuries caused there. The subterfuges invented to evade *Pennoyer's* antiquated territorialism, which failed to accommodate the needs of a federal system with a mobile population, produced a convoluted case law burdened with subtle distinctions and marred by inconsistent results. Realizing the confusion it had wrought, the Court ultimately decided to put jurisdiction on an entirely different foundation. According to *International Shoe Co. v. Washington*, a state may adjudicate a dispute whenever the defendant has sufficient "minimum contacts" with the forum so that "maintenance of the suit does not offend 'traditional notions of fair play and substantial justice'."[2]

While it reaffirmed that part of *Pennoyer* which subjected jurisdictional assertions to due process scrutiny, the *International Shoe* case aligned American with continental European legal thinking: it no longer premised jurisdiction solely on the magic act of service or attachment within the forum state, but on the defendant's forum nexus. At the same time, the U.S. Supreme Court recognized the distinction between "general" and "specific" jurisdiction. If the defendant's forum activities are, in the Court's words, "continuous and systematic," he can be sued on causes of action that are unrelated to these contacts; if they are merely isolated or sporadic they support, at best, jurisdiction to adjudicate causes of action that arise out of these very activities.

1. 95 U.S. 714 (1878).
2. 326 U.S. 310, 316 (1945).

3. A unitary principle?

Although it "civilized" and expanded the American law of jurisdiction, *International Shoe* left the *Pennoyer* rules intact. Plaintiffs could still acquire *in personam* jurisdiction over defendants by serving them with process and *quasi in rem* jurisdiction by attaching assets in the forum state. These rules were of course difficult to reconcile with the principle underlying *International Shoe*, namely that the defendant must have a sufficiently close nexus with the forum. Obviously, a defendant's fleeting presence in the state – or the presence of his bank account – is a rather tenuous contact. It hardly amounts to "fair play and substantial justice," for example, to proceed against a person who was served with process while flying through the forum state's airspace, as happened in *Grace v. MacArthur*[3]. At the same time, the more expansive jurisdictional principle established by *International Shoe* made the common law's traditional jurisdictional bases dispensable.

Indeed, *Shaffer v. Heitner*[4] seemed to overrule what remained of *Pennoyer* exorbitance. In *Shaffer* the Supreme Court held that the attachment of corporate stock in Delaware, the state of defendant's incorporation, could not confer *quasi in rem* jurisdiction for a derivative suit against the corporation's nonresident officers and directors who owned the sequestered shares. Even assuming that Delaware was in fact the "situs" of the equity interests which the Delaware court had purported to seize (none of the share certificates was shown to be physically within Delaware), the mere presence of such assets would not amount to "minimum contacts," that is, a sufficient nexus to justify the exercise of jurisdiction. *Shaffer*, however, did more than outlaw *quasi in rem* jurisdiction, which allowed a court effectively to determine personal rights by proceeding against property that had been attached in the forum's state, an alternative *Pennoyer* had offered to proceeding *in personam* against a defendant who could not be served with process there. According to an expansive dictum in Justice Marshall's majority opinion, to comport with due process *all* jurisdictional assertions must comply with the "minimum contacts" test laid down in *International Shoe*.

4. Back to *Pennoyer*?

By parity of reasoning, that should be equally true of "tag" (or "transient") jurisdiction based on the service of process on a defendant who is only temporarily present in the forum state. Old lore, however, dies hard. In *Burnham v. Superior Court*[5] the Supreme Court upheld personal jurisdiction over a New Jersey defendant who, while traveling in California to conduct business and to visit his children, was served with process in a suit for divorce and incidental relief brought by his wife, a California resident. Although the holding was unanimous, eight justices split evenly on the underlying rationale. According to Justice Scalia's opinion, in-

3. 170 F.Supp. 442 (E.D. Ark. 1959).
4. 433 U.S. 186 (1977).
5. 495 U.S. 604 (1990).

state service of process suffices – in and of itself – to confer jurisdiction, as *Pennoyer* had held. Justice Brennan's concurrence stopped short of reviving that old notion; it argued that the defendant's knowing and voluntary presence in the forum state is presumptively a weighty enough contact to pass due process muster. Since Stevens, the ninth justice, refused to take a stand, the doctrinal basis of American jurisdictional law remains unclear.

B. *The Principles Applied*

Leaving aside *Burnham's* possible resuscitation of *Pennoyer*, the basic principle informing American jurisdictional law as elaborated by the U.S. Supreme Court seems straightforward: a defendant can only be sued if he has sufficient "minimum contacts" with the forum. Attempts by state courts to exercise jurisdiction without such a nexus are believed to violate the 14th Amendment's due process clause, with the consequence that the resulting judgment is void and can be neither enforced in the forum nor recognized in a sister state. The defendant may, however, waive this constitutional protection by his general appearance or consent to jurisdiction.

Although this scheme may look simple, its practical application is beset by problems. Not only does the *Burnham* decision becloud the pertinent principles, but the very notion of "minimum contacts" lacks a definable content. A vacillating case law, split Supreme Court decisions, confused state "long-arm statutes" (as jurisdictional enactments are customarily called in American legal jargon) and a bloated legal literature reveal the dubious nature of the attempt to extract concrete rules from the nebulous *International Shoe* test. Without discussing all of its facets, the following observations deal with the application of the minimum contacts test to some specific categories of disputes.

Before addressing these specifics, it is important to note that the Supreme Court only sets the perimeters of jurisdiction; each state remains free to confine the adjudicatory powers of its courts to a narrower scope than that which the Court allows. In practice, however, most states do claim jurisdiction to the fullest permissible extent. Some, notably California, have enacted statutes that expressly extend the state courts' jurisdictional reach to the outer limit. In other states, the highest court has construed ostensibly less expansive local long-arm statutes as reflecting a legislative intent to claim the full measure of jurisdiction allowed by the Supreme Court.

1. Torts

The majority of jurisdictional decisions the Supreme Court has rendered during the past decades deal with tort actions. Several of them emphasize that a local accident does not just, in and of itself, suffice to trigger jurisdiction in tort cases; rather, the nonresident defendant must have created the forum nexus by some form of deliberate conduct. As the U.S. Supreme Court puts it, the defendant must have "purposefully availed himself of the benefits and protection of forum law, or his activities must have been "purposefully directed" at the forum.[6] Such "availment" or "direction" will usually be found if the defendant is an enterprise that exploits the forum's market. Thus, in products liability cases foreign manufacturers or sellers are, as a rule, subject to jurisdiction for injuries in the forum state. Deliberate marketing in large quantities may even make them amenable to general jurisdiction for accidents that occurred in another state.

The mere fact that the defendant's product caused an injury within the forum state is, however, insufficient to warrant the exercise of jurisdiction. In *Asahi Metal Industry Co. v. Superior Court* a Taiwanese tire manufacturer was sued in California by a motorcyclist injured in that state when a defective tire caused his motorcycle to veer off the road. The defendant filed a cross-complaint seeking contribution from Asahi, the Japanese supplier that had made the valve whose malfunction had allegedly prompted the tire to explode. The Supreme Court unanimously held that the 14th Amendment's due process clause prohibited California's exercise of jurisdiction over the cross-defendant, but the Justices differed on the rationale supporting this conclusion.

According to Justice O'Connor's plurality opinion, Asahi's sales of valves to the Taiwanese tire manufacturer did not meet the minimum contacts requirements because they were not "purposefully directed" at California. In contrast, Justice Brennan's concurrence maintains that this requirement is satisfied whenever the "stream of commerce" carries the manufacturer's product to the forum state. He did, however, agree with the plurality's alternative argument that, on the facts presented, "fair play and substantial justice" precluded the California court from asserting jurisdiction to adjudicate the cross-complaint. In this fashion, *Asahi* introduced a new element into the jurisdictional calculus: whereas *International Shoe* and later cases seemed to say that "minimum contacts" guarantee "fair play and substantial justice," courts must now determine whether this nebulous requirement is met irrespective of whatever contacts the litigation may have with the forum state.

As the conflicting opinions in *Asahi* show, even in the narrow and specific area of products liability American jurisdictional law is far from settled. Ostensibly, the U.S. Supreme Court has not gone as far as the European Community's Court of Justice, which has construed the Brussels Convention on Jurisdiction and the Recognition of Judgments in Civil and Commercial Matters to confer jurisdiction, in tort actions, on the courts of either the place of acting or the place of injury.[7] But in most products liability cases American courts tend to reach much the same conclusion. The majority of other tort actions are traffic accidents, and, as noted earlier, the U.S. Supreme Court permitted the state of injury to assert jurisdiction over nonresident motorists even before it expanded the jurisdictional reach in *International Shoe*. In a defamation case, the Court considered the circulation of a mere 10,000 to 15,000 copies of a national magazine to be "purposefully directed" at the forum state, allowing its courts to

6. *See, e.g., Asahi Metal Industry Co. v. Superior Court*, 480 U.S. 102 (1987); *World-Wide Volkswagen Corp. v. Woodson*, 444 U.S. 286 (1980).
7. *See Bier v. Mines de Potasse d'Alsace*, 1976 E.C.R. 1736, [1977] 1 C.M.L.R. 284.

award nationwide damages to the plaintiff's reputation, irrespective of where they occurred, against the nonresident publisher.[8]

Also, while *Asahi* might suggest a narrow reading of the phrase "minimum contacts" in tort cases, the facts of that case differed from those presented in a normal personal injury suit. As noted earlier, at issue was a cross-complaint for contribution, rather than an action brought by a victim against the valve's manufacturer. Moreover, as Justice O'Connor's plurality opinion emphasizes, one alien entity was suing another. She seized upon this aspect to find the assertion of jurisdiction unfair because of the burden of defending a suit in a foreign judicial system and the minimal "interests" of California and the cross-complainant, as compared to the United States foreign relations interest and comity in having the dispute decided there. Had the injured motorcyclist sued the Japanese component part manufacturer directly, the justices might well have found that he and the state of California were sufficiently "interested," so that the exercise of jurisdiction over the Japanese tire manufacturer accorded with "fair play and substantial justice." In other words, *Asahi* may stand less for a principle than for an exception tailored to the peculiar facts of the case.

On the whole, then, as a practical matter American tort jurisdiction is not much narrower than that which European courts can claim pursuant to the Brussels and Lugano Conventions. Indeed, in two respects (leaving aside "tag" and whatever may remain of *quasi in rem* jurisdiction) it is even broader. While the Brussels Convention limits jurisdiction over nonresident enterprises that maintain local branches to actions relating to the branches' activities, *International Shoe* teaches that a defendant's "continuous and systematic activities" in the forum state justify the assertion of general jurisdiction. Accordingly, a branch establishment – or even mere sales – may render a foreign enterprise amenable to suit for causes of action that are unrelated to its forum activities. Secondly, nonresident corporations can arguably generate "minimum contacts" through the forum activities of their subsidiaries ("derivative jurisdiction"). On the other hand, *Keeton* allows any court that has general or specific jurisdiction to award the full measure of damages, irrespective of where the defamation plaintiff's reputation was impaired. In marked contrast, the E.C. Court of Justice has held that only courts that have general jurisdiction may award worldwide damages; those that merely have specific jurisdiction can only require the defendant to pay for the damages incurred within the forum.[9]

2. Contracts

Since most commercial contract disputes are arbitrated rather than litigated, fewer cases deal with jurisdiction in contract than in tort actions. The leading Supreme Court decision may still be *McGee v. International Life Insurance Co.*,[10] a case involving a life insurance policy that a foreign insurer had issued to

8. *See Keeton v. Hustler Magazine, Inc.*, 465 U.S. 770 (1984).
9. *See Shevill v. Presse Alliance*, 1995 E.C.R. I-415.
10. 355 U.S. 220 (1957).

a deceased California resident. Holding that the California beneficiary could sue the insurer in California, the U.S. Supreme Court said that it is "sufficient for purposes of due process that the suit was based on a contract which had substantial connection with that state."[11]

The precedential value of this expansive language is, however, doubtful because *McGee* was decided before the Court adopted the "purposeful availment" and "purposeful direction" tests. In a more recent contract case, *Burger King Corp. v. Rudzewicz*,[12] which upheld Florida's jurisdiction in an action brought by a Florida franchiser against a Michigan franchisee, Justice Brennan emphasized the element of "purposeful direction." He also stressed the parties' stipulation of Florida law, which, as he maintained, reinforced the defendant's deliberate affiliation with the forum and the foreseeability of litigation there. Although these criteria are less than pellucid, lower court decisions suggest that jurisdiction will be more readily asserted over foreign sellers than foreign buyers, and that a single contract will more likely trigger jurisdiction if it embodies a long-term relationship.

Of course, drafters of interstate and international contracts are unlikely to leave the issue of jurisdiction to the vagaries of a confused, and often unfathomable, case law or to potentially exorbitant foreign jurisdictional assertions. Ever since *Pennoyer*, consent has been considered to be a sufficient basis of jurisdiction, which enables the parties to designate a forum (judicial or arbitral) in their agreement. For quite some time, however, it was doubtful whether a forum-selection clause could deprive ("oust") an otherwise competent tribunal of jurisdiction. In *The Bremen v. Zapata Off-Shore Co.*[13] the Supreme Court held that a freely bargained-for forum-selection clause in a contract dealing with an international business transaction should normally be respected by courts that, but for the clause, would have jurisdiction. Although *The Bremen*, an admiralty decision, does not bind state judges, the large majority of federal and state courts that had to deal with the issue have followed the U.S. Supreme Court's lead and dismissed actions brought outside the stipulated forum. In *Carnival Cruise Lines v. Shute*,[14] a decision of dubious wisdom, the Supreme Court further extended the principle of party autonomy beyond the confines established in *The Bremen*. It dismissed the suit an injured passenger brought outside the stipulated forum, even though the forum-selection clause was contained in a contract of adhesion rather than, as in *The Bremen* case, in a freely negotiated private international agreement.

3. Divorce

American courts have traditionally treated divorce jurisdiction as unique. By labeling the petition to dissolve a marital relationship a "status" matter, *Pennoyer*

11. 355 U.S. at 223.
12. 471 U.S. 462 (1985).
13. 407 U.S. 1 (1972).
14. 499 U.S. 585 (1991).

found a verbal formula to "explain" why it is unnecessary in divorce cases to serve process on the defendant within the forum state. The Supreme Court thereby enabled deserted spouses to obtain a divorce at the matrimonial domicile if the deserter could no longer be found there. Initially it seemed that only the state in which the "marital domicile" was located could adjudicate the marital status. In *Williams v. North Carolina (I)*,[15] however, the Supreme Court held that the courts at *either* party's domicile have jurisdiction to grant a divorce.

As the Court emphasized in *Shaffer v. Heitner*, the notion of "status jurisdiction" has survived *International Shoe*. Accordingly, minimum contacts between the forum and the respondent are not required. However, in addition to sundering the marital ties, divorce decrees also adjudicate other incidents of marriage, in particular property rights and support obligations. In an effort to reconcile status jurisdiction with tenets of due process as applied to *in personam* jurisdiction, in *Estin v. Estin*[16] the Supreme Court made divorce "divisible": although the court at the petitioner's domicile can dissolve the marriage, it cannot affect the respondent's property rights unless that spouse has "minimum contacts" with the divorce forum. (The concept of "divisible divorce" helps explain the recent *Burnham* decision: California being the petitioner's domicile, the California court could clearly decree a divorce, but the petitioner also proceeded *in personam* to settle the couple's property rights and obligations).

4. Additional jurisdictional prerequisites

In certain instances, jurisdictional prerequisites beyond the defendant's forum nexus must be met. Examples are divorce (where the petitioner, as a rule, has to comply with the divorce forum's statutory durational residence requirements), adoption, and child custody proceedings. With respect to adoption, the Restatement (Second) of Conflict of Laws section 78 (1971) attempts to summarize the case law as follows:

> A state has power to exercise judicial jurisdiction to grant an adoption if
>
> (a) it is the state of domicil of either the adopted child or the adoptive parent, and
> (b) the adoptive parent and either the adopted child or the person having legal custody of the child are subject to its personal jurisdiction.

For child custody matters section 3 of the Uniform Child Custody Jurisdiction Act sets forth a complex set of rules, which are designed to prevent jurisdictional overlap by designating a single "court of custody."

15. 317 U.S. 287 (1942).
16. 334 U.S. 541 (1948).

5. *Forum non conveniens*

American judges have long assumed a discretionary power to dismiss cases. The so-called *forum non conveniens* doctrine, which the U.S. Supreme Court endorsed more than 50 years ago in the interstate case of *Gulf Oil Corp. v. Gilbert*,[17] has since come to play an important role as an anti-forum-shopping device, especially in international litigation. In *Piper Aircraft Co. v. Reyno*[18] the Court held that a federal district judge had properly exercised its discretion to dismiss an action brought against the American manufacturers of an aircraft and a propeller by Scottish relatives of Scotsmen killed in the crash of a small commuter airplane in Scotland. According to Justice Marshall's opinion, while the plaintiff's home state is presumptively a convenient forum, the obverse presumption applies to suits brought by nonresident aliens.

The *Piper Aircraft* case has been a boon to American defendants. Foreign plaintiffs now face a motion to dismiss on *forum non conveniens* grounds even if they sue in the defendant's home state (presumably the most convenient place for anyone defending a lawsuit). Such reverse forum shopping is especially effective in federal courts. Although Justice Marshall's opinion left open the question whether state or federal law controls the judicial discretion to dismiss, federal courts are wont to apply federal rather than state standards, especially in actions brought by nonresident aliens.

Since American law (unlike the Brussels Convention) does not follow the first-in-time rule, the *forum non conveniens* doctrine is often used, in both domestic and international cases, to serve the function of preventing concurrent litigation. Another way to accomplish this result is for the forum to enjoin a party who sues in some other state or country from pursuing that action. By issuing such an antisuit injunction, a court in effect takes the position that it is the convenient forum. Although the foreign court need not recognize this injunction (according to the prevailing opinion it is not even entitled to full faith and credit within the United States), the sanctions for contempt of court will usually assure that the party whom the court enjoins will no longer pursue the foreign litigation.

As between federal courts, the *forum non conveniens* doctrine no longer applies. Instead, 28 U.S.C. section 1404(a) permits federal judges to transfer a case "for the convenience of parties and witnesses, in the interest of justice" to any other district in which the defendant was amenable to jurisdiction. *Stewart Organization, Inc. v. Ricoh Corp.*[19] construed this provision to require federal courts to take into account forum-selection clauses in deciding whether or not to grant the motion for a transfer. In effect, this decision allows the federal judiciary to honor such clauses even if they are invalid according to the law of the state where the action was brought.

17. 330 U.S. 501 (1947).
18. 454 U.S. 235 (1981).
19. 487 U.S. 22 (1988).

III. Choice of Law

A. The Rise and Fall of "Classical" American Conflicts Law

1. Story's contribution

As is true of jurisdiction, to understand current American choice-of-law approaches it is helpful to look at the subject's historical evolution. The common law of England, which the United States inherited from its mother country, had little to contribute. Although there were some 18th century English choice-of-law cases, the bulk of early American conflicts law was imported from continental Europe. Justice Joseph Story, the great Supreme Court justice and Harvard professor, had the necessary legal and linguistic erudition to promote the reception of civilian learning. His *Commentaries on the Conflict of Laws*, the first edition of which appeared in 1834, not only laid the foundation for the American law of conflicts but his treatise also influenced developments in both common law and civil law nations.

As his German counterpart, Friedrich Carl von Savigny, did later, Story advocated the resolution of choice-of-law problems by means of multilateral rules that allocate legal relationships to a particular state or nation. To this end, he divided legal institutions into broad categories – such as family law, property, and contracts – and selected for each category a connecting factor – such as the domicile of a person, the situs of a thing, or the place where an event happened – to link any given relationship with one or the other legal system. Thus Story introduced the multilateralist approach, which he (following Ulrich Huber) premised on the "comity" one sovereign owes another, into American law.

2. Beale's Restatement

The multilateralist philosophy also underlies the work of Joseph Beale, a Harvard law professor who served as the reporter for the influential Restatement of Conflict of Laws, which appeared in 1934, a century after the first edition of Story's *Commentaries*. By laying down rules that attempt to resolve conflicts problems by allocating legal relationships to one or the other state, the First Conflicts Restatement kept American conflicts law in line with the views prevailing in other common law nations, as well as in the civilian legal orbit. It soon became apparent, however, that Beale's Restatement had been published at the wrong time in American legal history.

3. The legal realists

The First Restatement's publication fell into an era characterized by the emergence of American "legal realism," a jurisprudential movement that had little tolerance for such dogmatic artifices as the notion of "vested rights" (with which Beale had replaced Story's reliance on comity), for systems derived from deductive reasoning, and for hard and fast rules. Deriding the simple-minded precepts Beale had deduced from a dubious theoretical foundation, scholars such as David Cavers, Walter Cook, Ernest Lorenzen, and Hessel Yntema attacked the First Restatement and proffered their own rather different approaches to the choice-of-law problem.

One year before the First Restatement appeared in print, Beale's erstwhile pupil Cavers published a landmark article in the *Harvard Law Review*, which rejected out of hand the traditional (in Cavers's words "jurisdiction-selecting") multilateral rules. He maintained that instead of relying on a blind, value-free choice-of-law mechanism, judges should look at the competing substantive rules and take into account considerations of justice and social expediency in making their selection. In his words, "the court is not idly choosing a law; it is determining a controversy. How can it choose wisely without considering how the choice will affect that controversy?"[20] In essence, Cavers's early article advocated both a unilateralist methodology geared to the reach of rules of decision and a result-oriented substantive law approach.

4. The Supreme Court

Initially, these scholarly debates had little effect on American practice. But while Beale's Restatement was still widely accepted by state and federal courts, its critics managed to garner support on the judiciary's highest rung. Until the mid-thirties, the U.S. Supreme Court followed the vested rights doctrine and appeared to assume that the classical conflicts rules were constitutionally compelled. The traditional learning was, however, put to the test and found wanting in a series of cases dealing with the application of state workers' compensation acts to interstate cases. In *Alaska Packers Ass'n v. Industrial Accident Commission*[21] and *Pacific Employers Insurance Co. v. Industrial Accident Commission*[22] the Court held that either the state of hiring or the state of injury can constitutionally grant relief, because both have a sufficient "interest" in effectuating the policies underlying their protective legislation. The Court's opinions further suggested that other contacts as well may suffice to justify application of the forum's statute to a multistate workers' compensation claim.

Alaska Packers and *Pacific Employers* signaled a change in the justices' thinking about the relationship between the Constitution and the law of conflicts. Rather than *require* a particular choice of law, these cases construed the Constitution's full faith and credit and due process clauses merely to *preclude* the application of local law in cases where the forum state lacks a reasonable connection with the controversy. Thus the Court read the constitutional provisions to enshrine a states' rights charter that leaves state tribunals free to apply their own rules of decision to any transaction in which the forum has a sufficient "interest."

20. David F. Cavers, "A Critique of the Choice-of-Law Problem," 47 *Harv. L. Rev.* 173, 189 (1933).
21. 249 U.S. 532 (1935).
22. 306 U.S. 493 (1939).

In practice, this case law enhanced the protection of an increasingly mobile American labor force by permitting interstate employees to forum shop for the highest award. As a matter of legal theory, the Court undermined the multilateralist doctrine: by focusing attention on the "interests" of states in effectuating the policies underlying the *lex fori*, it recognized the legitimacy of a unilateralist approach to choice of law.

B. The "Conflicts Revolution: Contracts

In spite of the U.S. Supreme Court's nudging, for quite some time state courts stuck to the traditional learning. With respect to contract choice of law, however, judges began to doubt the wisdom of the First Restatement's *lex loci contractus* rule, which has several obvious flaws. First of all, the place-of-contracting rule is ambiguous because not all legal systems agree on when – and therefore where – a contract is made. Secondly, it hardly makes sense to let the parties' rights and obligations turn on the technicalities of offer and acceptance. Finally, the connecting factor is difficult to apply when parties negotiate by means of letter, telephone, fax, or e-mail, in which case it may be impossible to determine which of the various communications constitute "the" offer, and which "the" acceptance.

Unsurprisingly, a number of courts preferred a more flexible approach to localizing contracts. Some looked for the contract's "center of gravity"; others used the term "grouping of contacts" to explain the case-specific factual analysis they applied.[23] Although it substitutes an amorphous formula for the customary rigid connecting factors, this approach arguably still remains faithful to multilateralism. However, courts also permitted the parties to stipulate the applicable law, a solution Beale had rejected as incompatible with the vested rights doctrine. Clearly, party autonomy is at odds with the notion that choice of law should be governed by a predetermined set of connecting factors. It can only be supported by teleological considerations, although paradoxically it protects the multilateralist values of certainty, predictability, and uniformity of result far better than any multilateral choice-of-law rule could.

Although they deviated from the First Restatement, the cases rejecting the *lex loci contractus* rule still remained within the traditional framework. They simply aligned American practice with that of Europe, where party autonomy has coexisted with multilateralism for so long that many conflicts scholars believe the two to be compatible. Likewise, the method of localizing contracts, absent a choice-of-law clause, by looking for their "closest connection" with a particular legal system has long been familiar to Europeans. It is applied on the Continent as well as in England, where it forms part of the so-called "proper law of contract." Although open-ended connecting factors do undercut the fundamental multilateralist goals of predictability and uniformity, by allocating contracts to a given legal system these flexible rules remain within the framework of the classical conflicts doctrine.

23. *See Auten v. Auten*, 308 N.Y. 155, 124 N.E.2d 99 (1954).

C. *The "Conflicts Revolution": Torts*

1. Guest statutes and other statuta odiosa

While the switch to the "grouping of contacts" approach and the recognition of party autonomy may be considered evolutionary rather than revolutionary, American courts clearly broke with the First Restatement's philosophy once they began to scuttle the *lex loci delicti*. To understand the reasons for this change, it is necessary to look at the substantive rules that produced the majority of American choice-of-law problems. The principal source was the so-called "guest statutes," legislation which about half of the states had adopted during the 1930s. These enactments barred recovery by guest passengers from a host driver unless they could show some aggravated form of negligence (usually termed "willful" or "reckless" conduct) on the defendant's part. A second source was the American common law doctrine of intrafamily immunity, which precluded tort actions against family members. Yet another staple of American conflicts law were statutes that capped recovery for wrongful death at fairly low amounts.

2. Escape devices

Judges in states that lacked similar barriers to the fair compensation of accident victims viewed these *statuta odiosa* with understandable distaste. The classical conflicts system did, however, offer several possibilities to avoid the undesirable consequences of applying the *lex loci delicti*. First of all, it permitted a certain leeway in pigeonholing the issue presented. By adroit characterization courts could convert a tort into a contracts problem or convert a substantive issue into a procedural one. These ploys allow judges to invoke the *lex loci contractus* or the *lex fori* instead of some substandard foreign law. Secondly, differences in connecting factors enabled judges to resort to the *renvoi* doctrine for the purpose of escaping the accident state's *statutum odiosum*. Finally, the public policy reservation allowed them to reject those foreign rules of decision that fall below the forum's standards of justice.

Numerous reported cases document the judicial recourse to such escape devices for the purpose of avoiding unfair results. To cite but one example: in *Haumschild v. Continental Casualty Co.*[24] a Wisconsin wife sued her husband for injuries she suffered when he caused a car accident in California. The husband invoked interspousal immunity, an outdated defense that had been abolished in Wisconsin, but not as yet in California. Characterizing the issue as one of family rather than tort law, the Wisconsin Supreme Court applied the law of the parties' common domicile, that is, the *lex fori*. A concurring judge, relying on an earlier California case, which had characterized the issue of intrafamily immunity as a domestic relations matter that was governed by the parties' home state law, argued that Wisconsin should simply accept this *renvoi*. The same result could of course have been reached by holding that California's interspousal immunity rule violates Wisconsin public policy.

24. 7 Wis. 2d 130, 95 N.W.2d 814 (1959).

As the *Haumschild* case and many other decisions demonstrate, the classical system's "General Part" provided a substantial measure of flexibility, which could be used to evade the consequences seemingly compelled by a rigid choice-of-law rule. Such result-oriented judicial manipulation did, however, undermine confidence in the classical multilateralist scheme. Scholars cogently criticized the hypocrisy of paying lip service to a choice-of-law methodology only to pervert it. At the same time, judicial recourse to such escape devices defeated the objectives the system meant to promote, that is, certainty, predictability, and uniformity of result. As the First Conflict Restatement lost credibility, the time seemed ripe for a fundamental reorientation of American conflicts law.

3. Novel choice-of-law approaches

By the end of the 1950s, practically all American conflicts scholars shared the opinion that it was time to abandon the First Restatement, but they could not agree on what should replace it. Three widely differing methodologies were being discussed:

(1) A *proper law* approach akin to the one courts had adopted for contracts. The Oxonian scholar John Morris and the Columbia law professor Willis Reese (who became the Reporter of the Restatement (Second) of Conflict of Laws (1971)), advocated the extension of this methodology to tort choice of law. While retaining a multilateralist framework, they urged the replacement of hard and fast connecting factors with flexible, open-ended impressionistic formulae such as the "closest connection," the "most significant contacts," or, as the Second Restatement now puts it, the "most significant relationship." In addition, these scholars preferred more narrowly drawn, fact- and issue-specific rules to the First Restatement's broad categories.

(2) A *unilateralist* approach geared to discerning the spatial reach of substantive rules. As early as 1946, Paul Freund suggested that the analysis of state interests, which the U.S. Supreme Court undertook in the workers' compensation cases to determine the propriety of applying forum law "extraterritorially," could serve as the basis for a new choice-of-law methodology. Seizing upon this idea, Brainerd Currie wrote a series of articles, later collected in a volume entitled *Selected Essays on the Conflict of Laws* (1963), in which he developed what he called a "governmental interest analysis" to replace the classical choice-of-law rules.

(3) A *teleological* approach that takes into account the quality of competing rules of decision. To be sure, none of the "revolutionaries" unequivocally endorsed teleology pure and unadulterated. Cavers later retracted the result-oriented approach he had advocated in his 1933 article and Freund did not further pursue the result-selective approach his article had also suggested. However, Yntema, Robert Leflar, Elliot Cheatham, and Reese compiled lists of choice-of-law desiderata that contained result-selective elements, which permitted courts to consider "justice in the individual case" or to favor application of the "better rule" in deciding multistate cases.

Several authors proposed eclectic approaches that combine two or more of the three basic ones. Thus Cavers' "principles of preference" are tentative near-rules with some teleological element. Leflar's "choice-influencing considerations" attempt to blend the traditional system's virtues with interest analysis and teleology. Arthur von Mehren and Donald Trautman proffered a "functional approach," which combines interest analysis with the multilateral notion of applying the law of the "most concerned state," and also contains a teleological component that allows courts to prefer "emerging" to "regressive" rules of decision. The Second Conflicts Restatement adopted an eclectic combination of tentative rules, the "most significant relationship" connecting factor, and choice-influencing "principles."

4. The New York breakthrough

By the early 1960s, scholarly condemnation of the First Restatement and the Supreme Court's states rights stance encouraged courts to experiment with novel approaches. The judicial "conflicts revolution" was set in motion by a series of New York state and federal court decisions. In 1961 the New York Court of Appeals decided *Kilberg v. Northeast Airlines Inc.*,[25] a tort action following the crash of a passenger plane in Massachusetts, which, at the time, limited damages for wrongful death to $15,000 per victim. Characterizing damages as "procedural" and invoking a "strong, clear and old" New York public policy against limiting wrongful death recovery, the court refused to honor this statutory cap. Judge Desmond's opinion also noted that, in air crash cases, the place of injury may be "entirely fortuitous," and that "modern conditions make it unjust and anomalous to subject the traveling citizens of this State to the varying laws of other States through and over which they move."[26]

One year later, the Second Circuit Court of Appeals, in *Pearson v. Northeast Airlines, Inc.*,[27] dealt with another lawsuit resulting from the same air crash. While it followed the state precedent, the federal appellate court based its decision on rather different grounds. Excoriating the "legal legerdemain" of characterizing damages as "procedural," Judge Kaufman's *en banc* opinion concluded that New York had a sufficient "interest" in the issue of recovery by its citizen against an airline doing business in the state to permit a New York court to apply forum law in preference to the Massachusetts monetary ceiling.

This federal-state court interplay set the stage for *Babcock v. Jackson*,[28] in which the Empire State's highest court at long last scuttled the *lex loci delicti* rule. That case held that an Ontario guest statute did not bar the action brought by a New York guest passenger against a New York driver whose car had hit a stone wall in the Canadian province. Eschewing the classical escape devices, Judge Fuld announced a new approach to tort choice of law. He wrote:

> The "center of gravity" or "grouping of contacts" doctrine adopted by this court in conflicts cases involving contracts impresses us as likewise

25. 9 N.Y.2d 34, 172 N.E.2d 526, 211 N.Y.S.2d 133 (1961).
26. 172 N.E.2d at 527.
27. 309 F.2d 553 (2d Cir. 1962).
28. 12 N.Y.2d 473, 191 N.E.2d 279, 240 N.Y.S.2d 743 (1963).

> affording the appropriate approach for accommodating the competing interests in tort cases with multi-State contacts. Justice, fairness and "the best practical result" ... may best be achieved by giving controlling effect to the law of the jurisdiction which, because of its relationship or contact with the occurrence or the parties, has the greatest concern with the specific issue raised in the litigation.[29]

As this brief paragraph shows, Judge Fuld's opinion throws together three distinct methodologies: (1) the proper law approach; (2) Currie's idea that it is possible to deduce the reach of substantive rules from state "concerns" (or "interests"); and (3) the objective of achieving desirable results in multistate cases.

D. Current Tendencies: New York

Little did it matter to Judge Fuld that the three approaches his seminal *Babcock* opinion embraced are at odds with one another. He dealt with an "easy case": any approach other than applying the *lex loci delicti* would have invoked New York law. In Currie's terminology, *Babcock* presented a "false conflict": Ontario had no interest in the recovery of a New York guest from a New York host whose liability is covered by a New York insurer. In Second Restatement parlance, all "significant relationships" (except for the place of the accident) were with New York, which was the parties' domicile as well as the car's normal situs and the place where the trip began and was to end. As far as teleology is concerned, the Ontario guest act – which, at the time, barred recovery even for willful conduct – clearly represented substandard law.

Such a happy coincidence, however, tends to be the exception rather than the rule. As the New York Court of Appeals soon found out, not all conflicts cases are "easy," and in complex situations *Babcock's* undiscerning eclecticism failed to offer guidance. Unsuccessfully attempting to clarify its approach to tort choice of law, the highest New York tribunal has ever since "hopped frenetically in tort cases from one theory to another, like an overheated jumping bean." Initially leaning toward a proper law approach,[30] in *Tooker v. Lopez*[31] the court then turned to interest analysis *à la* Currie. Subsequently, Chief Judge Fuld's majority opinion in *Neumeier v. Kuehner*[32] adopted, for guest statute cases, a set of near-rules that resemble Cavers's "principles of preference."

After handing down some opinions that suggested a return to the *lex loci delicti* rule, in *Schultz v. Boy Scouts of America, Inc.*[33] the Court of Appeals resuscitated the *Neumeier* rules, which Chief Judge Fuld believed to reflect the teachings of interest analysis, and extended them beyond the confines of guest

29. 191 N.E.2d at 283.
30. *See Dym v. Gordon*, 16 N.Y.2d 120, 209 N.E.2d 792, 262 N.Y.S.2d 463 (1965).
31. 24 N.Y.2d 569, 249 N.E.2d 394, 301 N.Y.S.2d 519 (1969).
32. 31 N.Y.2d 121, 286 N.E.2d 454, 335 N.Y.S.2d 64 (1972).
33. 65 N.Y. 189, 480 N.E.2d 679, 491 N.Y.S.2d 90 (1985).

statutes. It employed this odd mixture to immunize two charities from liability for child molestation committed by a Franciscan monk and scoutmaster. Quite incongruously, the majority opinion in *Schultz* also discusses the traditional public policy escape device, as does the later case of *Cooney v. Osgodd Machinery, Inc.*[34]

If anything can be learned from New York's choice-of-law experiments, it is that the abolition of rules without a clear understanding of what should replace them exacts a high price from the litigants, their counsel, judges, and society.

E. *Current Tendencies: California*

Eschewing eclecticism at the outset, the California Supreme Court avoided some of the confusion that continues to plague its New York counterpart. Judge Traynor's landmark opinion in *Reich v. Purcell*,[35] in which the California Supreme Court refused to apply a sister-state wrongful death limitation, omitted any reference to the proper law approach and ostensibly committed the state to Currie's interest analysis. However, *Bernhard v. Harrah's Club*[36] superimposed a multilateralist element on Currie's unilateralist methodology adopting the so-called "comparative impairment" doctrine propounded by William Baxter. That doctrine attempts to resolve "true conflicts," which result if the policies underlying the different rules of decision that vie for application are irreconcilable, by invoking the law of the state whose interests would be more impaired if the other state's law were applied.

In a subsequent case, *Offshore Rental Co. v. Continental Oil Co.*,[37] the California Supreme Court employed the comparative impairment test in a result-selective manner. Judge Tobriner's opinion preferred the "prevalent and progressive" Louisiana law to an "archaic and isolated" California Civil Code provision, which would have favored the plaintiff, a California corporation. It therefore refused to apply the *lex fori* and denied recovery for damages for the loss of the services of its vice president, who had been injured on the defendant's Louisiana premises. This decision is of course quite at odds with the pro-forum and pro-plaintiff bias of interest analysis. The majority opinion in the later case of *Wong v. Tenneco*[38] then reintroduced – incongruously and confusingly – notions of comity and territoriality. In that case the highest state court relied on these multilateral considerations to dismiss a California resident's action for fraud against a corporation doing business in California on the ground that the plaintiff's conduct in Mexico had been illegal. In addition, the majority opinion in *Wong* discussed the potential impact of California public policy, a traditional concept that does not mesh with interest analysis, an approach the *Wong* court professed to apply. Thus, although there are fewer cases, California choice of law remains as unsettled as that of New York.

34. 81 N.Y.2d 66, 612 N.E.2d 277, 595 N.Y.S. 919 (1993).
35. 67 Cal. 2d 551, 432 P.2d 727, 63 Cal. Rptr. 31 (1967).
36. 16 Cal. 3d 313, 546 P.2d 719, 128 Cal. Rptr. 215, *cert. denied*, 429 U.S. 859 (1976).
37. 22 Cal. 3d 157, 583 P.2d 721, 148 Cal. Rptr. 867 (1978).
38. 39 Cal. 3d 126, 702 P.2d 570, 216 Cal. Rptr. 412 (1985).

F. Current Tendencies: Other States

Following New York's and California's lead, a majority of states has abandoned the *lex loci delicti* rule. In most of them a "methodological pluralism" prevails, and as a result of unbridled judicial eclecticism, chaos and confusion reign. To cite but one example: it took a federal district judge 31 pages and an index – on a second try – to ascertain and apply the Pennsylvania approach to choice of law, only to have his scholarly decision reversed on appeal. The numerous convoluted and heavily footnoted judicial opinions that purport to resolve multistate tort problems by recourse to some mish-mash methodology are difficult to fathom and offer little guidance in subsequent cases. Most of them read like the literary endeavors of eager law clerks fresh out of school, rather than the work product of seasoned judges.

G. An Assessment of the Choice-of-Law Experiments

Understandably, foreign observers – as well as quite a few American judges and scholars – feel that the departure from the traditional multilateralist system has been a resounding failure. Some legal writers have argued that the U.S. Supreme Court should impose certain limits on the forum's unbridled power to apply the *lex fori* to interstate and international transactions and to assure a minimum of comity in the American federal system. So far, however, the Supreme Court has refused to intervene and to curtail state court experimentation. In three cases during the 1980s the Court deliberately refrained from constitutionalizing choice of law; it simply reiterated what had been said in the workers' compensation cases: as long as a state has contacts that create "interests," it may apply forum law to multistate cases.[39]

Yet, notwithstanding the critics' understandable concern about the disorder it wrought, there is something to be said in favor of the American "conflicts revolution." Not only does the effort to rethink conventional wisdom seem worthwhile, but the results the new learning produces in actual practice are frequently superior to those that would follow from the application of such hard and fast choice-of-law rules as the *lex loci delicti*. Instead of indiscriminately importing foreign *statuta odiosa*, such as guest statutes, interspousal immunity rules, and limitations on wrongful death recovery, the novel conflicts approaches serve as quality control devices that filter out substandard law. The reasons for their benign propensity are readily apparent.

1. The Second Restatement

The Second Restatement's impressionistic proper-law formula is sufficiently flexible to permit judges to localize transactions in the state whose law they prefer. More often than not that state happens to be the forum. Since counsel will rarely

39. *Allstate Insurance Co. v. Hague*, 449 U.S. 302 (1981), *Phillips Petroleum Co. v. Shutts*, 472 U.S. 797 (1985), and *Sun Oil Co. v. Wortman*, 486 U.S. 717 (1988).

advise a client to sue in a state that limits or bars recovery, a multistate tort case is, as a rule, brought in a forum favorable to the victim. Because jurisdiction, as noted earlier, usually requires "minimum contacts," the case is bound to have a sufficiently plausible connection to attribute to the forum a "significant relationship."

2. Interest analysis

Interest analysis has an even stronger homing tendency. Currie, who hypothesized that states are primarily interested in their residents, substituted the personal law principle for territorial contacts. Since parties usually sue where they live, interest analysis reinforces the forum preference inherent in any conflicts method that attempts to discern the spatial reach of substantive rules, which usually begins and ends with ascertaining the purport of domestic law. If, as in *Haumschild* and *Babcock*, both parties reside in the forum, that state is the only one interested; the case poses a "false conflict." If they are from different states, a "true conflict" may be presented, in which case Currie proposed the application of the *lex fori* on the ground that judges lack the power to accommodate conflicting state interests. Not surprisingly, even those courts that, while professing their allegiance to interest analysis, reject Currie's blunt forum bias, usually still end up applying the *lex fori*, the law that judges know best and find most congenial.

3. Leflar's considerations

In states that have adopted Leflar's "choice-influencing considerations," the homing trend is supported by item (E) of his list of choice-of-law desiderata, that is, the advancement of the forum's governmental interests. In some cases, however, courts that follow Leflar's teachings have gone as far as to apply superior foreign rules of decision by relying on the catalog's last consideration, which calls for the application of the better rule of law. Thus Leflar's list can serve to eliminate domestic as well as foreign *statuta odiosa*; it promotes teleology without the need for forum shopping.

H. The Revolution's Mixed Blessings

To the extent that current American conflicts law strengthens the position of multistate tort plaintiffs it is a welcome evolution away from the inflexible *lex loci delicti* principle, which all too often frustrated meritorious claims by invoking noxious foreign tort rules. Still, those who are concerned not merely about results, but also the manner in which results are reached, should be disquieted by the chaotic state of American conflicts jurisprudence. The opaque and often impenetrable judicial opinions and the surfeit of doctrines they espouse hardly instill confidence in the cogency of current choice-of-law thinking.

Moreover, as the New York Court of Appeals decision in *Schultz* demonstrates, the novel approaches do not even guarantee acceptable results. Beyond that, the unsettled state of American conflicts law impedes the efficient disposition of mass disaster litigation. To facilitate the adjudication of complex cases, such as air crashes or suits against the manufacturers of defective products, federal procedure permits the consolidation of actions filed in different districts before a single judge. Supreme Court case law, however, requires that judge to apply the law – including the choice-of-law rules – of the forum in which each case was brought initially. Given the unsettled state of American conflicts law, that task is daunting and the outcome of mass disaster cases is often less than satisfactory.

I. Specific Choice-of-Law Areas

As the foregoing discussion shows, tort choice of law has been in the forefront of the American "conflicts revolution." In that area, the "revolutionary" approaches will probably continue to play a role. The substantive issues that provoked the upheaval have largely vanished; limits on recovery formerly found in wrongful death act, guest statutes, and interspousal immunity have fallen by the wayside. The problem of *statuta odiosa*, however, has not. A wave of "tort reform" statutes has introduced new barriers to tort recovery, which, by balkanizing American tort law, continue to engender choice-of-law problems that invite recourse to the modern methodologies.

Outside the field of torts, however, the "revolution" has been less successful. While doctrinal writers, the Second Conflicts Restatement, and some judicial opinions suggest that interest analysis and other modern approaches apply across the board to all choice-of-law problems, some areas continue to lead a placid existence untroubled by the turmoil that characterizes tort choice of law.

1. Contracts

Contract issues are not as often litigated as torts. The parties to an agreement usually perform the obligations they have undertaken; should a dispute arise, arbitration is the preferred method of resolving it. Accordingly, although challenges to the First Conflicts Restatement's rigid *lex loci contractus* rule predated the attack on *lex loci delicti*, once courts and legislatures aligned American contract choice-of-law rules with those that have long prevailed in other nations, the turmoil has largely ceased. The most important reform in this area has been the acceptance of party autonomy, which allows individuals and enterprises to resolve conflicts on their own by means of choice-of-law clauses. Both section 1-105(1) of the Uniform Commercial Code and section 187 of the Second Restatement explicitly recognize this principle. While the UCC's current version still requires a "reasonable relation" between the contract and the law selected, the Code's revision can be expected to abolish this requirement. Party autonomy has also been endorsed by the U.S. Supreme Court. Chief Justice Burger's majority opinion in *The Bremen* (*see* pt. II.B.2) emphasized the parties' freedom not only to designate the forum for future disputes, but also to choose the law governing their agreement.

Absent a contractual choice, however, courts continue to differ on how to select the applicable law. Surprisingly, a number of states have retained the *lex loci contractus* rule, while others apply interest analysis or the Second Conflicts Restatement's proper law approach. With respect to matters covered by the Uniform Commercial Code, section 1-105(l) provides that "this Act applies to transactions bearing an appropriate relation to the state." Although this unilateral rule may look like a parochial attempt to broaden the sway of forum law, the drafters have proffered a teleological justification: they justified the Code's expansive purport by emphasizing its superior quality. Now that the Code has been adopted in all states, however, the revised version of this provision can be expected to incorporate the proper law approach.

Hence, as in multistate tort cases, multilateralism, unilateralism, and teleology co-exist in contract choice of law. Also, as is true of their opinions in tort cases, courts are wont to combine these discordant approaches in an eclectic fashion. Nevertheless, since contract issues are less frequently litigated, party autonomy reigns supreme. And since substantive contract law contains fewer *statuta odiosa*, this area has a much less "revolutionary" appearance than the cognate field of tort choice of law.

2. Property

Although it has been attacked by some academic writers, the situs rule by and large still dominates property choice of law. This is certainly true of immovables, where the "land taboo," a hallmark of the common law, has long overshadowed competing considerations. Specifically, Anglo-American courts have rejected the principle of "universal succession," according to which the decedent's personal law, rather than the *lex rei sitae*, controls the devolution of both his movable and immovable property. Similarly, the law of the situs, rather than the couple's domiciliary law, controls marital property rights in immovables.

The rules on movables are less categoric. Exceptions to the situs principle have been made for "general (or universal) assignments," such as the devolution of movables upon death, marriage, or insolvency. Similarly, in disputes between the parties to a conveyance, as long as rights of third parties are not at issue, courts often look to the law governing the transaction, rather than the *lex rei sitae*, to determine what interests the transaction has created.

Article 9 of the Uniform Commercial Code has laid to rest many of the problems posed by security interests in chattels that cross state and national borders. Instead of relying on traditional choice-of-law rules for the resolution of such *conflits mobiles*, the code establishes a recording mechanism for nonpossessory security interests and lays down common-sensical rules that assure a fair measure of certainty, predictability, and fairness.

3. Family Law

As compared to what has been happening in Europe, American domestic relations choice of law has remained tranquil. In the United States, the domiciliary nexus not only accords with common law tradition, but citizenship would of course be an inept connecting factor in a federal system in which domestic relations are governed by state rather than federal law. Hence, the United States, which has always been an immigration country, has avoided the massive influx of foreign law that continues to plague countries that determine a party's personal law by reference to the *lex patriae*. Since the parties – especially in domestic relations disputes – usually sue at home, as a rule the domiciliary nexus invokes the *lex fori* rather than foreign law. Also, domicile is a malleable concept and allows a judge to find palatable solutions in interstate cases by domiciling parties in the state whose law he favors.

a. *Marriage*. There is one important exception to the principle that the domiciliary nexus controls domestic relations choice of law: in most states the validity of a marriage depends on the *lex loci celebrationis*. This rule has been criticized for selecting a law with which the prospective spouses may have but a fleeting connection rather than that of the truly "interested" states of their (present or future) domiciles. There is, however, a ready explanation for the rule: by liberating husband and wife from the constraints their home states may impose, it promotes the freedom to marry. At the same time, since people (especially in dubious cases) usually celebrate their nuptials in a state whose law upholds their marriage, the seemingly value-blind *lex loci celebrationis* rule in effect validates marriages that otherwise might be void.

b. *Marital property*. American courts have long followed the principle of partial mutability. That is to say the spouses' marital property regime changes along with their domicile, yet property rights that accrued at the couple's previous domicile are recognized. This principle has served the United States well. Although the country's population is highly mobile and there are vast differences in the states' marital property regimes, which range from separate to community property, partial mutability has not caused insurmountable problems in practical application.

c. *Divorce*. As noted earlier (*see* pts. II.A.1, II.B.3), the U.S. Supreme Court has held that the courts at either spouse's domicile have jurisdiction to grant a divorce and the resulting decree is entitled to full faith and credit in all sister states. There is no choice of law; the divorce court applies the *lex fori* to all issues, including the grounds for divorce. Since each spouse is free to change his or her domicile at any time, this rule encourages forum shopping. Decades ago, when some states made the dissolution of a marriage exceedingly difficult, the rule facilitated consensual divorces in haven jurisdictions such as Nevada or Idaho.

40. 334 U.S. 541 (1948).

There are, however, certain limits to forum shopping. The principle according to which either party's domicile is necessary and sufficient does not cover all incidents of divorce. Rather, as mentioned earlier (*see* pt. II.B.3), in *Estin v. Estin*[40] the U.S. Supreme Court made divorce "divisible": to adjudicate the spouses' property rights and support obligations, the forum must have *in personam* jurisdiction over the respondent. Hence a change of domicile does not suffice to either diminish or augment the parties' personal rights and obligations.

d. *Other matters*. A number of state and federal enactments deal with various interstate and international family law problems. Statutes in most states establish durational residence requirements, whose constitutionality was upheld in *Sosna v. Iowa*.[41] The Uniform Reciprocal Enforcement of Support Act (URESA) attempts to safeguard the rights of support claimants against nonresident providers. The Uniform Child Custody Jurisdiction Act (UCCJA) discourages child-snatching by non-custodial parents. The Parental Kidnapping Prevention Act of 1980 federalizes the UCCJA by requiring full faith and credit recognition of custody decrees that meet the Act's jurisdictional standards. To curtail international kidnaping, the United States has ratified the 1980 Hague Convention on the Civil Aspects of International Child Abduction, which has been implemented by the International Child Abduction Act. *See* Chap. 11, pts. II.F, IX.

4. Succession

The conflicts revolution has had hardly any effect on the law of descent and distribution. Although some courts have used interest analysis language in succession cases, by and large the common law rules survive intact. According to these rules, the distribution of movables is governed by the law of the decedent's last domicile, and the descent of immovables by the *lex rei sitae*. To soften these hard and fast multilateral precepts, such traditional ploys as characterization and *renvoi* remain available, and at times courts still rely on them to prevent inequitable results in particular cases.

In the context of succession, the notion of "quasi-community property" bears mention. First introduced in California, it attempts to avoid disparities resulting from the fact that some states protect the interests of surviving spouses by succession rules and others by marital property law. Since marital property interests depend on the parties' domicile at the time when an asset is acquired, whereas succession is governed by the law of the decedent's last domicile, a move from a separate to a community property state may defeat the surviving spouse's protection. To cope with this difficulty, California enacted a statute (which has since been copied by other community property states) according to which assets that would have been community property had the couple been domiciled in California all along pass to the surviving spouse. Quasi-community property provisions have also been enacted for the division of assets upon divorce.

41. 419 U.S. 393 (1975); *see* Chap. 4, pt. X.C.2.a.

5. Corporations

According to American law, a corporation's "internal affairs," that is, such issues as the entity's existence and dissolution, as well as the rights and liabilities of management and shareholders, are governed by the law of the place of incorporation rather than that of the enterprise's principal place of business or its administrative headquarters. The jurisdictional counterpart of this choice-of-law rule was the "internal affairs doctrine," according to which only the state of incorporation could adjudicate cases concerning the corporation's existence and relations with management and shareholders. While most courts have since disavowed the idea that they lack jurisdiction to deal with the internal affairs of an entity incorporated in another state, they still tend to dismiss cases raising such issues on *forum non conveniens* grounds.

The American choice-of-law rule entails the freedom to incorporate in the state whose law is most favorable to management. The choice of, say, Delaware, as the place of incorporation may, however, frustrate policies of the state where most of the shareholders reside, or from which it derives the bulk of its profits, or where the entity is *de facto* headquartered. In response to this problem some states, notably New York and California, have enacted "outreach" statutes that purport to deal with certain internal affairs of such "pseudo-foreign" corporations.

State courts have generally upheld the constitutionality of these statutes. In *Edgar v. MITE Corp.*,[42] however, the Supreme Court struck down an Illinois anti-takeover statute that applied to foreign target corporations if the shares held by Illinois residents amounted to ten percent or more of that corporation's stock. Dicta in *CTS Corp. v. Dynamics Corp. of America*[43] further support the proposition that states may not subject corporate internal affairs to inconsistent regulations. According to Justice Powell's majority opinion (which upheld the constitutionality of an Indiana statute that protects local corporations against hostile takeovers), the state of incorporation is the only one "to create corporations, to prescribe their powers, and to define the rights that are acquired by purchasing their shares."[44]

Where internal affairs are not at issue, states have ample power to deal with foreign entities. So-called "qualification statutes" require nonresident corporations that do business within the state to register with the secretary of state's office, to pay a registration fee, to file copies of the articles of incorporation and bylaws, and to consent to the host state's jurisdiction. Failure to comply with these requirements entails severe sanctions, including penalties, the inability to own property in the host state and to sue in its courts, as well as the nullification of contracts and the loss of property rights.

42. 457 U.S. 624 (1982).
43. 481 U.S. 69 (1987).
44. 481 U.S. at 91.

6. The conflict of regulatory laws

Forty-five years ago, Judge Learned Hand's landmark opinion in *United States v. Aluminum Co. of America*[45] established the "effects doctrine" in the field of antitrust law. According to this case, acts committed abroad can render foreign parties liable for criminal penalties and civil sanctions if these acts affect American commerce. The doctrine has since become part and parcel of American "extraterritorial" antitrust enforcement. It has also been invoked to justify the application of other regulatory laws, in particular securities legislation, to foreign transactions and foreign parties.

The problem with the effects doctrine, as Judge Learned Hand noted, is its overbreadth. In an interdependent world economy, most important restraints on trade are bound to affect American commerce in some fashion. Courts and commentators have therefore attempted to restrict the objective territorial principle's sway. The Restatement (Third) of the Foreign Relations Law of the United States (1987) contains a series of complex provisions that attempt to moderate its unilateral thrust with the multilateralist notion of comity. These provisions would, *inter alia*, permit American courts to take into account the interests of foreign countries.

Whether the new Foreign Relations Law Restatement can successfully resolve the clash of territorial sovereignty with the exigencies of international trade and commerce is open to doubt. The real problem, as in most conflicts cases, is the lack of a supranational court and legislature, which leaves the regulation of events that are transnational in nature to national courts and national law. Progress here, as elsewhere in the conflict of laws, may lie in the realization that while, in the absence of worldwide agencies, the enforcement of regulatory laws in the international sphere must be left to national institutions, these agencies ought to take into account that they function, in effect, as organs of the world community.

IV. Recognition of Judgments

A. Sister-State Judgments

As between sister states, the recognition of judgments is assured by the Constitution's full faith and credit clause (art. IV, § 1). Mere recognition does not, of course, equal enforcement. But while the common law used to require a full-fledged second suit, by now most states have simplified the steps necessary to collect on sister-state judgments. The Uniform Enforcement of Foreign Judgments Act, and kindred legislation in states that have not adopted the Act, facilitates execution by providing for summary procedures. To make a federal judgment enforceable outside the state where it was rendered, mere registration with the local federal district court suffices.

45. 148 F.2d 416 (2d Cir. 1945).

To qualify for recognition, a judgment has to be final and on the merits. In addition, the foreign court must have had jurisdiction over the defendant, and the defendant must have been afforded due notice and an opportunity to be heard. If any of these three essential prerequisites is lacking, the judgment violates the due process clause; it is void where rendered and cannot be enforced elsewhere. The lack of jurisdiction can, however, be cured by the defendant's appearance or consent. Moreover, if the defendant contests jurisdiction, a ruling adverse to him becomes res judicata.[46]

B. Foreign Country Judgments

Except for decisions in tax and penal matters, a similarly liberal attitude prevails with respect to foreign country judgments, including default judgments. There is no *révision au fond*; American courts accord recognition as long as the foreign court had jurisdiction (in the American sense) and its procedure comported with due process. Attempts of judgment debtors to invoke the public policy reservation and similar defenses have been largely unsuccessful. Although the U.S. Supreme Court in *Hilton v. Guyot*[47] did require reciprocity, the precedential value of this decision has become doubtful in light of state decisions and legislation.

The Uniform Foreign Money-Judgments Recognition Act, which has been adopted by a majority of states – including such important ones such as New York and California – eliminates the reciprocity requirement. According to the prevailing opinion, the recognition of foreign country judgments is governed by state rather than federal law, so that *Hilton* has ceased to play much of a role in practice. To be sure, some states are less generous in recognizing foreign country judgments than others, and a few states have retained the reciprocity requirement. But even if the judgment debtor's American assets are located in such a state, the judgment creditor can vindicate his rights by first proceeding in a more liberal jurisdiction. Once he obtains a judicial declaration recognizing his foreign-country judgment in, say, New York, the Constitution's full faith and credit clause compels all sister states to honor the New York determination.

Future recognition practices may be influenced by an international convention the United States is currently negotiating within the framework of the Hague Conference on Private International Law and by federal legislation. The American Law Institute has recently approved a project dealing with the effect of such a convention on domestic law and the elaboration of a draft that may serve as the basis for a future federal statute.

46. *See Baldwin v. Iowa State Traveling Men's Ass'n*, 283 U.S. 522 (1931).
47. 159 U.S. 113 (1895).

C. Family Law Matters

As noted earlier (*see* pt. II.B.3.), state courts have jurisdiction to grant a divorce as long as either the petitioner or the respondent is domiciled in the divorce forum and their decisions are entitled to full faith and credit in all sister states. According to Supreme Court precedents, domicile, like any other jurisdictional fact, becomes res judicata if both parties are before the divorce court. Thus, the petitioner's allegation of domicile cannot be challenged in another state if the respondent entered an appearance. This rule was of considerable practical importance at a time when some states severely curtailed the possibility to obtain a divorce, because it sheltered decrees obtained collusively in haven jurisdictions such as Nevada.

According to the Supreme Court decision in *Estin v. Estin*, the adjudication of property and pecuniary issues incidental to a divorce are entitled to sister-state recognition only if the divorce forum had jurisdiction over the defendant (*see* pts. II.B.3., III.I.3). The recognition of support decrees is governed by the Uniform Reciprocal Enforcement of Support Act (URESA). Custody decrees are protected by the Uniform Child Custody Jurisdiction Act (UCCJA), which, like URESA, has been enacted in all states, and by a federal statute, the Parental Kidnapping Act.

Foreign country decrees dealing with family law matters are, as a rule, liberally recognized. *Hilton v. Guyot* never required reciprocity in status matters, nor does state law. Consensual divorces obtained in such haven jurisdictions as (formerly) certain Mexican states and (more recently) Haiti and the Dominican Republic are usually recognized by American courts as long as one of the parties actually appeared in the foreign forum and the other one was represented. A number of states also enforce foreign country support decrees in accordance with the liberal URESA provisions upon a showing that the foreign country accords reciprocity to the forum's support decrees.

Selected Bibliography

American Law Institute, *Restatement of the Law of Conflict of Laws* (1934).
—, *Restatement (Second) of the Law of Conflict of Laws* (1971).
—, *Restatement (Third) of the Foreign Relations Law of the United States* (1986).
Joseph H. Beale, 1-3 *A Treatise on the Conflict of Laws* (1935).
Gary B. Born, *International Civil Litigation in United States Courts* (3d ed. 1996).
Lea Brilmayer, *Conflict of Laws* (2d ed. 1995).
Robert C. Casad, 1-2 *Jurisdiction in Civil Actions* (2d ed. 1991 & Supp. 1997).
David F. Cavers, *The Choice-of-Law Process* (1965).
Walter Wheeler Cook, *The Logical and Legal Bases of the Conflict of Laws* (1942).
Brainerd Currie, *Selected Essays on the Conflict of Laws* (1963).
Albert A. Ehrenzweig, *A Treatise on the Conflict of Laws* (1962).
—, 1-3 *Private International Law* (1967, vol. 2 with Erik Jayme 1973).

Friedrich K. Juenger, *Choice of Law and Multistate Justice* (1992).
—, *Selected Essays on the Conflict of Laws* (2000).
Robert A. Leflar, Luther L. McDougal & Robert L. Felix, *American Conflicts Law* (4th ed. 1986).
Ernest G. Lorenzen, *Selected Articles on the Conflict of Laws* (1947).
Arthur Taylor von Mehren & Donald Theodore Trautman, *The Law of Multistate Problems* (1965).
Kurt H. Nadelmann, *Conflict of Laws: International and Interstate* (1972).
Ernst Rabel, 1-4 *The Conflict of Laws: A Comparative Study* (vol. 4 1958, vols. 1-3 2d ed. 1958-1964).
Eugene F. Scoles, Peter Hay, Patrick J. Borchers & Symeon C. Symeonides, *Conflict of Laws* (3d ed. 2000).
Robert A. Sedler, *Across State Lines: Applying the Conflict of Laws to Your Practice* (1989).
Gene R. Shreve, *A Conflict-of-Laws Anthology* (1997).
Joseph Story, *Commentaries on the Conflict of Laws* (2d ed. 1841).
George Wilfred Stumberg, *Principles of Conflict of Laws* (3d ed. 1963).
Symeon C. Symeonides, ed., *Private International Law at the End of the 20th Century: Progress or Regress?* (2000).
Russel J. Weintraub, *Commentary on the Conflict of Laws* (4th ed. 2001).
William M. Richman & William L. Reynolds, *Understanding Conflict of Laws* (2d ed. 1993).

Chapter 18
An American Case

*David S. Clark**

I. Introduction

Appellate judicial opinions play a central role in American law. In this sense they are the most important source of legal rules. Although the United States Constitution is at the top of the hierarchy of legal rules, and a legislature may normally overrule a court's lawmaking, American jurists instinctively believe that a statute or even the Constitution does not really provide a rule until it has been interpreted by a court.

The common law tradition of judge-made law supports this view. The American variation, however, is peculiar in several respects. Two characteristics will be mentioned here. First, no country in the world produces as many published judicial opinions as the United States. This is not a recent phenomenon. Joseph Story counted 150 volumes of American jurisprudence in 1821. By the end of the 19th century American courts reported 500,000 accumulated decisions and at the beginning of the 21st century that number stood at approximately 5.2 million cases. About 100,000 new cases are added to the public record stockpile annually. Under these circumstances, of course, no jurist can "know" the law. The system would have collapsed of its own weight long ago without the development of case digests and, more recently, searchable compact disc databases and Internet access to computer databases. *See* Chap. 3, pt. III.A.

Second, the appellate case is the principal element used for instruction of students at American law schools. Beginning at Harvard Law School in the 1870s, the case method of teaching law spread to other schools and as a "scientific" method helped to secure law's place at the university. Generations of law students, in a classroom atmosphere of question and answer, have learned to examine an appellate case for its relevant facts and to make arguments about legal rules and social policies to a professor sitting as the surrogate "court." The use of

* Maynard and Bertha Wilson Professor of Law, Willamette University College of Law; Vice President, American Society of Comparative Law.

David S. Clark and Tuğrul Ansay (eds.) Introduction to the Law of the United States, 451-473

cases has been defended for over a century on the ground that they teach a student the skill of thinking like a lawyer. The impact of this system is that it has pushed procedure and method to the fore and deemphasized substance. The daunting problem of too much "law" is thus largely ignored. Technique of argument is valued over knowledge of rules. *See* Chap. 2, pts. I.A, II.C.

The case that follows in part II is from the United States Supreme Court. In form and style it is similar to cases decided by federal courts of appeals or by high courts in the 50 American states. It involves the interpretation of the Fourth Amendment of the U.S. Constitution. *See* Chap. 15, pt. III. Read the case carefully for its use of legal argument. Part III of this chapter then presents a series of notes and questions that might approximate a classroom discussion of the issues raised by the Supreme Court's treatment of the dispute. This is the method by which students are introduced to American law. The techniques of argument that they learn are carried over to their practice as lawyers before courts, which write opinions then used in law schools to close the circle of learning.

II. THE CASE: UNITED STATES V. VERDUGO-URQUIDEZ

United States v. Verdugo-Urquidez

Supreme Court of the United States
494 U.S. 259, 110 S.Ct. 1056, 108 L.Ed.2d 222 (1990)
Rehearing denied, 494 U.S. 1092 (1990)
(Most footnotes omitted)

CHIEF JUSTICE REHNQUIST delivered the opinion of the Court.

The question presented by this case is whether the Fourth Amendment applies to the search and seizure by United States agents of property that is owned by a nonresident alien and located in a foreign country. We hold that it does not.

Respondent Rene Martin Verdugo-Urquidez is a citizen and resident of Mexico. He is believed by the United States Drug Enforcement Agency (DEA) to be one of the leaders of a large and violent organization in Mexico that smuggles narcotics into the United States. Based on a complaint charging respondent with various narcotics-related offenses, the Government obtained a warrant for his arrest on August 3, 1985. In January 1986, Mexican police officers, after discussions with United States marshals, apprehended Verdugo-Urquidez in Mexico and transported him to the United States Border Patrol station in Calexico, California. There, United States marshals arrested respondent and eventually moved him to a correctional center in San Diego, California, where he remains incarcerated pending trial.

Following respondent's arrest, Terry Bowen, a DEA agent assigned to the Calexico DEA office, decided to arrange for searches of Verdugo-Urquidez's Mexican residences located in Mexicali and San Felipe. Bowen believed that the searches would reveal evidence related to respondent's alleged narcotics trafficking activities and his involvement in the kidnaping and torture-murder of DEA Special Agent Enrique Camarena Salazar (for which respondent subsequently has been convicted in a separate prosecution. See *United States v. Verdugo-Urquidez*,

No. CR-87-422-ER (CD Cal., Nov. 22, 1988)). Bowen telephoned Walter White, the Assistant Special Agent in charge of the DEA office in Mexico City, and asked him to seek authorization for the search from the Director General of the Mexican Federal Judicial Police (MFJP). After several attempts to reach high ranking Mexican officials, White eventually contacted the Director General, who authorized the searches and promised the cooperation of Mexican authorities. Thereafter, DEA agents working in concert with officers of the MFJP searched respondent's properties in Mexicali and San Felipe and seized certain documents. In particular, the search of the Mexicali residence uncovered a tally sheet, which the Government believes reflects the quantities of marijuana smuggled by Verdugo-Urquidez into the United States.

The District Court granted respondent's motion to suppress evidence seized during the searches, concluding that the Fourth Amendment applied to the searches and that the DEA agents had failed to justify searching respondent's premises without a warrant. A divided panel of the Court of Appeals for the Ninth Circuit affirmed. 856 F.2d 1214 (1988). It cited this Court's decision in *Reid v. Covert*, 354 U.S. 1 (1957), which held that American citizens tried by United States military authorities in a foreign country were entitled to the protections of the Fifth and Sixth Amendments, and concluded that "The Constitution imposes substantive constraints on the federal government, even when it operates abroad." 856 F.2d, at 1218. Relying on our decision in *INS v. Lopez-Mendoza*, 468 U.S. 1032 (1984), where a majority of Justices assumed that illegal aliens in the United States have Fourth Amendment rights, the Ninth Circuit majority found it "difficult to conclude that Verdugo-Urquidez lacks these same protections." 856 F.2d, at 1223. It also observed that persons in respondent's position enjoy certain trial-related rights, and reasoned that "[i]t would be odd indeed to acknowledge that Verdugo-Urquidez is entitled to due process under the Fifth amendment, and to a fair trial under the Sixth amendment, ... and deny him the protection from unreasonable searches and seizures afforded under the Fourth amendment." *Id.*, at 1224. Having concluded that the Fourth Amendment applied to the searches of respondent's properties, the court went on to decide that the searches violated the Constitution because the DEA agents failed to procure a search warrant. Although recognizing that "an American search warrant would be of no legal validity in Mexico," the majority deemed it sufficient that a warrant would have "substantial constitutional value in this country," because it would reflect a magistrate's determination that there existed probable cause to search and would define the scope of the search. *Id.*, at 1230.

The dissenting judge argued that this Court's statement in *United States v. Curtiss-Wright Export Corp.*, 299 U.S. 304, 318 (1936), that "[n]either the Constitution not the laws passed in pursuance of it have any force in foreign territory unless in respect of our own citizens," foreclosed any claim by respondent to Fourth Amendment rights. More broadly, he viewed the Constitution as a "compact" among the people of the United States, and the protections of the Fourth Amendment were expressly limited to "the people." We granted certiorari, 490 U.S. 1019 (1989).

Before analyzing the scope of the Fourth Amendment, we think it significant to note that it operates in a different manner than the Fifth Amendment, which is not at issue in this case. The privilege against self-incrimination guaranteed by the Fifth Amendment is a fundamental trial right of criminal defendants. See *Malloy v. Hogan*, 378 U.S. 1 (1964). Although conduct by law enforcement officials prior to trial may ultimately impair that right, a constitutional violation occurs only at trial. *Kastigar v. United States*, 406 U.S. 441, 453 (1972). The Fourth Amendment functions differently. It prohibits "unreasonable searches and seizures" whether or not the evidence is sought to be used in a criminal trial, and a violation of the Amendment is "fully accomplished" at the time of an unreasonable governmental intrusion. *United States v. Calandra*, 414 U.S. 338, 354 (1974); *United States v. Leon*, 468 U.S. 897, 906 (1984). For purposes of this case, therefore, if there were a constitutional violation, it occurred solely in Mexico. Whether evidence obtained from respondent's Mexican residences should be excluded at trial in the United States is a remedial question separate from the existence *vel non* of the constitutional violation. *Calandra, supra*, at 354; *Leon, supra*, at 906.

The Fourth Amendment provides:

> The right of the people to be secure in their persons, houses, papers, and effects, against unreasonable searches and seizures, shall not be violated, and no Warrants shall issue, but upon probable cause, supported by Oath or affirmation, and particularly describing the place to be searched, and the persons or things to be seized.

That text, by contrast with the Fifth and Sixth Amendments, extends its reach only to "the people." Contrary to the suggestion of *amici curiae* that the Framers used this phrase "simply to avoid [an] awkward rhetorical redundancy," Brief for American Civil Liberties Union et al. as *Amici Curiae* 12, n.4, "the people" seems to have been a term of art employed in select parts of the Constitution. The Preamble declares that the Constitution is ordained and established by "the People of the United States." The Second Amendment protects "the right of the people to keep and bear Arms," and the Ninth and Tenth Amendments provide that certain rights and powers are retained by and reserved to "the people." See also U.S. Const., Amdt. 1 ("Congress shall make no law ... abridging ... *the right of the people* peaceably to assemble") (emphasis added); Art. I, § 2, cl. 1 ("The House of Representatives shall be composed of Members chosen every second Year *by the People of the several States*") (emphasis added). While this textual exegesis is by no means conclusive, it suggests that "the people" protected by the Fourth Amendment, and by the First and Second Amendments, and to whom rights and powers are reserved in the Ninth and Tenth Amendments, refers to a class of persons who are part of a national community or who have otherwise developed sufficient connection with this country to be considered part of that community. See *United States ex rel. Turner v. Williams*, 194 U.S. 279, 292 (1904) (Excludable alien is not entitled to First Amendment rights, because "[h]e does not become one of the people to whom these things are secured by our Constitution by an attempt to enter forbidden by law"). The language of these Amendments contrasts with the words "person" and "accused" used in the Fifth and Sixth Amendments regulating procedure in criminal cases.

What we know of the history of the drafting of the Fourth Amendment also suggests that its purpose was to restrict searches and seizures which might be conducted by the United States in domestic matters. The Framers originally decided not to include a provision like the Fourth Amendment, because they believed the National Government lacked power to conduct searches and seizures. See C. Warren, The Making of the Constitution 508-509 (1928); The Federalist No. 84, p. 513 (C. Rossiter ed. 1961) (A. Hamilton); 1 Annals of Cong. 437 (1789) (statement of J. Madison). Many disputed the original view that the Federal Government possessed only narrow delegated powers over domestic affairs, however, and ultimately felt an Amendment prohibiting unreasonable searches and seizures was necessary. Madison, for example, argued that "there is a clause granting to Congress the power to make all laws which shall be necessary and proper for carrying into execution all of the powers vested in the Government of the United States," and that general warrants might be considered "necessary" for the purpose of collecting revenue. *Id.*, at 438. The driving force behind the adoption of the Amendment, as suggested by Madison's advocacy, was widespread hostility among the former colonists to the issuance of writs of assistance empowering revenue officers to search suspected places for smuggled goods, and general search warrants permitting the search of private houses, often to uncover papers that might be used to convict persons of libel. See *Boyd v. United States*, 116 U.S. 616, 625-626 (1886). The available historical data show, therefore, that the purpose of the Fourth Amendment was to protect the people of the United States against arbitrary action by their own Government; it was never suggested that the provision was intended to restrain the actions of the Federal Government against aliens outside of the United States territory.

There is likewise no indication that the Fourth Amendment was understood by contemporaries of the Framers to apply to activities of the United States directed against aliens in foreign territory or in international waters. Only seven years after the ratification of the Amendment, French interference with American commercial vessels engaged in neutral trade triggered what came to be known as the "undeclared war" with France. In an Act to "protect the Commerce of the United States" in 1798, Congress authorized President Adams to "instruct the commanders of the public armed vessels which are, or which shall be employed in the service of the United States, to subdue, seize and take any armed French vessel, which shall be found within the jurisdictional limits of the United States, or elsewhere, on the high seas." § 1 of An Act Further to Protect the Commerce of the United States, ch. 68, 1 Stat. 578. This public naval force consisted of only 45 vessels, so Congress also gave the President power to grant to the owners of private armed ships and vessels of the United States "special commissions," which would allow them "the same license and authority for the subduing, seizing and capturing any armed French vessel, and for the recapture of the vessels, goods and effects of the people of the United States, as the public armed vessels of the United States may by law have." § 2, 1 Stat. 579; see U.S. Const., Art. I, § 8, cl. 11 (Congress has power to grant letters of marque and reprisal). Under the latter provision, 365 private armed vessels were commissioned before March 1, 1799, see G. Allen, Our Naval War with France 59 (1967); together, these enactments resulted in scores of seizures of foreign vessels under congressional authority. See M. Palmer, Stoddert's War: Naval Operations During the Quasi-War with France, 1798-1801, p. 235 (1987). See also An Act Further to Suspend the Commercial Intercourse Between the United States and France, ch.

2, 1 Stat. 613. Some commanders were held liable by this Court for unlawful seizures because their actions were beyond the scope of the congressional grant of authority, see, *e.g.*, *Little v. Barreme*, 2 Cranch 170, 177-178 (1804); cf. *Talbot v. Seeman*, 1 Cranch 1, 31 (1801) (seizure of neutral ship lawful where American captain had probable cause to believe vessel was French), but it was never suggested that the Fourth Amendment restrained the authority of Congress or of United States agents to conduct operations such as this.

The global view taken by the Court of Appeals of the application of the Constitution is also contrary to this Court's decisions in the *Insular Cases*, which held that not every constitutional provision applies to governmental activity even where the United States has sovereign power. See, *e.g.*, *Balzac v. Porto Rico*, 258 U.S. 298 (1922) (Sixth Amendment right to jury trial inapplicable in Puerto Rico); *Ocampo v. United States*, 234 U.S. 91 (1914) (Fifth Amendment grand jury provision inapplicable in Philippines); *Dorr v. United States*, 195 U.S. 138 (1904) (jury trial provision inapplicable in Philippines); *Hawaii v. Mankichi*, 190 U.S. 197 (1903) (provisions on indictment by grand jury and jury trial inapplicable in Hawaii); *Downes v. Bidwell*, 182 U.S. 244 (1901) (Revenue Clauses of Constitution inapplicable to Puerto Rico). In *Dorr*, we declared the general rule that in an unincorporated territory – one not clearly destined for statehood – Congress was not required to adopt "a system of laws which shall include the right of trial by jury, and that *the Constitution does not, without legislation and of its own force, carry such right to territory so situated.*" 195 U.S., at 149 (emphasis added). Only "fundamental" constitutional rights are guaranteed to inhabitants of those territories. *Id.*, at 148; *Balzac*, *supra*, at 312-313; see *Examining Board of Engineers, Architects and Surveyors v. Flores de Otero*, 426 U.S. 572, 599, n.30 (1976). If that is true with respect to territories ultimately governed by Congress, respondent's claim that the protections of the Fourth Amendment extend to aliens in foreign nations is even weaker. And certainly, it is not open to us in light of the *Insular Cases* to endorse the view that every constitutional provision applies wherever the United States Government exercises its power.

Indeed, we have rejected the claim that aliens are entitled to Fifth Amendment rights outside the sovereign territory of the United States. In *Johnson v. Eisentrager*, 339 U.S. 763 (1950), the Court held that enemy aliens, arrested in China and imprisoned in Germany after World War II could not obtain writs of habeas corpus in our federal courts on the ground that their convictions for war crimes had violated the Fifth Amendment and other constitutional provisions. The *Eisentrager* opinion acknowledged that in some cases constitutional provisions extend beyond the citizenry; "[t]he alien ... has been accorded a generous and ascending scale of rights as he increases his identity with our society." *Id.*, at 770. But our rejection of extraterritorial application of the Fifth Amendment was emphatic:

> "Such extraterritorial application of organic law would have been so significant an innovation in the practice of governments that, if intended or apprehended, it could scarcely have failed to excite contemporary comment. Not one word can be cited. No decision of this Court supports such a view. Cf. *Downes v. Bidwell*, 182 U.S. 241 [(1901)]. None of the learned

> commentators on our Constitution has even hinted at it. The practice of every modern government is opposed to it." *Id.*, at 784.

If such is true of the Fifth Amendment, which speaks in the relatively universal term of "person," it would seem even more true with respect to the Fourth Amendment, which applies only to "the people."

To support his all-encompassing view of the Fourth Amendment, respondent points to language from the plurality opinion in *Reid v. Covert*, 354 U.S. 1 (1957). *Reid* involved an attempt by Congress to subject the wives of American servicemen to trial by military tribunals without the protection of the Fifth and Sixth Amendments. The Court held that it was unconstitutional to apply the Uniform Code of Military Justice to the trials of the American women for capital crimes. Four Justices "reject[ed] the idea that when the United States acts *against citizens* abroad it can do so free of the Bill of Rights." *Id.*, at 5 (emphasis added). The plurality went on to say:

> "The United States is entirely a creature of the Constitution. Its power and authority have no other source. It can only act in accordance with all the limitations imposed by the Constitution. When the Government reaches out to punish a *citizen* who is abroad, the shield which the Bill of Rights and other parts of the Constitution provide to protect his life and liberty should not be stripped away just because he happens to be in another land." *Id.*, at 5-6 (emphasis added; footnote omitted).

Respondent urges that we interpret this discussion to mean that federal officials are constrained by the Fourth Amendment wherever and against whomever they act. But the holding of *Reid* stands for no such sweeping proposition: it decided that United States citizens stationed abroad could invoke the protection of the Fifth and Sixth Amendments. The concurring opinions by Justices Frankfurter and Harlan in *Reid* resolved the case on much narrower grounds than the plurality and declined even to hold that United States citizens were entitled to the full range of constitutional protections in all overseas criminal prosecutions. See *id.*, at 75 (Harlan, J., concurring in result) ("I agree with my brother FRANKFURTER that ... we have before us a question analogous, ultimately, to issues of due process; one can say, in fact, that the question of which specific safeguards of the Constitution are appropriately to be applied in a particular context overseas can be reduced to the issue of what process is 'due' a defendant in the particular circumstances of a particular case"). Since respondent is not a United States citizen, he can derive no comfort from the *Reid* holding.

Verdugo-Urquidez also relies on a series of cases in which we have held that aliens enjoy certain constitutional rights. See, *e.g.*, *Plyler v. Doe*, 457 U.S. 202, 211-212 (1982) (illegal aliens protected by Equal Protection Clause); *Kwong Hai Chew v. Colding*, 344 U.S. 590, 596 (1953) (resident alien is a "person" within the meaning of the Fifth Amendment); *Bridges v. Wixon*, 326 U.S. 135, 148 (1915) (resident aliens have First Amendment rights); *Russian Volunteer Fleet v. United States*, 282 U.S. 481 (1931) (Just Compensation Clause of Fifth Amendment); *Wong Wing v. United States*, 163 U.S. 228, 238 (1896) (resident aliens entitled to Fifth and Sixth Amendment rights); *Yick Wo v. Hopkins*, 118 U.S. 356, 369 (1886)

(Fourteenth Amendment protects resident aliens). These cases, however, establish only that aliens receive constitutional protections when they have come within the territory of the United States and developed substantial connections with this country. See, *e.g.*, *Plyler*, *supra*, at 212 (The provisions of the Fourteenth Amendment "'are universal in their application, *to all persons within the territorial jurisdiction* ...'") (quoting *Yick Wo*, *supra*, at 369); *Kwong Hai Chew*, *supra*, at 596, n.5 ("The Bill of Rights is a futile authority for the alien seeking admission for the first time to these shores. But *once an alien lawfully enters and resides in this country* he becomes invested with the rights guaranteed by the Constitution to all people within our borders") (quoting *Bridges*, *supra*, at 161 (concurring opinion) (emphasis added)). Respondent is an alien who has had no previous significant voluntary connection with the United States, so these cases avail him not.

JUSTICE STEVENS' concurrence in the judgment takes the view that even though the search took place in Mexico, it is nonetheless governed by the requirements of the Fourth Amendment because respondent was "lawfully present in the United States ... even though he was brought and held here against his will." *Post*, at 279. But this sort of presence – lawful but involuntary – is not of the sort to indicate any substantial connection with our country. The extent to which respondent might claim the protection of the Fourth Amendment if the duration of his stay in the United States were to be prolonged – by a prison sentence, for example – we need not decide. When the search of his house in Mexico took place, he had been present in the United States for only a matter of days. We do not think the applicability of the Fourth Amendment to the search of premises in Mexico should turn on the fortuitous circumstance of whether the custodian of its nonresident alien owner had or had not transported him to the United States at the time the search was made. ...

Respondent also contends that to treat aliens differently from citizens with respect to the Fourth Amendment somehow violates the equal protection component of the Fifth Amendment to the United States Constitution. He relies on *Graham v. Richardson*, 403 U.S. 365 (1971), and *Foley v. Connelie*, 435 U.S. 291 (1978), for this proposition. But the very cases previously cited with respect to the protection extended by the Constitution to aliens undermine this claim. They are constitutional decisions of this Court expressly according differing protection to aliens than to citizens, based on our conclusion that the particular provisions in question were not intended to extend to aliens in the same degree as to citizens. Cf. *Mathews v. Diaz*, 426 U.S. 67, 79-80 (1976) ("In the exercise of its broad power over naturalization and immigration, Congress regularly makes rules that would be unacceptable if applied to citizens").

Not only are history and case law against respondent, but as pointed out in *Johnson v. Eisentrager*, 393 U.S. 763 (1950), the result of accepting his claim would have significant and deleterious consequences for the United States in conducting activities beyond its boundaries. The rule adopted by the Court of Appeals would apply not only to law enforcement operations abroad, but also to other foreign policy operations which might result in "searches or seizures." The United States frequently employs armed forces outside this country – over 200 times in our history – for the protection of American citizens or national security. Congressional Research Service, Instances of Use of United States Armed Forces Abroad, 1798-1989 (E. Collier ed. 1989). Application of the Fourth Amendment to those circumstances could significantly disrupt the ability of the political branches to respond to foreign situations involving our national interest. Were respondent to prevail, aliens with no attachment to this country might well bring actions for damages to remedy claimed violation of the Fourth Amendment in foreign countries or in international waters. See *Bivens v. Six Unknown Federal Narcotics Agents*, 403 U.S. 388 (1971); cf. *Tennessee v. Garner*, 471 U.S. 1 (1985); *Graham v. Connor*, 490 U.S. 386 (1989). Perhaps a *Bivens* action might be unavailable in some or all of these situations due to "'special factors counselling hesitation,'" see *Chappell v. Wallace*, 462 U.S. 296, 298 (1983) (quoting *Bivens*, *supra*, at 396), but the Government would still be faced with case-by-case adjudications concerning the availability of such an action. And even were *Bivens* deemed wholly inapplicable in cases of foreign activity, that would not obviate the problems attending the application of the Fourth Amendment abroad to aliens. The Members of the Executive and Legislative Branches are sworn to uphold the Constitution, and they presumably desire to follow its commands. But the Court of Appeals' global view of its applicability would plunge them into a sea of uncertainty as to what might be reasonable in the way of searches and seizures conducted abroad. Indeed, the Court of Appeals held that absent exigent circumstances, United States agents could not effect a "search or seizure" for law enforcement purposes in a foreign country without first obtaining a warrant – which would be a dead letter outside the United States – from a magistrate in this country. Even if no warrant were required, American agents would have to articulate specific facts giving them probable cause to undertake a search or seizure if they wished to comply with the Fourth Amendment as conceived by the Court of Appeals.

We think that the text of the Fourth Amendment, its history, and our cases discussing the application of the Constitution to aliens and extraterritorially require rejection of respondent's claim. At the time of the search, he was a citizen and resident of Mexico with no voluntary attachment to the United States, and the place searched was located in Mexico. Under these circumstances, the Fourth Amendment has no application.

For better or for worse, we live in a world of nation-states in which our Government must be able to "functio[n] effectively in the company of sovereign nations." *Perez v. Brownell*, 356 U.S. 44, 57 (1958). Some who violate our laws may live outside our borders under a regime quite different from that which obtains in this country. Situations threatening to important American interests may arise halfway around the globe, situations which in the view of the political branches of our Government require an American response with armed force. If there are to be restrictions on searches and seizures which occur incident to such American action, they must be imposed by the political branches through diplomatic understanding, treaty, or legislation.

The judgment of the Court of Appeals is accordingly

Reversed.

JUSTICE KENNEDY, concurring.

I agree that no violation of the Fourth Amendment has occurred and that we must reverse the judgment of the Court of Appeals. Although some explanation of my views is appropriate given the difficulties of this case, I do not believe they depart in fundamental respects from the opinion of the Court, which I join.

In cases involving the extraterritorial application of the Constitution, we have taken care to state whether the person claiming its protection is a citizen, see, *e.g.*, *Reid v. Covert*, 354 U.S. 1 (1957), or an alien, see, *e.g.*, *Johnson v. Eisentrager*, 339 U.S. 763 (1950). The distinction between citizens and aliens follows from the undoubted proposition that the Constitution does not create, nor do general principles of law create, any juridical relation between our country and some undefined, limitless class of noncitizens who are beyond our territory. We should note, however, that the absence of this relation does not depend on the idea that only a limited class of persons ratified the instrument that formed our Government. Though it must be beyond dispute that persons outside the United States did not and could not assent to the Constitution, that is quite irrelevant to any construction of the powers conferred or the limitations imposed by it. As Justice Story explained in his Commentaries:

> "A government may originate in the voluntary compact or assent of the people of several states, or of a people never before united, and yet when adopted and ratified by them, be no longer a matter resting in compact; but become an executed government or constitution, a fundamental law, and not a mere league. But the difficulty in asserting it to be a compact between the people of each state, and all the people of the other states is, that the constitution itself contains no such expression, and no such designation of parties." 1 Commentaries on the Constitution § 365, p. 335 (1833) (footnote omitted).

The force of the Constitution is not confined because it was brought into being by certain persons who gave their immediate assent to its terms.

For somewhat similar reasons, I cannot place any weight on the reference to "the people" in the Fourth Amendment as a source of restricting its protections. With respect, I submit these words do not detract from its force or its reach. Given the history of our Nations concern over warrantless and unreasonable searches, explicit recognition of "the right of the people" to Fourth Amendment protection may be interpreted to underscore the importance of the right, rather than to restrict the category of persons who may assert it. The restrictions that the United States must observe with reference to aliens beyond its territory or jurisdiction depend, as a consequence, on general principles of interpretation, not on an inquiry as to who formed the Constitution or a construction that some rights are mentioned as being those of "the people."

I take it to be correct, as the plurality opinion in *Reid v. Covert* sets forth, that the Government may act only as the Constitution authorizes, whether the actions in question are foreign or domestic. See 354 U.S., at 6. But this principle is only a first step in resolving this case. The question before us then becomes what constitutional standards apply when the Government acts, in reference to an alien, within its sphere of foreign operations. We have not overruled either *In re Ross*, 140 U.S. 453 (1891), or the so-called *Insular Cases* (*i.e., Downes v. Bidwell*, 182 U.S. 244 (1901); *Hawaii v. Mankichi*, 190 U.S. 197 (1903); *Dorr v. United States*, 195 U.S. 138 (1901); *Balzac v. Porto Rico*, 258 U.S. 298 (1922)). These authorities, as well as *United States v. Curtiss-Wright Export Corp.*, 299 U.S. 304, 318

(1936), stand for the proposition that we must interpret constitutional protections in light of the undoubted power of the United States to take actions to assert its legitimate power and authority abroad. Justice Harlan made this observation in his opinion concurring in the judgment in *Reid v. Covert*:

> "I cannot agree with the suggestion that every provision of the Constitution must always be deemed automatically applicable to American citizens in every part of the world. For *Ross* and the *Insular Cases* do stand for an important proposition, one which seems to me a wise and necessary gloss on our Constitution. The proposition is, of course, not that the Constitution 'does not apply' overseas, but that there are provisions in the Constitution which do not *necessarily* apply in all circumstances in every foreign place. In other words, it seems to me that the basic teaching of *Ross* and the *Insular Cases* is that there is no rigid and abstract rule that Congress, as a condition precedent to exercising power over Americans overseas, must exercise it subject to all the guarantees of the Constitution, no matter what the conditions and considerations are that would make adherence to a specific guarantee altogether impracticable and anomalous." 354 U.S., at 74.

The conditions and considerations of this case would make adherence to the Fourth Amendment's warrant requirement impracticable and anomalous. Just as the Constitution in the *Insular Cases* did not require Congress to implement all constitutional guarantees in its territories because of their "wholly dissimilar traditions and institutions," the Constitution does not require United States agents to obtain a warrant when searching the foreign home of a nonresident alien. If the search had occurred in a residence within the United States, I have little doubt that the full protections of the Fourth Amendment would apply. But that is not this case. The absence of local judges or magistrates available to issue warrants, the differing and perhaps unascertainable conceptions of reasonableness and privacy that prevail abroad, and the need to cooperate with foreign officials all indicate that the Fourth Amendment's warrant requirement should not apply in Mexico as it does in this country. For this reason, in addition to the other persuasive justifications stated by the Court, I agree that no violation of the Fourth Amendment has occurred in the case before us. The rights of a citizen, as to whom the United States has continuing obligations, are not presented by this case.

I do not mean to imply, and the Court has not decided, that persons in the position of the respondent have no constitutional protection. The United States is prosecuting a foreign national in a court established under Article III, and all of the trial proceedings are governed by the Constitution. All would agree, for instance, that the dictates of the Due Process Clause of the Fifth Amendment protect the defendant. Indeed, as Justice Harlan put it, "the question of which specific safeguards ... are appropriately to be applied in a particular context ... can be reduced to the issue of what process is 'due' a defendant in the particular circumstances of a particular case." *Reid*, *supra*, at 75. Nothing approaching a violation of due process has occurred in this case.

JUSTICE STEVENS, concurring in the judgment.

In my opinion aliens who are lawfully present in the United States are among those "people" who are entitled to the protection of the Bill of Rights, including the Fourth Amendment. Respondent is surely such a person even though he was brought and held here against his will. I therefore cannot join the Court's sweeping opinion.* I do agree, however, with the Government's submission that the search conducted by the United States agents with the approval and cooperation of the Mexican authorities was not "unreasonable" as that term is used in the first Clause of the Amendment. I do not believe the Warrant Clause has any application to searches of noncitizens' homes in foreign jurisdictions because American magistrates have no power to authorize such searches. I therefore concur in the Court's judgment.

JUSTICE BRENNAN, with whom JUSTICE MARSHALL joins, dissenting.

Today the Court holds that although foreign nationals must abide by our laws even when in their own countries, our Government need not abide by the Fourth Amendment when it investigates them for violations of our laws. I respectfully dissent.

I

Particularly in the past decade, our Government has sought, successfully, to hold foreign nationals criminally liable under federal laws for conduct committed entirely beyond the territorial limits of the United States that nevertheless has effects in this country. Foreign nationals must now take care not to violate our drug laws, our antitrust laws, our securities laws, and a host of other federal criminal statutes. The enormous expansion of federal criminal jurisdiction outside our Nation's boundaries has led one commentator to suggest that our country's three largest exports are now "rock music, blue jeans, and United States law." Grundman, The New Imperialism: The Extraterritorial Application of United States Law, 14 Int'l Law. 257, 257 (1980).

The Constitution is the source of Congress' authority to criminalize conduct, whether here or abroad, and of the Executive's authority to investigate and prosecute such conduct. But the same Constitution also prescribes limits on our Government's authority to investigate, prosecute, and punish criminal conduct, whether foreign or domestic. As a plurality of the Court noted in *Reid v. Covert*, 354 U.S. 1, 5-6 (1957): "The United States is entirely a creature of the Constitution. Its power and authority have no other source. It can only act in accordance with all the limitations imposed by the Constitution." (Footnotes omitted.) See also *ante*, at 277 (KENNEDY, J., concurring) ("[T]he Government may act only as the Constitution authorizes, whether the actions in question are foreign or domestic"). In particular, the Fourth Amendment provides:

* The Court's interesting historical discussion is simply irrelevant to the question whether an alien lawfully within the sovereign territory of the United States is entitled to the protection of our laws. Nor is comment on illegal aliens' entitlement to the protections of the Fourth Amendment necessary to resolve this case.

> "The right of the people to be secure in their persons, houses, papers, and effects, against unreasonable searches and seizures, shall not be violated; and no Warrants shall issue but upon probable cause, supported by Oath or affirmation, and particularly describing the place to be searched, and the persons or thing to be seized."

The Court today creates an antilogy: the Constitution authorizes our Government to enforce our criminal laws abroad, but when Government agents exercise this authority, the Fourth Amendment does not travel with them. This cannot be. At the very least, the Fourth Amendment is an unavoidable correlative of the Government's power to enforce the criminal law.

A

The Fourth Amendment guarantees the right of "the people" to be free from unreasonable searches and seizures and provides that a warrant shall issue only upon presentation of an oath or affirmation demonstrating probable cause and particularly describing the place to be searched and the persons or things to be seized. According to the majority, the term "the people" refers to "a class of persons who are part of a national community or who have otherwise developed sufficient connection with this country to be considered part of that community." *Ante*, at 265. The Court admits that "the people" extends beyond the citizenry, but leaves the precise contours of its "sufficient connection" test unclear. At one point the majority hints that aliens are protected by the Fourth Amendment only when they come within the United States and develop "substantial connections" with our country. *Ante*, at 271. At other junctures, the Court suggests that an alien's presence in the United States must be voluntary and that the alien must have "accepted some societal obligations." *Ante*, at 273. At yet other points, the majority implies that respondent would be protected by the Fourth Amendment if the place searched were in the United States. *Ante*, at 266, 274-275.

What the majority ignores, however, is the most obvious connection between Verdugo-Urquidez and the United States: he was investigated and is being prosecuted for violations of United States law and may well spend the rest of life in a United States prison. The "sufficient connection" is supplied not by Verdugo-Urquidez, but by the Government. Respondent is entitled to the protections of the Fourth Amendment because our Government, by investigation him and attempting to hold him accountable under United States criminal laws, has treated him as a member of our community for purposes of enforcing our laws. He has become, quite literally, one of the governed. Fundamental fairness and the ideals underlying our Bill of Rights compel the conclusion that when we impose "social obligations," *ante*, at 273, such as the obligations to comply with our criminal laws, on foreign nationals, we in turn are obliged to respect certain correlative rights, among them the Fourth Amendment.

By concluding that respondent is not one of "the people" protected by the Fourth Amendment, the majority disregards basic notions of mutuality. If we expect aliens to obey our laws, aliens should be able to expect that we will obey our Constitution when we investigate, prosecute, and punish them. We have recognized this fundamental principle of mutuality since the time of the Framers. James Madison, universally recognized as the primary architect of the Bill of Rights, emphasized the importance of mutuality when he spoke out against the Alien and Sedition Acts less than a decade after the adoption of the Fourth Amendment:

> "[I]t does not follow, because aliens are not parties to the Constitution, as citizens are parties to it, that, whilst they actually conform to it, they have no right to its protection. Aliens are not more parties to the laws than they are parties to the Constitution; yet it will not be disputed that, as they owe, on the one hand, a temporary obedience, they are entitled, in return, to their protection and advantage." Madison's Report on the Virginia Resolutions (1800), reprinted in 4 Elliot's Debates 556 (2d ed. 1836).

Mutuality is essential to ensure the fundamental fairness that underlies our Bill of Rights. Foreign nationals investigated and prosecuted for alleged violation of United States criminal laws are just as vulnerable to oppressive Government behavior as are United States citizens investigated and prosecuted for the same alleged violations. Indeed, in a case such as this where the Government claims the existence of an international criminal conspiracy, citizens and foreign nationals may be codefendants, charged under the same statutes for the same conduct and facing the same penalties if convicted. They may have been investigated by the same agents pursuant to the same enforcement authority. When out Government holds these codefendants to the same standards of conduct, the Fourth Amendment, which protects the citizen from unreasonable searches and seizures, should protect the foreign national as well.

Mutuality also serves to inculcate the values of law and order. By respecting the rights of foreign nationals, we encourage other nations to respect the rights of our citizens. Moreover, as our Nation becomes increasingly concerned about the domestic effects of international crime, we cannot forget that the behavior of our law enforcement agents abroad sends a powerful message about the rule of law to individuals everywhere. As Justice Brandies warned in *Olmstead v. United States*, 277 U.S. 438 (1928):

> "If the Government becomes a lawbreaker, it breads contempt for law; it invites every man to become a law unto himself; it invites anarchy. To declare that in the administration of the criminal law the end justifies the means ... would bring terrible retribution. Against that pernicious doctrine, this Court should resolutely set its face." *Id.*, at 185 (dissenting opinion).

This principle is no different when the United States applies its rules of conduct to foreign nationals. If we seek respect for law and order, we must observe these principles ourselves. Lawlessness breads lawlessness.

Finally, when United States agents conduct unreasonable searches, whether at home or abroad, they disregard our Nation's values. For over 200 years, our country has considered itself the world's foremost protector of liberties. The privacy and sanctity of the home have been primary tenets of our moral, philosophical, and judicial beliefs.[1] Our national interest is defined by those values and by the need to preserve our own just institutions. We take pride in our commitment to a Government that cannot, on mere whim, break down doors and invade the most personal of places. We exhort other nations to follow our example. How can we explain to others – and to ourselves – that these long cherished ideals are suddenly of no consequence when the door being broken belongs to a foreigner?

The majority today brushes aside the principles of mutuality and fundamental fairness that are central to our Nation's constitutional conscience. The Court articulates a "sufficient connection" test but then refuses to discuss the underlying principles upon which any interpretation of that test must rest. I believe that by placing respondent among those governed by federal criminal laws and investigation him for violations of those laws, the Government has made him a part of our community for purposes of the Fourth Amendment.

B

In its effort to establish that respondent does not have sufficient connection to the United States to be considered one of "the people" protected by the Fourth Amendment, the Court relies on the text of the Amendment, historical evidence, and cases refusing to apply certain constitutional provisions outside the United States. None of these, however, justifies the majority's cramped interpretation of the Fourth Amendment's applicability.

The majority looks to various constitutional provisions and suggests that "'the people' seems to have been a term of art." *Ante*, at 265. But the majority admits that its "textual exegesis is by no means conclusive." *Ibid.*[2] One Member of the majority even states that he "cannot place any weight on the reference to 'the people' in the Fourth Amendment as a source of restricting its protections." *Ante*, at 276 (KENNEDY, J., concurring). The majority suggests a restrictive interpretation of those with "sufficient connection" to this country to be considered among "the people," but the term "the people" is better understood as a rhetorical counterpoint to "the Government," such that rights that were reserved to "the

1. President John Adams traced the origins of our independence from England to James Otis' impassioned argument against the British writs of assistance, which allowed revenue officers to search American homes wherever and whenever they wanted. Otis argued that "[a] man's house is his castle," 2 Works of John Adams 524 (C. Adams ed. 1850), and Adams declared that "[t]hen and there the child Independence was born." 10 Works of John Adams 248 (C. Adams ed. 1856).
2. The majority places an insupportable reliance on the fact that the drafters used "the people" in the Fourth Amendment while using "person" and "accused" in the Fifth and Sixth Amendments respectively, see *ante*, at 265-266. The Drafters purposely did not use the term "accused." As the majority recognizes, *ante*, at 264, the Fourth Amendment is violated at the time of an unreasonable governmental intrusion, even if the victim of unreasonable governmental action is never formally "accused" of any wrongdoing. The majority's suggestion that the Drafters could have used "person" ignores the fact that the Fourth Amendment then would have begun quite awkwardly: "The right of persons to be secure in their persons ...."

people" were to protect all those subject to "the Government." Cf. *New Jersey v. T.L.O.*, 469 U.S. 325, 335 (1985) ("[T]he Court has long spoken of the Fourth Amendment's strictures as restraints imposed upon 'governmental action'"). "The people" are "the governed."

In drafting both the Constitution and the Bill of Rights, the Framers strove to create a form of Government decidedly different from their British heritage. Whereas the British Parliament was unconstrained, the Framers intended to create a Government of limited powers. See B. Bailyn, The, Ideological Origins of the American Revolution 182 (1967); 1 The Complete Anti-Federalist 65 (H. Storing ed. 1981). The colonists considered the British Government dangerously omnipotent. After all, the British declaration of rights in 1688 had been enacted not by the people, but by Parliament. The Federalist No. 84, p. 439 (M. Beloff ed. 1987). Americans vehemently attacked the notion that rights were matters of "'favor and grace,'" given *to* the people *from* the Government. B. Bailyn, *supra*, at 187 (quoting John Dickinson).

Thus, the Framers of the Bill of Rights did not purport to "create" rights. Rather, they designed the Bill of Rights to prohibit our Government from infringing rights and liberties presumed to be pre-existing. See, *e.g.*, U.S. Const., Amdt. 9 (The enumeration in the Constitution of certain rights, shall not be construed to deny or disparage others retained by the people"). The Fourth Amendment, for example, does not create a new right of security against unreasonable searches and seizures. It states that "[t]he right of the people to be secure in their persons, houses, papers, and effects, against unreasonable searches and seizures, *shall not be violated* ...." The focus of the Fourth Amendment is on *what* the Government can and cannot do, and *how* it may act, not on *against whom* these actions may be taken. Bestowing rights and delineating protected groups would have been inconsistent with the Drafters' fundamental conception of a Bill of Rights as a limitation on the Government's conduct with respect to all whom it seeks to govern. It is thus extremely unlikely that the Framers intended the narrow construction of the term "the people" presented today by the majority.

The drafting history of the Fourth Amendment also does not support the majority's interpretation of "the people." First, the drafters chose not to limit the right against unreasonable searches and seizures in more specific ways. They could have limited the right to "citizens," "freemen," "residents," or "the American people." The conventions called to ratify the Constitution in New York and Virginia, for example, each recommended an amendment stating, "That every freeman has a right to be secure from all unreasonable searches and seizures ...." W. Cuddihy, Search and Seizure in Great Britain and the American Colonies, pt. 2, p. 571, n.129, 574, n.134 (1974). But the Drafters of the Fourth Amendment rejected this limitation and instead provided broadly for "[t]he right of the people to be secure in their persons, houses, papers, and effects." Second, historical materials contain no evidence that the drafters intended to limit the availability of the right expressed in the Fourth Amendment. The Amendment was introduced on the floor of Congress, considered by Committee, debated by the House of Representatives and the Senate, and submitted to the 13 States for approval. Throughout that entire process, no speaker or commentator, pro or con, referred to the term "the people" as a limitation.

The Court also relies on a series of cases dealing with the application of criminal procedural protections outside of the United States to conclude that "not every constitutional provision applies to governmental activity even where the United States has sovereign power." *Ante*, at 268. None of these cases, however, purports to read the phrase "the people" as limiting the protections of the Fourth Amendment to those with "sufficient connection" to the United States, and thus none gives content to the majority's analysis. The cases shed no light on the question whether respondent – a citizen of a nonenemy nation being tried in a United States federal court – is one of "the people" protected by the Fourth Amendment.

The majority mischaracterizes *Johnson v. Eisentrager*, 339 U.S. 763 (1950), as having "rejected the claim that aliens are entitled to Fifth Amendment rights outside the sovereign territory of the United States." *Ante*, at 269. In *Johnson*, 21 German nationals were convicted of engaging in continued military activity against the United States after the surrender of Germany and before the surrender of Japan in World War II. The Court held that "the Constitution does not confer a right of personal security or an immunity from military trial and punishment upon an *alien enemy* engaged in the hostile service of a government at war with the United States." 339 U.S., at 785 (emphasis added). As the Court wrote:

> "It is war that exposes the relative vulnerability of the alien's status. The security and protection enjoyed while the nation of his allegiance remains in amity with the United States are greatly impaired when his nation takes up arms against us.... But disabilities this country lays upon the alien who becomes also an enemy are imposed temporarily as an incident of war and not as an incident of alienage." *Id.*, at 771-772.

The Court rejected the German nationals' efforts to obtain writs of habeas corpus not because they were foreign nationals, but because they were enemy soldiers.

The *Insular Cases*, *Balzac v. Porto Rico*, 258 U.S. 298 (1922), *Ocampo v. United States*, 234 U.S. 91 (1914), *Dorr v. United States*, 195 U.S. 138 (1904), and *Hawaii v. Mankichi*, 190 U.S. 197 (1903), are likewise inapposite. The *Insular Cases* all concerned whether accused persons enjoyed the protections of certain rights in criminal prosecutions brought by territorial authorities in territorial courts. These cases were limited to their facts long ago, see *Reid v. Covert*, 354 U.S., at 14 (plurality opinion) ("[I]t is our judgment that neither the cases nor their reasoning should be given any further expansion"), and they are of no analytical value when a criminal defendant seeks to invoke the Fourth Amendment in a prosecution by the Federal Government in a federal court.

C

The majority's rejection of respondent's claim to Fourth Amendment protection is apparently motivated by its fear that application of the Amendment to law enforcement searches against foreign nationals overseas "could significantly disrupt the ability of the political branches to respond to foreign situations involving our national interest." *Ante*, at 273-274. The majority's doomsday scenario – that American Armed Forces conducting a mission to protect our national security with no law enforcement objective "would have to articulate specific facts giving them probable cause to undertake a search or seizure," *ante*, at 274 – is fanciful. Verdugo-Urquidez is protected by the Fourth Amendment because our Government, by investigating and prosecuting him, has made him one of "the governed." See *supra*, at 284, 287. Accepting respondent as one of "the governed," however, hardly requires the Court to accept enemy aliens in wartime as among "the governed" entitled to invoke the protection of the Fourth Amendment. See *Johnson v. Eisentrager*, *supra*.

Moreover, with respect to non-law-enforcement activities not directed against enemy aliens in wartime but nevertheless implicating national security, doctrinal exceptions to the general requirements of a warrant and probable cause likely would be applicable more frequently abroad, thus lessening the purported tension between the Fourth Amendment's strictures and the Executive's foreign affairs power. Many situations involving sensitive operations abroad likely would involve exigent circumstances such that the warrant requirement would be excused. Cf. *Warden v. Hayden*, 387 U.S. 294, 298 (1967). Therefore, the Government's conduct would be assessed only under the reasonableness standard, the application of which depends on context. See *United States v. Montoya de Hernandez*, 473 U.S. 531, 537 (1985) ("What is reasonable depends upon all of the circumstances surrounding the search or seizure and the nature of the search or seizure itself").

In addition, where the precise contours of a "reasonable" search and seizure are unclear, the Executive Branch will not be "plunge[d] ... into a sea of uncertainty," *ante*, at 274, that will impair materially its ability to conduct foreign affairs. Doctrines such as official immunity have long protected Government agents from any undue chill on the exercise of lawful discretion. See, *e.g.*, *Butz v. Economou*, 438 U.S. 478 (1978). Similarly, the Court has recognized that there may be certain situations in which the offensive use of constitutional rights should be limited. Cf. *Bivens v. Six Unknown Fed. Narcotics Agents*, 403 U.S. 388, 396 (1971) (precluding suits for damages for violations of the Fourth Amendment where there are "special factors counselling hesitation"). In most cases implicating foreign policy concerns in which the reasonableness of an overseas search or seizure is unclear, application of the Fourth Amendment will not interfere with the Executive's traditional prerogative in foreign affairs because a court will have occasion to decide the constitutionality of such a search only if *the Executive* decides to bring a criminal prosecution and introduce evidence seized abroad. When the Executive decides to conduct a search as part of an ongoing criminal investigation, fails to get a warrant, and then seeks to introduce the fruits of that search at trial, however, the courts must enforce the Constitution.

II

Because the Fourth Amendment governs the search of respondent's Mexican residences, the District Court properly suppressed the evidence found in that search because the officers conducting the search did not obtain a warrant.[3] I cannot agree with JUSTICE BLACKMUN and JUSTICE STEVENS that the Warrant Clause has no application to searches of noncitizens' homes in foreign jurisdictions because American magistrates lack the power to authorize such searches. See *post*, at 297 (BLACKMUN, J., dissenting); *ante*, at 279 (STEVENS, J., concurring in judgment). The Warrant Clause would serve the same primary functions abroad as it does domestically, and I see no reason to distinguish between foreign and domestic searches.

The primary purpose of the warrant requirement is its assurance of neutrality. As Justice Jackson stated for the Court in *Johnson v. United States*, 333 U.S. 10, 13-14 (1948) (footnotes omitted):

> "The point of the Fourth Amendment, which often is not grasped by zealous officers, is not that it denies law enforcement the support of the usual inferences which reasonable men draw from evidence. Its protection consists in requiring that those inferences be drawn by a neutral and detached magistrate instead of being judged by the officer engaged in the often competitive enterprise of ferreting out crime. Any assumption that evidence sufficient to support a magistrate's disinterested determination to issue a search warrant will justify the officers in making a search without a warrant would reduce the Amendment to a nullity and leave the people's homes secure only in the discretion of police officers.... When the right of privacy must reasonably yield to the right of search is, as a rule, to be decided by a judicial officer, not by a policeman or government enforcement agent."

See also *Welsh v. Wisconsin*, 466 U.S. 740, 748-749, and n.10 (1984); *Coolidge v. New Hampshire*, 403 U.S. 443, 449 (1971). A warrant also defines the scope of a search and limits the discretion of the inspecting officers. See *New York v. Burger*, 482 U.S. 691, 703 (1987); *Marron v. United States*, 275 U.S. 192, 196 (1927). These purposes would be served no less in the foreign than in the domestic context.

The Warrant Clause cannot be ignored simply because Congress has not given any United States magistrate authority to issue search warrants for foreign searches. See Fed. Rule Crim. Proc. 41(a). Congress cannot define the contours

3. The District Court found no exigent circumstances that would justify a warrantless search. After respondent's arrest in Mexico, he was transported to the United States and held in custody in southern California. Only after respondent was in custody in the United States did the Drug Enforcement Administration (DEA) begin preparations for a search of his Mexican residences. On the night respondent was arrested, DEA Agent Terry Bowen contacted DEA Special Agent Walter White in Mexico to seek his assistance in conducting the search. Special Agent White contacted Mexican officials the next morning and at 1 p.m. authorized Agent Bowen to conduct the search. A team of DEA agents then drove to Mexico, met with Mexican officials, and arrived at the first of respondent's two residences after dark. 856 F.2d 1214, 1226 (CA9 1988). The search did not begin until approximately 10 p.m. the day after respondent was taken into custody. App. to Pet. for Cert. 101a. In all that time, particularly when respondent and Agent Bowen were both in the United States and Agent Bowen was awaiting further communications from Special Agent White, DEA Agents could easily have sought a warrant from a United States Magistrate.

of the Constitution. If the Warrant Clause applies, Congress cannot excise the Clause from the Constitution by failing to provide a means for United States agents to obtain a warrant. See *Best v. United States*, 184 F.2d 131, 138 (CA1 1950) ("Obviously, Congress may not nullify the guarantees of the Fourth Amendment by the simple expedient of not empowering any judicial officer to act on an application for a warrant"), cert. denied, 340 U.S. 939 (1951).

Nor is the Warrant Clause inapplicable merely because a warrant from a United States magistrate could not "authorize" a search in a foreign country. Although this may be true as a matter of international law, it is irrelevant to our interpretation of the Fourth Amendment. As a matter of United States constitutional law, a warrant serves the same primary function overseas as it does domestically: it assures that a neutral magistrate has authorized the search and limited its scope. The need to protect those suspected of criminal activity from the unbridled discretion of investigating officers is no less important abroad than at home.

III

When our Government conducts a law enforcement search against a foreign national outside of the United States and its territories, it must comply with the Fourth Amendment. Absent exigent circumstances or consent, it must obtain a search warrant from a United States court. When we tell the world that we expect all people, wherever they may be, to abide by our laws, we cannot in the same breath tell the world that our law enforcement officers need not do the same. Because we cannot expect others to respect our laws until we respect our Constitution, I respectfully dissent.

JUSTICE BLACKMUN, dissenting.

I cannot accept the Court of Appeals' conclusion, echoed in some portions of JUSTICE BRENNAN's dissent, that the Fourth Amendment governs every action by an American official that can be characterized as a search or seizure. American agents acting abroad generally do not purport to exercise *sovereign* authority over the foreign nationals with whom they come in contact. The relationship between these agents and foreign nationals is therefore fundamentally different from the relationship between United States officials and individuals residing within this country.

I am inclined to agree with JUSTICE BRENNAN, however, that when a foreign national is held accountable for purported violations of United States criminal laws, he has effectively been treated as one of "the governed" and therefore is entitled to Fourth Amendment protections. Although the Government's exercise of *power* abroad does not ordinarily implicate the Fourth Amendment, the enforcement of domestic criminal law seems to me to be the paradigmatic exercise of sovereignty over those who are compelled to obey. In any event, as JUSTICE STEVENS notes, *ante*, at 279, respondent was lawfully (though involuntarily) within this country at the time the search occurred. Under these circumstances I believe that respondent is entitled to invoke protections of the Fourth

Amendment. I agree with the Government, however, that an American magistrate's lack of power to authorize a search abroad renders the Warrant Clause inapplicable to the search of a noncitizen's residence outside this country.

The Fourth Amendment nevertheless requires that the search be "reasonable." And when the purpose of a search is the procurement of evidence for a, criminal prosecution, we have consistently held that the search, to be reasonable, must be based upon probable cause. Neither the District Court nor the Court of Appeals addressed the issue of probable cause, and I do not believe that a reliable determination could be made on the basis of the record before us. I therefore would vacate the judgment of the Court of Appeals and remand the case for further proceedings.

III. Notes and Questions

1. There are nine justices on the United States Supreme Court. Chief Justice Rehnquist wrote the majority opinion on the issue of whether the U.S. Constitution's Fourth Amendment applies to the search and seizure by United States agents of property owned by a Mexican and located in Mexico. His opinion was accepted by Justices Kennedy, O'Connor, Scalia, and White. Those justices with significantly different views are free to write their own opinions, even if they agree with the Court's result. Thus Justice Kennedy filed a concurring opinion. With more reservations, Justice Stevens filed an opinion concurring only with the judgment (but not the reasons). Finally, Justice Brennan wrote a dissenting opinion, in which Justice Marshall joined, and Justice Blackmun filed a dissenting opinion.
2. In addition to arguments presented by the two parties, Chief Justice Rehnquist refers to the decision of the single-judge district court and the split opinion of the three-judge panel of the court of appeals. He also discusses the brief submitted, by "friends of the court" (*amici curiae*), the American Civil Liberties Union. Do they represent the "public interest" or a particular "private interest?"
3. Chief Justice Rehnquist uses several distinct methods to interpret the Fourth Amendment to the U.S. Constitution. First, he distinguishes its temporal application from that for certain Fifth Amendment rights. The Fifth Amendment operates at the time of trial, while the Fourth Amendment seeks to protect individuals from unreasonable governmental intrusions prior to trial.

Second, Rehnquist uses a contextual interpretation to examine the words "the people" in the Fourth Amendment; he ascribes meaning to this noun based on its use in other parts of the Constitution. He then contrasts this meaning to the words "person" and "accused" found in the Fifth and Sixth Amendments.

Third, Rehnquist presents an historical interpretation by examining the drafting history of the Fourth Amendment. What did the Framers intend this amendment to mean and whom was it to protect? Why is the 1798 "undeclared war" with France relevant?

4. The common law method of judicial decision-making is often associated with the doctrine of *stare decisis*. The Supreme Court normally considers itself bound by the holding of its prior decisions. Does Chief Justice Rehnquist

argue that the Court is bound by the earlier *Insular Cases* and *Johnson v. Eisentrager* to take a restrictive view of the extraterritorial applicability of the Fourth Amendment? How did the facts in *Reid v. Covert* distinguish it from the facts in this case? Why are resident aliens provided greater constitutional rights than nonresident aliens?

5. American judicial opinion writing frequently takes the form of a dialogue. Chief Justice Rehnquist is in conversation with the past. *Stare decisis* demands that focus. He is also in dialogue with the court of appeals. Since the justices normally discuss the cases they hear in a group, the chief justice anticipates and responds to an argument put forth by Justice Stevens, who concurs in the judgment.

6. Chief Justice Rehnquist presents some policy reasons why the majority's decision is correct. Are these reasons persuasive?

7. To whom should the defendant Verdugo-Urquidez took for protection against an unreasonable American search and seizure of his property in Mexico? What rules would apply? Mexican law? International law?

8. Justice Kennedy writes a concurring opinion. What are his grounds of agreement and disagreement with the majority? Is the Fourth Amendment inapplicable because its use would be "impracticable and anomalous?"

9. Justice Stevens, concurring in the result, states that the Fourth Amendment is applicable to aliens abroad, but that "the search conducted by the United States agents with the approval and cooperation of the Mexican authorities was not 'unreasonable'."

10. Justice Brennan, dissenting, argues that if a foreigner must obey U.S. laws in his own country, then the United States government should similarly comply with the U.S. Constitution abroad, including the Fourth Amendment. This argument is based primarily on policy – a kind of fairness – rather than on the language or history of the Fourth Amendment.

Where does the principle of mutuality originate? It is not in the Constitution. Is the principle, nevertheless, applicable in this case? Is it related to the "rule of law?" Is part of Justice Brennan's point that the United States Government should lead the world's nations by example?

11. Justice Brennan, in part I.B of his opinion, characterizes the majority's interpretation of the Fourth Amendment as "cramped." Is his rebuttal to the majority's interpretation persuasive? On all points or only on some points? Does it matter whether a person's right of security against unreasonable searches and seizures pre-existed the Bill of Rights? Did this right originate in a state of nature? Should Mexicans thus also possess this natural right?

12. Justice Brennan asserts that the Fourth Amendment's warrant clause applies to U.S. Government searches in Mexico, even though the territoriality principle in international law would deprive a U.S. warrant of legality in Mexico. How is this possible? Is Justice Blackmun's opinion on this issue persuasive?

13. A jury in federal district court convicted defendant Verdugo-Urquidez of murder and the court sentenced him to life imprisonment. The court of appeals held that if the United States authorized or sponsored a Mexican citizen's abduction from his country, without the Mexican government's consent, it breached the Mexican-American extradition treaty. If the Mexican government then formally

objected to the treaty violation, an American court would have no jurisdiction to try the Mexican national. *United States v. Verdugo-Urquidez*, 939 F.2d 1341 (9th Cir. 1991). In *Verdugo-Urquidez II* the court remanded the case to the district court to determine in an evidentiary hearing whether the United States had sponsored the defendant's abduction without the Mexican government's consent and whether the Mexican government continued to maintain its protest. If the findings were affirmative, Verdugo-Urquidez should be released to the Mexican authorities.

Often the police arrest someone primarily to gather evidence of a crime. If the arrest is illegal, such as the violation of an extradition treaty, all evidence obtained as a direct or indirect consequence of the arrest is excluded from the criminal trial as "fruit of the poisonous tree." *See* Chap. 15, pt. IV.A.

Index